The Baby Name Wizard

The Baby Name Wizard

Revised 3rd Edition

A MAGICAL METHOD FOR FINDING THE PERFECT NAME FOR YOUR BABY

LAURA WATTENBERG

HARMONY

BOOKS • NEW YORK

For Martin, and the daughters we named together

Contents

Acknowledgments

✳

For this third, expanded *Baby Name Wizard*, I owe thanks to all the visitors who contribute to BabyNameWizard.com and NameCandy.com. Your comments on blogs and in forums and the personal insights you've shared on name pages in our "Namipedia" remind me every day that there is always more to learn about names.

Thanks as well to the NameCandy.com blogging team, a wonderful community and sounding board: Alex Frons, Alyssa Domzal, Ashley Young, Catherine Holecko, Colleen Cusick, Hikma Abdulghani, Katie Luscombe, Lane Rogers, Laura Emerson, Martina Fugazzotto, Suzy Byrne, and Victoria Loustalot. Lane Rogers was also my invaluable second set of eyes for this edition, reviewing every name snapshot down to the last brother and sister suggestion.

Finally, I continue to owe debts to everyone I've thanked in past editions, most of all my incredible website partner Jennie Baird and my family. Taking inspired sibling name suggestions from my own kids is a special kind of joy.

The indispensable friends and advisers who helped me with the original *Baby Name Wizard* were joined by a wide new circle for this edition. Some of these new advisers I can thank by name, such as Katja Battarbee on Finnish names, Angela Kitmiridis on Greek names, Natalie Miller-Moore on "Name Madness," Allan Tulchin on French names, Fernanda Viégas on Brazilian names, and my own children—just old enough this time around to lend a helping hand. Many more, though, are distant and anonymous: the scores of readers from around the world who have written to me and posted at BabyNameWizard.com. I have learned from every suggestion, opinion, and observation, and I hope this book does justice to the wisdom you all have offered me.

Jennie Baird was the book's first champion. She instantly saw its potential, and her support helped make it a reality. I'm further indebted to the people who gave me input on the book concept and proposal and the publishing process: Sarah Blustain, Neil Cronin, Stacy Cronin, Ari

Juels, Daniel Max, Judith Miller, Dan Newman, Amey Stone, and Bonnie Wong. I am also indebted to Karl Arruda, Andrea Dunn, Catherine Miranda, Alina Plourde, Laura Raymond, Julie Steinberg, and Janine Sullivan, who offered valuable insights on specific name styles.

Thanks to my agent, Stephanie Rostan, whose enthusiasm and practical guidance made a potentially hair-raising process a pleasure. My editor, Tricia Medved, showed unfailing patience, grace, and courage in staring down a book with 1550 graphs, seven spellings of Kaitlyn, and one first-time author.

Finally, special thank-yous to Julie Miles, Bernard Miller, Ruth Miller, and Karen Richter for reviewing large swaths of the manuscript, and to Martin Wattenberg for doing absolutely all of the above.

Introduction to the Third Edition

It's always an awkward moment at a party. "What do you do?" asks a new acquaintance. "I'm a baby name expert," I say, because what else *can* I say? In the puzzled silence that follows, I hear the unspoken question: *What the heck is there to be expert about?*

It may be hard to believe that the subject of baby names is worthy of "expertise." Yet the closer you look at names, the deeper and more revealing they turn out to be. Names tie into every part of our history and culture, and they're changing fast. Those changes shed light on everything from politics and religion to sex and celebrity, as well as the evolving nature of the American family.

In this third edition of *The Baby Name Wizard*, I've expanded the coverage of names' cultural connections. Each name snapshot now includes a new feature called "In the World," which suggests prominent associations that come to people's minds when they hear a name. New maps of name trends show the different naming styles at work in different parts of the country. You may be surprised at some of the hot local fashions. (Hint: conservative naming and conservative politics do not go hand in hand.)

Newly added style categories include a Turn of the 21st Century style and subcategories for jazz names, science fiction and fantasy names, and the increasingly influential world of video game names. I've also expanded the popular brother and sister suggestions that accompany each name. You'll now see six to eight suggestions for each sex, freshly chosen for this edition.

Those are just the most obvious changes. No name list or snapshot is untouched. I've reviewed each entry and rewritten many of them. And of course, most important of all, you'll find *hundreds* of new names throughout the book.

Many thanks,
Laura Wattenberg

In Search of the Perfect Name: A Peek Behind the Wizard's Curtain

When my first daughter was a baby, I noticed a curious phenomenon. It seemed that every baby girl we met in Riverside Park in New York was named either Hannah or Olivia. But every one of their mothers said she had chosen the name to be unusual!

That was my introduction to the mysterious landscape of modern names. Like hairstyles and hemlines, names have fashions that change with each generation. Each name has a social meaning that evolves, shaped by the people who bear it and the world that surrounds it.

When the time came to choose a name for my second child, I set out to find a map of the name landscape. Name dictionaries were an obvious place to start, but names are far more than words. Knowing that Olivia comes from the Latin word for "olive" doesn't tell you whether there will be three other Olivias on your block. And learning that Elmo has the same root as "helmet" doesn't clue you in that Elmo is a furry red Muppet. What I wanted wasn't a dictionary but a practical guide to name fashions, history, and style.

Over the following years, I compiled a huge database of name information: Popularity data from cities and countries around the world. Birth announcements in Ivy League alumni magazines. Lists of Catholic saints. African-American sorority memberships. Soap opera cast lists. Colonial census records. Then I developed computer models to spot trends and identify style categories. My "Name Matchmaker," for instance, was a program designed to take any name and pinpoint others with a similar style and feeling. I knew I was on to something when I told the Matchmaker the names of my two daughters and the top boy's name match it suggested was the very name my husband and I had agreed on for a boy.

Of course, it takes a human to interpret the data and make the final judgments. It's my own call to say that a boy named Romeo matches a girl named Valentine. In the end, the point of all the research and technology is to produce a real-world guide to names, with the kind of information that's worth kibitzing over. A hearty dinnertime debate over the merits of a name like Cabot or Clark is the best compliment this book could receive.

Consider *The Baby Name Wizard* a field guide to American names. It's designed to help you understand what's out there, identify name styles, and spot trends. But above all, it's designed to guide you to the perfect fit for your own personal taste and style.

Rules of Thumb for Choosing a Name

✳

Rule #1: Personal taste isn't so personal

Not long ago, I heard an expectant mother beside herself with outrage. She had just learned that another woman in her small town had "stolen" her baby name! No, she admitted, she had never met the woman. But for years now she had been planning to name a baby Keaton, a name she had personally invented, and now there was another little Keaton right across town. Someone must have told that other mother her own secret, special name. Thief!

Chances are this was not really a case of name larceny. That mom had just run into a startling fact of baby name life: our tastes, which feel so personal, are communal creations. Keaton? Well, it's a surname ending in "-n," a style parents are flocking to for fresh ideas that sound like classic names. "K" in particular is a hot first letter. And don't forget that almost every parent today grew up watching Alex Keaton on *Family Ties*. So just like that outraged mom, thousands of parents across the country have independently "invented" the name for their kids.

We live in a shared culture, with communities and experiences that shape our likes and dislikes. That means overlapping taste—and as a rule, the closer two people are, the greater the overlap. Many of us have had a long-cherished name "stolen" by friends who had long cherished it themselves. It's frankly unnerving to discover that the quirky name you've always just happened to like is now a chart topper. Whatever happened to individual style?

Before you panic and name your son Aloysius, remember that communal taste is really a good thing. That shared perspective is exactly what gives names their style and nuance. It's also the context that lets you define your own style, meaningfully. Use the backdrop of your social group, your community, and your generation to choose names that make the kind of statement you're looking for. And if you do meet another Keaton, take it as a positive sign that your son will be fashionable. Parents are the ones who worry about a name standing out; kids are happy to fit in.

Rule #2: Not all last names are created equal

I can see a runway model wearing a sheath dress that's so gorgeous, I could just melt looking at it. But I know perfectly well that the same dress on my real-world figure would be a train wreck. Similarly, I know that the stylish Irish name Kennedy, paired with my last name Wattenberg, would sound like someone falling down stairs.

In names, as in clothes, the key is to choose the styles that flatter you. Run down this basic checklist before you make your final choice.

Rhythm and rhyme: A full name is like a little line of poetry with rhyme and meter. You may choose a name you love, only to test it out with your surname and find that it falls flat. (Nope, you can't "fix" it with a middle name. Soon enough that middle name will disappear from your daily usage, leaving the awkward combo to last a lifetime.) Watch out for singsong rhythms and tongue twisters. If your compositions aren't working, try looking for names that echo one or more of the sounds in your surname. For example, the shared "uh" sound makes Hunter Sullivan sound more natural than, say, Hunter Flannigan.

The "Justin Case" syndrome: A perfectly reasonable first name can meet a perfectly reasonable last name and create something perfectly ridiculous. When you have a candidate picked out, say the full name out loud repeatedly to look for hidden land mines. Include nicknames too— Benjamin Dover is one thing, Ben Dover quite another.

Meeting in the middle: Look carefully where the end of one name meets the beginning of another. Jonas Sanders will be heard as Jonah Sanders or Jonas Anders. Alexander Anderson sounds like a stutter.

Special cases: If your last name is a common word, it's especially important to avoid alliteration. Jenny Jumps and Walter Wall sound like characters from a children's picture book. If your last name is a common first name, take special care to choose first names that won't make you sound inside out. Nicholson Thomas, for instance, is asking for trouble. And if your last name just *is* trouble (Rump, Hogg, etc.), you can use the rhythm of a long, rolling first name to draw the emphasis away from it.

Rule #3: All naming is local

America is a sprawling, diverse country, and at any given time many different name trends are operating at once. Money, geography, ethnicity, and education all swirl together to form "microclimates" of style, with local spikes in the use of particular names.

You can look up Ezra and say, "Ah, popularity rank #342, I won't meet many Ezras." But if your friends have kids named Levi and Ezekiel, you should expect to see Ezras on your block. Not to say that's a bad thing. In that kind of community, Ezra won't risk teasing, whereas he might find it rough going in a sea of Kaydens and Madisyns. Use the Sister/Brother names, style categories, and maps in this book to help gauge how a name will fit into your social surroundings.

Rule #4: Other people's opinions matter

As a parent, the choice of a baby name is entirely up to you. Why should you listen to what anybody else has to say, let alone your crazy friends and relatives?

Some food for thought: the choice may be yours, but you are making it for someone else. You are just a trustee in this matter, assigned to handle the affairs of another person who is unable to act because he or she has not yet been born. And those crazy friends and relatives? They are going to be your baby's friends and relatives before long. Don't let them bully you, but don't completely ignore them either. As a group, they represent the society that's going to be hearing, and judging, your child's name for a lifetime. You don't have to flag down every passing car to ask for opinions, but it's worth choosing a few level-headed confidantes to air out your ideas.

If you don't want to open the floodgates on a public name debate, this book gives you some middle ground. As you browse through the pages, think of it as a conversation with a friend who has thought an awful lot about names—and who will shut up when you're done with her. For a name you're seriously considering, try reading the listed Sister/Brother names out loud too. They'll give you the best sense of how the name you like will come across to others.

Rule #5: Choose the name you would like to have yourself

This is the top piece of advice I give expectant parents. We all have many factors in mind when we choose a name. We may want to honor our relatives or our ethnic heritage. We may see baby naming as an opportunity for personal expression. Use whatever criteria you like to narrow your name choices, but before you fill in the birth certificate, stop and give the name this final test: if you were starting life today, knowing everything you know about the world, is this the name you would want to represent you? If so, you can feel confident that you're giving your child the best birthday present possible, one that will last a lifetime.

Family Matters: Namesakes, Traditions, and Conflicts

You're about to introduce a new member of your family. This is a special, magical time filled with special, magical dilemmas, conflicts, and frustrations.

Names carry unique significance in a family setting, representing connections with the past as well as a glimpse into the future. We carry reflections of our families with us in our names, as surnames and often first and middle names as well. Even if you don't directly name your child after relatives, you can still be blindsided by family issues you never thought about before you contemplated parenthood. Here's a primer on some of the top trouble spots:

Namesakes

The simplest namesake is a Junior. Dad is Johann Schmidt, his son is Johann Schmidt Jr., and his grandson is Johann III. If that's your family tradition and everyone buys into it, you're golden. Skip this section and start concentrating on finding different nicknames to use in each generation.

In most families, though, the ways we honor relatives are more fluid and up to individual discretion. We have first and middle names to play with, nicknames and variations. We may shy away from naming after living relatives, or we may have beloved relatives with atrocious names. Some common strategies for sticky situations:

The middle name cure-all: Middle names are America's polite dumping ground for outmoded names. We use the middle name to honor Aunt Mildred without actually raising a little Millie. Best of all, as middle names, many of those quirky choices, especially foreign names, start to sound stylish and distinctive. Some parents are tempted to overdo it, stuffing two or three names in the middle to cover all their obligations. Resist this impulse if you can; this is a three-name-max society and extra names bring practical headaches.

The not-quite namesake: If you don't want two Margarets to create confusion at family gatherings, or just can't bear to name your son after your husband's grandpa Selig, try echoing the namesake with a slightly different choice. Many families just follow the first letter of the name. For a closer match, consider alternative forms from different times and cultures. Margaret would probably be delighted to be honored with a little Margot or Margery. Digging even deeper, you can start with a name root or meaning and derive a new equivalent. Edna, for instance, is believed to come from the same root as Eden. And the Yiddish Selig means "happy," same as the Hebrew Asher. If you really want to go all out, consider an anagram. Baseball star Nomar Garciaparra was named for his father Ramon.

The "nicknamesake": This favorite trick lets you name your son after great-grandpa Archie while sidestepping his given name Archibald. Many traditional nicknames can arise from multiple given names. So Uncle Don might be a Donald, but nephew Little Don is a Donovan. And Archie? Try the simple, uncommon choice Archer. The "Nicknames" style section in this book (on page 433) is a great source of ideas for alternative "nicknamesakes."

That Name Is *Mine!*

You and your siblings were raised together. You share the same heritage, traditions, and life-shaping experiences. Is it any surprise you share the same favorite names?

So out of the thousands of names in the world, you and your sister have both zeroed in on Maeve as the one and only perfect choice for a little girl. The rule is simple here, gals: first come, first served. Unless some previous explicit agreement exists, whoever gives birth to a girl first has dibs on the name. In a small, close family, this dibs system might even extend to cousins or beyond.

Some exceptions: in a really big family, something's gotta give. Among your 10 brothers and sisters and 30 nieces and nephews, you may have to accept an occasional duplicate name. Also, try to stay flexible to respect the input of in-law families. Perhaps your husband and your sister's husband both have fathers named Charles. You can both use the name if it's important, but try to hammer out a deal to call one boy Charlie and the other Chaz.

The Last Frontier: Last Names

It's old news by now that many parents, married or not, have different last names. Even couples who share a name may choose a hyphenated or combined version or come up with other creative ways to incorporate the mother's birth name into their new family identity. More and more, those solutions have an impact on given names as well.

The middle maiden name: This is a simple, tried-and-true method to incorporate the mom's family heritage into a child's name. Most any surname sounds fine as a middle name, and the full name spoken aloud will sound like a hyphenated surname.

The last shall be first: Some families take a bolder step and use a family surname as the child's first name. With the current popularity of surname-style names, this option is more appealing than ever. Not that it's a new idea: family surnames are traditional choices in the South, and you can pick up an Edith Wharton novel to see the same trend in Gilded Age New York. But please do proceed with caution. Try to put aside your emotional attachments and realize that not every surname is destined for a first-name role. (Sorry, Fantuzis and Rosenblatts.)

For the hyphenated child: If your child will be using a double last name, take triple the care in selecting a first name. Choose a name that sounds good with the full hyphenated version *and* with each surname alone. During the course of a lifetime, your child may have reasons to slim the name down: to look good on a theater marquee, to merge names with a spouse, or to address a dozen other situations we can't yet imagine. A little extra flexibility can't hurt.

Tips and Tricks for Name-Blocked Parents

You've been thinking about names nonstop since you first saw that little plus sign on the stick, and yet you're utterly, hopelessly stuck. Don't panic: this is your emergency preparedness kit. First, let's do some triage.

Does nothing at all seem right? *Go to section A.*
Are you torn among your favorites? *Go to section B.*
Are you and your partner totally at odds and on the brink of violence? *Go to section C.*
Is your baby already born? *Go directly to section D.*

A: I hate everything

Nothing makes a choice harder than choices—lots of choices. You go to the store to buy a flashlight, they have one flashlight, you buy it, you're happy. If they have 20 flashlights, though, you agonize, and probably go home worried that you didn't make the best possible selection. Now suppose there are 10,000 flashlights, and you'll have to keep the one you choose with you for the rest of your life. Is it any wonder that picking a baby name can be stressful?

Luckily, this isn't an Indiana Jones–type situation, where there's only one right choice and the rest send you to eternal damnation. There are plenty of names that will give your child a great start in life. The trick is to clear your mind and narrow your options to a workable range.

This book offers several ways to help you pare down. You can choose a style category that intrigues you and decide to look only within that list. If it's a large category, pick out a couple of starting/ending letters that particularly appeal. Once you're down to a set of 20 or so names, choose the two best of the group. Voilà, there are two names you like! Alternatively, choose half a dozen names that kind of appeal to you, even though they're not "the answer." Look them up in the "Name Snapshots" section and write down the names suggested as brothers and sisters. There's your list. Spend some time with it, giving each name honest consideration. Chances are you'll find a name you and your child can be happy with.

B: So close, but which one?

Excellent work, you've come up with your short list. Think of it—you started with a whole world's worth of names and now you're down to just an elite handful! That's important to keep in mind: every name on your list is good. When you keep staring at the same four names, it's easy to start finding fault with them. Instead, think about what delights you about them. Try to find the thrill in each name on your list, the wondrous warmth of calling your child by that name. You may find that when you focus on that feeling, one name rises quickly to the top. If not, it's time to take each name out for a full day's test-drive. For one day, the baby is no longer "baby"—he's Sawyer/Beckett/Paxton. Make yourself believe it. Live in each name for a day, see how it holds up, and see which name you're most reluctant to leave behind.

If at the end you genuinely love two names equally, here's a potential tiebreaker: imagine your kindergartener asking how you chose her name. Is there one name you can spin a particularly compelling tale about? If so, then you're getting an extra bonus with that name, a dose of personal history and meaning.

Finally, a tip on what *not* to do: don't wait until you meet the baby, to see which name suits him. Many parents head to the birthing center with a list of three or four names, figuring that once the baby is in their arms the choice will become clear. It's a natural impulse, but it's often too much to expect. Realistically, what newborn is going to just *seem* like a Sebastian? In my experience, leaving the job to the baby increases parents' risk of postpartum name panic.

C: My partner is just impossible

The good news is, you and your partner have great name ideas. The bad news is, they're not the *same* ideas. Or does your partner have no ideas at all? Perhaps you're left in charge of flipping through books, coming up with suggestion after suggestion for him to veto? Before your baby-naming problem becomes a relationship problem, it's time to defuse the situation. Ratchet down the hostilities by taking pen to paper.

The simplest approach is to exchange lists. Go to separate rooms and each write down your six top choices. (No, writing Eleanor six times doesn't count.) Then trade papers and each choose the two names you find least objectionable. That's your short list.

Give a game effort to agree on one of the short-list names. If you can't, use it as your reference point for finding a compromise. Break down what exactly appeals to you about each name and see if you can find compromise names that share those qualities. If he likes the gentle grace of Olivia and she likes the exotic uniqueness of Xanthe, look for a rare but delicate alternative (Lavinia, Raphaela). You can also use the Brother/Sister suggestions in this book to come up with alternatives for specific names.

If you're up for something more adventurous, try a round of "Name Madness." A *Baby Name Wizard* reader came up with this ingenious playoff system to jump-start the naming process. It works like the NCAA basketball championship or the Wimbledon tennis tournament. Start with 32 name ideas, 16 boys and 16 girls. Rank them for "seeding" purposes and enter them on a "bracket" form. (You can re-purpose one from an office sports pool.) Put the girls on the left, the boys on the right, then start pair-wise eliminations until you're down to one name for each sex. The ultrasound determines the ultimate champion.

A Name Madness tournament might hold special appeal for the many women who tell me that their male partners just won't talk about names. Who can resist the competitive allure of a playoff bracket? At the very least, the process should bring a little fun back to your naming discussions.

D: The baby's here! But the name...

Congratulations on your new child! What an exciting time! So about that name. If you really haven't chosen at all, you can go back and try the ideas in sections A–C. But if you have a name and aren't happy with it, read on.

Namer's remorse is more common than you might think. Many parents find that a name seems different in reality than it did in their mind's eye. Perhaps your friends all froze in polite half-grimaces when you announced the name. Perhaps they all said, "Oh, Ariel like in *The Little Mermaid?*" when you were thinking "Ariel like in *The Tempest.*" Perhaps that creative spelling you dreamed up seems a lot less fun after you've spelled it for people 100 times. Or perhaps you're simply holding your baby, calling him by his new name, and it just feels wrong. If you're caught in the grips of namer's remorse, I have two important pieces of advice for you. Two opposite pieces of advice.

First, the vast majority of parents who have qualms about a name at age two weeks are fine with it by age two years. Your child will grow into her name in ways that are hard to even imagine at this stage. You chose the name for a reason, and that reason still holds. Also, try to recognize that this is an emotionally fraught time. You're short on sleep, your whole world has changed, and the name that spent months attached to an imaginary baby is suddenly attached to a real one. It may take some time for the name to feel natural and "yours," and that's okay. (In fact, it may take some time for the *baby* to feel natural and "yours," and that's okay too.)

Second, if you truly do want to change the baby's name, go ahead and do it. Yes, you've already sent out hundreds of birth announcements. Yes, it may be a little embarrassing to change your mind so publicly. So what? A couple of days' worth of ribbing from relatives is no big deal compared to giving your child the right name for a lifetime. If you like, you can even send out a follow-up round of humorous "On second thought . . ." announcements. Perhaps something like this:

BIRTH ANNOUNCEMENT, TAKE 2

On August 12th we were blessed with a beautiful baby boy. Before he was born, we had expected that his name would be Jayden. Once we met him, we discovered we were mistaken. Who knew? He's actually:

From the baby's perspective, the change shouldn't be a big deal. Infants get called by so many names—Baby, Sweetie, Little Muffin—that one more should fit in fine. In a few years, the name change will mellow in everyone's memories, and perhaps even become a cherished bit of your child's personal history.

In other words, you'll be fine either way. Honest.

Today's Top 25

"Mary's only #112? Then what *is* a common name?" Satisfy your curiosity with this rundown of America's 25 most popular names for boys and girls.

Rank	Boys	Girls
1	Jacob	Sophia
2	Mason	Isabella
3	William	Emma
4	Jayden	Olivia
5	Noah	Ava
6	Michael	Emily
7	Ethan	Abigail
8	Alexander	Madison
9	Aiden	Mia
10	Daniel	Chloe
11	Anthony	Elizabeth
12	Matthew	Ella
13	Elijah	Addison
14	Joshua	Natalie
15	Liam	Lily
16	Andrew	Grace
17	James	Samantha
18	David	Avery
19	Benjamin	Sofia
20	Logan	Aubrey
21	Christopher	Brooklyn
22	Joseph	Lillian
23	Jackson	Victoria
24	Gabriel	Evelyn
25	Ryan	Hannah

The Baby Name Map: Trends Across America

Why should you care about trends? You're picking a name because you love it, not because of what everybody else thinks. In fact, you're determined to buck the trends and pick a name off the beaten path! Well, if so, you're smack dab in the middle of the hottest naming trend of the 21st century.

If there's one thing American parents have in common today, it's that we want to sound nothing like one another. In fact, every year hundreds of American babies are named Unique. It reflects a society where individuality has become a cherished virtue. Parents look at the popular name charts and engage in a kind of reverse arms race, vying to *not* be #1.

Yet as much as we want to stand out, our tastes remain very much like those of our neighbors. You may carefully choose a name you believe to be unusual, only to find your own neighborhood playground packed with little Hazels or Aspens. It's increasingly hard to predict local style from national style.

In past generations, the average American baby received a name that was broadly used and liked. Imagine a naming midpoint, where half of kids have a more common name and half a less common name. In the 1900s, the midpoint names were Jessie and Jack—familiar top-50 favorites. In the 1950s, Diana and Gregory represented the average. And today? Try Lyric and Jaxson, names that appeal to certain tastes and communities but are virtually unimaginable to others. Fashion is fracturing.

Some style communities look to the past or plumb deeper into classic sources for names that sound fresh. That has led to the revival of old-timers like Julius and Cora and to new popularity heights for biblical rarities like Zechariah and mythological names like Athena.

In other communities, you're more likely to find parents turning surnames like Paxton and Brantley into first names or working the transformation on words like Serenity and Maverick. Still other groups of parents are taking their cues from overseas, importing names like Giovanni and Nadia. And then there are the parents who don't want to use a name *from* anywhere at all. They custom-fashion new names like Brayleigh and Zamarion.

The maps that follow show off the distinctive naming themes that shape the sound of the times in each state. They're not the most popular names per se, but the names that are most *disproportionately* popular in that region compared to the rest of the country. Take a look at the part of the country where you live—or where you hope to live—to get a sense of how your name taste fits in.

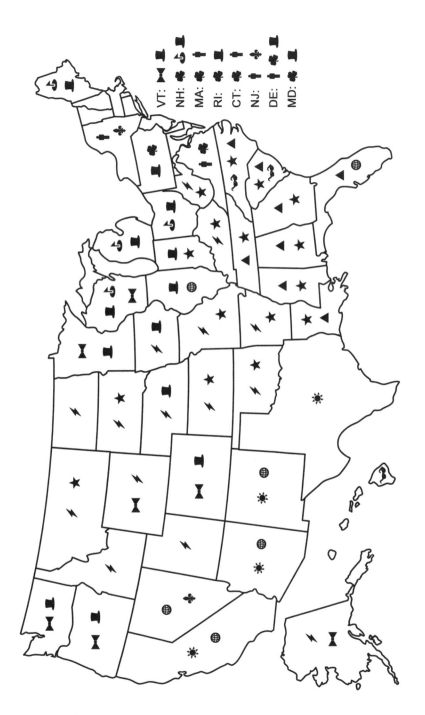

Local Color Map: Boys

 **Preppy Cowboys**
Examples: Bentley, Dalton, Trenton, Brantley, Easton

Quirky Classics
Examples: Ezra, Silas, Liam, Oliver, Asher, Elias

 Saintly Classics
Examples: Vincent, Nicholas, Lucas, Joseph, Anthony

 Shamrock Standards
Examples: Connor, Declan, Colin, Patrick, Ryan

 **Smooth Gents**
Examples: Owen, Miles, Blake, Nolan, Cole

 **Steady Guys**
Examples: Jack, Thomas, Matthew, Jake, Adam

 **Age of Aidens**
Examples: Ayden, Kayden, Braylon, Peyton, Jaylen

Classico
Examples: Diego, Jesús, Miguel, Andrés, Carlos

 **Global Elegance**
Examples: Sebastian, Xavier, Giovanni, Damian, Leonardo

 **Men of Action**
Examples: Ryker, Braxton, Maddox, Gage, Drake

 Old-School Prep
Examples: Carter, Brady, Parker, Wesley, Grant

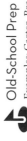 **Power Panache**
Examples: Zion, Kingston, Malachi, Titus, Jeremiah

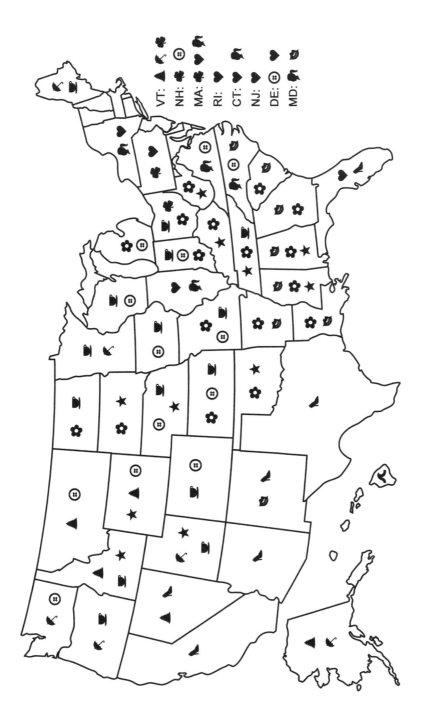

Local Color Map: Girls

 **Andro-Girly**
Examples: Aubree, Brooklynn, Ryleigh, Maci, Brynlee

 **Andro-Preppy**
Examples: Piper, Scarlett, Harper, Kendall, Reese

 **Classic Ladies**
Examples: Caroline, Eleanor, Julia, Charlotte, Catherine

 **Elegante**
Examples: Giselle, Ximena, Camila, Valeria, Natalia

 **Fresh Air**
Examples: Aspen, McKinley, Aurora, Willow, Juniper

 **High Gloss**
Examples: London, Serenity, Nevaeh, Paris, Jada, Angel

 **Island Breeze**
Examples: Kiani, Malia, Leilani, Kaia, Anela

 Neo-Cowgirls
Examples: Paisley, Oakley, Shelby, Presley, Josie

 Quirky Classics
Examples: Penelope, Hazel, Ivy, Josephine, Olive

 Romantic Flourish
Examples: Julianna, Valentina, Angelina, Gianna, Adrianna

 Shamrock Sleek
Examples: Maeve, Fiona, Keira, Nora, Brynn

 Sweet Little Ladies
Examples: Lydia, Clara, Ellie, Lucy, Cora

Getting Started: A Quick Guide to the Book

The *Wizard* is designed to guide you to names that fit your own personal taste and style. It's divided into three main sections: "Name Snapshots," "Name Styles," and the "Name Index."

Name Snapshots

The name snapshots are compact profiles of individual names. Use them to learn more about names you like and to set yourself on the path to more ideas. To get started, look up the snapshot of a name that interests you. You'll find a rundown of all the most pertinent facts about the name, including style designations, nicknames, variants, pronunciations, prominent examples, and a graph charting the popularity of the name over the course of the past century. One special feature, sisters and brothers, is designed to guide you to alternatives with a similar style and feeling. (A custom computer program helped identify the many elements that make up each name's trademark style.) If one of the sisters or brothers strikes your fancy, widen your search from there.

Key: Understanding the Name Snapshots

Each snapshot is a guide to the name's image and usage—and a starting point for finding new name ideas.

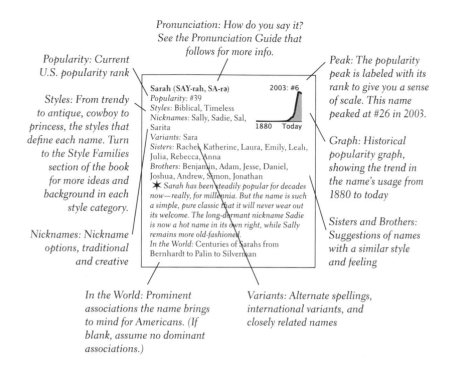

Pronunciation: How do you say it? See the Pronunciation Guide that follows for more info.

Popularity: Current U.S. popularity rank

Styles: From trendy to antique, cowboy to princess, the styles that define each name. Turn to the Style Families section of the book for more ideas and background in each style category.

Nicknames: Nickname options, traditional and creative

Sarah (SAY-rah, SA-rə)   2003: #6
Popularity: #39
Styles: Biblical, Timeless
Nicknames: Sally, Sadie, Sal,
Sarita   1880   Today
Variants: Sara
Sisters: Rachel, Katherine, Laura, Emily, Leah, Julia, Rebecca, Anna
Brothers: Benjamin, Adam, Jesse, Daniel, Joshua, Andrew, Simon, Jonathan
★ Sarah has been steadily popular for decades now—really, for millennia. But the name is such a simple, pure classic that it will never wear out its welcome. The long-dormant nickname Sadie is now a hot name in its own right, while Sally remains more old-fashioned.
In the World: Centuries of Sarahs from Bernhardt to Palin to Silverman

Peak: The popularity peak is labeled with its rank to give you a sense of scale. This name peaked at #26 in 2003.

Graph: Historical popularity graph, showing the trend in the name's usage from 1880 to today

Sisters and Brothers: Suggestions of names with a similar style and feeling

In the World: Prominent associations the name brings to mind for Americans. (If blank, assume no dominant associations.)

Variants: Alternate spellings, international variants, and closely related names

Name Styles

The styles are your introduction to the many flavors of American baby names. Distinctive styles can come from sounds (Kaylee and Kayden), ethnic origins (Francesca and Giovanni), cultural connections (Harlow and Gable), or historical usage patterns (Barbara and Donald). From biblical classics to modern meaning names, read about the styles that interest you and browse dozens of names that fit.

Name Index

The Name Index is the complete page reference for all the names in the book, including main snapshot entries, similar names lists, and style lists. Use it to look up rare names or to track down every mention of your favorite choice.

Pronunciation Guide

Each *Baby Name Wizard* name snapshot includes suggested pronunciations. When there's just one option listed, you can assume that's the most standard way to pronounce the name in American English. When there's more than one, the first is generally most common. If you prefer an unlisted pronunciation—or a more "authentic" pronunciation of a foreign name—think of the guide as a glimpse ahead at how others are likely to pronounce your child's name.

The pronunciations are designed to be readable rather than formally precise. If you're uncertain of a pronunciation, say it out loud a few times quickly and it should click into place.

Key to the Entries

ALL CAPS = stressed syllable

VOWEL SOUNDS

Written	*Sound*
a	a as in cat
ah	a as in father or o as in on
aw	aw as in dawn
ay	a as in ate or é as in café
er	er as in farmer
ə	a neutral, unstressed vowel as in sofa or upon
ee	e as in here
eh	e as in pet
i	i as in sit
iy	i as in bite or y as in my
oh	o as in tone
oo	oo as boot or u as in flute
ow	ow as in brown
oy	oy as in boy
uh	u as in but
uw	u as in put or oo as in wood

Written	*Sound*
ch	ch as in **ch**oose
g	g as in **g**ate
j	j as in **j**ump or g as in **g**iant
kh	unvoiced throat sounds that soften to an "h" in English, like jalapeño and **Ch**aim
ng	ng as in wal**king** or n as in a**n**chor
s	s as in **s**oft or c as in ra**c**e
z	z as in **z**ebra or s as in jean**s**
th	unvoiced th as in **th**in
dh	voiced th as in **th**ere
zh	s as in mea**s**ure or t as in equa**t**ion

Name Snapshots: Girls

Aaliyah (ah-LEE-ə)   2011: #46
Popularity: #46
Styles: African-American,
Lacy and Lissome, African
Nicknames: Liyah, LiLi, Aali   1880   Today
Variants: Aliya, Aliyah, Aleah
Sisters: Ayanna, Saniyah, Alexa, Aisha, Soraya, Rihanna
Brothers: Amari, Isaiah, Dakarai, Asante, Malachi, Mekhi
✷ The late R&B artist Aaliyah made this name a household word, and her image remains tied to it. Aaliyah is pure silken smoothness, practically a liquid name. It can be derived from a Swahili word meaning "most exalted," or the Hebrew term for "ascent."
In the World: Singer Aaliyah

Abby (A-bee)   2003: #163
Popularity: #296
Styles: Nicknames, New
Classics
Variants: Abbie, Abi   1880   Today
Sisters: Carly, Tessa, Molly, Jenna, Allie, Zoe, Sadie, Katy
Brothers: Drew, Seth, Alex, Jake, Micah, Cole, Ian, Aaron
✷ The name Abigail went through a long trek in the fashion desert, but its nickname never went away. In the 19th century Abbie breezed along happily with names like Tillie and Mattie. Today Abby is the most common spelling, popular as both nickname and given name. It's cute but not cutesy.
In the World: Advice columnist "Dear Abby"; Abby Sciuto of *NCIS*

Abigail (A-bi-gayl)   2003: #6
Popularity: #7
Styles: Antique Charm,
Biblical
Nicknames: Abby, Abbie, Gail   1880   Today
Variants: Abigale, Avigail
Sisters: Hannah, Olivia, Emily, Chloe, Molly, Madelyn, Lily, Bethany
Brothers: Caleb, Andrew, Elijah, Gabriel, Isaac, Jonah, Nathan, Owen
✷ Abigail was once considered a Puritan name and later became the stereotypical name for a servant or secretary. But this biblical classic has finally received a well-deserved makeover. It still has its colonial aura of simple purity but has shed its dowdy starch. Abbie remains charming, and the full Abigail is the mainstream of fashion. Grown-up Gail is a seldom heard nickname alternative.
In the World: Actress Abigail Breslin; presidential wife Abigail Adams

Ada (AY-də)   1880: #33
Popularity: #494
Styles: Ladies and
Gentlemen, Short and Sweet,
Saints, Why Not?   1880   Today

Variants: Adah
Sisters: Flora, Lena, Delia, Elsa, Belle, Eloise, Cleo, Iva
Brothers: Foster, Leo, Hugh, Jules, Walker, Silas, Casper, Ray
✷ A century ago, three-letter girls' names were the hottest thing going. Most of those names—Oda, Una, Osa—are best left in the past, but Ada is definitely worth a second look. It is one of the simplest, cleanest names for girls. The variant Adah is biblical, a wife of Esau.
In the World: Computer pioneer Ada Lovelace; Ada Wong of *Resident Evil*

Adair (ah-DAYR) 1995: #3875
Popularity: #5682
Styles: Celtic, Last Names First, Androgynous, Why Not? 1880 Today
Nicknames: Dare, Ada, Addie
Sisters: Tierney, Greer, Brodie, Gray, Laine, Rowan, Aisling, Mirren
Brothers: Torin, Greig, Niven, Ramsay, Carrick, Camden, Fraser, Colm
✷ Adair started out as a Scottish form of Edgar, but its smooth sound soon made it an option for girls as well as boys. Today Adair exudes confidence and sophistication as a girl's name. It still maintains an androgynous edge, but without mimicking boys' names.

Addison (A-di-sən) 2007: #11
Popularity: #13
Styles: Last Names First, Androgynous, The "-ens"
Nicknames: Addie 1880 Today
Variants: Addisyn, Addyson
Sisters: Emerson, Aubrey, Peyton, Riley, Finley, Carrigan, Mackenzie, Kendall
Brothers: Landon, Jackson, Brody, Cooper, Grayson, Carter, Brayden, Parker
✷ The newly feminine name Addison is a direct descendant of the super-hit Madison and close kin to old friend Allison. It's new yet familiar, a comfortable kind of innovation. Credit a *Grey's Anatomy* character for making Addison's transition from boyish to girly a quick one. Spelling variants like Addyson take the name in an even girlier direction.
In the World: Addison Montgomery of *Grey's Anatomy*

Adela (ah-DEH-lə) 1889: #454
Popularity: #1462
Styles: Lacy and Lissome, Antique Charm, Saints, Latino/Latina, Why Not? 1880 Today
Nicknames: Addie, Del
Variants: Adele, Adelia
Sisters: Flora, Rosalia, Adriana, Leora, Amalia, Viola, Evelyn, Delia
Brothers: Hugo, Roman, Julius, Edgar, Albin, Diego, Adrian, Rafael
✷ Check it out: a quaint, pretty, turn-of-the-century name that nobody's using. Say it out loud a few times; that soft, lilting sound feels nice, doesn't it? Adela could be a star in waiting, if celebrity-fueled sister Adele doesn't get there first.
In the World: Actress Adela Noriega

Adelaide (A-də-layd) 1884: #181
Popularity: #407
Styles: Ladies and Gentlemen, Saints, Antique Charm, Place Names 1880 Today
Nicknames: Addie, Ada, Della
Variants: Adelheid, Adelaida
Sisters: Josephine, Sadie, Annalise, Daphne, Aurelia, Daisy, Genevieve, Louisa
Brothers: August, Hugh, Porter, Charley, Felix, Everett, Theo, Oscar
✷ Adelaide is an adventurous revival with a stand-alone sound. It's antique and delicate-sounding, yet the best-known Adelaide is a cheeky dame from *Guys and Dolls*, and an Australian city gives it a down-under spin. Addie is pure cuteness for a little girl.
In the World: Australian city; Miss Adelaide of *Guys and Dolls*

Adele (ah-DEHL) 1914: #187
Popularity: #627
Styles: Ladies and Gentlemen, French
Nicknames: Del, Della, Addie 1880 Today
Variants: Adela
Sisters: Leona, Estelle, Camille, Marion, Flora, Geneva, Nola, Corinne
Brothers: Jules, Laurence, Emory, Forest, Willis, Louis, Clayton, Elliott
✷ Adele was just a quiet, respectable, mostly overlooked name . . . until *she* came along. The one-named singer Adele took the world by storm starting in 2011. Along the way, she infused this name with her soulful retro vibe.
In the World: Singer Adele; dancer Adele Astaire; a daughter of actress Molly Ringwald

Adeline (A-də-liyn) 1914: #166
Popularity: #288
Styles: Ladies and Gentlemen, Antique Charm
Nicknames: Addie, Ada 1880 Today
Variants: Adele, Adelina, Adaline
Sisters: Vivian, Eleanora, Lucille, Georgia, Josephine, Violet, Eloise, Annabelle
Brothers: Julius, Everett, Cyrus, Theodore, Leopold, Porter, Solomon, Maxwell
✷ "Sweet Adeline" used to be strictly for barbershop quartets, but the popularity of Madeline has eased her back into style. The name is still old-fashioned, but in an "aw, cute" way. Despite its formal looks, Adeline started out as a nickname, a French pet form of Adele.
In the World: Song "Sweet Adeline"

Adelyn (A-də-lin) 2011: #300
Popularity: #300
Styles: The "-ens"
Nicknames: Addie, Lyn
Variants: Adalyn, Adalynn,
Adelynn, Adeline

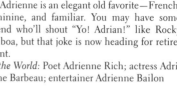

Sisters: Gracelyn, Brielle, Audrina, Emery, Raegan, Marlee, Lilah, Emmaline
Brothers: Landyn, Nolan, Jacoby, Paxton, Beckett, Archer, Madden, Grady
✸ First parents took a little off the top of Madison and uncovered the hit name Addison. Soon creative namers started giving the same new 'do to the more conservative sister in the Maddie family, Madelyn. If you prefer, though, you can call Adelyn a form of Adeline. (If you're looking for an uncommon name, you should know that the spelling Adalyn is equally popular, and double-"n" spellings are right behind them.)

Adina (ah-DEE-nə) 1974: #1007
Popularity: #1700
Styles: Biblical, Lacy and
Lissome, Jewish
Nicknames: Addie, Dina
Variants: Adinah
Sisters: Ilana, Shira, Aviva, Yael, Ariela, Atara, Delia, Risa
Brothers: Ari, Elan, Joah, Tobias, Doron, Asher, Coby, Noam
✸ This pretty Old Testament name is extremely uncommon yet feels timeless. It's a good choice to cross borders of language and style.
In the World: Actress Adina Porter; Rossini opera *Adina*

Adriana (ah-dree-AH-nə;
ay-dree-A-nə) 2006: #106
Popularity: #132
Styles: Lacy and Lissome,
Shakespearean, Latino/
Latina, Italian, New Classics
Nicknames: Dree, Adi, Ada
Variants: Adrianna, Adrian, Adrienne
Sisters: Gabriela, Liliana, Valeria, Miranda, Giovanna, Alessandra, Giselle, Natalia
Brothers: Raphael, Antonio, Leonardo, Emmanuel, Dominic, Alejandro, Quentin, Orlando
✸ This old feminine form of Adrian is a completely modern hit. It touches all the bases: antique and literary, Italian and sultry. Adriana's the name for a supermodel you can take home to Mom.
In the World: Model Adriana Lima; actress Adriana Barraza

Adrienne (ad-ree-EHN,
AYD-ree-ən) 1983: #140
Popularity: #669
Styles: French, New Classics,
African-American

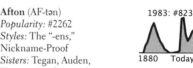

Nicknames: Dree, Adi, Ada
Variants: Adrianna, Adrian, Adrianne
Sisters: Danielle, Candice, Cristina, Simone, Meredith, Nicole, Julianne, Valerie
Brothers: Damon, Terrence, Nicholas, Derek, Andre, Christopher, Vincent, Geoffrey
✸ Adrienne is an elegant choice—French, feminine, and familiar. You may have some friend who'll shout "Yo! Adrian!" like Rocky Balboa, but that joke is now heading for retirement.
In the World: Poet Adrienne Rich; actress Adrienne Barbeau; entertainer Adrienne Bailon

Afton (AF-tən) 1983: #823
Popularity: #2262
Styles: The "-ens,"
Nickname-Proof
Sisters: Tegan, Auden,
Tierney, Marlowe, Adair,
Carson, Aislinn, Greer
Brothers: Eamon, Winslow, Sutton, Quinlan, Rhodes, Westley, Brennan, Locke
✸ Afton is a romantic, literary, old-fashioned girl's name, but it *sounds* like a contemporary androgynous invention. Intriguing combination, no? The name owes its romantic roots to Robert Burns's poem "Sweet Afton," about a river in Scotland.
In the World: Dozens of towns named Afton across the U.S.

Agatha (AG-ə-thə) 1899: #381
Popularity: #3201
Styles: Ladies and
Gentlemen, English
Nicknames: Aggie
Variants: Agata, Agathe
Sisters: Aurelia, Leonora, Wilhelmina, Agnes, Eudora, Winifred, Henrietta, Cordelia
Brothers: Horace, Edmund, Claude, Ambrose, Basil, Leopold, Godfrey, Clement
✸ Agatha is one of the weighty names long relegated to oil portraits of ancestors. It's still out on the fringes, but inching closer to consideration. As a middle name, it lightens up to sound pleasantly eccentric.
In the World: Mystery writer Agatha Christie; designer Ágatha Ruiz de la Prada

Name Snapshots: Girls **29**

Agnes (AG-nis) 1896: #38
Popularity: #2028
Styles: Porch Sitters
Nicknames: Aggie, Nessie
Variants: Inez, Inès, Annis 1880 Today
Sisters: Ida, Gladys, Viola,
Ethel, Hazel, Edna, Adele, Edith
Brothers: Otis, Homer, Archie, Edgar, Floyd,
Cyril, Claude, Luther
✳ It's hard for us to imagine the world in which
Agnes was a trendy, glamorous choice for a little
girl. For decades now it's been the most unfash-
ionable classic around. That hard "g" is like a
speed bump in the middle of the name. Some
parents feel that adds character, but if you're
looking for a smoother ride, you could try the
medieval form Annis or the French-styled pronunciation "ahn-yehs."
In the World: Dancer Agnes de Mille; currently
popular in Scandinavia

Aida (iy-EE-də, AY-də, IY-də) 2005: #1003
Popularity: #1504
Styles: Exotic Traditional,
Nickname-Proof, Literary
and Artistic 1880 Today
Variants: Ayda, Ada, Ida
Sisters: Lyra, Daria, Athena, Isis, Zara, Luz,
Asha, Mari
Brothers: Dante, Antony, Soren, Yannick,
Dorian, Tobin, Orlando, Taj
✳ Aida was the tragic heroine of Verdi's Egyp-
tian opera, and her name perfectly captures the
artful exoticism of the work. In the U.S., Aida
has usually been pronounced as two syllables,
an alternative spelling of Ida or Ada. The three-
syllable operatic pronunciation is more distinc-
tive and will be seen as more "correct" by opera
buffs.
In the World: Verdi opera *Aida;* Elton John/Tim
Rice musical based on the same story

Ailsa (AYL-sə) 2010: #6583
Popularity: #9095
Styles: Celtic, Nickname-
Proof, Why Not?
Sisters: Iona, Mirren, Maisie, 1880 Today
Sorcha, Skye, Marsaili,
Fiona, Isla
Brothers: Callum, Ewan, Graeme, Fraser,
Ramsay, Gregor, Struan, Keir
✳ The rocky isle of Ailsa Craig ("fairy rock")
lies in the channel between Scotland and
Northern Ireland. In Scotland, Ailsa has be-
come a familiar girl's name. In the U.S., unfa-
miliarity is one of its many virtues. It's
distinctive, Celtic, and easily pronounceable,
with a sound on the wildly stylish border be-
tween fashionable and quaint.

Aine (AWN-yə) 2003: #2438
Popularity: #3382
Styles: Celtic, Mythological
Variants: Áine, Anya
Sisters: Aiofe, Niamh, Oona, 1880 Today
Ariadne, Riona, Caoimhe,
Maeve, Sian
Brothers: Fionn, Oisin, Niall, Ruari, Colm,
Cormac, Cathal, Eoin
✳ Áine was the queen of the fairies in Celtic
mythology, and the name still sounds perfect for
a charming sprite. It's a favorite in contempo-
rary Ireland.
In the World: Name of several queens of medi-
eval Ireland

Ainsley (AYNZ-lee) 2011: #363
Popularity: #363
Styles: Last Names First,
Celtic, Bell Tones
Variants: Ainslee, Ansley 1880 Today
Sisters: Finley, Kendall,
Mckenna, Teagan, Briley, Madigan, Ellery,
Aubrey
Brothers: Keegan, Brodie, Kieran, Easton,
Brogan, Kane, Jacoby, Finnegan
✳ Ainsley is taken from an old Scottish sur-
name and was traditionally used more for boys
than girls. The name has taken off in the U.S.,
where it has become exclusively feminine. The
strong "A" sound is the big draw, a feminine
counterpart to Aidan.
In the World: TV news reporter Ainsley Ear-
hardt

Aisha (iy-EE-shə) 1977: #175
Popularity: #633
Styles: Muslim, African-
American
Nicknames: Isha 1880 Today
Variants: Iesha, Ayesha
Sisters: Jamila, Salima, Ayana, Tanisha,
Yasmin, Zahra, Safiya, Latifa
Brothers: Jamal, Kareem, Ahmad, Raheem,
Tariq, Sharif, Khalid, Rashad
✷ The name of Mohammed's favorite wife,
Aisha is a classic throughout the Muslim world.
Its sound is the prototype for African-American
standards like Lakeisha.
In the World: Actress Aisha Tyler

Aisling (ASH-ling, 2002: #2552
ASH-lin, AYZ-lin)
Popularity: #3117
Styles: Celtic
Nicknames: Ash 1880 Today
Variants: Ashling, Ashlyn,
Aislinn
Sisters: Ciara, Aine, Taryn, Caitlin, Alannah,
Niamh, Orla, Ainsley
Brothers: Ronan, Ciaran, Aidan, Liam, Niall,
Finlay, Eoghan, Conor
✷ Aisling is a modern Irish Gaelic name
coined from a word for "vision" or "dream." It's
been a top-50 name in Ireland for years but is
still unfamiliar to most Americans. So let's cut
to the chase: how do you pronounce it? As with
many Gaelic names, it all depends on which
part of Ireland you're from. Choose your favorite
from the variations listed above.

Alana (ah-LAH-nə) 2007: #143
Popularity: #186
Styles: Lacy and Lissome,
New Classics
Nicknames: Lani, Ali, Lana 1880 Today
Variants: Alanna, Alannah,
Alaina, Alayna
Sisters: Leila, Nadia, Fiona, Sienna, Malia,
Ariel, Talia, Maya
Brothers: Ronan, Asher, Eamon, Myles, Austin,
Judah, Colin, Liam
✷ This attractive invention is as sweet and fluid
as caramel syrup. It has such a natural feminin-
ity that it fits in comfortably with older classics.
The variant Alannah is especially popular in
Ireland, where it is taken from the Gaelic en-
dearment *a leanbh*, meaning "O child."
In the World: Actress Alana de la Garza; Alanna
of Trebond, a female knight in "The Song of the
Lioness" series

Alessandra 2006: #361
(ah-leh-SAHN-drə)
Popularity: #397
Styles: Italian, Lacy and
Lissome 1880 Today
Nicknames: Sandra, Sandy,
Alex, Allie, Lessa
Variants: Alejandra, Lisandra, Alessandria,
Alexandra
Sisters: Viviana, Francesca, Annabella, Liliana,
Cassandra, Daniella, Adrianna, Gabriella
Brothers: Matteo, Luca, Giovanni, Luciano,
Dante, Armando, Marco, Lorenzo
✷ This Italian classic is every bit as lush as the
familiar Russian form Alexandra. It just swaps
out snowy vistas for Mediterranean sunshine.
Alejandra is the popular Spanish version.
In the World: Italian ballerina Alessandra Ferri;
Brazilian model Alessandra Ambrosio

Alethea (ah-LEE-thee-ə, 1973: #522
ah-leh-THEE-ə)
Popularity: #4436
Styles: English, Lacy and
Lissome, Exotic Traditional 1880 Today
Nicknames: Thea, Lee
Variants: Alathea, Aletheia
Sisters: Liviana, Evangeline, Amabel, Charis,
Ophelia, Araminta
Brothers: Barnaby, Augustus, Emmanuel,
Tarquin, Caedmon, Aidric
✷ The closest match for Alethea isn't another
name, it's a word: "ethereal." This name isn't a
flight of fancy, though. It's an old, aristocratic
English name from the days when learned folk
would coin romantic girls' names from Greek
and Latin roots. (*Aletheia* is Greek for "truth.")
The passage of centuries has only burnished
that romantic glow.

Alexa (ah-LEHK-sə) 2006: #39
Popularity: #55
Styles: Lacy and Lissome
Nicknames: Lexi, Alex
Sisters: Violet, Ariana, 1880 Today
Jocelyn, Nadia, Ivy, Annika
Brothers: Austin, Zachary, Levi, Cole,
Maxwell, Gavin
✷ Alexa is a 20th-century invention that's built
like a classic. It first popped up in the '40s as a
glamorous, Hollywood-style creation akin to
Lana. It's still sleek, but powerful too—more
panther than kitten.
In the World: Singer Alexa Ray Joel (daughter of
Billy Joel and Christie Brinkley); the Internet
stats company Alexa

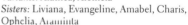
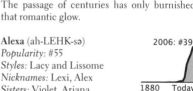

Name Snapshots: Girls 31

Alexandra (al-ik-ZAN-drə)   1993: #28
Popularity: #76
Styles: New Classics, Lacy
and Lissome, Slavic
Nicknames: Alex, Sandy,   1880   Today
Allie, Lexi, Sandra, Sasha,
Xander, Xandra, Shura
Variants: Aleksandra, Alexandria, Alejandra,
Alessandra
Sisters: Miranda, Natalia, Sophia, Charlotte,
Vanessa, Tatiana, Anastasia, Victoria
Brothers: Nicholas, Zachary, Julian, Sebastian,
Trevor, Maxwell, Gabriel, Nathaniel
✶Alexandra is the classic, regal, feminine
form of Alexander. The name is a relative new-
comer to English, and its roots in Russia and
Scandinavia add a luxurious hint of fur muffs
and winter palaces. The standard nicknames,
though, are decidedly American and down-to-
earth. If you prefer a Russian style, try Sasha or
Shura.
In the World: Centuries of Princess Alexandras
throughout Europe

Alexandria (al-ik-ZAN-dree-ə)   1993: #69
Popularity: #205
Styles: Lacy and Lissome,
Place Names, Turn of the 21st
Century   1880   Today
Nicknames: Alex, Lexi, Andi,
Sandy, Xander
Variants: Alexandrea
Sisters: Sierra, Christiana, Savannah, Marissa,
Angelica, Victoria, Cassandra, Arielle
Brothers: Trenton, Dakota, Austin, Charleston,
Devin, Jackson, Jericho, Trevor
✶Riding high on two trends, Alexandria takes
the popular "Alex-" root and turns it into a place
name. If you choose this five-syllable sensation,
be sure to choose a nickname too.
In the World: Cities around the world, including
in Egypt and Virginia; Miss World Alexandria
Mills

Alexia (ah-LEHKS-ee-ə)   2002: #128
Popularity: #275
Styles: Turn of the 21st
Century
Nicknames: Lexi, Alex, Xia   1880   Today
Variants: Alexea, Alessia
Sisters: Natalia, Juliana, Annika, Jasmine,
Livia, Avery, Giselle, Viviana
Brothers: Devin, Chance, Xavier, Parker,
Darius, Adrian, Jonas, Quinn
✶This feminine form of Alexis has taken off
around the world. It's a name you choose for
style rather than meaning. For what it's worth,
though, alexia (like amnesia or dyslexia) is a
neurological condition: loss of the ability to
read. Didn't know that? Don't worry, most peo-
ple your daughter meets won't either. Alessia is
a smooth Italian version of the name.
In the World: Italian singer Alexia (birth name
Alessia); Princess Alexia of the Netherlands

Alexis (ah-LEHK-sis)   1998: #6
Popularity: #26
Styles: Androgynous, Saints,
Turn of the 21st Century
Nicknames: Lexi, Alex   1880   Today
Variants: Alexys
Sisters: Chloe, Taylor, Paris, Marina, Alyssa,
Morgan, Sydney, Aubrey
Brothers: Connor, Landon, Aidan, Dylan,
Carter, Adrian, Darius, Mason
✶Alexis, a male name from ancient Greece,
used to be a sophisticated, unconventional
choice for American boys and girls. Then, in
1981, *Dynasty*'s female villain Alexis Car-
rington blew it wide open. The name is still as
attractive as ever, crackling and elegant. Its un-
conventional edge, though, is long gone.
In the World: Actress Alexis Bledel; Alexis Carrington of *Dynasty*

Alice (A-lis)   1880: #8
Popularity: #142
Styles: Antique Charm,
Ladies and Gentlemen
Nicknames: Allie, Elsie, Lisa   1880   Today
Variants: Alys, Alyce, Ailish,
Alicia, Alix, Alison
Sisters: Clara, Esther, Rose, Lucy, Anne,
Beatrice, Lydia, Grace
Brothers: Henry, Theodore, Julius, Leo,
Charlie, Oscar, Louis, George
✱This plain but charming classic is finally re-
turning after decades on the sidelines. The
image of diner waitresses and long-suffering
housewife Alice Kramden of *The Honeymoon-
ers* is disappearing. Now parents are rediscover-
ing the sweet enchantment of *Alice in
Wonderland*. The name has come back stron-
gest in the tony urban neighborhoods where
Lucy and Henry are hits.
In the World: Lewis Carroll's *Alice's Adventures
in Wonderland*; '70s sitcom *Alice*

Alicia (ə-LEE-shə,   1984: #40
ah-LEE-cee-ə)
Popularity: #259
Styles: Lacy and Lissome,
Latino/Latina, '70s–'80s,   1880   Today
Turn of the 21st Century
Nicknames: Ali, Licha
Variants: Alisha, Alecia, Alesha, Alycia, Elisha
Sisters: Marisa, Amanda, Nicole, Cassandra,
Jessica, Cristina
Brothers: Bryan, Andrew, Travis, Rafael, Justin,
Bradley
✱This Spanish form of Alice is decorous and
delicate, but choosing it is a lot like marrying
into a big family. Thousands of sound-alike Ale-
shas, Elishas, and Alycias come with the bar-
gain.
In the World: Singers Alicia Keys and Alicia Vil-
larreal; actresses Alicia Silverstone and Alicia
Witt

Alina (ah-LEE-nə)   2007: #193
Popularity: #265
Styles: Lacy and Lissome,
German and Dutch, Slavic
Variants: Elina, Alena,   1880   Today
Aleena
Sisters: Mira, Larissa, Anika, Marina, Katya,
Tatiana, Lilia
Brothers: Lukas, Barrett, Darian, Dominik,
Ari, Roman, Fabian
✱Alina slides smoothly into many guises. In
the right context, it can sound sensual, sophisti-
cated, or cheerfully girlish. It's used in several
different languages and can fit in anywhere.
Alina-with-an-A is generally taken to be a short
form of names like Adelina, while the similar
name Elina is a form of Helen, popular in Swe-
den and Finland.
In the World: Ballet dancers Alina Cojocaru and
Alina Somova

Alisa (ah-LEE-sə)   1970: #265
Popularity: #1016
Styles: Lacy and Lissome,
Slavic, Surfer '60s, '70s–'80s
Nicknames: Allie, Lise   1880   Today
Variants:
Sisters: Melanie, Andrea, Holly, Deanna,
Stacy, Lara
Brothers: Timothy, Brian, Andrew, Bradley,
Shawn, Jeffrey
✱The old standby Alice has many modern de-
scendants. Alisa is the brightest and cheeriest of
the lot, with a classic sound. See also Elisa,
which is similar-sounding but has a separate
origin.

Allegra (ah-LEHG-rə)   1997: #1192
Popularity: #2418
Styles: Lacy and Lissome,
Jewish, Exotic Traditional
Nicknames: Allie   1880   Today
Variants: Alegra
Sisters: Dalia, Aviva, Linnea, Zara, Charis,
Talia
Brothers: Asher, Gideon, Hugo, Noam, Roman,
Ari
✱Allegra is a dynamic choice, joyously femi-
nine and ready to take on the world. It's kin to
the Italian *allegro* ("cheerful") and was a popu-
lar choice of Sephardic Jews. One word of cau-
tion, though: it's also the name of an allergy
medicine, which could dismay some of the
sneezier members of your family.
In the World: Writer Allegra Goodman

Allie (A-lee)   1889: #145
Popularity: #198
Styles: Nicknames
Variants: Ally, Ali
Sisters: Cassie, Megan,   1880 Today
Gracie, Emma, Abby, Maddie
Brothers: Jake, Ryan, Drew, Austin, Evan, Andy
★ Allie is a particularly flexible nickname. It can be used as a diminutive for many different names, from offbeat antiques to ultra-modern creations. (Take a peek at the "Nicknames" section for ideas.) That gives Allie a timeless style that's not overly girlish. As a given name, it's cheerful and unpretentious.
In the World: TV shows *Ally McBeal* and *Kate and Allie;* actresses Ali Larter, Ali Landry, and Ali MacGraw

Allison (AL-i-sən)   1995: #34
Popularity: #40
Styles: New Classics
Nicknames: Allie, Ally
Variants: Alison, Allyson,   1880 Today
Alyson
Sisters: Lauren, Vanessa, Natalie, Jocelyn, Erin, Andrea, Jillian, Brooke
Brothers: Brandon, Zachary, Sean, Matthew, Ryan, Aaron, Justin, Evan
★ Alison looks like a surname, but it has always been a girl's given name. (It started off centuries ago as a French nickname for Alice.) Along the way, it merged with the English surname Allison. Today, with its multiple popular spellings, the name has left Alice in the dust and established itself as an American classic.
In the World: Actress Allison Janney; musician Alison Krauss

Alma (AHL-mə, AL-mə)   1894: #52
Popularity: #878
Styles: Ladies and
Gentlemen, Nickname-Proof,
Latino/Latina, German and   1880 Today
Dutch, Why Not?
Sisters: Vera, Elsa, Lena, Edith, Adela, Cora, Rhea
Brothers: Edgar, August, Louis, Casper, Anton, Conrad, Leon
★ Alma is the Spanish and Italian word for "soul," and thinking of it that way helps tip the name's style balance from fusty to warm and compassionate. It has other positive associations too, like a Latin goddess title meaning "nurturing" or "nourishing." Yet the name's first wave of popularity was sparked by a 19th-century battle (the one and only thing Alma has in common with Kimberly).
In the World: Singer Alma Cogan; socialite/muse Alma Mahler; the phrase "alma mater" (the school you graduated from)

Alondra (ah-LAHN-drə,   2005: #120
ah-LOHN-drə)
Popularity: #248
Styles: Latino/Latina
Nicknames: Lonnie   1880 Today
Variants: Alandra
Sisters: Adriana, Mariana, Julissa, Esmeralda, Natalia, Ximena, Fernanda, Perla
Brothers: Cesar, Fernando, Andres, Cristian, Omar, Adrian, Enrique, Armando
★ This glossy hit is Spanish for "lark." It's luxurious to pronounce—the name you want for an intimate evening on a moonlit beach. A huge favorite in Puerto Rico.
In the World: Conductor Alondra de la Parra

Althea (ahl-THEE-ə) 1920: #357
Popularity: #2515
Styles: Ladies and
Gentlemen, Mythological,
Why Not? 1880 Today
Nicknames: Thea
Variants: Althaea, Althaia
Sisters: Geneva, Carmela, Flora, Ione, Rosalia,
Leora, Avis, Eudora
Brothers: Jules, Foster, Truman, Willis,
Rudolph, Julius, Rex, Atticus
✳A cozy antique with origins in Greek my-
thology, Althea stands at the avant-garde of baby
name style for artists and PhDs. Americans
often identify the name with groundbreaking
African-American tennis star Althea Gibson.
The alternative spellings emphasize the name's
mythological roots.
In the World: Tennis player Althea Gibson;
Greatful Dead song "Althea"

Alyssa (ah-LI-sə) 1999: #11
Popularity: #37
Styles: Lacy and Lissome,
Turn of the 21st Century
Nicknames: Aly, Lissa 1880 Today
Variants: Alissa, Allyssa,
Alysa, Elissa
Sisters: Brianna, Alexis, Sydney, Marissa,
Arianna, Hayley, Jasmine
Brothers: Jordan, Austin, Devon, Javier, Dillon,
Tyler, Chase
✳Alyssa and its many variants are generally
described as variants of Alicia. They're better
understood as a phenomenon in their own
right—an attempt to capture the very essence of
lacy femininity in a name. The less traditional
the spelling, the lacier the effect.
In the World: Actress Alyssa Milano; figure
skater Alissa Czisny

Amanda (ah-MAN-də) 1987: #3
Popularity: #226
Styles: '70s–'80s, Lacy and
Lissome
Nicknames: Mandy, Manda 1880 Today
Sisters: Nicole, Jessica, Alicia,
Stephanie, Melissa, Andrea
Brothers: Jeremy, Andrew, Sean, Justin, Casey,
Aaron
✳Amanda is one of the picturesque Latinate
names that English writers used to dream up for
their heroines. (It's from the Latin for "lov-
able.") These old literary romantics have a dou-
ble appeal today. They're still ravishing, but by
surviving the centuries they've also developed
an air of authority. Amanda has become a global
name, used in many languages.
In the World: Actresses Amanda Seyfried,
Amanda Peet, and Amanda Bynes; rock musician Amanda Palmer

Amani (ah-MAH-nee) 2011: #560
Popularity: #560
Styles: African-American,
African, Muslim,
Androgynous 1880 Today
Nicknames: Mani
Sisters: Ayanna, Nia, Aliyah, Zuri, Kamaria,
Deja, Kenia, Safiya
Brothers: Jabari, Ahmad, Mekhi, Jelani, Taj,
Dakari, Kofi, Asante
✳Amani is taken from the Swahili word for
"peace." It first arrived in the U.S. as a boy's
name during the wave of Afrocentric names in
the 1970s. The name's delicate sound moved it
to the girls' side, where it has kept its momen
tum.
In the World: Football player Amani Toomer

Amaya (ah-MIY-ə) 2003: #181
Popularity: #210
Styles: Lacy and Lissome, Latino/Latina
Variants: Amaia, Amya
Sisters: Raina, Ariana, Mariah, Anahi, Galilea, Eliana
Brothers: Adan, Gael, Lukas, Cade, Rylan, Cruz
★Amaya is a Spanish surname with a honey-rich sound that's a natural for a girl's name. It comes from a Basque word meaning "end." If you don't care for that origin, it's also a Japanese name meaning "night rain." That's a good hint that this name crosses borders well. An MTV *Real World* cast member helped launch the name in the U.S.
In the World: Fashion designer Amaya Arzuaga; *Real World* personality Amaya Brecher

Amber (AM-ber) 1986: #13
Popularity: #260
Styles: '70s–'80s, Charms and Graces, Nickname-Proof
Sisters: Heather, Crystal, Amanda, Brittany, April, Summer
Brothers: Brandon, Travis, Corey, Heath, Eric, Shane
★Amber was occasionally heard a century ago when jewel names were in vogue. It really took off decades later thanks to the romantic novel *Forever Amber*, a mid-century sensation. As a result, the name's image is satin-and-lace sensual.
In the World: Actresses Amber Tamblyn, Amber Heard, and Amber Riley; models Amber Rose and Amber Valletta; AMBER alerts for abducted children

Amelia (ah-MEEL-ee-ə) 2011: #30
Popularity: #30
Styles: Antique Charm, English, Shakespearean
Nicknames: Amy, Mia, Mel, Lia, Millie
Variants: Aemilia, Amélie, Amalia, Emilia
Sisters: Sophia, Charlotte, Julia, Evelyn, Caroline, Lydia
Brothers: Oliver, Alexander, Emmett, Jasper, Owen, Henry
★Amelia was a shrinking violet for years, but now she's ready for her close-up. Parents are attracted to this gentle charmer as a twist on Emily or kindred spirit to Olivia. The up-and-coming nickname choice is Mia, as in the heroine of Meg Cabot's "Princess Diaries" books.
In the World: Aviator Amelia Earhart; "Amelia Bedelia" storybooks; "Amelia Peabody" mysteries

America (ah-MEHR-i-kə) 2002: #410
Popularity: #811
Styles: Modern Meanings, Place Names
Nicknames: Meri, Amy, Ricki
Sisters: Anastasia, Liberty, Miracle, Catalina, Sierra, Cielo
Brothers: Justice, Maverick, Abel, Phoenix, Alonso, Orion
★A combination of the craze for place names and a surge of patriotism sent this name into the mainstream in 2001. But the same power that attracts parents to the name makes it a challenge. The word "America" carries such a strong image that it takes a strong girl to make it her own. *Ugly Betty* star America Ferrera is one who has pulled it off.
In the World: Actress America Ferrera

Amira (ah-MEER-ə) 2008: #435
Popularity: #503
Styles: Lacy and Lissome, Jewish, Muslim
Nicknames: Mira, Mia, Mimi
Sisters: Aviva, Zaria, Mariam, Ariela, Ilana, Nadia
Brothers: Jaron, Ahmad, Eitan, Adin, Elijah, Zain
★This gentle name is a good global choice, easy to spell and pronounce in many languages. The name in fact has twin origins in Arabic and Hebrew, a peaceful coexistence that is a positive association in its own right.

Amity (AM-i-tee)   1979: #1125
Popularity: #4898
Styles: Charms and Graces,
Why Not?
Nicknames: Ami   1880   Today
Sisters: January, Melody,
Lavender, Tuesday, Avalon, Verity
Brothers: Storm, Heath, Tobin, Brecken,
Tanner, Leif
✳ Amity is rarely used as a name, but it's attractive in both sound and meaning—a pretty expression of goodwill. The one potential negative, *The Amityville Horror*, is blessedly fading from memory.

Amy (AY-mee)   1975: #2
Popularity: #143
Styles: Surfer '60s, '70s–'80s,
Nickname-Proof
Variants: Aimee, Amie   1880   Today
Sisters: Kelly, April, Stacy,
Tara, Christine, Julie, Robin, Holly
Brothers: Adam, Timothy, Brian, Eric, Jeffrey,
Kevin, Patrick, Scott
✳ Amy is bright, simple, and cheerily unpretentious. It was a monster hit in the '70s but doesn't sound dated. Think of the name's recent decline as merely a "stock market correction" back to its natural place as a modest, beloved classic. The French Aimee is equally traditional but showier.
In the World: Actresses Amy Adams, Amy Poehler, and Amy Irving; singers Amy Winehouse and Amy Grant; writer Amy Tan

Anaïs (a-niy-EES)   2006: #871
Popularity: #1415
Styles: French, Literary and
Artistic
Nicknames: Aïs, Ani   1880   Today
Variants: Anais
Sisters: Mireille, Anouk, Axelle, Fleur, Isadora,
Charis, Maëlle, Ariane
Brothers: Amiel, Olivier, Silvan, Aramis,
Ciprian, Amadeus, Soren, Bastien
✳ This Provençal form of Anne is associated with Anaïs Nin, the writer famed for her diaries and erotic stories. For those familiar with Nin, the name projects a sensual feminism. Over the past generation it has become a common name in France.
In the World: Writer Anaïs Nin

Analía (ah-nah-LEE-ah)   2009: #330
Popularity: #950
Styles: Latino/Latina
Nicknames: Ana, Lia, Ani
Variants: Anali   1880   Today
Sisters: Ximena, Dayana,
Eliana, Camila, Estrella, Nayeli, Yuliana,
Amaya
Brothers: Adriel, Mateo, Joaquin, Gael, Adan,
Armando, Yahir, Emiliano
✳ The 2009 telenovela *El Rostro de Analía* made this name an overnight sensation. It's built of classic, familiar parts, but the liquid flow of the name makes the effect perfectly contemporary. The first four letters, though, are hard for some to look past. The anagram Aliana, which sidesteps that issue, is also rising.
In the World: Telenovela *El Rostro de Analía*

Anastasia (a-na-STAY-zhə,   1998: #265
ah-nah-STAH-see-ə)
Popularity: #371
Styles: Lacy and Lissome,
Slavic, Greek, Saints   1880   Today
Nicknames: Nastia, Ana,
Annie, Stasia, Stacy, Stasi, Natasa, Tasia,
Tasoula
Variants: Anastácia
Sisters: Tatiana, Alexandra, Valentina,
Stefania, Katerina, Natalia
Brothers: Nicholas, Dimitri, Raphael, Lucas,
Roman, Maximilian
✳ This Greek/Russian enchantress radiates mystery and romance. The legend of the lost Romanov princess Anastasia is a big reason, but the gossamer name is simply a natural for shadowy beauties. That fantasy aura has made the name Anastasia a popular choice for the likes of the erotic novel *Fifty Shades of Grey* and an "international dating" website, but the name remains classic and handsome.
In the World: Princess Anastasia Romanova; Anastasia Steele of *Fifty Shades of Grey*

Andrea (AN-dree-ə, AHN-dree-ə) 1981: #24
Popularity: #81
Styles: New Classics, Lacy and Lissome
Nicknames: Andy, Andi, Drea, Dre, Dea
Variants: Andra
Sisters: Melanie, Alison, Daniela, Miranda, Rebecca, Natalie
Brothers: Brian, Adam, Jonathan, Daniel, Matthew, Jeffrey
✳ Like its male counterpart Andrew, Andrea is a classic that holds up well across the generations. It's soft and melodic, with a serious core. The full name has grown up to sound mature and grounded, while Andi is perpetually youthful and the "D" nicknames are distinctly contemporary.
In the World: TV journalist Andrea Mitchell; comedian Andrea Martin

Angel (AYN-jəl) 2002: #110
Popularity: #216
Styles: Modern Meanings, African-American
Nicknames: Angie
Variants: Angelle
Sisters: Faith, Destiny, Summer, Nevaeh, Hope, Essence
Brothers: Chance, Cassiel, Justice, Sincere, Emmanuel, Prince
✳ After centuries of Angela, Angelica, and Angelina, American parents decided to cut to the chase. "My little girl is an angel, and I'm calling her one!" A loving appellation that walks a line between confident and cutesy.
In the World: A wide array of pop songs from every era

Angela (AN-jə-lə) 1975: #5
Popularity: #189
Styles: Surfer '60s, Latino/Latina, German and Dutch, Slavic
Nicknames: Angie, Ange
Variants: Angelia, Angel
Sisters: Monica, Sonya, Stephanie, Tamara, Melissa, Teresa
Brothers: Gregory, Mark, Steven, Andre, Bradley, Patrick
✳ For years, Angela was *the* way to name your daughter with a touch of heaven. Today the options have exploded. Half a dozen different "Angel" names are popular, and Heaven itself is now a common name. But Angela's still a hit, and it remains the most modest, enduring, global choice.
In the World: Actresses Angela Bassett and Angela Lansbury; German chancellor Angela Merkel; activist Angela Davis

Angelica (an-JEHL-ik-ə) 1996: #97
Popularity: #373
Styles: Lacy and Lissome, Latino/Latina
Nicknames: Angie, Ange
Variants: Angelique, Angelika, Angeliki
Sisters: Cassandra, Alexandria, Gabriela, Christina, Arielle, Maricela, Veronica, Adriana
Brothers: Quinton, Julio, Emmanuel, Dimitri, Raphael, Armando, Alexander, Xavier
✳ Is there such a thing as demure extravagance? If so, you're looking at it. Angelica is a flamboyant name with a modest heart. It has declined from its popularity peak but maintains a timeless sound.
In the World: Actress Anjelica Huston; Mexican entertainer Angélica María

Angelina (an-jə-LEE-nə)   2005: #43
Popularity: #104
Styles: Antique Charm, Lacy
and Lissome
Nicknames: Angie, Lina,   1880   Today
Nina
Variants: Angeline, Angelia
Sisters: Juliana, Lorelai, Annabella, Natalia,
Arianna, Isabella
Brothers: Christian, Anthony, Nicholas,
Tristan, Josiah, Sebastian
★This flowery, old-fashioned diminutive of
Angela was popularized by actress Angelina
Jolie. Among the younger set, it's also known as
a ballet-dancing mouse. The French version
Angeline has the quaintest sound in the Angel
name family.
In the World: Actress Angelina Jolie; Angelina
Ballerina

Aniston (A-nis-tən)   2011: #1298
Popularity: #1298
Styles: Last Names First, The
"–ens"
Nicknames: Annie, Ani   1880   Today
Variants: Anniston
Sisters: Madigan, Blakely, Ellery, Larkin,
Carrington, Leighton, Marlowe, Arden
Brothers: Pierson, Colson, Carver, Briggs,
Sutton, Flynn, Beckham, Langston
★Actress Jennifer Aniston's uncommon sur-
name makes for a strikingly modern update on
Allison. The spelling Anniston is equally popu-
lar, owing to the familiar "Ann-" root and the
beloved nickname Annie.
In the World: Actress Jennifer Aniston

Anita (ah-NEE-tə)   1958: #82
Popularity: #1296
Styles: Solid Citizens, Latino/
Latina, African-American
Nicknames: Nita, Ani   1880   Today
Sisters: Elaine, Donna,
Yvonne, Gloria, Gwen, Bernadette, Regina,
Connie, Patricia
Brothers: Glenn, Roger, Dale, Philip, Jerome,
Allen, Russell, Douglas
★This Spanish-accented variant of Anna be-
came an American standard beginning in the
1930s. Parents have since turned to fresher in-
ventions, but Anita's crisp, bright sound is still
pleasant and fashionable.
In the World: Singer Anita Baker; Vampire
Hunter Anita Blake; law professor/sexual harass-
ment accuser Anita Hill

Aniya (ah-NEE-ə)   2005: #261
Popularity: #414
Styles: African-American,
Lacy and Lissome
Nicknames: Niya, Ani   1880   Today
Variants: Aniyah
Sisters: Iyanna, Kimora, Samara, Kiana,
Sariah, Lyric, Brionna, Zariah
Brothers: Amari, Davion, Malakai, Braydon,
Semaj, Jamir, Jakari, Tayshaun
★Aniya is more than a name. It's a sound, a
moment, a whole style of its own. Multiple
spellings of not only Aniya but Janiyah, Sani-
yah, Taniyah, and Zaniyah have made Ameri-
ca's top-1000 list. You can start with almost any
sound, include the "h," or leave it off. No matter
how you customize it, you can feel confident
the name will be in style.

Anna (AN-ə, AHN-ə)   1885: #2
Popularity: #38
Styles: Timeless, Antique
Charm, Biblical
Nicknames: Annie, Nan,   1880   Today
Anya, Anoushka, Anke,
Anouk
Variants: Ana, Anne
Sisters: Julia, Catherine, Lydia, Eva, Sarah,
Elizabeth
Brothers: Joseph, Alexander, Benjamin,
Edward, Samuel, Thomas
★Anna takes the timeless simplicity of Ann,
adds an old-fashioned gentleness, and then tops
it off with a sophisticated continental sheen.
That's an irresistible combination to the afflu-
ent, educated parents who have made this name
one of their top choices.
In the World: Actresses Anna Paquin and Anna
Kendrick; Tolstoy's Anna Karenina; editor Anna
Wintour

Annabelle (AN-ə-behl)   2011: #111
Popularity: #111
Styles: Antique Charm
Nicknames: Anna, Annie,
Belle   1880 Today
Variants: Annabel, Anabel,
Annabella, Amabel
Sisters: Madeline, Sophie, Charlotte,
Josephine, Adeline, Juliet
Brothers: Miles, Oliver, Jonas, Gabriel, Owen,
Bennett
✷ Not so long ago, Isabelle was the the only
"belle" of the ball. Annabelle is catching up
fast. It offers a lot of the same old-fashioned
charm and cranks the sweetness up to 11. For
spellings, women seem to prefer Annabel, men
Annabelle.
In the World: Edgar Allan Poe poem "Annabel
Lee"; actress Annabella Sciorra

Annabeth (A-nə-behth)   2011: #2080
Popularity: #2081
Styles: Why Not?
Nicknames: Annie, Ann,
Abby   1880 Today
Sisters: Jessamyn, Adeline,
Felicity, Tamsin, Juniper, Mirabel, Julianna,
Emmaline
Brothers: Campbell, Tobias, Walker, Finnegan,
Gibson, Pierce, Miles, Gideon
✷ Hordes of young readers know Annabeth as
the female lead in the book series "Percy Jackson and the Olympians." The name is built
from such comfortable ingredients that it probably feels familiar. In fact, though, Annabeths
are very rare in real life. Perhaps that will
change as Percy Jackson fans grow up into parents.
In the World: Actress Annabeth Gish; Annabeth
Chase of the "Percy Jackson and the Olympians" books

Annalise (an-ə-LEES;   2010: #525
German pronunciation,
ahn-ə-LEEZ-ə)
Popularity: #555
Styles: Antique Charm, Why   1880 Today
Not?
Nicknames: Ann, Annie, Lise, Annelie
Variants: Anneliese, Annelise, Annalisa
Sisters: Mirabelle, Julianna, Charlotte, Felicity,
Emmeline, Helena, Katerina, Lisbeth
Brothers: Pierce, Dominic, Matthias, Gideon,
Drew, Tobias, Carsten, Maxwell
✷ This compound name has an Old World
charm that should win it many new admirers.
Annalise's rhythm makes it an attractive counterpoint to popular lacy antiques like Isabella—a
great choice for sister names with a similar feeling but distinctive sounds.
In the World: Actress Anneliese van der Pol

Anne (AN)   1915: #52
Popularity: #593
Styles: Timeless, Why Not?
Nicknames: Annie, Nancy,
Nan, Annette, Anouk   1880 Today
Variants: Ann, Anna
Sisters: Katherine, Rose, Susan, Margaret,
Elizabeth, Jane
Brothers: Philip, Lawrence, Richard, Ray,
Martin, Paul
✷ Anne is one of the all-time classic names for
girls, yet it's teetering on the brink of obscurity.
Parents are tossing aside Anne in favor of her
sister Anna, who offers a little more continental
panache. Don't be too hasty to abandon a classic. For all of you tempted by the likes of Rose
and Claire, how about giving this warm, soft,
and simple name another chance?
In the World: Holocaust chronicler Anne Frank;
Queen Anne Boleyn; Raggedy Ann; actress
Anne Hathaway

Annette (an-NEHT) 1960: #62
Popularity: #1183
Styles: Mid-Century, French
Nicknames: Annie, Nettie
Variants: Annetta 1880 Today

Sisters: Suzanne, Connie, Yvonne, Lynette, Donna, Jeannine
Brothers: Dean, Tony, Randall, Ken, Rod, Barry
✴Thanks to Annette Funicello, this name has one foot back in 1964, nestled on a beach blanket. Even without Frankie 'n' Annette, though, this name wouldn't find many takers today. French pet forms are out . . . but Slavic and Germanic pet forms are in. Try Anya or Anika.
In the World: Actress Annette Funicello; actress Annette Bening

Annie (AN-ee) 1881: #8
Popularity: #386
Styles: Nicknames, Antique Charm, Guys and Dolls
Variants: Ani 1880 Today
Sisters: Molly, Kate, Lillie, Stella, Lucy, Ruby
Brothers: Charlie, Joe, Ben, Harry, Max, Sam
✴Annie is a fun-loving name, full of life. The classic American Annies are all over the cultural map but linked by a lively unpredictability: Annie Oakley, Annie Hall, Little Orphan Annie. Annie can be a nickname for longer names of every description (see the "Nicknames" style section). By choosing it as a full name, you're making fun your #1 priority.
In the World: Musical Annie; shooter Annie Oakley; singer Annie Lennox; photographer Annie Leibovitz

Annika (AN-i-kə, AHN-i-kə) 2003: #284
Popularity: #506
Styles: Lacy and Lissome, Nordic
Nicknames: Annie 1880 Today
Variants: Anika, Anneke
Sisters: Karina, Sofia, Alana, Greta, Britta, Linnea, Ingrid, Elin
Brothers: Finn, Gunnar, Kai, Alex, Lukas, Tristan, Soren, Asher
✴This pet form of Anna has the sound of a modern invention but the reserved demeanor of a Nordic classic. You'll hear it in countries from Finland to the Netherlands. Many English speakers met the name through golfer Annika Sörenstam, a Stockholm native who is a good model for Annika's strength and grace. The spelling Anika is also a Hindi name popular with Indian-American families.
In the World: Golfer Annika Sörenstam; actress/ singer Anika Noni Rose

Antoinette (an-twah-NEHT) 1917: #170
Popularity: #2283
Styles: French, Ladies and Gentlemen, African-American

Nicknames: Toni, Netta, Ann, Tonya
Variants: Antonietta
Sisters: Marguerite, Angeline, Eloise, Delphine, Lucienne, Marceline
Brothers: Armand, Claude, Laurent, Bertrand, Frederic, Gustave
✴In America, this name sounds ornate, old-fashioned, and, above all, French. In France, it sounds . . . exactly the same. The elaborate old French classics are rare on both sides of the Atlantic right now, with simpler choices like Charlotte and Camille taking their places.
In the World: Queen Marie Antoinette

Name Snapshots: Girls 41

Antonia (an-TOH-nee-ə)   1996: #394
Popularity: #1055
Styles: Timeless, Italian,
Latino/Latina, Saints, Why
Not?   1880   Today
Nicknames: Toni, Tonia, Tia,
Toña
Variants: Antonella, Antonietta
Sisters: Helena, Marina, Louisa, Simone,
Veronica, Celeste, Lucia, Eva
Brothers: Victor, Roberto, Ivan, Nicholas,
Theo, Julian, Carlo, Vincent
✱This overlooked classic is a fashion-forward
choice. It shares many of the charms of Olivia
but trades in that name's delicate lace for plush
velvet. It's familiar but uncommon, with an old-
world soul.
In the World: Willa Cather novel *My Antonia*;
author Antonia Fraser

Anya (AHN-ya)   2009: #362
Popularity: #432
Styles: Lacy and Lissome,
Slavic, Short and Sweet, Why
Not?   1880   Today
Variants: Anja, Aanya, Anka
Sisters: Mila, Nika, Alina, Stasia, Nadya, Lani,
Katya, Raya
Brothers: Luka, Eli, Alexi, Ivan, Ari, Roman,
Nico, Lev
✱Anya offers a lot of punch in a small package.
In Russian, it's the pet form of Anna, and it
makes a gently exotic twist on that popular stan-
dard.
In the World: Singer Anya Marina; TV host
Anya Monzikova

April (AY-pril)   1980: #25
Popularity: #395
Styles: Charms and Graces,
'70s–'80s, Nickname-Proof
Variants: Avril   1880   Today
Sisters: Erin, Amber, Holly,
Jamie, Crystal, Shannon
Brothers: Shawn, Heath, Casey, Chad, Dustin,
Shane
✱In the '70s and '80s, April was a huge hit
name, while calendar companions May and
June were out of sight. The tide is ready to turn
the other way now, but you still won't go wrong
with April. Months, seasons, and even days all
remain comfortably in style for girls.
In the World: April Fools' Day; the phrase "April
showers"

Arabella (a-rə-BEH-lə,   2011: #335
ah-rə-BEH-lə)
Popularity: #335
Styles: Lacy and Lissome,
English, Antique Charm   1880   Today
Nicknames: Bella, Bell, Ari
Variants: Arabel, Arabelle
Sisters: Liviana, Beatrix, Verity, Anastasia,
Liliana, Aurelia, Georgiana
Brothers: Beckett, Pierson, Atticus, Tristan,
Matthias, Gideon, Anderson
✱This perfectly lovely creation has been a fa-
vorite in literature for centuries. It used to be
rare in the real world, but the rise of names like
Isabella and Annabella has raised its profile. It's
not exactly common, but definitely fashionable.
The variant Arabel is trim and elegant.

Aria (AH-ree-ə)   2011: #157
Popularity: #157
Styles: Lacy and Lissome,
Modern Meanings
Variants: Arya   1880   Today
Sisters: Amaya, Lyra,
Cadence, Sienna, Layla, Eden
Brothers: Silas, Tristan, Case, Dante, Soren,
Isaiah
✱Aria is Italian for "air." In opera, it refers to
an expressive solo. Translate that into a name
and you get a dramatic, artistic image with a
light, clean sound.
In the World: Aria Montgomery of *Pretty Little
Liars*; anime/manga series "Aria"

Ariadne (a-ree-AD-nee,   2011: #1328
ah-ree-AHD-nee)
Popularity: #1328
Styles: Mythological, Exotic
Traditional, Saints, Why Not?   1880   Today
Nicknames: Ari
Variants: Arianne, Arianna
Sisters: Athena, Evadne, Persephone, Artemis,
Hermione, Ione
Brothers: Lucius, Evander, Elias, Caedmon,
Apollo, Phineas
✱In Greek myth, Ariadne was the clever hero-
ine who gave her beloved Theseus a thread to
find his way out of the Labyrinth. In keeping
with the tale, Ariadne is a name that sounds
both romantic and intelligent. Ariadne also ap-
pears in Celtic mythology, which gives the
name a British Isles flavor.
In the World: Opera *Ariadne auf Naxos*; Ariadne
in *Inception*

Arianna (ah-ree-AH-nə) — 2010: #54
Popularity: #52
Styles: Lacy and Lissome,
Italian
Nicknames: Ari
Variants: Ariana, Ariane,
Aryanna, Ariadne
Sisters: Gabriella, Liliana, Valeria, Alessandra,
Giselle, Alexia, Gianna, Natalia
Brothers: Sebastian, Lucas, Gabriel, Dominic,
Tristan, Adrian, Antonio, Julian
✳ Ariana belongs to the satin-and-lace world of
ultra-feminine names. It's smooth, supple, and
surprisingly serious. It's also traditional—the
Italian form of Ariadne. The spelling Ariana is
equally popular.
In the World: Media executive Arianna Huffington; actress Ariana Grande

Ariel (AY-ree-əl, AH-ree-əl, — 1991: #66
ah-ree-EHL)
Popularity: #220
Styles: Shakespearean,
Jewish, Namesakes
Nicknames: Ari
Variants: Arielle, Ariela
Sisters: Talia, Avery, Miranda, Ilana, Noelle,
Sierra
Brothers: Micah, Damian, Bryce, Ian, Judah,
Asher
✳ Ariel is a name with two lives. It is a charming Shakespearean and Hebrew name—and it is
the name of Disney's *Little Mermaid*. Parents
who like the first association tend to be turned
off by the second, but if you don't mind the mermaids, Ariel remains ethereal and lovely.
In the World: Spirit Ariel in Shakespeare's *The
Tempest*; Disney's *Little Mermaid*

Ariela (ah-ree-EH-lə) — 2009: #1801
Popularity: #1924
Styles: Lacy and Lissome,
Jewish, Why Not?
Nicknames: Ari, Ella
Variants: Ariella
Sisters: Aviana, Melina, Shira, Allegra, Lilia,
Rafaela
Brothers: Gideon, Noel, Avi, Atticus, Noam,
Dario
✳ It just doesn't get much smoother than Ariela, a name like a spoonful of honey. It's a feminine elaboration on the Hebrew name Ariel that
sounds the same in many languages as it does in
English: uncommon but attractive. A good
cross-cultural choice.

Armani (ahr-MAH-nee) — 2011: #727
Popularity: #727
Styles: Fanciful, Androgynous
Nicknames: Mani
Sisters: Lexus, Arista, Unique,
Nautica, Charisma, Chanel
Brothers: Valentino, Adonis, Triton, Maximus,
Gianni, Aramis
✳ Before you dismiss this designer name as a
flight of fancy, remember that Tiffany wasn't
used as a first name 60 years ago either. Luxury
labels are a natural target for glamour seekers,
and Armani has been chosen for thousands of
girls and boys alike. Its popularity was boosted
by its resemblance to the African name Amani,
which is a good choice if you like the sound but
don't want the price tag showing.
In the World: Giorgio Armani fashion house

Artemisia (ahr-teh-MEE-zhə) — 2000: #11,791
Popularity: #16,960
Styles: Exotic Traditional,
Lacy and Lissome, Literary
and Artistic, Classical
Nicknames: Artie, Mimi,
Misa
Variants: Artemis
Sisters: Rosalba, Seraphina, Araminta,
Melisande, Silvana, Ariadne
Brothers: Tarquin, Barnabas, Peregrine,
Maximilian, Calix, Leander
✳ This ruffled wedding gown of a name hides
a serious streak beneath its frills. It's associated
with a warrior queen of ancient Greece and
with Italian baroque painter Artemisia Gentileschi. A nickname is a must.
In the World: Painter Artemisia Gentileschi

Arya (AHR-yə) — 2011: #711
Popularity: #711
Styles: Fantastical, Lacy and
Lissome, Short and Sweet
Variants: Aria
Sisters: Lyra, Zara, Eowyn,
Isla, Evolet, Ariela, Esme, Mila
Brothers: Niko, Draven, Axel, Case, Kian,
Ryker, Caspian, Ronan
✳ The fantasy epic *A Game of Thrones* and its
sequels take place in a different but familiar
world, with different but familiar name styles.
The name Arya is that fantasy world's crossover
hit. (It already existed in some real-world cultures, but hadn't caught on with U.S. parents.)
It's so smooth and trim that only a fellow fantasy
buff will guess at its otherworldly origins.
In the World: Arya Stark of *A Game of Thrones*

Ashanti (ah-SHAHN-tee)   2002: #115
Popularity: #1049
Styles: African-American,
African, Turn of the 21st
Century   1880   Today
Nicknames: Ash, Asha, Shanti
Variants: Asante
Sisters: Imani, Aaliyah, Malaika, Danisha,
Ajani, Shaniyah
Brothers: Jabari, Omari, Malik, Jamal, Bakari,
Mekhi
★An overnight sensation in 2002, singer
Ashanti jumped straight from the pop charts to
the name charts. The name's a natural, with its
jazzy sound and echoes of African history. To
some, though, it will sound like an ethnicity
rather than a name.
In the World: Singer Ashanti; the Ashanti peo-
ple of Ghana

Ashby (ASH-bee)   2011: #4213
Popularity: #4225
Styles: Last Names First,
Androgynous, Why Not?
Nicknames: Ash   1880   Today
Sisters: Amory, Alden,
Quincy, Laine, Berkeley, Channing, Larkin,
Ellery
Brothers: Kingston, Decker, Brooks, Brody,
Larson, Hogan, Patton, Rourke
★Ashby was once a fancy boy's name, taken
from an English surname/place name rooted in
the ash tree. All of that applies to Ashley too.
Ashley is now an all-American girl, but Ashby
still has some of its preppy surname flavor.

Ashley (ASH-lee)   1987: #2
Popularity: #42
Styles: '70s–'80s, Last Names
First
Nicknames: Ash   1880   Today
Variants: Ashleigh, Ashlie,
Ashlee, Ashly, Ashli
Sisters: Amber, Brittany, Heather, Kelsey,
Jessica, Courtney
Brothers: Brandon, Justin, Tyler, Ryan, Austin,
Corey
★The sudden, immense popularity of Ashley
in the '80s ushered in a whole generation of
names. School rosters are now packed full of
androgynous surnames with a dash of aristo-
cratic hauteur. Yet the grandmomma of them
all, Ashley, has been so widely used that it has
shed its patrician edge to become the girl next
door.
In the World: Actresses Ashley Judd, Ashley Tis-
dale, and Ashley Olsen

Ashlyn (ASH-lin)   2005: #126
Popularity: #171
Styles: The "-ens," Bell Tones
Nicknames: Ash
Variants: Ashlynn, Aisling   1880   Today
Sisters: Kylie, Brooklyn,
Alexia, Camryn, Payton, Mckenzie
Brothers: Landon, Bryson, Tucker, Keaton,
Rylan, Chance
★This little hit has been cooked up from the
top ingredients of the past generation. Take a
pinch of Ashley, a splash of Kaitlyn, and you've
got a pleasingly familiar concoction with a fresh
flavor. More mashups like Amberlyn and Grace-
lyn have been following in its wake. See also
Aisling.

Ashton (ASH-tən)   1986: #267
Popularity: #1050
Styles: Last Names First, The
"-ens," Androgynous
Nicknames: Ash   1880   Today
Variants: Ashtyn
Sisters: Tyler, Devon, Ansley, Chandler,
Camryn, Addison
Brothers: Peyton, Drake, Gavin, Tanner,
Chase, Brennan
★Like a successful TV show, Ashley has gen-
erated spin-offs. Androgynous Ashton recap-
tures Ashley's surname roots in a trendy
Madison-like style. The name was tilting hard
toward the feminine until actor Ashton Kutcher
tilted it back.

Asia (AY-zhə)   1997: #195
Popularity: #658
Styles: Place Names,
African-American,
Nickname-Proof, Turn of the   1880   Today
21st Century
Sisters: Sierra, Raven, Isis, Jasmine, Paris, Jade,
India
Brothers: Dante, Quinton, Amari, Phoenix,
Cairo, Fabian, Jericho
★Asia is the biggest of places, but a tidy little
name. The aura of the continent helps it feel
more ambitious than other similarly soft, petite
choices.
In the World: The continent; '80s rock band
Asia

Aspen (AS-pin)   2011: #519
Popularity: #519
Styles: Place Names, Country and Western, The "-ens," Charms and Graces, Nickname-Proof
Sisters: Willow, Skye, Haven, Rowan, Sedona, Linden
Brothers: Colton, River, Flint, Trace, Orion, Quinlan
✶Aspen has a crisp, boyish sound and the popular hooks of a nature name and a place name. Not just any place name, mind you, but a beautiful and glamorous mountain resort. It's certainly not a timeless name, but it's perfect for this moment.
In the World: Aspen, Colorado

Astrid (AS-trid)   2005: #936
Popularity: #1056
Styles: Nordic, Exotic Traditional, German and Dutch
Nicknames: Asta
Sisters: Greta, Dagny, Sigrid, Linnea, Freya, Tove, Elsa, Ingrid
Brothers: Anders, Gunnar, Axel, Stellan, Wolf, Torsten, Niels, Linus
✶A cool and funky Nordic classic, Astrid is playfully clunky, like thick-soled clogs. Swedish author Astrid Lindgren, creator of Pippi Longstocking, is a perfect model for the name's spirit.
In the World: Writer Astrid Lindgren; Astrid Hofferson of *How to Train Your Dragon*

Athena (ah-THEE-nə)   2011: #313
Popularity: #313
Styles: Exotic Traditional, Nickname-Proof, Mythological, Greek
Nicknames: Thena
Sisters: Ariadne, Thalia, Paloma, Aurora, Isis, Artemis
Brothers: Titus, Apollo, Ulysses, Orion, Justus, Andreaas
✶This is a real power name, as in lightning-bolts-from-the-sky powerful. The Greek goddess of wisdom and victory, Athena is finally getting her overdue consideration as an English given name. You can also try the more reserved Roman equivalent, Minerva.
In the World: Video game series "Athena"

Aubrey (AW-bree)   2011: #20
Popularity: #20
Styles: Last Names First, Androgynous
Nicknames: Bree
Variants: Aubrie, Aubree
Sisters: Marley, Addison, Avery, Sydney, Payton, Emery
Brothers: Easton, Parker, Bentley, Nolan, Blake, Mason
✶Aubrey is oh-so-close to Audrey, which almost persuades you it's a classic girl's name. In fact, it's one of the fancy boys' names that American parents used to associate with British prep school lads. Like many of those names, it has found new life on the girls' side. Next up: Chauncey?
In the World: Singer/reality TV personality Aubrey O'Day; (male) artist Aubrey Beardsley

Aubrianna (aw-bree-A-nə)   2011: #867
Popularity: #867
Styles: Lacy and Lissome
Nicknames: Aubri, Bree
Variants: Aubriana, Audrianna
Sisters: Miabella, Gracelyn, Abriella, Aviana, Janessa, Lilianna
Brothers: Davion, Xander, Mason, Kane, Brayden, Alexavier
✶The elegant old men's name Aubrey has become feminine thanks to its resemblance to the all-girl classic Audrey. For some parents, though, Aubrey isn't quite feminine enough. A growing number have added the suffix "-anna" to create a new name with a classic shape.

Audra (AW-drə)   1967: #246
Popularity: #1347
Styles: '70s–'80s, Ladies and Gentlemen, Nickname-Proof, Why Not?
Sisters: Sonia, Rosanna, Greta, Dionne, Theda, Candace
Brothers: Jarvis, Clinton, Luke, Brooks, Avery, Carsten
✶This pretty, old-fashioned name had its revival 25 years ahead of the pack. Audra is the only name you'll find in both the Ladies and Gentlemen and '70s–'80s categories. The result is a name that can fit with many different styles but truly stands alone.
In the World: Actresses Audra McDonald and Audra Lindley

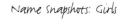

Audrey (AW-dree)   1928: #60
Popularity: #43
Styles: Timeless, Nickname-Proof
Variants: Audry, Audra   1880   Today
Sisters: Iris, Claire, Avery, Evelyn, Piper, Charlotte, Abigail, Vivian
Brothers: Calvin, Parker, Nolan, Jack, Carson, Elliot, Luke, Owen
✱ Back in the '30s, Audrey was a trendy choice alongside kindred spirits Shirley and Beverly. But Audrey had a clean, classic sound that never lost its luster. (Thanks surely go to actress Audrey Hepburn, who hasn't lost her luster either.) Today Audrey is a timeless alternative to fading favorites Ashley and Courtney.
In the World: Actresses Audrey Hepburn, Audrey Tautou, and Audrey Meadows; writer Audrey Niffenegger

Audrina (aw-DREE-nə)   2011: #318
Popularity: #318
Styles: Lacy and Lissome
Nicknames: Audri, Drina
Variants: Audriana   1880   Today
Sisters: Ariella, Addison, Felicity, Lilliana, Jaslene, Brielle
Brothers: Kingston, Jacoby, Jameson, Bentley, Donovan, Brogan
✱ For all that we talk about celebrity babies, the "ordinary" people of reality TV have tremendous name-style clout. When Audrina Patridge debuted on the series *The Hills*, she transformed this name from obscure and fusty to it-girl trendy.
In the World: TV personality Audrina Patridge

Augusta (aw-GUHST-ə)   1883: #108
Popularity: #4543
Styles: Ladies and Gentlemen, Saints, Place Names, Classical, Exotic Traditional   1880   Today
Nicknames: Gussie, Gus
Sisters: Aurelia, Octavia, Viola, Agatha, Magnolia, Georgiana, Emeline, Cordelia
Brothers: Ulysses, Ambrose, Richmond, Cornelius, Lucian, Clement, Merritt, Bartholomew
✱ Augusta is one of the true grandes dames. You won't have to worry about being taken lightly with this name. In fact, you might worry about scaring people away. Yet Augusta is really not such a big leap from hit names like Amelia, and it's awfully handsome. The nickname Gussie was once a big hit in its own right.
In the World: Augusta, Georgia, home of the Masters golf tournament; several 18th- and 19th-century princesses

Aurea (AW-ree-ə, OH-ree-ə)   1963: #2545
Popularity: #6329
Styles: Saints, Lacy and Lissome, Why Not?
Variants: Aurelia   1880   Today
Sisters: Twila, Margot, Flora, Lilia, Verena, Adria
Brothers: Royce, Alban, Stanton, Rex, Tobin, Vance
✱ Aurea is seldom heard today, but the name has the supple flow of a modern hit. It also has a deep history dating back to medieval saints. It comes from the Latin word for "golden."

Aurelia (oh-REE-lee-ə)   1908: #399
Popularity: #1034
Styles: Ladies and Gentlemen, Saints, Classical, Why Not?   1880   Today
Nicknames: Lia, Ria
Variants: Aurea, Aurélie
Sisters: Lavinia, Aurora, Adelaide, Eleanora, Emmeline, Theodora, Beatrix, Viola
Brothers: Lucius, Sebastian, Rupert, Hugh, Edison, Augustus, Conrad, Elias
✱ Aurelia is a romantic relic of ancient Rome. The name's ladylike comportment led it to a Victorian-era revival, but it's seldom thought of today. Consider it an exotic twist on Amelia—proper yet seductive. It shares Aurea's "golden" origins.

Aurora (oh-ROH-rə) 2011: #183
Popularity: #183
Styles: Timeless, Exotic Traditional, Mythological
Nicknames: Rory 1880 Today
Variants: Aurore
Sisters: Valentina, Lorelei, Athena, Juliet, Scarlett, Penelope, Camilla, Paloma
Brothers: Orlando, Roman, Atticus, Gideon, Titus, Eliot, Magnus, Orion
✴ Aurora was the Roman goddess of the dawn, and the name sounds the part. Ethereal yet strong, you can picture it equally on a theater marquee and an executive office. Wherever you see it, you're sure to remember it. Disney alert: this is the name given to the animated Sleeping Beauty.
In the World: Disney movie *Sleeping Beauty;* the Aurora Borealis (Northern Lights); a top-10 name in Italy

Autumn (AW-tuhm) 1998: #77
Popularity: #69
Styles: Modern Meanings, Charms and Graces, Nickname-Proof, New 1880 Today
Classics
Sisters: Sienna, Jasmine, Sage, Haven, Meadow, Amber, Harmony, Willow
Brothers: Trevor, Devin, Austin, Parker, Tanner, Chance, Holden, Logan
✴ The name May was the peak of fashion in 1900, June in 1930, April in 1970. Now those dewy Spring months have given way to Summer and Autumn. With an image of cozy sweaters and falling leaves, Autumn is the warm and wistful season choice.
In the World: Actress Autumn Reeser

Ava (AY-və) 2007: #4
Popularity: #5
Styles: Antique Charm, Short and Sweet, Nickname-Proof, Saints 1880 Today
Variants: Eva, Avah
Sisters: Chloe, Mia, Bella, Aubrey, Olivia, Zoe, Lily, Maya
Brothers: Noah, Liam, Owen, Eli, Aidan, Max, Ethan, Jack
✴ Ava is a tiny little name, yet voluptuous. Bombshell actress Ava Gardner is the main reason, along with the va-va-voom "V" sound. Starting in the late '90s, Ava began a dramatic rise to the top of the popularity charts. If you're looking for that classic Hollywood style but a less common name, consider Lana.
In the World: Actress Ava Gardner

Avery (AY-və-ree) 2011: #18
Popularity: #18
Styles: Androgynous, Last Names First
Nicknames: Ava 1880 Today
Variants: Averie
Sisters: Aubrey, Riley, Lily, Ava, Piper, Emery
Brothers: Carter, Evan, Mason, Conor, Brady, Aidan
✴ Light and nimble as a bird, Avery is a lyrical successor to Ashley and Courtney. Like those names, it took the historical path of surname to male name to female name. Unlike Ashley and Courtney, it remains a popular choice for boys as well . . . so far. See also Avery in "Name Snapshots: Boys."

Aviana (ay-vee-AH-n-ə, 2011: #762
ah-vee-AH-n-ə)
Popularity: #762
Styles: Lacy and Lissome, Why Not? 1880 Today
Nicknames: Ava
Variants: Avianna
Sisters: Alessia, Mariela, Viviana, Zara, Chiara, Noelia, Livia, Galilea
Brothers: Matteo, Paxton, Jacoby, Luca, Quinn, Maddox, Gideon, Nico
✴ Ava and Ariana are stylish hit names, and Aviana is a natural combo. This name, though, is more than the sum of its parts. The word "avian" refers to birds and birdlike qualities, and it lends Aviana a gravity-defying boost (except when the avian flu is in town).
In the World: Daughter of actress Amy Adams

Avis (AY-vis) 1912: #238
Popularity: Very rare
Styles: Ladies and Gentlemen, Nickname-Proof, Short and Sweet, Why Not? 1880 Today
Sisters: Ione, Cleo, Alys, Sybil, Petra, Minerva, Fay, Zora
Brothers: Milo, Jules, Theron, Ulysses, Felix, Ivor, Wolf, Axel
✴ Simple yet surprising, Avis is a contender for the "quirky classic" mantle now that Zoe and Iris have gone mainstream. It has been a girl's name since the Middle Ages but has never been common enough to be tied to one time period. The Avis car rental company's "We're #2" campaign is one major obstacle.
In the World: Avis car rental company

Aviva (ah-VEE-və) 2011: #2125
Popularity: #2126
Styles: Lacy and Lissome,
Jewish, Why Not?
Nicknames: Viv, Avi 1880 Today
Sisters: Ariela, Shira, Tali,
Yael, Tova, Atara, Allegra, Ilana
Brothers: Boaz, Elan, Asher, Raz, Judah, Ari,
Lazar, Ronen
✷Aviva is a modern Hebrew favorite that
means "springtime," and the name fairly bursts
with life—forward and backward.

Avonlea (A-vən-lee) 2011: #2703
Popularity: #2706
Styles: Literary and Artistic,
Place Names, Why Not?
Nicknames: Avi, Ava 1880 Today
Sisters: Evangeline, Arabella,
Briar, Guinevere, Marilla, Cambria
Brothers: Ellington, Caspian, Emerson, Rhett,
Dashiell, Tennyson
✷This name sounds like a modern composi-
tion, akin to Emberlee or Heavenleigh. But
every girl who ever dreamed big dreams with
Anne of Green Gables will recognize Avonlea
as a romantic and literary kindred spirit.
In the World: Setting for Lucy Maud Montgom-
ery's "Anne of Green Gables" series

Avril (AV-ril, ahv-REEL) 2008: #1499
Popularity: #1532
Styles: French, Charms and
Graces, Namesakes
Variants: April, Averil, Averill 1880 Today
Sisters: Soleil, Azure, Honor,
Fleur, Meadow, Bijou
Brothers: Bond, Regis, Leaf, Aidric, Blaise,
River
✷This name is now known as the French form
of April, associated with Canadian singer Avril
Lavigne. However, it does have a separate his-
tory as an English name. On that parallel track,
Avril is a relative of Averill, a Scottish first and
last name.
In the World: Singer Avril Lavigne

Ayanna (iy-AHN-ə) 2003: #361
Popularity: #635
Styles: Lacy and Lissome,
African-American, African
Nicknames: Yanni 1880 Today
Variants: Ayana, Aiyana
Sisters: Tamia, Amani, Saniyah, Aryella,
Larissa, D'asia, Mireya, Asha
Brothers: Jaylon, Darian, Jabari, Xavier,
Ahmad, Zion, Asante, Savion
✷This fluid creation echoes the sound of clas-
sic names in a modern form. While Ayanna's
feminine style sounds universal, the name has
African roots and has been chosen most fre-
quently by African-American parents. Similar-
sounding Japanese and Indian names are more
often spelled Ayana.

Aylin (AY-lin, iy-LEEN, IY-lin) 2011: #485
Popularity: #485
Styles: The "-ens", Latino/
Latina
Variants: Aylín, Aileen, Ailyn 1880 Today
Sisters: Jaida, Lexi, Rylan,
Skylar, Kaya, Adelyn, Maci, Aspen
Brothers: Cason, Kane, Gavyn, Keegan,
Colton, Bryce, Kyler, Devon
✷Three distinct names and pronunciations
share this spelling. "IY-lin" is Turkish, "iy-
LEEN" is Latina, and "AY-lin" is a slimmed-
down sibling of Kaylin and Jaylin. Use
whichever you prefer, but have patience with
people who guess wrong when pronouncing
your daughter's name. (The listed sibling sug-
gestions are for "AY-lin.")
In the World: Cuban actress/model Aylín
Mújica; Turkish singer Aylin Aslım

Azaria (ah-ZAHR-ee-ə) 2011: #872
Popularity: #872
Styles: Lacy and Lissome
Nicknames: Zara
Variants: Azariah 1880 Today
Sisters: Aviana, Keziah,
Isannah, Delilah, Ariela, Zahava
Brothers: Malachi, Samson, Isaak, Ezra,
Gideon, Jabez
✷Azariah (pronounced "ah-zah-RIY-ə") is a
common name in the Bible, borne by dozens of
different men. It means "whom God helps." But
you don't want that creaky old name for a boy,
you want the cool modern name "ah-ZAHR-
ee-ə" for a girl . . . and you want to claim the
biblical origin too! Many parents feel the same
way; the name is uncommon but rising.
In the World: Vanished Australian infant Azaria
Chamberlain

Bailey (BAY-lee) 1998: #60
Popularity: #88
Styles: Androgynous, Last
Names First, Bell Tones
Nicknames: Bay 1880 Today
Variants: Bailee, Baylee,
Bayleigh
Sisters: Kelsey, Avery, Payton, Sydney, Taylor,
Macy
Brothers: Jackson, Chase, Logan, Tanner,
Parker, Brennan
✷ In the standard spelling Bailey, this name is
boyish in a clear, sunny way. Creative rework-
ings like Baylee emphasize the prettiness of the
sound over the surname origin.
In the World: Actress Bailee Madison

Barbara (BAHR-brə, 1938: #2
BAHR-ber-ə)
Popularity: #764
Styles: Solid Citizens
Nicknames: Barb, Barbie, 1880 Today
Babs, Bobbie
Variants: Barbra
Sisters: Patricia, Marilyn, Gloria, Shirley,
Joanne, Beverly, Carolyn, Nancy
Brothers: Richard, Donald, Kenneth, Franklin,
Roger, Lawrence, Raymond, Gerald
✷ Barbara is a completely familiar name.
There's hardly an adult in America who has
grown up without Barbaras around—relatives,
teachers, neighbors. But today this handsome
name is going to be a tough sell. Barbara was so
vastly popular for such a short time that it's stub-
bornly glued to its era.
In the World: TV journalist Barbara Walters;
singer Barbra Streisand; politician Barbara Jordan

Beatrice (BEE-ə-tris, 1910: #36
BEE-tris, bay-ə-TREES)
Popularity: #707
Styles: Ladies and
Gentlemen, French, English, 1880 Today
Shakespearean, Why Not?
Nicknames: Bea, Bebe, Tricia, Tris
Variants: Beatrix, Beatriz
Sisters: Clementine, Eleanor, Violet, Eloise,
Charlotte, Genevieve
Brothers: Theodore, Oliver, Frederick, Louis,
Felix, Everett
✷ Beatrice is the properest of proper ladies, the
kind of formidable figure who would never
show a bare ankle in public. Is it impudent to
suggest she could be a real crowd-pleaser? The
name is light and pretty, and on a little girl it
turns positively cute. It's also the name of one of
Shakespeare's most appealing heroines. Beatrice ("Tris") Prior, the protagonist of the "Divergent" series, has added a fresh option to the
nickname list.
In the World: Actress Bea Arthur; Princess Beatrice of York; Beatrice Prior of "Divergent"; Beatrice Baudelaire of Lemony Snicket's "A Series
of Unfortunate Events" books

Beatrix (BEE-ə-triks, 2011: #1590
BEE-triks)
Popularity: #1593
Styles: Exotic Traditional,
Saints, English, Why Not? 1880 Today
Nicknames: Trixie, Bea
Variants: Beatrice, Beatriz
Sisters: Felicity, Isadora, Juniper, Evangeline,
Ariadne, Imogen, Bryony, Eloise
Brothers: Alistair, Atticus, Phineas, Barnaby,
Jasper, Beckett, Thaddeus, Tarquin
✷ Beatrice's exotic sister is just as genteel on
the surface but hints at surprises beneath. The
nickname Trixie may be an added temptation
toward the saucy side.
In the World: Children's author/illustrator Bea-
trix Potter; Queen Beatrix of the Netherlands

Belinda (bə-LIN-də) 1961: #142
Popularity: #1042
Styles: Surfer '60s, Lacy and Lissome
Nicknames: Lin, Lindy, Bel 1880 Today
Sisters: Angelia, Deanna, Renee, Cynthia, Suzanne, Tabitha, Janine, Tamara
Brothers: Craig, Terence, Timothy, Keith, Roderick Marc, Darren, Geoffrey
★ Belinda hit it big in the '60s at the same time as the rhyming name Melinda. Its roots, though, run deeper. The name has been in steady use since the Renaissance. If you like Belinda's essence but not its '60s overtones, Elodia and Rosalinda are antique alternatives, and Belina is an uncommon saint's name.
In the World: Singer Belinda Carlisle; Mexican entertainer Belinda

Bella (BEHL-ə) 2010: #48
Popularity: #60
Styles: Antique Charm
Variants: Belle
Sisters: Lily, Sofia, Luna, 1880 Today
Chloe, Eva, Eliza
Brothers: Eli, Julian, Owen, Miles, Carson, Jonas
★ In the 1990s, the names Isabella and Ella both started soaring to the top of America's wish list. It took years before parents noticed the charming little name halfway in between. Bella is an old-fashioned sweetie, with an updated sheen thanks to the heroine of the "Twilight" saga. It's Italian for "beautiful."
In the World: Bella Swan of the "Twilight" series; politician Bella Abzug; actress Bella Thorne

Bellamy (BEHL-ə-mee) 2011: #3115
Popularity: #3121
Styles: Last Names First, Why Not?
Nicknames: Bell, Belle, Bella, 1880 Today
Amy
Sisters: Amory, Madigan, Larkin, Marlowe, Everly, Tierney, Alden, Waverly
Brothers: Pierson, Cabot, Merrick, Brogan, Seaver, Prescott, Flynn, Brennan
★ Bellamy is a surname that sounds sunny and feminine as a first name. The old-fashioned nickname Bella should win over your more traditional-minded relatives. The meaning is appealing too, coming from the French for "fair friend."
In the World: Actress Bellamy Young; country duo The Bellamy Brothers

Belle (BEHL) 1880: #90
Popularity: #1556
Styles: Charms and Graces, Brisk and Breezy, Country and Western, Why Not? 1880 Today
Variants: Bella
Sisters: Mae, Flora, Lucie, Eve, Calla, Phoebe, Georgia, Bess
Brothers: Foster, Ellis, August, Sam, Roy, Emmett, Jude, Cal
★ This sweetheart of a name means "beautiful" and walks with a spring in its step. It's all around us as part of names like Isabelle and Annabelle, but extremely uncommon on its own. Most parents opt for a longer given name or for the Italian-styled Bella. "Just plain Belle," though, has a spirit all its own. The heroine of Disney's *Beauty and the Beast* showed off its sweetness and strength.
In the World: Western outlaw Belle Star; the phrase "Southern belle"; Belle of *Beauty and the Beast*.

Bertha (BER-thə) 1883: #7
Popularity: #3481
Styles: Porch Sitters, German and Dutch
Nicknames: Bertie 1880 Today
Variants: Berta
Sisters: Helga, Gertrude, Edna, Myrtle, Hilda, Ethel, Beulah, Hester
Brothers: Roscoe, Herman, Otto, Lester, Floyd, Emil, Otis, Luther
★ The Germanic classic Bertha was once one of the hottest names in America, but when the phrase "Big Bertha" entered the language during World War I, this poor name was doomed. (The phrase originally referred to the largest German artillery.) If you're looking for a namesake for your beloved Granny Bertha, try Bella or Bethany.
In the World: The phrase "Big Bertha" has been applied to large specimens of golf clubs, slot machines, and more

Bess (BEHS)　　　1887: #157
Popularity: #13,487
Styles: Guys and Dolls,
Nicknames
Variants: Bessie
Sisters: Evie, Nell, Josie,
Mabel, Della, Lotte, Tillie, Mae
Brothers: Ben, Ike, Charley, Teddy, Doc, Nat,
Archie, Sam
✱ Yes, it's yet another nickname for Elizabeth,
but don't tune out yet. Bess sounds soft and
cute, but adult. That puts it in select company
and makes it a strong choice to revive as either a
full or pet name. The diminutive Bessie was far
more common in the past.
In the World: Blues singer Bessie Smith; opera
Porgy and Bess; beauty queen Bess Myerson

Beth (BEHTH)　　　1964: #65
Popularity: #3330
Styles: Surfer '60s,
Nicknames, Jewish
Sisters: Lynn, Amy, Laurie,
Susan, Kim, Sarah, Stacy, Jill
Brothers: Jon, Brad, Tim, Jeffrey, Mark, Greg,
David, Josh
✱ Beth is one of the many nicknames of Eliza-
beth that have broken free to take on lives of
their own. It was a hit in the '60s but holds up
much better than other nicknames of that time.
Beth has been especially popular with Jewish
families, who take it from the Hebrew word for
"house" (as in Bethel, "house of God").
In the World: Beth March of Louisa May Al-
cott's *Little Women*

Bethany (BEH-thə-nee)　　　1987: #87
Popularity: #352
Styles: Biblical, '70s–'80s,
Turn of the 21st Century
Nicknames: Beth
Sisters: Tabitha, Rachel,
Meredith, Candace, Lindsay, Rebekah
Brothers: Nathan, Timothy, Jared, Trevor,
Joshua, Zachary
✱ This New Testament place name has the
sound and rhythm of a classic girl's name but
remains pleasantly individual. That feeling of
individuality is rising as the often-confused
names Brittany and Stephanie decline in popu-
larity.
In the World: Surfer Bethany Hamilton; actress
Bethany Joy Lenz

Betsy (BEHT-see)　　　1959: #228
Popularity: #1644
Styles: Mid-Century,
Nicknames
Variants: Betsey, Betty, Bess,
Elizabeth
Sisters: Penny, Sue, Kathy, Trudy, Debbie, Joy,
Nancy, Susie
Brothers: Jimmy, Mickey, Ted, Danny, Benjy,
Andy, Ricky, Jay
✱ Betsy is perennially girlish. If you meet a real
Betsy, though, chances are she's not a young girl
but a mom or a grandma. That disconnect has
the name in fashion limbo for now, but its fun-
damental charm will eventually bring it back.
In the World: Flag seamstress Betsy Ross; Maud
Hart Lovelace's "Betsy-Tacy" books; designer
Betsey Johnson

Betty (BEH-tee)　　　1930: #2
Popularity: #1392
Styles: Solid Citizens,
Nicknames
Nicknames: Bette, Betts
Variants: Bette, Bettie, Bettye
Sisters: Sally, June, Nancy, Patty, Dorothy,
Polly
Brothers: Bob, Ted, Bill, Eddie, Don, Walt
✱ From Betty Grable to Betty Crocker, this
name is a symbol of wholesome, all-American
womanhood. Yet that very symbolism seems to
be scaring off today's parents. Even the tradi-
tionalists who've dusted off chestnuts like Lucy
and Sadie have left Betty by the wayside. Maybe
it's a tad too domestic, suggesting a lifetime
spent in an apron. Or maybe we're just not quite
ready. Look for a new batch of Bettys down the
road.
In the World: Comedian Betty White; food icon
Betty Crocker; Betty of *Archie Comics*; rock
band Betty

Beverly (BEHV-er-lee)   1937: #14
Popularity: #1722
Styles: Solid Citizens
Nicknames: Bev
Variants: Beverley, Beverlee   1880   Today
Sisters: Rosalyn, Gloria, Rosemary, Vivian, Jeannette, Pamela, Constance, Lorraine
Brothers: Douglas, Wayne, Gerald, Russell, Raymond, Stewart, Randolph, Lawrence
✱ Beverly? Come on, really, Beverly? Yes, really. With its ladylike sound nestled around that strong "v," Beverly is a worthwhile alternative to powerhouses Evelyn and Olivia. Plus it's a converted surname, which is a hot style. If you're still not sold, try chopping off the "B" to make Everly.
In the World: Author Beverly Cleary; opera singer Beverly Sills; posh neighborhood Beverly Hills

Bianca (bee-AHN-kə)   1991: #89
Popularity: #282
Styles: Italian, Latino/Latina, Shakespearean
Nicknames: Bibi   1880   Today
Variants: Blanca
Sisters: Giada, Adriana, Marisa, Ariel, Angelica, Viviana
Brothers: Sergio, Marco, Giovanni, Fabian, Lorenzo, Dante
✱ Bianca is Italian for "white," a counterpart to the French Blanche and the Spanish Blanca. It's one of the handsome exotic names that Shakespeare favored for his plays in Italian settings. In recent decades the name's image has shifted toward glamour, influenced by Nicaraguan jetsetter Bianca Jagger.
In the World: Bianca Jagger; many soap opera characters

Billie (BIL-ee)   1930: #79
Popularity: #2227
Styles: Guys and Dolls, Nicknames, Androgynous
Variants: Billy   1880   Today
Sisters: Tommie, Frankie, Bobbie, Lu, Dixie, Vonnie, Evie, Sammie
Brothers: Jimmie, Bennie, Mac, Jackie, Louie, Teddy, Buddy, Joe
✱ There were tons of these boyish names in the '20s and '30s—little girl Freddies, Johnnies, Sammies, and Bobbies. The great Billie Holiday helps make this one special. It's not exactly fashionable, but charming nonetheless.
In the World: Singer Billie Holiday; actresses Billie Piper and Billie Burke; a daughter of actress Rebecca Gayheart

Blair (BLAYR)   1988: #423
Popularity: #973
Styles: Brisk and Breezy, Androgynous, Celtic
Variants: Blaire   1880   Today
Sisters: Bryn, Devin, Kendall, Darby, Blake, Adair, Lacey, Sloane
Brothers: Brooks, Chase, Easton, Spencer, Westley, Dalton, Reid, Tate
✱ Do you consider this Scottish surname the preppiest girl's name around? You're not alone. The rich prep school queen Blair Warner in the '80s sitcom *The Facts of Life* established the prototype; the rich prep school queen Blair Waldorf of *Gossip Girl* followed in her footsteps. Real-life Blairs, though, remain uncommon and welcome.
In the World: The *Gossip Girl* and *Facts of Life* characters; actress Blair Brown

Blake (BLAYK)   2011: #815
Popularity: #815
Styles: Androgynous, Brisk and Breezy
Sisters: Devyn, Shea, Brynn,   1880   Today
Carson, Reilly, Drew
Brothers: Garrison, Brett, Wesley, Barrett, Keane, Reid
✱ Blake has the makings of a bright, preppy name for a girl ready to form a power-name clique with Paige and Brooke. Actress Blake Lively is a natural candidate to make that happen. Yet this name has had flurries on the feminine side before, and it keeps coming back male.
In the World: Actress Blake Lively

Blanche (BLANCH) 1884: #52
Popularity: #15,032
Styles: Ladies and
Gentlemen, French
Variants: Blanca 1880 Today
Sisters: Maude, Estelle,
Delta, Magnolia, Pearl, Lucille
Brothers: Alphonse, Crawford, Gustave,
Lafayette, Raleigh, Armand
✷ Blanche could be one of the most formal of
names, French and fusty. But the immortal
character Blanche DuBois in Tennessee Wil-
liams's *A Streetcar Named Desire* turned that
image inside out and gave the name a wild
Southern spin. The sitcom *The Golden Girls*
played off that in naming its saucy belle Blanche
Devereaux. Today the name is half wallflower,
half diva.
In the World: Blanche DuBois of *A Streetcar
Named Desire*; Blanche Devereaux of *The
Golden Girls*; various medieval royals

Blythe (BLIYDH) 1974: #1075
Popularity: #1883
Styles: Brisk and Breezy, Last
Names First, Why Not?
Variants: Blithe 1880 Today
Sisters: Darcy, Greer, Charis,
Tamsin, Marlowe, Lark
Brothers: Flynn, Teague, Gareth, Blaine,
Graeme, Calder
✷ The word "blithe" means "carefree." It's a
lively, sophisticated little word that many associ-
ate with Noel Coward's *Blithe Spirit*—a lively,
sophisticated little play. The spelling Blythe
wraps all those good vibes up into an elegant
English surname. This is an uncommon and
stylish name.
In the World: Actress Blythe Danner; big-eyed
Blythe dolls

Bonnie (BAHN-ee) 1942: #34
Popularity: #1117
Styles: Mid-Century, Charms
and Graces, Nickname-Proof
Variants: Bonny 1880 Today
Sisters: Janet, Peggy, Donna,
Sandra, Betsy, Joy
Brothers: Jerry, Dennis, Bruce, Roger, Barry,
Glen
✷ Bonnie is taken from the Scottish word
meaning "pretty." The name's good feelings and
cutie-pie style made it a longtime favorite. That
kind of genial style is out right now, and the
name has quietly drifted off the rader. It's not
trendy, but it's likable.
In the World: Outlaws Bonnie and Clyde; song
"My Bonnie Lies Over the Ocean"

Brandy (BRAN-dee) 1978: #37
Popularity: #1514
Styles: '70s–'80s
Variants: Brandi, Brandie
Sisters: Misty, Tasha, Krista, 1880 Today
April, Nikki, Shawna
Brothers: Jamie, Dustin, Corey, Brandon,
Shane, Brent
✷ Brandy may be the only common English
name that comes from an alcoholic beverage.
(Sherry is borderline.) The name took off in the
'70s on the heels of a popular song ("Brandy,
you're a fine girl, what a good wife you would
be . . ."). It's now more likely to remind people
of the TV and singing star Brandy, but she
wasn't able to keep it from falling out of fashion.
In the World: Singer/actress Brandy Norwood;
song "Brandy (You're a Fine Girl)"

Bree (BREE) 1977: #616
Popularity: #954
Styles: Brisk and Breezy, Nicknames
Variants: Brie 1880 Today
Sisters: Alexis, Nika, Joss, Paige, Carly, Bryn
Brothers: Blake, Tristan, Cole, Reed, Topher, Kai
★ The name Bree is pure positive energy, like a bright spree. It can be a nickname for names from Bridget to Sabrina, but its use as a given name dates to the 1971 film classic *Klute*. That makes Bree the only name launched by a screen prostitute (granted, an Academy Award–winning one). If that origin doesn't thrill you, you can call it a form of the Irish Gaelic word *brígh*, meaning "force." The spelling Brie is best left to cheese.
In the World: Bree Van de Kamp of *Desperate Housewives*; actress Bree Turner

Brenda (BREHN-də) 1950: #14
Popularity: #530
Styles: Mid-Century, Celtic, Nickname-Proof
Sisters: Sheila, Colleen, 1880 Today
Janice, Pamela, Cheryl, Paula
Brothers: Bruce, Douglas, Garry, Duane, Kelvin, Dwight
★ *Brenda Starr, Girl Reporter* made her debut in the Sunday funnies in 1940. She was the perfect modern girl, looking like Rita Hayworth and living like Lois Lane. Her fresh Scottish first name fairly bounded from the page. For 30 years that image of Brenda held, but a name can stay modern for only so long.
In the World: Singer Brenda Lee; actresses Brenda Song and Brenda Vaccaro

Brenna (BREH-nə) 1995: #235
Popularity: #510
Styles: Celtic, Nickname-Proof
Variants: Brynna 1880 Today
Sisters: Cara, Tierney, Nia, Alanna, Keelin Mara
Brothers: Logan, Trevor, Conor, Bryce, Tynan, Kane
★ Brenna is a slimmed-down version of Brenda. Thin is in, and this name's smooth silhouette keeps it current, if not exactly trendy. Like close relative Brianna, Brenna is usually described as Irish in origin but has never been common in Ireland.

Brianna (bree-AN-ə, 2000: #15
bree-AHN-ə)
Popularity: #45
Styles: Lacy and Lissome, Turn of the 21st Century 1880 Today
Nicknames: Bree
Variants: Briana, Breanna, Brianne, Breanne, Bryanna, Abrianna
Sisters: Alyssa, Brooklyn, Kayla, Alexis, Brittany, Marissa
Brothers: Tyler, Donovan, Brandon, Chandler, Bryce, Dalton
★ This feminine take on Brian has several popular spellings. It followed on the heels of Brittany and seems to appeal to the same group of parents—you'll meet a lot of sisters named Brittany and Brianna. Briella is the new hot member of this name family.
In the World: Actress Brianna Brown; rapper Brianna Perry

Briar (BRY-er) 2011: #1938
Popularity: #1939
Styles: Charms and Graces, Literary and Artistic, Nickname-Proof 1880 Today
Sisters: Auden, Willow, Scout, Brynn, Winter, Honor
Brothers: Blake, Calder, Sawyer, Rowan, Dashiell, River
★ A briar is a prickly thicket, the last kind of plant you'd expect parents to think of when naming a baby girl. Briar has powerful friends, though: the Brothers Grimm. When they told the story of Sleeping Beauty as "Briar Rose," they endowed the name with lasting romance and mystery. Today Briar is starting to catch the eye of adventurous parents. Expect the written name to be read as "Brian," though.
In the World: Fairy tale "Briar Rose"

Bridget (BRI-jit) 1973: #112
Popularity: #472
Styles: Celtic, Surfer '60s, '70s–'80s
Nicknames: Bree, Bridie, Britt 1880 Today
Variants: Brigid, Brighid, Brigit, Brigitte, Birgit
Sisters: Shannon, Lesley, Deirdre, Holly, Erin, Kelly
Brothers: Brian, Casey, Scott, Brendan, Jeffrey, Sean

✶ Bridget is a great American success story. In the 19th century, when poor Irish immigrants were struggling to gain a foothold in the U.S., this classic Irish name was shunned as a name of the servant class. Generations later, Bridget is still as Irish as you can get, but today's parents eagerly seek out that touch of the Emerald Isle. The name has become a beloved modern classic.
In the World: Book/film *Bridget Jones's Diary*; actresses Bridget Fonda and Bridget Moynahan

---

Brielle (bree-EHL) 2011: #126
Popularity: #126
Styles: Bell Tones
Nicknames: Bree
Variants: Briella 1880 Today
Sisters: Audrina, Cadence, Adalynn, Savanna, Baylee, Gracelyn
Brothers: Easton, Jace, Caden, Braylen, Drake, Jaxon

✶ Parents have found their way to Brielle by building up and chopping down. Some constructed it out of the raw materials of favorites like Brianna and Danielle; others trimmed Gabrielle down to its smooth core. With all of those popular ancestors, the name feels more traditional than it really is.

Brinley (BRIN-lee) 2011: #525
Popularity: #525
Styles: Bell Tones, Last Names First
Nicknames: Brin, Bryn 1880 Today
Variants: Brynlee, Brinlee, Brynleigh
Sisters: Rylie, Peyton, Braelyn, Oakley, Brielle, Paisley
Brothers: Easton, Bridger, Bentley, Raylan, Jaxon, Ryker

✶ Never heard of the name Brinley? You must not live near Utah. The state is a naming world unto itself, and while the rest of the country wasn't looking, Utah parents made Brinley a major in-state hit. It has spread since, but Utah remains the epicenter. The spelling Brinley gives the name a surname style, while Brynlee is more like a composite name (such as Katelynne) that emphasizes the nickname Bryn.

Briony (BREE-ə-nee) 2011: #7386
Popularity: #7445
Styles: Charms and Graces, English, Why Not?
Nicknames: Bree 1880 Today
Variants: Bryony
Sisters: Verity, Tamsin, Anthea, Romilly, Juniper, Briar, Amity, Jessamyn
Brothers: Gareth, Barnaby, Winslow, Piers, Bennet, Alistair, Calder, Corin

✶ Briony (or "bryony") is a climbing vine. The Victorian craze for botanical names somehow passed this one by, but it quietly surfaced in 20th-century England. (A character in the book and film *Atonement* is one example.) With its contemporary sound and quaint, quirky style, this could be a jackpot name.
In the World: Briony of *Atonement*

Brisa (BREE-sah) 2010: #463
Popularity: #807
Styles: Latino/Latina
Nicknames: Bri, Bree
Sisters: Perla, Abril, Dulce, 1880 Today
Tessa, Jazmin, Maia, Rocío, Rubi
Brothers: Mateo, Angel, Cruz, Alexis, Diego, Cristian, Lucas, Marco

✶ Brisa is Spanish for "breeze," and that essence translates charmingly. This is a name with broad and flexible appeal.

Bristol (BRIS-təl)   2011: #434
Popularity: #434
Styles: Place Names,
Namesakes, Nickname-Proof
Sisters: Shiloh, Ireland,   1880   Today
London, Juneau, Leighton,
Reagan, Harlow, Aspen
Brothers: Kingston, Bentley, Madden,
Lexington, Beck, Tate, Jericho, Boston
✹ When America met the Palin family of
Alaska, the name Bristol instantly struck a
chord. The sound was familiar—Crystal with a
splash of Britney—and the androgynous place-
name style was perfectly contemporary. But un-
like other Palin family names (Piper, Willow),
the popularity of Bristol seems to run along par-
tisan political lines.
In the World: Sarah Palin's daughter Bristol
Palin; Bristol, England; Bristol, Connecticut
(home of ESPN)

Britt (BRIT)   1973: #882
Popularity: #8647
Styles: Nordic, Brisk and
Breezy
Variants: Britta   1880   Today
Sisters: Lise, Katrine, Bree,
Anika, Mari, Blake
Brothers: Leif, Brant, Anders, Niels, Rune,
Lance
✹ This Scandinavian name (a nickname for
Birgit) has a brittle style that's icy but enticing.
Keep in mind that many people will assume it's
short for Brittany. The form Britta might help
avoid that confusion.
In the World: Actress Britt Ekland; singer Britt
Nicole

Brittany (BRIT-ə-nee,   1989: #3
BRIT-nee)
Popularity: #419
Styles: '70s–'80s, Place
Names   1880   Today
Nicknames: Britt
Variants: Britany, Brittanie, Brittni, Britny,
Britney
Sisters: Whitney, Chelsea, Tiffany, Ashley,
Brianna, Courtney
Brothers: Brandon, Cory, Jordan, Austin, Tyler,
Casey
✹ This glittering place name became part of
the rhythm of the '80s and '90s. It wasn't just
Brittany, but Britney, Brittni, and countless
variations. The result was a name that went
from fresh invention to overexposure in record
time (with a big assist from singer Britney
Spears).
In the World: Singer Britney Spears; actress Brit-
tany Murphy

Brooke (BRUWK)   1996: #45
Popularity: #86
Styles: Brisk and Breezy, New
Classics
Variants: Brook   1880   Today
Sisters: Paige, Bailey, Lauren,
Autumn, Jenna, Natalie
Brothers: Drew, Evan, Blake, Connor, Cole,
Trevor
✹ Brooke started out in high style, thanks to
society grande dame Brooke Astor. It then hit
the mainstream in the late '70s with the double
whammy of teen actress Brooke Shields and a
popular character on the soap *All My Children.*
That populist appeal hasn't hurt the name's dig-
nity a bit. Brooke doesn't have a long history as
a name, but it still feels like a classic.
In the World: Actress Brooke Shields; socialite
Brooke Astor; TV host Brooke Burke

Brooklyn (BRUWK-lin)   2011: #21
Popularity: #21
Styles: Place Names, The
"-ens"
Nicknames: Brook, Lyn   1880   Today
Variants: Brooklynn
Sisters: London, Peyton, Aspen, Berkeley,
Gracelyn, Alexa, Sydney, Bristol
Brothers: Camden, Kingston, Cooper,
Grayson, Trenton, Chase, Bryson, Hudson
★ Place names like Paris and Savannah take a
lot of their style from the places themselves.
Brooklyn, though, is more the sum of its parts: a
composite of the familiar girls' names Brooke
and Lynn. In fact, the less parents think about
the borough of Brooklyn, the more they seem to
like the name. Its popularity increases the far-
ther you go from New York.
In the World: Model Brooklyn Decker; actress
Brooklyn Sudano; all things Brooklyn, New
York

Bryce (BRIYS)   1998: #1151
Popularity: #1774
Styles: Brisk and Breezy,
Androgynous
Sisters: Quincy, Laine, Blake,   1880   Today
Channing, Carson, Drew
Brothers: Bowen, Drake, Garrison, Chandler,
Blaise, Connor
★ Bryce is an overwhelmingly male name. It's
so popular for boys that it has launched spin-offs
like Brycen, while it's scarcely a blip on the
screen for girls. So why list it as a girl's name?
Because Reese was overwhelmingly male too,
until Reese Witherspoon came along. Actress
Bryce Dallas Howard has a few parents consid-
ering this name for their daughters.
In the World: Actress Bryce Dallas Howard

Brylee (BRIY-lee)   2011: #408
Popularity: #408
Styles: Bell Tones
Nicknames: Bry
Variants: Briley, Brylie,   1880   Today
Bryleigh
Sisters: Brooklynne, Makenna, Caylee, Skylar,
Brynlee, Ashtyn
Brothers: Brycen, Keaton, Grayson, Gaige,
Bradyn, Jayce
★ Brylee marries two of the sounds that con-
temporary-style namers love most: the "Br-" of
Brayden and Brianna and the "-lee" of Kaylee
and Rylee. Don't place too much store in the
popularity ranking for this name. Its use is di-
vided up among several popular spellings.

Brynn (BRIN)   2011: #190
Popularity: #190
Styles: Brisk and Breezy,
Celtic
Variants: Bryn   1880   Today
Sisters: Grier, Emlyn, Carys,
Briar, Rowan, Bly
Brothers: Dylan, Cole, Pryce, Brennan, Rhys,
Gray
★ This Welsh name, which means "hill," is
poised for a breakthrough in the U.S. Its
strength is its swiftness, which leaves competi-
tors like Brianna and Brooklynn looking fussy
by comparison. In the U.K., it is primarily a
male name.
In the World: Bryn Mawr College; a daughter of
reality TV star Bethenny Frankel

Cadence (KAY-dəns)   2005: #207
Popularity: #279
Styles: Modern Meanings,
Bell Tones
Nicknames: Cady, Kay   1880   Today
Variants: Caydence,
Kadence, Kaydence
Sisters: Avery, Campbell, Aria, Harmony,
Sienna, Taryn
Brothers: Brayden, Chance, Cooper, Landon,
Hunter, Garrett
★ A cadence is a rhythmic flow of sounds, as in
a poem or a marching song. In the space of a few
years in the early 2000s, it also became a popu-
lar name. A movie character (from *American
Wedding*) was a launching pad, and fashionable
nicknames worked as turbo-boosters. Creative
spellings move the name away from its musical
roots into Kaitlyn territory.
In the World: Cadence of *American Wedding*;
"My Little Pony" Princess Cadence; rapper Cadence Weapon

Caitlin (KAYT-lin, kat-LEEN)
1988: #44
Popularity: #392
Styles: Bell Tones, The "-ens," Celtic, Turn of the 21st Century
1880　Today
Nicknames: Cait
Variants: Kaitlyn, Katelyn, Kaitlynn, Caitlyn
Sisters: Megan, Courtney, Erin, Morgan, Brianne, Ciara
Brothers: Brendan, Conor, Trevor, Donovan, Kieran, Casey
✴ This Irish Gaelic form of Catherine has a chiming-bell quality that parents love. If you want a truly Gaelic aura, though, look elsewhere. If you tally up its many spellings, Caitlin has been one of America's most common baby names over the past generation. Catriona (pronounced "Katrina") is a less familiar Irish spin on Catherine.
In the World: Writers Caitlin Davies and Caitlín R. Kiernan

Calista (kah-LIS-tə)
1999: #519
Popularity: #1169
Styles: Lacy and Lissome
Nicknames: Callie, Cali
Variants: Callista, Kalista, Caliste
1880　Today
Sisters: Thalia, Celeste, Ariane, Galilea, Livia, Dafne, Allegra, Cassia
Brothers: Trajan, Marius, Soren, Brice, Atticus, Dominic, Dashiell, Carsten
✴ This graceful name is Greek for "most beautiful" and is worthy of that mantle. Actress Calista Flockhart of *Ally McBeal* fame raised awareness of the name, but it had the goods to fly on its own.
In the World: Actress Calista Flockhart

Calla (KA-lə)
1881: #623
Popularity: #1911
Styles: Short and Sweet, Charms and Graces, Why Not?
1880　Today
Nicknames: Callie
Sisters: Willa, Dahlia, Luna, Coral, Mercy, Cassia
Brothers: Rowan, Elias, Quinn, Corin, Forest, Simeon
✴ Calla has seldom been used as a name, but oh, is it ever ready. The dewdrop elegance of calla lilies gives the name instant luster. Calla has a chance to modernize the old favorite Callie, much as Jenna did for Jennie and Tessa for Tessie.

Callie (KA-lee)
1880: #122
Popularity: #212
Styles: Timeless, Nicknames
Variants: Cali, Caleigh, Kallie, Kali
1880　Today
Sisters: Josie, Maggie, Lina, Ivy, Katie, Chloe
Brothers: Ben, Jack, Ethan, Clay, Will, Sam
✴ Callie is a malleable little name that parents arrive at from different angles. Some like it as a cozy old-fashioned nickname, like Josie or Maggie. (It's traditionally short for Caroline, but you can find other options in the "Nicknames" style list.) Others make it a modern full name with spellings like Kali.
In the World: Actress Callie Thorne; Callie Torres of *Grey's Anatomy*; screenwriter Callie Khouri

Cameron (KAM-er-ən, KAM-rin)
1999: #176
Popularity: #442
Styles: Celtic, Androgynous
Nicknames: Cammie, Cami
1880　Today
Variants: Camryn, Kameron
Sisters: Emerson, Carson, Cadence, Logan, Riley, Quinn
Brothers: Donovan, Brogan, Reid, Connor, Brennan, Kane
✴ Actress Cameron Diaz single-handedly opened this name to girls, much to the chagrin of thousands of male Camerons. It works nicely as a girl's name but loses the Scottish swagger that makes it such a smash for boys. If your real love is the nickname Cammie, check out all of your options in the "Nicknames" section.
In the World: Actress Cameron Diaz

Camilla (kah-MIL-ə)   2011: #458
Popularity: #458
Styles: Timeless, English,
Saints
Nicknames: Cami, Millie,   1880 Today
Milla
Variants: Camille, Camila
Sisters: Amelia, Louisa, Daphne, Helena,
Juliet, Annabel
Brothers: Theo, Vincent, Colin, Bennett,
Oliver, Julian
✷ Camilla is a timeless, graceful name with a
right-now sound. In England the association
with Prince Charles's wife Camilla runs strong,
but in the U.S. the name's own ladylike poise
shines through. If it reminds you of a flower,
you're thinking of the similar but unrelated
name Camellia.
In the World: royal spouse Camilla Parker-
Bowles; actress Camilla Belle; TV host Camila
Alves

Camille (kah-MEEL)   2011: #240
Popularity: #240
Styles: Timeless, French,
Literary and Artistic
Nicknames: Cami   1880 Today
Variants: Camilla, Camila
Sisters: Vivienne, Celeste, Juliet, Adele,
Giselle, Daphne
Brothers: Tristan, Noel, Graham, Quentin,
Julian, Blaise
✷ Ah, how romantic! The French classic Ca-
mille has a creative, artistic image, equal parts
flower petals thrown in a stream and cigarettes
smoked at a sidewalk café. For all that romance,
Camille is simple, trim, and very usable. The
English Camilla and Spanish Camila are
equally stylish.
In the World: Alexandre Dumas's novel/play *Ca-
mille*; social critic Camille Paglia; artist Ca-
mille Claudel

Campbell (KAM-bəl)   2006: #662
Popularity: #936
Styles: Last Names First,
Androgynous
Nicknames: Cammie, Cam   1880 Today
Sisters: Parker, Cadence,
Cameron, Emerson, Kendall, Leighton
Brothers: Connor, Logan, Jackson, Ryland,
Archer, Remington
✷ The surname Campbell, familiar from a
century of soup cans, is traditionally masculine
but without any classic male markers. Add in
the nickname Cammie and you have a major
draw for parents of girls. A few have tried to
feminize it with the spelling "Campbelle," but
that makes the silent "p" jump back into play.
In the World: Campbell's Soup; newscaster
Campbell Brown

Camryn (KAM-rin)   1999: #158
Popularity: #294
Styles: The "-ens"
Nicknames: Cami, Cam
Variants: Kamryn   1880 Today
Sisters: Ashlyn, Hadley,
Mckenzie, Kendall, Rylie, Joslyn
Brothers: Dawson, Brennan, Cade, Paxton,
Colton, Brogan
✷ In 1998 actress Camryn Manheim won an
Emmy and gave a memorable, much-publicized
acceptance speech. Her first name, previously
unusual, instantly shot up the charts. Parents
sensed the name's potential as a solution to the
gender confusion of Cameron and as a match
for the style of mega-hit Kaitlyn.
In the World: Actress Camryn Manheim

Candace (KAN-dis) 1982: #103
Popularity: #1540
Styles: '70s–'80s, Mid-
Century, Biblical
Nicknames: Candy   1880 Today
Variants: Candice, Candis
Sisters: Meredith, Lesley, Valerie, Christina,
Jacqueline, Bethany
Brothers: Geoffrey, Mitchell, Lance, Derek,
Terrance, Wesley
✳ Candace sounds comfortably modern and
American. It has already ridden two U.S. popu-
larity waves, one in the 1940s sparked by a
minor movie character, and another sparked by
one of those 1940s babies, actress Candice Ber-
gen. Yet the name has a more regal style than
most all-American girl names, owing perhaps to
its grand history. Candace was a traditional
name for ancient queens of Ethiopia, and it's
mentioned as such in the Bible.
In the World: Actress Candice Bergen; writer
Candace Bushnell

Caprice (kah-PREES) 1966: #943
Popularity: #5534
Styles: Modern Meanings,
Nickname-Proof
Sisters: Ember, Lark, Honor, 1880 Today
Promise, Halo, Avalon
Brothers: Arrow, Roan, Indigo, Talon, Calder,
Orion
✳ A caprice is a whim, an impulse, a lark. Oh,
and a Chevy. It's shaped conveniently like a
classic French name and could be an inspired
choice for a girl. In England the name is linked
to model/reality TV star Caprice Bourret.
In the World: Chevrolet Caprice; model/reality
TV star Caprice Bourret

Carissa (kah-RIS-ə) 1992: #239
Popularity: #920
Styles: Lacy and Lissome,
Turn of the 21st Century
Nicknames: Cari, Rissa   1880 Today
Variants: Charissa, Karissa,
Charis, Karis
Sisters: Brianna, Arielle, Carina, Mariella,
Cassandra, Serena
Brothers: Devon, Elijah, Trevor, Chandler,
Zachary, Colby
✳ Carissa is constructed from the Greek word
charis ("grace") on the lacy model of Clarissa.
Reflections of the word "caress" give the name a
rosewater sweetness. Also consider the name
Charis, which in fact has a longer history
as an English given name.
In the World: Surfer Carissa Moore; sportscaster
Charissa Thompson

Carla (KAHR-lə) 1962: #78
Popularity: #747
Styles: Surfer '60s, Italian
Nicknames: Carly
Variants: Karla   1880 Today
Sisters: Sandra, Michele,
Belinda, Teresa, Sonya, Dina
Brothers: Marc, Craig, Randy, Barry, Keith,
Jeffrey
✳ Carla was a big hit of the '60s, but it doesn't
sound like the other "cute" names of that time.
Its style and strength are more like the sturdy
classics of earlier generations. That has helped
Carla (and especially Karla) stick around while
many other '60s names have vanished. Clara is
a fashionable anagram.
In the World: Model/singer Carla Bruni; actress
Carla Gugino

 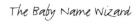

Carly (KAHR-lee)   1995: #122
Popularity: #251
Styles: New Classics, Nicknames
Variants: Karli, Carlie
Sisters: Tessa, Abby, Mallory, Jenna, Brooke, Casey
Brothers: Cole, Jesse, Connor, Dylan, Blake, Tyler
✷ Carly started to be heard as a given name when Carly Simon topped the pop charts in the '70s. It held on strong and is now much more common than the formal Carla. (Caroline beats both, though.) On the model of Ms. Simon, Carly is sweet and pretty with a strong independent streak. The TV series *iCarly* helped keep that image going into the 21st century.
In the World: Sitcom *iCarly*; singers Carly Simon and Carly Rae Jepsen

Carmen (KAHR-min)   1968: #142
Popularity: #349
Styles: Latino/Latina, Timeless, Literary and Artistic, Nickname-Proof
Variants: Carmel
Sisters: Maria, Ana, Yolanda, Diana, Pilar, Luz, Alicia, Margarita
Brothers: Ramon, Mario, Ruben, Roberto, Julio, Raul, Victor, Manuel
✷ This classic has a passionate soul, thanks to Bizet's operatic heroine. Yet the name is too straightforward to wallow in melodrama. Computer game globe-hopper Carmen Sandiego may be a better model for Carmen's modern cross-cultural potential.
In the World: TV show/computer game *Where in the World Is Carmen Sandiego?*; TV personality Carmen Electra; singer Carmen McRae

Carol (KAR-əl)   1945: #5
Popularity: #1258
Styles: Solid Citizens, Androgynous
Nicknames: Carrie
Variants: Carole, Carroll, Karol
Sisters: Ellen, Barbara, Rita, Judith, Susan, Joan
Brothers: Gary, Donald, Paul, Richard, Franklin, Raymond
✷ To understand the name Carol, think of it as the 1940s Courtney. An uncommon male name is embraced as a modern, androgynous choice for women and becomes a runaway hit. By now Carol sounds neither modern nor androgynous and is fading away. More traditional feminine forms of the name, like Caroline and Carolina, have risen to take its place.
In the World: Comedian Carol Burnett; singers Carole King and Carol Channing

Carolina (ka-rə-LIYN-ə, kah-roh-LEE-nah)   2004: #254
Popularity: #429
Styles: Place Names, Antique Charm, Country and Western, Latino/Latina, Italian
Nicknames: Carrie, Carol, Callie
Variants: Caroline
Sisters: Veronica, Catalina, Savannah, Paulina, Virginia, Sierra
Brothers: Walker, Elias, Jackson, Adrian, Emilio, Jonas
✷ Usually, adding an "-a" to the end of a girl's name makes it frillier. In this case, it makes it sassier. Carolina's a lady, make no mistake, but she's not shy and she's nobody's fool. Most Americans will pronounce Carolina like the U.S. states, but the Spanish/Italian version is equally stylish.
In the World: Designer Carolina Herrera; Brazilian actress Carolina Dieckmann

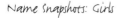

Name Snapshots: Girls   61

Caroline (KA-rə-liyn) 1881: #73
Popularity: #87
Styles: Timeless, Antique Charm
Nicknames: Carrie, Carol, Callie 1880 Today
Variants: Carolina
Sisters: Julia, Charlotte, Grace, Josephine, Victoria, Isabel
Brothers: Samuel, Harrison, Benjamin, Henry, Simon, Alexander
✹ Elegant Caroline is a global favorite. The name is stately and serene and appeals to a wide cross-section of parents. Compare that with seemingly similar names like Pauline and Francine, which have sunk like stones. The stressed "een" sound, dominant for much of the century, is out of favor, while "iyn" is in. Less common "iyn" options include Clementine, Adeline, and Coraline.
In the World: Song "Sweet Caroline"; presidential daughter Caroline Kennedy; tennis player Caroline Wozniacki

Carolyn (KA-rə-lin) 1942: #10
Popularity: #741
Styles: Solid Citizens
Nicknames: Carrie, Lyn, Callie 1880 Today
Variants: Caroline, Carolynn
Sisters: Janet, Kathryn, Judith, Patricia, Sharon, Donna
Brothers: Kenneth, Richard, Dennis, Philip, Allen, Douglas
✹ Carolyn is an appealingly grown-up name. Neither frilly nor boyish, it sounds like an attractive, responsible woman with a good head on her shoulders. Over the past generation, Carolyn has given way to the older French form Caroline.
In the World: Advice columnist Carolyn Hax; actress Carolyn Jones; pseudonymous Nancy Drew author Carolyn Keene

Carrie (KA-ree) 1880: #20
Popularity: #1490
Styles: '70s–'80s, Nicknames
Variants: Karrie, Cari, Kari
Sisters: Jessie, Liza, Holly, 1880 Today
Cassie, Tara, Stacy
Brothers: Sean, Casey, Ryan, Jamie, Clint, Jesse
✹ Perhaps you love Carrie because it's a perky turn-of-the-century nickname. Or perhaps you're a little tired of it because of the Carries, Karis, and Kerries who swarmed through the '70s. The latter view seems to be winning out right now. The name has fallen out of fashion, despite the influence of style queen Carrie Bradshaw on *Sex and the City*. Callie is one alternative that's still going strong.
In the World: Horror novel/film *Carrie*; singer Carrie Underwood; actress Carrie Fisher; Carrie Bradshaw of *Sex and the City*

Carson (KAHR-sən) 1999: #560
Popularity: #1317
Styles: Last Names First, The "-ens," Androgynous, Literary and Artistic 1880 Today
Nicknames: Cari
Sisters: Logan, Harper, Campbell, Flannery, Carrington, Parker
Brothers: Holden, Cooper, Spencer, Jake, Deacon, Colt
✹ As a boy's name, Carson is rollickingly masculine. It wouldn't be a likely girl's choice save for the model of novelist Carson McCullers (born Lula Carson Smith.) That literary model helps make this a chic choice and gives you a good answer for relatives who moan, "That's a *boy's* name!"
In the World: Writer Carson McCullers

Carys (KA-ris)   2006: #1225
Popularity: #1579
Styles: Celtic, Why Not?
Nicknames: Carrie
Variants: Cerys, Charis, Karis   1880   Today
Sisters: Eleri, Maris, Tegan,
Bryn, Lowri, Bethan
Brothers: Rhys, Steffan, Ellis, Cadogan, Price,
Bevan
✷ Carys is a modern Welsh name, coined from
the Welsh root meaning "love." Charis is an
older English/Greek name, coined from the
Greek word for "grace." That's two impeccable
origins sharing one stylish sound (rhyme it with
Paris). The Welsh version is often spelled Cerys
in Wales, but the equally acceptable "a" spelling
is clearer to Americans.
In the World: A daughter of actors Michael
Douglas and Welsh-born Catherine Zeta-Jones

Casey (KAY-see)   1987: #81
Popularity: #620
Styles: '70s–'80s,
Androgynous, Celtic,
Country and Western   1880   Today
Nicknames: Case
Variants: Kacey, Kasey, Kaycee, Kacie
Sisters: Kerry, Shannon, Lesley, Reilly,
Courtney, Kendall
Brothers: Shane, Conor, Kyle, Donovan,
Dustin, Jarrett
✷ Back in the days of train engineer Casey
Jones, Casey was pure Irish manliness. But
names with a "-y" ending are all targets for gen-
der crossover, and today a baby Casey—in one
spelling or another—is as likely to be a girl as a
boy. The original spelling is particularly ener-
getic and self-confident.
In the World: Singer Kasey Chambers; come-
dian Casey Wilson

Cassandra (kə-SAN-drə,   1990: #49
kə-SAHN-drə)
Popularity: #411
Styles: Mythological, Lacy
and Lissome, '70s–'80s, Turn   1880   Today
of the 21st Century
Nicknames: Cass, Cassie, Sandra
Variants: Casandra, Kassandra
Sisters: Alexandria, Miranda, Christina,
Angelica, Bethany, Sabrina
Brothers: Nicholas, Christopher, Desmond,
Anthony, Jonathon, Zachary
✷ Isn't it amazing what a classical pedigree can
do? Most names with this much flounce sound
like pure frill. But thanks to its tragic mytho-
logical weight, Cassandra is sumptuous and se-
rious. It's one name that your practical
mother-in-law and princess-obsessed niece
might agree on.
In the World: Singer Cassandra Wilson; writer
Cassandra Clare

Cassia (KAS-ee-ə, KASH-ə)   1998: #2888
Popularity: #4350
Styles: Charms and Graces,
Lacy and Lissome, Classical,
Why Not?   1880   Today
Nicknames: Cass, Cassie
Variants: Keziah
Sisters: Livia, Arista, Acadia, Linden, Sylvie,
Corinna
Brothers: Carsten, Stone, Torin, Conall, Silvan,
Lake
✷ Cassia is a spice, a form of cinnamon. Its
pretty sound begs for adoption as a girl's name.
The original Hebrew version Keziah (keh-ZAI-
uh) was the name of one of Job's daughters in
the Bible.

Cassidy (KA-si-dee)   1999: #99
Popularity: #283
Styles: Last Names First,
Country and Western, Turn
of the 21st Century   1880   Today
Nicknames: Cass, Cassie
Sisters: Mckenzie, Landry, Camryn, Kennedy,
Delaney, Savannah
Brothers: Carson, Dillon, Bryce, Cooper,
Tanner, Jackson
✷ The cowboy Cassidys (Butch and Hopalong)
still enliven this name. A young Cassidy is more
likely to be a city gal than a ranch hand, but the
energetic, self-assured spirit of the name owes
plenty to its cowboy days.
In the World: Outlaw Butch Cassidy; actress
Cassidy Freeman; '70s teen idol Shaun Cassidy

Cassie (KA-see) 1982: #137
Popularity: #1170
Styles: Nicknames, Antique
Charm, '70s–'80s

1880 Today

Nicknames: Cass
Variants: Cassey
Sisters: Josie, Lacie, Jenna, Trista, Nikki, Carlie
Brothers: Cody, Drew, Jeremy, Brett, Shaun, Travis
✸This popular nickname is cute but confident—sassy, brassy Cassie. It's a rare example of a name that has already come and gone twice, leaving it with a style that's more timeless than trendy. Clip it even shorter and you have the supremely confident nickname Cass.
In the World: Singer Cassie (Ventura)

Catalina (ka-tə-LEE-nə, 2009: #600
kah-tah-LEE-ə)
Popularity: #646
Styles: Latino/Latina, Exotic
Traditional, Place Names,
Antique Charm

1880 Today

Nicknames: Cat, Catie, Lina
Sisters: Juliana, Carolina, Paloma, Victoria, Violeta, Mariana, Natalia, Valentina
Brothers: Rafael, Joaquin, Julio, Lorenzo, Fernando, Andres, Pablo, Santiago
✸This Spanish form of Catherine makes a distinctive alternative to Caitlin or Katrina. Its traditional elegance also meshes nicely with turn-of-the-century favorites like Isabelle. For Californians, it may sound like a place name, thanks to scenic Catalina Island.
In the World: Catalina Island; actress Catalina Sandino Moreno

Catherine (KA-thrin, 1914: #18
KA-thə-rin)
Popularity: #161
Styles: Timeless

1880 Today

Nicknames: Cat, Cathy, Cate
Variants: Katherine, Catharine, Kathryn, Katerina, Carina
Sisters: Charlotte, Elizabeth, Josephine, Margaret, Anna, Cecelia
Brothers: Joseph, Edward, Louis, George, Henry, Charles
✸Catherine is the French form of the classic regal name. This spelling was also the U.S. favorite in the 19th century, so it now carries a gently old-fashioned luster. If you're choosing between "C" and "K," think of Catherine as a pearl and Katherine as a sapphire.
In the World: Catherine, Duchess of Cambridge; actress Catherine Zeta-Jones; empress Catherine the Great

Cecile (sə-SEEL) 1902: #222
Popularity: #5360
Styles: French, Ladies and
Gentlemen

1880 Today

Nicknames: Ceil, Sissy
Variants: Cecilia, Cécile
Sisters: Celeste, Marguerite, Adele, Camille, Marion, Estelle
Brothers: Jules, Clement, Hugo, Foster, Edmond, Gaston
✸Cecile has the soft grace of comeback queens Lillian and Eleanor, heard through a French translator. The form Cecilia has more fashion momentum at the moment, though. Try Cecile and French sisters like Camille, Simone, and Celeste as middle names, especially after names with first-syllable stress such as Isabel and Abigail.
In the World: Actress Cécile de France; composer Cécile Chaminade

Cecilia (sə-SEEL-yə, sə-SEE-lee-ə)   1904: #190

Popularity: #241
Styles: Timeless
Nicknames: Sissy, Ceil, Celia, Ceci
Variants: Cecelia, Cecily, Cicely, Cecile, Cecilie
Sisters: Antonia, Josephine, Vivian, Helena, Catherine, Eliza
Brothers: Harrison, Charles, Everett, Simon, Thomas, Theodore
✳ Shh . . . this soft, sibilant selection is sentimental yet serious. Some suggest it suffers from a surplus of "s" sounds, but it's oh-so-sweet and satisfying. Sweet Cecilia is currently a high-status name in the U.S., but modest and understated (as truly high-status choices often are).
In the World: Opera singer Cecilia Bartoli; Simon & Garfunkel song "Cecilia"; writer Cecelia Ahern

Cecily (SEHS-i-lee)   1989: #497

Popularity: #1912
Styles: Antique Charm, English, Saints, Why Not?
Nicknames: Ceil
Variants: Cicely, Cecilia, Cecile
Sisters: Violet, Davina, Briony, Annalise, Verity, Amalia
Brothers: Gareth, Colman, Crispin, Barnaby, Albin, Benedict
✳This pretty form of Cecilia is especially quaint and delicate, but you wouldn't want to cross a Cecily. That lady's tougher than she looks. The name's rhythm and style make it a great sister for Olivia or Isabella. The variant Cicely is also the name of an herbaceous plant.
In the World: Actress Cicely Tyson; painter Cecily Brown; illustrator Cicely Mary Barker

Celeste (seh-LEST)   2004: #204

Popularity: #453
Styles: Timeless, French, Nickname-Proof, Why Not?
Variants: Celestine
Sisters: Simone, Penelope, Emmeline, Camille, Audra, Elise
Brothers: Noel, Elliot, Duncan, Hugo, Bennett, Vincent
✳ Celeste is elegant, confident, and womanly. This French-American classic is a fabulous example of a name that sounds mature but not a bit boring. It also reaches for the sky in a subtler way than Heaven or Star. A high-impact choice.
In the World: Queen Celeste of *Babar the Elephant*; actress Celeste Holm; Mama Celeste frozen pizza

Celia (SEE-lee-ə, SEEL-yə)   1895: #158

Popularity: #735
Styles: Timeless, Shakespearean, Why Not?
Nicknames: Cissy, Ceil
Variants: Caelia
Sisters: Lydia, Helena, Alice, Celeste, Antonia, Nina
Brothers: Vincent, Oliver, Joseph, Simon, Anton, Samuel
✳ Sweet, serious Celia is an attractive name with surprisingly few takers. As a given name, it dates back to ancient Rome with a stopover at Shakespeare, but you can also use it as a nickname for Cecelia.
In the World: Singer Celia Cruz; actress Celia Imrie

Celine (seh-LEEN)   1998: #455

Popularity: #1191
Styles: French
Variants: Céline
Sisters: Giselle, Delphine, Sylvie, Simone, Amelie, Noelle, Sabine
Brothers: Blaise, Julien, Luc, Marcel, Fabrice, Adrien, Etienne
✳ Singer Céline Dion has been both a blessing and a curse to this name. She introduced its silken charms to a whole new audience, but she was so strongly identified with the name that her image was hard to shake. By now, though, the name has been familiar for long enough that it no longer sounds like an homage.
In the World: Singer Céline Dion

Chanel (shə-NEHL) 1991: #382
Popularity: #827
Styles: '70s–'80s, Fanciful
Variants: Chanelle
Sisters: Cristal, Desiree, 1880 Today
Madison, Shante, Vanessa,
Armani
Brothers: Jordan, Aramis, Halston, Cortez,
Marquis, Westley
★A natural sister for Tiffany—your family will be a living stroll down Fifth Avenue. (Prada and Armani update the theme.) Chanel has a sleek French essence inherited from fashion icon Coco Chanel, but it is not used as a first name in France. For an authentic Gallic alternative, try Chantal.
In the World: Chanel fashion house; model Chanel Iman

Chantal (shawn-TAHL) 1990: #551
Popularity: #2679
Styles: French, Saints,
African-American
Nicknames: Tali, Chan 1880 Today
Variants: Chantel, Chantelle,
Shantel
Sisters: Lisette, Simone, Arianne, Sabine, Soleil, Brigitte
Brothers: Marcel, Blaise, Dominique, Mathieu, Quentin, Etienne
★This '50s French classic started to catch on in the U.S. in the '80s, but it's still uncommon and maintains a distinctly French character. Alternate spellings shift the style from French toward African-American.
In the World: Singer Chantal Kreviazuk; jockey Chantal Sutherland

Charity (CHA-ri-tee) 1975: #183
Popularity: #852
Styles: Charms and Graces,
Antique Charm, Nickname-
Proof, Why Not? 1880 Today
Sisters: Harmony, Felicity, Willow, Daphne, Juniper, Mercy
Brothers: Jasper, Pierce, Gideon, Tobias, Vance, Jericho
★With its generous spirit and girly style, Charity may be the cheeriest of the virtue names. The dance hall girl of the musical *Sweet Charity* was one negative association, but that's slowly fading away.
In the World: Actress Charity Wakefield; musical *Sweet Charity*

Charlene (shahr-LEEN, 1949: #100
chahr-LEEN)
Popularity: #1631
Styles: Mid-Century,
African-American 1880 Today
Nicknames: Charlie
Variants: Charline, Charleen, Sharleen, Carlene, Charlaine
Sisters: Marsha, Gayle, Marlene, Charmaine, Francine, Rosanne
Brothers: Jerome, Bruce, Gerard, Wayne, Ronald, Barry
★This feminine form of Charles was a standard through much of the 20th century. It has now yielded the fashion high ground back to 19th-century favorite Charlotte.
In the World: Writer Charlaine Harris; actress Charlene Tilton; comedian Charlyne Yi

Charlie (CHAHR-lee) 2011: #376
Popularity: #376
Styles: Nicknames, Guys and
Dolls, Androgynous
Variants: Charley 1880 Today
Sisters: Georgie, Tess, Libby, Frankie, Mae, Rosie, Billie, Mattie
Brothers: Jack, Deacon, Max, Duke, Lawson, Archer, Beck, Sam
★Charlie is the #1 friendliest boy's name. On a girl, it's equally friendly, with an added rebellious charm. Parents who love that moxie often find formal versions like Charlotte a little too staid, so they go with Charlie on the birth certificate. As a given name, it's lovable, but not very flexible.
In the World: *Charlie's Angels*; Revlon's "Charlie" perfumes; a daughter of actress Rebecca Romijn

Charlotte (SHAHR-lət) 1943: #47
Popularity: #27
Styles: Antique Charm,
English, Timeless, New
Classics
Nicknames: Lottie, Lotte,
Charlie
Sisters: Caroline, Amelia, Georgia, Isabelle,
Josephine, Phoebe
Brothers: Emmett, Henry, Oliver, Owen,
Samuel, Jasper
✷ Charlotte was once an intensely Southern
name. A *Sex and the City* character helped propel its transformation in the 2000s into a top
choice of the coastal urban elite. It's a dignified
classic with a warm and cuddly side: a crowd-
pleaser.
In the World: Charlotte of *Sex and the City;*
writer Charlotte Brontë; Charlotte, North Caro-
lina; singer Charlotte Church

Chastity (CHAS-ti-tee) 1974: #311
Popularity: #3709
Styles: Charms and Graces
Nicknames: Chas, Chassie
Variants: Chasity
Sisters: Patience, Clemency,
Honesty, Mercy, Verity, Temperance
Brothers: Peregrine, Concord, Moses, Tobias,
Honor, Constant
✷ Of all the virtue names, Chastity may have
the most contemporary sound. Parents shy away
from it nonetheless, reluctant to include any direct reference to sex (or the lack thereof) in their
daughter's name. Some parents have tried to
keep the sound but drop the sex with the hybrid
Chasity. You might try Charity instead.
In the World: TV personality Chaz Bono, for-
merly Chastity Bono

Chaya (KHIY-ə) 2011: #715
Popularity: #715
Styles: Jewish, Short and
Sweet
Variants: Chava
Sisters: Shira, Tova, Rivka,
Noa, Avigail, Ilana
Brothers: Hillel, Ezra, Yakov, Ari, Noam,
Yehuda
✷ Chaya is a runaway hit name among reli-
gious Jews. It comes from the Hebrew word for
"life," making it the female equivalent of
Chaim. Unlike Chaim, Chaya is starting to at-
tract non-Jewish parents as well. It's light, wom-
anly, and life-affirming.

Chelsea (CHEHL-see) 1992: #15
Popularity: #222
Styles: Place Names,
Nickname-Proof, Turn of the
21st Century
Variants: Chelsey, Chelsie
Sisters: Lindsay, Amanda, Courtney,
Channing, Devon, Mallory
Brothers: Austin, Spencer, Clayton, Jared,
Holden, Shane
✷ Chelsea is an English place name, a bor-
ough of London. American and Australian par-
ents flocked to it in the '80s and '90s as a creative
girl's name with a jet-setting kick. The London
association faded as the name became popular,
but Chelsea's distinctive spelling still connects
it to its roots.
In the World: Presidential daughter Chelsea
Clinton; comedian Chelsea Handler

Cheryl (SHEHR-əl) 1958: #13
Popularity: #2709
Styles: Mid-Century
Nicknames: Cher
Variants: Cherryl, Sheryl,
Cheryle, Sherrill, Sherrell
Sisters: Pamela, Kathleen, Marsha, Denise,
Sandra, Cynthia
Brothers: Barry, Mark, Randall, Gregory, Dana,
Douglas
✷ Cheryl was the Kaitlyn of the '50s: a popular
sensation that inspired a frenzy of creative spell-
ing. It first appeared in the '20s with a hard "ch"
sound like "cherry." Once that softened to a
"sh," on the model of the French *chérie,* the
name really hit its stride. Like many sudden sen-
sations, Cheryl passed out of fashion in a hurry
and is now a rarity.
In the World: Singers Sheryl Crow and Cheryl
Cole; actress Cheryl Ladd; model Cheryl Tiegs;
dancer Cheryl Burke

Cheyenne (shiy-AN, shiy-EHN)
1996: #68
Popularity: #274
Styles: Place Names, Country and Western, Turn of the 21st Century

1880 Today

Variants: Cheyanne, Shyanne
Sisters: Sierra, Cassidy, Savannah, Aspen, Brielle, Shelby
Brothers: Cody, Shane, Bridger, Dakota, Chance, Tanner

✱ Like Dakota, Cheyenne gives us the mind-bender of parents naming their kids after Indians to make them sound like cowboys. Or in this case, cowgirls. In the classic spelling, this is a rare, pure Wild West name for girls. Variations like Shyanne morph it into a modern invention.
In the World: Cheyenne, Wyoming; golfer Cheyenne Woods; singer Cheyenne Kimball; (male) actor Cheyenne Jackson

Chloe (KLOH-ee)
2010: #9
Popularity: #10
Styles: Antique Charm, Nickname-Proof, Short and Sweet

1880 Today

Variants: Chloë, Chloé, Khloe
Sisters: Ava, Maya, Zoe, Claire, Sophie, Lila, Piper, Phoebe
Brothers: Luke, Eli, Owen, Wyatt, Liam, Caleb, Mason, Noah

✱ Chloe, an appellation of the Greek goddess Demeter, was the top girl's name in England for years. It was a more modest hit in the U.S. until reality TV star Khloe Kardashian gave the name a glossy boost (and an unlikely but popular alternate spelling). If you love the classical sound and style of the original but crave a less common name, consider Daphne or Ione.
In the World: Reality TV star Khloe Kardashian; Chloé fashion house; actresses Chloë Moretz and Chloë Sevigny

Christiana (kris-tee-AH-nə)
1996: #699
Popularity: #1324
Styles: Lacy and Lissome, Why Not?
Nicknames: Chris, Christie, Chrissy

1880 Today

Variants: Christiane, Cristiana, Christina
Sisters: Alexandria, Graciela, Evangeline, Celeste, Cassandra, Angelica
Brothers: Adrian, Charleston, Tomas, Alexander, Maximilian, Raphael

✱ A mouthful, but perhaps the most sophisticated of all the Christine variations. The variant Christiane was a big hit in France in the '40s and Germany in the '60s.
In the World: Newscaster Christiane Amanpour; actress Cristiana Oliveira

Christina (kris-TEE-nə)
1978: #15
Popularity: #271
Styles: Timeless, '70s–'80s
Nicknames: Chris, Chrissy, Christie, Tina

1880 Today

Variants: Christine, Cristina, Kristina, Christiana
Sisters: Rebecca, Victoria, Stephanie, Cassandra, Danielle, Veronica
Brothers: Matthew, Alexander, Patrick, Joel, Nathaniel, Anthony

✱ Christina is a survivor of the '70s storm of Christy names. Its timeless elegance is as strong as ever, and a lavish girl's classic like this one will always find takers.
In the World: Singer Christina Aguilera; actresses Christina Ricci and Christina Hendricks; poet Christina Rossetti

Christine (kris-TEEN)
1968: #14
Popularity: #731
Styles: Surfer '60s, '70s–'80s, French
Nicknames: Chris, Christie, Chrissy

1880 Today

Variants: Christina, Kristine, Kristin
Sisters: Denise, Teresa, Jacqueline, Melinda, Kimberly, Stephanie
Brothers: Steven, Jeffrey, Mark, Timothy, Michael, Gregory

✱ Before there was Kristin, or Christa, or Kirsten, there was this French/English standard. The Chris craze has yielded to crazes for Kay, Bree, and beyond, but Christine still sounds sharp. The name's warm, true sound transcends its historical trendiness.
In the World: Christine Daaé of *The Phantom of the Opera*; sitcom *The New Adventures of Old Christine*

Christy (KRIS-tee)   1975: #53
Popularity: #1672
Styles: Nicknames, '70s–'80s
Nicknames: Chris
Variants: Christie, Christi,   1880 Today
Kristi, Kristie, Kristy
Sisters: Kerri, Mindy, Tricia, Stacey, Jody, Tara
Brothers: Jamey, Brent, Chad, Derrick, Torrey,
Shawn
✷ Add up all the spellings, and there were
more girls named Christy in the '70s than Sarah
or Mary. And that doesn't even count the Kris-
tens, Christines, and Kristas who go by this
nickname. Why did parents love Christy so?
The name has a sparkle to it, like sunshine on
fresh Christmas snow. Unfortunately, the '70s
date-stamp is now just as strong as the sparkle.
In the World: Models Christie Brinkley and
Christy Turlington; actress Kristy McNichol;
skater Kristi Yamaguchi

Ciara (see-EHR-ə, KEER-ə)   2005: #150
Popularity: #528
Styles: African-American,
Celtic
Variants: Ciera, Sierra, Keira,   1880 Today
Kira, Chiara, Kiara
Sisters: Nia, Fiona, Taryn, Caitlin, Alexis,
Brenna, Aine, Tegan
Brothers: Conor, Rohan, Keenan, Desmond,
Shane, Devon, Brendan, Bryce
✷ Ciara is two names: a popular Irish name
pronounced "KEE-rə" and an African-Ameri-
can name, popularized by the one-named
singer Ciara and pronounced "see-EH-rə." It's
attractive either way, and if you love the spell-
ing, you can stick to your guns and live with the
mispronunciations. If it's just the sound you
want, though, Keira or Sierra might save some
hassles. For the pronunciation "kee-AH-rə,"
consider the Italian name Chiara. See also
Kiara and Keira.
In the World: Singer Ciara Harris

Cindy (SIN-dee)   1957: #19
Popularity: #638
Styles: Mid-Century,
Nicknames, Surfer '60s
Variants: Cinda, Cindi,   1880 Today
Cyndi
Sisters: Lisa, Sandy, Terri, Kim, Denise, Vicky
Brothers: Randy, Kenny, Rick, Steve, Danny,
Greg
✷ Cindy is a prototype for the perky breed of
girls' names. Its femininity is the high-spirited
kind, like a cheerleader rather than a damsel or
diva. While the name is still rooted in its mid-
century prime, it sounds as sunny and pleasant
as ever—especially in its traditional role as a
nickname for Cynthia or Lucinda.
In the World: Model Cindy Crawford; singer
Cyndi Lauper; photographer Cindy Sherman

Claire (KLAYR)   2011: #50
Popularity: #50
Styles: Timeless, French,
Brisk and Breezy
Variants: Clare, Clara   1880 Today
Sisters: Audrey, Elise, Brooke,
Camille, Grace, Sophie, Juliet, Charlotte
Brothers: Julian, Grant, Cole, Benjamin, Davis,
Graham, Vincent, Luke
✷ Claire is straightforward, in the best kind of
way: sweet, pretty, and smart. This classic is
now enjoying a burst of popularity, especially
among urban professional parents who appreci-
ate its dressed for-success strength. The tradi-
tional English spelling is Clare, the French is
Claire.
In the World: Actresses Claire Danes and Claire
Forlani; Claire's accessory stores

Clara (KLAYR-ə, KLA-rə)   1884: #8
Popularity: #151
Styles: Ladies and
Gentlemen, Antique Charm,
Nickname-Proof   1880 Today
Sisters: Eliza, Cora, Lydia,
Eleanor, Amelia, Ada
Brothers: Leo, Miles, Emmett, Oscar, Charles,
Henry
✷ Clara is trim and cute but every inch a lady.
This name has the sweet heirloom style that has
made Emma and Lily smash hits. It's on its way
up.
In the World: Red Cross founder Clara Barton;
silent film star Clara Bow; pianist/composer
Clara Schumann

Clarice (kla-REES) 1913: #258
Popularity: #3989
Styles: Ladies and
Gentlemen, Nickname-Proof
Variants: Clarisse, Clarissa 1880 Today
Sisters: Petra, Adele, Iona,
Margery, Sybil, Corinne
Brothers: Roland, Laurence, Conrad, Wallace,
Lyle, Clifton
✳ Clarice has the form of a '50s French favorite, but it dates from the Middle Ages. It was a romantic choice then, used in tales of heraldry. Today the derivative Clarissa is more romantic, and Clarice is still recovering from the creepy voice of Anthony Hopkins talking to Jodi Foster's FBI agent Clarice in *The Silence of the Lambs*.
In the World: Clarice Starling of *The Silence of the Lambs*; children's book *Clarice Bean*; writer Clarice Lispector

Clarissa (kla-RIS-ə) 1995: #239
Popularity: #597
Styles: Lacy and Lissome,
New Classics
Nicknames: Rissa 1880 Today
Variants: Clarice
Sisters: Angelica, Cassandra, Vanessa, Larissa, Arielle, Christiana, Gabrielle, Julianna
Brothers: Garrett, Brendan, Christian, Spencer, Blake, Trevor, Kendrick, Lucas
✳ Clarissa is a pretty, almost-but-not-quite-prissy name, scented with flowers and the dust of 19th-century romantic novels. While this name has no real nicknames, Clarissas inevitably end up with one anyway. If you're particular about that, you're best off choosing one early.
In the World: TV series *Clarissa Explains It All*; Samuel Richardson's novel *Clarissa*; Clarissa of Virginia Woolf's novel *Mrs. Dalloway*

Claudia (KLAW-dee-ə, 1952: #111
KLOW-dee-ə)
Popularity: #609
Styles: Timeless, Classical,
German and Dutch, Italian, 1880 Today
Biblical
Nicknames: Claudie
Variants: Klaudia, Claudette
Sisters: Martina, Veronica, Candace, Antonia, Bettina, Portia, Celeste, Renata
Brothers: Anton, Vincent, Ivan, Victor, Mario, Marcus, Lorenzo, Roman
✳ Claudia has been an English name for centuries, but it still sounds appealingly foreign. Whether in the classical form of a female counterpart to Claudius or the impeccable form of German model Claudia Schiffer, the name conveys a stately grace.
In the World: Model Claudia Schiffer; actress Claudia Cardinale

Clementine 1890: #384
(KLEHM-ehn-tiyn)
Popularity: #1507
Styles: Ladies and
Gentlemen, French, Country 1880 Today
and Western
Nicknames: Clemmie, Tina
Sisters: Eloise, Beatrice, Penelope, Dorothea, Millicent, Susannah
Brothers: Hugo, Rupert, Theodore, Felix, Leopold, Conrad
✳ One part fusty and one part cute as a button, darling Clementine has tons of potential now that Madeline and friends have paved the way. This name is one good nickname away from star status.
In the World: Song "Oh My Darling, Clementine"; "Clementine" children's book series; clementine citrus fruit

 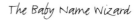

Cleo (KLEE-oh)   1907: #171
Popularity: #2162
Styles: Guys and Dolls,
Exotic Traditional, Short and
Sweet, Why Not?   1880   Today
Variants: Clio
Sisters: Avis, Rhea, Ruby, Lola, Ione, Eden,
Evie, Zora
Brothers: Rex, Fletcher, Bruno, Nat, Archie,
Milo, Murphy, Oscar
✷ Chloe is the modern darling, a stylish favorite in English and French. A tiny twist gives you Cleo, which is a little quirkier but every bit as charming . . . and completely undiscovered. The spelling Cleo is short for Cleopatra; Clio was the Greek muse of history. The name may strike a chord with cartoon fans as the goldfish in *Pinocchio* and a dog in the "Clifford" series.
In the World: Jazz singer Cleo Laine; psychic "Miss Cleo"; Cleo the goldfish in *Pinocchio*; daughter of actor David Schwimmer

Colette (koh-LEHT)   1966: #372
Popularity: #1039
Styles: Mid-Century, French,
Saints, Literary and Artistic
Sisters: Nanette, Patrice,   1880   Today
Yvonne, Roxanne, Chantal,
Jeannine
Brothers: Marcel, Gerard, Blaise, Michel,
Denis, Christophe
✷ Coquettish with literary underpinnings, this name could satisfy your serious and girly sides both at once. The name was a mid-century hit in both France and the U.S., thanks to the novelist known by the single name Colette (born Sidonie-Gabrielle Colette).
In the World: *Gigi* author Colette; singer Colette Carr

Colleen (kah-LEEN)   1964: #94
Popularity: #1456
Styles: Celtic, Mid-Century,
Nickname-Proof
Sisters: Sheila, Maureen,   1880   Today
Denise, Shannon, Brenda,
Leslie
Brothers: Keith, Glenn, Brian, Patrick, Randall,
Barry
✷ Colleen is an Irish word for "girl," but the name sounds more like an American mom than a Celtic lass. It's a 20th-century creation seldom used in Ireland or England.
In the World: Writer Colleen McCullough; actress Colleen Dewhurst

Connie (KAH-nee)   1955: #35
Popularity: #2356
Styles: Mid-Century,
Nicknames
Sisters: Debbie, Julie, Karen,   1880   Today
Bonnie, Janice, Annette
Brothers: Barry, Dean, Allen, Jerry, Dennis,
Glenn
✷ Connie is a pure mid-century classic, with squeaky-clean sweetness personified by singing star Connie Francis. Unlike most hits of that period, Connie still has most of the sparkle that sent it to the top. Instead of being outmoded, it sounds cheerfully retro . . . as a nickname. Try it as a short form of Constance, Connolly, Cornelia, or Consuela.
In the World: Singer Connie Francis; newscaster Connie Chung; actresses Connie Britton, Connie Stevens, and Connie Sellecca

Constance (KAHN-stehns)   1950: #85
Popularity: #1583
Styles: Solid Citizens,
Charms and Graces
Nicknames: Connie   1880   Today
Sisters: Anita, Rosemary,
Judith, Bonnie, Lorraine, June
Brothers: Glenn, Lawrence, Mark, Jerome,
Randolph, Philip
✷ Virtue names are in full flower today, but dear Constance has been left behind. Unlike cousins Patience and Faith, Constance was extremely popular during the 20th century, so she lacks the element of surprise. She does, though, have the classic nickname Connie, which gives her a chance to kick up her heels.
In the World: Actresses Constance Marie, Constance Bennett, and Constance Zimmer

Cora (KOH-rə)   1880: #15
Popularity: #204
Styles: Ladies and
Gentlemen, Antique Charm
Nicknames: Corrie   1880   Today
Sisters: Alma, Eliza, Adeline,
Lucy, Clara, Iva, Sadie
Brothers: Leo, Hugh, Eli, Sam, Everett, Porter
✷ Cora was one of the trendiest hits of the 1870s–'80s. For a long time, the name's image stayed back in that era. We pictured a Cora sitting, tightly corseted, in a stiff formal portrait. Today she's ready to cut loose. That trim shape and strong "o" sound are luring in a new generation.
In the World: Cora Crawley of *Downton Abbey*; 19th-century courtesan Cora Pearl

Coral (KOHR-əl) 1888: #486
Popularity: #1508
Styles: Charms and Graces,
Why Not?
Nicknames: Cori 1880 Today
Sisters: Ember, Opal, Calla,
Mercy, Raine, Honor
Brothers: Jasper, Stone, Simeon, Lake, Hayes,
Turner
✷ Coral is one of the rarest names in the gem family, and one of the most modern-sounding. Images of sea and sand make this a perfect contemporary nature name.

Coraline (COH-rə-liyn, 2010: #1039
COH-rə-leen)
Popularity: #1089
Styles: Ladies and
Gentlemen, Literary and 1880 Today
Artistic, Why Not?
Nicknames: Cora, Corrie, Lina, Coral
Sisters: Christabel, Emmeline, Juniper,
Clementine, Delia, Adelaide
Brothers: Casper, Julius, Dashiell, Eliot,
Burgess, Hugh
✷ Let's start with the good: this is a sweet old 19th-century name with strong nicknames. Now the bad: it will constantly be confused with Caroline, and nobody will know which way to pronounce it. If you feel the good outweighs the bad, I don't think you're alone.
In the World: Children's fantasy/horror book and film *Coraline*

Cordelia (kohr-DEEL-yə, 1880: #204
kohr-DEE-lee-ə)
Popularity: #1318
Styles: Ladies and
Gentlemen, English, 1880 Today
Shakespearean
Nicknames: Corrie, Delia, Dell
Sisters: Emmeline, Harriet, Beatrice, Ophelia,
Coraline, Augusta
Brothers: Augustus, Edgar, Ambrose, Leopold,
Rupert, Conrad
✷ Cordelia was King Lear's virtuous daughter, a worthy literary exemplar. Yet conniving sister Regan has the hit name of the moment. The naming life can be so unfair. You can help resuscitate this respectable name or just use Delia, a lighter but equally traditional option.
In the World: Cordelia of *King Lear*; Cordelia Chase of *Buffy the Vampire Slayer*

Corinne (koh-RIN, 1926: #249
koh-REEN)
Popularity: #797
Styles: Timeless, French
Nicknames: Cory, Cora 1880 Today
Variants: Corinna, Corrine
Sisters: Adrienne, Simone, Martina, Camille,
Claudia, Yvonne, Candace, Patrice
Brothers: Noel, Vincent, Clinton, Byron,
Marcel, Anton, Clay, Quentin
✷ This French standard is a model of decorum. It's feminine without frills or flash and immune to the winds of fashion. The English Corinna is equally classic with a more poetic spirit.
In the World: Singer Corinne Bailey Rae; song "Corrine, Corrina"

Courtney (COHRT-nee) 1990: #17
Popularity: #418
Styles: Last Names First,
Androgynous, '70s–'80s
Nicknames: Court 1880 Today
Variants: Kourtney, Cortney
Sisters: Lindsay, Kelsey, Shannon, Whitney,
Heather, Chelsea
Brothers: Dustin, Taylor, Corey, Kyle, Travis,
Brandon
✷ Fifty years ago, Courtney was a fancy-pants boy's name derived from a Norman baronial name. (Neville and Aubrey are similar examples.) More recently, it emerged as part of a new group of girls' names that became the sound of the '80s and '90s. Like its companions Brittany and Ashley, Courtney is still widely used but no longer on the cusp of fashion.
In the World: Actresses Courtney Cox and Courtney Thorne-Smith; reality TV star Kourtney Kardashian

Crystal (KRIS-təl)   1982: #9
Popularity: #343
Styles: Modern Meanings,
'70s–'80s, Charms and
Graces   1880   Today
Nicknames: Kris, Chrystie
Variants: Kristal, Chrystal, Krystal, Krystle,
Cristal
Sisters: Amber, Nicole, Heather, Jessica,
Candice, April
Brothers: Dustin, Chad, Brent, Casey, Travis,
Shaun
✳ Crystal was a staple of the '70s and '80s, a
shimmering choice that perfectly fit the sound
of the times. Today that shimmer is down to an
ember, as the name is approaching generational
limbo. The original spelling is holding up bet-
ter than the creative variants; it has old roots as
a gem name from the era of Ruby and Opal.
In the World: Singer Crystal Gayle; many fan-
tasy uses, including *Dark Crystal* film and
"Crystal Saga" game

Cynthia (SIN-thee-ə)   1957: #7
Popularity: #430
Styles: Mid-Century
Nicknames: Cindy, Tia,
Cinda, Thea   1880   Today
Variants: Cinzia, Cíntia

Sisters: Teresa, Pamela, Deborah, Christine,
Stephanie, Belinda
Brothers: Gregory, Mark, Timothy, Curtis,
David, Stephen
✳ This '50s favorite has held up beautifully.
The name Cynthia comes from a title for the
goddess Artemis, and its classical feminity has
kept it current. The nickname Cindy has not
been as fortunate, but Tia is a fashionable alter-
native.
In the World: Designer Cynthia Rowley; actress
Cynthia Nixon

Daisy (DAY-zee)   1880: #48
Popularity: #166
Styles: Charms and Graces,
Antique Charm, Nickname-
Proof   1880   Today
Sisters: Poppy, Rosie, Belle,
Violet, Sadie, Lucy
Brothers: Jack, Charlie, Max, Harry, Milo,
Oliver
✳ Daisy is the cutest and lightest of the classic
flower names. Its innocent, old-fashioned
charm is hard to resist. The images of Daisy
Mae of Dogpatch and Daisy Duke of Hazzard
County keep the name from getting airs.
In the World: Daisy Duke of *The Dukes of Haz-
zard*; Daisy Mae of *Li'l Abner*; TV host Daisy
Fuentes; *Driving Miss Daisy*; Daisy of *The
Great Gatsby*

Dakota (dah-KOH-tə)   2006: #190
Popularity: #297
Styles: Place Names, Country
and Western
Nicknames: Koty   1880   Today

Sisters: Sedona, Oakley,
Montana, Shenandoah, Laramie, Bryce
Brothers: Maverick, Chayton, Ridge, Jedidiah,
Coty, Sawyer
✳ Dakota was one of the hottest new boys'
names of the 1990s. It was a rugged individualist, as craggy as the Dakota Badlands. Then a
funny thing happened. The best-known Dakota
of the following decade was a girl: actress Dakota Fanning. The name quickly moved over to
meet her and has become completely androgynous.
In the World: Actresses Dakota Fanning and Dakota Blue Richards

Dale (DAYL)   1952: #237
Popularity: Very rare
Styles: Solid Citizens, Brisk
and Breezy, Androgynous
Sisters: Lynne, Janis, Carol,   1880   Today
Gwen, Hollis, Kaye
Brothers: Garry, Dwight, Von, Randolph,
Glynn, Stewart
✳ Dale has been primarily a boy's name for
many years, but it's worth reconsidering for
girls. It's swift and androgynous in a modern
style. The image of Western star Dale Evans rid-
ing the range with Roy Rogers could give it a
little cowgirl power.
In the World: Actresses Dale Evans and Dale
Dickey

Dalia (DAH-lee-ə)   1994: #485
Popularity: #955
Styles: Lacy and Lissome,
Jewish, Muslim, Nickname-
Proof, Why Not?   1880   Today
Variants: Dahlia
Sisters: Ilana, Nadia, Dima, Amira, Maryam,
Liora, Ariel
Brothers: Jaron, Ari, Bilal, Eitan, Samir, Kamil,
Dov
★This soft, gentle name is a cross-cultural
gem, used in languages from Hebrew to Span-
ish to Arabic. The floral spelling Dahlia is pri-
marily British but starting to rise in the U.S. For
a more old-fashioned spin on the name, con-
sider Delia.

Dana (DAY-nə)   1971: #44
Popularity: #610
Styles: Surfer '60s,
Androgynous, Nickname-
Proof   1880   Today
Variants: Dayna
Sisters: Jody, Carla, Tracy, Tamara, Kerry,
Leslie
Brothers: Derek, Scott, Troy, Craig, Darren,
Marc
★The name Dana was just for boys a century
ago, but the rise of Donna and Diana in the '50s
made it a tempting choice for girls. After a peak
from the '60s to the '80s, the name entered a
quiet period, and now it is neither in nor out of
fashion.
In the World: Actress Dana Delany; political
commentator Dana Perino; agent Dana Scully
of *The X-Files*

Danica (DA-ni-kə)   2007: #307
Popularity: #463
Styles: Slavic
Nicknames: Dani, Nika
Variants: Danika   1880   Today
Sisters: Milana, Daria,
Sienna, Anya, Willow, Alina, Katya, Nadia
Brothers: Lukas, Damian, Dominik, Maxim,
Griffin, Quinn, Devon, Roman
★When auto racer Danica Patrick hit the top
five in the Indy 500, she also drove her name
into the American mainstream. In languages
like Serbian and Slovak, it's pronounced "DAH-
nee-tsah."
In the World: Auto racer Danica Patrick; actress/
math advocate Danica McKellar

Daniela (dan-YEH-lə)   2003: #112
Popularity: #168
Styles: Italian, Slavic, Latino/
Latina, Lacy and Lissome,
New Classics   1880   Today
Nicknames: Dani, Ella
Variants: Daniella, Danielle, Danila
Sisters: Adriana, Gabriela, Lidia, Nadia,
Valeria, Juliana
Brothers: Lucas, Marco, Nicolas, Julian, Colin,
Dominik
★This fluid twist on Daniel, common in
Southern and Eastern Europe, sounds just per-
fect to American ears. It has a hint of glamour
without veering far from the tried and true. The
double-"l" spelling Daniella, influenced by the
French version Danielle, is less traditional but
nearly as popular.
In the World: Actresses Daniela Ruah, Daniela
Romo, and Daniella Monet

Danielle (dan-YEHL)   1987: #14
Popularity: #207
Styles: '70s–'80s, French
Nicknames: Dani
Variants: Daniela, Daniella   1880   Today
Sisters: Nicole, Michelle,
Stephanie, Melissa, Lindsay, Amanda, Erica,
Justine
Brothers: Kyle, Jeremy, Derek, Dustin, Jared,
Nicholas, Brandon, Scott
★Danielle and Michelle led a solid group of
French favorites through the '70s and '80s. Dan-
ielle was the most romantic of the bunch, wear-
ing its French form like a designer gown. Today
the familiar French names are starting to give
way to Italian and Slavic variants. Danielle is
still popular, but Daniela has taken the lead.
In the World: Writer Danielle Steel

Daphne (DAF-nee) 1962: #266
Popularity: #450
Styles: Timeless, Mythological, English, Nickname-Proof, Why Not? 1880 Today
Variants: Dafne, Daphna
Sisters: Phoebe, Violet, Arabella, Juliet, Noelle, Camilla
Brothers: Graham, Duncan, Miles, Jude, Noel, Elliot
✳ Daphne is an easy name to fall in love with. It has a soft-focus beauty, as befits a Greek nymph. But soft-headed Daphne is not: there's a keen intelligence radiating through the gauzy romance.
In the World: Writer Daphne du Maurier; actress Daphne Zuniga; style icon Daphne Guinness; Daphne of *Scooby-Doo*

Darcy (DAHR-see) 1968: #349
Popularity: #1552
Styles: Last Names First, Literary and Artistic, Surfer '60s, Nickname-Proof 1880 Today
Variants: Darcie, D'Arcy
Sisters: Carey, Dana, Auden, Laney, Kirby, Marlo
Brothers: Campbell, Tobin, Dexter, Bennet, Dorian, Byron
✳ This '60s choice hasn't aged a bit. It's still a vivid, British-style alternative to Marcie or Tracy. It's also a more romantic alternative thanks to Mr. Darcy of Jane Austen's *Pride and Prejudice.*
In the World: Fitzwilliam Darcy of *Pride and Prejudice*

Daria (DAH-ree-ə) 1998: #740
Popularity: #1684
Styles: Italian, Saints, Slavic, Nickname-Proof, Why Not? 1880 Today
Sisters: Katia, Milena, Lilia, Charis, Mira, Dasia
Brothers: Alban, Maxim, Carlo, Gideon, Donato, Tobin
✳ Daria is the female form of Darius and is equally saintly and accessible. It has the smooth European styling of hits like Gabriela and Nadia, as well as an MTV animated series to its credit. Yet you never meet a real-life Daria . . . isn't it time?
In the World: Animated series *Daria*; model Daria Werbowy

Darlene (dar-LEEN) 1958: #49
Popularity: #1231
Styles: Mid-Century, Solid Citizens
Nicknames: Darli, Darla, 1880 Today
Lena
Variants: Darla, Darleen, Darline
Sisters: Sheila, Janice, Brenda, Gwen, Joanne, Donna, Maureen, Paula
Brothers: Gerald, Barry, Darryl, Wayne, Kenny, Randall, Rodger, Bruce
✳ The name Darlene was coined as an endearment—the word "darling" shaped into name form. It's a sweet sentiment, but the sound of the name hasn't been fashionable for some time. Cheri is a French-accented take on the same theme.
In the World: Singers Darlene Love and Darlene Zschech; Darlene of sitcom *Roseanne*

Davina (də-VEE-nə) 1976: #767
Popularity: #1696
Styles: Lacy and Lissome, Celtic, English, Why Not?
Nicknames: Vina, Davy, Dina 1880 Today
Variants: Davinia, Davia
Sisters: Fiona, Jamesina, Lilias, Nicola, Arabella, Iona, Elspeth, Ailsa
Brothers: Duncan, Alistair, Callum, Trevor, Evander, Ross, Ivar, Keir
✳ Davina is a Scottish feminine form of David that American parents have somehow overlooked. It could be your solution to honoring Grandpa Dave or your long-sought perfect Scottish sister for Fiona.
In the World: British TV host Davina McCall

Dawn (DAWN) 1970: #16
Popularity: #2067
Styles: Charms and Graces, Surfer '60s, Brisk and Breezy
Variants: Dawna 1880 Today
Sisters: Robin, Lynn, Dina, Beth, Kelly, Jody, Denise, Renee
Brothers: Todd, Darrin, Kris, Troy, Kerry, Dirk, Shawn, Scott
✳ The sunrise image of Dawn is tender and lovely. The name was so trendy in the '60s and '70s, though, that it can be hard to hear that ethereal essence (especially if you remember Dawn Dolls, the Barbie competitors in minidresses and go-go boots). Today Dawn is most popular as a middle name, particularly with meaning names like Summer. For a more exotic twist, consider Aurora, the goddess of the dawn.
In the World: Comedian Dawn French; actress Dawn Wells; singer Dawn Upshaw

Dayana (diy-AH-nah, diy-A-nə)
2009: #420

Popularity: #446
Styles: Latino/Latina
Nicknames: Yana
1880 Today
Variants: Dayanara, Dayane, Daiana, Diana
Sisters: Eliana, Amaya, Ximena, Romina, Camila, Sarai, Luciana, Vanessa
Brothers: Fernando, Cruz, Rodrigo, Diego, Daniel, Alonso, Giovanni, Adrian
✸ Dayana is an alternate spelling of Diana, with a purpose. It makes the intended pronunciation clear in languages like Spanish, where Diana starts with a "dee" sound. The effect is more contemporary and glamorous than the original. A series of beauty queens and fashion models named Dayana (and elaborations like Dayanara) have reinforced the glamour.
In the World: Past Miss Universes Dayana Mendoza and Dayanara Torres

Deanna (dee-AN-ə)
1970: #90

Popularity: #817
Styles: '70s–'80s, Lacy and Lissome
Nicknames: Dee
1880 Today
Variants: Deana, Deanne
Sisters: Kathryn, Belinda, Candace, Tamara, Sonia, Corinna
Brothers: Geoffrey, Byron, Marc, Darren, Timothy, Brett
✸ Your grandma may think of the golden-age Hollywood star Deanna Durbin. You'll think of . . . what? This name won't be pinned down easily. You can convince yourself it's lacy or simple, creative or old-fashioned. A flexible choice.
In the World: Actress Deanna Durbin; Deanna Troi of *Star Trek: The Next Generation*

Debbie (DEH-bee)
1959: #20

Popularity: #4682
Styles: Mid-Century, Nicknames
Nicknames: Deb
1880 Today
Variants: Debby, Debi
Sisters: Kathy, Laurie, Julie, Cindy, Pam, Becky
Brothers: Ricky, Steve, Doug, Randy, Jerry, Mike
✸ Actress Debbie Reynolds helped form our image of a wholesome 1950s America, and her bubbly stage name (she was born Mary Frances) became a favorite for two decades. The '70s "adult" film *Debbie Does Dallas* played off that all-American girl image. Today the biblical distinction of the full name Deborah is the stronger draw.
In the World: Actress Debbie Reynolds; singers Debbie Harry and Debbie Gibson; the phrase "Debbie Downer"; Little Debbie snacks

Deborah (DEHB-rə)
1954: #3

Popularity: #808
Styles: Mid-Century, Biblical
Nicknames: Deb, Debbie
Variants: Debra, Débora, Devorah
1880 Today
Sisters: Susan, Rebecca, Cynthia, Diane, Judith, Theresa
Brothers: Stephen, Gregory, Daniel, Philip, Michael, David
✸ Deborah was ahead of its time. In the '50s, when cheery little names like Nancy, Karen, and Linda were the rage, this graceful Old Testament name elbowed its way to the top of the charts. Deborah tends to be ignored today because of overfamiliarity, but it's as gracious as ever.
In the World: Actresses Deborah Kerr, Debra Messing, and Debra Winger; singer Deborah Cox

Deirdre (DEER-drə)
1961: #333

Popularity: #5946
Styles: Celtic, Surfer '60s, Why Not?
Nicknames: Dee, DiDi
1880 Today
Variants: Deidre, Diedre
Sisters: Brigid, Fiona, Maura, Lesley, Siobhan, Dara
Brothers: Craig, Rory, Brian, Keane, Declan, Casey
✸ Deirdre was a beautiful heroine of Irish legend. The name enjoyed a brief jump in popularity in the '60s, but never became American enough to undermine its delicate Irish spirit.
In the World: Actress Deidre Hall

Delaney (deh-LAY-nee) 2004: #169
Popularity: #235
Styles: Last Names First
Nicknames: Laney, Lane, Dell
Sisters: Riley, Avery, Rowan, Mckenna, Cassidy, Kendall
Brothers: Jackson, Cameron, Parker, Drake, Donovan, Connor
✴ Parents first discovered the Irish/English surname Delaney in the form of TV stars Kim Delaney and Dana Delany. By now, the name has left that small-screen origin in the dust. It's smart, polished, and well liked.
In the World: Actresses Kim Delaney and Dana Delany

Delia (DEEL-yə, DEE-lee-ə) 1883: #128
Popularity: #1010
Styles: Ladies and Gentlemen, Nickname-Proof, Why Not?
Sisters: Nora, Eliza, Susana, Celeste, Rhea, Willa
Brothers: Jasper, Solomon, Vincent, August, Reuben, Hugh
✴ Delia has the grace of the feminine classics with an extra, frisky step. Its sweet lightness makes it sound like a nickname for a grand dame like Cordelia or Bedelia. In fact, its full-name roots are broad and deep. Delia was an ancient Greek festival and a byname of the goddess Artemis. It has been used as a given name in English for centuries.
In the World: dELiA*s clothing stores; writer Delia Ephron; cooking expert Delia Smith

Delilah (di-LIY-lə) 2011: #172
Popularity: #172
Styles: Biblical, Exotic Traditional
Nicknames: Del, DeDe, Lilah
Sisters: Evangeline, Scarlett, Jemima, Salome, Lorelei, Josephine
Brothers: Judah, Lincoln, Gideon, Elias, Xavier, Phineas
✴ Delilah is one of the few biblical girls' names that sound glamorous and sensual. That allure, though, is tinged with guile. The dirty dealings of Samson's lover Delilah historically limited the name's appeal. But what's a little treachery compared to the power of a hit song? "Hey There Delilah" by The Plain White T's was one of the top hits of 2007 and freed many parents to use this name they'd always secretly loved.
In the World: Song "Hey There Delilah"; radio host Delilah

Della (DEHL-ə) 1881: #60
Popularity: #1732
Styles: Guys and Dolls, Why Not?
Nicknames: Dell
Sisters: Flora, Nellie, Dora, Mabel, Celia, Mae
Brothers: Charlie, Harry, Zeke, Reuben, Archie, Guy
✴ Like Ella, Della is a sunny Jazz Age favorite associated with a singer (Della Reese). Unlike the popular favorite Ella, the name Della hasn't been heard from in years. It may sound a little dowdy, but so did Ella not so long ago. Della also gives you the option of the winning nickname Dell.
In the World: Singer Della Reese; secretary Della Street of *Perry Mason*

Delphine (dehl-FEEN) 1930: #428
Popularity: #5202
Styles: French, Fantastical, Why Not?
Nicknames: Del, Della, Fifi
Variants: Delphina, Delfina
Sisters: Celestine, Elodie, Cecile, Sylvie, Genevieve, Vivienne
Brothers: Lucien, Armand, Florian, Regis, Gustave, Olivier
✴ This near-forgotten French classic has traffic-stopping good looks. Delphine is coming off a spike of popularity in its native land and should have tons of potential here as well.

Denise (deh-NEES) 1964: #25
Popularity: #603
Styles: French, Mid-Century, Surfer '60s, Nickname-Proof
Variants: Denyse
Sisters: Michelle, Renee, Cynthia, Robin, Pamela, Danielle
Brothers: Brian, Mark, Darren, Gregory, Steven, Keith
✴ In the '50s and '60s, this French feminine form of Dennis became an American standard. Modern and energetic, it was a perfect choice for the generation that launched the sexual revolution. Today Denise is no longer modern but a reliable, familiar favorite.
In the World: Actress Denise Richards; opera singer Denyce Graves

Desiree (deh-zi-RAY)　　　1983: #95
Popularity: #594
Styles: Modern Meanings,
'70s–'80s, French, African-
American　　　　　　　1880　Today
Nicknames: Rae, Desi
Variants: Désirée, Desirae
Sisters: Dominique, Natasha, Scarlett, Athena,
Cassandra, Angelique
Brothers: Quinton, Derrick, Andre, Marquis,
Damien, Emmanuel
✹ *Désirée* is French for "desired," indicating a
wished-for child. It's an altogether different
kind of desire that inflames the name today,
though. This may be the most purely sensuous
name you can give a girl.
In the World: Short story "Désirée's Baby"; busi-
ness leader Desirée Rogers

Destiny (DEHS-ti-nee)　　　2000: #24
Popularity: #91
Styles: Modern Meanings,
Turn of the 21st Century
Nicknames: Dez, Dessie　　1880　Today
Variants: Destinee
Sisters: Trinity, Genesis, Harmony, Jasmine,
Autumn, Serenity
Brothers: Chance, Justice, Dakota, Sincere,
Skyler, Maverick
✹ Destiny is a blast of inspirational energy
packaged in the style of a traditional girl's name.
Its popularity peak coincided with the chart-
topping years of R&B group Destiny's Child.
Destiny's particular hook is its forward gaze, a
contrast to the here-and-now celebration of
names like Miracle. Journey is a less common
choice with a similar sense of purpose.
In the World: Destiny's Child; many appear-
ances in comic books and video games

Devin (DEH-vin)　　　1991: #238
Popularity: #1425
Styles: Androgynous, The
"-ens," Nickname-Proof
Variants: Devyn, Devan,　　1880　Today
Devon, Deven
Sisters: Darby, Ashton, Kelsey, Carson, Brenna,
Taryn
Brothers: Chandler, Dalton, Keaton, Colby,
Tanner, Austin
✹ Devin was discovered at the same time for
boys and for girls. It eventually settled in as a
popular boy's name, with half a dozen common
spellings. If you're looking for a gender-bender,
no problem . . . but if you're just looking for a
fresh invention with no baggage for a girl, keep
looking.
In the World: Pop singer Dev (Devin Star Tailes)

Diamond (DIY-mənd)　　　1999: #150
Popularity: #760
Styles: Modern Meanings,
Charms and Graces,
African-American　　　　1880　Today
Nicknames: Di
Sisters: Raven, Essence, Emerald, Jasmine,
Destiny, Jade
Brothers: Marquis, Jett, Justice, Messiah,
Phoenix, Prince
✹ This name describes itself: glittering, strong,
sharp, and flashy. It's a jazzy choice that de-
serves its recent popularity, but the glitz isn't for
everyone. If your tastes are more modest, there's
always Pearl.
In the World: Dozens of associations, from jew-
elry to baseball to playing cards

Diana (diy-AN-ə)　　　1946: #42
Popularity: #203
Styles: Timeless,
Mythological, Shakespearean
Nicknames: Di　　　　1880　Today
Variants: Diane, Dayana
Sisters: Laura, Jacqueline, Christina, Juliet,
Daphne, Rebecca
Brothers: Philip, Christopher, Thomas,
Gregory, Stephen, Alexander
✹ The exquisite goddess of the moon, the
huntress. The image of the Roman goddess
Diana still fits this name well. It's strong, lovely,
and timeless. The late Princess of Wales is a
powerful association but does not dominate the
name.
In the World: Diana, Princess of Wales; singer
Diana Ross; editor Diana Vreeland; Wonder
Woman, alias Diana Prince

Diane (diy-AN)   1955: #14
Popularity: #1662
Styles: Mid-Century, French
Nicknames: Di
Variants: Dianne, Dyan,   1880 Today
Diana
Sisters: Sharon, Pamela, Denise, Lynn, Donna, Valerie
Brothers: Gary, Stephen, Allen, Kenneth, Douglas, Gregory
★ Diane is a '50s-era name that has matured into a classic. It has a smooth sound and a nice no-nonsense attitude. While Diane is French (a form of the Roman goddess name), it is most common in the English-speaking world. The English version Diana stays closer to the name's mythological essence.
In the World: Actresses Diane Keaton and Diane Lane; designer Diane von Furstenberg; Senator Dianne Feinstein

Dina (DEE-nə)   1969: #199
Popularity: #1338
Styles: Surfer '60s, Italian,
Jewish
Nicknames: Dee   1880 Today
Variants: Deena
Sisters: Carla, Sonya, Jodi, Dawn, Dori, Alisa
Brothers: Kris, Darin, Troy, Marc, Toby, Vince
★ This lively cross-cultural name was most often heard in the '60s and '70s, when similar choices like Tina and Gina were huge. For a twist, you could consider updating the name to the sunny Dia, following the model of Tia and Gia.
In the World: Actress Dina Merrill; reality TV personality Dina Manzo

Dinah (DIY-nə)   1955: #485
Popularity: #3535
Styles: Biblical, Guys and
Dolls
Nicknames: Di   1880 Today
Variants: Dina
Sisters: Merry, Adah, Jemima, Susannah, Etta, Liza
Brothers: Lionel, Hiram, Rubin, Lemuel, Dell, Mahlon
★ This is a simple, pretty biblical name, familiar but uncommon. It used to hold the stigma of a "slave name," but that association is finally fading. (A second association, "Dinah won't you blow," is still holding some parents back.) The name has started to pop up on stylish TV and movie characters. It should have a brighter future in the decades to come.
In the World: Singers Dinah Shore and Dinah Washington; Dinah of the song "I've Been Working on the Railroad"

Dixie (DIK-see)   1938: #167
Popularity: #846
Styles: Guys and Dolls,
Nicknames, Country and
Western   1880 Today
Sisters: Delta, Hallie, Reba, Maxie, Dinah, Melba
Brothers: Duke, Buddy, Roy, Woody, Tex, Roscoe
★ You'll find Georgias and Carolinas north of the Mason-Dixon Line, but Dixie is one name that's strictly a Southern belle. As a nickname for the southeastern U.S., its connotations are constantly evolving. As a name for a person, it has the kind of sassy kick that even Northern urbanites love. This could make a heck of a nickname, if you're willing to stretch a little for a formal version (Candice or Madison, maybe?).
In the World: The Dixie Chicks band; actress Dixie Carter; song "I Wish I Was in Dixie"; Dixie cups

Dolly (DAHL-ee)   1886: #283
Popularity: #8697
Styles: Country and Western,
Namesakes, Guys and Dolls,
Nicknames   1880   Today
Sisters: Reba, Polly, Dixie,
Nell, Rosie, Delta, Tillie, Lacy
Brothers: Barney, Mack, Ollie, Eddie, Buck,
Major, Wiley, Earl
✷ Dolly, a jolly old nickname for Dorothy, was
adopted as the name of a cute child's toy. As a
result, the name is mighty hard to take seriously
today. In contemporary use, it has become
nearly a "one-woman name" referring to coun-
try legend Dolly Parton.
In the World: Singer Dolly Parton; musical
Hello, Dolly!; Dolly Madison baked goods;
Dolly, the cloned sheep

Dolores (də-LOH-ris)   1930: #13
Popularity: #3827
Styles: Latino/Latina, Porch
Sitters
Nicknames: Dolly, Lola,   1880   Today
Lolita
Variants: Doloris, Deloris
Sisters: Phyllis, Consuelo, Norma, Lois,
Socorro, Laverne
Brothers: Roland, Eugene, Refugio, Placido,
Murray, Garland
✷ This Spanish name was a glamorous favorite
in the '30s. More recently, it has been rejected
for sounding too . . . well, dolorous. It's rather
downbeat in both sound and meaning. (Dolores
is Spanish for "sorrows," as in the Virgin Mary
appellation "Mary of the Sorrows.")
In the World: Actress Dolores del Rio; film *Do-
lores Claiborne*; Dolores Umbridge of the
"Harry Potter" series

Dominique (doh-mi-NEEK)   1985: #83
Popularity: #1171
Styles: French, Androgynous,
African-American
Nicknames: Nikki, Dom   1880   Today
Variants: Dominica,
Dominga
Sisters: Angelique, Emmanuelle, Desiree,
Nicolette, Simone, Veronique
Brothers: Fabrice, Antoine, Marcel, Damien,
Andre, Valentin
✷ Dominique is sultry, but serious. You imme-
diately recognize the name as a distinguished
classic. (It's common for both men and women
in France.) Yet it also personifies our image of a
romantic evening in Paris, with perhaps a hint
of danger attached. It's like that little black dress
you can wear to a power meeting, then out to a
hot date afterward.
In the World: Gymnasts Dominique Dawes and
Dominique Moceanu; actress Dominique
Swain

Donatella (dahn-ə-TEHL-ə)   2010: #6848
Popularity: #8262
Styles: Italian, Exotic
Traditional, Why Not?
Nicknames: Dona   1880   Today
Sisters: Valentina, Giovanna,
Serafina, Paloma, Graziella, Alessandra
Brothers: Massimo, Fabrizio, Leonardo,
Giancarlo, Giorgio, Tommaso
✷ This romantic name is waiting to be swept
off its feet by parents who appreciate its wom-
anly beauty. It's a classic of northern Italy, and
modestly familiar in the U.S. thanks to fashion
designer Donatella Versace. It also inherits
some of the artistic aura of the masculine ver-
sion of the name, Donatello.
In the World: Designer Donatella Versace; restaurateur Donatella Arpaia

Donna (DAHN-ə)   1959: #5
Popularity: #1201
Styles: Mid-Century,
Nickname-Proof
Variants: Dona
Sisters: Sandra, Lisa, Janice,
Diane, Karen, Anita
Brothers: Bruce, Gary, Douglas, Gerald,
Kenneth, Allen
★ If you take the time to give Donna some thought, you'll see the charms that kept it near the top of the charts for 40 years. It has a trim, all-American sound with hints of both Italy (it's Italian for "lady") and Scotland (a feminine form of Donald). To most parents, though, it's just too familiar to be interesting today.
In the World: Singer Donna Summer; designer Donna Karan; actress Donna Reed; Ritchie Valens's song "Donna"

Dora (DOH-rə)   1881: #46
Popularity: #2247
Styles: Ladies and
Gentlemen, Latino/Latina,
Nickname-Proof
Sisters: Rosa, Adela, Blanca,
Pearl, Iva, Frida
Brothers: Edgar, Archie, Alonzo, Fred, Julius,
Abe
★ Dora was at its peak in the 1870s, when it was a fashionable offshoot of Theodora, Dorothy, and Isadora. Today the longer versions hold more interest, but Dora still works well as a nickname. For your kids, cartoon heroine Dora the Explorer will be the name's touchstone.
In the World: Dora the Explorer

Doris (DOHR-is, DAWR-is)   1929: #6
Popularity: #2425
Styles: Solid Citizens,
Mythological
Nicknames: Dorrie, Dora
Variants: Dorris
Sisters: Lois, Norma, Maxine, Phyllis, Sybil,
Wilma
Brothers: Vernon, Eugene, Lyle, Gordon,
Eldon, Arnold
★ The "-is" ending was trendy for girls in the '20s. Names like Doris, Phyllis, Mavis, and Lois stormed into style together, then receded together. Now they're stuck together in generational limbo. If the sound intrigues you, fresher examples include Hollis, Glynis, Iris, Tanis, Carys, and Dilys.
In the World: Actress Doris Day; heiress Doris Duke; writer Doris Lessing; historian Doris Kearns Goodwin

Dorothea (doh-rə-THEE-ə)   1913: #176
Popularity: #7866
Styles: Ladies and
Gentlemen, Why Not?
Nicknames: Dot, Dottie,
Dora, Thea
Variants: Dorothy
Sisters: Beatrice, Geneva, Althea, Eleanora,
Angeline, Josefa
Brothers: Jules, Benedict, Merritt, Richmond,
Frederick, Everett
★ Dorothea sounds like the responsible older sister of today's carefree antique revival names. She's just as attractive but more reserved. That's the sort who could be a pleasant surprise for those who take the time to appreciate her charms. See also Theodora.
In the World: 19th-century social activist Dorothea Dix; photojournalist Dorothea Lange

Dorothy (DOH-rə-thee, DOH   1923: #2
Popularity: #937
Styles: Solid Citizens
Nicknames: Dot, Dottie,
Dodie, Dolly, Dee
Variants: Dorothea
Sisters: Margery, Vivian, Rosemary, Virginia,
Eloise, Sylvia
Brothers: Ray, Lawrence, Clifford, Ellis,
Theodore, Russell
★ Dorothy's popularity has been plummeting ever since Judy Garland's Dorothy followed the Yellow Brick Road. It was a monster hit until then, and its deep-seated sweetness still shines. This name has comeback potential. It may surprise people, but in a nice way.
In the World: Dorothy Gale of *The Wizard of Oz*; writer Dorothy Parker; actress Dorothy Dandridge

Drew (DROO)   1999: #613
Popularity: #1355
Styles: Androgynous, Brisk
and Breezy
Sisters: Devin, Shea, Harper,
Alex, Rory, Blake
Brothers: Luke, Ian, Grant, Zane, Hunter,
Chase
★ Actress Drew Barrymore's upbeat, accessible charm made this name an option for girls. It's still predominantly male, though, and almost certain to stay that way. That steady boyishness turns out to be the name's greatest allure for parents of boys and girls alike.
In the World: Actress Drew Barrymore

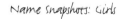

Ebony (EH-bə-nee)   1982: #132
Popularity: #2010
Styles: African-American,
Modern Meanings, Charms
and Graces, Nickname-Proof   1880   Today
Variants: Eboni
Sisters: Raven, Brandi, Keisha, Amber, Crystal,
Natasha
Brothers: Dion, Jamal, Courtney, Darnell,
Jermaine, Donte
✱ Ebony is a nature name, a tropical tree with
dark wood prized for rarefied uses like violin fittings. It is a feminine name, with the effortless
grace of Emily. But above all it is an African-American name. The suggestion of dark-hued
beauty made Ebony a favorite of black parents
for a generation.
In the World: Ebony magazine

Eden (EE-dən)   2011: #181
Popularity: #181
Styles: Modern Meanings,
The "-ens," Short and Sweet
Nicknames: Edie   1880   Today
Sisters: Syke, Jordan, Esme,
Wren, Rowan, Grace
Brothers: Noah, Eli, Zion, Luca, Roan, Kai
✱ A demure glimpse of paradise. If you feel
that names like Heaven and Miracle lay it on a
little thick, try this gentle little choice that feels
like a classic.
In the World: The Garden of Eden; Eden Natural Foods; young reality TV star Eden Wood

Edith (EE-dith)   1889: #29
Popularity: #771
Styles: Ladies and Gentlemen
Nicknames: Edie
Variants: Edythe, Edita   1880   Today
Sisters: Alice, Clara, Olive,
Esther, Ida, Flora
Brothers: Arthur, Hugh, Julius, Theodore, Roy,
Edgar
✱ Try to put the image of Edith Bunker from
All in the Family out of your mind. Instead,
focus on the 19th-century decorum of novelist
Edith Wharton. This name isn't for everybody,
but its sound is ready for a comeback. (It's almost a remix of Ethan.) The nickname Edie is a
bonus.
In the World: Writer Edith Wharton; Edith
Bunker of *All in the Family*; singer Édith Piaf

Edna (EHD-nə)   1893: #14
Popularity: #2020
Styles: Porch Sitters
Nicknames: Eddie, Edie
Sisters: Agnes, Irma, Hilda,   1880   Today
Gladys, Vera, Ethel
Brothers: Otis, Herman, Floyd, Ernest, Virgil,
Lester
✱ It's little and arguably cute, but Edna is
many years away from a comeback. Its sound is
too dense for current fashion. If you want to
name a child in honor of an Edna, Eden comes
from the same Hebrew root.
In the World: Writers Edna St. Vincent Millay
and Edna Ferber

Eileen (iy-LEEN)   1943: #68
Popularity: #748
Styles: Solid Citizens, Celtic,
Nickname-Proof
Variants: Ilene, Aileen, Aylín   1880   Today
Sisters: Sheila, Colleen,
Janice, Glenda, Roberta, Lorraine
Brothers: Gordon, Kenneth, Lyle, Douglas,
Lawrence, Stuart
✱ Most of us identify Eileen as an Irish name,
but for many years its popularity crossed all ethnic boundaries. America is full of grown-up Eileens with last names like Cohen and
Rodriguez. Now that the name is no longer
broadly fashionable, its Gaelic roots are reappearing. It still sounds great with a traditional
Irish surname.
In the World: Designer Eileen Fisher; song
"Come On, Eileen"; actress Eileen Davidson;
astronaut Eileen Collins

Eirlys (AYR-lis, IYR-lis)   rarely used
Popularity: Very rare
Styles: Celtic
Sisters: Eleri, Carys, Seren,   1880   Today
Glynis, Alys, Lowri
Brothers: Bevan, Rhodri,
Carwyn, Gethin, Rhys, Idris
✱ This Welsh name is unfamiliar in the U.S.,
but it has a fashionable sound and none of those
special Welsh consonants that spark panic in
the uninitiated. Just put the stress on the first
syllable and you're in good shape.

Elaine (eh-LAYN) 1945: #44
Popularity: #697
Styles: Solid Citizens
Nicknames: Laney, Ellie
Variants: Elayne 1880 Today
Sisters: Marianne, Carole,
Jeanne, Constance, Joyce, Lorraine
Brothers: Laurence, Kenneth, Stuart, Roland,
Lionel, Randolph
✳ Elaine has a no-nonsense attitude but a ro-
mantic core. Despite the name's French sound,
its English roots run deep, including the mother
of Galahad in Arthurian legend. This name has
slipped quietly off the style radar and entered
the "pleasant surprise" category. One factor in
its decline was the sitcom *Seinfeld*, perhaps the
only TV hit that ever made its character names
less popular.
In the World: Elaine of *Seinfeld*; actress/singers
Elaine Paige and Elaine Stritch

Eleanor (EHL-ə-nohr) 1915: #28
Popularity: #150
Styles: Antique Charm,
Ladies and Gentlemen
Nicknames: Nell, Ellie, Nora, 1880 Today
Lana, Nory
Variants: Elinor, Eleanora, Leonor
Sisters: Amelia, Evelyn, Josephine, Violet,
Adeline, Beatrice
Brothers: Charles, Henry, Theodore, Everett,
Samuel, Edward
✳ Our unscientific survey ranks Eleanor and
Lillian as the names men and women disagree
on most. Women find them gentle and
dignified—elegant ladies with a backbone. Men
just think they sound old. How could men be so
wrong . . . er, I mean, what an unfortunate dif-
ference of opinion. If you can talk him into Eleanor, there's a great selection of nicknames he
can pick from.
In the World: First lady Eleanor Roosevelt; Eleanor of Aquitaine; Elinor Dashwood of *Sense
and Sensibility*

Eleanora (ehl-ə-NOHR-ə) 1916: #486
Popularity: #2473
Styles: Ladies and
Gentlemen, Lacy and
Lissome, Antique Charm 1880 Today
Nicknames: Nora, Ellie, Elle
Variants: Eleanor
Sisters: Amelia, Josphine, Viola, Dorothea,
Lavinia, Eloise
Brothers: Theodore, Julius, Leopold, Ellsworth,
Edmond, Thornton
✳ Eleanor has carved out a niche with its wom-
anly toughness, à la Eleanor Roosevelt. Adding
an "-a" to the end subtly reshapes the name's
style. Eleanora still sounds strong and stylish,
but more antique and more classically femi-
nine, even romantic.

Elena (eh-LAY-nə) 2011: #160
Popularity: #160
Styles: Timeless, Latino/
Latina, Italian, Slavic
Nicknames: Ellie, Elle, Lena 1880 Today
Variants: Alaina, Alayna
Sisters: Sofia, Eva, Teresa, Lucia, Daniela, Ana
Brothers: Simon, Antonio, Nicholas, Carlos,
Julian, Lukas
✳ Helen's face launched a thousand ships, and
her name has launched a thousand variations.
The international favorite Elena is the softest
and most timeless.
In the World: Supreme Court justice Elena
Kagan; Elena Gilbert of *The Vampire Diaries*;
actress Elena Anaya

Eleni (eh-LAY-nee, 1993: #1005
eh-LEH-nee)
Popularity: #1479
Styles: Greek, Why Not?
Nicknames: Ellie, Leni, Elle 1880 Today
Variants: Elene
Sisters: Melina, Xenia, Demi, Georgia, Kyriaki,
Evangelia
Brothers: Nikos, Elias, Kostas, Aris, Dimitri,
Markos
✳ Eleni is the modern Greek form of Helen. It
offers the rare package of a traditional, globally
feminine sound without an "-a" ending. An
everyday classic in Greece, Eleni comes across
as uncommon but approachable in the U.S.
In the World: Tremendously popular in Greece;
Eleni Andros Cooper of soap *Guiding Light*

Eliana (ehl-ee-AH-nə,   2011: #156
ay-lee-AH-nə)
Popularity: #156
Styles: Lacy and Lissome,
Italian, Latino/Latina, Jewish   1880   Today
Nicknames: Liana
Variants: Éliane, Aeliana, Elliana, Elianna
Sisters: Talia, Mira, Evangeline, Viviana,
Giselle, Lilia
Brothers: Abel, Elliot, Matteo, Elijah, Joaquin,
Asher
✳ Eliana is one of those fluid names so naturally feminine that many cultures are drawn to them. It came to the Romance languages from the Roman name Aelianus. It can also be one of the many forms of Helen (notice the resemblance to Elaine) or a Hebrew name meaning "my God has answered." It should be welcome in any company.
In the World: Brazilian TV host Eliana

Elin (EH-lin, EE-lin,   2011: #659
EE-ə-lin)
Popularity: #659
Styles: Nordic, Celtic
Nicknames: Eli, Lina   1880   Today
Variants: Ellen, Helen
Sisters: Malin, Freya, Seren, Maja, Siri, Enya
Brothers: Erik, Anton, Wynn, Rhys, Marius,
Soren
✳ Here's a first: a name trend sparked by a divorce. When golfer Tiger Woods's marriage to Elin Nordegren fell into very public shambles, one unexpected by-product was parents' saying, "Elin, what a pretty name!" It's a Scandinavian and Welsh form of Ellen with a sleek modern shape. The Swedish pronunciation is three syllables, but most Americans pronounce it as two.
In the World: Tiger Woods's former wife Elin Nordregen; a top-100 name in Sweden, Switzerland, and Wales

Elisa (eh-LEE-sə)   1981: #312
Popularity: #533
Styles: Timeless, Lacy and
Lissome, Italian, Latino/
Latina   1880   Today
Nicknames: Elli, Lisa, Elle,
Lissie
Variants: Elise, Eliza
Sisters: Marisa, Elena, Lea, Corina, Serena,
Liana
Brothers: Brent, Casey, Mario, Ruben, Erik,
Jaime
✳ Alyssa is an American favorite, but Elisa spans the globe. This short form of Elisabeth is used in half a dozen languages and is popular across Europe. It may blend in with the crowd a bit, but it's an uncommonly flexible name, comfortable in any time or place.

Elise (ə-LEES, eh-LEE-zə)   2011: #162
Popularity: #162
Styles: Timeless, French,
German and Dutch
Nicknames: Ellie, Lise, Lisa   1880   Today
Variants: Elyse, Élise, Else,
Lise, Elisabeth
Sisters: Camille, Sabine, Elsa, Astrid, Noelle,
Celeste
Brothers: Simon, Elliott, Quentin, Bennett,
Lucas, Julian
✳ The name Elise has always been around, but suddenly we're sitting up and taking notice. Its timelessness is soothing, its elegance unforced. For a fully French flavor, write it with an accent: Élise. For a Germanic version, use the three-syllable pronunciation.
In the World: Beethoven's "Für Elise"; actress Elise Neal

Eliza (eh-LIY-zə)   1880: #85
Popularity: #255
Styles: Antique Charm
Nicknames: Liza, Liz, Ellie
Sisters: Lydia, Charlotte,   1880   Today
Amelia, Lucy, Phoebe,
Caroline
Brothers: Oliver, Henry, Jasper, Simon, Isaac,
Emmett
✳ This short form of Elizabeth can sound elegant or feisty, like the two incarnations of Eliza Doolittle in *My Fair Lady*. A stylish choice that's not too common.
In the World: Eliza Doolittle of *My Fair Lady*; actress Eliza Dushku

Elizabeth (eh-LI-zə-behth) 1880: #4
Popularity: #11
Styles: Timeless, Biblical
Nicknames: Beth, Bess, Betsy,
Betty, Bette, Buffy, Eliza,
Elle, Elsie, Elsa, Izzy, Liz,
Lisa, Liza, Lizbeth, Lise, Liddy, Libby
Variants: Elisabeth, Elspeth, Elisabeta,
Elisheba, Elisheva, Isabel
Sisters: Katherine, Anna, Margaret, Caroline,
Julia, Josephine, Sarah, Victoria
Brothers: James, William, Joseph, Edward,
Andrew, Christopher, Thomas, Alexander

1880   Today

✴ Elizabeth is the chameleon name. It changes into a remarkable array of nicknames, letting you tweak the style to fit any personality. This abundance dates back to the days when Elizabeth was such a ubiquitous name in England that many alternatives were needed to tell women apart. You can feel confident that this classic can handle its ongoing modern popularity with ease.
In the World: Queens Elizabeth I and II; centuries of women in all walks of life

Ella (EH-lə) 1880: #13
Popularity: #12
Styles: Antique Charm, Guys and Dolls
Nicknames: Ellie
Sisters: Ava, Ruby, Mia,
Sophie, Lucy, Grace
Brothers: Max, Owen, Ethan, Luke, Samuel,
Noah

1880   Today

✴ Ella has emerged from the pack of soft, cute grandma names to become the height of style. Its secret weapon is jazz legend Ella Fitzgerald, who breathes swinging life into the name. "A tisket/A tasket/A green and yellow basket/I found a name so short and sweet/I just could not resist it."
In the World: Singer Ella Fitzgerald; fashion brand Ella Moss; Cinderella novel *Ella Enchanted*

Elle (EHL) 2011: #412
Popularity: #412
Styles: Short and Sweet, Brisk and Breezy, Why Not?
Sisters: Eden, Britta, Blair,
Jolie, Reese, Esme
Brothers: Ian, Tate, Jude, Easton, Kai, Liam

1880   Today

✴ Elle has emerged as a more modern, glossy take on Ella. The gloss owes to the fashion-forward combo of model Elle McPherson, the magazine *Elle*, and Elle Woods, the heroine of *Legally Blonde*. Despite that lineage, the name is too simple to sound pretentious. It's most often pronounced as one syllable.
In the World: *Elle* magazine; model Elle McPherson; Elle Woods of *Legally Blonde*

Ellen (EH-lin) 1884: #59
Popularity: #699
Styles: Solid Citizens
Nicknames: Ellie, Elle, Nell
Variants: Elin
Sisters: Janet, Susan, Patricia,
Kathy, Judith, Gail, Carolyn, Diane
Brothers: Roger, Glenn, Kenneth, Paul,
Martin, Ray, Lawrence, Peter

✴ Ellen is a straight arrow that has flown true for generations. Sure, the name doesn't jump off the page, but that modesty can be an asset. The splashiest names are often the first to sound dated. Despite its drop in popularity, Ellen still sounds timeless.
In the World: Comedian/talk show host Ellen DeGeneres; actresses Ellen Page, Ellen Pompeo, and Ellen Burstyn

Ellery (EH-lə-ree) 2011: #1215
Popularity: #1216
Styles: Last Names First, Literary and Artistic, Why Not?
Nicknames: Ella, Elle, Ellie
Sisters: Larkin, Emory, Hollis, Carrington,
Berkeley, Connolly
Brothers: Campbell, Watson, Bennett, Merrick,
Bowen, Sutton

✴ Fictional detective Ellery Queen was dreamed up in 1929 as a fancified intellectual. A *male intellectual*. But fancy-sounding surnames have jumped the fence, and many now sound more natural for girls than for boys. Ellery's musical rhythm and girlish nicknames make an especially attractive package.
In the World: Fictional detective Ellery Queen

Elodie (EH-loh-dee,   1883: #692
ay-lo-DEE)
Popularity: #1855
Styles: French, Saints, Exotic
Traditional, Why Not?   1880   Today
Nicknames: Ella, Ellie, Dia
Variants: Élodie, Elodia, Alodia
Sisters: Delphine, Amelie, Vivienne, Salome, Arianne, Sylvie
Brothers: Mathias, Jules, Elias, Lucien, Jude, Blaise
✴ This downy beauty has been a chart-topper in France for years and is ready for import. The only drawback is confusion with the more familiar American name Melody.
In the World: Actresses Élodie Bouchez and Elodie Yung

Eloise (EH-loh-eez)   1921: #164
Popularity: #449
Styles: Ladies and
Gentlemen, French, Literary
and Artistic, Why Not?   1880   Today
Nicknames: Ellie, Ella, Elsie, Lo, Lulu
Variants: Eloisa, Heloise
Sisters: Adeline, Dorothea, Hermione, Matilda, Beatrice, Clementine
Brothers: Hugo, Elliott, Jules, Winslow, Foster, Conrad
✴ For the past 50 years, Eloise has been a precocious children's book character who lives at the Plaza Hotel in New York. Real-world Eloises are few and far between (in the U.S., anyway). The name shows real promise now as a sweet heirloom name, following in the footsteps of fellow kid-lit superstar Madeline.
In the World: Kay Thompson's series of "Eloise" books

Elora (eh-LOH-rə)   2011: #1306
Popularity: #1310
Styles: Lacy and Lissome,
Fantastical
Sisters: Lyra, Eowyn, Thalia,   1880   Today
Rinoa, Avalon, Melia
Brothers: Atreyu, Taven, Orion, Soren, Neo, Locke
✴ A baby girl named Elora was the subject of prophesy in the 1988 fantasy film *Willow*. Most Eloras alive today were named with that inspiration in mind. If you love the name's dreamy sound but don't want to pin it to the movie, try saying that it's a form of Eleanor, or that it comes from the Hebrew for "my light," like Leora.
In the World: Elora Danan of *Willow*

Elsa (EHL-sə)   1895: #215
Popularity: #578
Styles: Antique Charm,
German and Dutch, Nordic,
Why Not?   1880   Today
Nicknames: Elsie
Variants: Else
Sisters: Lena, Sophie, Greta, Ingrid, Mina, Eva
Brothers: Oscar, Leo, August, Hans, Felix, Casper
✴ Elsa sounds like an antique, but the name has never really gone out of style. This German and Swedish name (a pet form of Elisabeth) has always been quietly used in the U.S. It's a slightly more formal alternative to Ella.
In the World: Actresses Elsa Lanchester and Elsa Pataky; Elsa the lioness of *Born Free*

Elsie (EHL-see)   1896: #31
Popularity: #480
Styles: Guys and Dolls,
Nicknames
Sisters: Millie, Ada, Pearl,   1880   Today
Sadie, Lottie, Tessie
Brothers: Sam, Harry, Mack, Gus, Roy, Otto
✴ While many cutie-pie nicknames have regained their youth, Elsie has remained a little dowdy. Borden Dairy's Elsie the Cow is one reason. The name is sweet and huggable, though, and ready for rediscovery as a nickname if not a given name.
In the World: Elsie the Cow; "Elsie Dinsmore" children's books

Ember (EHM-ber)   2011: #669
Popularity: #671
Styles: Modern Meanings,
Why Not?
Nicknames: Emmy   1880   Today
Sisters: Luna, Eden, Winter, Indigo, Ivy, Promise
Brothers: Quill, River, Arrow, Roan, Shadow, Flint
✴ Amber is a rich, golden substance and name. A huge 1980s Amber wave took the edge off that golden glow, though. A tiny vowel shift to Ember restores the name's drama, with a flourish. Where Amber glows gently, Ember smolders, ready to ignite.
In the World: Book and film *City of Ember*

Emerson (EH-mer-sən)   2011: #275
Popularity: #276
Styles: Last Names First,
Androgynous
Nicknames: Emmy   1880   Today
Variants: Emersyn
Sisters: Cameron, Auden, Campbell, Madelyn,
Elliott, Mckenzie
Brothers: Jackson, Porter, Nolan, Carter,
Easton, Tucker
✳The name Emerson is a showdown between
name beginnings and endings. The "Em-"
opening is a feminine favorite (Emma, Emily);
the "-son" ending is masculine, in the most lit-
eral sense. The feminine influence pulled
ahead during Emily's peak, but today the name
is used equally for boys and for girls.
In the World: Philosopher Ralph Waldo Emerson; a daughter of actress Teri Hatcher

Emery (EH-mer-ee)   2011: #272
Popularity: #272
Styles: Last Names First,
Androgynous
Nicknames: Emmy   1880   Today
Variants: Emory
Sisters: Madelyn, Finley, Avery, Raine, Ashby,
Hayden
Brothers: Nolan, Spencer, Madden, Brooks,
Easton, Asher
✳Emory and Emery are two forms of the same
name. Until recently, they'd also been used the
same: as an old but uncommon male name
gradually gaining as a girl's name. Now, though,
the twins are parting ways. Emory retains its an-
drogynous surname style, while Emery has
taken off as an update of Emily (see also Emory
in "Snapshots: Boys").
In the World: Emery boards; rock band Emery;
a daughter of actress Angie Harmon

Emily (EH-mə-lee)   1999: #1
Popularity: #6
Styles: Timeless
Nicknames: Emmy, Millie,
Em   1880   Today
Variants: Emilie, Amelie,
Emilee, Emilia, Amelia
Sisters: Rachel, Victoria, Katie, Sarah, Abigail,
Julia
Brothers: Benjamin, Jacob, Nicholas, Nathan,
Evan, Andrew
✳You've just got to like Emily. It's bright and
friendly, traditional and unpretentious, with
fabulous literary heritage. So sure enough, ev-
erybody does like it, enough to have made this
simple classic the #1 name in the English-
speaking world for the early 21st century. That
run at #1 scared some parents away, but the
name retains its charm.
In the World: Writer Emily Brontë; poet Emily
Dickinson; etiquette expert Emily Post; actresses Emily Blunt, Emily Watson, and Emily
Deschanel

Emlyn (EHM-lin)   2010: #5376
Popularity: #6174
Styles: Celtic, The "-ens,"
Androgynous, Why Not?
Sisters: Seren, Wynne,   1880   Today
Mabyn, Bethan, Eleri,
Anwen
Brothers: Rhys, Evan, Price, Cadogan, Steffan,
Maxen
✳Emlyn is a classic Welsh men's name. It's
never been familiar in the U.S., and American
parents who come across it are more likely to
hear feminine potential—a natural blend of
Emily and Kaitlyn.

Emma (EH-mə)   1881: #3
Popularity: #3
Styles: Antique Charm,
Nickname-Proof
Sisters: Sophie, Grace, Anna,   1880   Today
Lucy, Ella, Claire, Lily
Brothers: Owen, Samuel, Jack, Noah, Henry,
Benjamin, Ethan
✳A breath of gentle simplicity, Emma has re-
turned to the heights of popularity it reached a
century ago. It's a smash in Europe too, one of
the top favorites in countries from France to
Sweden. You now meet enough young Emmas
that the name no longer feels so quaint, but it's
still soft and sweet without silliness.
In the World: Jane Austen's novel *Emma*; ac-
tresses Emma Thompson, Emma Stone, Emma
Roberts, and Emma Watson

Emmeline (EH-mə-leen;   2011: #1422
EH-mə-liyn; EH-mə-lin)
Popularity: #1426
Styles: Antique Charm,
Ladies and Gentlemen,   1880   Today
English, Why Not?
Nicknames: Emme, Emmy, Lina
Variants: Emmaline, Emeline
Sisters: Adelaide, Josephine, Cordelia, Elinor,
Jessamine, Annelise, Imogen
Brothers: Harrison, Theodore, George,
Bancroft, Henry, Bayard, Prescott
✳ Today's parents might have been tempted to
invent this name by combining Emma and
Caroline, but luckily they didn't have to. Em-
meline is an age-old classic with centuries of
respectability behind it. It has every making of a
hit . . . except clear pronunciation. There is no
popular consensus on the "right" version, no
matter what a dictionary (or your friends) might
say. Just choose the one you like best and correct
people—politely.
In the World: Suffragist Emmeline Pankhurst; a
daughter of actor Christian Bale

Erica (EH-ri-kə)   1983: #33
Popularity: #481
Styles: '70s–'80s, Nickname-
Proof
Variants: Erika, Ericka   1880   Today
Sisters: Jessica, Danielle,
April, Erin, Tara, Heather
Brothers: Jeremy, Dustin, Shawn, Derek, Jared,
Brett
✳ Erica swept in on the coattails of Eric and
soon established itself as part of the basic Amer-
ican naming stock. It's clean and energetic, with
a girl-next-door familiarity. For extra '80s
points, Erica is also Latin for "heather."
In the World: Actresses Erica Durance and
Erika Christensen; musician Erykah Badu;
writer Erica Jong

Erin (EH-rin)   1983: #18
Popularity: #233
Styles: Celtic, '70s–'80s,
Nickname-Proof, The "-ens"
Variants: Éireann, Eryn   1880   Today
Sisters: Shannon, Tara,
Megan, Erica, Allison, Kelly
Brothers: Ryan, Kyle, Sean, Kevin, Brendan,
Casey
✳ Erin is derived from a poetic name for Ire-
land. It's not an Irish name per se, but rather a
loving nod to Irish heritage. Thanks to its sim-
plicity, it has been embraced by families of
every ethnicity.
In the World: The phrase "Erin go Bragh," ex-
pressing Irish pride; film *Erin Brockovich*;
sportscaster Erin Andrews

Esme (EHZ-may)   2010: #921
Popularity: #981
Styles: Short and Sweet,
Exotic Traditional, Why Not?
Variants: Esmé, Esmée,   1880   Today
Ismay
Sisters: Isla, Tanith, Astrid, Ariadne, Honor,
Clio
Brothers: Axel, Roman, Milo, Phineas,
Dashiell, Wolf
✳ This rare bird used to be a bit of a secret,
prized by the literary and artistic elite. Then it
was given to one of the vampires in the "Twi-
light" saga. Okay, the secret may be out, but
please don't panic and abandon your favorite
name. Esme remains chic and uncommon,
only now people will know how to spell it. The
name has old French roots but is seldom used in
France; it is most common in Scotland and the
Netherlands.
In the World: Esme Cullen of the "Twilight"
series; J. D. Salinger story "For Esmé—with
Love and Squalor"

Esmeralda 1998: #134
(ehz-mə-RAHL-də,
ehs-meh-RAHL-dah)
Popularity: #332
Styles: Antique Charm, 1880 Today
Latino/Latina
Nicknames: Esme
Sisters: Alondra, Esperanza, Perla, Adriana,
Estefania, Dulce, Angelica, Carolina
Brothers: Cesar, Fernando, Javier, Alejandro,
Julio, Emilio, Mario, Cristian
✸ This name, Spanish for "emerald," is associated with the sweet gypsy girl of *The Hunchback of Notre Dame*. With a Spanish pronunciation, it's lilting and romantic; with an English accent, it's an offbeat antique.
In the World: Esmeralda of the many incarnations of the Hunchback story; telenovela *Esmeralda*

Esperanza 2000: #528
(eh-spay-RAHN-sah)
Popularity: #879
Styles: Latino/Latina, 1880 Today
Charms and Graces
Nicknames: Pelancha
Sisters: Liliana, Graciela, Rocío, Lidia,
Esmeralda, Rosa, Estrella, Alejandra
Brothers: Adolfo, Manuel, Miguel, Fernando,
Felipe, Salvador, Rafael, Eduardo
✸ This luminous classic has recently staged a welcome comeback. Esperanza is Spanish for "hope" and makes a perfect vessel for romantic dreams.
In the World: Musician Esperanza Spalding; young adult novel *Esperanza Rising*

Essence (EHS-ins) 1998: #455
Popularity: #1023
Styles: Modern Meanings,
African-American 1880 Today
Sisters: Justice, Eternity,
Jasmine, Raven, Diamond,
Miracle, Promise, Cherish
Brothers: Sincere, Tyree, Marquise, Darian,
Talon, Davonte, Jaylon, Terrell
✸ Essence is an upbeat meaning name, spurred on by the image of *Essence* magazine. This name looks fabulous on paper and sounds great in your mind, but be sure to try speaking it out loud, fast, with your surname. It's awfully hard to say.
In the World: *Essence* magazine; actress Essence Atkins; basketball player Essence Carson

Estella (eh-STEHL-ə) 1883: #106
Popularity: #1051
Styles: Ladies and
Gentlemen, Literary and
Artistic, Why Not? 1880 Today
Nicknames: Ella, Estee
Variants: Estelle, Stella, Estela, Estrella
Sisters: Delia, Lavinia, Emeline, Helena,
Adela, Viola
Brothers: Edmund, Richmond, Hugh, Merritt,
Everett, Truman
✸ An old-fashioned name with the appealing meaning "star." Most people you ask will tell you Estella is a lovely choice, a romantic charmer on the model of Isabella. A few (mostly menfolk) will say they can't picture the name on anyone under 70. The nickname Ella might help split the difference.
In the World: Estella of *Great Expectations*; actress Estella Warren

Esther (EHS-ter) 1896: #27
Popularity: #236
Styles: Ladies and
Gentlemen, Biblical, Jewish
Nicknames: Estee, Hettie, 1880 Today
Etta, Essie
Variants: Ester
Sisters: Miriam, Edith, Leora, Ruth, Alice,
Rose
Brothers: Saul, Arthur, Julius, Solomon,
Simon, Reuben
✸ One of the great biblical heroines, Esther was also one of the classic 1900s girls' names. As the name slid from fashion, its timeless biblical style had to fight against dowdiness. Today, as parents scramble for biblical names for girls, Esther is making a quiet comeback. It's a gently surprising alternative to names like Abigail and Hannah.
In the World: Swimming film star Esther Williams; models Esther Cañadas and Esther Baxter

Ethel (EH-thəl) 1894: #7
Popularity: #8281
Styles: Porch Sitters
Sisters: Edna, Hazel, Hilda, Agnes, Edith, Gladys 1880 Today
Brothers: Wilbur, Earl, Horace, Fred, Elmer, Leroy
✳ Ethel is an Old English name element meaning "noble." Originally, it was combined with other name pieces to produce winners like Ethelbert and Etheldreda. Around the 1870s, that Dark Ages sound surprisingly came into vogue, and Ethel began a 50-year run as a wildly popular full name for girls. Like the similar name Hilda, it has now essentially disappeared.
In the World: Singer/actresses Ethel Merman and Ethel Waters

Etta (EH-tə) 1880: #72
Popularity: #2250
Styles: Guys and Dolls
Nicknames: Ettie
Sisters: Minnie, Della, Lula, 1880 Today
Bessie, Evie, Dora
Brothers: Arlo, Mose, Archie, Roscoe, Mack, Louie
✳ Cute and jazzy, Etta is the kind of old-fashioned name that we think of as a fun-loving grandma. So far, that's kept it off most parents' short lists. But as other cuddly classics like Mollie and Ella rise to the top, Etta is getting closer to a comeback. It could also work as a nickname for lacy choices like Violetta or Marietta.
In the World: Singer Etta James (given name Jamesetta)

Eva (EE-və, AY-və) 1886: #32
Popularity: #83
Styles: Antique Charm, Short and Sweet, Latino/Latina, German and Dutch 1880 Today
Nicknames: Evie, Evita
Variants: Eve, Aoife, Ava
Sisters: Lena, Clara, Lucy, Rosa, Anna, Sophie, Julia
Brothers: Henry, Leo, Oscar, Felix, Sam, Oliver, Emmett
✳ This Latin form of Eve has always been the preferred version in the U.S., especially a century ago, when it reigned alongside Ada and Iva. That history makes Eva the traditional choice, while Eve travels in faster circles.
In the World: Actresses Eva Longoria, Eva Green, and Eva Mendes; Argentine first lady Eva Perón

Evangeline (eh-VAN-jə-leen, 2011: #286
eh-VAN-jə-liyn)
Popularity: #286
Styles: Antique Charm, Exotic Traditional 1880 Today
Nicknames: Eva, Evie, Lina, Angie, Vangie, Evan
Variants: Evangelina, Evangelia
Sisters: Genevieve, Annabelle, Seraphina, Beatrix, Madeleine, Josephine
Brothers: Alexander, Emerson, Maximilian, Dominick, Matthias, Benedict
✳ Name your favorite adjective—Evangeline fits. It's traditional, distinctive, romantic, and sophisticated. It's also a treasure trove of nickname potential, the name of an attractive actress (Evangeline Lilly of *Lost*), the title of a celebrated Longfellow poem, and . . . well, Evangeline has it all going on. The name comes from the Latin for "gospel," and many will hear it as a link to Christian evangelism.
In the World: Actress Evangeline Lilly; the wishing star in Disney's *The Princess and the Frog*

Eve (EEV) 2011: #546
Popularity: #546
Styles: Timeless, Biblical, Short and Sweet, English 1880 Today
Nicknames: Evie, Evita
Variants: Eva, Chava
Sisters: Leah, Ivy, Hope, Juliet, Lily, Zoe, Kate, Claire
Brothers: Noel, Simon, Ari, Eliot, Samuel, Noah, Bennett, Asher
✳ While Adam has settled in comfortably as a modern classic, his old garden mate Eve is seldom heard from. (In the U.S., anyway—it's a standard in the U.K.) The name's image is complex: simple yet sophisticated, sweet with a dangerous edge. Pixar played off the name's Eden imagery in naming the robotic EVE in the film *WALL-E*.
In the World: Rapper Eve; film *All About Eve*; EVE of *WALL-E*; actresses Eve Arden and Eve Plumb

Evelyn (EH-və-lin) 1919: #11
Popularity: #24
Styles: Antique Charm, The
"-ens"
Nicknames: Evie 1880 Today
Variants: Evelynn, Evaline,
Evalyn, Evelin
Sisters: Vivian, Charlotte, Lillian, Claire,
Madeline, Violet
Brothers: Oliver, Emmet, Henry, Jack, Owen,
Samuel
★That was quick! For years, Evelyn was one of
the ladies your grandma played bridge with.
Suddenly, it's the most stylish name on the
block. This sweetheart of a name has the
rhythm to win over fans of Addison and Payton
and the style to charm admirers of Eleanor and
Clara.
In the World: (Male) writer Evelyn Waugh; real-
ity TV star Evelyn Lozada

Everly (EH-ver-lee) 2011: #1098
Popularity: #1099
Styles: Last Names First,
Why Not?
Nicknames: Evie, Ever 1880 Today
Variants: Everleigh, Everlee
Sisters: Marlowe, Oakley, Harper, Bellamy,
Larkin, Presley
Brothers: Brighton, Hendrix, Pippin, Carver,
Holden, Gibson
★Everly is familiar as a surname, thanks to the
classic rock act The Everly Brothers. But Everly
is actually an uncommon last name, with al-
most no history as a first name. So, even as
familiar as it is, it sounds completely contempo-
rary. The "Eve-" root and the echo of Beverly
make it more purely female than most sur-
names.
In the World: The Everly Brothers; film thriller
Everly

Faith (FAYTH) 2002: #48
Popularity: #71
Styles: Charms and Graces,
Country and Western
Sisters: Lily, Grace, Hope, 1880 Today
Paige, Autumn, Joy
Brothers: Caleb, Owen, Gabriel, Noah,
Carson, Luke
★Faith is pure and pretty, with an uplifting
meaning. It was quietly timeless until the ascent
of singer Faith Hill. She jump-started the name
with a country twist.
In the World: Singers Faith Hill and Faith
Evans; George Michael song "Faith"; phrases
such as "have faith"

Fallon (FA-lən) 1982: #376
Popularity: #1193
Styles: The "-ens," Celtic,
Nickname-Proof
Sisters: Rhiannon, Siobhan, 1880 Today
Brenna, Felicia, Tegan,
Shannon
Brothers: Garret, Cameron, Killian, Donovan,
Eamon, Trevor
★This Irish surname was a brief baby-name
phenomenon in the '80s, thanks to a character
on the prime-time soap *Dynasty*. (Fellow char-
acters Krystle, Blake, and Alexis had even bigger
impacts.) It's an uncommon but attractive
choice today, and comedian Jimmy Fallon has
helped to restore its surname style.
In the World: Comedian Jimmy Fallon; Fallon
Carrington Colby of *Dynasty*

Farrah (FAR-ə) 1977: #177
Popularity: #544
Styles: '70s–'80s, Namesakes,
Nickname-Proof
Sisters: Shanna, Trisha, 1880 Today
Tennille, Christa, Jaclyn,
Nikki
Brothers: Torrey, Heath, Jarrett, Clint, Shaun,
Dusty
★The name Farrah was mostly heard from in
the '70s, which leaves all the Farrahs out there
with the sad certainty that they were named
after one of *Charlie's Angels*. (Farrah Fawcett's
star run on the TV show was 1976–77.) Luckily,
it's a perfectly pleasant, attractive name.
In the World: Actress Farrah Fawcett

Fatima (fah-TEE-mah) 2006: #228
Popularity: #281
Styles: Muslim, Latino/
Latina
Nicknames: Tima 1880 Today
Variants: Fatimah, Fátima
Sisters: Mariam, Ximena, Pilar, Loreto,
Yasmin, Samira
Brothers: Ismael, Omar, Hassan, Manuel,
Amir, Cruz
★A favorite Muslim name, after Mohammed's
daughter, Fatima has also been well used by
Catholics in honor of the famed visitation of
Our Lady of Fátima in Portugal. English-speak-
ing parents occasionally hesitate on this name
because of the letters "fat."
In the World: The Hand of Fatima amulet (also
called a Hamsa)

Felicia (feh-LEESH-ə) 1986: #90
Popularity: #1446
Styles: '70s–'80s, Lacy and
Lissome
Variants: Felisha, Felice, 1880 Today
Felícia
Sisters: Monica, Deanna, Leticia, Adrienne,
Katrina, Natasha
Brothers: Travis, Lance, Derrick, Shannon,
Damon, Terrence
✴ Felicia is as flamboyantly feminine as you
can get, with a sunny boost from its meaning
("lucky"). The name is as attractive as ever,
though it's no longer the exotic surprise it was in
the '60s. In fact, demure sister Felicity has taken
the lead.
In the World: Actresses Phylicia Rashad and Fe-
licia Day; Felicia of the "Darkstalkers" video
game series

Felicity (feh-LIS-i-tee) 1999: #390
Popularity: #666
Styles: English, Charms and
Graces, NicknameSaints,
Why Not? 1880 Today
Nicknames: Fliss, Flick, Fizz,
Felix, Lici
Variants: Felice
Sisters: Verity, Lorelei, Juliet, Dahlia, Arabella,
Briony
Brothers: Colin, Sebastian, Oliver, Duncan,
Barnaby, Crispin
✴ America has never fully opened its arms to
names like Verity, Amity, and Felicity. What are
we waiting for? They represent admirable quali-
ties, and they're mighty catchy too. Felicity,
which means "happiness," has been well used
as a name in the U.K. A late '90s TV show made
it familiar in the U.S., but it remains uncommon, with a winking sense of fun.
In the World: Collegiate TV drama *Felicity*; actresses Felicity Huffman and Felicity Kendal

Fern (FERN) 1916: #152
Popularity: #4244
Styles: Charms and Graces
Sisters: Nell, Ivy, Flora, Avis,
Hazel, Olive 1880 Today
Brothers: Ward, Stuart,
Forrest, Ellis, Carl, Roy
✴ Leafy and lacy, a fern is a graceful botanical
image for a girl's name. The name also holds a
timeless place in children's literature as the
main human character in *Charlotte's Web*. In
the early 1900s, Fern was especially popular as a
middle name, which would be a perfect way to
revive it.
In the World: Author Fern Michaels; Fern Ara-
ble of *Charlotte's Web*

Fifi (FEE-fee) 1926: #3046
Popularity: Very rare
Styles: Nicknames, French,
Fanciful
Sisters: Gigi, Babette, Coco, 1880 Today
Bijou, Fleur, Lilou
Brothers: Rémy, Pippin, Dino, Fabrice, Kip,
Gilles
✴ Frivolous? Fluffy? Fit for a poodle? Okay,
okay . . . but Fifi could be cute for a little girl.
It's a French nickname for Josephine, so the
practical parent can just choose that venerable
classic. Then, if your daughter doesn't seem like
a natural Fifi (and how many of us do?), she can
simply slip into something a little more com-
fortable.
In the World: Children's TV series *Fifi and the
Flowertots*; the perfume industry's FiFi Awards

Finley (FIN-lee) 2011: #364
Popularity: #364
Styles: Last Names First,
Celtic, Androgynous
Nicknames: Fin 1880 Today
Variants: Finlay
Sisters: Hadley, Rowan, Sawyer, Landry,
Addison, Rory
Brothers: Hudson, Gavin, Cole, Cullen,
Maddox, Sullivan
✴ It takes most names generations to achieve
what Finley has done in just a few short years. It
has transitioned from a quirky and decidedly
Scottish men's name and surname to an Ameri-
can girl next door.
In the World: Daughters of musician Lisa Marie
Presley, actress Angie Harmon, and actor Dan-
iel Baldwin

Finola (fin-NO-lə)   2007: #6539
Popularity: #11,415
Styles: Celtic
Nicknames: Nola
Variants: Fenella, Fionnuala   1880   Today
Sisters: Niamh, Siobhan,
Grania, Aoife, Sinéad, Catriona
Brothers: Cormac, Declan, Colm, Kieran,
Eoin, Ronan
✱ Finola is a hard-core Celtic classic for families who really want Irish heritage and not just a trendy Irish sound. It comes from the Gaelic Fionnghuala, a swan maiden of Celtic myths.
In the World: Actress Finola Hughes

Fiona (fee-OH-nə)   2010: #257
Popularity: #267
Styles: English, Celtic, Lacy
and Lissome
Nicknames: Fi   1880   Today
Sisters: Isla, Teagan, Kiera,
Nora, Daphne, Brynn
Brothers: Liam, Finlay, Malcolm, Rowan, Ian,
Graham
✱ It's baffling why this Scottish U.K. standby didn't hit the U.S. sooner. It's a romantic knockout with a playful spirit. But just as stylish American parents were starting to catch on to the name, along came the *Shrek* movies with their ogre princess Fiona to nudge it into the mainstream. It's still not too common, though . . . and still a knockout.
In the World: Fiona of *Shrek;* singer Fiona Apple; actress Fiona Shaw

Flannery (FLA-nə-ree)   2006: #5703
Popularity: #9875
Styles: Last Names First,
Celtic, Literary and Artistic,
Nickname-Proof   1880   Today
Sisters: Tierney, Carrigan,
Carson, Bellamy, Madigan, Connolly
Brothers: Brennan, Garrick, Sawyer, Declan,
Cullen, Tynan
✱ Flannery is an Irish surname with a puckish sound. It owes its new life as a first name to writer (Mary) Flannery O'Connor. This name has no natural nicknames, which you might think is a plus . . . until you find that you're calling your daughter "Flann" despite yourself.
In the World: Writer Flannery O'Connor

Fleur (FLOOR)   1972: #4791
Popularity: #15,356
Styles: Charms and Graces,
French
Variants: Flor, Flora   1880   Today
Sisters: Clemence, Aurora,
Dahlia, Poppy, Lilou, Anouk
Brothers: Florian, Piers, Regis, Bastien, Luc,
Frost
✱ Fleur is French for "flower." In theory, that sounds impossibly romantic and a little showy. In practice, this one-syllable name is gentle and even understated. It's popular in Belgium and the Netherlands, and uncommon but rising in France.
In the World: Fleur Delacour of the "Harry Potter" series

Flora (FLOH-rə)   1880: #68
Popularity: #1724
Styles: Charms and Graces,
Ladies and Gentlemen,
Saints, Mythological, Why   1880   Today
Not?
Nicknames: Flo, Flossie
Variants: Fleur
Sisters: Louisa, Olive, Vera, Clio, Adela, Rhea
Brothers: Leo, Felix, Victor, Julius, Casper,
Hugh
✱ When Lily, Rose, and Daisy were at their peaks, so was this name: the Roman goddess of flowers. More than any of the others, Flora keeps its 19th-century flavor.

Florence (FLOH rchns)   1893: #7
Popularity: #2474
Styles: Ladies and
Gentlemen, Place Names
Nicknames: Flo, Flossie,   1880   Today
Florrie
Variants: Florencia, Florentia, Floris
Sisters: Dorothy, Louise, Adelaide, Estelle,
Virginia, Harriet
Brothers: Albert, Clarence, Walter, Ernest,
Arthur, Thornton
✱ In the 19th century, Florence was a hero name. Florence Nightingale was the founder of modern nursing and the most admired woman of her time. She made this formerly obscure old name wildly fashionable. (Nightingale was named Florence after the city where she was born.) Today Florence has returned to obscurity; Flora is a more promising option.
In the World: Nursing pioneer Florence Nightingale; actress Florence Henderson; band Florence + The Machine

Name Snapshots: Girls   93

Frances (FRAN-sis)   1918: #8
Popularity: #789
Styles: Solid Citizens, Ladies
and Gentlemen
Nicknames: Fran, Francie, 1880 Today
Frankie, Fanny
Variants: Francesca
Sisters: Helen, Patricia, Evelyn, Martha,
Dorothy, Alice
Brothers: Richard, Warren, Henry, Louis,
Frederick, Arthur
✳ Like her old pals Helen and Dorothy, Frances is fighting an uphill style battle. But also like those others, this is a name that will come back—maybe sooner than you expect. For now, Francesca is the more common source for Fran.
In the World: Actress Frances McDormand; writer Frances Hodgson Burnett; daughter of musician Kurt Cobain

Francesca (fran-CHEHS-kə)   1996: #353
Popularity: #500
Styles: Italian, Lacy and
Lissome, Why Not?
Nicknames: Fran, Frankie, 1880 Today
Francie, Cesca, Cecca, Cicca
Variants: Frances, Francisca, Franziska
Sisters: Giovanna, Adriana, Chiara, Paola,
Daniella, Alessandra
Brothers: Marco, Lorenzo, Antonio, Sergio,
Dante, Mario
✳ One of the most vividly Italian girls' names, Francesca is sumptuous and womanly. In Europe its popularity has spread far beyond Italy. The boyish "Frankie" is the hot nickname choice in the U.S., while the "C" names, especially Cesca, are popular elsewhere.
In the World: Tennis player Francesca Schiavone; photographer Francesca Woodman

Freya (FRAY-ə, FRIY-ə)   2011: #1176
Popularity: #1179
Styles: Mythological, Nordic,
English, Why Not?
Variants: Freja, Freyja, Freia 1880 Today
Sisters: Zara, Dania, Maren,
Imogen, Maia, Gemma
Brothers: Anders, Theo, Marius, Torin, Felix,
Alec
✳ Freya was the radiant, powerful Norse goddess of love. Her name, which packs its own feminine power punch, is a favorite both in her Nordic homelands and in the United Kingdom. As for Americans, they don't dislike the name; most are simply unaware of it. Perhaps your daughter will change that?
In the World: Freya lingerie/swimwear; model Freja Beha Erichsen; writer Freya Stark

Gabriela (ga-bree-EHL-ə)   2003: #102
Popularity: #165
Styles: Slavic, Latino/Latina,
Lacy and Lissome
Nicknames: Gaby, Gabi, Gab 1880 Today
Variants: Gabriella, Gabrielle
Sisters: Natalia, Daniela, Adriana, Giselle,
Valeria, Juliana
Brothers: Sebastian, Nicholas, Tristan, Xavier,
Lukas, Damian
✳ This seductive name has three equally traditional forms: the Slavic/Spanish Gabriela, the Italian Gabriella, and the French Gabrielle. All three have shot up in popularity, with their brother Gabriel racing alongside. That makes for a crowded field but doesn't diminish Gabriela's charms. It remains one of the warmest and richest of the lacy names.
In the World: Poet Gabriela Mistral; tennis player Gabriela Sabatini; actress Gabriella Wilde

Gabrielle (ga-bree-EHL) 1998: #47
Popularity: #119
Styles: French, Turn of the 21st Century
Nicknames: Gabby, Gabi, Gab
Variants: Gabriella, Gabriela
Sisters: Natalie, Alexandra, Danielle, Jocelyn, Madeleine, Sophie
Brothers: Collin, Garrett, Tristan, Zachary, Christian, Nathaniel
✶This old French classic earns high marks on both style and substance. It's a mature, well-built name with plenty of polish. If you like the name's sophistication, though, the lightweight nicknames might give you pause.
In the World: Representative Gabrielle Giffords; actress Gabrielle Union; Gabrielle of *Desperate Housewives*

Gaia (CIY·ə) 2011: #3130
Popularity: #3130
Styles: Mythological, Short and Sweet
Sisters: Vega, Dafne, Lyra, Oriana, Juno, Freya
Brothers: Orion, Evander, Bodhi, River, Atticus, Raz
✶The Greek goddess of the Earth, Gaia is an otherworldly name with the magic of legend. It's also a cute, simple little name. That makes it a natural sister for Zoe, which is Greek for "life."
In the World: GaiaOnline website; "Gaia Hypothesis" of Earth as a living entity; daughter of actress Emma Thompson

Gail (GAYL) 1951: #36
Popularity: #8289
Styles: Mid-Century, Brisk and Breezy
Variants: Gale, Gayle
Sisters: Janis, Kay, Donna, Margo, Gwen, Kathleen, Lynne
Brothers: Keith, Gary, Alan, Dennis, Gregory, Dean, Bruce
✶Most of the mid-century nicknames were dimple-cute: Trudy, Peggy, Vicki. Gail was smooth and mature, with a briskness that plays well today. It's seldom heard, though, and could be a strong choice alone or as a nickname for Abigail.
In the World: Writers Gail Collins and Gail Carson Levine; wrestler Gail Kim

Gemma (JEHM-mə) 2011: #356
Popularity: #356
Styles: Saints, English, Italian
Nicknames: Gem
Variants: Jemma
Sisters: Gillian, Zara, Felicity, Violet, Clare, Dahlia
Brothers: Rowan, Alec, Rupert, Colin, Fraser, Tobias
✶This Italian name, meaning "gem," was a '70s–'80s favorite in England that could arrive with fanfare in the U.S. Cute and tidy, it reflects current trends without following them.
In the World: Actresses Gemma Arterton, Gemma Jones, and Gemma Atkinson; Libba Bray's "Gemma Doyle" fantasy trilogy

Genesis (JEH-nə-sis) 2011: #82
Popularity: #82
Styles: Modern Meanings, Latino/Latina
Nicknames: Genny
Sisters: Serenity, Cadence, Journey, Scarlett, Giselle, Phoenix, Estrella, Trinity
Brothers: Emmanuel, Justice, Josiah, Matthias, Giovanni, Maverick, Lukas, Jericho
✶ Genesis is an origin or beginning, especially the beginning of the Bible. That's a splashy combination of word name and religious name and a perfect sister for Trinity. The name's overall rhythm sounds masculine, but the "Jen" sound makes it a pure girl's name.
In the World: First book of the Bible; actress Genesis Rodriguez, rock band Genesis; Hyundai Genesis sedan

Name Snapshots: Girls 95

Geneva (jeh-NEEV-ə) 1924: #110
Popularity: #1439
Styles: Ladies and
Gentlemen, Place Names,
Why Not? 1880 Today
Nicknames: Genie, Jenny,
Evie
Variants: Genevra, Ginevra
Sisters: Marian, Violet, Dorothea, Verona,
Willa, Silvia, Althea, Eleanora
Brothers: Everett, Conrad, Clinton, Rudolph,
Foster, Theodore, Edmond, Jules
✳ One part imposing elegance and one part
sauciness, Geneva is ready for a new turn in the
spotlight. You can consider it a place name
(after the Swiss city) or a form of Genevieve or
Guinevere. The Italian form Ginevra is the full
name of Ginny Weasley in the "Harry Potter"
series.
In the World: Geneva watches; the Geneva
Conventions, which set standards for the treat-
ment of war victims

Genevieve (JEH-neh-veev; 1915: #77
zhawn-VYEHV)
Popularity: #232
Styles: Exotic Traditional,
Antique Charm, French, 1880 Today
Saints
Nicknames: Ginny, Genny, Gen, Eve
Variants: Geneviève, Genoveva, Geneva
Sisters: Evangeline, Vivienne, Eleanor,
Beatrice, Victoria, Melisande, Violet,
Josephine
Brothers: Raphael, Quentin, Benedict,
Mathias, Dominic, Nicholas, Maximilian,
Roman
✳ If your top priority in a name is elegance,
look no further. Genevieve is the patron saint of
Paris, a fact that perfectly illustrates the name's
timeless grace. (And if you're worried about
your Gen blending in with the many Jennifers
in her class, relax—they're all Isabellas nowa-
days.)
In the World: Actresses Geneviève Bujold and
Genevieve Cortese; interior design show *Dear
Genevieve*

Georgia (JOHR-jə) 1882: #81
Popularity: #305
Styles: Place Names, Country
and Western, Antique
Charm, Greek 1880 Today
Nicknames: Georgie
Variants: Georgina, Georgiana, Georgette,
Jorja
Sisters: Charlotte, Lillie, Josephine, Stella,
Lucy, Scarlett, Ruby, Caroline
Brothers: Charlie, Maxwell, Emmett, Henry,
Luke, Theo, Walker, Eli
✳ Like Carolina, this name has the sound of a
proper lady but the style of a red-hot mama. It
also has a worldly elegance—Georgia is more
common in England and Greece than in the
U.S. It's a strong classic that pleases many audi-
ences.
In the World: Artist Georgia O'Keeffe; songs
"Georgia on My Mind" and "Sweet Georgia
Brown"

Gertrude (GER-trood) 1896: #23
Popularity: #7504
Styles: Porch Sitters, German
and Dutch
Nicknames: Gert, Trudy, 1880 Today
Gertie
Variants: Gertrud, Gertruda, Gertrudis
Sisters: Mildred, Hilda, Florence, Bertha,
Myrtle, Agnes
Brothers: Herman, Bertram, Claude, Horace,
Lester, Ernst
✳ There was a craze for Germanic names in
the 19th century, much like the Irish craze now.
Imagine how opulent Gertrude must have
sounded, how refined and continental! Can't
imagine it? You're not alone, and that craze
won't be coming back around for a good long
time.
In the World: Writer Gertrude Stein; actress
Gertrude Lawrence; swimmer Gertrude Ederle

Gia (JEE-ə) 2011: #299
Popularity: #299
Styles: Short and Sweet
Sisters: Livia, Giada, Nina,
Adriana, Elle, Paola 1880 Today
Brothers: Nico, Marco, Luca,
Tonio, Aldo, Matteo
✳ This little winner puts an Italian spin on the
petite names of the moment. It's a perfectly re-
spectable full name (though not used as one in
Italy), and it can also serve as a nickname for
ornate imports like Giovanna.
In the World: Model Gia Carangi; a child on
The Real Housewives of New Jersey

Giada (JAH-dah, jee-AH-də) 2010: #751
Popularity: #776
Styles: Italian
Variants: Jada
Sisters: Chiara, Giulia, Paola, Livia, Mariella, Liliana
Brothers: Luca, Giovanni, Nico, Dario, Enzo, Matteo

★The Italian form of Jade, Giada was virtually unknown in the U.S. until Italian-born chef Giada De Laurentiis hit the Food Network. Parents quickly picked up on the name as a stylish alternative to both Jada and Gianna. (It's gotten hot in Italy too.) The Italian pronunciation is two syllables.
In the World: TV chef Giada De Laurentiis

Gianna (jee-AH-nə, JAHN-ə) 2011: #63
Popularity: #63
Styles: Italian
Nicknames: Gia, Gigi
Variants: Giana
Sisters: Arianna, Gabriella, Ava, Lucia, Gemma, Chiara
Brothers: Dante, Luca, Marco, Dominic, Carlo, Matteo

★A few years ago, Gianna was a foreign name you couldn't even find in an American baby name book. Today it's a smash. The name is like the distilled essence of Italy, with all the lushness of names like Francesca and Alessandra concentrated into six smooth letters. The Italian pronunciation is two syllables, but English speakers usually make it three. See also Giovanna.

Gillian (JI-lee-ən, GI-lee-ən) 1999: #303
Popularity: #1267
Styles: English, Turn of the 21st Century
Nicknames: Jill, Gilly
Variants: Jillian
Sisters: Abigail, Chloe, Felicity, Gemma, Regan, Fiona
Brothers: Trevor, Gavin, Colin, Garrett, Reid, Connor

★This English favorite is soft and serious, a rare and coveted combination. It has never been too common in the U.S., despite a brief rise during the heyday of The X-Files with star Gillian Anderson. In the U.K. it's most often pronounced with a hard "G," but in the U.S. the "G" is usually soft. See also Jillian.
In the World: Actresses Gillian Anderson and Gillian Jacobs; singer Gillian Welch

Gina (JEE-nə) 1967: #54
Popularity: #1408
Styles: Surfer '60s, Italian
Variants: Gena, Geena
Sisters: Angela, Lisa, Dawn, Toni, Dana, Carla
Brothers: Kurt, Joey, Troy, Darrin, Dino, Randy

★This Italian nickname was an all-American favorite alongside Dina and Tina in the '60s. With a bit of distance, it's starting to sound Italian again. If you want an even bigger dose of Italian sound, you could go with the full name Luigina (like actress Gina Lollobrigida). Not tempted? Then try Georgina, Regina, Angelina, Giovanna, or Virginia.
In the World: Actresses Gina Lollobrigida, Gina Gershon, Geena Davis, and Gena Rowlands; MMA fighter Gina Carano

Ginger (JIN-jer) 1971: #187
Popularity: #1686
Styles: Charms and Graces, Surfer '60s, Nicknames
Nicknames: Ginny
Sisters: Marcy, Dawn, Trina, Sandy, Robin, Holly
Brothers: Tad, Scotty, Dirk, Gregg, Kip, Toby

★If it weren't for Gilligan's Island . . . if it weren't for Ginger Spice . . . wouldn't this be a great name? It's a nature name with extra "snap," but with its history, it's a little tough to take seriously. To hedge your bets, try it as a nickname for Virginia.
In the World: Actress Ginger Rogers; Ginger of Gilligan's Island; a nickname for redheads (sometimes pejorative)

Giovanna (joh-VAHN-ə) 2005: #680
Popularity: #786
Styles: Italian, Lacy and Lissome, Why Not?
Nicknames: Gianna, Gia, Vanni, Vanna
Sisters: Francesca, Chiara, Viviana, Alessandra, Giada, Adriana
Brothers: Lorenzo, Giancarlo, Vincenzo, Rocco, Dario, Leonardo

★Giovanna, the feminine form of Giovanni (John), is the sumptuous Italy of our dreams. Long considered "too foreign" to be an American hit, it's now a fashionable import. The short form Gianna is even more popular.

Giselle (ji-ZEHL, zhee-ZEHL   2007: #134
Popularity: #152
Styles: French, Nickname-
Proof, Latino/Latina
Variants: Gisele, Gisela   1880   Today
Sisters: Candice, Damaris,
Natalia, Liliana, Fleur, Camille
Brothers: Tristan, Xavier, Emmanuel, Joaquin,
Mateo, Nicolas
✳ This French classic is drenched in romantic glamour. It's a famous ballet, an international supermodel, and even a Disney Princess. Is that over the top? Remarkably, no. The name's simple, demure style—swift as a gazelle—still outweighs all the glitz.
In the World: Model Gisele Bündchen; ballet *Giselle;* Princess Giselle of *Enchanted*

Gladys (GLA-dis)   1901: #11
Popularity: #2287
Styles: Porch Sitters, Celtic
Sisters: Muriel, Lois, Thelma,
Hazel, Agnes, Vera   1880   Today
Brothers: Lloyd, Otis, Morris,
Earl, Cyril, Hubert, Mervin
✳ In the late 1800s, the Welsh name Gladys became an international sensation. Back then, Gladys sounded like a sensuous, exotic heroine. Try Gwyneth or Carys for a similar effect today.
In the World: Singer Gladys Knight; nosy neighbor Gladys Kravitz of *Bewitched*

Glenda (GLEHN-də)   1944: #79
Popularity: #3341
Styles: Mid-Century, Celtic
Nicknames: Glen
Variants: Glinda   1880   Today
Sisters: Marcia, Carol, Lynda,
Sondra, Glynis, Kathleen
Brothers: Douglas, Wayne, Kerry, Stuart,
Ronald, Bruce
✳ Americans aren't the only ones who invent new names. Glenda is a Welsh name, but not a traditional one—it was born in the 20th century. As a result, it's currently in a no-man's-land of fashion, neither classic nor contemporary. One possible freshener is Glenna, on the model of Brenda/Brenna. (If you're thinking of the Good Witch of the North, who travels in a bubble, she's Glinda.)
In the World: Actress Glenda Jackson; Glinda of *The Wizard of Oz*

Gloria (GLOH-ree-ə)   1945: #23
Popularity: #571
Styles: Solid Citizens,
Nickname-Proof
Variants: Glory   1880   Today
Sisters: Barbara, Elaine,
Patricia, Marilyn, Beverly, Joyce
Brothers: Donald, Roger, Gerald, Richard,
Lawrence, Raymond
✳ Gloria is a name of the 20th century. It was born in a George Bernard Shaw play at the dawn of the century, and by the year 2000 the name was fading away. It's easy to see the velvety elegance that enticed generations of parents, but Gloria is entering grandma territory now. It's a strong revival possibility a generation or two down the line, once its roots as the Latin for "glory" start shining through again.
In the World: singers Gloria Estefan and Gloria Gaynor; actress Gloria Swanson; activist Gloria Steinem; several stick-in-your-mind "Gloria" songs

Glynis (GLI-nis)   1963: #596
Popularity: Very rare
Styles: English, Celtic
Nicknames: Glyn
Variants: Glynnis   1880   Today
Sisters: Bronwyn, Carys,
Elspeth, Bethan, Eirlys, Lowri
Brothers: Vaughn, Griffith, Wynn, Ivor,
Gethin, Steffan
✳ This Welsh name is an individualist. It's not unfashionable, exactly—it just opts out of the fashion race altogether. Glynis could be a gentle way to stand out from the crowd.
In the World: Actress Glynis Johns

Golda (GOHL-də)   1894: #295
Popularity: #4245
Styles: Ladies and
Gentlemen, Jewish
Nicknames: Goldie   1880   Today
Variants: Zahava
Sisters: Frieda, Esther, Leora, Belle, Sadie,
Bluma
Brothers: Rueben, Moss, Asa, Haskell, Otto,
Abe
✳ Golda may sound old-a, but it has a chance at a second youth now that similar names like Bella and Cora are on the upswing. Zahava is a modern Hebrew name with the same golden meaning.
In the World: Israeli prime minister Golda Meir; actress Goldie Hawn

Grace (GRAYS)   1890: #13
Popularity: #16
Styles: Antique Charm,
Charms and Graces
Nicknames: Gracie   1880   Today
Variants: Grazia, Gratia
Sisters: Sophie, Claire, Lydia, Charlotte, Anna,
Lily
Brothers: Owen, Henry, August, Emmett,
Maxwell, Samuel
✖This lovely classic is bursting with positive
meanings: beauty, refinement, mercy, and
blessings. It was neglected for much of the 20th
century, but today it's a full-bore hit—even
more than its high rank suggests. Grace is a
powerhouse as a *middle* name, where its artful
simplicity complements more elaborate first
names.
In the World: Actress Grace Kelly; singer Grace
Jones; song "Amazing Grace"; phrases like
"grace under pressure" and "fall from grace"

Gracelyn (GRAYS-lin)   2011: #480
Popularity: #482
Styles: The "-ens"
Nicknames: Gracie
Variants: Gracelynn, Gracyn   1880   Today
Sisters: Madelyn, Sydney,
Abrielle, Mckenna, Emersyn, Avalyn
Brothers: Griffin, Kayden, Maddox, Grady,
Bryce, Rylan
✖The name Gracelyn repackages the timeless
elegance of Grace in a thoroughly modern
wrapper. If Grace seems an unlikely choice for
this treatment, consider the influence of Grace-
land, the estate of Elvis Presley.

Gracie (GRAY-see)   2005: #94
Popularity: #136
Styles: Guys and Dolls,
Nicknames
Sisters: Lillie, Bella, Rosie,   1880   Today
Ivy, Molly, Sadie
Brothers: Max, Jake, Eli, Cole, Grady, Levi
✖This pet form plays up the cuteness and
dizzy-dame fun, but loses some of the grace that
is, of course, the very core of Grace. It's a lovable
nickname, but you don't lose anything by put-
ting the formal version on the birth certificate.
In the World: Comedian Gracie Allen; a daugh-
ter of singers Faith Hill and Tim McGraw

Graciela (grah-cee-EHL-a)   1998: #574
Popularity: #1584
Styles: Latino/Latina, Lacy
and Lissome, Why Not?
Nicknames: Gracie, Chela,   1880   Today
Ella
Variants: Graziella
Sisters: Silvia, Mariela, Lidia, Cristina,
Gabriela, Susana, Lucia, Marcela
Brothers: Guillermo, Arturo, Mario, Alberto,
Aldo, Felipe, Gustavo, Francisco
✖ Graciela is the Spanish equivalent of Gracie,
and it is as opulent as Gracie is impish. It's an
uncommon choice that sounds like the peak of
fashion. A promising alternative to the popular
Gabriela.
In the World: Cuban jazz singer Graciela;
singer/actress Graciela Beltrán

Greer (GREER)   1996: #2228
Popularity: #3171
Styles: Solid Citizens, Brisk
and Breezy, Celtic,
Androgynous   1880   Today
Variants: Grier
Sisters: Brynn, Tatum, Emlyn, Bly, Shea, Adair
Brothers: Flynn, Blane, Quinlan, Shaw,
Carrick, Gray
✖ Eileen Greer Garson was one of the biggest
movie stars of the 1940s. She dropped her given
name and went by Greer, which was her moth-
er's maiden name. Ever since, Greer has been
an unsual combination of masculine sound and
womanly style. As a surname, it's Scottish, a
form of Gregor. It could be useful as a namesake
if you have Gregorys in your family tree.
In the World: Actresses Greer Garson and Greer
Grammer, daughter of actor Kelsey Grammer

Greta (GREH-tə)   1932: #318
Popularity: #684
Styles: Ladies and
Gentlemen, German and
Dutch, Nordic, Why Not?   1880   Today
Nicknames: Gretchen, Gretel
Sisters: Elsa, Ingrid, Lena, Thea, Anneliese,
Astrid
Brothers: Conrad, Bennett, Niels, Karl, Stefan,
Lars
✖ Swedish film star Greta Garbo was the inter-
national epitome of sophistication. Her name,
originally a pet form of Margareta, is a bit old-
fashioned now but still worldly and sophisti-
cated. A good choice for understated elegance.
In the World: Actresses Greta Garbo, Greta Ger-
wig, and Greta Scacchi; commentator Greta
Van Susteren

Gretchen (GREH-chən) 1973: #191
Popularity: #1059
Styles: German and Dutch,
Nickname-Proof
Variants: Greta, Gretel 1880 Today
Sisters: Heidi, Lisbeth,
Ingrid, Tamara, Christa, Elke
Brothers: Kurt, Stefan, Tobias, Niels, Karl,
Erich
✶ Gretchen is a German nickname, a pet form
of Margarete/Greta. It retains some of that nick-
name style in English, but its grinding-gear
sound is the opposite of the light, girlish nick-
names that rule the roost today. On the plus
side, Gretchen's crunchy consonants lend the
name a style-defying confidence, and it grows
up well.
In the World: Singer Gretchen Wilson; actress
Gretchen Mol

Guadalupe 1997: #210
(gwah-dah-LOO-pay)
Popularity: #353
Styles: Latino/Latina,
Androgynous 1880 Today
Nicknames: Lupe, Lupita,
Pita
Sisters: Carmen, Rosario, Pilar, Carolina,
Belèn, Luz, Mercedes, Luisa
Brothers: Pedro, Jesus, Francisco, Jorge, Pablo,
Santiago, Raul, Ricardo
✶ Guadalupe is the quintessential Mexican
name. It celebrates the 16th-century appear-
ance of the Virgin Mary to a poor Indian named
Juan Diego. Our Lady of Guadalupe grew to
become a national symbol of Mexico, represent-
ing the fusion of Spanish Catholicism with na-
tive Mexican cultures. The name is used for
both boys and girls but is predominantly female
in the U.S.
In the World: Actress Lupe Vélez; singer Lupita
D'Alessio

Guinevere (GWI-nə-veer) 2011: #2092
Popularity: #2094
Styles: Exotic Traditional,
Literary and Artistic
Nicknames: Guin, Vera 1880 Today
Variants: Jennifer
Sisters: Emeline, Morgana, Gwendolyn,
Rhiannon, Eowyn, Melisande
Brothers: Alastair, Caedmon, Evander, Gavin,
Graeme, Caradoc
✶ Most of us hear Guinevere, the name of
King Arthur's queen, as purely the stuff of leg-
end. But those legends have made the name as
familiar as it is romantic. An old Cornish ver-
sion of Guinevere has already found some tak-
ers; perhaps you've heard of the name Jennifer?
In the World: Legendary wife of King Arthur;
actress/screenwriter Guinevere Turner

Gwen (GWEHN) 1959: #295
Popularity: #1217
Styles: Mid-Century, Solid
Citizens, Celtic, Saints
Sisters: Margo, Dale, Kaye, 1880 Today
Nora, Glenda, Janis
Brothers: Kent, Von, Barry, Gregg, Rex, Hal
✶ Gwen's appeal is its dispatch. It doesn't put
on airs, nor does it try to masquerade as a boy's
name. It's upfront and female, like it or not.
(You'll find that many do like it very much.)
Singer Gwen Stefani has pumped up the name's
grrl power. If you want to turn down that watt-
age, try it as a nickname for Gwendolyn or
Gwyneth.
In the World: Singer Gwen Stefani; *Spider-Man*
character Gwen Stacy; TV journalist Gwen Ifill

Gwendolyn (GWEHN-də-lin) 1953: #112
Popularity: #572
Styles: Solid Citizens, Celtic,
African-American
Nicknames: Gwen, Wendy 1880 Today
Variants: Gwendolen,
Gwendoline
Sisters: Bronwyn, Constance, Bernadette,
Rosemary, Muriel, Glenda
Brothers: Stuart, Clark, Randolph, Llewellyn,
Clifford, Vaughn
✶ The Welsh classic Gwendolyn bucks fash-
ion. Such a heaping helping of consonants is
decidedly old-school. While the name's heft
will scare some away, it's actually Gwendolyn's
biggest asset. This is a substantial name, full of
character and impossible to forget.
In the World: Poet Gwendolyn Brooks

Hadassah (hah-DAH-sah) 2011: #804
Popularity: #804
Styles: Biblical, Jewish
Sisters: Shoshana, Miriam,
Yael, Esther, Allegra, 1880 Today
Elisheva
Brothers: Mordecai, Reuben, Hillel, Asher,
Boaz, Abram
✳ Hadassah is the original Hebrew name of the biblical Esther. Like many Old Testament names, Hadassah is finding a new audience among Christian parents eager for creative biblical name ideas for girls. They're hearing the name afresh, in all its whispery femininity. In the Jewish world it's a classic, but more more old-fashioned than fashionable.
In the World: Jewish women's volunteer organization Hadassah

Haley (HAY-lee) 1996: #30
Popularity: #159
Styles: Last Names First, Bell
Tones, Nickname-Proof,
Turn of the 21st Century 1880 Today
Variants: Hailey, Hayley,
Haylie, Hailee, Haleigh
Sisters: Kelsey, Brianna, Taylor, Sydney, Kayla, Shelby
Brothers: Tyler, Logan, Dillon, Chandler, Payton, Dalton
✳ This former surname became popular in Britain in the '60s thanks to child actress Hayley Mills. Americans didn't catch on until the '90s, but then took to the name like mad. The spelling Hailey is equally popular, and creative variants abound.
In the World: Actresses Hayley Mills, Hailee Steinfeld, and Haylie Duff; Hailie Mathers, daughter of rapper Eminem

Hallie (HA-lee) 1894: #210
Popularity: #602
Styles: Guys and Dolls
Variants: Halle
Sisters: Addie, Nora, Josie, 1880 Today
Evie, Nell, Tillie
Brothers: Joe, Harry, Mack, Cyrus, Sam, Nat
✳ Hallie is the antique answer to Haley, an old-fashioned cutie with time-tested tenderness. If you'd prefer to use it as a nickname, Harriet is a traditional source. The similar name Halle, familiar thanks to actress Halle Berry, has separate origins as a Scandinavian name.

Halo (HAY-loh) 2010: #1489
Popularity: #1675
Styles: Modern Meanings,
Fantastical
Sisters: Nova, Skye, Aura, 1880 Today
Cielo, Aeris, Tru, Ember
Brothers: Draven, Pax, Roan, Creed, Sparrow, Zion, Locke
✳ This smooth, vowel-strong name packs a world of images into its four letters. As a symbol of sacred glory, it's a creative alternative to Heaven or Angel. But a comic-book superheroine named Halo gives the name a tougher edge, and a violent video game series makes it positively deadly. Meanwhile, a 2008 Beyoncé song recast the angelic meaning as an aura of romantic love. Can your daughter make the name her own?
In the World: Video game series "Halo"; Beyoncé ballad "Halo"

Hannah (HA-nə, HAH-nə) 2000: #2
Popularity: #25
Styles: Antique Charm,
Biblical, Nickname-Proof
Variants: Hanna, Hana 1880 Today
Sisters: Abigail, Sarah,
Emma, Olivia, Grace, Leah
Brothers: Joshua, Caleb, Noah, Samuel, Jacob, Ethan
✳ Looking for a warm, old-fashioned biblical name? Male choices abound, but for girls' names it's slim pickings. Hannah is one that hits the bull's-eye. It's simple and sweet and sounds great with almost any type of surname. Hannah has been hugely popular in the past generation, especially in cold-climate states, where warmth is always in fashion.
In the World: TV series *Hannah Montana*; film *Hannah and Her Sisters*; political theorist Hannah Arendt

Harley (HAHR-lee) 2003: #312
Popularity: #436
Styles: Last Names First,
Androgynous, Fantastical
Variants: Harlee, Harleigh 1880 Today
Sisters: Macy, Parker,
Leighton, Shelby, Bailey, Skylar
Brothers: Gunner, Brock, Drake, Ryker,
Keaton, Jacoby
✱A handful of parents may be inspired by
comic-book villainess Harley Quinn, but for
most this name is all about Harley-Davidson
motorcycles. If you live to hit the open road on
your hog, jump on the name. But if you just like
the sound of it, consider a similar alternative
with a little less horsepower.
In the World: Harley-Davidson motorcycles;
Harley Quinn of comic-book fame; soap opera
character Harley Cooper; writer/actress Harley
Jane Kozak

Harlow (HAR-loh) 2011: #621
Popularity: #621
Styles: Last Names First,
Why Not?
Sisters: Harper, Scarlett, 1880 Today
Monroe, Lola, Shiloh, Everly
Brothers: Flynn, Hudson, Gable, Archer,
Hendrix, Winslow
✱Jean Harlow was a platinum-blond bomb-
shell, a screen sensation of the 1930s. Her image
suffuses this name, resulting in a contemporary
surname with an aura of old-time glamour.
In the World: Actress Jean Harlow; a daughter of
musician Joel Madden and reality TV star Ni-
cole Richie

Harmony (HAHR-mə-nee) 2011: #223
Popularity: #224
Styles: Modern Meanings,
Nickname-Proof
Sisters: Autumn, Cadence, 1880 Today
Journey, Willow, Summer,
Liberty
Brothers: Landon, Ryder, Chance, Justice,
Holden, Phoenix
✱It's only fitting that Harmony should have a
meaning with two parts that work together. It
suggests beautiful music as well as the even
more beautiful image of peace. Just don't use it
as a sister for Melody, or Harmony will always
feel like she's playing second fiddle.

Harper (HAR-per) 2011: #54
Popularity: #54
Styles: Last Names First,
Literary and Artistic,
Androgynous 1880 Today
Sisters: Emerson, Marlowe,
Piper, Juniper, Flannery, Scarlett
Brothers: Lincoln, Holden, Calder, Archer,
Truman, Sawyer
✱*To Kill a Mockingbird* may be America's fa-
vorite novel. The book's unique blend of the
colloquial and the sophisticated rubs off on
baby names too. That's true of character names
like Atticus and Scout as well as the name of the
book's author, (Nelle) Harper Lee. Harper may
look like just another surname, but it's as literary and American as Huck Finn.
In the World: Writer Harper Lee; many celebrity babies, including a daughter of David and
Victoria Beckham

Harriet (HA-ree-ət) 1880: #73
Popularity: #2186
Styles: Ladies and Gentlemen
Nicknames: Hattie, Ettie
Variants: Harriett 1880 Today
Sisters: Flora, Estelle,
Millicent, Adeline, Georgiana, Marian
Brothers: Edmund, Willis, Frederick, Foster,
Gilbert, Arthur
✱ Let's go out on a limb and call for a Harriet
revival. The name has been out of commission
for generations, but its whimsical charm could
fit adorably on a little girl. The renewal of simi-
lar names like Charlotte and Eleanor should
help pave the way.
In the World: Abolitionist Harriet Tubman; chil-
dren's novel *Harriet the Spy*; writer Harriet
Beecher Stowe

Haven (HAY-vin) 2009: #567
Popularity: #570
Styles: Modern Meanings,
The "-ens," Androgynous,
Why Not? 1880 Today
Sisters: Journey, Eden, Raine,
Winter, Ember, Wren
Brothers: Gideon, Harper, Sage, Bowen, River,
Ronan
✴This strong new name is ready to blossom. It has the auspicious meaning and glossy style of favorites like Heaven and Raven, but doesn't sound gaudy. Perhaps the meaning itself is the reason; there's a warmth and restraint to the idea of a haven, or sanctuary. While the other names strut, this one glides.
In the World: Supernatural TV series *Haven*; a daughter of actress Jessica Alba

Hayden (HAY-din) 2008: #126
Popularity: #185
Styles: The "-ens,"
Androgynous, Bell Tones,
Nickname-Proof 1880 Today
Variants: Haidyn
Sisters: Payton, Emerson, Ainsley, Marley,
Teagan, Camryn
Brothers: Ryder, Easton, Landon, Dawson,
Baylor, Hudson
✴Hayden was always the most traditionally masculine of the "-ayden" names. The most famous Haydens were football coaches and Darth Vader himself, Hayden Christensen. But one little cheerleader can change everything. When actress Hayden Panettiere hit it big on the TV series *Heroes*, this name instantly entered the androgynous realm.
In the World: Actress Hayden Panettiere

Hazel (HAY-zəl) 1897: #18
Popularity: #211
Styles: Charms and Graces,
Antique Charm, Nickname-
Proof 1880 Today
Sisters: Alice, Stella, Pearl,
Violet, Millicent, Iris, Olive
Brothers: August, Milo, Julius, Felix, Otto,
Casper, Everett
✴In some places, the idea of naming a little girl Hazel is still unthinkable. But this name is ultra-fashionable in certain circles, and it could get hotter. The parents who love Hazel today are the same cutting-edge tastemakers who led names like Ruby and Lillian back from the desert in the '90s.
In the World: *Hazel* TV series and comic strip about a maid; a daughter of actress Julia Roberts

Heather (HEH-dher) 1975: #3
Popularity: #708
Styles: '70s–'80s, Charms and
Graces, Nickname-Proof
Sisters: Shannon, Holly, 1880 Today
Amber, Erica, Kristin, April
Brothers: Ryan, Justin, Jeremy, Chad, Travis,
Lance
✴This flower name is tender and pretty, but America had a national Heather overdose in the '70s and '80s. (Remember the movie *Heathers*, where all the popular girls in school had the same name?) If Heather's floral essence is the reason you love the name, also consider Calla, Violet, and Laurel.
In the World: Actresses Heather Locklear, Heather Graham, and Heather Morris; movie *Heathers*

Heaven (HEH-vən) 2005: #245
Popularity: #317
Styles: Modern Meanings,
The "-ens," Fanciful
Variants: Nevaeh 1880 Today
Sisters: Trinity, Eden,
Miracle, Serenity, Harmony, Star
Brothers: Chance, Phoenix, Zion, Clarion,
Judah, Prince
✴This name is a bit fanciful and a lot for any girl to live up to. But Heaven does have a lovely sound for a girl's name, and perhaps your little angel can rise to the challenge. Parental advisory: it's also an extremely popular stage name for strippers and porn stars.
In the World: Song "Stairway to Heaven"; phrases like "heaven help us" and "Heaven on Earth"

Heidi (HIY-dee) 1974: #60
Popularity: #331
Styles: Surfer '60s, '70s–'80s,
German and Dutch, Literary
and Artistic 1880 Today
Sisters: Wendy, Sonya, Holly,
Gretchen, Christa, Marcie
Brothers: Eric, Kurt, Jeffrey, Heath, Troy, Dirk
✴Heidi is a nickname for the ever-popular Adelheid and Heidrun—and of course, the heroine of a classic children's story. Heidi's heady heyday was in the '60s and '70s, and it may sound too cutesy to some today. But it may also give you a jolly little alternative to Zoe and Chloe.
In the World: Children's novel *Heidi*; model Heidi Klum; reality TV personality Heidi Montag

Helen (HEH-lehn) 1917: #2
Popularity: #427
Styles: Solid Citizens, Ladies
and Gentlemen
Nicknames: Ella, Lena, Ellie 1880 Today
Variants: Helena, Helene,
Ellen
Sisters: Margaret, Jane, Alice, Dorothy,
Frances, Ruth
Brothers: Edward, Louis, Arthur, George,
Walter, Carl
✳ If you like your names both classic and classical, Helen is an impeccable choice. A little boring? Perhaps, but less so every day. Think of it this way: in recent years, there have been 20 Madisons born for every Helen. When your daughter looks around her classroom, which of those names will seem more interesting?
In the World: Helen of Troy; deaf-blind writer Helen Keller; actresses Helen Hayes, Helen Mirren, and Helen Hunt

Helena (heh-LAY-nə, 1884: #201
HEH-li-nə, heh-LEE-nə)
Popularity: #588
Styles: Antique Charm,
Shakespearean, Saints, 1880 Today
Timeless, Why Not?
Nicknames: Lena
Variants: Helene
Sisters: Celia, Antonia, Josephine, Daphne,
Adela, Camilla
Brothers: Edgar, Duncan, Casper, Anton,
Porter, Edmund
✳ Helena borrows Helen's understated manner but ties it up in a poetic bow. The name is a standard in Shakespeare's romantic comedies, and that age-old lyricism still serves it well. Pronunciation varies by geography. The eastern half of the U.S. (and England) usually says "heh-LAY-nə." As you get closer to Helena, Montana, people are more likely to say "HEHL-in-ə," while a smaller group goes with "heh-LEEN-ə," as in St. Helena, California.
In the World: Actress Helena Bonham-Carter; model Helena Christensen; Helena Rubenstein cosmetics

Henrietta (hehn-ree-EH-tə) 1880: #106
Popularity: #4249
Styles: Ladies and
Gentlemen, English
Nicknames: Etta, Hettie, 1880 Today
Ettie, Hattie, Hennie, Nettie
Variants: Henriette
Sisters: Georgianna, Wilhelmina, Cornelia,
Estella, Celestine, Mathilda
Brothers: Archibald, Horace, Rupert,
Ferdinand, Sylvester, Crawford
✳ In England, Henrietta is a fearsomely aristocratic name. In America, it's an old-fashioned girl—soft, sweet, and hopelessly out of date. If you're looking for something unexpected but not strange, note how familiar and natural the name sounds despite the fact that it's hard to name real-life Henriettas, past or present.
In the World: Medical research subject Henrietta Lacks

Hermione (her-MIY-ə-nee) 2006: #2478
Popularity: #3039
Styles: Saints, Mythological,
Exotic Traditional,
Shakespearean, Literary and 1880 Today
Artistic
Sisters: Ariadne, Guinevere, Imogen, Beatrix,
Persephone, Isadora
Brothers: Lysander, Caedmon, Inigo, Atticus,
Phineas, Tarquin
✳ Hermione is a grand mythological name, glowing with dignity but darned hard to pronounce. Luckily, today's kids have all been schooled in the name via the "Harry Potter" books and films. Every 10-year-old on the block will think this is a cool pick.
In the World: Hermione Granger of the "Harry Potter" series; actresses Hermione Gingold and Hermione Norris

Hilda (HIL-də) 1899: #87
Popularity: #3774
Styles: Porch Sitters, German and Dutch
Nicknames: Hildy
Variants: Hilde 1880 Today
Sisters: Elsa, Vera, Mildred, Bertha, Leona, Irma
Brothers: Herman, Emil, Felix, Bertram, Ernst, Otto

★ Hilda is in dire straits as a name, a relic of a long-ago Teutonic craze. If you want to resurrect it, you could do well with the Scandinavian spelling Hilde, which roots the name in modern Europe. The nickname Hildy still sounds surprisingly sharp.
In the World: Mystic Hildegard von Bingen; Spitfire Hildy of *His Girl Friday*; Labor secretary Hilda Solis

Hillary (HI-lə-ree) 1992: #132
Popularity: #1368
Styles: Androgynous, Last Names First, Nickname-Proof
Variants: Hilary, Ilaria 1880 Today
Sisters: Kelsey, Mallory, Devin, Aubrey, Meredith, Lesley
Brothers: Bryant, Dalton, Wesley, Kyle, Heath, Peyton

★ The big American Hillary wave began in the '70s, part of a craze for gently androgynous surnames (Whitney, Lindsay, Mallory). But Hillary hit a wall in the early '90s when Hillary Clinton emerged on the national scene. Ms. Clinton, born in the '40s, simply aged the name before its time. A younger generation of Hillarys, led by entertainer Hilary Duff, wasn't quite enough to retilt the balance.
In the World: Hillary Clinton; actresses Hilary Duff and Hilary Swank

Hollis (HAH-lis) 1953: #769
Popularity: #2867
Styles: Last Names First, Androgynous
Nicknames: Holly 1880 Today
Sisters: Jensen, Ellis, Adair, Channing, Emory, Alden
Brothers: Barton, Rogers, Vaughn, Hilton, Prentiss, Farrell

★ One of the few androgynous surnames from an earlier age, Hollis has a long, quiet history as a girl's name. It could sound pleasantly contemporary given the chance.
In the World: Book/film *Pictures of Hollis Woods*; golfer Hollis Stacy

Holly (HAH-lee) 1983: #48
Popularity: #426
Styles: Charms and Graces, Nickname-Proof, Surfer '60s, '70s–'80s
Variants: Hollie, Holli
Sisters: April, Heather, Kelly, Robin, Shannon, Heidi
Brothers: Brian, Scott, Jared, Lance, Casey, Eric

★ This charming botanical is generations removed from Lily and Daisy, but gives off the same good vibes. The name's '70s–'80s surge doesn't mask its essential style. A natural for girls born in the Christmas season.
In the World: Holly Golightly of *Breakfast at Tiffany's*; actress Holly Hunter; *Playboy* star Holly Madison

Honor (AHN-er) 2009: #1995
Popularity: #1992
Styles: Charms and Graces, Modern Meanings, Exotic Traditional
Variants: Honorée, Honora, 1880 Today
Honoria
Sisters: Winter, Amity, Halo, Sage, Tru, Ember
Brothers: River, Dashiell, Leif, Atticus, Quill, Roan

★ This is one virtue name that's more stately than sweet. Honor may sound a little "out there" to most Americans, but it has a long and respectable history as a girl's name. In 19th-century England, Honor was a likely sister to Patience and Prudence.
In the World: A daughter of actress Jessica Alba

Hope (HOHP) 2000: #146
Popularity: #231
Styles: Timeless, Charms and Graces
Sisters: Faith, Camille, 1880 Today
Mercy, Juliet, Daphne, Leah
Brothers: Reid, Elliot, Simon, Carter, Bennett, Noah

★ The name Hope is warmth, pure and simple. It has the positive energy of modern inspiration names like Destiny, but it's also charmingly modest, in keeping with its Puritan origins. Hope is now fashionable in a suitably modest way.
In the World: Actress Hope Davis; soccer player Hope Solo; the phrase "hope springs eternal"

Ida (IY-də) 1880: #7
Popularity: #2083
Styles: Ladies and
Gentlemen, Saints, German
and Dutch, Nordic 1880 Today
Sisters: Cora, Ruth, Flora,
Mae, Ada, Elsa
Brothers: Albert, Louis, Gus, Casper,
Frederick, Leon
✶ Ida is still out of the picture in the U.S., but in trendsetting pockets of Europe she's the toast of the town. And why not? The name is bright and sweet with only a little dowdiness to overcome. To change your mind-set, try reading Tennyson's poem "The Princess," which helped kick off the last Ida craze.
In the World: Comic opera *Princess Ida* (based on the Tennyson poem); journalist Ida B. Wells; actress Ida Lupino

Iliana (i-lee-AHN-ə) 2007: #655
Popularity: #696
Styles: Lacy and Lissome,
Slavic, Latino/Latina, Greek,
Why Not? 1880 Today
Nicknames: Illy, Ilia, Yana,
Ana
Variants: Ileana
Sisters: Melina, Lilia, Thalia, Galilea, Dasia, Irina
Brothers: Alvaro, Dimitri, Andreas, Viktor, Leonel, Nikolai
✶ Iliana is a supremely lyrical name, and you can sense its international style even if you're not *quite* sure where it comes from. Could it be Spanish, or Greek, or maybe Slavic? Yes, actually, all of those. Is it a form of Helen, or perhaps a feminine version of Elias? Yep, both. That all makes for a name that's traditional, yet easily molded to your own tastes.
In the World: Actress Ileana Douglas

Ily (IY-lee) 2011: #3156
Popularity: #3173
Styles: Bell Tones, Short and
Sweet, Modern Meanings,
Why Not? 1880 Today
Sisters: Nevaeh, Halo, Ember,
Lyra, Zoe, Tru
Brothers: Pax, Teo, Galen, Noah, Bodhi, Canyon
✶ Ily is a deceptively simple name. It holds a secret message: the textspeak acronym for "I Love You." That sweet but hidden statement makes the name a more modest alternative to adoring options like Heaven and Princess. And no, you don't have to name her brother Rofl.
In the World: Textspeak for "I Love You"

Imani (i-MAH-nee) 1998: #253
Popularity: #393
Styles: African-American,
African
Variants: Iman 1880 Today
Sisters: Ayana, Kamari, Zuri,
Malaika, Aliyah, Jamila
Brothers: Jabari, Dakarai, Asante, Omari, Malik, Jelani
✶This strong and elegant Swahili name, which means "faith," is shaping up to be an African-American classic. It's a favorite of Ivy League parents and was the name of a pioneering black fashion doll.
In the World: Model Iman; singer Imani Coppola; actress Imani Hakim

Imogen (IM-oh-jehn) 2011: #1870
Popularity: #1874
Styles: Exotic Traditional,
English, Shakespearean
Variants: Imogene, Innogen 1880 Today
Sisters: Beatrix, Hermione,
Phoebe, Poppy, Eloise, Verity
Brothers: Barnaby, Alistair, Archie, Felix, Fraser, Gareth
✶ How powerful a cultural force is William Shakespeare? Even his mistakes become classic names. Imogen is a mistranscription of Innogen, which appeared in Shakespeare's play *Cymbeline.* It has been a name ever since and is currently fashionable in the U.K.
In the World: Musician Imogen Heap; writer Imogen Lloyd Webber; comedian Imogene Coca

India (IN-dee-ə) 2001: #297
Popularity: #1001
Styles: Place Names, Lacy
and Lissome, African-
American, English 1880 Today
Sisters: Alexandria, Serena,
Paris, Zara, Clio, Geneva
Brothers: Devon, Brice, Jericho, Rohan,
Neville, Justus
✳ While most of the top place names of the
moment have a country-western twang, this one
shimmers with silk and spices. India is a sophis-
ticated name that feels timeless, despite its re-
cent burst of popularity. As a British name, it
has a history connected with British rule of co-
lonial India, but that aspect of the name is
muted on this side of the Atlantic.
In the World: Singer India.Arie; India Wilkes of
Gone with the Wind; a daughter of actor Chris
Hemsworth

Indigo (IN-di-goh) 1992: #1875
Popularity: #2787
Styles: Modern Meanings,
Androgynous
Nicknames: Indy 1880 Today
Sisters: Juniper, Phoenix,
Halo, Calico, Sonnet, Tru
Brothers: Orion, Shadow, Fox, Reef, Quill,
Sparrow
✳ Indigo is a color of the rainbow, a plant-
based dye, and a magnet for parents seeking a
dynamically unconventional name. Despite the
"-o" ending, girl Indigos outnumber boys.
In the World: Folk-rock duo Indigo Girls; actress
Indigo; a daughter of actor Lou Diamond Phil-
lips

Ingrid (ING-grid) 1967: #381
Popularity: #856
Styles: Nordic, German and
Dutch, Timeless
Nicknames: Inga 1880 Today
Sisters: Greta, Astrid, Margit,
Petra, Dagny, Elsa
Brothers: Lars, Stefan, Gunner, Erik, Hans,
Konrad
✳ Ingrid will never be a top-10 smash, but its
simple formality will always win some fans. It's
a model of elegant restraint, the essence of
Northern Europe.
In the World: Actress Ingrid Bergman; singer
Ingrid Michaelson

Ione (iy-OH-nee) 1908: #329
Popularity: #5231
Styles: Exotic Traditional,
Celtic, Mythological, Why
Not? 1880 Today
Nicknames: Nonie
Variants: Iona
Sisters: Clio, Isla, Althea, Avis, Charis, Ariadne
Brothers: Ivor, Theron, Felix, Ulysses, Tavish,
Linus
✳ It's breezy, exotic, and traditional. What
more can you ask? How about not one but two
trendy origins: Ione's a Celtic name and a sea
nymph from Greek mythology. Occasional pro-
nunciation difficulties are just the entry fee to
this kind of quirky cool.
In the World: Actress Ione Skye

Ireland (IY-er-lənd) 2009: #815
Popularity: #1006
Styles: Place Names
Variants: Irelyn
Sisters: Phoenix, London, 1880 Today
Cadence, Promise, Aspen,
Winter
Brothers: Everest, Brighton, Killian, Jericho,
Brogan, Kingston
✳ If you want to honor your Irish heritage,
there's no more direct way. Ireland has a nice
strut to its step, but it's a mouthful and has no
natural nickname. Some parents sidestep those
drawbacks by using Ireland as a middle name.
Others attempt to "namify" it with spellings like
Irelyn, but those dilute the name's impact.
In the World: Daughter of actors Alec Baldwin
and Kim Basinger

Irene (iy-REEN) 1916: #17
Popularity: #689
Styles: Solid Citizens, Greek,
Mythological
Nicknames: Rene 1880 Today
Variants: Irina, Eirene, Irini,
Irena
Sisters: Helen, Frances, Ruth, Esther, Sylvia,
Adele
Brothers: Frank, Lawrence, Carl, Alvin, Harry,
Raymond
✳ Irene is still a sweetheart, but most new par-
ents don't give the name a second thought. It's
comfy, warm, and out of fashion. The key is the
"-een" ending, which is becoming an endan-
gered species. You could try extending it to
three syllables like its original source Eirene,
the Greek word for "peace."
In the World: Song "Goodnight, Irene"; singer
Irene Cara; actress Irene Dunne

Iris (IY-ris) 1928: #200
Popularity: #303
Styles: Timeless, Charms and
Graces, Mythological,
Shakespearean, Nickname-   1880 Today
Proof
Sisters: Hazel, Violet, Ione, Flora, Sybil, Juliet
Brothers: Arlo, Everett, Reuben, Rex, Leo,
Calvin
✳ As a flower, the iris is a lovely curiosity with
delicate, meandering forms that you could
never confuse with a lily or rose. As a name, too,
this is the classic individualist of the flower fam-
ily.
In the World: Writer Iris Murdoch; designers
Iris Apfel and Iris Van Herpen

Isabel (I-zə-behl) 2003: #83
Popularity: #128
Styles: Antique Charm,
French, Latino/Latina
Nicknames: Izzy, Bella, Isa,   1880 Today
Chavela
Variants: Isabelle, Isobel, Isabella
Sisters: Charlotte, Madeline, Sophie, Amelia,
Lilian, Abigail
Brothers: Lucas, Simon, Owen, Isaac, Oliver,
Nicholas
✳ Originally a Spanish form of Elizabeth, Isa-
bel has a regal heritage and 19th-century charm
that sent it roaring up the charts. As with similar
names like Annabel, different endings convey
different images: Isabel is chic, Isabelle is girly,
and Isabella trails flowers in its wake.
In the World: Writer Isabel Allende; actresses
Isabelle Huppert, Isabelle Adjani, and Isabel
Lucas; designer Isabel Marant

Isabella (i-zə-BEHL-ə, 2010: #1
ee-sah-BEH-lah)
Popularity: #2
Styles: Antique Charm, Lacy
and Lissome, Shakespearean,   1880 Today
Italian
Nicknames: Izzy, Bella
Variants: Isabela, Izabella, Isabel, Isobel,
Isabelle
Sisters: Adriana, Gabriella, Olivia, Juliana,
Angelina, Liliana
Brothers: Sebastian, Nicholas, Christian,
Isaiah, Gabriel, Alexander
✳ Isabella offers a warmly traditional route to a
lacy, ultra-feminine name. It's like a parental
love note: adoring, but not quite overindulgent.
That approach has won the name the hearts of a
generation. See also Isabel.
In the World: Actress Isabella Rossellini; Isa-
bella ("Bella") Swan of the "Twilight" series;
Isabella Stewart Gardner Museum

Isadora (i-zə-DOHR-ə) 1882: #634
Popularity: #1543
Styles: Exotic Traditional,
Literary and Artistic, Antique
Charm   1880 Today
Nicknames: Dora, Izzy
Variants: Isidora
Sisters: Seraphina, Genevieve, Beatrix,
Mahalia, Hermione, Tallulah
Brothers: Dashiell, Atticus, Hugo, Calder,
Phineas, Inigo
✳ Isadora is a respectable lady's name with an
untamed spirit, thanks to flamboyant dancer
Isadora Duncan. It could be an adventurous
parent's alternative to Isabella.
In the World: Dancer Isadora Duncan; daughter
of singer Bjork and artist Matthew Barney

Isannah (i-SAHN-ə)
Popularity: Very rare
Styles: Lacy and Lissome, rarely used
Why Not?
Nicknames: Isa — 1880 Today
Sisters: Priscilla, Damaris,
Shiloh, Phyllida, Bethany, Tabitha
Brothers: Matthias, Gideon, Josiah, Phineas,
Jericho, Thaddeus
✱ Paul Revere had 16 children. Fifteen of them had common, traditional names. The sole exception was the exotically named Isannah. Generations later, writer Esther Forbes spotted that name in the Revere family tree and used it for a character in her Revolutionary War tale *Johnny Tremain.* There's your historical and literary precedent. Now feel free to use the name just because it's pretty.
In the World: Isannah of *Johnny Tremain*

Isis (IYsis) 2005: #522
Popularity: #636
Styles: Exotic Traditional,
Nickname-Proof,
Mythological — 1880 Today
Sisters: Athena, Clio, Delilah,
Halo, Selena, Anais
Brothers: Orion, Blaze, Maximus, Ajax, Taj,
Phoenix
✱ The simplicity of this Egyptian goddess name reins it in from the realm of the fanciful. An accessible, dynamic fashion statement.

Isla (IY-lə) 2011: #268
Popularity: #268
Styles: Celtic, English, Short
and Sweet
Variants: Ila — 1880 Today
Sisters: Fiona, Zara, Iona,
Esme, Niamh, Orla, Nora, Skye
Brothers: Liam, Rowan, Rhys, Conor, Finlay,
Duncan, Callum, Theo
✱ First things first: the "s" is silent, as in "island." In fact, the name comes from an island, the Scottish isle of Islay. That leaves Isla with an abundance of fashion riches, from a quirky Celtic style to a fluid, Lila-like sound. This name is a U.K. hit, and American parents are finally catching on too, thanks to actress Isla Fisher.
In the World: Actress Isla Fisher; Spanish for "island" (pronounced EES-lah)

Ivy (IY-vee) 2011: #265
Popularity: #266
Styles: Charms and Graces,
Antique Charm, Short and
Sweet, Timeless, Nickname- — 1880 Today
Proof
Sisters: Luna, Zoe, Phoebe, Eden, Willow,
Eve, Iris, Ruby
Brothers: Jasper, Eli, Emmett, Felix, Oliver,
Miles, Liam, Owen
✱ Ivy is as stylish a name as you'll find in America today. Its botanical meaning places it with the turn-of-the-century sweethearts, but unlike demure Lily and Rose, Ivy is vigorous and self-assured. If there's one thing holding the name back, it's "poison ivy."
In the World: Poison ivy; Ivy League colleges; "Ivy and Bean" children's books

Jacey (JAY-see) 2006: #747
Popularity: #873
Styles: Bell Tones
Variants: Jaycee
Sisters: Miley, Jada, — 1880 Today
Kaydence, Laney, Kayla,
Emery
Brothers: Tyler, Cody, Jayden, Devin, Tanner,
Keegan
✱ This peppy little entry echoes fashionable nicknames (Josie) and surnames (Lacey). Jacey itself, though, is neither—a contemporary creation.
In the World: Kidnap survivor Jaycee Dugard

Jacqueline (JA-kə-lin) 1964: #37
Popularity: #200
Styles: Timeless, French
Nicknames: Jackie, Jacqui
Variants: Jaclyn, Jacquelyn — 1880 Today
Sisters: Marianne, Diana,
Valerie, Cynthia, Adrienne, Julianne
Brothers: Terrence, Vincent, Philip,
Christopher, Jerome, Anthony
✱ This French classic bears the lasting stamp of first lady Jacqueline Kennedy. Luckily, hers is a versatile image: elegant, honorable, pretty, and strong. All of those qualities apply to her name too.
In the World: Jacqueline Kennedy Onassis; actresses Jacqueline Bisset and Jaclyn Smith

Jada (JAY-də)   2005: #76
Popularity: #167
Styles: Short and Sweet, Bell
Tones, African-American,
Turn of the 21st Century   1880   Today
Variants: Jayda, Jaida, Jade
Sisters: Kayla, Macy, Ella, Jasmine, Eden, Mia
Brothers: Liam, Devon, Isaiah, Kai, Joah, Eli
✳ This fun and pretty Spanish variation on
Jade got a boost from actress Jada Pinkett Smith.
It sounds an awful lot like other trendy names
from Jaden to Kayla, but Jada has so much per-
sonality that it has carved out its own niche.
In the World: Actress Jada Pinkett Smith

Jade (JAYD)   2002: #86
Popularity: #113
Styles: Brisk and Breezy,
Charms and Graces, Modern
Meanings   1880   Today
Variants: Jayde, Jada
Sisters: Jasmine, Amber, Autumn, Skye, Paris,
Raine
Brothers: Drake, Jett, Jordan, Chase, Braxton,
Quinn
✳ A recent addition to Pearl and Ruby's family,
with a sultry character all her own. Jade has the
feminine allure of longer frilly names, but she's
no shrinking violet—she looks you right in the
eye. Sexy-tough.
In the World: Jade Jagger, daughter of singer
Mick Jagger; 1995 thriller *Jade*

Jaelyn (JAY-lin)   2008: #332
Popularity: #417
Styles: The "-ens," Bell Tones
Nicknames: Jae
Variants: Jaylin, Jailyn,   1880   Today
Jalynn, Jaylyn, Jalyn, Jaylynn
Sisters: Rylie, Kamryn, Jayda, Baylee, Raegan,
Jazmyn
Brothers: Landen, Aydin, Jayce, Kyler, Jaxton,
Colton
✳ This kind of name is "sneaky popular." It
spreads out across so many spellings that you
don't realize just how common it is. A dozen
different spellings are in use, many of them for
boys and girls alike. When you add in all the
Jaylas and Jaidyns, any Jaelyn had better brace
herself for a lifetime of misspellings.

Jamie (JAY-mee)   1976: #18
Popularity: #437
Styles: '70s–'80s,
Androgynous
Variants: Jaime, Jayme,   1880   Today
Jaimie, Jami
Sisters: Kerry, Leigh, Shannon, Tricia, Nikki,
Casey
Brothers: Shaun, Corey, Jeremy, Brent, Heath,
Dustin
✳ Jamie is a grown-up tomboy, upbeat and ca-
pable. Two perfect examples: actress Jamie Lee
Curtis and *Bionic Woman* Jaime Sommers,
whose TV heroics turbo-charged the name in
the '70s. Jamie is almost always a full given
name for girls, but if you're looking for a longer
version, you can try Jamila or even Jessamine.
In the World: Actresses Jamie Lee Curtis, Jaime
Pressly, Jamie-Lynn Spears, and Jamie-Lynn
Sigler

Jamila (jah-MIL-ə,   1977: #468
jah-MEE-lə)
Popularity: #2165
Styles: African-American,
Muslim, Why Not?   1880   Today
Variants: Jamilah
Sisters: Naima, Samira, Zahra, Amina,
Yasmeen, Soraya, Halima, Tahira
Brothers: Sharif, Tariq, Zaid, Khalil, Amir,
Bashir, Taj, Malik
✳ Jamila comes from the Arabic word for
"beautiful," and it's worthy of the meaning.
This name has never really broken through to
broad popularity and could be a stylish choice.
In the World: Basketball player Jamila Wideman

Jane (JAYN)   1945: #36
Popularity: #368
Styles: Solid Citizens,
Timeless
Nicknames: Janie, Jenny   1880   Today
Variants: Jayne
Sisters: Anne, Martha, Kate, Rose, Margaret,
Alice
Brothers: Paul, Mark, Thomas, Ned, Martin,
Peter
✳ Plain Jane is the gold standard for simplicity,
and that's a terrific distinction. The founders of
Jane magazine banked on the name's directness
to cement their image. It's straight-shooting and
genuine.
In the World: Writer Jane Austen; humanitarian
Jane Addams; actresses Jane Russell, Jane
Fonda, Jane Seymour, Jane Lynch, and Jane
Curtin

Janessa (jə-NEH-sə, jayn-EH-sə) 2009: #548
Popularity: #640
Styles: Lacy and Lissome
Nicknames: Jan, Jane, Janie, Jay, Nessa
Variants: Jenessa
Sisters: Audriana, Brielle, Julissa, Alannah, Jazlyn, Kendra, Janae, Alexia
Brothers: Braxton, Kaleb, Gavyn, Quinn, Kyler, Braydon, Jayce, Kellan
✱ Janessa is built of traditional feminine ingredients, but it doesn't sound a bit traditional. This is the very model of the modern "mashup" name. (Can't you picture fans swooning over a celebrity couple Jake and Vanessa called Janessa?) Yet the name is carving out a niche of its own. It's notable for being used equally by families of all races.

Janet (JA-nət) 1952: #19
Popularity: #951
Styles: Mid-Century, Solid Citizens
Nicknames: Jan
Variants: Janette, Janis
Sisters: Linda, Diane, Judith, Carolyn, Donna, Gwen
Brothers: Douglas, Glenn, Roger, Kenneth, Jerry, Dwight
✱ This is one '50s name that still has legs. Janet's no-nonsense sound may not be stylish, but it's strong. Girls' names ending in "-t" project self confidence, even when wrapped in softness (à la Violet). Prime model: *Schoolhouse Rock* heroine Interplanet Janet.
In the World: Singer Janet Jackson; actress Janet Leigh; writer Janet Evanovich; *Rocky Horror Picture Show* song "Dammit Janet"

Janice (JA-nis) 1946: #22
Popularity: #1246
Styles: Solid Citizens, Mid-Century
Nicknames: Jan
Variants: Janis
Sisters: Sandra, Carolyn, Joanne, Sharon, Dianne, Elaine
Brothers: Roger, Allen, Gerald, Larry, Ronald, Dennis
✱ Janice teamed up with Janet to flood the country with little Jans in the '50s. Today the spelling Janis may be the stronger candidate thanks to the legendary singer Janis Joplin.
In the World: Singer Janis Joplin; model/reality TV star Janice Dickinson; comic strip *Arlo & Janis*

Janine (jə-NEEN) 1965: #232
Popularity: #4255
Styles: Surfer '60s
Nicknames: Jan, Nina
Variants: Jeannine, Janina
Sisters: Deanne, Michele, Tamera, Sherry, Suzanne, Rhonda
Brothers: Craig, Scotty, Darren, Joel, Kurt, Randall
✱ This is the French Jeannine, slimmed down to '60s style. Janine is a traditional variant of the name in France, but it sounds purely American. That's working against the name, since authentically foreign names are more fashionable today.
In the World: Actress Janine Turner; comedian Janeane Garofalo

January (JA-nyoo-eh-ree) 1978: #638
Popularity: #5578
Styles: Charms and Graces, Why Not?
Nicknames: Jan
Sisters: Bryony, Amity, Willow, Tuesday, Juniper, Amethyst
Brothers: Jericho, Birch, Caspian, August, Storm, Everest
✱ Parents love the image of sunshine for their daughters. We have the flowering months of April, May, and June and the warm, cozy seasons of Summer and Autumn. But frosty January has a feminine form and a confident style and can be a symbol of new beginnings. The name's tiny late-'70s surge came from the protagonist of a film called *Once Is Not Enough*.
In the World: Actress January Jones (named after the *Once Is Not Enough* character)

Jasmine (JAZ-min) 1993: #23
Popularity: #74
Styles: Modern Meanings,
Charms and Graces,
African-American, Turn of   1880   Today
the 21st Century
Nicknames: Jaz
Variants: Jessamine, Jasmin, Jazmin, Jasmyn,
Yasmin, Yasmine
Sisters: Summer, Alexa, Jade, Destiny, Sierra,
Ariel
Brothers: Donovan, Kobe, Xavier, Chase,
Devin, Jordan
★ Jasmine is a fragrant, exotic companion to
Lily and Rose. This name (in the form Yasmin)
has long been popular in the Arab world and
makes a lush new presence in the list of Ameri-
can standards. Disney deserves an assist here, as
Aladdin's Princess Jasmine helped raise the
name's profile.
In the World: Princess Jasmine of *Aladdin*;
singer Jasmine Villegas; actress Jasmine Guy

Jayden (JAY-dən) 2007: #172
Popularity: #292
Styles: The "-ens," Bell
Tones, Androgynous
Nicknames: Jade   1880   Today
Variants: Jaden, Jaiden,
Jaidyn, Jadyn
Sisters: Rylie, Jayla, Ashlyn, Harley, Baylee,
Camryn
Brothers: Bryson, Dixon, Jace, Tavion, Corbin,
Kyler
★ This fast riser was equally new, and equally
trendy, for girls and boys in the late 1990s. A de-
cade later, boy Jaydens and Jadens had taken
control. Some less common spellings like
Jaidyn remain unisex. See also Jayden in "Snap-
shots: Boys."

Jayla (JAY-lə) 2006: #99
Popularity: #149
Styles: Bell Tones, African-
American
Variants: Jaylah   1880   Today
Sisters: Keira, Arianna,
Ashlyn, Janiya, Kailyn, Briella
Brothers: Jayden, Braxton, Ryder, Josiah,
Davion, Myles
★ This lively confection merges the hits Jada,
Kayla, and Jalyn. Unlike some such crossbreeds
(Jazlyn, Shirlene), Jayla comes across as com-
pletely natural. It has taken off faster than a
prize Labradoodle.

Jazlyn (JAZ-lin) 2008: #378
Popularity: #400
Styles: The "-ens"
Nicknames: Jaz
Variants: Jaslyn, Jaslene,   1880   Today
Jazlynn, Jazzlyn
Sisters: Alexis, Lizeth, Shanyce, Ximena, Jada,
Gracelyn
Brothers: Dameon, Xavier, Jaxon, Joaquin,
Gunner, Zander
★ There's something about the name Jasmine
that puts parents in a creative mood. Maybe the
"jazz" sound inspires improvisation? Thou-
sands of families have customized the name
into new creations, like sparkly Jazlyn. Several
variants of this name are Latina favorites.
In the World: Reality TV model Jaslene Gonza-
lez

Jean (JEEN) 1930: #14
Popularity: #2944
Styles: Solid Citizens
Nicknames: Jeanie
Variants: Jeanne   1880   Today
Sisters: Ann, Rita, Vivian,
Gloria, Frances, Joyce
Brothers: Gordon, Carl, Raymond, Warren,
Paul, Robert
★ The male John morphs into the female Jean,
Jane, and Joan. Right now Jane sounds the snap-
piest, Joan is the most mature, and Jean the
most flexible. Jean is actually a Scottish form of
the name; the French spelling Jeanne is a bit
dressier.
In the World: Comics hero Jean Grey; actresses
Jean Harlow and Jean Simmons; model Jean
Shrimpton; blue jeans

Jeanette (jə-NEHT) 1939: #82
Popularity: #1749
Styles: Solid Citizens, French
Nicknames: Jean, Jeanie
Variants: Jeannette, Janette, 1880 Today
Jannette
Sisters: Marianne, Constance, Roberta,
Lorraine, Rosalie, Arlene
Brothers: Russell, Franklin, Clifford, Roland,
Laurence, Bernard
✹ In the '40s and '50s, names ending in the
French diminutive "-ette" were favorite choices
for modern girls. Names like Nanette, Paulette,
and Jeanette sounded so much perkier than old-
fashioned Edna and Florence. Today that mod-
ern role has been taken up by new androgynous
creations like Jadyn and Ryleigh.
In the World: Actress Jeanette MacDonald;
writer Jeanette Winterson; Jeannette Rankin,
first woman in Congress

Jenna (JEHN-nə) 1985: #50
Popularity: #170
Styles: Short and Sweet,
'70s–'80s, Turn of the 21st
Century 1880 Today
Nicknames: Jen
Variants: Jena
Sisters: Tessa, Carly, Megan, Alana, Jillian,
Kendra
Brothers: Devin, Jared, Blake, Colin, Trevor,
Chase
✹ The new century's answer to Jenny, Jenna
captures that old favorite's upbeat spirit while
shedding its '70s style. It's a multigenerational
crowd-pleaser. Parental advisory: look for Jenna
on the web and you'll get a heavy dose of one
particularly well-known Jenna, a porn star.
In the World: Actresses Jenna Fischer and Jenna
Elfman; presidential daughter Jenna Bush;
adult film star Jenna Jameson

Jemima (jə-MIY-mə) 1885: #695
Popularity: #3843
Styles: Biblical, Namesakes,
English
Nicknames: Jem 1880 Today
Sisters: Dinah, Jerusha,
Georgia, Henrietta, Claribel, Mahala
Brothers: Jethro, Barnaby, Homer, Amos, Cecil,
Reuben
✹ Alas, lovely Jemima is still buried under the
image of a kerchiefed "mammy" figure dishing
out pancakes. (The advertising icon Aunt
Jemima actually got a modern makeover years
ago. She now looks more like a bridge partner
for Betty Crocker.) It's a big hurdle, but this bib-
lical classic is so perfectly lovable that it could
be well worth taking the plunge. It has been
more fashionable in England, where the
mammy image doesn't weigh on the national
conscience.
In the World: Aunt Jemima breakfast foods; actress Jemima Kirke; Beatrix Potter story *Jemima
Puddle-Duck*

Jennifer (JEH-nə-fer) 1974: #1
Popularity: #134
Styles: '70s–'80s
Nicknames: Jen, Jenny, Jennie
Variants: Jenifer, Gennifer, 1880 Today
Guinevere
Sisters: Kimberly, Melissa, Heather, Amy,
Stephanie, Christina, Jessica, Michelle
Brothers: Brian, Christopher, Jason, Eric,
Bradley, Jeffrey, Matthew, Timothy
✹ Hi, Jen! Looking up your name? Yep, Jenni-
fer is one of the most common names selected
by expectant mothers. It's actually an old Cor-
nish form of Guinevere, and if you think of it
that way, you can imagine how intriguing it
sounded to the '50s parents who first started
using the name in the U.S. Today, though, it
sounds purely American.
In the World: Performers Jennifer Lopez and
Jennifer Hudson; actresses Jennifer Aniston,
Jennifer Lawrence, Jennifer Love Hewitt, Jennifer Garner, and Jennifer Connelly

Jenny (JEH-nee)   1972: #119
Popularity: #761
Styles: Nicknames
Nicknames: Jen
Variants: Jennie   1880   Today

Sisters: Kristy, Jodi, April,
Mindy, Amy, Kelly, Tara, Angie
Brothers: Shawn, Jason, Jamie, Brian, Toby,
Chad, Eric, Jeremy
✶ Jenny, like Jennifer, sounds like pure 1970s.
The name's real heyday, though, was in the 19th
century, when singer Jenny Lind was an interna-
tional sensation. (Think of the name as the
1850s Britney.) Back then, Jenny was a nick-
name for Jane or Jean, but the subsequent Jen-
nifer glut has numbed us to that possibility.
In the World: Actresses Jenny McCarthy and
Jennie Garth; Jenny Craig weight-loss program

Jeri (JEH-ree)   1957: #300
Popularity: #7921
Styles: Surfer '60s,
Nicknames
Variants: Geri, Jerry, Jerri,   1880   Today
Jerrie, Gerri, Gerry
Sisters: Toni, Randi, Kris, Jody, Cindi, Gwen,
Rikki, Jan
Brothers: Russ, Bart, Rob, Curt, Todd, Steve,
Kenny, Greg
✶ The girl's name Jeri, in every imaginable
spelling, was a staple of the '50s and '60s. As a
boy's name (Jerry), it had been a staple of the
'30s and '40s. Today the name has hit a quiet
period, and parents of girls are turning instead
to surnames and place names like Jersey for an-
drogynous options.
In the World: Actress Jeri Ryan; Spice Girl Geri
Halliwell

Jessamine (JEH-sə-min)   1891: #1006
Popularity: #12,603
Styles: English, Charms and
Graces, Why Not?
Nicknames: Jess, Jessie   1880   Today
Variants: Jessamyn, Jessamy
Sisters: Briony, Amabel, Emmaline, Camellia,
Felicity, Dahlia
Brothers: Corin, Barnaby, Auberon, Crispin,
Sterling, Atticus
✶ To a botanist, Jessamine and Jasmine blos-
soms are one and the same. To a baby namer,
though, they have distinct personalities. Jessa-
mine is English, delicate, and antique. Jasmine
is jazzier—as its sound and its Disney Princess
pedigree suggest—and more closely linked to
the Persian original Yasmin. Jessamyn is a favorite contemporary variation.
In the World: Writer Jessamyn West

Jessica (JEH-si-kə)   1987: #1
Popularity: #120
Styles: Shakespearean,
'70s–'80s, Turn of the 21st
Century   1880   Today

Nicknames: Jessie, Jess
Sisters: Amanda, Stephanie, Lauren, Melissa,
Nicole, Samantha
Brothers: Matthew, Christopher, Ryan, Jeremy,
Justin, Brandon
✶ Everything parents have always loved about
Jessica still applies. It's a delicately feminine
name with a Shakespearean heritage and a
peppy nickname. It's an impeccable choice, but
not one that will attract much notice—it's been
so popular for so long that it gets taken for
granted. Less common lacy classics include Ce-
cilia, Juliana, and Veronica.
In the World: Actresses Jessica Biel, Jessica Alba,
Jessica Lange, Jessica Paré, and Jessica Tandy;
singer Jessica Simpson

Jessie (JEH-see) 1882: #37
Popularity: #690
Styles: Nicknames
Nicknames: Jess
Variants: Jessye, Jesse, Jessi 1880 Today
Sisters: Carrie, Maggie, Cassie, Lizzie, Katie, Jennie
Brothers: Alex, Jamie, Jeremy, Ben, Drew, Andy
✳ We know Jessie as a nickname for Jessica, but the name was a hit on its own back when Jessica was still a Shakespearean oddity. In Scotland, it was a pet form of Jean or Janet; in the U.S., a girlish full-name favorite. Today we can't separate Jessie from the recent swarm of Jessicas, so the name is getting a rest.
In the World: Toy Story cowgirl Jessie; singer Jessie J; teen sitcom *Jessie*

Jewel (JOOL) 1904: #198
Popularity: #946
Styles: Charms and Graces, Modern Meanings
Variants: Jewell 1880 Today
Sisters: Sienna, Jade, Star, Meadow, Lyric, Raven
Brothers: Hart, Sterling, Forrest, Flint, Arrow, Storm
✳ Jewel flourished in the age of Ruby and Pearl, yet it harmonizes with modern affirmation names like Angel and Destiny. That makes it the most forward-looking of the classic gem and flower names. The singer Jewel briefly brought the name back to parents' attention, but it remains uncommon.
In the World: Singer Jewel; actress Jewel Staite

Jezebel (JEH-zə-behl) 2007: #3522
Popularity: #4466
Styles: Namesakes, Biblical
Nicknames: Jez, Bel, Belle
Sisters: Salome, Bathsheba, 1880 Today
Delilah, Cleopatra, Lorelei, Electra
Brothers: Damien, Jericho, Hannibal, Samson, Adonis, Maxim
✳ Jezebel was a queen of ancient Israel who turned the throne away from the Lord, used violent tyranny to force idolatry on the populace, and ultimately met a gruesome end. She was so irredeemably bad that her name has become a common word for a shameless, wicked woman. It's mighty catchy, though, and nowadays that's what matters. Just ask Delilah.
In the World: Women's website Jezebel; Bette Davis film *Jezebel*

Jill (JIL) 1966: #49
Popularity: #3135
Styles: Surfer '60s, Brisk and Breezy, Why Not?
Sisters: Beth, Jody, Robin, 1880 Today
Lisa, Marcy, Lynn
Brothers: Mark, Scott, Jeremy, Kip, Greg, Keith
✳ Jill could be the 1960s' first revival candidate. The name's directness gives it a kind of grown-up girl power: fun and fearless. Plus the phrase "Jack and Jill," dating back 600 years, shows that the image of Jill as a spirited lass is genuinely timeless.
In the World: Jack and Jill; clothier J. Jill; actresses Jill Clayburgh and Jill Hennessy

Jillian (JI-lee-in) 1982: #96
Popularity: #221
Styles: The "-ens," New Classics
Nicknames: Jill, Jilly 1880 Today
Variants: Gillian
Sisters: Mallory, Jocelyn, Lauren, Brooke, Lindsay, Allison
Brothers: Drew, Garrett, Ryan, Jared, Blake, Trenton
✳ Jill was a '50s–'60s favorite, beloved but plain. So in the '70s and '80s, parents turned it into the fancier Jillian. That version turned out to have staying power, even into the age of Madelyn and Addison. The traditional spelling Gillian has always been preferred in the U.K.
In the World: Fitness trainer Jillian Michaels

Jo (JOH) 1954: #53
Popularity: #8341
Styles: Mid-Century, Nicknames
Nicknames: Joey 1880 Today
Sisters: Kay, Gail, Peggy, Meg, Janis, Lynn
Brothers: Del, Ted, Jerry, Hal, Gene, Bill
✳ Since the publication of *Little Women* in 1868, Jo has been linked to the independent, artistic tomboy Jo March. It was purely a nickname at first, but it became a popular given name in the '30s (sometimes as part of a compound name like Jo Anne). Today that fad has passed, but the name is still full of energy. If you're considering Jo as a nickname, see the "Nicknames" style section for given name ideas.
In the World: Jo March of *Little Women*; singer Jo Stafford; Jo of the sitcom *The Facts of Life*

Joan (JOHN)   1932: #5
Popularity: #2742
Styles: Solid Citizens
Nicknames: Joanie, Jo
Variants: Jeanne, Jean, Joanne

Sisters: Carol, Barbara, Joyce, Elaine, Judith, Ann
Brothers: Donald, Bill, Richard, Glenn, Paul, Franklin
✷ Joan is somewhat plain, but not quite plain enough. Parents who really want to make a back-to-basics style statement choose Jane. Joan, the beloved favorite of the '30s and '40s, is simply perceived as too ordinary to be interesting. It's not the first time that's happened to this boom-or-bust name. There was such a glut of Joans in the Middle Ages that the name acquired a "common" reputation and virtually disappeared for centuries.
In the World: French icon Joan of Arc; actresses Joan Crawford and Joan Collins; singer Joan Jett; Joan of *Mad Men*

Joanna (joh-AN-ə)   1984: #88
Popularity: #326
Styles: Timeless, Biblical
Nicknames: Jo, Joey, Jody, Joanie
Variants: Johanna, Joanne

Sisters: Susana, Rachel, Tabitha, Veronica, Bethany, Candace
Brothers: Marcus, Joel, Wesley, Andrew, Daniel, Clayton
✷ While other female forms of John like Joan and Jane wax and wane, Joanna remains modest and timeless. It was a 19th-century favorite, held steady through the Joanne-dominated 1950s, and now fits with soft favorites like Daniela and Adriana. The more European-styled Johanna currently has a bit more fashion momentum.
In the World: Actresses Joanna Lumley and Joanna Kerns; musician Joanna Newsom

Joanne (joh-AN)   1934: #45
Popularity: #2085
Styles: Solid Citizens
Nicknames: Jo, Joey, Joanie
Variants: Joann, Jo Anne, Joan

Sisters: Marlene, Beverly, Janice, Yvonne, Carole, Marcia
Brothers: Ronald, Duane, Stuart, Allen, Barry, Gordon
✷ Joanne comes from an Old French form of Joan, but sounds more like the compound names of the '40s (Ruthann, Maryjo). Joanna, a similar but separate name, has a more timeless appeal.
In the World: Actress Joanne Woodward; Jo-Ann Fabrics stores

Jocelyn (JAH-sə-lin)   1883: #179
Popularity: #70
Styles: New Classics, The "-ens"
Nicknames: Joss, Jo, Josie
Variants: Joselyn, Joslyn, Yoselin

Sisters: Gabrielle, Autumn, Sabrina, Jillian, Kendall, Daniela
Brothers: Damian, Blake, Cameron, Cooper, Reid, Brendan
✷ The name Jocelyn is the hero that names like Madison want to grow up like. A man's name for centuries, it has turned completely feminine yet kept its style intact. It's a familar, traditional choice in a trendy vein.

Jodi (JOH-dee)   1997: #40
Popularity: #2606
Styles: Surfer '60s, '70s–'80s, Nicknames
Variants: Jody, Jodie

Sisters: Teri, Lori, Kris, Cindy, Stacy, Toni
Brothers: Brad, Scotty, Jamie, Greg, Toby, Curt
✷ This boyish '60s star still charms us with its good humor. As a nickname, it's pitch-perfect. As a full name, though, it's more limited. Picture actress Jodie Foster as Johanna instead . . . doesn't it suit her dignity better? Other formal options include Judith, Jordan, and Josephine.
In the World: Actress Jodie Foster; writer Jodi Picoult

Johanna (joh-HA-nə, yo-HAH-nə)
1890: #548

Popularity: #520
Styles: Timeless, German and Dutch, Nordic
Nicknames: Jo, Joey, Jody, Joanie, Hanna
Variants: Johana, Joanna
Sisters: Elena, Margaret, Celia, Lydia, Caroline, Lucia
Brothers: Simon, Nathaniel, Thomas, Clayton, Elliott, Noel
✴ This is the Central and Northern European form of Joanna and a timeless choice in the U.S. A bit more formal than the gentle Joanna, it's a good match for brawny surnames.
In the World: *Heidi* author Johanna Spyri

Jordan (JOHR-din)
1997: #40

Popularity: #196
Styles: The "-ens," Last Names First, Androgynous, Place Names, Turn of the 21st Century
Nicknames: Jordy, Jody, Jo
Variants: Jordin, Jordyn, Jordana
Sisters: Morgan, Taylor, Bailey, Logan, Sydney, Payton
Brothers: Tanner, Dalton, Connor, Dillon, Trevor, Landon
✴ You like the punch of an androgynous surname, but you want something familiar enough to not sound pretentious. You've found it: Jordan is a solid hit for girls and boys alike. The spelling Jordin is also a popular feminization, thanks to *American Idol* champion Jordin Sparks.
In the World: Singer Jordin Sparks; TV series *Crossing Jordan*

Josefa (joh-SEH-fə)
1881: #116

Popularity: #8800
Styles: Ladies and Gentlemen, Slavic, Latino/Latina, Why Not?
Nicknames: Jo, Josie, Jody, Posy
Variants: Josepha
Sisters: Adela, Thora, Cecile, Petra, Viola, Honora
Brothers: Silvan, Alonzo, Basil, Anton, Emory, Edgar
✴ Josefa is a traditional name in many languages and was once common in the U.S. It's barely familiar today, though, as Josephine became our standard feminine form of Joseph. That has left Josefa sounding fresh, more like a discovery than a revival.
In the World: Josefa Ortiz de Domínguez, who fought for Mexico's independence from Spain

Josephine (JOH-seh-feen)
1916: #21

Popularity: #182
Styles: Antique Charm, Saints
Nicknames: Jo, Josie, Joey, Josette, Fifi, Jody, Posy
Variants: Josephina, Josefina
Sisters: Charlotte, Genevieve, Eleanor, Violet, Helena, Evangeline
Brothers: Theodore, Jasper, Frederick, Everett, Oliver, August
✴ How many names can be all this for you: elegant as an empress, familiar as an old friend, and ready to kick back with fun little nicknames? The answer is exactly three: Victoria, Catherine, and Josephine. The first two are perennially popular, but the third still manages to sound creative. Ahhh.
In the World: Entertainer Josephine Baker; Joséphine, wife of Napoleon Bonaparte

Josie (JOH-zee)   1881: #116
Popularity: #256
Styles: Guys and Dolls,
Nicknames
Variants: Josey   1880 Today
Sisters: Carly, Eliza, Ruby,
Addie, Stella, Ivy, Lucy, Sadie
Brothers: Leo, Harry, Emmett, Nate, Jackson,
Charlie, Sam, Jasper
✳ Here's a surprise: in the '60s and '70s, when
Josie and the Pussycats were first shaking their
tails in the pages of *Archie Comics,* the name
Josie was at its absolute low point of popularity.
This is not a Surfer '60s name but an 1800s
name—a lighter spin on the then wildly popular
Josephine. It's back now, and welcome, though
the full Josephine is still the more versatile
choice.
In the World: Josie and the Pussycats; model
Josie Maran

Journey (JUWR-nee)   2011: #372
Popularity: #372
Styles: Modern Meanings
Variants: Sojourner
Sisters: Haven, Aria, Clarity,   1880 Today
Raine, Eden, Ember, Paloma,
Skye
Brothers: Justice, Deacon, Bodhi, Beckett,
Phoenix, Judah, River, Jacoby
✳ Journey is a contemporary choice that even a
traditionalist can admire. It combines the femi-
ninity of a classic virtue name with the punch of
a modern meaning name. It also strikes a bal-
ance between the humility of Patience and Pru-
dence and the assurance of Destiny and
Miracle: sending your child out on the path to
greatness, but knowing it's up to her to get there.
In the World: '80s band Journey; *Journey* adventure films (based on the book *Journey to the
Center of the Earth*)

Joy (JOY)   1974: #109
Popularity: #507
Styles: Mid-Century, Charms
and Graces, Brisk and Breezy,
Why Not?   1880 Today
Sisters: Merry, June, Margo,
Gail, Rosemary, Laurel, Holly, Jill
Brothers: Rex, Dean, Roger, Neil, Rudy,
Johnny, Clark, Von
✳ What could be a more natural name for the
soft little bundle in a new parent's arms? Joy is a
sweet, loving choice for a baby and matures
smoothly into womanhood. Like other sweet
one-syllable messages (Grace, Rose), Joy is cur-
rently most popular as a middle name.
In the World: Comedian Joy Behar; musician
Joy Williams; various *Joy of . . .* books

Joyce (JOYS)   1941: #13
Popularity: #969
Styles: Solid Citizens
Variants: Jocosa
Sisters: Elaine, Janice, Carol,   1880 Today
Rita, Gayle, Lorna,
Constance, Gloria
Brothers: Roger, Gerald, Donald, Duane,
Lawrence, Stuart, Raymond, Russell
✳ Joyce is incorruptible. She's a pillar of the
community, a sympathetic ear, a refuge in hard
times. She's also likely to be your grandma's age.
This is a classic name currently in a slump.
Look for a comeback in your grandchildren's
generation.
In the World: Author Joyce Carol Oates; actress
Joyce DeWitt; psychologist Dr. Joyce Brothers

Judith (JOO-dith)   1940: #4
Popularity: #838
Styles: Biblical, Solid
Citizens
Nicknames: Judy, Jude, Jodi   1880 Today
Variants: Judita
Sisters: Elaine, Carolyn, Janet, Deborah,
Nancy, Carol, Patricia, Sharon
Brothers: Kenneth, Roger, Peter, Stuart,
Dennis, Philip, Allen, Richard
✳ In the '30s and '40s, Old Testament names
were at their lowest ebb. Judith bucked the trend
to become one of the most stylish hits of the day.
Today we tend to group it with dated cohorts
like Carol and Barbara, but you'd do well to
focus on Judith's biblical style instead. It's a
strong and now uncommon alternative to Abi-
gail and Hannah.
In the World: Actresses Judith Light and Judith
Anderson; gender theorist Judith Butler

Judy (JOO-dee)   1946: #11
Popularity: #2054
Styles: Mid-Century,
Nicknames
Nicknames: Jude   1880   Today
Variants: Judie, Judi, Jody
Sisters: Connie, Janet, Sue, Gail, Linda, Kathy,
Gwen, Sandra
Brothers: Roger, Jerry, Alan, Steve, Garry,
Danny, Ken, Rick
✴ Swept up in a generational turnover, this
name has virtually disappeared. The Judy Gar-
land–era flock of little Judys may be graying,
but the name is still warm and charming. Your
best bet today is choosing it as a nickname for
the sturdier classic Judith.
In the World: Singer/actress Judy Garland;
Judge Judy TV series; actress Judi Dench; the
phrase "Judy, Judy, Judy"

Julia (JOO-lee-ə)   1880: #26
Popularity: #57
Styles: Timeless,
Shakespearean, Antique
Charm   1880   Today
Nicknames: Julie, Jules, Jill
Variants: Julie, Giulia
Sisters: Anna, Lydia, Caroline, Eva, Celia,
Catherine, Grace, Amelia
Brothers: Samuel, Henry, Oliver, Emmett,
Simon, Isaac, Leo, Joseph
✴ This warm and handsome classic was a 19th-
century standby. By the 1950s, the French form
Julie had taken over, leaving Julia sounding
slightly old-fashioned. Today that very quaint-
ness is part of its appeal. Julia is currently the
height of fashion throughout Europe.
In the World: TV chef Julia Child; actresses
Julia Roberts, Julia Louis-Dreyfus, and Julia
Stiles; poet Julia Ward Howe

Juliana (joo-lee-AN-ə)   2011: #147
Popularity: #147
Styles: Lacy and Lissome,
Saints, Latino/Latina
Nicknames: Julie, Jules   1880   Today
Variants: Julianna, Julianne,
Giuliana
Sisters: Victoria, Natalia, Liliana, Adriana,
Felicity, Mariana, Angelina, Camilla
Brothers: Mason, Nathaniel, Evan, Nicolas,
Parker, Adrian, Owen, Elliot
✴ Juliana has been quietly used for centuries
alongside timeless sister Julia. It's ornamental
with a gentle, poetic touch. The name started to
catch fire in the 1990s, in a wave of fashion for
the lacy classics, but it has never been overused.
In the World: Actress Julianna Margulies; musi-
cian Juliana Hatfield

Julianne (joo-lee-AN)   1985: #364
Popularity: #768
Styles: New Classics
Nicknames: Julie, Jules
Variants: Juliana, Juliann,   1880   Today
Julienne
Sisters: Candace, Noelle, Lilliana, Brenna,
Laurel, Adrienne
Brothers: Corbin, Myles, Kendall, Drew,
Bennett, Dorian
✴ Julianne is a 20th-century creation: the tra-
ditional Juliana reimagined in the age of com-
pound names like Rosanne and Maribeth. Its
smooth elegance helped keep it popular long
past the other compound names' heydays.
In the World: Actress Julianne Moore; per
former Julianne Hough

Julie (JOO-lee)   1969: #12
Popularity: #396
Styles: Surfer '60s, Mid-
Century, French
Nicknames: Jules   1880   Today
Variants: Julia
Sisters: Denise, Cindy, Christine, Laura, Amy,
Lisa
Brothers: Jeffrey, Mark, Eric, Steven, Timothy,
Keith
✴ Together, the Latin Julia and the French
Julie make up a timeless classic. The stately
Julia was the favorite a hundred years ago. Then
Julie's cute, nickname-like sound took over mid-
century. Today stately gentleladies are back in,
and Julie's handing off the baton.
In the World: Actresses Julie Andrews and Julie
Christie; film *Julie and Julia*; TV host Julie
Chen; director Julie Taymor

Juliet (joo-lee-EHT)   2011: #252
Popularity: #252
Styles: Timeless, Shakespearean
Nicknames: Julie, Jules   1880   Today
Variants: Juliette
Sisters: Annabelle, Daphne, Harper, Camilla, Charlotte, Aurora
Brothers: Bennett, Duncan, Graham, Gavin, Tobias, Raphael
✳ Juliet is simple, traditional, and drenched in romance. Unlike her star-crossed lover Romeo, Juliet doesn't sound too showy. The name conjures a ravishing image in an understated, thoughtful way.
In the World: Romeo and Juliet; actresses Juliette Binoche and Juliette Lewis; singer Juliet Simms

June (JOON)   1925: #39
Popularity: #470
Styles: Charms and Graces, Solid Citizens, Brisk and Breezy, Why Not?   1880   Today
Variants: Juno
Sisters: Rose, Eva, Marian, Joy, Dale, May
Brothers: Rex, Harris, Carl, Hal, Clark, Ray
✳ Sweet simplicity is in—just ask Grace and Faith. But so far parents have skipped over June, which offers the same attractions as either a first or middle name.
In the World: Singer June Carter Cash; TV mom June Cleaver; stylist June Ambrose

Junia (JOO-nee-ə)   1883: #920
Popularity: #7197
Styles: Biblical, Classical
Nicknames: June, Junie
Variants: Juno   1880   Today
Sisters: Sabina, Aquila, Damaris, Tamar, Sapphira, Claudia
Brothers: Titus, Justus, Philemon, Bartholomew, Jabez, Matthias
✳ In Romans 16:7, Junia is described as "of note among the apostles." If you don't find her in your Bible, it's because commentators in the Middle Ages decided that such a description of a woman must be wrong. They scratched out Junia and came up with the masculine Junias in its place. Many translators today are reversing that decision. Call this one a traditional name that bucks tradition.

Juniper (JOO-ni-per)   2011: #968
Popularity: #970
Styles: Charms and Graces, Why Not?
Nicknames: June, Junie   1880   Today
Sisters: Briar, Verity, Clementine, Clover, Lavender, January
Brothers: Jericho, Reef, Lennox, Jasper, Barnaby, Archer
✳ You've never met a Juniper. Perhaps the name strikes you as a little silly. And yet you rather like it, don't you? It's fun and lively and makes you smile. That quality, along with a nice conventional nickname to fall back on, has placed this name on the short lists of more and more parents. Juniper has a history as a male saint's name, but today it's all girl.

Juno (JOO-noh)   2011: #2813
Popularity: #2830
Styles: Mythological, Shakespearean
Nicknames: Junie   1880   Today
Variants: June
Sisters: Calliope, Halo, Lyra, Vesper, Clio, Ione
Brothers: Ajax, Oberon, Linus, Hugo, Magnus, Samson
✳ In languages like Italian and Spanish, an "-o" ending signals masculinity. But when you put an "-o" on an English girl's name, it doesn't sound boyish (unlike, say, "-son" or "-man" names). It sounds quirky, individualistic, and confident. That description fits the title character of the 2007 film *Juno* to a tee.
In the World: Roman goddess Juno; film *Juno;* actress Juno Temple

Justice (JUHS-tis)   1995: #261
Popularity: #529
Styles: Modern Meanings, African-American, Nickname-Proof, Androgynous   1880   Today
Sisters: Journey, Skye, Haven, Sage, Essence, Liberty
Brothers: Clarion, Phoenix, Storm, Zion, Arrow, River
✳ Like Destiny, this name is a power punch of affirmation. But Justice takes a step past self-empowerment to embrace a broader social agenda. It's a message name, for better and worse. A big load for a little girl, but tremendous upside.
In the World: Film *Poetic Justice;* daughters of musicians John Mellencamp, Ziggy Marley, and Zac Brown

Justine (juhs-TEEN) 1987: #175
Popularity: #1349
Styles: '70s–'80s, Nickname-
Proof, French
Variants: Justina
Sisters: Danielle, Chelsea,
Monique, Kirsten, Jenna, Whitney
Brothers: Travis, Jared, Corey, Bryant, Kurtis,
Derrick
✶ While most similar-sounding names (Ja-
nine, Francine) were on the way out by the '80s,
Justine was just hitting its stride. The booming
popularity of Justin for boys helped, as did the
actress Justine Bateman of *Family Ties*. Today,
though, Justine is fading back into the pack.
The Latin form Justina may sound more con-
temporary.
In the World: Actress Justine Bateman; tennis
player Justine Henin; notorious Marquis de
Sade novel *Justine*

Kaitlyn (KAYT-lin) 2000: #30
Popularity: #100
Styles: Bell Tones, The
"-ens," Turn of the 21st
Century
Nicknames: Kait, Katie, Kay
Variants: Caitlin, Katelyn, Kaitlynne, Caitlyn,
etc.
Sisters: Kylie, Megan, Allyson, Mckenna,
Hailey, Ashlyn
Brothers: Tyler, Brayden, Dylan, Kieran, Riley,
Kameron
✶ Caitlin is Gaelic and traditional, but Kaitlyn
is a phenomenon. There's something about the
name that struck a chord with "kreative" nam-
ers in the U.S., who placed a dozen different
spellings of it in the top thousand girls' names.
In the years to come, expect to meet countless
Kaitlyns, no two spelled the same.

Kara (KAH-rə, KA-rə) 1991: #106
Popularity: #340
Styles: New Classics, Short
and Sweet, Nickname-Proof
Variants: Cara
Sisters: Jenna, Abby, Tori,
Tessa, Kendra, Sasha
Brothers: Damon, Erik, Korey, Trent, Abel,
Brett
✶ Spelled Cara, this name means "dear" in
Italian. Spelled Kara, it means you like cute lit-
tle names that start with K. Most people you
meet will share your opinion. Kara's been a
quiet favorite for two generations, but alterna-
tives Keira and Kaia are luring many parents
away.
In the World: Music executive Kara DioGuardi

Karen (KA-rin) 1956: #7
Popularity: #287
Styles: Mid-Century,
Nickname-Proof, Nordic
Variants: Karin, Karyn,
Carin, Karon, Karren
Sisters: Laura, Susan, Kathy, Julie, Donna,
Sharon
Brothers: Mark, Gregory, David, Scott,
Stephen, Kenneth
✶ Every Kaitlyn, Megan, and Devin in the
land should tip her hat to Karen. When this
Scandinavian form of Katherine took off 60
years ago, it established a whole new sound for
the all-American girl.
In the World: Singers Karen Carpenter and
Karen O; actress Karen Black

Karina (kah-REEN-ə) 1995: #109
Popularity: #337
Styles: Lacy and Lissome,
Nordic, Turn of the 21st
Century
Nicknames: Kari
Variants: Carina, Karena
Sisters: Marissa, Annika, Kelsey, Hayley,
Breanna, Alexa
Brothers: Donovan, Colby, Zachary, Stefan,
Darius, Trey
✶ The pure happiness of this name is conta-
gious. Karina's easy femininity, a twist on earlier
favorites Karen and Christina, makes it a natu-
ral for American parents. It's a natural around
the world too, with versions emerging in many
different languages. The spelling Carina may
have the deepest roots, from an early Orthodox
saint to a constellation in the southern sky.
In the World: Dancer Karina Smirnoff; musician Karina Pasian

Kate (KAYT)   1880: #79
Popularity: #175
Styles: Nicknames, Timeless
Variants: Cate
Sisters: Claire, Leah, Lily,   1880   Today
Eve, Abby, Hope
Brothers: Alex, Jack, Adam, Simon, Luke,
James
✷When Catherine Middleton married England's Prince William, the palace put out a directive that her former nickname, Kate, was to be abandoned. Fat chance. To the public she remained Kate, exemplifying the name's image. Kate is impeccably classic, with a clean, crisp style that works for any generation.
In the World: Kate Middleton (Catherine, Duchess of Cambridge); musical *Kiss Me, Kate*; actresses Kate Winslet, Kate Hudson, and Kate Beckinsale

Kateri (kah-TEH-ree)   1980: #1721
Popularity: #3729
Styles: Saints
Sisters: Shadi, Halona,
Winema, Mahala, Chenoa,   1880   Today
Nayeli
Brothers: Sakari, Chayton, Kohana, Wayra,
Seattle, Enapay
✷An Iroquois form of Katherine, this is a highly individual name with cross-cultural strength. Kateri Tekakwitha, a 17th-century Mohawk Christian, was beatified by Pope John Paul II.
In the World: Mohawk saint Kateri Tekakwitha

Katherine (KATH-rin)   1988: #27
Popularity: #61
Styles: Timeless
Nicknames: Kat, Kate, Kathy,
Katie, Kay, Kit, Kitty, Kari,   1880   Today
Katia
Variants: Katharine, Catherine, Kathryn, Katerina, Katrina, Karen
Sisters: Elizabeth, Caroline, Julia, Rebecca, Sarah, Anna
Brothers: James, Christopher, Alexander, William, Andrew, Thomas
✷ If you want a name to stay fashionable until your daughter is a grandma, you can't find a better bet than Katherine. This is a name of saints, queens, and empresses, with countless versions and derivatives. Several different spellings are traditional, but Katherine is the most timeless. Katharine (with the extra "a") has patrician associations. See also Catherine.
In the World: Actresses Katharine Hepburn and Katherine Heigl; singer Katherine Jenkins

Kathleen (kath-LEEN)   1949: #9
Popularity: #632
Styles: Mid-Century, Celtic
Nicknames: Kathy, Kat
Sisters: Pamela, Sharon,   1880   Today
Maureen, Brenda, Susan,
Janice
Brothers: Douglas, Kenneth, Bruce, Garry, Patrick, Neil
✷ Kathleen is the Anglicized form of the Gaelic Caitlin. For many years it was a favorite of Irish families in America, but today most parents have redirected their affections to the Gaelic original. The result, surprisingly, is to make Kathleen sound even better. Its retro style now makes it a comfort name, glowing with warmth.
In the World: Actress Kathleen Turner; politician Kathleen Sebelius; opera singer Kathleen Battle

Kathy (KA-thee)   1958: #14
Popularity: #1344
Styles: Mid-Century,
Nicknames
Nicknames: Kat   1880   Today
Variants: Cathy, Kathie,
Kathi
Sisters: Julie, Linda, Karen, Sandy, Judy, Debra
Brothers: Jerry, Ricky, Ken, Steve, Barry, Greg
✷This is a name that's full of heart and free of pretense. The recent dominance of "Kate" sounds (like Kaitlyn) has left Kathy as the charmingly old-fashioned option. It's now rarely used as a given name, but it's still a worry-free nickname.
In the World: Actress Kathy Bates; TV host Kathie Lee Gifford; comedian Kathy Griffin; comic strip *Cathy*

Katia (KAH-tyə)   1996: #772
Popularity: #1614
Styles: Slavic, Why Not?
Nicknames: Kat, Katie
Variants: Katya, Katja   1880   Today
Sisters: Anya, Milena, Daria,
Vika, Annika, Lilia
Brothers: Lukas, Gabe, Andrei, Lev, Torin, Maxim
✷ Just a single vowel separates Katia and Katie, but it makes a literal world of difference. Katia's heart lies across the globe in Russia, and Katie's at home right here in the U.S. Both can be used as nicknames for Katherine, Ekaterina, and their many variants.

Katie (KAY-tee)   1986: #38
Popularity: #192
Styles: Nicknames, Timeless
Variants: Katy, Kate, Cate
Sisters: Abby, Emily, Lauren,   1880 Today
Molly, Sara, Maggie
Brothers: Alex, Jake, Andrew, Jesse, Ben, Will
★ Many parents skip right past Katherine and choose this cute, unpretentious nickname. It's a sure way to avoid having your daughter called Kathy or Kat against your wishes, but it forces her to sound girlish—even when she might prefer womanly. For a middle path, consider the given name Kate. That's the stylish nom du jour for Hollywood stars and British princesses.
In the World: Singer Katy Perry; newscaster Katie Couric; actress Katie Holmes

Katrina (kah-TREEN-ə)   1980: #90
Popularity: #1063
Styles: Namesakes, '70s–'80s,
German and Dutch
Nicknames: Trina, Kat, Katia   1880 Today
Variants: Catrina, Catriona,
Katerina, Katrine
Sisters: Christa, Monika, Nicole, Candice, Erika, Marisa
Brothers: Derrick, Brent, Shaun, Jeremy, Lance, Travis
★ This lively contraction of Katherine has a Scandinavian form and a Celtic rhythm. (It's used as an English version of the Gaelic Catriona.) It has a buoyant sound, classic yet cheerleader-ready. But this sunny name now has a tragically dark side. It's up to you, as you read this, to determine whether the specter of the devastating Hurricane Katrina of 2005 still overwhelms the name.
In the World: Hurricane Katrina; actress Katrina Bowden; band Katrina and the Waves

Kay (KAY)   1939: #76
Popularity: #3456
Styles: Solid Citizens,
Nicknames
Variants: Kaye   1880 Today
Sisters: Jo, Gail, Sue, June, Peggy, Rue, Dale
Brothers: Dean, Van, Rex, Hale, Barry, Gene, Royce
★ Kay is one of the trendiest *nicknames* in America. It's the short form for such hits as Kayla, Kaylee, Kaylin, and Makayla. That completely transforms the perception of this name, a '40s fireball that was once a glamorous pet name for Katherine. *Washington Post* publisher Katharine ("Kay") Graham was a legendary example.
In the World: Entertainer and Eloise creator Kay Thompson; Senator Kay Bailey Hutchison; actress Kay Francis

Kayla (KAY-lə)   1991: #12
Popularity: #59
Styles: Bell Tones, African-
American, Turn of the 21st
Century   1880 Today
Nicknames: Kay
Variants: Kaila, Kaela, Kaylah, Cayla
Sisters: Alyssa, Haley, Kelsey, Brianna, Jenna, Taylor
Brothers: Tyler, Blake, Devon, Jordan, Cody, Keenan
★ This name is pure sunshine. It was introduced on the soap opera *Days of Our Lives* in the 1980s and instantly took off as parents reveled in its clean, bright sound—a harbinger of an entire Bell Tones generation. Kayla no longer sounds new, but the simple purity of its sound should help it age well.
In the World: Kayla of *Days of Our Lives*; actress Kayla Ewell

Kaylee (KAY-lee)   2009: #26
Popularity: #36
Styles: Bell Tones
Nicknames: Kay
Variants: Kayleigh, Kaylie,   1880   Today
Kayley, Kailee, Kailey,
Kayleen
Sisters: Rylee, Kasey, Hayden, Jayla, Avery,
Skylar
Brothers: Kyler, Brayden, Chase, Landon,
Colton, Grayson
✻ This name sits squarely at the center of a
trend that has given an entire generation of kids
a trademark sound. The sounds "kay" and "lee"
are enormously popular building blocks used in
dozens of names, and the name Kaylee itself is
found in every spelling you can imagine.
In the World: Actress Kaley Cuoco; murder vic-
tim Caylee Anthony

Kaylin (KAY-lin)   2009: #372
Popularity: #413
Styles: Bell Tones, The "-ens"
Nicknames: Kay
Variants: Kailyn, Kaylyn,   1880   Today
Kaylynn, Kaelyn, Kalyn
Sisters: Kylie, Jasmyn, Haley, Kyra, Ashlyn,
Jayla
Brothers: Braydon, Keaton, Skyler, Tate,
Greyson, Kane
✻ Halfway between Kayla and Kaitlyn falls
this pleasant compromise. Kaylin keeps Kayla's
smooth sound but shapes it into Kaitlyn's trendy
boyish rhythm.

Keira (KEE-rə)   2006: #109
Popularity: #176
Styles: Celtic, Nickname-
Proof
Variants: Ciara, Kyra, Kira,   1880   Today
Kiera
Sisters: Fiona, Jayla, Rylee, Kendall, Tegan,
Alana
Brothers: Ronan, Camden, Bryce, Quinn,
Declan, Liam
✻ The Gaelic original Ciara is hot in Ireland,
but actress Keira Knightley has made Keira *the*
spelling of the name in the rest of the world. It
has soared especially high in her native En-
gland.
In the World: Actresses Keira Knightley and
Kyra Sedgwick

Keisha (KEE-shə)   1976: #233
Popularity: #2578
Styles: African-American,
'70s–'80s, Nickname-Proof
Variants: Kesha, Kisha,   1880   Today
Lakeisha, Lakesha, Keshia
Sisters: Tasha, Felicia, Cristy, Tonya, Kristal,
Shonda
Brothers: Torrey, Kevin, Kenny, Shad, Jarrod,
Derrick
✻ Keisha was everywhere in the '70s and '80s.
It popped up in different spellings, with and
without suffixes. And for pure '80s cred, you
can't beat a cute kid from *The Cosby Show*. This
energetic name faded surprisingly fast, perhaps
a victim of its own popularity.
In the World: The Cosby Show actress Keshia
Knight Pulliam; singer Ke$ha

Kelly (KEH-lee)   1977: #10
Popularity: #336
Styles: Surfer '60s, Celtic,
'70s–'80s
Variants: Kelli, Kellie, Kelley   1880   Today
Sisters: Stacy, April, Kristen,
Shannon, Tara, Kimberly
Brothers: Brian, Jeffrey, Sean, Bradley, Kevin,
Todd
✻ Kelly is the original androgynous Irish sur-
name (see Riley, Mckenzie, etc.). While it's still
quite popular, this standby has been swamped
by thousands of little Kaylees, Kylies, and Kel-
seys. As a result, Kelly now has an image that
would have been unimaginable back in its '60s
heyday: it's the mature, traditional alternative.
In the World: Singers Kelly Clarkson and Kelly
Rowland; TV host Kelly Ripa; reality TV personality Kelly Osbourne

Kelsey (KEHL-see) 1992: #23
Popularity: #254
Styles: Androgynous, Last
Names First, Nickname-
Proof, Bell Tones, Turn of the 1880 Today
21st Century
Variants: Kelsie
Sisters: Lindsey, Mallory, Kendra, Haley,
Taylor, Sydney
Brothers: Tyler, Dalton, Kyle, Austin, Jarrett,
Keaton
✳ Kelsey was a mild-mannered boy's name
(think actor Kelsey Grammer) that suddenly ex-
ploded as a girl's name. With its energetic,
faintly androgynous style, it pals around com-
fortably with Courtney and Shelby. One of the
hottest names of the '90s, Kelsey is now cooling
off.
In the World: Chef Kelsey Nixon; actress Kelsey
Chow; basketball player Kelsey Griffin

Kendall (KEHN-dəl) 2011: #123
Popularity: #123
Styles: Last Names First,
Celtic, Androgynous
Variants: Kendal 1880 Today
Sisters: Logan, Kelsey,
Harper, Carrigan, Kennedy, Rowan
Brothers: Donovan, Brennan, Reid, Tanner,
Grayson, Sullivan
✳ An unexpected gender crossover, Kendall
has a particularly boyish sound (like a Ken doll,
not a Barbie). Its big draw is a surname sound
without the usual "-n," "-r," and "-y" endings.
Also consider Kimball, which offers a similar
sound and a handy feminine nickname.
In the World: Reality TV personality Kendall
Jenner

Kendra (KEHN-drə) 1987: #77
Popularity: #293
Styles: '70s–'80s, New
Classics, African-American,
Nickname-Proof 1880 Today
Sisters: Kelsey, Jenna,
Katrina, Ericka, Amber, Alicia
Brothers: Kyle, Jared, Brendan, Marcus, Ryan,
Derrick
✳ This is a Welsh/Gaelic/Norse/Anglo-Saxon
name meaning "knowledge/champion/magi-
cal/high hill/water baby/royal power." In other
words, nobody knows where it came from, so
don't worry yourself about it. Kendra *sounds* like
a modern blend of Kenneth and Sandra, which
makes it a solid mainstream choice.
In the World: Playboy star Kendra Wilkinson

Kennedy (KEH-nə-dee) 2011: #90
Popularity: #90
Styles: Last Names First,
Celtic, Androgynous
Nicknames: Kenna 1880 Today
Variants: Kennedi
Sisters: Delaney, Cassidy, Tatum, Reagan,
Mckenzie, Addison
Brothers: Connor, Parker, Jackson, Carter,
Donovan, Lincoln
✳ Americans first took up this Irish boy's name
in the '60s to honor President John F. Kennedy.
Today Kennedy is a hit for girls, driven more by
its Celtic cadence than politics. Its masculine-
sounding "Ken-" root makes it more nickname-
resistant than most long surnames.
In the World: President John F. Kennedy and his
political family; MTV VJ Kennedy

Kenya (KEHN-yə) 1973: #275
Popularity: #802
Styles: Place Names,
African-American
Variants: Kenia 1880 Today
Sisters: Latifah, Samara,
Jamaica, Milan, India, Zaria
Brothers: Zaire, Kendrick, Kareem, Jamal,
Cairo, Tyron
✳ The nation of Kenya has a catchy name
that's been a natural target for African-Ameri-
can parents seeking to reflect their African
roots. The reflection is so direct, though, that it
can sound more like a country than a girl. The
spelling Kenia is standard in many other lan-
guages, and more traditionally namelike in En-
glish.
In the World: Actress Kenya Moore

Kerri (KEH-ree) 1975: #166
Popularity: #3782
Styles: '70s–'80s
Variants: Kerry, Keri
Sisters: Shannon, Kristi, 1880 Today
Trisha, Stacie, Tonya, Jodi
Brothers: Heath, Torrey, Shawn, Brent, Jamie,
Kraig
✳ Remember Kerri Strug, the Olympic gym-
nast who charmed the country back in the '90s
with her courageous performance on an injured
leg? That's the classic Kerri: cute, spunky, and
born in 1977. Yet Kerri's just a stone's throw
from current hits like Kira and Kylie and could
fit in comfortably with any age group. If you like
the idea of it as a nickname, try Kerrigan.
In the World: Gymnast Kerri Strug; singer Keri
Hilson; actresses Kerry Washington and Keri
Russell

Name Snapshots: Girls 125

Kia (KEE-ə)   1993: #647
Popularity: #4838
Styles: Short and Sweet
Variants: Kiya
Sisters: Bria, Kari, Anika,   1880   Today
Taryn, Jena, Tyra
Brothers: Jaron, Shea, Keenan, Joah, Kiefer,
Teo
✷ This miniature name would be irresistible to
many parents, except for the association with a
low-priced line of cars. An alternative spelling
could help break that link; Kiya was the wife of
an ancient Egyptian pharoah.
In the World: Kia Motors

Kiana (kee-AH-nə)   1996: #190
Popularity: #628
Styles: Bell Tones, Lacy and
Lissome, African-American,
Turn of the 21st Century   1880   Today
Variants: Quiana
Sisters: Kamia, Jada, Malia, Janae, Marisa,
Sierra
Brothers: Braden, Davion, Kaleb, Jalen, Skylar,
Kobe
✷ Kiana is an attractive member of a mix-and-
match name family that includes Kiara, Tiana,
and Tiara. A tropical breeze sets Kiana apart: it
is especially popular in Hawaii, where it has the
sound of a traditional name.
In the World: Fitness expert Kiana Tom

Kiara (kee-AH-rə)   1999: #78
Popularity: #320
Styles: Lacy and Lissome,
Celtic, Saints, African-
American, Nickname-Proof   1880   Today
Variants: Ciara, Kiera, Kira,
Chiara, Ceara
Sisters: Nadia, Aliyah, Tiana, Kayla, Tegan,
Dasia
Brothers: Keenan, Rohan, Darius, Devon,
Kilian, Quinn
✷ Kiara's newfound popularity has come from
many directions. Some parents choose it as an
Irish Gaelic name, pronounced "KEE-ra" or
"KEE-a-ra." Pronounced "kee-AH-ra," it can be
a Kenyan name, a version of the Italian Chiara,
or the cub in Disney's *Lion King II*. That's
enough associations that no one of them really
sticks. If you choose the name, choose it be-
cause you love the sound. See also Keira and
Ciara.
In the World: Kiara of *Lion King II*

Kiki (KEE-kee)   1975: #2057
Popularity: #10,733
Styles: Nicknames, Nordic
Sisters: Vivi, Suki, Britt,
Zuzu, Tove, Anni, Romy, Siri   1880   Today
Brothers: Timo, Xander,
Niko, Tycho, Finn, Rafe, Soren, Marko
✷ It's easy to file this name with the ooh-la-la
sisters Fifi and Mimi, but Kiki is made of sterner
stuff. It's Scandinavian (a nickname for Kris-
tina) and has artistic associations and an inde-
pendent spirit. As a nickname, it could free you
from the overcommon Kristy.
In the World: Singer Kiki Dee; artist Kiki Smith;
movie *Kiki's Delivery Service*

Kim (KIM)   1960: #34
Popularity: #3309
Styles: Mid-Century,
Nicknames
Sisters: Kris, Liz, Joni, Lynn,   1880   Today
Dee, Jill
Brothers: Rod, Kip, Von, Bret, Wes, Kurt
✷ We usually hear Kim as a nickname for Kim-
berly, but it used to be given just as often as a full
name. In the '50s, it sounded crisp and modern,
like *Vertigo* actress Kim Novak. It's still snappy
today, though more conventional. Some uncon-
ventional uses could be as a nickname for Kim-
ball, Kimberlin, or Kimora.
In the World: All-purpose celebrity Kim Kardashian; singer Lil' Kim; actresses Kim Novak,
Kim Basinger, and Kim Cattrall

Kimberly (KIM-ber-lee)   1967: #2
Popularity: #67
Styles: Surfer '60s
Nicknames: Kim, Kimber
Variants: Kimberley   1880   Today
Kimberlee
Sisters: Stephanie, Tracy, Michelle, Leslie,
Melissa, Kelly
Brothers: Jeffrey, Brian, Timothy, Kevin, Scott,
Gregory
✷ Kimberly has been a favorite for decades
thanks to its bright sound, like a tinkling of
bells. The name's enormous popularity in the
'60s and '70s is now starting to drag it down, as
every new parent knows at least a couple of
Kims. The variant spelling Kimberley was origi-
nally the standard version, honoring a battle in
the Boer Wars.
In the World: Actresses Kimberly Williams,
Kimberly Caldwell, and Kimberly Elise; Kim-
berly-Clark Corporation

Kimora (ki-MOH-rə)   2008: #291
Popularity: #607
Styles: African-American
Nicknames: Kim
Sisters: Kaliyah, Rihanna,   1880   Today
Amari, Kelis, Tiana, Kateri
Brothers: Davion, Semaj, Omarion, Trevin,
Mehki, Keyon
✷ Model and fashion designer Kimora Lee
Simmons introduced America to this name.
Her image fit the name perfectly: a multiracial
stunner with a unique look and a flamboyantly
stylish attitude.
In the World: Model/fashion designer Kimora
Lee Simmons

Kinley (KIN-lee)   2011: #194
Popularity: #194
Styles: Last Names First
Sisters: Ainsley, Rylie, Adelyn,
Briley, Leighton, Marley   1880   Today
Brothers: Jackson, Kaden,
Tiernan, Parker, Bryson
✷ Kinley is a surname, a trimmed version of
McKinley. Starting around 2010, it was sud-
denly the name everyone wanted. What sparks
such a naming storm? Well, Kinley fits in with a
generation of Kaylees and Kylies, without blend-
ing in. And its traditional surname form works
for parents leery of "made-up" names.
In the World: A child pageant entrant on the re-
ality series Toddlers & Tiaras

Kinsey (KIN-zee)   2011: #837
Popularity: #839
Styles: Last Names First
Nicknames: Kin
Sisters: Hadley, Parker,   1880   Today
Kaylin, Macy, Finley,
Mckenna
Brothers: Keaton, Skylar, Brennan, Jacoby,
Paxton, Dayton
✷ You can thank mystery writer Sue Grafton
for this name, introduced in her popular series
about detective Kinsey Millhone. It's a fresh al-
ternative to the more popular Kelsey. Parental
advisory: keep in mind the Kinsey Reports on
sexual behavior.
In the World: Kinsey Millhone of Sue Grafton's
"alphabet" mystery series; the "Kinsey scale" of
sexual orientation

Kirsten (KIR-stin)   1991: #154
Popularity: #850
Styles: Nordic, The "-ens,"
'70s–'80s, Turn of the 21st
Century   1880   Today
Nicknames: Kirsty, Kirstie
Variants: Kerstin, Kirstin, Kiersten
Sisters: Megan, Katelyn, Sabrina, Allyson,
Jenna, Lauren
Brothers: Brendan, Erik, Kendall, Travis,
Dustin, Jamison
✷ Kirsten, the Danish and Norwegian form of
Christine, first hit America in the same 1970s
wave that brought so many Kristens and Kristas.
(It hit Scotland much earlier, thanks to its kin-
ship with the traditional Scottish pet name
Chirsty.) Like most Christine variants, it's now
more common among mothers than babies.
In the World: Actress Kirsten Dunst; Senator
Kirsten Gillibrand

Krista (KRIS-tə)   1986: #93
Popularity: #1279
Styles: '70s–'80s
Nicknames: Kris
Variants: Christa   1880   Today
Sisters: Erica, Katrina, Jaclyn,
Tara, Stacy, Kendra
Brothers: Brett, Casey, Kevin, Shaun, Derek,
Corey
✷ Krista was a card-carrying member of the
'70s "Kris" brigades. It was a quiet choice at the
time, but it turned out to be a trendsetter. Krista
helped set the blueprint for later favorites like
Tessa and Jenna, and those names in turn
helped to keep Krista sounding more contem-
porary than other names of its generation.
In the World: Actresses Christa Miller and
Christa Allen

Kristen (KRIS-tin)   1982: #33
Popularity: #661
Styles: '70s–'80s, The "-ens"
Nicknames: Kris, Kristie,
Krissy   1880   Today
Variants: Kristin, Kristina,
Kirsten, Christen
Sisters: Nicole, Lindsay, Candice, April, Jillian,
Heather
Brothers: Justin, Chad, Brandon, Shane, Ryan,
Jason
✷ Every possible form of Christine was a hit in
the '70s and '80s. One of the biggest was Kris-
ten, which sounds so much like a Scandinavian
girl's classic that it's hard to believe it's a modern
creation.
In the World: Actresses Kristen Stewart, Kristen
Bell, Kristen Wiig, Kristin Scott Thomas, Kris-
tin Davis, and Kristin Chenoweth

Kyla (KIY-lə)   2004: #162
Popularity: #285
Styles: Bell Tones
Variants: Kylah
Sisters: Macy, Jada, Ashlyn,   1880   Today
Ayla, Laney, Teagan, Tyra,
Lexi
Brothers: Keegan, Braden, Gage, Kade, Rylan,
Kian, Brady, Trey
✷ This is what name dictionaries like to call "a
euphonious invention." Which is a euphonious
way to say that folks made it up 'cause it sounds
nice. Kyla's as modern as Skylar and as feminine
as Kayleigh and should grow up well.
In the World: Actress Kyla Pratt; singer Kyla La
Grange

Kylie (KIY-lee)   2003: #52
Popularity: #58
Styles: Bell Tones
Variants: Kylee, Kiley,
Kyleigh   1880   Today
Sisters: Tayla, Macie, Khloe,
Kailyn, Alexa, Jada
Brothers: Tanner, Kolby, Hayden, Kellan,
Chase, Ashton
✷ This was an Australian name, but it fit per-
fectly into American tastes. So when American
parents encountered the name via Aussie enter-
tainer Kylie Minogue, they jumped on it. There
is no standard spelling in the U.S., but Kylie and
Kylee are the most common.
In the World: Entertainer Kylie Minogue; real-
ity TV personality Kylie Jenner

Kyra (KEE-rə, KIY-rə)   2005: #179
Popularity: #388
Styles: Short and Sweet, Bell
Tones, Nickname-Proof
Variants: Kira, Keira   1880   Today
Sisters: Ayla, Macy, Ariana,
Eden, Kiley, Tessa
Brothers: Kyle, Connor, Easton, Chase, Keaton,
Brayden
✷ This springy, attractive name is usually pro-
nounced "KEE-ra," but you'll also hear "KY-ra"
(like Tyra). If you want to clarify the "KEE" pro-
nunciation, try spelling it Kira. And just to
muddy the waters even more, see also Kiera,
Kiara, and Ciara.
In the World: Actress Kyra Sedgwick

Lacey (LAY-see)   1983: #128
Popularity: #440
Styles: Last Names First, Bell
Tones
Nicknames: Lace   1880   Today
Variants: Lacy, Lacie, Laci
Sisters: Lindsey, Blair, Danielle, Hillary, Kirby,
Meredith
Brothers: Drew, Bryant, Kendall, Jameson,
Colby, Weston
✷ The name Merry is merry and Joy is joyous,
so shouldn't Lacey be lacy? In fact, this sur-
name is closer to the sleek style of Lindsay and
Whitney. It has a patrician element, exempli-
fied by the *Doonesbury* comic-strip congress-
woman Lacey Davenport. Spellings like Laci
move the name from the patrician surnames
column toward the modern inventions.
In the World: Actress Lacey Chabert

Lana (LAH-nə)   1948: #188
Popularity: #486
Styles: Mid-Century, Short
and Sweet, Slavic, Why Not?
Sisters: Sonia, Mila, Harlow,   1880   Today
Ava, Vivien, Sondra, Isla,
Kaye
Brothers: Grant, Flynn, Spencer, Rand, Gavin,
Kent, Deacon, Reed
✷ It's the purest old Hollywood legend. Young
Julia Turner is discovered at a soda fountain and
transformed into glamorous star Lana Turner.
The name was perfect for her sweater-girl
image: youthful in form, sultry in demeanor.
The golden Hollywood glow it cast back then
still works its magic today.
In the World: Actress Lana Turner; Lana Lang
of *Superman*; singer Lana Del Rey

Landry (LAN-dree)   2011: #1144
Popularity: #1147
Styles: Last Names First,
Country and Western,
Androgynous, Saints, Why   1880   Today
Not?
Sisters: Autry, Logan, Anniston, Layne, Shelby,
Oakley
Brothers: Gannon, Brant, Cade, Lawson,
Deacon, Colt
✳The call has gone out: "Bring unto us your
surnames ending in '-y'! We shall forge of them
an army of girls' names." Landry is a very old
French surname and saint's name, but Ameri-
cans don't hear it that way. We hear a com-
pletely modern name with a touch of cowgirl
sass. The name is found most often where mem-
ories of Dallas Cowboys coach Tom Landry run
deep.
In the World: Football coach Tom Landry;
Landry Clarke, a male character on *Friday
Night Lights*

Laney (LAY-nee)   2005: #480
Popularity: #523
Styles: Last Names First, Bell
Tones, Why Not?
Variants: Lainey   1880   Today
Sisters: Kiley, Jacey, Tessa,
Larkin, Marin, Finley
Brothers: Keaton, Rowan, Flynn, Calder,
Barrett, Griffin
✳Laney is new but tantalizingly familiar. It
could be a twist on Lonnie, a nickname for
Elaine, or a merger of Lacey and Lindsay. It's a
strong, clean sound with power-name potential.

Lara (LAH-ra)   1969: #222
Popularity: #924
Styles: New Classics, Slavic,
Fantastical
Sisters: Sonia, Lisa, Darcy,   1880   Today
Kara, Tanya, Christa
Brothers: Damon, Toby, Andre, Bryan, Jamie,
Marc
✳This variation on Laura and Larissa emerged
in the '60s when round, full sounds were getting
trimmed down to pocket size. It was starting to
fade from view until the *Tomb Raider* heroine
Lara Croft briefly reenergized the name.
In the World: Lara Croft of *Tomb Raider*; ac-
tresses Lara Dutta and Lara Flynn Boyle;
"Lara's Theme" from *Doctor Zhivago*

Larissa (lah-RIS-a)   1994: #363
Popularity: #853
Styles: Lacy and Lissome,
Slavic, African-American
Nicknames: Lara, Rissa   1880   Today
Variants: Larisa
Sisters: Juliana, Natasha, Tatiana, Gabriella,
Ayanna, Marissa
Brothers: Darius, Jovan, Dominik, Quinton,
Damian, Maxwell
✳If Larissa hadn't existed, it would have been
invented in the '80s. It sounds like a natural ex-
tension of Melissa, Clarissa, and other frilly
classics. In fact, Larissa is a Slavic classic in its
own right, as well as an ancient Greek town and
a moon of Neptune.
In the World: Model Larissa Riquelme; actress
Larisa Oleynik

Lark (LAHRK)   1950: #1124
Popularity: #5805
Styles: Charms and Graces,
Modern Meanings, Brisk and
Breezy, Why Not?   1880   Today
Sisters: Bay, Wren, Winter,
Skye, Blythe, Caprice, Linden, Ember
Brothers: Reef, Hart, Phoenix, Frost, Arrow,
Silvan, Indigo, Birch
✳Lark has two common meanings in English:
a cheery songbird and a spontaneous, light-
hearted adventure. Both suit a girl's name to a
tee. This is a catchy name with some surprise
to it.

Latasha (lah-TAH-sha)   1980: #141
Popularity: #10,047
Styles: African-American,
'70s–'80s
Nicknames: Tasha   1880   Today
Variants: Latosha, Letasha
Sisters: Tamika, Latonya, Cherise, Kendra,
Marquita, Sharonda
Brothers: Stephon, Bryant, Demond, Darnell,
Jermaine, Cedric
✳The "La-" prefix that dominated the African-
American name scene for years lost its luster
in the 21st century, leaving favorites like Lata-
sha in the lurch. The more recent hot sound:
"Ja-," as in Jakayla and Janiyah.

LaToya (lah-TOY-ə) 1984: #60
Popularity: Very rare
Styles: African-American
Nicknames: Toya
Sisters: Latasha, Sheena, 1880 Today
Quiana, Cherise, Tameka,
Sharonda
Brothers: Jamaal, Torrance, Courteney,
Jermaine, Dedrick, Darnell
✶This name is generally attributed to LaToya
Jackson, who was born in 1956. Her name hit
the spotlight in the '70s when her Jackson 5
brothers became singing sensations. It was a
splashy hit but has now virtually disappeared.
In the World: Singer LaToya Jackson; *American
Idol* singer LaToya London; artist LaToya Ruby
Frazier

Laura (LAW-rə) 1968: #11
Popularity: #273
Styles: Timeless
Nicknames: Laurie, Lori,
Lolly 1880 Today
Variants: Laurel, Lauren
Sisters: Sarah, Julia, Kate, Rebecca, Amy,
Christina
Brothers: Peter, Daniel, Matthew, Gregory,
Martin, Stephen
✶One of the steadiest choices around the
world, Laura has a smooth sound that has made
it a favorite in song and story for centuries—
from Petrarch to *General Hospital*—and it's a
hit in almost every European language. This
author has spent many happy years with the
name, for which she thanks her parents.
In the World: "Little House" writer Laura In-
galls Wilder; radio show *Dr. Laura*; actress
Laura Linney

Laurel (LAW-rəl) 1956: #241
Popularity: #927
Styles: New Classics, Charms
and Graces, Why Not?
Nicknames: Laurie 1880 Today
Sisters: Margo, Julianne,
Willow, Daphne, Rosemary, Candace
Brothers: Duncan, Mitchell, Heath, Vance,
Forrest, Wesley
✶This attractive botanical name mirrors the
classic softness of Laura but gives that standard
an unexpected twist. It has never been com-
mon: there are over a dozen Laurens (and a
handful of Lauras) born for every Laurel. That
makes the name distinctive, but brace for its
being constantly misheard.
In the World: Writer Laurell Hamilton; designer
Laurel Burch; comedians Laurel and Hardy

Lauren (LAW-rin) 1989: #9
Popularity: #62
Styles: The "-ens," '70s–'80s,
Turn of the 21st Century
Nicknames: Laurie 1880 Today
Variants: Loren
Sisters: Nicole, Jessica, Allison, Megan,
Brooke, Natalie
Brothers: Ryan, Matthew, Sean, Justin,
Christopher, Evan
✶This Laura variant first hit the scene in the
1940s in the glamorous form of actress Lauren
Bacall. It rode along quietly for many years,
then suddenly burst into popularity in the '80s.
In this tight-knit name family, Lauren is the
modern girl, Laura the most traditional, and
Laurel the most creative.
In the World: Actresses Lauren Bacall and Lau-
ren Graham; reality TV star Lauren Conrad;
model Lauren Hutton

Lavender (LAV-in-der) 2009: #4178
Popularity: #4278
Styles: Charms and Graces
Sisters: Amethyst, Verity,
Linden, Juniper, January, 1880 Today
Dahlia
Brothers: Frost, Lake, Phoenix, Lysander, Gray,
Lennox
✶This elegant color and botanical name is
ready to become a girl's name. It's quirky but not
silly, and familiar to the younger set via a char-
acter in the "Harry Potter" books.
In the World: Lavender Brown of the "Harry
Potter" series

Lavinia (lah-VIN-ee-ə) 1886: #360
Popularity: #3851
Styles: Ladies and
Gentlemen, Mythological,
Exotic Traditional, Lacy and 1880 Today
Lissome, Why Not?
Nicknames: Liv, Vin
Sisters: Rafaela, Ariadne, Aurelia, Octavia,
Verena, Linnea
Brothers: Leander, Benedict, Jules, Augustus,
Caspian, Bartholomew
✷ Traditional, feminine, and extremely rare,
Lavinia is a name with enormous potential. In
Virgil's *Aeneid*, Lavinia was the wife of Aeneas
and foremother of the Roman people. The
name has continued to be a favorite in literature
from Shakespeare to Dickens to Eugene
O'Neill. Its melodious beauty comes across just
as well in the real world.
In the World: Despite the name's place in history and use in many languages, there are no
strong popular associations

Layla (LAY-lə) 2011: #33
Popularity: #33
Styles: Lacy and Lissome,
Muslim
Variants: Laila, Leila 1880 Today
Sisters: Alana, Emery, Amira,
Alexa, Chloe, Nadya
Brothers: Evan, Julian, Pryce, Zayn, Elias,
Chase
✷ From an Arabic (and Hebrew) term for
"night," Layla is a tender murmur of a name.
This name is closely related to Lila, a name with
several subtly different versions. It's the most
contemporary-sounding of the family, à la
Kayla, and is associated with the iconic Eric
Clapton song.
In the World: Song "Layla"; boxer Laila Ali;
story "Layla and Majnun"

Lea (LAY-ə) 1970: #397
Popularity: #553
Styles: French, Short and
Sweet, Timeless
Variants: Léa, Leia, Lia 1880 Today
Sisters: Cara, Elisa, Julie,
Ana, Hope, Noelle
Brothers: Abel, Barrett, Tomas, Clay, Nolan,
Joel
✷ Léa, the French form of Leah, is one of the
hottest names in France. Without the accent,
it's a popular Hawaiian name, from a goddess.
In either form, the name has a smooth, elusive
delicacy, like a fine chocolate. (Add an "i,"
though, and it's in a galaxy far, far away.)
In the World: Actresses Lea Thompson and Lea
Michele; singer Lea Salonga

Leah (LEE-ə, LAY-ə) 2009: #28
Popularity: #29
Styles: Timeless, Biblical
Nicknames: Lee
Variants: Lea 1880 Today
Sisters: Rachel, Lauren,
Hope, Sarah, Katie, Emily
Brothers: Joel, Adam, Nathan, Seth, Luke,
Noah
✷ This is one of the simplest and sweetest biblical names for girls. Leah is similar in feeling to
Hannah, but its popularity has grown more
slowly and quietly. See also Lea.
In the World: Actress Leah Remini

Leanna (lee-AN-nə) 1989: #383
Popularity: #688
Styles: Lacy and Lissome
Nicknames: Lee
Variants: Liana, Leanne 1880 Today
Sisters: Carina, Elisa, Iliana,
Noelle, Sabina, Arielle
Brothers: Tobias, Elliot, Cullen, Duncan,
Blaine, Kendall
✷ Leanna started life as a minor offshoot of
Leanne, but it's now the more popular and fashionable choice. The extra syllable softens Leanne's country twang into a more universal
femininity.

Leanne (lee-AN)
Popularity: #1624
Styles: Surfer '60s, Country and Western, '70s–'80s
Nicknames: Lee
Variants: Lianne, LeAnn, Lee Ann, Leanna
Sisters: Danielle, Annmarie, Rochelle, Stacey, Jolene, Lynette
Brothers: Clint, Geoffrey, Casey, Jarvis, Kurtis, Shane

1969: #321

✴ This combination name, first heard in the '40s, has an infectious cheer but is now a step behind current fashion. It has always been most popular in the South and Southwest, and that association has been reinforced by country singers LeAnn Rimes and Lee Ann Womack.
In the World: Singers LeAnn Rimes and Lee Ann Womack

Leigh (LEE)
Popularity: #3554
Styles: '70s–'80s, Brisk and Breezy
Sisters: Kerry, Beth, Jamie, Britt, Erin, Darcy
Brothers: Brant, Shawn, Derek, Lance, Brett, Casey

1969: #202

✴ Leigh's time as a full given name is mostly past, but it has been absorbed deep into our naming culture. This spelling now pops up to "personalize" names like Bayleigh, Carleigh, and Myleigh. As a middle name, it has the sound flexibility of Lee without the '50s style.
In the World: Actress Rachel Leigh Cook; actresses Vivian Leigh, Janet Leigh, and Chyler Leigh

Leighton (LAY-tən)
Popularity: #526
Styles: Last Names First, The "-ens," Androgynous
Variants: Leyton
Sisters: Emerson, Reece, Campbell, Carrington, Finley, Madigan
Brothers: Kingston, Madden, Bennett, Remington, Weston, Briggs

2011: #525

✴ *Gossip Girl* was a rare hit TV show where the names of the cast were more creative and influential than the names of the characters. Case in point: Leighton, the English place name and surname borne by actress Leighton Meester. Its style secret is taking the super-popular feminine suffix "-leigh" and moving it up to star billing.
In the World: Actress Leighton Meester

Leila (LAY-lə, LIY-lə)
Popularity: #230
Styles: Lacy and Lissome, Muslim, Antique Charm
Variants: Layla, Laila, Lila
Sisters: Sonia, Liliana, Thea, Hallie, Nina, Celia
Brothers: Jesse, Hayden, Isaac, Chase, Myles, Jonas

1891: #179

✴ Leila is a 50-50 name, half Layla and half Lila. Both pronunciations are lilting and lovely, and this spelling is sweetly traditional. But if you know, deep down, that constant mispronunciations would drive you nuts, consider one of the less ambiguous spellings.
In the World: See the listings under Layla or Lila, depending on your chosen pronunciation

Leilani (lay-LAH-nee)
Popularity: #244
Styles: Exotic Traditional
Nicknames: Lani
Sisters: Maile, Noelani, Kalea, Willow, Lorelei, Kyrielle
Brothers: Makani, Nainoa, Kalani, Raiden, Titus, Gideon

2011: #244

✴ Leilani is the one Hawaiian name that has been widely embraced in America. It jumped to the mainland in the '30s thanks to the Bing Crosby tune "Sweet Leilani." Today it still wafts in on a soft island breeze.
In the World: Song "Sweet Leilani"; basketball player Leilani Mitchell

Lena (LEE-nə, LAY-nə)
Popularity: #360
Styles: Antique Charm, German and Dutch, Short and Sweet, Guys and Dolls
Nicknames: Leni
Variants: Lina
Sisters: Lydia, Annie, Stella, Cora, Eva, Nell, Clara, Lucy
Brothers: Harry, Leo, Oscar, Sam, Oliver, Theo, Charlie, Max

1883: #42

✴ Lena is a nice old-fashioned nickname for some nice old-fashioned names (Helena, Magdalena). If it doesn't sound old-fashioned to you, thank the timeless style of singer Lena Horne. This name is experiencing a huge revival in Europe and is worthy of the same in the U.S.
In the World: Entertainer Lena Horne; actress Lena Headey; filmmaker Lena Dunham

Leona (lee-OH-nə)   1905: #69
Popularity: #929
Styles: Ladies and Gentlemen
Nicknames: Lee, Leonie
Variants: Léonie   1880   Today

Sisters: Adele, Louisa, Flora, Estelle, Iona, Vera
Brothers: Rudolph, Emil, Willis, Clifford, Luther, Gilbert
✶ If you love old-fashioned names, here's one that still has its full antique style. Leona is a slow-paced name, not exactly fashionable but warm and handsome. The variation Leonie is currently hot in France and Germany.
In the World: Singer Leona Lewis; notorious businesswoman Leona Helmsley

Leora (lay-OHR-ə)   1904: #354
Popularity: #2694
Styles: Ladies and
Gentlemen, Jewish, Why
Not?   1880   Today

Variants: Liora
Sisters: Delia, Adela, Geneva, Flora, Iona, Cleo, Viola, Shira
Brothers: Julius, Asa, Theo, August, Reuben, Asher, Emmett, Solomon
✶ Leora means light, and it glowed brightly in the 19th century. The name then quietly disappeared, though it does pop up today as a modern Hebrew name.

Leslie (LEHZ-lee, LEHS-lee)   1969: #64
Popularity: #245
Styles: New Classics, Celtic,
Androgynous, Nickname-
Proof   1880   Today

Variants: Lesley
Sisters: Hilary, Dana, Erin, Meredith, Kerry, Melanie
Brothers: Keith, Brendan, Ian, Garrett, Mark, Craig
✶ Leslie has had nine lives. Initially a Scottish surname, it crossed over to become a male first name. In the '50s, it caught on as a girl's name with other peppy choices like Cindy and Denise. Today the old Scottish surname roots are driving its popularity once more. In Australia this spelling remains mostly masculine, while Lesley is feminine.
In the World: Actresses Leslie Caron, Leslie Mann, Leslie Uggams, Leslie Bibb, and Lesley Ann Warren; singer Lesley Gore

Leticia (leh-TEE-shə)   1976: #232
Popularity: #1369
Styles: Lacy and Lissome,
African-American, Latino/
Latina   1880   Today
Nicknames: Tish, Tisha, Letty, Leti
Variants: Letitia, Latisha, Laetitia, Laticia, Lettice
Sisters: Felicia, Roxanna, Esmeralda, Angelica, Silvia, Larissa
Brothers: Demetrius, Rolando, Cedric, Lamont, Hector, Armando
✶ One pronunciation gives you a whole spectrum of names. At one end is Laetitia: archaic, Roman, and white. At the other end, Latisha: modern, American, and black. Nestled in the middle is Leticia, an international spelling with broad appeal.
In the World: Etiquette expert Letitia Baldrige; model/actress Laetitia Casta; actress Leticia Calderón

Lexi (LEK-see)   2010: #241
Popularity: #253
Styles: Nicknames
Sisters: Cassie, Ava, Abby,
Nika, Tessa, Demi   1880   Today
Brothers: Noah, Tanner, Will, Xander, Drew, Quinn
✶ When you look at the graph of the name Lexi, pay attention to the timeline more than the raw numbers. There are far more Lexis with the given name Alexis, Alexandra, Alexa, etc., than "just Lexi." If you're torn between Lexi and Alex for your daughter's nickname, Alex gets higher ratings from my readers for sounding smart and strong, Lexi for sounding young, friendly, and sexy.
In the World: Golfer Lexi Thompson

Lia (LEE-ə) 2010: #356
Popularity: #378
Styles: Nicknames, Short and Sweet, Italian
Variants: Lía, Léa, Leah 1880 Today
Sisters: Kira, Holly, Lana, Liv, Ali, Mila
Brothers: Evan, Logan, Eli, Matteo, Nico, Abel
★A name is both a sound and a visual image. You can pronounce Leah and Lia the same, but the image makes a world of difference. Where Leah is a gentle antique, Lia looks global and contemporary. It's heard in many languages, either on its own (as a local form of Leah) or as a nickname for any name with the letters "lia."
In the World: Radio host Lia Knight of *The Lia Show*

Líadan (LEE-ə-din, LEE-din) 2010: #11,158
Popularity: #15,844
Styles: Celtic, The "-ens"
Nicknames: Lee
Variants: Líadáin 1880 Today
Sisters: Rhian, Sibhan, Aisling, Niamh, Aoife, Grainne
Brothers: Cillian, Niall, Oisin, Colm, Ruari, Finian, Lorcan
★Americans love Irish names, yet few of Ireland's Gaelic favorites make it across the ocean. The reason: spelling. We're scared off by treats like Caoimhe (KEE-və) and Sadhbh (SIYV). Líadan is one old, traditional Irish name that shouldn't spark too much terror in English speakers.

Libby (LI-bee) 2010: #797
Popularity: #922
Styles: Guys and Dolls, Nicknames
Variants: Liddy 1880 Today
Sisters: Tillie, Clara, Abby, Tess, Evie, Liza, Maggie
Brothers: Sam, Ned, Henry, Rollo, Harvey, Nate, Joe
★Libby is an age-old nickname, which oddly enough makes it sound new. Today's nicknames are usually trimmed straight from the front of the name. In centuries past, though, nicknames took on shapes all their own, like Peggy for Margaret. Libby makes a pleasantly individual form of Elizabeth or Isabel.
In the World: Libby's foods; swimmer Libby Trickett

Liberty (LI-ber-tee) 2004: #410
Popularity: #568
Styles: Modern Meanings, Country and Western
Nicknames: Libby 1880 Today
Sisters: Harmony, Faith, Serenity, America, Sierra, Journey
Brothers: Justice, Phoenix, Lincoln, Sawyer, Chance, River
★This meaning name surfaces at historical moments when Americans contemplate their freedoms. Lots of little Liberties were born at the end of World War I, during the 1976 bicentennial celebration, and again in the wake of the 9/11 attacks. With the modern fashion for positive meaning names like Destiny and Serenity, Liberty now works as both a philosophical statement and a style statement.
In the World: Liberty Bell; Statue of Liberty; the phrase "Life, Liberty, and the Pursuit of Happiness"

Lila (LIY-lə) 1930: #170
Popularity: #163
Styles: Short and Sweet, Antique Charm, Nickname-Proof 1880 Today
Variants: Lyla, Lilah
Sisters: Eva, Zoe, Ella, Violet, Naomi, Ivy
Brothers: Jack, Emmett, Eli, Leo, Grady, Jasper
★Lila is a name you want to say tenderly. It's simple and old-fashioned, yet seductive. It was sadly neglected for decades but has recently shot back into style. The variant spelling Lilah is rising just as fast, propelled by the biblical aura of the (unrelated) name Delilah. See also Leila.
In the World: Singer Lila Downs; daughter of model Kate Moss

Lilia (LIL-ee-ə) 2011: #859
Popularity: #859
Styles: Lacy and Lissome, Slavic, Latino/Latina, Why Not? 1880 Today
Nicknames: Lil
Variants: Lília, Lilya, Liliya, Lillia
Sisters: Dania, Mariela, Anya, Ariela, Malin, Noelia, Mila, Katia
Brothers: Lukas, Maxim, Ari, Adriel, Viktor, Emilio, Dimitri, Mateo
★Lilia is a stylish twist on the familiar. It's the Russian form of Lily, with a sound that's universally feminine. Be prepared for English speakers to accidentally add an "-n" to the end.
In the World: TV journalist Lilia Luciano

Liliana (li-lee-AH-nə, li-lee-A-nə) 2011: #115
Popularity: #115
Styles: Lacy and Lissome, Latino/Latina, Italian
Nicknames: Lili, Lily
Variants: Lilliana, Lilyana, Lilianna
Sisters: Viviana, Luciana, Camila, Sabrina, Natalia, Mariella
Brothers: Marco, Adrian, Vincent, Santiago, Lorenzo, Xavier
★ This form of Lilian is used in most Romance languages and has a gracious style that makes it universal. It strikes a rare balance between creative and traditional. In fact, Liliana could be the solution to a lot of naming dilemmas, especially for parents who worry that Lily is too cute to stand alone but that Lillian is too severe for a little girl.

Lillian (LI-lee-ən) 1898: #10
Popularity: #22
Styles: Antique Charm
Nicknames: Lillie, Lil
Variants: Lilian, Liliana
Sisters: Clara, Violet, Sophia, Madeline, Eleanor, Vivian
Brothers: Henry, Oliver, Everett, Isaac, Maxwell, Samuel
★ A true turn-of-the-century classic. Graceful and dignified, Lillian is the perfect lady—and Lillie gives you a feisty alter ego. If you find that not everyone agrees with this assessment, see the discussion under Eleanor.
In the World: Writer Lillian Hellman; stage star Lillian Russell; catalog merchant Lillian Vernon

Lillie (LI-lee) 1882: #36
Popularity: #467
Styles: Antique Charm, Guys and Dolls, Nicknames
Sisters: Sadie, Annie, Lucy, Stella, Mollie, Ruby
Brothers: Charlie, Leo, Sam, Archie, Harry, Nate
★ Choosing between Lily and Lillie? The sound's the same, but Lily leans sweet and demure while Lillie is more of a live wire. Lillie also gives you the two-for-one option of a classically demure given name (Lillian) with the nickname as a vivacious alter ego.
In the World: Victorian actress/singer Lillie Langtry

Lily (LI-lee) 2011: #15
Popularity: #15
Styles: Charms and Graces, Antique Charm
Nicknames: Lil
Variants: Lillie, Lilly, Lilia
Sisters: Emma, Claire, Violet, Sophie, Chloe, Isabel
Brothers: Charlie, Noah, Luke, Max, Henry, Owen
★ Lily has become the darling of upscale parents. It's lively and delicate, with a classic femininity that doesn't feel forced. The name's antique patina is fading, though, as it grows into its new status as a 21st-century favorite.
In the World: Singer Lily Allen; designer Lilly Pulitzer; actress Lily Collins; Lily Potter, mother of wizard Harry Potter

Linda (LIN-də) 1948: #1
Popularity: #592
Styles: Mid-Century
Nicknames: Lynn, Lindy
Variants: Lynda
Sisters: Sandra, Janet, Donna, Kathy, Susan, Diane
Brothers: Roger, Dennis, Gary, Stephen, Glenn, Alan
★ Linda is legendary in baby naming lore as the first name to pass Mary into the #1 spot. Its heyday is now long past—chances are you're looking up Linda because it's your mom's name rather than a top choice for your baby. But it's still a very pretty name (in fact, it's Spanish for "pretty"), and to your child's generation it will sound sweetly old-fashioned.
In the World: Actresses Linda Evans, Linda Blair, Linda Carter, Linda Lavin, and Linda Cardellini; singer Linda Ronstadt

Linden (LIN-din) 2010: #2887
Popularity: #3231
Styles: The "-ens," Charms and Graces, Androgynous
Nicknames: Lin, Lindy
Sisters: Arden, Calla, Larkin, Ashby, Wren, Bay
Brothers: Tobin, Calder, Shepherd, Birch, Archer, Perrin
★ A linden is a flowering tree. It could be a nature lover's reinterpretation of Linda, just as Laurel is for Laura. It may be mistaken for the unrelated surname Lyndon, as in President Lyndon Johnson.

Lindsay (LIND-zee) 1983: #36
Popularity: #653
Styles: Last Names First,
'70s–'80s
Nicknames: Lin 1880 Today
Variants: Lindsey, Lyndsay,
Lynsey, Linsey
Sisters: Whitney, Courtney, Kristen, Heather,
Hillary, Kelsey
Brothers: Shaun, Wesley, Brandon, Tyler,
Dustin, Travis
✴ In the wake of the '70s *Bionic Woman* icon
Lindsay Wagner, this surname became a standard overnight. While Lindsay's popularity has plummeted, the name is still fashionable in sound and style. Kinsey, Laney, and Ainsley are among the hot new names walking in Lindsay's footsteps.
In the World: Actresses Lindsay Lohan and Lindsay Wagner; tennis player Lindsay Davenport

Linnea (li-NAY-ə, LI-nee-ə) 2006: #1411
Popularity: #1649
Styles: Nordic, Exotic
Traditional, Lacy and
Lissome, Why Not? 1880 Today
Nicknames: Linn, Nea
Variants: Linnéa, Linnaea
Sisters: Elsa, Astrid, Lavinia, Elina, Britta,
Ronia
Brothers: Leif, Anders, Elias, Magnus, Aric,
Soren
✴ This Swedish classic is pretty and serious, an attractive combination that should appeal far beyond its Scandinavian base. It even has both pretty and serious roots: the name is taken from a flower native to Sweden, which in turn was named for the great botanist Carl Linnaeus.

Lisa (LEE-sə) 1965: #1
Popularity: #703
Styles: Surfer '60s,
Nickname-Proof
Variants: Liza, Leesa, Elisa 1880 Today
Sisters: Amy, Robin, Julie,
Beth, Teresa, Jill
Brothers: David, Jon, Kevin, Todd, Jeffrey,
Chris
✴ Lisa was the #1 girl's name of the 1960s. Unlike girlfriends like Lori and Tina, though, it's not trapped in that era. Lisa is a classic with plenty of history: it was a common name for girls back in Renaissance Florence (think "Mona Lisa"). It's not trendy right now, but clean and faultless.
In the World: Actresses Lisa Kudrow and Lisa Bonet; singers Lisa Marie Presley and Lisa Loeb; cartoon daughter Lisa Simpson

Lise (LEEZ, LEES, LEE-zə) 1959: #814
Popularity: Very rare
Styles: Brisk and Breezy,
French, Nordic, Why Not?
Variants: Lisette 1880 Today
Sisters: Britt, Maia, Sylvie,
Claire, Linnea, Marin
Brothers: Soren, Rune, Brice, Karl, Stellan,
Niels
✴ This international form of Lisa is disarmingly simple and uncommon. It gives you a fresh sound with traditional roots. The exact pronunciation is up to you.
In the World: Physicist Lise Meitner; Lise Charmel lingerie

Liv (LIV) 2011: #953
Popularity: #956
Styles: Nicknames, Nordic,
Short and Sweet
Sisters: Siri, Maja, Lise, Alva, 1880 Today
Tove, Elin, Malin, Britt
Brothers: Finn, Kai, Leif, Axel, Nils, Stefan,
Mio, Anton
✴ When is a nickname not a nickname? When it's a Scandinavian classic on its own. Liv has been a girl's name since the days of the Vikings. It also means "life" in Swedish, Danish, and Norwegian. Nonetheless, you should be prepared for the constant question: "Is that short for Olivia?"
In the World: Actresses Liv Tyler and Liv Ullmann

Livia (LIV-ee-ə)   2011: #751
Popularity: #751
Styles: Lacy and Lissome,
Classical, Italian
Nicknames: Liv   1880   Today
Sisters: Cassia, Dania, Sofia,
Anika, Eleni, Serena, Sylvie, Melia
Brothers: Marius, Tobin, Dario, Anders, Eliot,
Trajan, Nico, Bram
★ No, it's not just a headless version of Olivia.
The name Livia goes back millennia; it was the
the name of a powerful empress of Rome. Stylis-
tically, it's a perfect balance of trim and roman-
tic, classic and contemporary. It's a hit in
Northern Europe and attractive around the
globe. But okay, yes, a lot of people will think it's
just a headless Olivia. Sorry about that.
In the World: Livia Drusilla, wife of Augustus;
popular in Scandinavia, where Liv is a traditional full name

Liviana (li-vee-AHN-ə)   2010: #4688
Popularity: #4967
Styles: Lacy and Lissome,
Classical, Why Not?
Nicknames: Liv, Livvi, Vivi   1880   Today
Sisters: Laelia, Avila, Aemilia,
Sephora, Artemisia, Raphaela
Brothers: Evander, Severin, Florian, Piers,
Aeneas, Calix
★ Is this you? You don't like "made-up" names.
You want your daughter's name to be traditional
and serious, something that will command re-
spect. But deep down, you're a sucker for lace
and frills and you can't wait until her hair is
long enough to do up in ribbons. It's okay, you
can have it both ways. Liviana dates all the way
back to ancient Rome—and the nicknames are
cute too.
In the World: Designer Liviana Conti

Liza (LIY-zə)   1973: #392
Popularity: #1947
Styles: '70s–'80s, Nicknames,
Guys and Dolls
Sisters: Evie, Nell, Corrie,   1880   Today
Reva, Ella, Roxie
Brothers: Cal, Luke, Charley, Miles, Beau,
Colt
★ Entertainer Liza Minelli singlehandedly res-
cued this Elizabeth variant from the dustbin,
and she's done us all a favor. Liza is cute and
confident, a terrific combination. If it feels a
generation behind to you, try thinking of it as
Lila with a "z."
In the World: Entertainer Liza Minelli; song
"Li'l Liza Jane"; actress Liza Weil

Lizbeth (LIZ-behth)   2002: #133
Popularity: #540
Styles: Nicknames, Latino/
Latina
Nicknames: Liz   1880   Today
Variants: Lisbeth, Lizeth,
Lizabeth, Elspeth
Sisters: Katrine, Astrid, Sherlyn, Lotte, Frida,
Lizette
Brothers: Gunnar, Leonel, Aldo, Soren, Bram,
Marcos
★ This contracted name cleverly splits the dif-
ference between the formality of Elizabeth and
the plainness of Liz. It was a 2000s favorite, es-
pecially in Latino families. More recently, the
Germanic "s" spelling has become familiar,
thanks to Lisbeth Salander, the Girl with the
Dragon Tattoo. Elspeth is a similar Scottish
contraction.
In the World: Lisbeth Salander of *The Girl with
the Dragon Tattoo*; actress Lizbeth MacKay

Logan (LOH-gən)   1996: #257
Popularity: #524
Styles: Last Names First,
Androgynous, Celtic
Sisters: Kendall, Reilly,   1880   Today
Cameron, Bailey, Rowan,
Tegan
Brothers: Hudson, Cooper, Reid, Kendrick,
Brogan, Kane
★ Logan sounds so virile on a boy that it's a sur-
prise that it works well for girls too. The models
are Morgan and Jordan, which set the stage for
this whole name style. It also helped that a char-
acter on the soap opera *The Bold and the Beauti-
ful* was referred to by her last name, Logan.
In the World: Actress Logan Browning; Brooke
Logan of *The Bold and the Beautiful*

Lois (LOH-is)   1929: #17
Popularity: #2612
Styles: Solid Citizens,
Biblical
Sisters: Rita, Marjorie, Avis,   1880   Today
Gloria, Rhoda, June
Brothers: Lionel, Roy, Hal, Gordon, Lyle,
Clyde
✷ It's a long shot, but here's hoping Lois makes
a reappearance. Right now the name sounds
like a nosy old neighbor kibbitzing over a back-
yard fence. But think about the ageless zest of
Lois Lane, tracking down Superman! Better
yet, think of Lois as a trim little biblical classic
that hasn't been heard in years. Or fire up your
competitive spirit: British parents have already
rediscovered this name. Do you want to fall behind?
In the World: Lois Lane of *Superman;* comic
strip *Hi and Lois;* writer Lois Lowry

Lola (LOH-la)   1904: #99
Popularity: #243
Styles: Guys and Dolls
Sisters: Mae, Cleo, Georgia,
Rubi, Kiki, Roxie   1880   Today
Brothers: Alonzo, Max,
Oscar, Ike, Leo, Rocco
✷ It's Lolita, all grown up! Lola has that same
dangerous sensuality, but she's a strong, mature
woman who knows what she wants—and is
going to have fun getting it. That's old-fash-
ioned grrl power. In song, a Lola is in-your-face
feminine: "Whatever Lola wants, Lola gets";
"Her name was Lola, she was a showgirl"; and
the Kinks' not-quite-feminine "lo-lo-lo-lo Lola."
In the World: Dancer Lola Folana; the many
Lola songs; a hot name for Hollywood babies

London (LUHN-dən)   2011: #94
Popularity: #94
Styles: The "-ens,"
Androgynous, Place Names
Variants: Londyn   1880   Today
Sisters: Haven, Brooklyn,
Paris, Jasmine, Aspen, Quinn
Brothers: Kingston, Lexington, Maddox,
Jagger, Paxton, Grayson
✷ This place name has a breezy, fashionable
sound that's just a bit glitzy. It's a natural alter-
native to Paris for parents who feel that name
has been a tad overexposed. London is used for
both boys and girls; as a boy's name, it's a little
more playful, a little less showy.
In the World: All things London, England; Lon-
don Tipton of *The Suite Life of Zack and Cody*

Lorelei (LOH-rə-liy)   2011: #499
Popularity: #499
Styles: Exotic Traditional,
Mythological, Why Not?
Nicknames: Lori, Rory, Lolo   1880   Today
Variants: Lorelai
Sisters: Evangeline, Penelope, Aurora, Violet,
Ariadne, Paloma
Brothers: Evander, Roman, Japheth, Atticus,
Gideon, Bram
✷ In old German legend, Lorelei was a beauti-
ful siren who lured sailors onto the rocky banks
of the Rhine. In *Gentlemen Prefer Blondes,* Lo-
relei was Marilyn Monroe, and the risky rocks
were diamonds. In the TV show *Gilmore Girls,*
the perils were rocky relationships. That last
Lorelai—spelled Lorelai—has finally brought
some attention to this neglected classic.
In the World: Lorelai of *Gilmore Girls;* Lorelei
Lee of *Gentlemen Prefer Blondes* (and a porn
star named for her)

Loretta (loh-REH-tə)   1938: #62
Popularity: #1877
Styles: Solid Citizens
Nicknames: Lori, Etta
Sisters: Roberta, Jeanette,   1880   Today
Dorothy, Maxine, Ramona,
Pauline
Brothers: Wallace, Marvin, Gordon, Lyle,
Wendell, Franklin
✷ In the '30s, this name sounded lush and
womanly, like actress Loretta Young. Our movie
stars are skinnier and more girlish today, and the
name is out of style.
In the World: Singer Loretta Lynn; actresses Lo-
retta Young, Loretta Swit, and Loretta Devine

Lori (LOH-ree)   1963: #8
Popularity: #1765
Styles: Surfer '60s
Variants: Laurie, Lorri
Sisters: Tina, Cindy, Beth,   1880   Today
Marcy, Lisa, Jill, Tracy, Jodi
Brothers: Jeff, Greg, Chris, Randy, Tim, Scott,
Robbie, Ken
✷ This nickname was a top-20 smash in the
'60s. It is now completely out of the picture, as
today's parents are making the root Laura lon-
ger (Lauren, Laurel) rather than shorter.
In the World: Actress Lori Loughlin; perfor-
mance artist Laurie Anderson

Lorraine (loh-RAYN)　　　1928: #39
Popularity: #1860
Styles: Solid Citizens, Place
Names
Nicknames: Lori, Rain　　1880　Today
Variants: Loraine
Sisters: Constance, Marjorie, Pauline,
Rosemary, Beverly, Therese
Brothers: Gene, Franklin, Vernon, Clifford,
Lionel, Stanton
✳ Lorraine comes from the name of a French
province (the one thing it has in common with
Brittany). You won't meet many young Lor-
raines, but the name's still worth a look. When
your daughter's an artsy 15-year-old, she'll love
the chance to adopt the nickname Rain.
In the World: Playwright Lorraine Hansberry;
actress Lorraine Bracco; quiche lorraine

Lottie (LAWT-ee)　　　1883: #76
Popularity: #3944
Styles: Guys and Dolls,
Nicknames
Variants: Lotte, Lotty　　1880　Today
Sisters: Belle, Ruby, Stella,
Tessie, Lillie, Thea
Brothers: Archie, Ike, Gus, Charley, Otto, Abe
✳ This bubbly nickname paints a lovable pic-
ture of a young girl. Today it's a bit too cute to
stand on its own but charming as an everyday
nickname. The usual full name is Charlotte;
you can also consider Lieselotte or simply Lotte,
a common full name in Scandinavia and the
Netherlands.
In the World: A hot name in the U.K.; model
Lottie Moss

Louisa (loo-EE-zə)　　　1881: #119
Popularity: #1225
Styles: Ladies and
Gentlemen, Saints, Literary
and Artistic, Why Not?　　1880　Today
Nicknames: Lou, Lulu
Variants: Lovisa, Louise, Luisa
Sisters: Josefa, Adela, Eleanor, Charlotte,
Georgia, Estella
Brothers: Conrad, Jules, Hugh, Foster,
Edmund, Emerson
✳ Louisa has always been a quiet shadow of the
French Louise. Today it's the version with all
the potential. Louisa's ladylike rhythm lightens
its rich sound and sets it up well for the 21st cen-
tury. The impression is of old-fashioned warmth
with intelligence, personified by *Little Women*
author Louisa May Alcott.
In the World: Writer Louisa May Alcott

Louise (loo-EEZ)　　　1912: #17
Popularity: #1698
Styles: Ladies and
Gentlemen, French,
Nicknames: Lou, Lulu　　1880　Today
Variants: Luise, Louisa
Sisters: Marion, Lucille, Frances, Harriet,
Estelle, Lenore
Brothers: Claude, Harvey, Luther, Albert,
Ernest, Arthur
✳ During the long and dignified life of Louise,
the name lost its continental elegance and set-
tled into a cozy matronliness. It still has an old-
fashioned charm but would be a retro choice in
the U.S. today. In the U.K., though, the name is
back in every guise: Louise and Louisa, the
similar-sounding Eloise, and even compound
names like Ella-Louise.
In the World: Louise of the sitcom *The Jeffer-
sons;* film *Thelma and Louise;* actresses Louise
Brooks and Louise Fletcher

Lourdes (LOOR-dəs,　　　1968: #554
LUWRDZ)
Popularity: #1832
Styles: Latino/Latina, Exotic
Traditional　　1880　Today
Nicknames: Lulu, Lola
Sisters: Rosario, Silvia, Milagros, Pilar,
Soledad, Luz
Brothers: Salvador, Cruz, Manuel, Nestor,
Domingo, Santos
✳ Lourdes, France, was the site of a famous ap-
parition of the Virgin Mary. Like many names
associated with the Virgin, it has been most
popular in Spanish. The unusual rhythm of
Lourdes makes it a particularly unconventional
choice.
In the World: Lourdes Leon, daughter of singer
Madonna

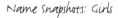

Lucia (loo-SEE-ə , LOO-shə, 2011: #242
loo-CHEE-ə)
Popularity: #242
Styles: Timeless, Italian,
Saints 1880 Today
Nicknames: Lucy, Lu, Lulu,
Lux
Variants: Lucy, Luce
Sisters: Eva, Clara, Sofia, Emilia, Luna,
Camilla
Brothers: Julian, Ezra, Roman, Elliot, Carlo,
Jonas
✳ Lucia has a swinging international style and
cute, trendy nicknames. That's two great names
for the price of one, name shoppers! What's
more, the name comes in a fashionable array of
pronunciations. All three listed are traditional;
the Spanish "loo-SEE-ə" is currently the most
popular. (It's red-hot in Spain too.)
In the World: Entertainer Lucía Méndez; opera
Lucia di Lammermoor

Lucille (loo-SEEL) 1915: #29
Popularity: #455
Styles: Ladies and
Gentlemen, French, Country
and Western 1880 Today
Nicknames: Lucy
Variants: Lucile, Lucilla, Lucia
Sisters: Estelle, Leonor, Sylvia, Irene, Clarice,
Virginia
Brothers: Maurice, Earl, Clarence, Eugene,
Luther, Roy
✳ Thanks to comedian Lucille Ball, we tend to
picture this name in the '40s and '50s. In fact,
Lucille's day was largely past by that point. The
name belongs to the earlier age of Estelle and
Eleanor—she's their brassy Southern cousin,
come to shake things up a little.
In the World: Comedian Lucille Ball; poet Lu-
cille Clifton; blues guitarist B. B. King's nick-
name for his guitars

Lucinda (loo-SIN-də) 1881: #153
Popularity: #1385
Styles: Mid-Century
Nicknames: Lucy, Cindy,
Cinda 1880 Today
Variants: Lucia
Sisters: Estella, Susannah, Josephine, Georgia,
Rosalind, Louisa
Brothers: Randolph, Dwight, Luther, Fletcher,
Stewart, Willis
✳ Lucinda is an old literary offshoot of Lucia,
used by Cervantes and Molière. It sounds a little
bit heavy today, but lovely Lucy lightens it right
up. Singer Lucinda Williams adds a honky-tonk
edge.
In the World: Singer Lucinda Williams; film
Oscar and Lucinda

Lucy (LOO-see) 1881: #44
Popularity: #72
Styles: Antique Charm, Guys
and Dolls
Variants: Lucie, Lucia 1880 Today
Sisters: Ruby, Ella, Sadie,
Gracie, Lena, Stella, Alice, Molly
Brothers: Leo, Sam, Oscar, Charlie, Max, Jack,
Henry, Oliver
✳ Lucy's a stealth U.S. hit among affluent,
trendsetting urbanites who appreciate the
name's sweetness and lack of pretension. In the
rest of the world, forget stealth: Lucy (or Lucie)
is a smash everywhere from New Zealand to
France to Scotland to the Czech Republic.
Lucy is a traditional full name, but if you prefer
it as a nickname, consider Lucinda, Lucia, or
Luciana.
In the World: Sitcom *I Love Lucy*; Lucy Van Pelt
of comic strip *Peanuts*; Beatles song "Lucy in
the Sky with Diamonds"

Luna (LOO-nə)   2011: #278
Popularity: #278
Styles: Short and Sweet,
Mythological, Antique
Charm   1880   Today
Sisters: Isla, Lyra, Ivy,
Daphne, Stella, Aurora, Zara, Maia
Brothers: Jasper, Miles, Leo, Wolf, Liam, Jules,
Ronan, Orion
✳ Misty, magical Luna is the goddess of the
moon. That's a voluptuous image, yet the name
is just four little letters with a modest sound.
This name has enormous potential, but the
Luna who has raised the name's profile may also
be a drawback: "Harry Potter" character Luna
Lovegood, occasionally known as Looney.
In the World: Luna Lovegood of the "Harry Pot-
ter" series; Luna energy bars; a hot name in
French-speaking countries

Luz (LOOS)   1999: #463
Popularity: #870
Styles: Latino/Latina, Short
and Sweet
Nicknames: Lucha   1880   Today
Sisters: Rocío, Sol, Ana,
Esperanza, Camila, Perla, Carmen, Paz
Brothers: Mario, Omar, Salvador, Pablo, Javier,
Victor, Rafael, Luis
✳ The Spanish word for "light" makes a deli-
cate, airy classic. It became a name via the Vir-
gin Mary title Nuestra Señora de la Luz ("Our
Lady of Light"). The only thing holding it back
from broader English use is that it sounds like
the word "loose."
In the World: Actresses Luz Elena González
and Luz María Aguilar

Lydia (LI-dee-ə)   1883: #75
Popularity: #96
Styles: Timeless, Biblical,
Antique Charm, Classical
Nicknames: Liddy, Lida   1880   Today
Variants: Lidia
Sisters: Julia, Cecilia, Grace, Eliza, Phoebe,
Clara
Brothers: Henry, Simon, Oliver, Harrison,
Samuel, Leo
✳ Lydia is an elegant classic with ancient ori-
gins but a light touch. It is increasingly fashion-
able, but still a long way from overused. Your
grandparents may grumble about the song
"Lydia the Tattooed Lady," but that will mean
nothing to your daughter's classmates. (Besides,
tattooed ladies are cool now, right?)
In the World: TV chef Lidia Bastianich; actress
Lydia Cornell; song "Lydia the Tattooed Lady"

Lynn (LIN)   1956: #58
Popularity: #1861
Styles: Mid-Century, Surfer
'60s, Brisk and Breezy
Variants: Lynne, Lyn   1880   Today
Sisters: Jill, Beth, Cathy,
Diane, Lisa, Gail, Dana, Jan
Brothers: Alan, Dean, Troy, Gary, Tim, Jon,
Scott, Mark
✳ Lynn was a mid-century mainstay, a boyish
counterpart to Linda. It's uncommon on its own
today, but is still part of the sound of the times
thanks to hits like Brooklynn and Ashlynn. For
first-name options that stand alone, Lynn's
sound is echoed in the Welsh names Brynn and
Wynne.
In the World: Actresses Lynn Redgrave, Lynn
Whitfield, and Lynn Collins

Lyra (LIY-rə)   2011: #1028
Popularity: #1030
Styles: Short and Sweet,
Fantastical, Nickname-Proof,
Why Not?   1880   Today
Sisters: Arya, Esme, Elodie,
Zara, Briar, Vega
Brothers: Triton, Nico, Sirius, Caspian, Leo,
Axel
✳ The constellation Lyra, the lyre, makes for a
light, artistic name. It may be most familiar as
the name of the heroine of *The Golden Com-
pass*, but the name isn't dominated by that as-
sociation.
In the World: Lyra Belacqua of *The Golden
Compass*

Lyric (LEE-rik)   2011: #325
Popularity: #325
Styles: Modern Meanings,
Fanciful, African-American
Sisters: Cadence, Aria,   1880   Today
Phoenix, Justice, Indigo,
Journey
Brothers: Jett, Orion, Tyme, Falcon, Quill,
Chance
✳ Lyric is a bit self-conscious as a name, but its
intensity and verve are undeniable. Unlike most
names lifted from the world of music (Melody,
Harmony), this name is no marshmallow. It's
pretty but tough, and utterly modern. Its exact
date of birth is 1994, in the film *Jason's Lyric*.
In the World: Film *Jason's Lyric*

Mabel (MAY-bəl) 1891: #15
Popularity: #1226
Styles: Guys and Dolls
Nicknames: May, Mabs
Variants: Maybelle, Mable 1880 Today
Sisters: Pearl, Sadie, Della,
Ida, Alice, Nell
Brothers: Otto, Mack, Major, Archie, Harry,
Roscoe
✴ If you're seriously considering Mabel, I don't
have to tell you that it hasn't been heard from in
half a century. Or that it sounds to many people
like a sassy diner waitress from a Technicolor
film. If you're considering Mabel, you know all
that and you like it. You see the sweetness be-
hind the sass, and you hear the name's contemporary sound. You're starting to have company,
especially in the U.K.
In the World: Silent film star Mabel Normand; a
daughter of actor Bruce Willis

Mackenzie (mə-KEHN-zee) 2001: #40
Popularity: #68
Styles: Last Names First,
Androgynous, Celtic
Nicknames: Kenzie 1880 Today
Variants: McKenzie,
Makenzie
Sisters: Delaney, Madison, Camryn, Kennedy,
Riley, Kerrigan
Brothers: Carson, Spencer, Donovan, Brennan,
Connor, Jackson
✴ Mackenzie Phillips, sitcom star of the '70s,
was named by her rock-star dad John in honor of
singer Scott McKenzie. It was an unconven-
tional, aggressively androgynous choice at the
time. A generation later, the name is thriving in
the mainstream. It's the standard-bearer for a
whole crop of elaborate Celtic surnames for
girls.
In the World: Actresses Mackenzie Phillips,
Mackenzie Foy, and Mackenzie Rosman

Macy (MAY-see) 2003: #219
Popularity: #295
Styles: Last Names First,
Short and Sweet, Bell Tones
Variants: Macey, Macie, 1880 Today
Maci
Sisters: Kiley, Logan, Eden, Delaney, Tatum,
Mckenna, Haley, Emery
Brothers: Payton, Colby, Keaton, Lane, Tate,
Brennan, Tucker, Easton
✴ Macy is the newest member of the girls' sur-
name family that includes Tracy, Lacey, and
Stacy. It is by far the most contemporary of the
group, with a tough edge that the others can't
match. The alternate spelling Maci was popu-
larized by a star of the reality series Teen Mom.
In the World: Macy's department stores; singer
Macy Gray; Maci Bookout of Teen Mom

Maddie (MA-dee) 2009: #1160
Popularity: #1286
Styles: Nicknames
Variants: Maddy
Sisters: Carlie, Emmy, Chloe, 1880 Today
Bree, Abby, Molly
Brothers: Cole, Bryce, Liam, Carter, Mason,
Jake
✴ Madeline too old-fashioned? Madison too
trendy? Some parents are skipping the choice
and going straight for the nickname. It's full of
charm, but be sure you really want your daugh-
ter to be "just Maddie" for life. (You're not just
wimping out on the full name decision . . .
right?)
In the World: A daughter of singer Jamie-Lynn
Spears; Maddie Hayes of TV show Moonlight-
ing

Madeline (MA-də-lin, MA-də-liyn)   1998: #50
Popularity: #85
Styles: Antique Charm, Literary and Artistic
1880   Today
Nicknames: Maddy
Variants: Madeleine, Madalyn, Madelynn, Maddalena
Sisters: Isabel, Caroline, Annalise, Claire, Abigail, Charlotte, Juliet, Annabelle
Brothers: Maxwell, Owen, Caleb, Carson, Oliver, Nathaniel, Samuel, Alexander
✳ Madeline is a classic that still sounds charmingly old-fashioned, even though it's more popular in the 21st century than ever before. Ludwig Bemelmans's beloved children's books helped fuel the vogue for the name. Note that a little Maddy risks confusion with Madisons on the playground.
In the World: Picture book *Madeline*; diplomat Madeleine Albright; author Madeleine L'Engle; actress Madeline Zima

Madison (MA-di-sən)   2001: #2
Popularity: #8
Styles: Last Names First, The "-ens," Place Names
1880   Today
Nicknames: Maddie
Variants: Maddison, Madisen, Madisyn, Madyson
Sisters: Taylor, Mckenzie, Brooklyn, Morgan, Hailey, Peyton
Brothers: Mason, Austin, Tyler, Dylan, Hunter, Logan
✳ When the mermaid in the 1984 movie *Splash* chose this name from a Manhattan street sign, it was a big joke. But it seems the film's youngest fans weren't laughing—they were taking notes. A decade later, Madison was a rising star on its way to the top of the charts. It hits a trendy trifecta of place name, presidential surname, and androgyny, all with a traditional girl's nickname.
In the World: President James Madison; Madison of *Splash*; actress Madison Pettis

Madigan (MA-di-gehn)   2002: #2374
Popularity: #3856
Styles: Last Names First, Celtic, Androgynous, Why Not?
1880   Today
Nicknames: Maddie
Sisters: Mirren, Lanigan, Connolly, Sheridan, Marlowe, Larkin
Brothers: Callahan, Riordan, Flynn, Quinlan, Brannigan, Carrick
✳ Nestled between favorites Madeline and Madison lies this name that you'd never even considered. Finding yourself tempted? The Irish "-gan" names are a great place to look for unexpected alternatives to the popular "-son" surnames. Like Madigan, many of them trim down to comfy nicknames. Try Carrigan, Merrigan, Kerrigan, or Lanigan.

Madonna (mah-DAHN-ə)   1933: #536
Popularity: #15,915
Styles: Fanciful
Nicknames: Maddie, Madge, Donna
1880   Today
Sisters: Assunta, Santina, Grazia, Domenica, Loreto, Annunziata
Brothers: Fortunato, Celestino, Pasquale, Primo, Angelo, Salvatore
✳ Want proof positive that it takes more than just celebrity to launch a celebrity baby name? Over the past generation, there has been no bigger star than Madonna. Her name? Forget about it. The name that sounds so flamboyant on the singer is really a reverent but old-fashioned Catholic name, 75 years past its prime time.
In the World: Appellation of the Virgin Mary; singer Madonna; song "Lady Madonna"

Mae (MAY) 1892: #52
Popularity: #803
Styles: Guys and Dolls,
Charms and Graces, Country
and Western, Why Not? 1880 Today
Variants: May
Sisters: Pearle, Belle, Flora, Bess, Nellie, Cleo
Brothers: Archie, Mack, Gus, Fletcher, Roy,
Reuben
✴ Read the entry for May, then crank up the
volume a notch for the spirit of Mae West, the
brassiest dame of them all. This attractive spell-
ing was the dominant one in the 1800s and
could be again today.
In the World: Entertainer Mae West; astronaut
Mae Jemison; actress Mae Whitman

Maëlle (MAH-ehl) 2010: #3223
Popularity: #4850
Styles: French, Celtic, Why
Not?
Variants: Maelle, Maëlys 1880 Today
Sisters: Axelle, Lilou, Eliane,
Maite, Amelie, Sabine
Brothers: Bastien, Mathis, Blaise, Fabien,
Yannick, Olivier
✴ A fashionable hit in France, Maëlle has yet
to find its way to the United States. It will inspire
a lot of mispronunciations, but also a lot of oohs
and aahs. If you're looking for new Celtic op-
tions, this is actually a Breton name, a form of
the Celtic men's name Mael.

Maeve (MAYV) 2010: #535
Popularity: #590
Styles: Celtic, Brisk and
Breezy, Why Not?
Variants: Méabh, Medb 1880 Today
Sisters: Fiona, Niamh, Nora,
Brynn, Aine, Shea
Brothers: Finn, Declan, Teague, Ronan,
Ciaran, Niall
✴ Here's a strong, classic, and intensely Irish
name. Think of it as the Celtic Claire, with all
of that name's gentle seriousness. Maeve is an
ancient name (from a legendary Irish warrior
queen), but it's only now catching on in elite
pockets of the U.S.
In the World: Writer Maeve Binchy

Maggie (MA-gee) 1880: #46
Popularity: #228
Styles: Nicknames, Timeless
Nicknames: Mags
Variants: Margie 1880 Today
Sisters: Callie, Josie, Ellie,
Sadie, Kate, Abby, Lizzie, Annie
Brothers: Ben, Charlie, Jack, Sam, Max, Will,
Andy, Jake
✴ Margaret is as classic as they come, but a lit-
tle bit stern. Maggie, though, is pure sweetness.
As with Annie and Molly, the nickname's fun-
loving style has brought it front and center while
the traditional source is taking a backseat.
In the World: Actresses Maggie Smith, Maggie
Gyllenhaal, and Maggie Grace; song "Maggie
May"; infant Maggie on *The Simpsons*

Magnolia (mag-NOH-lee-ə) 1909: #418
Popularity: #1275
Styles: Charms and Graces,
Country and Western
Nicknames: Maggie, Nola, 1880 Today
Meg
Sisters: Georgia, Winona, Clementine,
Shenandoah, Violet, Carolina
Brothers: Richmond, Furman, Crawford,
Harlan, Raleigh, Houston
✴ If you're a true son or daughter of the South,
this old-fashioned beauty is bound to catch your
eye. It's a bit of a showboat, but simple nick-
names like Maggie and Nola take some of the
pressure off.
In the World: Magnolia blossoms; 1999 film
Magnolia

Maisie (MAY-zee) 2011: #1590
Popularity: #1597
Styles: Celtic, Nicknames
Variants: Mazie, Maisy,
Mayzie 1880 Today
Sisters: Tilly, Sadie, Poppy,
Phoebe, Effie, Pippa, Daisy, Evie
Brothers: Archie, Jamie, Liam, Jay, Charlie,
Fergus, Leo, Alfie
✴ This is a name so impish and cute that you
just want to pinch its cheeks. Maisie is an old
Scottish nickname for Margaret (or the Gaelic
form Mairead) and would make a charming al-
ternative to Maggie. As a full name, it's consid-
ered borderline "cutesy" in the U.S., but
fashionable in the U.K.
In the World: Dr. Seuss book *Daisy-Head
Mayzie*; "Maisy Mouse" picture book series

Maite (MIY-teh, MIY-tay, mah-ee-TEH)   2011: #1016
Popularity: #1018
Styles: Latino/Latina, French, Nicknames   1880 Today
Variants: Maïté
Sisters: Lilou, Giselle, Lizeth, Maricris, Axelle, Ivelisse
Brothers: Josué, Hugo, Rene, Olivier, Nicolas, Mateus
✳ Maite is a contraction of Maria Teresa. It used to be just a nickname, but no more. The trim and stylish Maite is now an established given name around the world. In fact, it's gaining ground even as the classics Maria and Teresa decline. Etymological bonus: *maite* also means "I love" in Basque.
In the World: Mexican actress Maite Perroni; Venezuelan TV host Maite Delgado

Makayla (mah-KAY-lə)   2008: #37
Popularity: #56
Styles: Bell Tones
Nicknames: Kay, Kayla
Variants: Michaela, Makaila,   1880 Today
Mikaela, Mikayla, McKayla
Sisters: Alyssa, Makenzie, Skylar, Madyson, Brianna, Ryleigh
Brothers: Hayden, Tyler, Zane, Kaleb, Jaxon, Kane
✳ Makayla is a creative modern spelling that has far outpaced the traditional Michaela. It's closer in spirit to surnames like Mckenna and innovations like Kaylee
In the World: Olympic gymnast McKayla Maroney

Malaika (mah-LIY-kə)   1972: #1378
Popularity: #2800
Styles: African, African-American, Why Not?
Sisters: Kamaria, Safiya,   1880 Today
Aminata, Naima, Shivani, Rehema
Brothers: Rashid, Dakarai, Sharif, Kiran, Khalid, Rohan
✳ Malaika is a true name of the world. It's the Swahili word for "angel" (from an Arabic root), it's the name of an Indian TV star, and it could catch the eye of the same American parents who are drawn to names like Mikayla.
In the World: Oft-recorded song "Malaika"; model/actress Malaika Arora Khan

Malia (mah-LEE-ə, MAHL-yə, MAH-lee-ə)   2009: #191
Popularity: #314
Styles: Lacy and Lissome, Bell Tones   1880 Today
Nicknames: Lia
Variants: Maleah, Mahlia
Sisters: Kiana, Melina, Leilani, Kamea, Rania, Maile
Brothers: Elias, Kaleo, Myles, Kai, Quinn, Nikos
✳ Presidential daughter Malia Obama introduced this name from her father's native Hawaii to the whole country. Parents quickly fell in love with its sunny poetry. Ms. Obama has also taught us to pronounce Malia on the second syllable: "mah-LEE-ə." The name has other separate origins, though, including a Greek resort town, stressed on the first syllable. Take your pick, but expect the Hawaiian pronunciation to dominate.
In the World: Presidential daughter Malia Obama; surfer/model Malia Jones

Mallory (MA-lə-ree)   1986: #83
Popularity: #290
Styles: Last Names First, Nickname-Proof
Sisters: Jillian, Kelsey, Aubrey,   1880 Today
Meredith, Cassidy, Lindsey
Brothers: Cameron, Bryant, Dalton, Mitchell, Jameson, Jarrett
✳ Mallory was an obscure, mostly male name until the '80s, when its melodious sound and a character on the sitcom *Family Ties* boosted it into the female mainstream. Mallory's classic feminine rhythm has made it a lasting favorite, a middle ground between the old world of Valerie and the new world of Finley and Trinity.
In the World: Mallory of *Family Ties*; model Mallory Snyder

Mara (MAH-rə) 1997: #568
Popularity: #842
Styles: Biblical, Short and
Sweet, Nickname-Proof
Variants: Marah 1880 Today
Sisters: Lena, Brenna, Reese,
Leah, Abigail, Alanna
Brothers: Eli, Nathan, Logan, Owen, Jared,
Asher
✳ Mara came into style in sync with Maya and
Mia, but its personality is quieter and more
timeless. Mara is a biblical name too. Few peo-
ple realize that fact, which may be just as well,
given that in the Bible the name is chosen as a
symbol of a bitter life.
In the World: Actresses Rooney Mara and Mara
Wilson; designer Mara Hoffman

Marcella (mahr-SEH-lə, 1922: #155
mahr-CHEH-lə)
Popularity: #1351
Styles: Italian, Saints, Lacy
and Lissome, Why Not? 1880 Today
Nicknames: Marcie, Markie,
Ella, Chela
Variants: Marcela, Marcelle
Sisters: Marianna, Gabriella, Rosaria, Paula,
Carmella, Antonia
Brothers: Bruno, Salvatore, Marcus, Anthony,
Carlo, Mario
✳ Choose your favorite Marcella: pronounced
"mahr-CHEL-a," it's lavishly Italian and a par-
ticular favorite in Rome. As "mar-SEL-a," it's a
soft-spoken old American favorite. The Spanish
single-"l" spelling tilts the name toward the lat-
ter pronunciation.
In the World: Singer Marcella Detroit; cook-
book author Marcella Hazan

Marcia (MAHR-shə) 1951: #74
Popularity: #3415
Styles: Mid-Century
Nicknames: Marcie
Variants: Marsha 1880 Today
Sisters: Paula, Connie,
Donna, Janice, Glenda, Carol
Brothers: Gerald, Larry, Dwight, Allen, Jerry,
Bruce
✳ Marcia's soft sound made it a mid-century
sweetheart but now sends parents running the
other way. It's a pleasant enough name, just
swimming against the fashion tide. If you're
looking for a trendier way to feminize Mark, try
Marcella.
In the World: Actresses Marcia Cross and Mar-
cia Gay Harden; TV daughter Marcia Brady

Marcy (MAR-see) 1971: #256
Popularity: #5433
Styles: Surfer '60, Nicknames
Variants: Marci, Marcie
Sisters: Trina, Jodi, Shelly, 1880 Today
Ginger, Lori, Cindy
Brothers: Robbie, Kris, Scotty, Greg, Toby,
Kenny
✳ Marcy is one of the youthful '60s names that
belong in an endless summer. That decade
marked a transition point in the name, as a re-
ceding wave of Marcia-called-Marcys met a ris-
ing tide of just-Marcys. Today the name would
be most fashionable as a nickname once again.
Formal options include Martha, Marcella, and
Marceline.
In the World: Marcie of comic strip *Peanuts*;
band Marcy Playground

Maren (MA-rin) 2008: #961
Popularity: #1092
Styles: The "-ens," Nordic,
Why Not?
Variants: Marin 1880 Today
Sisters: Freya, Malin, Linnea,
Rowen, Anika, Liv
Brothers: Soren, Espen, Elias, Anders, Axel,
Torben
✳ Karen was once just a Scandinavian form of
Katherine. Maren is currently just a Scandina-
vian form of Marina, but that could change in
the blink of an eye. It resembles many classic
American girls' names yet sounds fresh and con-
temporary. Note that the stress is on the first syl-
lable, unlike Marin County, California.

Margaret (MAHR-grit)   1916: #4
Popularity: #187
Styles: Ladies and
Gentlemen, Solid Citizens
Nicknames: Meg, Peg,   1880   Today
Margie, Maggie, Madge,
Maisie, Greta, Gretchen, Megan, May, Maj,
Meta
Variants. Margarita, Marguerite, Margit,
Margot, Margret, Margery
Sisters: Catherine, Helen, Mary, Eleanor,
Cecilia, Martha
Brothers: Edward, Charles, Robert, Paul,
Henry, George
✷ Margaret, Katherine, and Elizabeth are the
timeless English trio. They're long but not
showy, with bushels of nickname options to wel-
come your personal touch. Yet unlike her style
sisters, Margaret has been slipping out of notice
the past 40 years. Time to bring on the Maggies!
Or Megs, or Gretas, or Maisies. . . .
In the World: Generations of Margarets, from
British PM Margaret Thatcher to Judy Blume's
Are You There God? It's Me, Margaret

Margarita   1966: #382
(mahr-gah-REE-tah)
Popularity: #1376
Styles: Latino/Latina, Solid
Citizens, Slavic   1880   Today
Nicknames: Rita, Marita,
Marguita
Variants: Margherita, Marguerite, Margaretha
Sisters: Martina, Tania, Angelita, Paulina,
Marcela, Tereza
Brothers: Ivan, Rodolfo, Tomas, Valentin,
Alfonso, Gilberto
✷ Margarita is an old-fashioned classic with a
flirtatious style, ingredients that should add up
to a smash. But if the ingredients that spring to
your mind are tequila and lime, you've hit on
the problem. Here's hoping the name's gracious
style overcomes its alcoholic associations.
In the World: Margarita cocktails; song "Mar-
garitaville"; actress Margarita Levieva

Margo (MAHR-goh)   1951: #295
Popularity: #1997
Styles: Mid-Century,
Nickname-Proof, Why Not?
Variants: Margot, Margaux   1880   Today
Sisters: Janis, Sonja, Gwen,
Candace, Lana, Audra
Brothers: Dana, Vaughn, Dwight, Kip, Russell,
Craig
✷ The unusual "-o" ending gives Margo char-
acter and makes the name virtually trend-proof.
It's one classic that will never get lost in the
crowd. The European spelling Margot can be
pronounced with a silent or spoken "t." Mar-
gaux is a French village and wine appellation.
In the World: Ballet dancer Margot Fonteyn;
actresses Margot Kidder, Margo Harshman,
and Margaux Hemingway

Marguerite (mahr-gə-REET)   1897: #78
Popularity: #2637
Styles: Ladies and
Gentlemen, French, Saints,
African-American   1880   Today
Nicknames: Margot
Variants: Margarita
Sisters: Antoinette, Estelle, Beatrice, Eugenie,
Blanche, Cecile
Brothers: Claude, Maurice, Laurence,
Edmond, Emile, Armand
✷ The French form of Margaret was once an
everyday choice in America. It's been gone long
enough to shake off its slumber and reemerge
with renewed grace and polish.
In the World: Writers Marguerite Duras and
Marguerite Henry; actress Marguerite Moreau

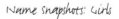

Maria (mah-REE-ə)   1966: #44
Popularity: #92
Styles: Timeless, Biblical,
Latino/Latina, Italian, Greek
Nicknames: Ria, Mimi, Mai,   1880 Today
Mia, Mari, Masha, Mieke
Variants: María, Marie, Mary, Mariah, Marja,
Mariya, Maija
Sisters: Anna, Christina, Julia, Carmen,
Victoria, Teresa
Brothers: David, Roberto, Michael, Victor,
Daniel, Stephen
✳Timeless Maria is a classic favorite in lan-
guages from Spanish to Swedish, Polish to Por-
tuguese. In the U.S., it is most commonly
associated with Spanish and Italian, but it
makes a handsome choice for girls of any heri-
tage. Once upon a time, Maria was pronounced
mah-RIY-ə in the U.S.; if you want that pronunciation today, add an "-h" to the end.
In the World: Subject of many familiar songs,
including the *West Side Story* classic and "My
Maria"

Mariah (mah-RIY-ə)   1996: #63
Popularity: #98
Styles: Antique Charm, Lacy
and Lissome, Nickname-
Proof   1880 Today
Variants: Maria
Sisters: Angelina, Hannah, Sierra, Jasmine,
Abigail, Michaela
Brothers: Isaiah, Caleb, Austin, Levi, Riley,
Noah
✳An antique variation on Maria, this name
was seldom heard before singer Mariah Carey
came on the scene. It is traditional, though, and
a pretty choice whether or not you're a fan of
Carey's. It's also the surest way to get people to
use the old-fashioned English pronunciation of
Maria.
In the World: Singer Mariah Carey

Marian (MA-ree-ən)   1928: #71
Popularity: #1474
Styles: Ladies and
Gentlemen, Solid Citizens,
Nickname-Proof, Why Not?   1880 Today
Variants: Marion
Sisters: Vivian, Sylvia, Beatrice, Adele, Valerie,
Louisa, Margery, June
Brothers: Hugh, Edmund, Forrest, George,
Harris, Peter, Curtis, Clark
✳In theory, Marion and Marian are the same
name. Marian is just a variant spelling, and the
two names have been used side by side for cen-
turies. Yet stylistically, there's a distinction.
Marian has been less common in the U.S. and
is associated with the English Maid Marian of
Robin Hood and May Queen lore. That makes
the "a" spelling a bit fresher and more romantic.
In the World: Maid Marian; singer Marian Anderson

Mariana (mah-ree-AH-nə)   2005: #165
Popularity: #298
Styles: Lacy and Lissome,
Saints, Latino/Latina,
Shakespearean   1880 Today
Nicknames: Mari, Ana
Variants: Marianna
Sisters: Natalia, Evelina, Adriana, Marcela,
Liliana, Valeria
Brothers: Nicolas, Fabian, Alonso, Lucas,
Marco, Adrian
✳A lyrical Latina hit with big potential for
girls of all backgrounds. With its familiar
"Mari-" root, Mariana's like an old friend after a
diet and makeover. And if anyone asks how you
thought of it, tell them you've been reading
Shakespeare—it's a favorite choice in his come-
dies.

Marianne (ma-ree-AN, mah-ree-AHN)
Popularity: #1848
Styles: Solid Citizens, French
Nicknames: Mari
Variants: Mariamne
1957: #139

1880 Today
Sisters: Therese, Patricia, Yvonne, Rosalind, Kathryn, Margot
Brothers: Cornell, Gerard, Laurence, Von, Stuart, Randolph
★ Marianne, the national emblem of France, has been a familiar English name for centuries. To mid-century American parents, Marianne sounded more like a sophisticated continental twist on Marion—exactly how the Spanish/Italian Mariana sounds today.
In the World: Singer Marianne Faithfull; writer Marianne Williamson; Marianne Dashwood of *Sense and Sensibility*

Maribel (MAR-i-behl, mah-ree-BEHL)
Popularity: #1140
Styles: Latino/Latina, Why Not?
1980: #316
1880 Today
Sisters: Graciela, Beatriz, Marisol, Luz, Damaris, Jacinta
Brothers: Orlando, Noel, Felipe, Armando, Rafael, Javier
★ This pretty and delicate Spanish name could be high on the list of Isabel and Annabel fans. A composite name built from Maria, it could also be a creative way to honor a relative with any name in the Mary family.
In the World: Actresses Maribel Verdú and Maribel Guardia

Marie (mah-REE)
Popularity: #599
Styles: Solid Citizens, French, Biblical
Nicknames: Manon
Variants: Maria, Mary
1899: #8
1880 Today
Sisters: Ellen, Irene, Rose, Nancy, Alice, Jane
Brothers: Carl, Frank, Louis, Roy, Albert, Paul
★ This cheerful French form of Maria was the source, ages ago, for the English name Mary. Marie itself has been adopted so thoroughly into our language that it no longer sounds especially French. These days the name is most often bumped down a slot and selected as a middle name.
In the World: Scientist Marie Curie; Marie Antoinette, Queen of France; singer Marie Osmond

Mariela (mah-ree-EHL-ə)
Popularity: #1227
Styles: Lacy and Lissome, Latino/Latina, Why Not?
Variants: Mariella, Mariel
1992: #472
1880 Today
Sisters: Graciela, Viviana, Camila, Dalia, Julieta, Romina
Brothers: Agustin, Javier, Alejandro, Marcelo, Santiago, Mateo
★ Mariela is a Spanish diminuitive of Mary. This graceful name should appeal across cultures, like popular favorites Gabriela and Natalia. It's a hit in South America, but only gently familiar in the U.S.

Marietta (ma-ree-EH-tə)
Popularity: #6026
Styles: Lacy and Lissome, Place Names, Italian
Nicknames: Etta, Mara, Mia
Variants: Marieta, Mariette
1938: #399
1880 Today
Sisters: Georgianna, Annetta, Marcella, Geneva, Josephina, Adelia
Brothers: Richmond, Merritt, Houston, Forrest, Rowland, Hardy
★ This pet form of Maria has a grandmotherly style with a sweet ruffle of lace. It's also the name of a Georgia city, a connection that has done wonders for the name Savannah.
In the World: Marietta, Georgia

Marilla (mah-RIL-ə)
Popularity: Very rare
Styles: Lacy and Lissome, Ladies and Gentlemen, Why Not?
Nicknames: Rilla
Variants: Amarilla, Marillis
1882: #740
1880 Today
Sisters: Diantha, Verena, Josefa, Dulcie, Lavinia, Adelia
Brothers: Mahlon, Sampson, Gaston, Hubbard, Albin, Richmond
★ Back in the 19th century, you were more likely to meet a Marilla than a Marissa. That fact will sound natural to fans of *Anne of Green Gables*, who associate the name with the beloved character Marilla Cuthbert. Marilla sounds perfectly contemporary today, with a lively sweetness. It does rhyme with gorilla, though.
In the World: Marilla Cuthbert of *Anne of Green Gables*

Marilyn (MAR-ə-lin)   1936: #13
Popularity: #545
Styles: Solid Citizens
Variants: Marilynn, Marylyn
Sisters: Beverly, Elaine,   1880   Today
Gloria, Joyce, Rosalyn,
Joanne
Brothers: Franklin, Gene, Donald, Russell,
Richard, Gerald
✴ Doesn't Marilyn have a perfectly contemporary sound? It's a smooth hybrid of Madison, Kaitlyn, and Caroline—what could be trendier? Of course, we can't really hear it that way because every Marilyn we know is eligible for AARP membership. As attractive as the name is, most of us are stuck picturing it as an awkward mixture of Grandma's canasta partners and Marilyn Monroe in her heyday.
In the World: Actress Marilyn Monroe; opera singer Marilyn Horne; "Ask Marilyn" columnist Marilyn vos Savant

Marina (mah-REE-nə)   1994: #218
Popularity: #618
Styles: Timeless,
Shakespearean, Italian,
Greek, Saints   1880   Today
Nicknames: Mari, Marni,
Mia, Mina, Rina
Variants: Maren
Sisters: Lucia, Camille, Adriana, Silvia, Renata, Miranda
Brothers: Roman, Quentin, Raphael, Adrian, Graham, Vincent
✴ This sophisticated name has near-universal appeal. It gives you classical origins, Shakespearean pedigree, and a romantic association with the sea. Need more? How about global style? Marina is used as a Scottish form of Mary, and Saint Marinas have hailed from Spain, Turkey, and Japan. A little Marina will fit in handsomely the world over.
In the World: Singer Marina and the Diamonds; actress Marina Sirtis

Marion (MA-ree-ən)   1917: #45
Popularity: #1815
Styles: Solid Citizens, Ladies
and Gentlemen, French,
Nickname-Proof   1880   Today
Variants: Marian
Sisters: Louise, Helen, Adele, Vivian, Frances, Irene
Brothers: Warren, Laurence, Gordon, Vernon, Hugh, Claude
✴ Marion, an old French diminutive of Marie, has been an English girl's name since medieval times. Its popularity has ebbed and flowed through the centuries and across the globe. In the U.S., the name is in a down phase, as we sleep off an early-20th-century binge. See also Marian.
In the World: Actresses Marion Davies, Marion Ross, and Marion Cotillard; author Marion Zimmer Bradley

Marisol (mah-ree-SOHL)   1996: #234
Popularity: #574
Styles: Latino/Latina
Nicknames: Mari, Mai, Misa
Sisters: Araceli, Maribel, Luz,   1880   Today
Tania, Maritza, Raquel
Brothers: Esteban, Gustavo, Agustin, Raul, Mauricio, Rodrigo
✴ To an English speaker, Marisol has a dark, silky sophistication. To a Spanish speaker, though, this name is anything but dark: it's the very sea and sun (*mar y sol*). Marisol's actual origin is probably Maria + Soledad ("solitude"), but the sun can't help shining through.
In the World: Actress Marisol Nichols; TV personality Marisol González

Marissa (mah-RIS-ə)   1994: #53
Popularity: #257
Styles: Lacy and Lissome,
Turn of the 21st Century
Nicknames: Mari, Missy   1880   Today
Variants: Marisa
Sisters: Angelica, Gabriela, Lindsay, Brianna, Miranda, Cassandra
Brothers: Trevor, Brendan, Devin, Garrett, Spencer, Donovan
✴ Marissa is a lively, lacy favorite born in the 20th century. It stepped up in the '90s to take the torch from '70s–'80s lacy queen Melissa. The spelling Marisa gives it a Spanish/Italian slant, while the double-"s" version plays up the frills.
In the World: Actresses Marisa Tomei and Marisa Berenson; model Marisa Miller; tech exec Marissa Mayer

Marjorie (MAHR-jə-ree)   1921: #16
Popularity: #1778
Styles: Solid Citizens, Why Not?
Nicknames: Marj, Margie, Jorie, Jo   1880   Today
Variants: Margery, Marjory
Sisters: Vivian, Dorothy, Therese, Virginia, Corinna, Rosemary
Brothers: Hugh, Russell, Edmund, Lawrence, Clifton, Harris

✳ Marjorie boomed, ebbed, then vanished during the 20th century, yet it doesn't sound as old as its graph suggests. The name's rhythm has stayed current across the generations in names from Stephanie to Emily to Cassidy. Also consider the antique spelling Margery (as in the nursery rhyme "See-Saw, Margery Daw"), which lets you choose from Margaret's smorgasbord of nicknames.
In the World: Film *Marjorie Morningstar;* nursery rhyme "See-Saw, Margery Daw"

Marlene (mahr-LEEN,   1936: #39
mahr-LAY-nə)
Popularity: #883
Styles: Mid-Century, German and Dutch, French   1880   Today
Nicknames: Marly, Marlee, Lena
Variants: Marlène, Marlena, Marlen
Sisters: Yvonne, Margot, Sondra, Janice, Greta, Marianne
Brothers: Jerome, Roland, Franklin, Manfred, Karl, Dwight

✳ Marlene is a German name, a contraction of Maria Magdalene made famous by actress Marlene Dietrich. For Dietrich, it was three gentle syllables. If you know an American Marlene, though, she most likely pronounces it to rhyme with Darlene. The pronunciation is key: the American version is fading, while the German is more fashionable.
In the World: Actress Marlene Dietrich

Marley (MAHR-lee)   2008: #145
Popularity: #258
Styles: Last Names First, Nickname-Proof
Sisters: Harper, Sienna, Tatum, Macy, Lyla, Aubrey   1880   Today
Brothers: Sawyer, Madden, Micah, Ryder, Judah, Holden

✳ Reggae legend Bob Marley's surname, like his music, is a balance of sunny and serious. It was never truly popular until 2008, when the film *Marley & Me* arrived. The Marley in that film, a male *dog*, inspired a remarkable number of female human namesakes. I know, you just liked the name, and who can blame you? If you tell your daughter her name was inspired by the song "Three Little Birds" instead, I won't give you away.
In the World: Film *Marley & Me;* reggae star Bob Marley; actress Marley Shelton

Marlowe (MAHR-loh)   2011: #2221
Popularity: #2238
Styles: Last Names First, Literary and Artistic, Why Not?   1880   Today
Variants: Marlo
Sisters: Auden, Harper, Winslow, Blythe, Channing, Jensen, Adair
Brothers: Sawyer, Whitman, Beckett, Locke, Carver, Holden, Tennyson

✳ The sound of this name is the same as '60s *That Girl* Marlo Thomas, but the spelling gives you a dramatic style shift. Marlowe suggests Raymond Chandler's hard-boiled detective Philip Marlowe. (Picture Humphrey Bogart in *The Big Sleep.*) That places Marlowe in a similar Hollywood era as the hot new name Harlow, but with a little extra toughness.
In the World: Fictional detective Philip Marlowe; actress Marlo Thomas; playwright Christopher Marlowe; a daughter of actress Sienna Miller

Martha (MAHR-thə) 1880: #16
Popularity: #772
Styles: Ladies and
Gentlemen, Biblical
Nicknames: Marty, Mattie,   1880 Today
Patsy, Marcie
Variants: Marta
Sisters: Alice, Margaret, Anne, Edith, Frances, Rosa
Brothers: Albert, Charles, Walter, George, Harry, Edward
✷ Parents who find themselves drawn to names like George should give Martha a second look. It has that same no-frills appeal that frees you from the shackles of passing fashion.
In the World: Lifestyle mogul Martha Stewart; first first lady Martha Washington; the island Martha's Vineyard

Martina (mahr-TEEN-ə) 1984: #576
Popularity: #1725
Styles: Timeless, Slavic,
Italian, German and Dutch,
Latino/Latina 1880 Today
Nicknames: Marty, Tina
Variants: Martine
Sisters: Claudia, Renata, Ingrid, Johanna, Elena, Susana
Brothers: Rafael, Stefan, Tomas, Andreas, Roberto, Ivan
✷ This dignified classic has Latin origins and Renaissance style. But do you hear a twang? That could be either the country twang of singer Martina McBride or the twang of a tennis ball hitting the racket of center-court legend Martina Navratilova. Those two Martinas, regularly referred to by first name only, shape the name's modern image.
In the World: Singer Martina McBride; tennis players Martina Navratilova and Martina Hingis (named after Navratilova)

Mary (MAY-ree, MA-ree) 1880: #1
Popularity: #112
Styles: Timeless, Biblical
Nicknames: Molly, Mamie,
May, Mitzi, Polly 1880 Today
Variants: Maria, Marie, Mari, Maire
Sisters: Martha, Catherine, Rose, Margaret, Alice, Anne
Brothers: John, Edward, Charles, Paul, Robert, George
✷ The most popular girl's name of the 20th century. And the 19th, and the 18th . . . but the Grand Old Name is remarkably uncommon in century 21. Modern parents have shied away from Mary precisely because of its past popularity. Ironically, that now gives you the opportunity to choose the name as a distinctive fashion statement. It is warm, pretty, and the ultimate "back to basics" classic.
In the World: Potent imagery ranging from the Virgin Mary to Bloody Mary to the nursery rhyme "Mary, Mary, Quite Contrary"

Matilda (mah-TIL-də) 1880: #100
Popularity: #769
Styles: Ladies and
Gentlemen, Saints, Why
Not?   1880 Today
Nicknames: Tilda, Tillie,
Tilly, Mattie
Variants: Mathilda, Mathilde, Mafalda
Sisters: Beatrice, Amelia, Adelaide, Flora, Penelope, Louisa
Brothers: Casper, August, Felix, Hugh, Edmund, Foster
✷ This is a powerful old classic name, borne by the wife of William the Conqueror. In France and Scandinavia, Matilda/Mathilde is a hot name, a stylish sister for Sophie or Isabel. It's also popular in the U.K. and Australia, along with the nickname Tilly. In the U.S., though, a bit of Matilda's dusty antique image still lingers. Consider this a chance to be ahead of the curve.
In the World: Book/film *Matilda*; song "Waltzing Matilda"; daughter of actors Heath Ledger and Michelle Williams

Mattea (mah-TAY-ə) 2006: #1872
Popularity: #3101
Styles: Lacy and Lissome,
Why Not?
Nicknames: Mattie, Tea   1880 Today
Sisters: Chiara, Linnea,
Mika, Ariela, Katya, Aviana
Brothers: Enzo, Bram, Teo, Nico, Tobin,
Maxim
✳ An old Italian offshoot of Matthew, Mattea sounds trendy yet is virtually unknown. Its only tiny spike was inspired by the surname of country singer Kathy Mattea. This could be a snappy discovery.
In the World: Singer Kathy Mattea; a daughter of actress Mira Sorvino

Maude (MAWD) 1882: #20
Popularity: #11,743
Styles: Ladies and Gentlemen
Nicknames: Maudie
Variants: Maud   1880 Today
Sisters: Olive, Flora, Iris,
Blanche, Louise, Matilda
Brothers: August, Luther, George, Arthur,
Hugh, Otto
✳ Maude is a dignified classic with two strikes against it. First is its bluntness, which doesn't sound particularly feminine to modern ears. Second is the '70s Bea Arthur sitcom with its stick-in-your-head theme song ("And then there's Maude . . ."). Maude remains distinguished, but it's far from fashionable.
In the World: Maude TV series; actress Maud Adams; film Harold and Maude

Maura (MAW-rə, MOHR-ə, 1964: #468
MOW-rə)
Popularity: #1305
Styles: Celtic, Saints,
Nickname-Proof   1880 Today
Variants: Máire, Moya, Mary
Sisters: Bridget, Nora, Kathleen, Brenna,
Deirdre, Maeve
Brothers: Patrick, Rory, Bryan, Connor,
Murphy, Shane
✳ Maura is a Celtic classic especially favored by Irish-American parents. Its style is gentle and serious, more contemporary than the familiar related name Maureen. For an even more contemporary style, you could go with the Irish version Máire—if you dare.
In the World: Actress Maura Tierney; musician Máire Brennan

Maureen (moh-REEN) 1948: #88
Popularity: #2839
Styles: Mid-Century, Celtic
Nicknames: Mo, Reenie
Variants: Maurine   1880 Today
Sisters: Glenda, Eileen,
Margaret, Teresa, Kathleen, Patricia
Brothers: Darrell, Barry, Kerry, Phillip,
Douglas, Kenneth
✳ In the '40s–'50s heyday of Irish screen beauty Maureen O'Hara, this name was the glamorous favorite of Irish-American families. Its decline was swift enough to pin the name to that generation, but Maureen still has a great Irish spirit, especially paired with a perfect surname like O'Hara. Also consider the svelter Maura.
In the World: Actresses Maureen O'Hara, Maureen McCormick, and Maureen O'Sullivan; columnist Maureen Dowd

Maxine (mak-SEEN) 1923: #76
Popularity: #1434
Styles: Solid Citizens
Nicknames: Maxie
Sisters: Lorraine, Vivian,   1880 Today
Marjorie, Sylvia, Rita,
Laverne
Brothers: Vernon, Lyle, Bernard, Marvin,
Leon, Stanley
✳ Maxine was a glamour name in the '20s, and it's easy to see why. It sounded modern and brassy in a world full of Marthas and Ediths. Today, in a world of Madisons and Savannahs, even that foxy "x" can't quite keep Maxine around.
In the World: Politician Maxine Waters; writer Maxine Hong Kingston

May (MAY) 1880: #57
Popularity: #2173
Styles: Charms and Graces,
Why Not?
Variants: Mae   1880 Today
Sisters: Belle, Flora, Lena,
Pearl, Lottie, Dove
Brothers: Nat, Archie, Theo, Ben, Mack,
Charley
✳ This wee and lovely turn-of-the-century name has escaped most parents' notice. May's sunlit optimism makes a natural alternative (or sister) to meaning names like Hope and Faith. Also be sure to consider the spelling Mae (see separate entry), which is less rooted to the common word.
In the World: Spider-Man's Aunt May; phrases like "May Day" and "may or may not"

 *Name Snapshots: Girls* 153

Maya (MIY-ə) 2006: #57
Popularity: #64
Styles: Short and Sweet,
Nickname-Proof, Nordic,
Jewish 1880 Today
Variants: Maia, Maja, Mya
Sisters: Jada, Nina, Zoe, Asha, Annika, Naomi,
Ava
Brothers: Noah, Max, Dylan, Riley, Kiran,
Liam, Eli
✱ Maya is a hit name that seemed to rise out of
nowhere . . . or everywhere. It's Sanskrit, mean-
ing "illusion," and Hebrew, meaning "water."
It's a Scandinavian form of Maria; a Greek
nymph; a Mexican civilization. And in the case
of writer Maya Angelou, it's short for Margue-
rite. Perhaps it's no surprise, then, that everyone
finds something to like about this name.
In the World: Writer Maya Angelou; actress
Maya Rudolph; artist Maya Lin; the Maya peoples of Mexico and Central America

Mckenna (mə-KEHN-ə) 2002: #177
Popularity: #239
Styles: Last Names First,
Celtic
Nicknames: Kenna 1880 Today
Variants: Makenna
Sisters: Cassidy, Savannah, Madigan, Camryn,
Macy, Delaney
Brothers: Logan, Donovan, Tucker, Easton,
Connor, Brennan
✱ Mckenna is a twin sister to Mckenzie, but
not identical. Like most twins, they mirror
each other but carve out their own niches of
style. Where Mckenzie is playful and boyish,
Mckenna is more traditionally feminine, on the
model of cousin Makayla. The pet form Kenna
could stand on its own as a given name too.

McKinley (mə-KIN-lee) 2011: #451
Popularity: #451
Styles: Last Names First,
Androgynous
Nicknames: Kin, Kinley 1880 Today
Variants: Kinley
Sisters: Kennedy, Logan, Kerrigan, Reagan,
Delaney, Campbell
Brothers: Finnegan, Brogan, Dempsey,
Sullivan, Baylor, Quinlan
✱ McKinley is a craggy Scottish spin on presi-
dential surnames. Even craggier is Mount
McKinley, a rugged symbol of American wil-
derness. Despite all the crags, this name is more
common for girls than for boys today. It's both a
twist on Mackenzie and an elaboration of Kin-
ley.
In the World: President William McKinley;
Mount McKinley, the highest peak in the U.S.

Meadow (MEH-doh) 2007: #764
Popularity: #892
Styles: Modern Meanings,
Charms and Graces
Sisters: Ember, Willow, 1880 Today
Serenity, Winter, Eden,
Avonlea, Sage
Brothers: Canyon, River, Bodhi, Phoenix,
Arrow, Storm, Falcon
✱ This nature name is a gentle free spirit. It
had a flower-child aura until the TV series *The
Sopranos* gave the name a Jersey gangster spin.
In the World: Meadow Soprano of *The Sopranos*

Megan (MEH-gən, MAY-gən, 1985: #10
MEE-gən)
Popularity: #164
Styles: Celtic, Turn of the
21st Century, The "-ens" 1880 Today
Nicknames: Meg
Variants: Meagan, Meghan, Meaghan
Sisters: Lauren, Allison, Jenna, Danielle,
Nicole, Caitlin
Brothers: Ryan, Trevor, Ian, Jeremy, Colin, Kyle
✱ Megan started off in Wales as a pet form of
Margaret, but it has found huge popularity as a
U.S. given name. It's a long-established hit, yet
feels perpetually youthful. The alternate spell-
ing Meaghan, which gives the name an Irish
look, is in fact a modern American creation.
Also consider Bethan, a similar Welsh take on
Elizabeth.
In the World: Actresses Megan Fox, Megan
Hilty, Meagan Good, and Meaghan Martin

Mehitabel (meh-HIT-ə-behl) rarely used
Popularity: Very rare
Styles: Exotic Traditional, Biblical, Literary and Artistic
Nicknames: Bella, Mel, Hettie
Variants: Mehetabel
Sisters: Hermione, Phyllida, Leocadia, Amabel, Melisande, Zippporah
Brothers: Ichabod, Algernon, Phineas, Barnaby, Horatio, Ishmael
✶This name may be unrealistic for most families. But if you just love Madeline and Isabel and just can't bear the thought of a popular name, this whimsical rarity is an option. Mehitabel is chiefly known—among those who know it at all—as an alley cat who keeps company with a literary cockroach named Archy. *In the World: archy and mehitabel* by Don Marquis

Melanie (MEH-lə-nee) 1973: #43
Popularity: #89
Styles: New Classics, French
Nicknames: Mel, Melly
Variants: Melany, Melania
Sisters: Andrea, Stephanie, Gabrielle, Leslie, Amanda, Natalie
Brothers: Timothy, Bryan, Kevin, Bradley, Eric, Damon
✶Melanie is a rare medieval French saint's name. What, that's not your image of Melanie? Then thank *Gone with the Wind*, which brought the name to America's notice. It has been a standard ever since, thoroughly likable and unaffected. *In the World:* Actress Melanie Griffith; singer Melanie Fiona; Melanie Wilkes of *Gone with the Wind*

Melia (meh-LEE-ə, MEE-lee-ə, MEEL-yə) 2006: #1212
Popularity: #1517
Styles: Lacy and Lissome, Mythological
Variants: Meliya, Maleia
Sisters: Lilia, Nalani, Danae, Milana, Serena, Eleni
Brothers: Luca, Kai, Orion, Micah, Leander, Teo
✶The name Melia is smooth and warm, like water flowing in the sunshine. Its various origins back up that image. In Greek mythology, Melia was a nymph of a freshwater spring. In Hawaii, it is a popular name based on a tropical flower. The Hawaiian name is "meh-LEE-ə," other versions typically "MEE-lee-ə." See also Malia.

Melina (meh-LEEN-ə) 2009: #456
Popularity: #580
Styles: Lacy and Lissome, Greek, Why Not?
Nicknames: Mel, Lina
Variants: Malina
Sisters: Liana, Thalia, Mariela, Athena, Cassandra, Ariela
Brothers: Matteo, Nikos, Ari, Enzo, Gideon, Andreas
✶From the Greek word for "honey," Melina is as smooth and sweet as its meaning suggests. Despite its attractive and accessible sound, this name has never been widely used in the U.S. Melina Kanakaredes, an American actress of Greek heritage, has recently helped make it familiar. *In the World:* Actresses Melina Mercouri and Melina Kanakaredes; wrestler Melina Perez

Melinda (meh-LIN-də) 1973: #72
Popularity: #1253
Styles: '70s–'80s, Lacy and
Lissome
Nicknames: Mindy, Mel, 1880 Today
Lindy
Variants: Malinda
Sisters: Deanna, Melissa, Candace, Stacey,
Felicia, Lesley
Brothers: Jeffrey, Brent, Mark, Brian, Timothy,
Randall
✻ Melinda is a mellifluous name created in the
1800s when the "-inda" ending was the height of
romance. Its popularity peaked in the 1970s,
and the nickname Mindy (à la sitcom *Mork and
Mindy*) is still planted firmly in the Me Decade.
If you're looking for nickname alternatives, Mel
is the rising choice and Lindy a quiet charmer.
Also consider Melina, which shares the same
Greek root and smooth style.
In the World: Actress Melinda Clarke; philan-
thropist Melinda Gates; singer Melinda Doolittle

Melisande (MEH-li-sahnd) 1972: #7276
Popularity: Very rare
Styles: Exotic Traditional,
Why Not?
Variants: Mélisande, 1880 Today
Melisende, Millicent
Sisters: Amandine, Artemisia, Guinevere,
Mariamne, Evangeline, Iolanthe
Brothers: Peregrine, Montague, Tristram,
Evander, Barnabas, Florian
✻ Melisande is the French source of the name
that became Millicent in English. The name's
ethereal beauty has lured writers to bestow it on
fairy tale princesses, nymphs, and mysterious
forest maidens. For all that fairy tale style,
though, Melisande does not sound fanciful. It's
delicate but serious.
In the World: Opera and play *Pelléas et Mélisande*; Melisende, a medieval queen of Jerusa-
lem

Melissa (mə-LIS-ə) 1979: #2
Popularity: #184
Styles: '70s–'80s, Lacy and
Lissome
Nicknames: Missy, Mel, Lissa 1880 Today
Variants: Melisa, Malissa
Sisters: Michelle, Amy, Jennifer, Jessica,
Stephanie, Amanda
Brothers: Brian, Jeffrey, Christopher, Eric,
Jeremy, Shawn
✻ Melissa was the lacy sound of the '70s. It's
still as sweet as ever, and a host of new hits pay
homage to the name's delicate rhythm. To-
gether, Carissa, Alyssa, Larissa, and Marissa
make up a Melissa tribute band.
In the World: Actresses Melissa Joan Hart, Me-
lissa McCarthy, and Melissa Gilbert; singers
Missy Elliott and Melissa Etheridge

Melody (MEH-loh-dee) 1960: #153
Popularity: #201
Styles: New Classics, Modern
Meanings
Nicknames: Mel 1880 Today
Variants: Melodie
Sisters: Kimberly, Crystal, Melinda, Holly,
Summer, Janelle
Brothers: Damon, Bradley, Lance, Kelvin,
Andre, Bryan
✻ This name waltzed into America's hearts
hand in hand with Melanie. The two sound
similar enough to be confused, but the musical
associations of Melody make it at once frothier
and more tender.
In the World: Singers Melody Gardot and Me-
lody Thornton; actress Melody Thomas Scott

Mercedes (mer-SAY-deez) 1993: #171
Popularity: #758
Styles: Latino/Latina
Nicknames: Meche, Mercy,
Sadie 1880 Today
Sisters: Guadalupe, Paulina,
Yesenia, Mariela, Milagros, Esmeralda
Brothers: Salvador, Fernando, Cristian,
Gerardo, Vicente, Francisco
✻ This lovely name, meaning "mercies,"
comes from a title for the Virgin Mary. Of
course, you could just as well say, "This lovely
car, meaning 'status,' comes from Germany."
The automotive association is now so strong
that people may consider this a brand name like
Lexus or Armani. Other reverent names to con-
sider include Milagros, Altagracia, and Socorro.
In the World: Mercedes-Benz automobiles; ac-
tresses Mercedes McCambridge and Mercedes
Ruehl

Mercy (MER-cee)   2011: #1028
Popularity: #1031
Styles: Charms and Graces,
Timeless, Why Not?
Nicknames: Merce, Merry   1880 Today
Variants: Merce
Sisters: Charity, Poppy, Flora, Amity, Daphne,
Calla
Brothers: Judah, Silas, Barrett, August, Ezra,
Gideon
✳This Puritan favorite has been mysteriously
overlooked by modern parents. Its generous
spirit compares well with current favorites Faith
and Hope, and its sound is effortlessly contem-
porary.

Meredith (MEH-rə-dith)   1980: #140
Popularity: #596
Styles: New Classics,
Androgynous
Nicknames: Merry, Mere   1880 Today
Sisters: Alison, Julianne,
Mallory, Bethany, Channing, Sabrina
Brothers: Kendall, Bradley, Drew, Mitchell,
Brendan, Jamison
✳ Here's a good one to consider if you and your
partner are deadlocked on names. Looking for a
hushed, gentle name to whisper to your sweet
baby? Meredith. A modern-sounding choice
with an androgynous edge? Meredith. A com-
fortable old favorite with a cute nickname? You
get the idea. A name for all seasons.
In the World: TV journalist Meredith Viera; actress Meredith Baxter; character Meredith Grey
of *Grey's Anatomy*

Merry (MEH-ree)   1954: #469
Popularity: #8020
Styles: Mid-Century, Charms
and Graces
Variants: Meri   1880 Today
Sisters: Bonnie, Trudy,
Melody, Cinda, Joy, Gayle
Brothers: Danny, Nick, Teddy, Mickey, Skip,
Dean
✳ Merry's upbeat meaning charmed parents
two generations ago, when jolly names like
Cherry and Bonnie were frequently heard. It
was especially favored for births in the Christ-
mas season. Joy is another happy Yuletide op-
tion.
In the World: Merry-go-round; Merry Christ-
mas!

Meta (MAY-tə, MEH-tə)   1890: #227
Popularity: #12,894
Styles: Nicknames, Nordic,
German and Dutch, Short
and Sweet   1880 Today
Sisters: Mina, Lida, Josefa,
Leonie, Lilla, Tilda
Brothers: Lonzo, Nils, Mose, Anton, August,
Otto
✳A German nickname for Margareta, Meta
was stylish in the 1890s. It's unfamiliar enough
today that it may sound more like a prefix than a
name.
In the World: Words like "metaphysical";
phrases like "that's so meta"

Mia (MEE-ə)   2011: #9
Popularity: #9
Styles: Short and Sweet,
Nickname-Proof, Nordic
Variants: Mia   1880 Today
Sisters: Ava, Lila, Chloe, Liv,
Jada, Zoe
Brothers: Max, Oliver, Ian, Mason, Noah,
Liam
✳This little charmer of a name was quietly
stylish until the ascent of soccer star Mia
Hamm. Today, forget quiet—picture a raucous
playroom full of little Mias. Like Hamm her-
self, the name suggests a modern all-American
girl: the delightful dynamo.
In the World: soccer star Mia Hamm; actress
Mia Farrow; "Princess Diaries" protagonist Mia
Thermopolis

Michaela (mi-KAY lə)   1997: #100
Popularity: #409
Styles: Antique Charm, Turn
of the 21st Century
Nicknames: Mickey, Kayla,   1880 Today
Kaelie, Mica, Mischa, Mike
Variants: Micaela, Michela, Makayla, Mikayla
Sisters: Daniella, Alexandria, Karina, Annalise,
Madeline, Olivia
Brothers: Devin, Maxwell, Joshua, Carson,
Spencer, Caleb
✳This feminine form of Michael was ex-
tremely uncommon until the countless Mikes
of the mid-century started having daughters.
Then TV's *Dr. Quinn, Medicine Woman* put it
over the top. The original spelling Michaela
still has an antique flavor, but it's been over-
taken by the trendy modern variant Makayla
(see separate entry).
In the World: Michaela of *Dr. Quinn, Medicine
Woman*; actress Michaela Conlin

Michelle (mi-SHEHL) 1969: #2
Popularity: #144
Styles: '70s–'80s, French
Nicknames: Missy, Chelle, Shelly
Variants: Michele
Sisters: Kimberly, Melissa, Stephanie, Jennifer, Christine, Danielle
Brothers: Kevin, Mark, Bradley, Eric, Jeffrey, Matthew
✷ Michelle is no longer the French "belle" the Beatles sang about in the '60s. The name has enjoyed such steady use in the U.S. that it now sounds like an all-American girl. Make that an all-American woman: standard-bearers like Michelle Obama and Michelle Pfeiffer make this a grown-up name to be reckoned with.
In the World: First lady Michelle Obama; actresses Michelle Pfeiffer, Michelle Williams, and Michelle Rodriguez; skater Michelle Kwan

Mila (MEE-lə) 2011: #174
Popularity: #174
Styles: Slavic, Short and Sweet
Variants: Milla
Sisters: Anya, Nika, Alina, Maia, Annika, Ivy, Katya, Luna
Brothers: Luka, Ari, Viktor, Ronan, Owen, Kai, Maxim, Nico
✷ In various Slavic languages, Mila is a short form of names like Ludmila, Miloslava, and Milena. In English, it stands alone: Mia turned surprisingly sumptuous with the addition of a single "l." The name has risen steadily in the U.S., in step with the career of Ukrainian-born actress Milena ("Mila") Kunis.
In the World: Actresses Mila Kunis and Milla Jovovich

Milagros (mee-LAH-grohs) 2008: #725
Popularity: #987
Styles: Latino/Latina
Nicknames: Mili, Millie, Mila
Sisters: Rocio, Damaris, Monserrat, Graciela, Lourdes, Evangelina
Brothers: Santos, Agustin, Moises, Marcelo, Cruz, Ezequiel
✷ The English name Miracle, in the singular, celebrates the miracle that is a child. The Spanish Milagros, plural, is a grateful homage to divine miracles—or a plea for them. ("Our Lady of the Miracles" is one of the many titles of the Virgin Mary.) The word *milagro* can also refer to religious charms left as votive offerings at holy places.
In the World: Model Milagros Schmoll

Milan (mi-LAHN) 2011: #606
Popularity: #608
Styles: Place Names, African-American
Variants: Milania
Sisters: Aspen, Vienna, London, Asia, Marin, Sasha, Bristol, Venice
Brothers: Devon, Boston, Cairo, Maxim, Jovan, Dante, Camden, Kingston
✷ To much of the world, Milan is a classic Slavic name, stressed on the first syllable and decidedly masculine. But Milan is also the English rendering of the Italian fashion capital Milano. That has attracted American parents of girls, who see the name as a glossy sister to Paris and London.
In the World: Milan, Italy; a daughter of boxer Mike Tyson

Mildred (MIL-drid) 1913: #6
Popularity: #2586
Styles: Porch Sitters
Nicknames: Millie
Sisters: Bernice, Hilda, Gladys, Irma, Myrtle, Gertrude
Brothers: Lester, Wilfred, Herman, Orville, Milton, Willard
✷ This Old English name means "gentle strength." I know, I know, you don't really care. I'm just trying to send some kind thoughts toward a name that was once the pinnacle of fashion but now personifies dowdiness. If you love the nickname Millie, try Amelia, Camille, or Millicent.
In the World: Film *Mildred Pierce*; singer Mildred Bailey

Milena (mee-LEH-nə,   2011: #1061
mi-LAY-nə)
Popularity: #1064
Styles: Slavic, Italian, Why
Not?
Nicknames: Mila, Milanka
Variants: Milana
Sisters: Natalya, Ivana, Daria, Eliana, Alessia,
Renata
Brothers: Aldo, Dimitri, Matteo, Andre, Marek,
Viktor
✴This lyrical Slavic name has spread to many
languages, but English speakers have yet to
catch on. What's holding you back? It has the
smooth grace of a modern invention, but sounds
(and is) impeccably traditional. Milena is a
form of the male name Milan, but its use in
Italy owes to a Queen Milena, not to the city of
Milano.
In the World: Actresses Milena Govich and
Milena ("Mila") Kunis; Milena Vukotić, a
queen of Montenegro

Miley (MIY-lee)   2008: #128
Popularity: #316
Styles: Bell Tones
Variants: Mylee, Mylie,
Myleigh
Sisters: Bailey, Macy, Ashlyn,
Teagan, Cadence, Hayden
Brothers: Brayden, Rylan, Jacoby, Keegan,
Drake, Landon
✴When Destiny Hope Cyrus was a toddler,
her dad nicknamed her "Smiley Miley." The
Miley part stuck. As the teen star of *Hannah
Montana*, Cyrus chose Miley as her legal name,
and scores of parents followed suit for their
daughters. This name hews to the sound of an-
drogynous surnames like Riley, but it's all girl.
In the World: Actress Miley Cyrus

Millicent (MI-li-sənt)   1927: #434
Popularity: #2725
Styles: Ladies and Gentlemen
Nicknames: Millie
Variants: Melisande
Sisters: Dorothea, Harriet,
Winifred, Adelaide, Elinor, Eloise
Brothers: Frederick, Theodore, Clarence,
Sylvester, Albert, Julius
✴This is the queen of the old-lady names. It
may be hard to picture a Millicent in little girl's
pigtails instead of white hair . . . but if you man-
age, it's a surprisingly adorable image. This is a
long shot that could pay off handsomely.
In the World: Editor/politician Millicent Fen-
wick

Mimi (MEE-mee)   1961: #806
Popularity: #3863
Styles: Mid-Century,
Nicknames
Sisters: Mitzi, Nanette, Gigi,
DeeDee, Suzette, Kiki
Brothers: Rudy, Dino, Skip, Guy, Monty, Tad
✴This nickname became well known as the
heroine of the opera *La Bohème* (and later, its
stepchild *Rent*). Like Fifi and Gigi, it tends to
make Americans giggle a bit, but it still makes a
fun, freewheeling nickname. You can use it as a
pet form of almost any name starting with "M."
In the World: Mimi of *La Bohème*; actress Mimi
Rogers; nickname of singer Mariah Carey

Mindy (MIN-dee)   1979: #81
Popularity: #1950
Styles: '70s–'80s, Nicknames
Sisters: Kristy, Trisha, Marcie,
April, Brandy, Holly
Brothers: Shaun, Jamey,
Chad, Corey, Dusty, Scott
✴Mindy swept through America in the '70s,
usually as a nickname but often enough on its
own. This kind of spun-sugar name is sweet for
a girl but can be insubstantial for a grown
woman. The current preference is to stick with
Melinda or Miranda on the birth certificate.
In the World: Sitcom *Mork and Mindy*; actresses
Mindy Kaling and Mindy Cohn; singer Mindy
McCready

Minerva (mi-NER-və)   1880: #193
Popularity: #3953
Styles: Ladies and
Gentlemen, Mythological,
Exotic Traditional,
Fantastical
Nicknames: Mina, Minnie
Sisters: Augusta, Lavinia, Evangeline,
Hermione, Aurora, Octavia
Brothers: Ulysses, Ambrose, Horatio, Augustus,
Linus, Philo
✴Minerva doesn't sound like a young girl's
name. It has a stern, gray-haired demeanor.
Yet the name's mythical, magical style (the
Roman goddess of wisdom) helps it shine above
other old-lady names. Both sides, stern and fan-
tastical, are embodied by Professor Minerva
McGonagall of "Harry Potter" fame.
In the World: Minerva McGonagall of the
"Harry Potter" series; cartoon seductress Mi-
nerva Mink

Mira (MEER-ə, MIY-rə) 2011: #785
Popularity: #787
Styles: Slavic, Short and
Sweet, Nickname-Proof, Why
Not? 1880 Today
Variants: Myra, Meera
Sisters: Lilia, Anya, Riya, Katya, Daria, Milena
Brothers: Enzo, Maxim, Lukas, Kiran, Pavel,
Lev
✷ Like many simple, feminine names, Mira
arose independently in different cultures.
Whether you call the name Slavic, Hindi, or
Italian, the current preferred pronunciation is
with a strong "e" sound. If you prefer the strong
"i" sound, consider the spelling Myra to avoid
confusion and gain a Scottish flavor.
In the World: Actress Mira Sorvino; director
Mira Nair

Miracle (MI-rə-kəl) 2007: #451
Popularity: #495
Styles: Modern Meanings,
Fanciful
Nicknames: Mira 1880 Today
Sisters: Essence, Heaven,
Cherish, Blessing, Genesis, Serenity
Brothers: Justice, Sincere, Zion, King, Phoenix,
Chance
✷ Miracle has only recently been adopted as
an English given name. It's a passionate, emo-
tional choice, and some people may be discom-
fited by its intensity. Unlike the Spanish
Milagros, which is a general celebration of di-
vine miracles, the name Miracle tends to focus
on the baby girl herself. It's often chosen in
cases where the child represents a triumph over
adversity, such as infertility or premature birth.
In the World: Phrases such as "Miracle on Ice"
and "Miracle Mile"; Miracle Whip sandwich
spread

Miranda (mi-RAN-də) 1995: #57
Popularity: #199
Styles: New Classics, Lacy
and Lissome, Shakespearean
Nicknames: Mandy, Randi, 1880 Today
Mindy, Mira, Mimi
Variants: Maranda, Myranda
Sisters: Alexandra, Daniela, Gabrielle,
Melanie, Adriana, Vanessa
Brothers: Colin, Spencer, Matthew, Ian,
Nathaniel, Trevor
✷ For The Tempest, Shakespeare conjured up
this name to sound beautiful, strong, and all-
around "admirable." (It's based on the same
Latin root as that word.) Darned if the Bard
didn't know what he was doing too. Four centu-
ries later, that image is still holding strong.
In the World: Actress Miranda Cosgrove; singer
Miranda Lambert; model Miranda Kerr; Mi-
randa of Sex and the City

Miriam (MEER-ee-əm) 1917: #134
Popularity: #342
Styles: Biblical, Timeless,
Jewish
Nicknames: Miri, Mira, 1880 Today
Mimi, Mim
Variants: Miryam, Maryam, Myriam
Sisters: Esther, Naomi, Cecilia, Ruth, Vivian,
Leora
Brothers: Reuben, Saul, Julius, Abraham, Asa,
Solomon
✷ As parents scramble to unearth more biblical
name ideas, there's one place they're not turn-
ing to: the 20th century. The handful of Old
Testament girls' names that came and went in
your parents' and grandparents' generations re-
main "undiscovered." Miriam is a distinguished
name with an attractive rhythm and stylish
nickname options if you can look past the
grandma aura.
In the World: Singer Miriam Makeba

Mirren (MIR-in)   2010: #14848
Popularity: Very rare
Styles: Celtic, The "-ens,"
Why Not?
Variants: Máirín   1880   Today
Sisters: Tamsin, Emlyn,
Lilias, Keelin, Nola, Tierney, Tegan, Seren
Brothers: Ewan, Kerr, Niven, Eamon, Forbes,
Lachlan, Callum, Struan
✻ Think that a creative "-en" name has to be
newly invented or androgynous? Think again.
Mirren is traditionally feminine, a Scottish
form of Marian. It's a hot choice in Scotland but
an attractive unknown in the U.S. (If you think
of Mirren as a surname, that owes solely to ac-
tress Helen Mirren. Her Russian immigrant
family created the name by anglicizing
Mironov.)

Misha (MEE-sh)   1991: #1249
Popularity: #2387
Styles: Short and Sweet
Variants: Mischa, Mishka
Sisters: Lana, Sasha, Maya,   1880   Today
Danya, Jolie, Natasha
Brothers: Lukas, Davin, Jovan, Andre, Ruslan,
Maxim
✻ Misha is the standard nickname for Mikhail,
making it the Russian equivalent of Mike. It's
also the standard Russian name for a storybook
bear, much as we use Leo for lions. In non-
Slavic languages, the name is more often given
to girls, thanks to the "-a" ending. Like the simi-
lar import Sasha, it's simple but lush.
In the World: Actress Mischa Barton

Misty (MIS-tee)   1977: #40
Popularity: #2437
Styles: '70s–'80s, Modern
Meanings
Variants: Misti   1880   Today
Sisters: Brandy, Tawny,
Crystal, Tonya, Nikki, Fawn
Brothers: Dusty, Lance, Jamie, Stoney, Tad,
Brock
✻ In 1971, when names like Mindy and Kristy
were just taking off, along came a film called
Play Misty for Me. Kismet! Over the next two
decades, thousands of girls were named Misty.
Then the mist blew over, suddenly and com-
pletely. Most parents now consider Misty too
lightweight for a grown woman.
In the World: Beach volleyball player Misty
May-Treanor; horse novel *Misty of Chinco-
teague*

Molly (MAH-lee)   1991: #74
Popularity: #78
Styles: Guys and Dolls,
Nicknames, Antique Charm
Variants: Mollie   1880   Today
Sisters: Lily, Ruby, Tess,
Katie, Emma, Sophie
Brothers: Jake, Max, Henry, Jonah, Ben,
Charlie
✻ Molly was traditionally a nickname for
Mary, but it's now riding high on its own. Par-
ents love it because it's energetic, unpreten-
tious, and just plain adorable.
In the World: Actress Molly Ringwald; *The Un-
sinkable Molly Brown*; model Molly Sims; a
street drug

Monica (MAH-ni-kə)   1973: #40
Popularity: #406
Styles: '70s–'80s, Surfer '60s,
Saints
Nicknames: Mo, Mona   1880   Today
Variants: Monique, Monika
Sisters: Ericka, Andrea, Leslie, Vanessa,
Melinda, Adrienne
Brothers: Derrick, Bradley, Darren, Jeremy,
Marcus, Jared
✻ Monica was a top-100 name for American
girls for three decades straight. Then came the
1998 Monica Lewinsky scandal, and the name's
popularity plummeted. At the time, it seemed
like Monica would be forever tainted. But a de-
cade later, Monica sounded like Monica again:
a classic, global name. Its popularity, though,
has not rebounded.
In the World: infamous intern Monica Lewinsky; one-named singer Monica; actress Monica
Bellucci; tennis player Monica Seles

Monique (moh-NEEK)   1980: #93
Popularity: #1677
Styles: French, '70s–'80s,
African-American
Nicknames: Mique, Nikki,   1880   Today
Mo
Variants: Monica
Sisters: Desiree, Yvette, Adrienne, Natasha,
Michelle, Raquel
Brothers: Andre, Terrance, Antoine, Jarvis,
Derrick, Germaine
✻ The French form of Monica, Monique was a
huge mid-century hit in France. In the U.S., it
became popular in the '60s alongside Monica.
It's a smoother, glam version of that favorite.
In the World: Comedian Mo'Nique; actress Mo-
nique Coleman; designer Monique Lhuillier

Montana (mahn-TA-nə)   1998: #510
Popularity: #1984
Styles: Place Names, Country
and Western, Androgynous
Sisters: Cheyenne, Savannah,   1880   Today
Landry, Cadence, Dakota,
Sedona
Brothers: Bridger, Canyon, Trace, Maverick,
Dallas, Colton
✻ Parents flirted with Montana as a cowboy-ready boy's name, but it seems to have settled down on the girls' side. It's tough but flouncy, an unusual combination that's not for everyone. Great for a country singer, though.
In the World: The state of Montana

Morgan (MOHR-gin)   1995: #23
Popularity: #75
Styles: Androgynous, Celtic,
The "-ens," Nickname-Proof,
Turn of the 21st Century   1880   Today
Variants: Morgana
Sisters: Jordan, Kelsey, Megan, Sydney, Taylor,
Haley, Mckenzie, Brenna
Brothers: Trevor, Dylan, Connor, Kyle, Devin,
Tanner, Brendan, Cameron
✻ Whew, that was fast! It seems only yesterday that Morgan was an uncommon Welsh name with a masculine swagger. Now it's a popular standard—and feminine, like King Arthur's nemesis Morgan le Fay. (To kids, Morgan le Fay is the magical librarian from "The Magic Treehouse" series. Doesn't ring a bell, expectant parents? Just wait six years and you'll see!)
In the World: Actress Morgan Fairchild; financial firm Morgan Stanley

Muriel (MYOO-ree-əl)   1922: #112
Popularity: #6450
Styles: Ladies and
Gentlemen, Solid Citizens,
Celtic, Nickname-Proof   1880   Today
Variants: Meriel, Muir
Sisters: Sybil, Avis, Lenore, Imogene, Opal,
Iona
Brothers: Lyle, Wallace, Boyd, Archibald,
Kermit, Fergus
✻ Muriel is a distinguished Celtic classic, but it feels mighty old-fashioned. The problem is the "yoo" sound—consider how much more youthful Mariel sounds. You can stick with the name and trust that its virtues will shine through, or consider the traditional variant Meriel, or just Muir, meaning "sea."
In the World: Author Muriel Spark; poet Muriel Rukeyser; film *Muriel's Wedding*

Myra (MIY-rə)   1880: #156
Popularity: #792
Styles: Solid Citizens,
Nickname-Proof
Sisters: Rhoda, Vera, Olive,   1880   Today
Iva, Lorna, Rena
Brothers: Guy, Willis, Doyle, Wendell, Clyde,
Roy
✻ Names like Kyra and Mira are stylish and rising fast, so Myra should be right in the mainstream of fashion, right? Alas, no. This is a case where the little graph really tells the name's story. Myra is still linked to its 1940s surge, making it sound generations older than those similar names.
In the World: Book/film *Myra Breckinridge*

Nadia (NAH-dyə, NAH-dee-ə)   2005: #178
Popularity: #269
Styles: Slavic, Lacy and
Lissome, Nickname-Proof,
Muslim, New Classics   1880   Today
Variants: Nadya
Sisters: Mira, Daniela, Anya, Amina, Sasha,
Katya
Brothers: Andre, Roman, Lukas, Dominik,
Omar, Maxim
✻ In the 1976 Olympics, Romanian gymnast Nadia Comaneci became the world's sweetheart. Her first name (traditionally short for Nadezhda) also vaulted into America's consciousness, and today it still carries her image of petite foreign beauty.
In the World: Gymnast Nadia Comaneci; singer Nadia Ali; composer Nadia Boulanger

Nadine (nay-DEEN)   1933: #234
Popularity: #1459
Styles: Porch Sitters, French
Nicknames: Dina
Variants: Nadia   1880   Today
Sisters: Arlene, Jeanette,
Maxine, Marcelle, Eveline, Leonor
Brothers: Roland, Marlin, Lionel, Jerome,
Regis, Loren
✻ Nadine is one of the many French-styled names of the '20s and '30s that are seldom heard today. It sounds more intriguing when you realize that it's a French form of Nadia.
In the World: Writer Nadine Gordimer; Chuck Berry song "Nadine"

Nahla (NAH-lə)   2011: #859
Popularity: #861
Styles: Muslim
Variants: Nala
Sisters: Zahra, Safiya, Nadya,   1880   Today
Basma, Layla, Amira
Brothers: Zaid, Samir, Kamil, Taj, Bilal, Amir
✱ Nahla comes from the Arabic for "honey-bee," which suits the name just right. It has a smooth sweetness in a trim little form. Note that the female lead in the movie *The Lion King* is called Nala, which has made that identical-sounding name a popular choice for cats and dogs.
In the World: A daughter of actress Halle Berry; Nala of *The Lion King*

Nancy (NAN-see)   1947: #7
Popularity: #541
Styles: Nicknames, Solid Citizens
Nicknames: Nan   1880   Today
Variants: Nancie
Sisters: Sally, Joyce, Betty, Judy, Gloria, Peggy
Brothers: Tommy, Eddie, Bill, Larry, Ted, Gene
✱ Nancy is a nickname (for Ann) that still sounds right for the little girl in the *Nancy* comic strip. In real life, though, many Nancys are now sporting gray hair. By their sheer numbers, they've forced their name to grow up with them. Looking forward, it's easy to imagine the girls who grew up with the "Fancy Nancy" picture books reviving this name for the next generation.
In the World: *Nancy* comic strip; "Fancy Nancy" books; first lady Nancy Reagan; politician Nancy Pelosi; "Nancy Drew" books

Naomi (nay-OH-mee)   2011: #93
Popularity: #93
Styles: Timeless, Biblical, Nickname-Proof
Variants: Noemí, Noémie,   1880   Today
Noêmia, Noomi
Sisters: Miriam, Violet, Cecilia, Eve, Lydia, Iris, Vivian, Delilah
Brothers: Asher, Eli, Simon, Felix, Moses, Max, Solomon, Micah
✱ Naomi doesn't sound like anything else. That's its secret weapon. The name is traditional and timeless, but because it can't get lost in a crowd of similar alternatives, it still has the ability to surprise. The biblical Naomi was the recipient of the all-time greatest tribute to a mother-in-law ("whither thou goest, I will go").
In the World: Actress Naomi Watts; model Naomi Campbell; social critics Naomi Wolf and Naomi Klein; singer Naomi Judd

Natalia (nah-TAHL-yə,   2006: #94
nah-TAHL-ee-ə)
Popularity: #108
Styles: Slavic, Lacy and
Lissome, Saints, Latino/   1880   Today
Latina
Nicknames: Natasha, Talia
Variants: Natalya, Natalie
Sisters: Anastasia, Catalina, Gabriela, Juliana, Valeria, Tatiana
Brothers: Alexander, Diego, Dominik, Sebastian, Ivan, Roman
✱ Natalia is an elegant Russian classic from which the familiar nickname "Natasha" springs. It's also the fashionable Spanish take on Natalie and wide open to all ethnicities.
In the World: Model Natalia Vodianova; ballerina Natalia Makarova

Name Snapshots: Girls   163

Natalie (NAT-ə-lee)   2005: #18
Popularity: #14
Styles: New Classics, French
Nicknames: Nat, Tali
Variants: Natalia, Nathalie, 1880   Today
Nataly
Sisters: Allison, Brooke, Gabrielle, Samantha,
Bethany, Melanie, Miranda, Lauren
Brothers: Evan, Lucas, Jonathan, Christian,
Gabriel, Ian, Zachary, Colin
★This steady favorite is especially popular for
Christmas babies, thanks to its meaning "birth-
day of the Lord." It's taken from the French
form of the saint's name Natalia. Natalie sounds
more classically American, Natalia more dra-
matic.
In the World: Actresses Natalie Portman and
Natalie Wood; singers Natalie Cole, Natalie Im-
bruglia, and Natalie Merchant

Natasha (nah-TAH-shə)   1982: #71
Popularity: #489
Styles: Slavic, '70s–'80s,
African-American
Nicknames: Tasha   1880   Today
Sisters: Sonya, Monika,
Nicole, Dominique, Nadia, Tatiana
Brothers: Dominik, Erik, Terrence, Dimitri,
Jarrett, Lukas
★Natasha is so Slavic and seductive that it's
tempting to say it with a cartoon Russian accent.
Yet it's now so firmly established as an American
favorite that you'll never have to repeat it or
spell it out. For the most authentically Russian
version, try the full name Natalia with Natasha
as its nickname.
In the World: Singer Natasha Bedingfield; actresses Natasha Richardson and Natasha Hen-
stridge; cartoon villainess Natasha of *The Rocky
and Bullwinkle Show*

Nayeli (nah-YAY-lee)   2001: #175
Popularity: #382
Styles: Latino/Latina
Nicknames: Eli
Variants: Nayely, Nallely   1880   Today
Sisters: Anahi, Ximena,
Dayana, Sarai, Idalis, Citlali, Nyasia, Yareli
Brothers: Adriel, Gael, Yahir, Jairo, Ismael,
Cesar, Emilio, Misael
★A red-hot name of the 21st century, Nayeli is
a Latina name, but not a Spanish one. It comes
from the Zapotec language of Mexico. In parts
of the U.S., this name will be utterly unfamiliar,
but its supple grace translates beautifully.

Nell (NEHL)   1886: #144
Popularity: #4496
Styles: Guys and Dolls,
Nicknames, Why Not?
Nicknames: Nellie, Nelly   1880   Today
Variants: Nelle, Nella
Sisters: Evie, Bess, Reba, Cleo, Tess, Mae
Brothers: Nat, Charley, Theo, Abe, Jess, Ben
★Nell is a nickname for Eleanor or Helen, and
its pet form Nellie was once a wildy fashionable
name in its own right. Today the trim Nell hits
the spot, carrying on the sweet essence of Nellie
in a more mature form.
In the World: Singer Nelly Furtado; actress Nell
Carter; Little Nell of Charles Dickens's *The Old
Curiosity Shop*; Jodie Foster film *Nell*

Nevaeh (neh-VAY-ə, neh-VAY)   2010: #25
Popularity: #35
Styles: Modern Meanings
Sisters: Trinity, Ily, Genesis,
Treah, Eden, Lilah   1880   Today
Brothers: Josiah, Zion, Galen,
Messiah, Malachi, Gideon
★This unique name rose out of the mist in
2001 to become a popular sensation. It's created
from an anagram—"heaven" backward—and
many parents are captivated by the concept.
Think of it as a loving secret message to a child.
Be aware, though, that the appeal is far from
universal. Nevaeh may be the most stylistically
divisive name in America, inspiring strong feel-
ings pro and con.

Nia (NEE-ə)   2000: #307
Popularity: #490
Styles: African-American,
Short and Sweet, Celtic,
African, Nickname-Proof   1880   Today
Variants: Nyah, Niamh
Sisters: Kira, Zara, Halle, Anya, Zuri, Macy,
Elle, Laila
Brothers: Ian, Kobe, Rohan, Taj, Noel, Devin,
Nico, Reese
★Nia's like a compact SUV or a shot of
espresso. It's a trim little burst of personality,
perfectly suited to the moment. It has two inde-
pendent origins: from a Swahili word meaning
"goal" and from the Welsh form of the name
Niamh.
In the World: Actresses Nia Long, Nia Vardalos,
and Nia Peeples

Niamh (NEEV) 2008: #2552
Popularity: #2990
Styles: Celtic, Mythological
Variants: Neve, Nia
Sisters: Aoife, Roisin, Sinéad, 1880 Today
Aine, Siobhan, Ciara
Brothers: Cian, Eoghan, Conor, Cathal, Fionn, Niall

✳An ancient Celtic goddess name, Niamh is a hot choice in Ireland and Scotland today. It's pronounced "NEEV," and in the U.S. you'd best be prepared to spell and pronounce it over and over again. The most common Anglicized spelling, Neve, comes with a bit of confusion of its own. The best-known Neve is actress Neve Campbell—whose name actually comes from her mother's Dutch surname and is pronounced "NEHV."

Nicole (ni-KOHL) 1983: #7
Popularity: #116
Styles: French, '70s–'80s,
Turn of the 21st Century
Nicknames: Nikki 1880 Today
Variants: Nichole, Nicola
Sisters: Danielle, Amanda, Stephanie, Jessica, Marisa, Natalie
Brothers: Brandon, Sean, Eric, Trevor, Andre, Jared

✳Michael, Daniel, Nicholas. Michelle, Danielle, Nicole. When the male names became popular, their French feminine forms soon followed. And just as Nicholas continues to be a strong choice for boys, Nicole is still a favorite for its round, crisp sound. The Italian-styled version Nicola, common in England, is stressed on the first syllable.
In the World: Actress Nicole Kidman; TV personality Nicole Richie; singer Nicole Scherzinger

Nika (NEE-kə) 2009: #2542
Popularity: #2958
Styles: Slavic, Nicknames,
Short and Sweet, Why Not?
Variants: Nike, Nica 1880 Today
Sisters: Mira, Anya, Romy,
Sela, Tali, Katya, Daria, Lina
Brothers: Lev, Teo, Maxim, Ari, Viktor, Marek, Bram, Lazar

✳Nika is typically short for Veronika, or any other "-nika" name of your liking. (Annika is the popular choice today.) You can also call it a form of Nike, the Greek goddess of victory, and thus part of the Nicole family. Like many Slavic nicknames, it sounds appealingly modern as a full name in English.

Nina (NEE-nə) 1887: #114
Popularity: #304
Styles: Timeless, Nickname-
Proof, Short and Sweet
Sisters: Celia, Iris, Nora, 1880 Today
Julia, Eva, Anna, Ivy, Clara
Brothers: Simon, Felix, Foster, Sam, Ross, Emmett, Ellis, Leo

✳This name seems to exist outside of the normal constraints of fashion—you just can't pin it down. Nina has origins in languages ranging from Russian to Hebrew to Swahili. It can be a nickname or a full name. It's never trendy, yet never goes out of style. It's sweet and strong and sassy. So what is it, really? Perhaps a refreshingly clean slate for your daughter's own unique personality.
In the World: Singer Nina Simone; actress Nina Dobrev

Noelle (noh-EHL) 2011: #357
Popularity: #357
Styles: French
Nicknames: Noe
Variants: Noël 1880 Today
Sisters: Simone, Paloma,
Eden, Sylvie, Camille, Nathalie
Brothers: Quentin, Julian, Nicolas, Miles, Damien, Roman

✳This is the *usual* feminine form of the name Noel, which is *usually* given to babies born around Christmas. But don't let either "usual" hold you back. For spellings, Noelle is soft and classic, but Noël is equally chic. And despite the yuletide connotations, the name is welcome and stylish any time of year.
In the World: Christmas associations like the carol "The First Noel"

Noemi (noh-EH-mee, noh-ay-MEE) 2001: #553
Popularity: #685
Styles: Latino/Latina, Italian, Biblical
Variants: Noemí, Noémie, Naomi
Sisters: Camila, Ester, Marisol, Lidia, Sarai, Silvia
Brothers: Ezequiel, Moises, Ariel, Neftali, Efrain, Abel
★This form of Naomi is still unfamiliar to many English speakers and may trip up some tongues. Yet it's one of the sunniest names on the planet, and a favorite in languages from Italian and Spanish to Hungarian (and French, in the spelling Noémie). The stress is on the middle syllable in French and Italian, and on the final syllable in Spanish.
In the World: Italian singer Noemi

Nola (NOH-lə) 1894: #249
Popularity: #888
Styles: Ladies and Gentlemen, Short and Sweet, Why Not?
Variants: Nuala
Sisters: Iva, Willa, Evie, Iona, Cleo, Delia
Brothers: Emory, Gray, Leon, Charley, Foster, Boyd
★Nola's roots are Irish—it's short for Finola. Nola's sound, though, is quirky and old-fashioned. Think of it as the point where Lucy and Stella meet Caitlin and Kiera. But Nola has yet another side too, as the popular abbreviation for New Orleans, Louisiana. If you want to emphasize that southern side, you can try Nola as a nickname for Magnolia.
In the World: NOLA (New Orleans, LA)

Nora (NOH-rə) 1881: #55
Popularity: #137
Styles: Antique Charm, Celtic, Nickname-Proof
Variants: Norah
Sisters: Clara, Lucy, Eliza, Nina, Stella, Molly
Brothers: Owen, Charlie, Angus, Jack, Murphy, Nolan
★ Nora is a nickname for Eleanora, Leonora, or Honora. In the U.S., though, simple Nora has always been more popular than those three stately sisters put together. The name hit its peak in the 1880s and spent the 20th century in gentle decline. Recently, it's begun to reemerge as a stylish, upscale choice for families of Irish descent.
In the World: Writers Nora Ephron and Nora Roberts; singer Norah Jones; film *Nick and Norah's Infinite Playlist*

Norma (NOHR-mə) 1931: #22
Popularity: #1933
Styles: Solid Citizens, Nickname-Proof
Sisters: Rita, Lois, Arlene, Loretta, Ramona, Joyce
Brothers: Arnold, Gordon, Marvin, Ralph, Stanley, Howard
★ Norma Shearer was one of Hollywood's biggest stars of the 1930s, a buoyant modern woman with a wardrobe to die for. Today she's overlooked and largely forgotten. The same fate has befallen her name, which has gone from the top of the heap to an afterthought. Its doughy style just doesn't appeal to today's parents.
In the World: Actress Norma Shearer; song "Goodbye Norma Jean"; designer Norma Kamali; film *Norma Rae*

Nyla (NIY-lə) 2011: #315
Popularity: #315
Styles: Short and Sweet, African-American
Sisters: Layla, Zuri, Nia, Anya, Amaya, Jade
Brothers: Kobe, Rylan, Luca, Kaleb, Tyson, Joah
★This lithe little name has built quite a following. It's simple and sultry, with echoes of hits like Tyra and Nia . . . but perhaps a bit synthetic, like Nylon. In non-naming contexts, Nyla is occasionally used as shorthand for New York + Los Angeles.
In the World: N.Y.L.A. shoes

Oakley (OHK-lee) 2011: #1431
Popularity: #1436
Styles: Last Names First,
Country and Western,
Androgynous, Why Not? 1880 Today
Sisters: Landry, Shiloh,
Larkin, Paisley, Sedona, Berkeley
Brothers: Colton, Nash, Lawson, Cooper,
Bentley, Ryder
✳ Picture Western sharpshooter Annie Oakley
shooting a playing card edge-on, in a pair of de-
signer Oakley sunglasses. That's the kind of
freewheeling cool that is attracting parents of
boys and girls alike to this surname.
In the World: Sharpshooter Annie Oakley; Oak-
ley eyewear

Octavia (ahk-TAY-vee-ə) 1880: #305
Popularity: #2510
Styles: Exotic Traditional,
Classical, African-American,
Why Not? 1880 Today
Nicknames: Tavi
Sisters: Augusta, Marguerite, Ophelia,
Drusilla, Zora, Minerva, Olympia, Lavinia
Brothers: Ulysses, Demetrius, Alonzo, Cassius,
Tycho, Napoleon, Aeneas, Titus
✳ Octavia and Olivia start the same and end
the same. They're both traditional, ladylike, and
Shakespearean. But where Olivia is a romantic,
Octavia is made of sterner stuff. Don't let the
sternness scare you. This is one impressive
name, suggesting an impressive woman be-
hind it.
In the World: Actress Octavia Spencer; author
Octavia Butler

Olga (OHL-gə) 1916: #126
Popularity: #2757
Styles: Slavic
Nicknames: Olya
Sisters: Vera, Ludmila, Anya, 1880 Today
Nadezhda, Ksenia, Irina
Brothers: Boris, Alexei, Igor, Vladimir, Nikolai,
Pavel
✳ Olga is a cultured classic with an elegant
lilt . . . in Russian. The Russian pronunciation
centers on a soft "l," a velvety sound that's hard
to reproduce in English. The American pronun-
ciation mires the name in leaden Soviet style.
In the World: Gymnast Olga Korbut; Olga linge-
rie

Olive (AH-liv) 1886: #84
Popularity: #416
Styles: Charms and Graces,
Ladies and Gentlemen
Nicknames: Ollie, Liv 1880 Today
Variants: Olivia
Sisters: Hazel, Pearl, Alice, Opal, Esther, Iris
Brothers: Leo, Oscar, August, Milo, Casper,
Julius
✳ Olivia sounds like a 19th-century revival,
but it was staid sister Olive who really won
hearts back in Victorian days. Today the name
is aggressively contrarian, an emblem of anti-
style—which, of course, makes it extra stylish.
It's quite adorable on a toddler too.
In the World: Olive Oyl of *Popeye*; a hot celeb-
rity baby name

Olivia (oh-LI-vee-ə) 2011: #4
Popularity: #4
Styles: Antique Charm,
Shakespearean, Lacy and
Lissome 1880 Today
Nicknames: Liv, Livvy
Variants: Livia, Olive, Olivié
Sisters: Isabella, Sophia, Grace, Madeline, Ava,
Annabelle
Brothers: Owen, Alexander, Ethan, Nathaniel,
Lucas, Noah
✳ Starting in the '90s, thousands of parents si-
multaneously discovered the lovely and under-
used name Olivia. It's a faultless choice, with its
antique charm and hip nickname. Today Olivia
is no longer an underused discovery but a huge
popular hit. If you wish it weren't so common,
just remember that in this case "popular" truly
means "well loved."
In the World: Actresses Olivia de Havilland
and Olivia Wilde; singer Olivia Newton-John;
"Olivia the Pig" books

Orly (OHR-lee)
Popularity: #6053
Styles: Jewish, Short and Sweet, Latino/Latina
Sisters: Tali, Reyna, Romi, Eliana, Luz, Sarai
Brothers: Elan, Ariel, Noam, Abel, Esai, Vidal

2009: #5355

1880 — Today

✴ This sunny sprite of a name means "my light" in Hebrew. You can think of it as a contemporary remix of Leora. Or, if you prefer, you can follow a path to Orly from the Roman name Aurelius. (That's the version behind Paris-Orly Airport.) Whichever Orly you choose, expect some people to see it as textspeak for "Oh, RealLY?"
In the World: Orly Airport; the O RLY? owl (Internet meme)

Paige (PAYJ)
Popularity: #107
Styles: Brisk and Breezy, Turn of the 21st Century
Variants: Page
Sisters: Brooke, Shelby, Jenna, Logan, Haley, Shea
Brothers: Blake, Chase, Tanner, Grant, Dalton, Bryce

1995: #58

1880 — Today

✴ Cheerfully preppy, Paige is a sunlit alternative to Brooke and Brett. The "i" is essential to the preppy style. As Page, the name's roots as a servantly surname show through. An especially popular middle name choice.
In the World: TV host Paige Davis; *Charmed* character Paige Matthews

Paisley (PAYZ-lee)
Popularity: #195
Styles: Modern Meanings, Fanciful, Bell Tones
Sisters: Cadence, Brinley, Audrina, Presley, Brielle, Oakley
Brothers: Keegan, Brantley, Parker, Quaid, Easton, Rylan

2011: #195

1880 — Today

✴ It's cute, it's charming, it sounds like a girl's name. It also has country singer Brad Paisley in its corner. So Paisley has made the jump from fabric pattern to baby name. Many folks will be tickled by the choice, but be prepared for grumbling from those—including most of your parents' generation—who liken it to Plaid and PolkaDot.
In the World: Singer Brad Paisley; the paisley pattern

Paloma (pah-LOH-mah)
Popularity: #830
Styles: Exotic Traditional, Latino/Latina, Why Not?
Sisters: Catalina, Lorelei, Frida, Isadora, Iliana, Athena, Aurora
Brothers: Atticus, Leonardo, Maxim, Matthias, Orlando, Gideon, Justus

2010: #698

1880 — Today

✴ Ripe and romantic, Paloma (Spanish for "dove") is also a sign of peace. Accessory designer Paloma Picasso, daugher of Pablo, has added a layer of luxury to the name.
In the World: Designer Paloma Picasso; singer Paloma Faith

Pamela (PA-mə-lə)
Popularity: #967
Styles: Mid-Century
Nicknames: Pam
Variants: Pamella, Pamala
Sisters: Sandra, Diane, Cheryl, Brenda, Sharon, Deborah, Cynthia, Paula
Brothers: Douglas, Barry, Dennis, Gregory, Kenneth, Darrell, Bruce, Roger

1954: #12

1880 — Today

✴ Think of the Breck Girl, the advertising icon with the flowing locks. For 40 years she was the timeless, glamorous, American beauty. Then one day she disappeared and became a retro sweetheart looked back on with fondness. The name Pamela has followed her along that same path.
In the World: Actresses Pamela Anderson and Pam Grier; diplomat/socialite Pamela Harriman

Paola (POW-lə)
Popularity: #479
Styles: Italian
Nicknames: Pao
Variants: Paula
Sisters: Gianna, Daniela, Viviana, Noemi, Eliana, Francesca
Brothers: Emilio, Sergio, Luca, Marco, Matteo, Alberto

1999: #299

1880 — Today

✴ Simple men's classics like John, Frank, and Paul are slipping from the charts, but they're not forgotten. We see them resurrected in their Italian feminine forms: Gianna, Francesca, and Paola are 21st-century hits.

Paralee (PA-rə-lee) 1881: #470
Popularity: Very rare
Styles: Country and Western,
Ladies and Gentlemen, Why
Not? 1880 Today
Sisters: Marietta, Evaline,
Delta, Mamie, Lucille, Florida, Cordelia,
Larue
Brothers: Frazier, Wiley, Lafayette, Barney,
Lemuel, Hardy, Lonzo, Hubbard
✳ Here's an old-timer who looks like a spring chicken. The name Paralee was a favorite in the South during the 19th and early 20th centuries, but has since vanished. Its sound is now surprisingly modern, yet the echoes of Southern grandmas past set it apart from a roomful of Natalees, Baylees, and Emmalees.
In the World: Found most often in a cluster of states bounded by Texas, Missouri, and Georgia

Paris (PA-ris) 2004: #157
Popularity: #338
Styles: Place Names,
Nickname-Proof,
Androgynous 1880 Today
Sisters: Kingston, Myles,
Dante, London, Jericho, Talon, Justus, Jett
Brothers: Skye, Justice, Aspen, Nadia, Phoenix, Sienna, Presley, Venice
✳ The ultimate place name, Paris risks the "pretentious" label but gets by thanks to its simple sound. It's self-assured, but not arrogant—though ubiquitous socialite Paris Hilton has tilted the name toward the flashy side.
In the World: Socialite Paris Hilton; Paris, the "City of Light"

Parker (PAHR-ker) 2011: #366
Popularity: #366
Styles: Last Names First,
Androgynous
Sisters: Campbell, Riley, 1880 Today
Sawyer, Addison, Finley,
Elliot
Brothers: Jackson, Hunter, Deacon, Paxton, Maddox, Hudson
✳ Parker is still solidly male, but magnetic actress Parker Posey has lured the name toward the girls' side. If you want a more feminine name in the same genre, Piper is one possibility.
In the World: Actress Parker Posey

Patience (PAY-shehnts) 2006: #578
Popularity: #843
Styles: Charms and Graces,
Antique Charm
Nicknames: Pat, Patty 1880 Today
Sisters: Mercy, Honor, Amity, Temperence, Charity, Promise
Brothers: Tobias, Peregrine, Gideon, Matthias, Josiah, Phineas
✳ The fashion for virtue names has brought back this quintessential Puritan classic. The modesty and restraint of Patience are apparent, but this name has a surprising elegance too. Its sound is graceful, and Patience is a sophisticated virtue that's often in short supply these days.
In the World: Phrases like "patience is a virtue"; another word for solitaire games

Patricia (pah-TRI-sh-ə) 1951: #3
Popularity: #667
Styles: Solid Citizens
Nicknames: Pat, Patty, Patsy,
Trish, Tricia, Tia, Trixie 1880 Today
Variants: Tricia, Patrice, Patrizia
Sisters: Carolyn, Gloria, Marianne, Barbara, Janet, Sharon, Judith, Theresa
Brothers: Kenneth, Richard, Philip, Donald, Raymond, Martin, Paul, Lawrence
✳ Patricia is one of the true mid-century classics. The full name's dignity is timeless, but nickname Patty is pure 1940s (like the youngest of the singing Andrews Sisters). Get creative with nicknames or stick with the full Patricia, and you may have a trend-busting winner.
In the World: Actresses Patricia Neal, Patricia Heaton, and Patricia Arquette

Paula (PAW-la) 1963: #42
Popularity: #821
Styles: Mid-Century,
Nickname-Proof
Variants: Paola 1880 Today
Sisters: Sandra, Pamela, Connie, Marcia, Susan, Donna
Brothers: Barry, Randall, Douglas, Wayne, Jerry, Patrick
✳ It's hard to find fault with this name, which is a straightforward feminine form of the equally straightforward Paul. It's just not attracting much notice at the moment, just like Roberta, Carla, and their straightforward kin. Italian sister Paola is one eye-catching alternative.
In the World: Singer/reality TV star Paula Abdul; chef Paula Deen; TV journalist Paula Zahn; actress Paula Patton

Name Snapshots: Girls 169

Paulina (paw-LEEN-ə) 2002: #364
Popularity: #759
Styles: Slavic, Latino/Latina,
Shakespearean, Saints
Nicknames: Lina 1880 Today
Variants: Pauline
Sisters: Mariana, Natalia, Daniela, Melania,
Viviana, Tatiana, Bianca, Gabriela
Brothers: Adrian, Dominik, Rodrigo, Tomas,
Orlando, Ivan, Dimitri, Lorenzo
✳ This old Latin name was an unlikely come-
back queen of the 1990s, when other "Paul"
names were fading. The reasons: Mexican pop
star Paulina Rubio and Czech model Paulina
Porizkova.
In the World: Singer Paulina Rubio; model Pau-
lina Porizkova

Pauline (paw-LEEN) 1915: #32
Popularity: #2697
Styles: Porch Sitters, French
Variants: Paulina
Sisters: Louise, Jeanette, 1880 Today
Marion, Frances, Lucille,
Helene
Brothers: Maurice, Herbert, Rudolph,
Clarence, Bernard, Claude
✳ Back around the First World War, Pauline
was a huge hit—bigger than now-beloved old-
timers like Emma, Clara, and Julia. By the end
of the Roaring Twenties, the name had started a
nosedive that took it completely out of the run-
ning. In the past generation, Pauline has had to
watch from the sidelines as sidekick Paulina has
taken center stage.
In the World: Film critic Pauline Kael; Pauline
Fossil of book/film *Ballet Shoes*

Pearl (PERL) 1890: #24
Popularity: #814
Styles: Charms and Graces,
Guys and Dolls
Variants: Perla 1880 Today
Sisters: Mae, Flora, Hazel,
Olive, Mabel, Fern, Daisy, Louise
Brothers: Harry, Mack, Major, Otto, Harvey,
Clyde, Oscar, Ernest
✳ Once upon a time, Pearl sounded as light
as Lily, as romantic as Rose, and as radiant as
Ruby. Yet today's parents seem to feel that it's as
old as Olive. Pearl still has great charm—it just
takes a little daring to use. That makes it a par-
ticularly appealing middle name choice.
In the World: Entertainer Pearl Bailey; writer
Pearl Buck; band Pearl Jam

Peggy (PEH-gee) 1937: #31
Popularity: #5633
Styles: Mid-Century,
Nicknames
Nicknames: Peg 1880 Today
Sisters: Betsy, Nancy, Donna,
Fran, Penny, Becky
Brothers: Jimmy, Bob, Billy, Tommy, Ted,
Danny
✳ Thanks to Buddy Holly's "Peggy Sue," this
name gives off the sunny glow of a mythical,
clean-scrubbed 1950s. (Compare it to the more
serious style of the full name Margaret.) Despite
the cute nickname style, Peggy sounds like a
grown-up, and a smart, likable one at that. The
Mad Men character Peggy has reinforced that
image.
In the World: Peggy of *Mad Men*; song "Peggy
Sue"; Peggy Hill of *King of the Hill*; Peg Bundy
of *Married . . . With Children*

Penelope (peh-NEHL-ə-pee) 2011: #169
Popularity: #169
Styles: Mythological,
Timeless
Nicknames: Penny, Pip, 1880 Today
Nellie, Nell
Sisters: Felicity, Phoebe, Marjorie, Beatrix,
Eleanor, Lorelei, Rosemary
Brothers: Theodore, Benedict, Vaughn, Milo,
Elliott, Tobias, Linus
✳ Penelope is an individualistic classic. Its gal-
loping Greek pronunciation makes it memora-
ble yet keeps it from becoming too popular.
Spanish actress Penelope Cruz has led a mini-
revival of the name.
In the World: Actresses Penelope Cruz and Pe-
nelope Ann Miller; author Penelope Lively;
2006 film *Penelope*; a hot name for celebrity
babies

Penny (PEH-nee)   1963: #87
Popularity: #1398
Styles: Mid-Century,
Nicknames, English
Nicknames: Pen   1880   Today
Sisters: Suzy, Connie, Cindy,
Pam, Sandy, Jan
Brothers: Rick, Ken, Barry, Jay, Steve, Tony
✳ Penny, a nickname for Penelope, is best
known and loved as a coin: "Bright as a
penny" . . . "Pennies from Heaven" . . . "Pick it
up, all the day you'll have good luck." The
thought of a shiny penny brings a smile to your
face, and that gives this name a fairy-tale charm
that transcends its '50s style. The full Penelope
is the fashionable given name, though.
In the World: Actress/director Penny Marshall;
Penny of *The Big Bang Theory*; many "penny"
songs and phrases

Petra (PEHT-rə)   1894: #429
Popularity: #1755
Styles: Ladies and
Gentlemen, German and
Dutch   1880   Today
Sisters: Josefa, Willa, Sibyl,
Iona, Avis, Rhea
Brothers: Emil, Jules, Casper, Emory, Anton,
Bertram
✳ This name won't be for everyone. It's stately
rather than spry, but it has a quiet sweetness that
should win a few hearts. Like Peter, Petra comes
from the Greek word for "rock"; the ancient city
of Petra is carved out of rock cliffs.
In the World: Tennis player Petra Kvitová; a
character in the children's novel *Chasing Ver-
meer*

Peyton (PAY-tən)   2009: #42
Popularity: #53
Styles: Last Names First,
Androgynous, The "-ens,"
Nickname-Proof   1880   Today
Variants: Payton
Sisters: Kendall, Parker, Hayden, Riley, Paige,
Addison
Brothers: Logan, Walker, Ashton, Garrett,
Mason, Paxton
✳ Most androgynous names come across very
differently for the two sexes. Picture a male and
a female Sidney, for instance. Payton, though, is
remarkably consistent: it's modern and sleekly
preppy, with a hint of a Southern drawl, for girls
and boys alike.
In the World: Actress Peyton List; Peyton Saw-
yer of *One Tree Hill*

Philomena (fi-lo-MEEN-ə)   1915: #355
Popularity: #3745
Styles: Exotic Traditional,
Saints, Ladies and
Gentlemen   1880   Today
Nicknames: Mena, Phil
Variants: Filomena
Sisters: Celestine, Aurelia, Theodora,
Sophronia, Leocadia, Augusta
Brothers: Ferdinand, Leander, Benedict,
Constantine, Florian, Ambrose
✳ Quite common a hundred years ago, the
name Philomena has virtually disappeared
from our culture. It may seem like a curiosity
today, but it's a handsome one. (It comes from
Greek roots meaning "love" and "strength.")
The Italian spelling Filomena tilts the style
from antique to exotic.

Phoebe (FEE-bee)   1883: #219
Popularity: #310
Styles: Antique Charm, Short
and Sweet, Nickname-Proof,
Shakespearean, Biblical   1880   Today
Variants: Phebe
Sisters: Daphne, Lydia, Sophie, Esme, Piper,
Zoe
Brothers: Emmett, Oliver, Jasper, Milo, Eli,
Owen
✳ An absolute sweetheart of a name, Phoebe
carries its girlish sound with graceful maturity.
The sophisticated spelling is the key—a Phoebe
wouldn't have a chance. The eccentric Phoebe
from the sitcom *Friends* may be the first Phoebe
in many folks' minds, but it's not a dominant
association.
In the World: Characters on the TV series
Friends and *Charmed*; actress Phoebe Cates;
singer Phoebe Snow

Phyllis (FI-lis) 1929: #24
Popularity: #6470
Styles: Solid Citizens,
Mythological
Nicknames: Phyl 1880 Today
Variants: Phyllida
Sisters: Shirley, Doris, Beverly, Marilyn,
Rosalie, Gloria
Brothers: Wendell, Gordon, Donald, Gilbert,
Norris, Leonard
✷ Phyllis has appealing ingredients: classical
roots (a tragic lover in Greek mythology) and a
contemporary rhythm. But the name just can't
shake its grandma aura. Its mythological spirit is
better captured now by names like Avis and
Luna, or by Phyllida, another form of the same
Greek root.
In the World: Comedian Phyllis Diller; singer
Phyllis Hyman; conservative activist Phyllis
Schlafly

Pia (PEE-ə) 1983: #1462
Popularity: #2587
Styles: Nordic, Short and
Sweet
Variants: Pía 1880 Today

Sisters: Britta, Mari, Nika,
Liv, Una, Mina
Brothers: Teo, Kai, Axel, Nico, Soren, Aric
✷ This adorable little name, a form of Pius, is
an international bundle of cheer. You'll meet
girls named Pia everywhere from South America to Scandinavia. Not in the U.S., though,
despite the popularity of the similar name Mia.
There's no escaping the reason: "me" is a much
more positive association than "pee." That
won't matter much after grade school, though.
In the World: Singer/actress Pia Zadora; *American Idol* contestant Pia Toscano

Piper (PIY-per) 2011: #110
Popularity: #110
Styles: Last Names First
Nicknames: Pip, Pippi, Pippa
Sisters: Harper, Willow, 1880 Today
Phoebe, Larkin, Scarlett, Ivy
Brothers: Griffin, Jack, Sawyer, Liam, Miles,
Finn
✷ A piper plays the pipes, or a flute. (Picture
the Pied Piper.) That makes Piper an occupa-
tional surname, but it stands apart from that
crowded field. Piper's sound and meaning are
bright and lively, and unlike most surnames,
this one is purely, unapologetically female. The
effect is surname style without any hint of pom-
posity—a high-status name.
In the World: Actresses Piper Laurie and Piper
Perabo; Piper of *Charmed*; Piper Aircraft; a
daughter of Sarah Palin

Pippa (PI-pə) 2011: #2565
Popularity: #2588
Styles: Short and Sweet,
English
Nicknames: Pip 1880 Today
Variants: Philippa
Sisters: Dulcie, Isla, Zara, Tamsin, Poppy,
Gemma
Brothers: Jonty, Finn, Barnaby, Toby, Ivor, Kit
✷ This little Brit nickname is as lively as they
come, a kicky Carnaby Street creation. It was
virtually a British-only secret for many years,
until Pippa Middleton turned heads at her sis-
ter's wedding to England's Prince William. The
full version Philippa is every bit as British, but as
formal as Pippa is fun.
In the World: Royal sister-in-law Pippa Middleton; actress Pippa Black

Polly (PAH-lee) 1881: #222
Popularity: #3567
Styles: Solid Citizens,
Nicknames
Sisters: Dottie, Nan, Kitty, 1880 Today

Poppy, Tillie, Rosie
Brothers: Louie, Ned, Pete, Archie, Hal,
Barney
✷ Polly is cozy, sunny, and jolly. Like Molly, it
was once a common nickname for Mary, but
unlike Molly, it has slipped into obscurity.
Today you're most likely to encounter Polly as a
name for dolls or parrots. (The identification of
Polly with parrots goes back at least 400 years.)
On a girl, it's old-fashioned and endearing.
In the World: Polly Pocket dolls; actress Polly
Walker; the phrase "Polly wants a cracker"; film
Along Came Polly

Poppy (PAHP-ee) 2011: #1638
Popularity: #1640
Styles: Charms and Graces, English, Why Not?
Sisters: Mercy, Clover, Ruby, Dahlia, Maisie, Romy
Brothers: Harry, Albert, Alfie, Jem, Flynn, Theo
1880 Today
✳ Poppy is one of the oh-so-cute names beloved by English parents and ignored by their American counterparts. It's not a cutesy nickname, though, just a sweet flower. If Lily can bloom in the U.S., why not Poppy too?
In the World: Actress Poppy Montgomery

Portia (POHR-shə) 1988: #734
Popularity: #2726
Styles: English, Shakespearean, Nickname-Proof, Classical, Exotic Traditional
1880 Today
Sisters: Silvia, Anthea, Imogen, Cassia, Nicola, Cecily
Brothers: Galen, Marius, Tarquin, Corin, Piers, Lysander
✳ This Shakespearean standard has a noble elegance that few names can match. Parents who love its literary style, though, will be dismayed when it is constantly confused with the sports car Porsche.
In the World: Actress Portia de Rossi; the heroine of *The Merchant of Venice*

Precious (PREH-shəs) 1998: #381
Popularity: #1222
Styles: Modern Meanings
Sisters: Treasure, Princess, Charity, Unique, Harmony, Bliss, Jubilee, Miracle
1880 Today
Brothers: Sincere, Messiah, Wisdom, Zion, Peerless, Orion, Prince, Justice
✳ This name is a sweet sentiment to show a new daughter how much she is loved. It's a pure idea, but a complicated name. In the U.S., the name Precious can come across as uncomfortably cutesy for a grown woman. And then there's the long shadow of the movie *Precious*, in which the name is borne by a ghetto teenager whose parents showered her with horrifying abuse, not love. If you're looking for the buoyancy with fewer complications, consider names like Promise, Essence, or Star.
In the World: 2009 film *Precious*; Precious Ramotswe of *The No. 1 Ladies' Detective Agency*

Presley (PREHS-lee) 2011: #227
Popularity: #227
Styles: Namesakes, Last Names First, Androgynous
Variants: Pressley
1880 Today
Sisters: Harley, Everly, Scarlett, Cassidy, Piper, Marley
Brothers: Cash, Kingston, Jagger, Paxton, Lennon, Beckham
✳ If it's a boy, we'll call him Jagger. And if it's a girl . . . ah, of course! If Peyton and Ainsley are too tame for your taste, Presley is a surname that cranks up the volume. If you just like the name but not the Elvis (really?), add an "s" and make it Pressley.
In the World: Singer Elvis Presley

Priscilla (pri-SIL-ə) 1940: #127
Popularity: #487
Styles: Timeless, Biblical
Nicknames: Cilla, Prissy, CeCe
1880 Today
Variants: Prisca
Sisters: Susana, Patricia, Constance, Cecilia, Penelope, Tabitha
Brothers: Nathaniel, Thaddeus, Philip, Simon, Paul, Timothy
✳ Priscilla has a prim reputation, thanks to the pet form Prissy and a storied history as a Puritan name. Today the name is smart but exceedingly formal. If you can scare up a good nickname, it could be a stylish choice. Ironically, formal Priscilla itself started off life as a pet form of Prisca. The biblical Priscilla is referred to by both names.
In the World: Actress Priscilla Presley; film *Priscilla, Queen of the Desert*; Mayflower Pilgrim Priscilla Alden

Quinn (KWIN) 2011: #188
Popularity: #188
Styles: Brisk and Breezy, Androgynous
Variants: Quin
1880 Today
Sisters: Reese, Parker, Avery, Rowan, Skye, Blake
Brothers: Drake, Xavier, Connor, Jude, Jameson, Paxton
✳ Until recently, the name Quinn was reliably masculine. Who would think to name a girl after "The Mighty Quinn"? The makers of the TV series *Glee*, that's who. The show's pretty blond cheerleader Quinn instantly pushed the name into the androgynous column.
In the World: Quinn Fabray of *Glee*; TV series *Dr. Quinn, Medicine Woman*

Rachel (RAY-chəl) — 1985: #13
Popularity: #117
Styles: Timeless, Biblical, Nickname-Proof
Variants: Rachael, Rochelle, Raquel
Sisters: Sarah, Lauren, Emily, Rebecca, Megan, Abigail
Brothers: Andrew, Benjamin, Joshua, Matthew, Aaron, Nathan
✴ Rachel is a biblical classic, but it doesn't sound like a quaint heirloom. It was one of the favorite names of the late 20th century, hitting its peak with the '90s *Friends* character Rachel and her eponymous hairstyle. Today Rachel's biblical roots and decades of popularity make it one of the most flexible and risk-free names you can choose.
In the World: Rachel of TV series *Friends*; chef Rachael Ray; conservationist Rachel Carson; actress Rachel McAdams

Rae (RAY) — 1892: #311
Popularity: #2992
Styles: Guys and Dolls
Variants: Ray
Sisters: Roxie, Nell, Mae, Cleo, Delta, Bess
Brothers: Lon, Abe, Major, Ike, Earl, Wiley
✴ Rae has always been a flexible name, used equally as a nickname, middle name, and compound element (Rae Ann, Raelyn, Carly Rae). It makes an airy little first name too.
In the World: Actress Rae Dawn Chong

Rafaela (rah-fiy-EHL-ə) — 1903: #789
Popularity: #2915
Styles: Exotic Traditional, Lacy and Lissome, Latino/ Latina, Why Not?
Nicknames: Rafi, Rae
Variants: Rafaela, Raffaella, Raphaela
Sisters: Antonia, Luisa, Arabella, Mariana, Valentina, Serafina
Brothers: Emmanuel, Domenic, Marco, Nicolas, Matthias, Sergio
✴ The feminine form of Raphael is familiar in many languages, but not in English. English-speaking parents have overlooked this lyrical classic, leaving it with great untapped fashion potential. Several spellings are equally traditional. The Spanish/Portuguese Rafaela is the sleekest, the Italian Raffaella the most dramatic, and the German/English Raphaela the most delicate and antique.
In the World: Rafaella sportswear; entertainer Raffaella Carrà; Saint Raphaela Mary

Raine (RAYN) — 2011: #1883
Popularity: #1891
Styles: Brisk and Breezy, Modern Meanings, Why Not?
Variants: Rayne, Rain
Sisters: Blythe, Ember, Skye, Tru, Indigo, Eden
Brothers: Hart, Beckett, River, Sawyer, Pryce, Ronan
✴ Raine is a not-quite nature name. It gains spirit from the flows of water and weather without actually saying "cloudburst." Raine's misty/ mystical side has made it a favorite of romance and fantasy authors, while its restraint makes it a real-world possibility.
In the World: Rayne, half-vampire protagonist of the "BloodRayne" video game series

Ramona (rah-MOH-nə) — 1928: #117
Popularity: #1335
Styles: Solid Citizens, Literary and Artistic
Nicknames: Rae, Mona
Sisters: Priscilla, Lorna, Therese, Bernadette, Phyllis, Glenda
Brothers: Stuart, Wendell, Jerome, Lionel, Marlin, Gilbert
✴ Ramona was a romantic choice for many years, thanks to a popular novel in the 1880s and a popular song in the 1920s. Then, in 1968, Beverly Cleary published the children's classic *Ramona the Pest*, and this dignified name was saddled with a teasing tagline that has been hard to shake.
In the World: Beverly Cleary's series of Ramona Quimby books; Helen Hunt Jackson novel *Ramona*

Randi (RAN-dee) — 1982: #235
Popularity: #2298
Styles: Surfer '60s, Nicknames
Variants: Randy
Sisters: Mindy, Rikki, Darcy, Leanne, Marci, Tricia
Brothers: Brad, Kenny, Robbie, Kris, Toby, Dusty
✴ Like Toni and Jerri, Randi was an attempt to make a male name feminine with a wave of the magic "-i." It was a hot trend in the '60s, and you see its descendants in new feminized "y" creations like Ryleigh, Jordyn, and Sydnie. Today Randi is mostly heard as a nickname for Miranda.
In the World: Radio host Randi Rhodes

Raquel (rah-KEHL)   1970: #215
Popularity: #642
Styles: Latino/Latina
Nicknames: Rocky, Raqui,
Kelly   1880   Today
Variants: Raquelle
Sisters: Roxana, Marisol, Angelica, Luz, Perla, Reyna
Brothers: Alberto, Raul, Jaime, Ramiro, Salvador, Enrique
✳ The Spanish form of Rachel, this name acquired a sensuous vibe in the U.S. thanks to the voluptuous star Raquel Welch. It's also simple and classic and plays well to both Spanish- and English-speaking audiences.
In the World: Actress Raquel Welch

Raven (RAY-vehn)   1993: #139
Popularity: #591
Styles: Modern Meanings,
The "-ens," Charms and
Graces, African-American,   1880   Today
Turn of the 21st Century
Nicknames: Rae
Sisters: Jasmine, Skye, Devon, Journey, Eden, Jade
Brothers: Phoenix, Gage, Donovan, Jett, Storm, Talon
✳ How do you like your romantic heroines, lacy and proper or glossy and bold? If bold is your style, Raven has a dramatic flair that begs for the spotlight. It's strong and supremely confident.
In the World: Actress Raven-Symoné; Edgar Allan Poe poem "The Raven"

Reagan (RAY-gən)   2011: #122
Popularity: #122
Styles: Last Names First,
Androgynous, The "-ens"
Nicknames: Rae   1880   Today
Variants: Raegan
Sisters: Ashlyn, London, Camden, Aubrey, Kennedy, Payton
Brothers: Jackson, Colton, Ryder, Thatcher, Easton, Drake
✳ From Jefferson and Madison to Carter and Reagan, presidential surnames are hotter than ever. In most cases, parents are focusing on style more than politics, but Reagan is an exception. The name started popping up when Bill Clinton was elected, apparently as a name of Republican nostalgia. It jumped up again following Ronald Reagan's death, and it remains most popular in parts of the country that vote heavily Republican.
In the World: President Ronald Reagan; actress Reagan Gomez-Preston

Reba (REE-bə)   1915: #234
Popularity: #6261
Styles: Guys and Dolls,
Country and Western,
Nicknames   1880   Today
Variants: Reva
Sisters: Rae, Dolly, Nell, Cleo, Willa, Iva
Brothers: Joe, Wiley, Roy, Walker, Nat, Arch
✳ A charming 1900s flirt, Reba could tempt the same parents who are drawn to Ruby and Lily. The name also has a country style thanks to singer Reba McEntire.
In the World: Singer Reba McEntire

Rebecca (rə-BEH-kə)   1974: #10
Popularity: #148
Styles: Timeless, Biblical
Nicknames: Becky, Becca,
Reba   1880   Today
Variants: Rebekah, Rebeca,
Rebekka, Rivka
Sisters: Rachel, Amanda, Stephanie, Veronica,
Sarah, Tamara
Brothers: Daniel, Jeremy, Michael, David,
Aaron, Benjamin
✳ Graceful Rebecca has long been a literary
favorite. Recently, biblical "rediscoveries" like
Abigail and Hannah have been more popular,
but Rebecca remains an unquestioned classic.
The spelling Rebekah is sometimes chosen to
emphasize the biblical style, evoking names like
Deborah, Leah, and Delilah.
In the World: Gothic romance *Rebecca*; *Rebecca
of Sunnybrook Farm*; actress Rebecca
Romijn

Rebekah (rə-BEHK-ə)   1996: #146
Popularity: #438
Styles: Biblical
Nicknames: Becky, Bekka,
Reba   1880   Today
Variants: Rebecca, Rebekka,
Rivka
Sisters: Abigail, Deborah, Elisabeth, Elisha,
Rachael, Bethany
Brothers: Jeremiah, Nathan, Jakob, Micah,
Zachariah, Nathanael
✳ Most alternative name spellings that swap
out a "c" for a "k" have a modern "kreative"
style. This version of Rebecca is an exception.
Since it's the most common form in religious
texts, the spelling Rebekah emphasizes the
name's biblical origins.

Reese (REES)   2011: #130
Popularity: #130
Styles: Androgynous, Brisk
and Breezy
Variants: Reece   1880   Today
Sisters: Quinn, Shea, Rylee,
Tatum, Brynn, Rowan
Brothers: Carter, Drew, Rylan, Jackson, Cole,
Jude
✳ This was a preppy boy's name until actress
Reese Witherspoon hit the movie screen with
100 watts of charm. Witherspoon (whose given
name is Laura) is a perfect Reese: trim, attrac-
tive, and tough.
In the World: Actress Reese Witherspoon;
Reese's Peanut Butter Cups

Regan (REE-gin, RAY-gin)   2001: #389
Popularity: #930
Styles: The "-ens,"
Nickname-Proof,
Shakespearean, Celtic   1880   Today
Variants: Reagan
Sisters: Morgan, Nia, Fallon, Logan, Kiara,
Tatum, Kendal, Taryn
Brothers: Brennan, Conor, Rowan, Damian,
Griffin, Kane, Gavin, Dylan
✳ This Shakespearean name has found a new
audience because of its Celtic surname style
(and its role in a horror film). It's a worthy alter-
native to Megan, but parents considering this
name should take a quick look at its origins in
the play *King Lear.* An ungrateful daughter who
double-crosses her dad . . . hmm, maybe Megan
isn't so bad after all? The variant Reagan is a
political homage.
In the World: The possessed child of *The Exor-
cist*

Regina (reh-JEE-nə,   1964: #83
reh-JIY-nə)
Popularity: #561
Styles: Mid-Century, Saints,
African-American   1880   Today
Nicknames: Gina, Reggie
Sisters: Paula, Yvonne, Anita, Tamara, Annette,
Vonda
Brothers: Roderick, Phillip, Gerard, Darryl,
Lyndon, Dwight
✳ Regina is Latin for "queen," and it's a tasteful
way to anoint your daughter with regal majesty.
That's assuming you pronounce it "re-JEE-
na" . . . as "re-JY-na," it's far, far too close to a
part of the female anatomy.
In the World: Singers Regina Spektor and Re-
gina Belle; actress Regina King

Renata (rə-NAH-tə)   1980: #335
Popularity: #757
Styles: Italian, Slavic, Why
Not?
Nicknames: Ren   1880   Today
Variants: Renate, Renée
Sisters: Daria, Milena, Lavinia, Marina,
Annelise, Charis, Livia, Silvana
Brothers: Carlo, Maxim, Victor, Roman,
Marius, Vance, Anton, Rex
✳ The original Latin form of Renée, Renata
has classic gravity and poise that travels well. It's
been quietly used in many languages, including
Czech, Italian, German, and Polish.
In the World: Currently popular in South Amer-
ica; writer Renata Adler

Renée (reh-NAY)   1967: #62
Popularity: #834
Styles: Surfer '60s, French,
Nickname-Proof
Variants: Renee, Renae,   1880   Today
Renata
Sisters: Robin, Denise, Christine, Tanya,
Nicole, Stacy, Tamara, Michelle
Brothers: Craig, Marc, Jeffrey, Randy, Scott,
Timothy, Eric, Keith
✶This French name means "reborn." Various
forms of the name have been used since the
time of the early Christians, for whom it signi-
fied a spiritual rebirth. Renée's airy sound sent it
soaring in the '60s, and it became so common
that both its French origins and religious mean-
ing took a backseat. Today you'll meet Renées of
every background and persuasion.
In the World: Actress Renée Zellweger; opera
singer Renée Fleming

Renesmee (rə-NEHZ-may)   2010: #3386
Popularity: #4416
Styles: Fantastical
Nicknames: Nessie
✶The young heroes of the   1880   Today
vampire "Twilight" romance
created the name Renesmee for their daughter.
Like the girl herself, the name was half-human,
half-vampire. It's built from the names of her
two grandmas, undead Esme and warmblood
Renée. This is a rare name for which I list no
sibling suggestions. You have two choices: scour
character lists of your favorite books, or combine two names from your own family tree.
In the World: Renesmee Cullen of the "Twilight" series

Reva (REE-və)   1921: #351
Popularity: #3569
Styles: Guys and Dolls, Why
Not?
Variants: Riva   1880   Today
Sisters: Roma, Cleo, Delta,
Iva, Zora, Nola
Brothers: Conway, Arlo, Truman, Dewey,
Mack, Alton
✶Like Reba, this is an old-time country gal
name. The one-letter switch, though, makes it
sharp enough for any setting. Reva has always
been a stand-alone name (created when Vera
and Iva were the height of fashion), but you
could also try it as a nickname for Rebecca.
In the World: Reva Shayne of soap *Guiding
Light*

Rhea (REE-ə)   1893: #360
Popularity: #1186
Styles: Antique Charm,
Mythological, Short and
Sweet, Why Not?   1880   Today
Sisters: Nola, Cleo, Ione,
Viola, Delia, Iva
Brothers: Jules, Hugh, Winslow, Theo,
Fletcher, Royce
✶Rhea grafts the old-time warmth of names
like Bella and Lucy onto the breeziness of new
favorites Mia and Zoe. A compromise that
should satisfy many tastes.
In the World: Actress Rhea Perlman; model
Rhea Durham; R&B singer Rhea

Rhiannon (ree-AH-nən)   1999: #423
Popularity: #1454
Styles: Celtic, Mythological
Nicknames: Rhi
Variants: Rhian, Riannon   1880   Today
Sisters: Guinevere, Aeron,
Ffion, Niamh, Ariadne, Eilonwy, Bronwyn,
Briallen
Brothers: Cadogan, Gareth, Maxen, Rohan,
Evander, Trystan, Orion, Maddox
✶Rhiannon was a goddess in Welsh mythol-
ogy. Her name generally wasn't used by humans
until the past century, which contributes to its
romantic essence. The Fleetwood Mac song
about a shadowy, elusive Rhiannon reinforces
the image.
In the World: Fleetwood Mac's song "Rhian-
non"

Rhoda (ROH-də)   1881: #159
Popularity: #5000
Styles: Solid Citizens,
Biblical, Nickname-Proof
Sisters: Alma, Lenora,   1880   Today
Clarice, Polly, Martha, Vera
Brothers: Willis, Stewart, Casper, Clifton,
Emory, Hugh
✶The '70s sitcom *Rhoda* is most Americans'
touchstone for this name. If you can suppress
that image, you might find that Rhoda surprises
you. It's a quiet name from the New Testament
that reached its peak in the 19th century along-
side Willa, Petra, and Zelda.
In the World: Sitcom *Rhoda*; writer Rhoda
Broughton

Rhonda (rahn-də) 1965: #37
Popularity: #6741
Styles: Surfer '60s
Nicknames: Ronnie
Variants: Ronda   1880 Today
Sisters: Carla, Denise, Yvette,
Rochelle, Gina, Shelly
Brothers: Darryl, Todd, Gregg, Reggie,
Terrence, Keith
✷The year: 1965. The song: "Help Me,
Rhonda" by the Beach Boys. At that moment,
the name was a cool, contemporary invention
riding a wave of popularity. That wave quickly
crested, and the name is now beached. None-
theless, its grown-up sound makes it a stronger
choice than other, more lightweight '60s hits.
In the World: song "Help Me, Rhonda"; actress
Rhonda Fleming

Rihanna (ree-AH-nə) 2008: #311
Popularity: #729
Styles: African-American,
Lacy and Lissome,
Namesakes   1880 Today
Variants: Rihana
Sisters: Janiyah, Audrina, Kelis, Brianna,
Sienna, Kimora
Brothers: Omarion, Braylon, Rowan, Mekhi,
Jamari, Kayden
✷Rihanna *resembles* an Arabic name meaning
"sweet basil" and the Welsh goddess name Rhi-
annon. Rihanna *is* a singer from Barbados, and
that's what matters most to this name. Robyn
Rihanna Fenty was hitting top-40 charts around
the world before her 18th birthday. The U.S.
baby name charts weren't far behind.
In the World: Singer Rihanna

Riley (RIY-lee, RIY-ə-lee) 2010: #40
Popularity: #47
Styles: Last Names First,
Androgynous, Celtic
Variants: Reilly, Rylie,   1880 Today
Ryleigh, Rylee
Sisters: Avery, Kennedy, Morgan, Rory, Bailey,
Regan
Brothers: Cooper, Logan, Jackson, Brady,
Dylan, Carson
✷This classic Irish boy's name is a hot choice
for girls too. In the feminine version, the boyish-
ness dominates and Riley's Celtic style slips to
the background. This is a case where alternative
spellings really change the nature of the name:
Reilly is pure surname, and Ryleigh is closer in
spirit to Kayleigh than Riley. See also Rylee.
In the World: Actress Riley Keough (grand-
daughter of Elvis Presley)

Rita (REE-tə) 1930: #42
Popularity: #1370
Styles: Solid Citizens, Italian
Sisters: Jean, Lois, Anita, Iris,
Bonnie, Faye   1880 Today
Brothers: Gene, Alvin, Ray,
Leon, Russell, Warren
✷There's an eternal appeal to punchy, pint-
sized girls' names. Kira and Mia fill the bill
today, just as Rita did back in the '20s. Like
many of these miniature hits, Rita has nick-
name roots—it's short for Margarita. Rita now
has a vintage style, but isn't staging a come-
back . . . yet.
In the World: Actresses Rita Hayworth, Rita
Moreno, and Rita Wilson; writers Rita Mae
Brown and Rita Dove; singers Rita Coolidge
and Rita Ora

Roberta (rə-BER-tə) 1937: #66
Popularity: #2959
Styles: Solid Citizens, Italian
Nicknames: Bobbi, Robbie
Sisters: Loretta, Carolyn,   1880 Today
Ramona, Joan, Constance,
Paula
Brothers: Gene, Donald, Franklin, Gordon,
Lyle, Raymond
✷Time was, to make a feminine form of a
name you had to add a vowel at the end. Nowa-
days you can just switch around the vowels in-
side, and . . . voilà! Ryley and Camaryn are girls.
That could be one reason why Roberta has
come to sound so dated. (Just say no to Robyrt,
though. Stick with Robyn.)
In the World: Singer Roberta Flack

Robin (RAH-bin) 1961: #27
Popularity: #1529
Styles: Surfer '60s, Charms
and Graces, Androgynous,
Nickname-Proof   1880 Today
Variants: Robyn
Sisters: April, Beth, Jody, Denise, Shawn,
Stacy, Holly, Renee
Brothers: Craig, Randy, Brian, Darren, Chris,
Brad, Jeffrey, Kevin
✷Robin is an old boys' nickname, but the
image of robins in springtime enlivens the girl's
version. That sweetness keeps it fresher than
other '60s favorites. It could fit in with old-tim-
ers like May and Hope or upstarts like Eden and
Lark.
In the World: Actresses Robin Wright and Robin
Givens; male Robins include Robin Hood and
Batman's sidekick

Romilly (RAHM-ə-lee) rarely used
Popularity: Very rare
Styles: English, Why Not?
Nicknames: Millie
Sisters: Sidony, Philippa, Rosabel, Poppy, Jessamine, Briony
Brothers: Corin, Barnaby, Broderick, Pippin, Carrick, Piers

1880 Today

✴ Only anglophiles and name-ophiles are likely to know this name. It's a rare place name/surname with a gently aristocratic edge. It has been given occasionally to both boys and girls in the U.K. for many years. Happily, this is a case where unfamiliar does not equal weird. You'll find that most Americans are intrigued by the name and sense that there's history behind it.
In the World: British newsreader Romilly Weeks; Gaia Romilly Wise, daughter of actress Emma Thompson

Romy (ROH-mee) 1964: #1331
Popularity: #2884
Styles: Nicknames, Why Not?
Nicknames: Ro
Variants: Romi
Sisters: Nelly, Joss, Sukey, Edie, Miri, Harlow, Zara, Laney
Brothers: Rafe, Milo, Nate, Cole, Beck, Joss, Deacon, Flynn

1880 Today

✴ Romy is an old nickname for Rosemary, with a sound that's youthful and new. You can also call it a form of the modern Hebrew name Romi ("high, exalted"). It's nestled right in that style sweet spot—unusual yet not a bit strange.
In the World: Actress Romy Schneider; film *Romy and Michele's High School Reunion*

Ronia (ROH-nyə) 2005: #7877
Popularity: Very rare
Styles: Nordic, Literary and Artistic, Why Not?
Nicknames: Roni
Variants: Ronya, Ronja
Sisters: Freya, Dania, Runa, Malin, Briar, Siri, Annelie, Linnea
Brothers: Soren, Bram, Stellan, Leif, Espen, Linus, Anders, Magnus

1880 Today

✴ Swedish author Astrid Lindgren gave this name to the heroine of her 1981 adventure tale, *Ronia the Robber's Daughter.* The beloved book launched the name Ronia as a modern Scandinavian standard. Few Americans will recognize the literary homage, but the image of feminine strength should translate smoothly.
In the World: Astrid Lindgren's *Ronia the Robber's Daughter*

Rosa (ROH-zə) 1880: #52
Popularity: #624
Styles: Ladies and Gentlemen, Italian, Latino/Latina
Nicknames: Rosie
Variants: Rose, Rosita
Sisters: Clara, Alma, Esther, Flora, Ada, Dora, Lucy, Georgia
Brothers: Louis, Harry, Oscar, Roy, Sam, Edgar, Joe, Reuben

1880 Today

✴ The Spanish and Italian form of Rose, Rosa has a floral sweetness all its own. It's a bit less dainty and more womanly than the English version. It also gives you an appealing hero in civil rights pioneer Rosa Parks.
In the World: Civil rights pioneer Rosa Parks; wrestler/model Rosa Mendes; revolutionary Rosa Luxemburg

Rosabella (ROH-zə-BEH-lə) 2011: #3426
Popularity: #3468
Styles: Lacy and Lissome
Nicknames: Rosie, Bella
Variants: Rosabel, Rosabelle
Sisters: Audrianna, Liviana, Mirabelle, Ariella, Graciela, Lilliana, Annalise
Brothers: Lysander, Aldric, Tommaso, Orlando, Ariston, Silvan

1880 Today

✴ Rosabella has the look and feel of an Italian name, but it's seldom heard in Italy. The name was a 19th-century romantic creation in English, and it still sounds purely romantic.

Rosalind (RAH-zə-lind)   1942: #292
Popularity: #2842
Styles: Solid Citizens,
Shakespearean
Nicknames: Rosie, Rosa,   1880   Today
Lindy, Sal
Variants: Rosalyn, Rosalinda, Rosaline
Sisters: Marianne, Lorna, Gwendolyn,
Jeanette, Beverly, Lorraine, Ramona,
Constance
Brothers: Randolph, Bernard, Gilbert, Roland,
Franklin, Stewart, Lawrence, Gerard
✱ Rosalind was the essence of romance in the
16th century, a heroine of Shakespeare and
Spenser. In the 20th century, actress Rosalind
Russell added a brassy edge. And for the 21st
century? Rosalind's heavy sound scares parents
away, but its romantic strength could lure them
back. If you're drawn by the Old England style,
also consider Rosamond.
In the World: Actress Rosalind Russell; Rosalind
of Shakespeare's *As You Like It*

Rosanna (roh-ZA-nə)   1983: #434
Popularity: #3875
Styles: Italian, Lacy and
Lissome
Nicknames: Rosie   1880   Today
Variants: Roseanna, Rosanne,
Roxanna
Sisters: Marcella, Corinna, Annette, Janelle,
Catrina, Audra, Georgina, Deanna
Brothers: Derrick, Shannon, Bradley, Roderick,
Carlo, Brant, Randall, Gerard
✱ Try to separate Rosanna from Roseanne in
your mind. Roseanne is currently stuck in the
'50s, and the image of "domestic goddess" co-
median Roseanne Barr hasn't helped. Rosanna,
though, is a 19th-century literary beauty. It
could be considered alongside Juliana and Dan-
iela.
In the World: 1980s Toto song "Rosanna"; actress Rosanna Arquette

Rose (ROHZ)   1908: #16
Popularity: #291
Styles: Charms and Graces,
Ladies and Gentlemen
Nicknames: Rosie   1880   Today
Variants: Rosa
Sisters: Grace, Alice, Alma, Pearl, Eva, Ruby,
Violet, Mae
Brothers: Harry, Louis, Roy, George, Joseph,
Oscar, Sam, Carl
✱ Rose is an eternal symbol of beauty, as a
flower or a name. It was the queen of the flower
names that blossomed for a generation starting
in the 1880s. Today it's seldom heard, yet it's
easily the most popular name in America. Yes,
you read that mind-bender right. Rose is a
mega-hit *middle* name, but as a first name it retains the unexpected charm of a Victorian heirloom.
In the World: Burlesque star Gypsy Rose Lee;
actresses Rose McGowan and Rose Byrne

Rosemary (ROHZ-meh-ree)   1946: #75
Popularity: #654
Styles: Solid Citizens,
Charms and Graces, Why
Not?   1880   Today
Nicknames: Romy, Rosie,
Rose, Roxie
Variants: Rosemarie
Sisters: Marjorie, June, Penelope, Dorothy,
Cecilia, Beverly, Joy, Marianne
Brothers: Vaughn, Russell, Clark, Stanton,
Royce, Calvin, Forrest, Clifton
✱ After decades on the outs, this name's day is
due. It has an old-fashioned femininity and an
exceptional nickname assortment. Rosie lures
you with sweetness, Roxie is saucy, and Romy
sounds snappy and contemporary.
In the World: Singer Rosemary Clooney; horror
film *Rosemary's Baby*

Rowan (ROH-ən)   2007: #451
Popularity: #535
Styles: Androgynous, The
"-ens," Charms and Graces,
Celtic
Nicknames: Ro
Sisters: Brynn, Willow, Piper, Rory, Emlyn,
Wren
Brothers: Finn, Griffin, Kieran, Stone, Quill,
Tobin
★ Rowan is a traditional Anglo-Irish men's
name. Its growing use for girls, though, isn't
simply a case of cross-gender appropriation.
Rowan has a second origin in the rowan tree
and its wood, long associated with tales of
magic. That gives the name a romantic aura
unique among modern unisex names.
In the World: Rowan Mayfair of the "Vampire
Chronicles" series; a daughter of actress Brooke
Shields

Roxanne (rahk-SAN)   1954: #158
Popularity: #1027
Styles: Mid-Century
Nicknames: Roxie
Variants: Roxana, Roxane
Sisters: Lynette, Rochelle,
Valerie, Carla, Pamela, Janine
Brothers: Curtis, Terrence, Barry, Darryl,
Phillip, Randall
★ Roxanne has a long and storied history,
going back to the wife of Alexander the Great.
Unfortunately, that heritage is currently buried
by the name's outmoded '50s image. The Latin
version Roxana feels more up to date. Also see
Roxie for a brassy twist on the name.
In the World: Police song "Roxanne"; Roxane of
Cyrano de Bergerac; film *Roxanne* (based on
Cyrano de Bergerac)

Roxie (RAHK-see)   1881: #177
Popularity: #2155
Styles: Guys and Dolls
Variants: Roxy
Sisters: Lola, Goldie, Trixie,
Cleo, Josie, Della
Brothers: Ike, Roscoe, Fritz, Gus, Buck, Archie
★ Roxie Hart, the fame-seeking missile from
the musical *Chicago*, is a great mascot for this
name's Jazz Age sass. If you're looking for a for-
mal version for less sassy occasions, consider
Roxana, Rosalia, or Rosemary.
In the World: Roxie Hart of *Chicago*; actress
Roxie Roker; Roxy fashion brand; various Roxy
theaters and clubs

1880   Today

Ruby (ROO-bee)   1911: #22
Popularity: #109
Styles: Charms and Graces,
Guys and Dolls, Antique
Charm, Nickname-Proof
Variants: Rubi
Sisters: Ella, Lucy, Sadie, Hazel, Stella, Molly
Brothers: Jack, Oscar, Sam, Max, Harry, Leo
★ While Violet and Pearl were blushing in the
parlor, Ruby was kicking up her heels at the
music hall. She's the spitfire of this old-fash-
ioned name family.
In the World: Actress Ruby Dee; song "Ruby
Tuesday"; civil rights icon Ruby Bridges; pro-
gramming language Ruby

1880   Today

Rue (ROO)   1900: #1562
Popularity: #8983
Styles: Short and Sweet, Brisk
and Breezy, Fantastical
Sisters: Clover, Bly, Arya,
Prairie, Rilla, Dove
Brothers: Dune, Wynn, Taran, Frost, Cullen,
Sage
★ This rare name used to call up *Golden Girls*
actress Rue McClanahan, as well as the word
meaning "regret." But a beloved (if doomed)
character in *The Hunger Games*, named for the
medicinal plant rue, has given it new life. Rue
has great potential as a simple but creative mid-
dle name.
In the World: Actress Rue McClanahan; Rue of
The Hunger Games; the phrase "you'll rue the
day"

Ruth (ROOTH)   1915: #5
Popularity: #362
Styles: Solid Citizens,
Biblical
Nicknames: Ruthie
Variants: Ruta
Sisters: Helen, Esther, Rose, Irene, Miriam,
Vera, Alice, Fern
Brothers: Carl, Roy, Louis, Raymond, Joseph,
Sam, Arthur, Frank
★ Yoo-hoo! Over here! An underused biblical
classic, yours for the taking! Ruth has the
hushed dignity of Hannah, yet remains uncom-
mon and gently surprising.
In the World: Supreme Court justice Ruth
Bader Ginsburg; sex therapist "Dr. Ruth"

1880   Today

Ryan (RIY-in)   1986: #340
Popularity: #575
Styles: Androgynous, The
"-ens," Celtic
Variants: Ryann, Rian,   1880   Today
Rianna
Sisters: Teagan, Reese, Logan, Kendall, Devin,
Rylee
Brothers: Parker, Reid, Christian, Brendan,
Garrett, Trevor
✶ Starting in the '80s, parents took a run at
turning this top boy's favorite into a girl's name.
It has a clean, modern appeal, but remains pri-
marily masculine. The frequent alternative
spelling Ryann clarifies the sex but clouds the
pronunciation.
In the World: Actress Ryan Simpkins; singer
Ryan Starr

Rylee (RIY-lee)   2010: #102
Popularity: #102
Styles: Bell Tones,
Androgynous
Nicknames: Ry   1880   Today
Variants: Ryleigh, Rylie
Sisters: Jaycee, Raegan, Taylor, Chloe, Macie,
Skylar
Brothers: Caden, Tanner, Logan, Gage, Ryder,
Trenton
✶ This name is almost pure sound, completely
distinct from the traditional Irish name Riley.
There are plenty of similar-looking names like
Baylee, Kaylee, and Brylee, but Rylee has a par-
ticularly clean, direct sound.

Sabrina (sah-BREE-nə)   1997: #53
Popularity: #261
Styles: New Classics
Nicknames: Bree, Sabi
Sisters: Miranda, Bethany,   1880   Today
Samantha, Gabrielle,
Tabitha, Cassandra
Brothers: Brendan, Spencer, Colin, Casey,
Garrett, Evan
✶ This is an old name out of Celtic legend, but
rendered eternally youthful by *Sabrina, the
Teenage Witch.* Positively sparkly.
In the World: TV show *Sabrina, the Teenage
Witch;* Audrey Hepburn film *Sabrina*

Sadie (SAY-dee)   1881: #69
Popularity: #124
Styles: Nicknames, Guys and
Dolls, Antique Charm,
Jewish   1880   Today
Sisters: Lucy, Sophie, Clara,
Josie, Lillie, Stella
Brothers: Sam, Harry, Max, Eli, Jack, Leo
✶ Sadie is a nickname for Sarah, and it once
held a place in the roster of nickname classics
alongside Betsy, Molly, and Maggie. Then it
vanished. So now it's old-fashioned, and utterly
charming to a new generation of parents. Folks
old enough to remember the last round of Sa-
dies may still consider it exclusively an old-lady
name.
In the World: Actress Sadie Frost; Sadie Hawkins
Day events (when girls invite boys)

Sage (SAYJ)   2004: #358
Popularity: #461
Styles: Brisk and Breezy,
Modern Meanings, Charms
and Graces, Androgynous,   1880   Today
Why Not?
Sisters: Sierra, Rowan, Bay, Piper, Willow,
Raine
Brothers: Chance, Holden, Lane, River,
Paxton, Reed
✶ Sage is a fragrant herb, which gives the name
softness. It means "wise," which gives it depth.
And it's a swift single syllable, which gives it
snap. That balance makes this a modern name
choice with an old soul.
In the World: Sportscaster Sage Steele; daughter
of actress Toni Collette

Sally (SA-lee)   1938: #54
Popularity: #1163
Styles: Solid Citizens,
Nicknames
Nicknames: Sal   1880   Today
Variants: Sallie
Sisters: Betty, Peggy, Nancy, Sue, Polly, Jo,
Rosie, Janie
Brothers: Tommy, Billy, Bobby, Ted, Sammy,
Ray, Jimmy, Joe
✶ Sally is Charlie Brown's sister in *Peanuts.*
The name fits the retro sweetness of that comic
strip's eternal childhood. Sally has fallen far out
of style, but with Lucy staging a comeback, this
name looks like a good bet. It's also a nickname
for the classic favorite Sarah.
In the World: Actress Sally Field; astronaut Sally
Ride; student loan company Sallie Mae

Samantha (sah-MAN-thə) 1991: #5
Popularity: #17
Styles: New Classics
Nicknames: Sam, Sammy
Sisters: Natalie, Jessica,
Alexandra, Stephanie,
Sabrina, Vanessa, Miranda, Cassandra
Brothers: Brandon, Zachary, Nicholas, Joshua,
Justin, Drew, Matthew, Garrett
✱ Through the magic of reruns, generations of
girls have grown up *Bewitched* by TV's subur-
ban sorceress Samantha Stephens. The televi-
sion show sparked the initial popularity of the
name Samantha, and it continues to reflect our
impression of Sam: clever, attractive, and fun. A
more recent TV model was Kim Cattrall's Samantha on *Sex and the City*.
In the World: TV host Samantha Brown; Samantha Stephens of *Bewitched*; Samantha
Jones of *Sex and the City*

Samira (sah-MEE-rə) 2003: #792
Popularity: #1151
Styles: Muslim, Lacy and
Lissome
Nicknames: Sammie, Mira
Sisters: Amina, Zahra, Safiya,
Yasmin, Salima, Nabila
Brothers: Khalid, Hassan, Jaleel, Bilal, Tariq,
Bashir
✱ The lyrical beauty of this Islamic name
could win it fans from all cultures. It is the fem-
inine form of the popular name Samir, mean-
ing "evening conversationalist."
In the World: Singer Samira Said

Sandra (SAHN-drə, SAN-drə) 1940: #6
Popularity: #614
Styles: Mid-Century, Italian
Nicknames: Sandy
Variants: Saundra
Sisters: Linda, Diane,
Kathleen, Brenda, Donna, Sharon
Brothers: Stephen, Bruce, Daniel, Kenneth,
Douglas, Terry
✱ Sandra was a stylish hit from the '40s to the
'60s, with the wholesome image of actress San-
dra Dee. Of course, that was just Miss Dee's
stage name. She jettisoned a long, clunky eth-
nic name that simply wouldn't do. Her original
name? Alexandra, which is now all the rage,
while Sandra is sliding.
In the World: Actresses Sandra Bullock and San-
dra Oh; Supreme Court justice Sandra Day
O'Connor; cook Sandra Lee

Saoirse (SEER-shə) 2011: #1938
Popularity: #1951
Styles: Celtic
Sisters: Caoimhe, Órlaith,
Niamh, Aoife, Áine, Sinéad,
Grainne, Aoibheann
Brothers: Tadhg, Fionn, Cathal, Diamuid,
Darragh, Oisin, Cillian, Odhran
✱ This name is pure Irish Gaelic, but that
doesn't mean it's traditional. Saoirse is the
Gaelic word for "freedom," which patriotic Irish
parents adopted as a girl's name starting in the
20th century. Most Americans who know the
name met it in the form of actress Saoirse
Ronan.
In the World: Actress Saoirse Ronan

Sara (SAR-ə, SAY-rə) 1981: #26
Popularity: #131
Styles: Timeless
Nicknames: Sadie, Sally
Variants: Sarah
Sisters: Lauren, Abby,
Amanda, Erin, Rachel, Katie
Brothers: Ryan, Matthew, Eric, Adam, Sean,
Andrew
✱ Sara is a traditional variant of Sarah that
sharpens and lightens the name. It is more con-
temporary, less biblical.
In the World: Actresses Sara Paxton and Sara
Gilbert; singer Sara Evans

Sarah (SAY-rah, SA-rə) 1981: #4
Popularity: #39
Styles: Biblical, Timeless
Nicknames: Sally, Sadie, Sal,
Sarita
Variants: Sara
Sisters: Rachel, Katherine, Laura, Emily, Leah,
Julia, Rebecca, Anna
Brothers: Benjamin, Adam, Daniel, Nicholas,
Andrew, Simon, Jonathan, Nathan
✱ Sarah has been steadily popular for decades
now—really, for millennia. But the name is
such a simple, pure classic that it will never wear
out its welcome. The long-dormant nickname
Sadie is now a hot name in its own right, while
Sally remains more old-fashioned.
In the World: Centuries of Sarahs, from Bern-
hardt to Palin to Silverman

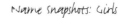

Sarai (sah-RIY) 2009: #400
Popularity: #443
Styles: Biblical, Nickname-
Proof, Exotic Traditional,
Jewish, Latino/Latina 1880 Today
Variants: Sarahi
Sisters: Atara, Eden, Noemi, Adira, Reyna,
Vashti
Brothers: Simeon, Ariel, Gideon, Omar, Ezra,
Abel
✳ In the Bible, Abram and Sarai were the origi-
nal names of the couple whom God blessed and
renamed Abraham and Sarah. Abram has a
familar sound in English, but Sarai has always
been rare and exotic. In the past generation that
has begun to change. It is still uncommon, but
fashionable.

Sasha (SAH-shə) 1988: #147
Popularity: #374
Styles: New Classics, Slavic
Variants: Sascha
Sisters: Nadia, Tessa, Talia, 1880 Today
Kendra, Jasmine, Katya,
Mischa, Larissa
Brothers: Lukas, Gabriel, Andrei, Roman,
Maxim, Drew, Stefan, Blake
✳ Sasha is Russia's version of Alex, a hugely
popular unisex nickname for Alexander and Al-
exandra. In English, Sasha is decidedly femi-
nine. Alex tones down the steamy side of
Alexandra; Sasha heats it up.
In the World: Presidential daughter Sasha
Obama; actress Sasha Alexander; adult film per-
former Sasha Grey

Savannah (sah-VAN-ə) 1996: #43
Popularity: #41
Styles: Place Names, Country
and Western
Nicknames: Savvy, Vanna 1880 Today
Variants: Savanna
Sisters: Sierra, Cheyenne, Alexandria, Shelby,
Cassidy, Angelina
Brothers: Austin, Hunter, Noah, Spencer,
Bryce, Carson
✳ The name Savannah took off after the book
Midnight in the Garden of Good and Evil made
Savannah, Georgia, a hot spot. The city's quirky
Southern charm, coupled with the name's vel-
vety, sassy sound, made Savannah a major hit.
In the World: Newscaster Savannah Guthrie

Scarlett (SCAHR-leht) 2011: #80
Popularity: #80
Styles: Exotic Traditional,
Literary and Artistic, Country
and Western, Modern 1880 Today
Meanings, Nickname-Proof
Variants: Scarlet
Sisters: Georgia, Ivy, Sienna, Violet, Ruby,
Piper
Brothers: Sawyer, Wyatt, Jude, Holden,
Jackson, Beckett
✳ Scarlett is a sassy spitfire, thanks to proto-
types like Scarlett O'Hara, Scarlett Johansson,
and Miss Scarlett from the board game "Clue."
This name packs a wallop, and for a girl with a
red-hot personality, it can be a smashing suc-
cess. It has risen fast throughout the English-
speaking world.
In the World: Scarlett O'Hara of *Gone with the
Wind*; actress Scarlett Johansson

Selah (SAY-lah, SEE-lə) 2011: #579
Popularity: #579
Styles: Biblical, African-
American
Variants: Sela 1880 Today
Sisters: Eden, Irie, Zaria,
Shekinah, Journey, Shiloh
Brothers: Judah, Asher, Zion, Tesfah, Malakai,
Justice
✳ The Hebrew word *selah* appears throughout
the Book of Psalms. Its precise meaning is mys-
terious, but it is interpreted as a pause to breathe
and reflect on the important words just uttered.
The term has also been adopted by the Rastafari-
ans, often as a kind of "amen." Sela, as in actress
Sela Ward, is an unrelated biblical place name.
In the World: Singer Selah Sue; Christian music
group Selah; a daughter of singer Lauryn Hill

Selena (sə-LEE-nə, seh-LAY-nə 1995: #91
Popularity: #321
Styles: Lacy and Lissome,
Latino/Latina
Variants: Selina, Selene 1880 Today
Sisters: Valeria, Thalia,
Alexandra, Destiny, Carolina, Aurora
Brothers: Tristan, Luca, Adrian, Victor, Jonah,
Elias
✳ Selena is a Latinized form of Selene, a
Greek moon goddess. The late singing star
Selena put her own stamp on the name, setting
its literary style to a Tejano beat. It's a youthful
take on international elegance.
In the World: Singer Selena; actress/singer
Selena Gomez (named for the singer)

Sephora (seh-FOH-rə) 2010: #3929
Popularity: #4029
Styles: Exotic Traditional
Variants: Zipporah, Tzipora
Sisters: Solange, Athena, 1880 Today
Elodie, Alethea, Charis,
Seraphina, Paloma, Serena
Brothers: Matthias, Caedmon, Samson, Justus,
Phineas, Japheth, Simeon, Leander
✴ Sephora is a form of the name Zipporah, the biblical wife of Moses. This smooth, elegant name would be on more parents' lists if the cosmetics chain Sephora hadn't gotten there first.
In the World: Cosmetics retailer Sephora

Seraphina (sehr-ə-FEE-nə) 2011: #1462
Popularity: #1468
Styles: Saints, Exotic
Traditional
Nicknames: Sera, FiFi, Fina 1880 Today
Variants: Serafina
Sisters: Francesca, Gabriela, Raphaela,
Delphina, Philomena, Valentina
Brothers: Xavier, Jedidiah, Sebastian, Matthias,
Phineas, Maximilian
✴ The seraphim are a fiery order of angels in the Bible. The name Seraphina comes from those celestial beings and captures their essence well. The name is feathery-light, yet more intense than other gauzy creations. It has always been rare in English, but the Italian and Spanish version Serafina was once moderately common.
In the World: A daughter of actors Jennifer Garner and Ben Affleck

Serena (seh-REEN-ə) 2000: #209
Popularity: #448
Styles: Lacy and Lissome,
Saints, Classical, Italian
Variants: Serina, Sarina, 1880 Today
Serene
Sisters: Tatiana, Marina, Camille, India,
Alexis, Daria
Brothers: Damon, Antony, Darius, Julian,
Quentin, Marco
✴ Serena means "calm" and was the name of an early saint. Serena also sounds lavish and is the name of a charismatic tennis star. You can have it both ways with this snazzy classic.
In the World: Tennis player Serena Williams; Serena van der Woodsen of *Gossip Girl*

Serenity (seh-REH-ni-tee) 2011: #66
Popularity: #66
Styles: Modern Meanings,
Charms and Graces,
Fantastical 1880 Today
Variants: Serena
Sisters: Honesty, Genesis, Trinity, Lavender,
Rayne, Whisper, Eternity, Journey
Brothers: Strider, Phoenix, Zion, Emmanuel,
Caspian, Storm, Truth, River
✴ Serenity's meaning and rhythm combine for an image of gentle grace. It's deceptively long, though, and you'll have to be creative with nicknames. The anime series "Sailor Moon" launched the name into popular use, and a TV/movie spaceship sent it into orbit.
In the World: 2005 sci-fi film *Serenity*; Princess and Queen Serenity of "Sailor Moon"

Shakira (shah-KEE-rə) 2002: #534
Popularity: #2301
Styles: Latino/Latina,
Muslim
Nicknames: Kira 1880 Today
Variants: Shakirah
Sisters: Samira, Nadya, Jamila, Yesenia,
Araceli, Thalia, Layla, Alondra
Brothers: Omar, Tariq, Ismael, Nestor, Efren,
Alvaro, Mustafa, Ariel
✴ Ready for a global ride? The Latin diva Shakira is Colombian, but her heritage is Lebanese and her name Arabic. (The singer's publicists translate it as "woman full of grace"; the more standard translation is "thankful.") In the U.S., the name has been used occasionally by Arab- and African-Americans and became a hot choice for Latinas in the singer's wake.
In the World: Singer Shakira

Shana (SHAY-nə, SHAH-nə) 1977: #184
Popularity: #3315
Styles: '70s–'80s, Nickname-Proof
Variants: Shayna, Shauna, Shawna, Shanna, Shonna
Sisters: Trisha, Rachelle, Nikki, Krista, Misty, Brianna
Brothers: Corey, Jarrod, Brant, Torrey, Erik, Dustin
✳ With six popular variations, Shana rose out of nowhere to become one of the top names of the '70s and '80s. The "SHAH-nə" variants disappeared just as quickly, but "SHAY-nə" stuck around longer. (Shayna is also the Yiddish word for "pretty.") It's not hard to see the appeal of the name, which is like a whispered midnight endearment, but there were too many Shanas too soon.
In the World: Model/actress Shanna Moakler

Shannon (SHA-nən) 1976: #17
Popularity: #706
Styles: Celtic, Androgynous, '70s–'80s, Nickname-Proof
Sisters: Megan, Kelly, Colleen, Erin, Stacy, Tara
Brothers: Ryan, Kyle, Casey, Shane, Jared, Heath
✳ Shannon is a soft, smooth spitfire of a name. Like Erin, it's an homage to Ireland rather than a traditional Irish name. (The River Shannon forms a spine through the country.) The name is now in decline from its '70s–'80s glory days, but none the worse for wear.
In the World: Actresses Shannen Doherty, Shannon Elizabeth, and Shannyn Sossamon

Sharon (SHA-rən) 1946: #9
Popularity: #823
Styles: Mid-Century
Nicknames: Shari
Variants: Sharen, Sharyn, Sharron
Sisters: Donna, Janice, Pamela, Cheryl, Diane, Kathleen, Sandra, Lynne
Brothers: Gary, Dennis, Alan, Bruce, Kenneth, Roger, Stephen, Glenn
✳ Here's an inspiring example for parents torn between creativity and tradition: a 20th-century Bible name. Sharon is a place name in the Bible and wasn't widely adopted as a personal name until the 1920s. It then became a staple for 50 years. Today the name is in a down phase, but it has established a permanent spot in the first-name ranks.
In the World: Actress Sharon Stone; reality TV star Sharon Osbourne

Shawn (SHAWN) 1970: #168
Popularity: #10,228
Styles: Surfer '60s, Androgynous, Celtic
Variants: Shawna, Shaun, Sean, Sian
Sisters: Kerry, Shannon, Leigh, Robyn, Jodi, Tracey
Brothers: Craig, Darin, Scotty, Todd, Jeff, Troy
✳ Back in the '60s and '70s, parents tweaked the masculine Sean into the more feminine Shawn, on the model of names like Dawn and Fawn. The continuing popularity of the male name has helped this name grow up with its style intact. If you want to update the sound to 21st-century style, consider Siân, a traditional Welsh girl's name equivalent to Jean.
In the World: Singer Shawn Colvin; gymnast Shawn Johnson; actress Sean Young

Shayla (SHAY-lə) 1999: #267
Popularity: #509
Styles: Bell Tones, Lacy and Lissome, African-American
Nicknames: Shay
Variants: Shyla, Sheyla, Shaylee
Sisters: Kiana, Skyla, Hayley, Janae, Samara, Breanne
Brothers: Jaylen, Keaton, Colby, Brayden, Tate, Skyler
✳ Shayla is a name so smooth and slinky that it almost purrs. It's not overtly sexy, though, and on a little girl sounds like a sweet term of endearment.
In the World: Romance novelist Shayla Black

Shea (SHAY) 2005: #762
Popularity: #1346
Styles: Brisk and Breezy,
Celtic, Androgynous, Why
Not? 1880 Today
Variants: Shay, Shae
Sisters: Bryn, Rory, Quinn, Logan, Blythe,
Drew, Kendall, Reese
Brothers: Keane, Brogan, Donovan, Bryce,
Flynn, Ian, Dane, Pierce
✖ Why weigh yourself down with a big, clunky
name? Shea hits all the Celtic surname high-
lights in a single whisper-soft syllable. It's most
familiar to Americans as an Irish surname, but it
is also the Anglicized version of a traditional
Gaelic given name. (Séaghdha, if you must
know.)
In the World: Shea Stadium (former home of
the New York Mets and Jets); shea butter mois-
turizer

Sheila (SHEE-lə) 1963: #50
Popularity: #1291
Styles: Mid-Century, Celtic,
Nickname-Proof
Variants: Síle 1880 Today
Sisters: Brenda, Colleen,
Sherry, Paula, Kathleen, Glenda
Brothers: Barry, Glenn, Rodger, Shannon,
Mark, Keith
✖ Sheila was once a quintessential Irish name,
the Gaelic form of Cecilia. It then became so
broadly popular that it lost its Celtic connec-
tions. (A glimpse into Caitlin's future?) In Aus-
tralia, Sheila is even a generic slang term for a
girl. You could update it with the Gaelic spell-
ing Síle, or try Celia.
In the World: Musician Sheila E.

Shelby (SHEHL-bee) 1991: #33
Popularity: #218
Styles: Last Names First,
Country and Western, Turn
of the 21st Century 1880 Today
Nicknames: Shell
Variants: Shelbi, Shelbie
Sisters: Haley, Jordan, Sydney, Kelsey, Jenna,
Cassidy
Brothers: Jackson, Tanner, Bryce, Dillon,
Shane, Dalton
✖ Shelby sounds thoroughly modern, but the
name has been used for girls since the '30s.
Back then it was a twist on the trendsetting hit
Shirley. Today Shelby is a Southern belle, most
popular in the deep South and rugged West.
In the World: Singer Shelby Lynne; actress
Shelby Young; Shelby of *Steel Magnolias*

Sherry (SHEH-ree) 1963: #49
Popularity: #2641
Styles: Surfer '60s, Mid-
Century
Variants: Sherri, Sherrie, 1880 Today
Sheri, Cheri, Shari
Sisters: Carla, Laurie, Jeri, Sheila, Sandy,
Deena
Brothers: Randy, Kent, Jeffrey, Gregg, Darren,
Todd
✖ Sherry's girlish style comes at you from many
directions. It's a cute nickname for Shirley or
Sheryl. It sounds like an endearment, similar to
the French *chérie*. And it's sweet like a Spanish
sherry wine. The name faded from view in the
'80s; in its place came Shelby, which is similarly
sweet with a surname twist.
In the World: TV host Sherri Shepherd; actress
Sherry Stringfield; psychologist/author Sherry
Turkle

Shiloh (SHIY-loh) 2009: #595
Popularity: #625
Styles: Biblical, Place Names,
Country and Western
Sisters: Scarlett, Delilah, 1880 Today
Willow, Aspen, Harlow, Selah
Brothers: Jericho, Levi, Deacon, Tobias, Zion,
Winslow
✖ Shiloh is a place name in the Bible and was
adopted as the name of towns in many U.S.
states. The Shiloh that dominated the name for
generations was Shiloh, Tennessee, site of a hor-
rific Civil War battle. Incredibly, a single celebrity baby has managed to overwrite that sad
legacy. Shiloh Jolie-Pitt, born in 2006, re-
launched Shiloh as a sweet biblical name for
girls.
In the World: Battle of Shiloh; book/film *Shiloh*
(about a dog); daughter of actors Angelina Jolie
and Brad Pitt

Name Snapshots: Girls 187

Shirley (SHER-lee)   1935: #2
Popularity: #1263
Styles: Solid Citizens
Variants: Shirlee
Sisters: Barbara, Phyllis,   1880   Today
Norma, Marilyn, Beverly,
Arlene
Brothers: Donald, Gene, Franklin, Gordon,
Stuart, Stanley
★ This is a name we can no longer judge on its own merits. There are so many Shirleys with AARP cards now (thanks to 1930s kiddie superstar Shirley Temple) that it's hard to picture the name any other way. It will take another generation or two before we can appreciate the name's sweetness anew.
In the World: Actresses Shirley Temple and Shirley MacLaine; singer Shirley Bassey; writer Shirley Jackson

Shoshana (shoh-SHAH-nə)   1997: #1247
Popularity: #1818
Styles: Jewish, Lacy and
Lissome, Biblical
Nicknames: Sue, Shosh,   1880   Today
Shoshi
Variants: Shoshanna, Susanna
Sisters: Hadassah, Ilana, Allegra, Miriam,
Aviva, Elisheva
Brothers: Boaz, Shimon, Gavriel, Asher,
Eliezer, Hillel
★ Shoshana is Hebrew for "lily," and the source of the English Susanna. This is a gentle old name, like leaves rustling in the wind. It's quaint in Israel, but youthful and sophisticated in the U.S.
In the World: Designer Shoshanna Lonstein; actress Shoshana Bean

Sienna (see-EHN-ə)   2007: #169
Popularity: #225
Styles: Charms and Graces,
Lacy and Lissome,
Nickname-Proof   1880   Today
Variants: Siena
Sisters: Savannah, Willow, Dahila, Shiloh,
Rowan, Luna
Brothers: Cole, Lucas, Pierce, Conor, Kai,
Sawyer
★ Sienna is a clay used in pigments. Treated with fire, it becomes burnt sienna, a lush reddish-brown tint familiar to every child with a 64-pack of Crayolas. Siena, with one "n," is a historic Italian city. Both are lovely inspirations for a name, but the Sienna minivan may actually have inspired more namesakes.
In the World: Actresses Sienna Miller and Sienna Guillory; Toyota Sienna minivans

Sierra (see-EHR-ə)   1998: #51
Popularity: #277
Styles: Country and Western,
Place Names, Nickname-
Proof, Lacy and Lissome,   1880   Today
Turn of the 21st Century
Variants: Cierra
Sisters: Savannah, Autumn, Cheyenne,
Alexandria, Dakota, Mariah
Brothers: Tanner, Jackson, Logan, Cody,
Dillon, Shane
★ The name Sierra is taken from the word for a jagged ridge of mountains. It suggests a bond with nature's rugged beauty. The effect is subtle, though, since the name sounds traditionally feminine.
In the World: Sierra Nevada mountains; Sierra Club; film *High Sierra*; actress Sierra McCormick

Simone (si-MOHN)   1988: #311
Popularity: #649
Styles: French, African-
American, Nickname-Proof,
Timeless, Why Not?   1880   Today
Variants: Simonne
Sisters: Celeste, Noelle, Juliet, Selene,
Daphne, Camille
Brothers: Vincent, Quentin, Julian, Byron,
Raphael, Blaise
★ Silky but serious, Simone is a fine example of mature elegance. The prominent Simones of the past have left the name with echoes of their combined intellectual and artistic flair.
In the World: Writer/philosopher Simone de Beauvoir; singer Nina Simone; actress Simone Signoret

Siobhan (shi-VAWN)   1979: #628
Popularity: #3241
Styles: Celtic
Nicknames: Vannie
Variants: Siobhán, Shevaun,   1880   Today
Chevonne
Sisters: Aoife, Saoirse, Aislinn, Sinéad,
Catriona, Aine, Caoimhe, Niamh
Brothers: Ciaran, Eoin, Tadhg, Niall, Oisin,
Lorcan, Ruari, Colm
✱ Here's an opportunity to vex every relative
who has to write your child a birthday card.
Siobhan has a soft, easy sound, but it's devilish
to spell. To pacify those who find the name baf-
fling, just explain it's Irish for Joan.
In the World: Irish singer Siobhan Fahey; *Amer-
ican Idol* contestant Siobhan Magnus

Siri (SEE-ree)   2009: #1801
Popularity: #1919
Styles: Nordic, Namesakes
Variants: Sigrid, Siiri
Sisters: Maja, Liv, Sofie,   1880   Today
Freya, Anni, Maren
Brothers: Soren, Anders, Marius, Odin, Viggo,
Espen
✱ Siri is a pet form of the Nordic classic Sigrid,
and a popular given name in Sweden, Norway,
and Denmark. In the U.S., it was almost un-
known until a Danish-born tech executive be-
stowed it on his virtual "daughter": a talking
intelligent assistant for smartphones. Over-
night, Siri went from girl to app as iPhone users
talked with "her" in place of typing. That's a big
burden for this otherwise stylish name.
In the World: Apple virtual assistant Siri

Skye (SKIY)   2004: #400
Popularity: #476
Styles: Modern Meanings,
Brisk and Breezy, Place
Names, Celtic   1880   Today
Variants: Sky
Sisters: Sage, Rhys, Ewan, Finn, Brodie, Talon,
Bryce, Keane
Brothers: Bryn, Shea, Piper, Niamh, Isla,
Quinn, Aspen, Raine
✱ This attractive creation has a fresh-faced
femininity and, naturally, a sunny demeanor.
It's still a creative choice for a full name, but
you'll meet quite a few Skylars who go by Sky.
The spelling Skye is taken from the name of a
Scottish island. It is one of several isle names
(Iona, Ailsa) popular for girls in Scotland.
In the World: Soap opera character Skye Chan-
dler; singer Skye Sweetnam; actress Skye (Sky-
lar) Townsend

Skyla (SKIY-lə)   2011: #517
Popularity: #517
Styles: Bell Tones
Sisters: Kaydence, Alexa,
Sienna, Paisley, Mckenna,   1880   Today
Aspen
Brothers: Jaxon, Tristan, Chance, Talon,
Boston, Storm
✱ This name is part Skylar, part skylark, and all
girl. Its high-gloss finish has made it a favorite
for names of fashion accessories and aspiring
entertainers' stage names. If your Skyla should
someday dream of her name in lights, she'll be
all set.

Skylar (SKIY-ler)   1999: #131
Popularity: #145
Styles: Androgynous, Last
Names First
Nicknames: Sky   1880   Today
Variants: Skyler, Skyla
Sisters: Kennedy, Bailey, Sawyer, Avery, Reese,
Payton
Brothers: Dawson, Tucker, Griffin, Landon,
Drake, Mason
✱ America met this girl's name in 1997 in two
very differerent incarnations. On TV, Skylar
was the name of a new *Baywatch* babe. In the
movies, she was the cerebral Harvard student in
Good Will Hunting. Amazingly, the name fits
both images equally well—perfect for the brainy
cheerleader. Skylar/Skyler is used equally for
boys and girls; the "a" spelling tends to lean
feminine, the "e" spelling masculine.
In the World: Singer Skylar Grey; actress Skyler
Samuels

Sloane (SLOHN)   2011: #510
Popularity: #511
Styles: Brisk and Breezy, Last
Names First
Variants: Sloan   1880   Today
Sisters: Blair, Whitney,
Emory, Greer, Campbell, Reese
Brothers: Sutton, Tate, Chandler, Grant,
Briggs, Trip
✱ This surname comes across as prosperous
and confident, bordering on arrogant. Think of
it as Paige's swank big sister. In fact, in England
"Sloane" (or "Sloane Ranger") is a generic term
for the prosperous and confident set, a counter-
part to the American "preppie."
In the World: Tennis player Sloane Stephens;
Sloan McQuewick of *Entourage;* Sloane Peter-
son of *Ferris Bueller's Day Off*

Sofia (soh-FEE-ə) 2011: #19
Popularity: #19
Styles: Antique Charm,
Nordic, Greek, Italian,
Latino/Latina 1880 Today
Nicknames: Sofie, Sofi
Variants: Sofía, Sophia, Zofia
Sisters: Camila, Natalia, Lucia, Giselle,
Valeria, Lilia
Brothers: Lucas, Xavier, Julian, Elias, Roman,
Marco
✴ All forms of Sophia have soared, but this spelling has carved out its own distinct niche. While Sophie/Sophia has a cuddly side, Sofia is pure chic jet-setter. Feel free to fly it anywhere: this name is fashionable from Buenos Aires to Stockholm, Quebec to Milan.
In the World: Actresses Sofía Vergara and Sofia Black-D'Elia; director Sofia Coppola

Sonia (SOHN-yə) 1973: #174
Popularity: #770
Styles: Surfer '60s, '70s–'80s,
Slavic, Latino/Latina,
Nickname-Proof 1880 Today
Variants: Sonya, Sonja
Sisters: Tamara, Veronica, Sandra, Raquel,
Paula, Lara
Brothers: Macus, Damon, Joel, Ivan, Byron,
Rafael
✴ Sonia started life as a Russian diminutive of Sophia, but in English it's well established as a full name. It sounds luxurious, simple, and classic, a power combination. Real-life Sonias have shown a lot of power too. The spelling Sonia is the most timeless; Sonya is more Slavic but more '60s too.
In the World: Supreme Court justice Sonia Sotomayor; Indian politician Sonia Gandhi; skater Sonja Henie

Sookie (SOO-kee) 2010: #10,370
Popularity: #16,409
Styles: Nicknames,
Fantastical
Variants: Sukie, Sukey, Susan 1880 Today
Sisters: Poppy, Libby, Dovie,
Buffy, Zuzu, Lottie
Brothers: Rollie, Pip, Xander, Dobbin, Lex,
Hodge
✴ Sookie is an old-time nickname for Susan. (Remember the nursery rhyme, "Polly put the kettle on/Sukey take it off again?" Well, Polly and Sukey were Mary and Susan.) Today, for millions of fans, Sookie means Sookie Stackhouse of *True Blood*. As popular as the character and her name are, though, you won't find Sookie much as a given name. You can use it as a nickname for Susan, Susanna, or any of their many variants.
In the World: Sookie Stackhouse of *True Blood*

Sophia (soh-FEE-ə) 2011: #1
Popularity: #1
Styles: Antique Charm
Nicknames: Sophie, Sonya
Variants: Sofia, Sophie, Zofia 1880 Today
Sisters: Alexandra, Charlotte,
Lillian, Isabella, Olivia, Amelia
Brothers: Nicholas, Samuel, Lucas, Isaac,
Julian, Maxwell
✴ The ultimate in Sophi-stication. Sophia sounds serious, mature, and intelligent, and it's also just plain pretty: a feminine power name. Yes, it has become wildly popular, but that's the price you pay for perfection. This version of the name has the most stately grace; see also sweet, old-fashioned Sophie and globally chic Sofia.
In the World: Actresses Sophia Loren and Sophia Bush

Sophie (SOH-fee)　　　　2011: #51
Popularity: #51

1880　Today

Styles: Antique Charm, Guys and Dolls, French, German and Dutch
Variants: Sophia, Sofie
Sisters: Ruby, Lena, Grace, Lucy, Phoebe, Lillie, Sadie, Ella
Brothers: Max, Oliver, Leo, Emmett, Theo, Owen, Jack, Henry
✳ Sophie has a nickname style, but it's perfectly traditional as a given name. It's the French and German form of Sophia, and a century ago it was the more standard American version too. Back then, the name bridged the gap between immigrant names like Sigrid and dance-hall sweethearts like Lillie. Today Sophie and Sophia are equally chic.
In the World: Very popular in the U.K.; writer Sophie Kinsella; "Red Hot Mama" Sophie Tucker; actress Sophie Marceau

Stacy (STAY-see)　　　　1971: #32
Popularity: #984

Styles: Surfer '60s, '70s–'80s, Androgynous
Variants: Stacey, Stacie
Sisters: Kerry, Trina, Darcy, Leigh, Tara, Marcy, Shannon, Lesley
Brothers: Scott, Jamie, Shawn, Chad, Toby, Todd, Brian, Corey
✳ Stacy and Tracy were the original sparkly surnames for girls. Their sunny demeanor still shines, but parents are now looking for fresher choices with the same spirit. Macy and Riley are two recent heirs to the throne.
In the World: Wrestler/actress Stacy Keibler; "Malibu Stacy" doll from *The Simpsons*

Stefania (steh-FAHN-ya)　　　　1916: #1168
Popularity: #3801

Styles: Italian, Lacy and Lissome, Slavic, Greek, Why Not?
Nicknames: Stefi, Stevie
Variants: Estefania, Stephania
Sisters: Alessandra, Milana, Daniela, Katerina, Claudia, Simona, Renata, Mariella
Brothers: Carlo, Dimitri, Donato, Anton, Alexi, Luca, Maxim, Dario
✳ This variation puts a new shine on Stephanie, just as Daniela has done for Danielle. Note that the stress is on the second syllable.
In the World: Italian actress Stefania Sandrelli

Stella (STEH-lə)　　　　1889: #55
Popularity: #73

Styles: Antique Charm, Guys and Dolls
Sisters: Sadie, Lena, Lucy, Clara, Ruby, Violet, Georgia, Eva
Brothers: Oliver, Leo, Jack, Jasper, Henry, Ben, Emmett, Charlie
✳ Stella is a 'tweener. On one side, you have Ella: trim, jazzy, and ultra-fashionable. On the other side, Estella: stately, graceful, and antique. Stella takes some from each, which results in a modest, charming compromise. Do be prepared for a lifetime of Marlon Brando imitations ("Hey, Stellllaaaa!!").
In the World: Designer Stella McCartney; Stella of *A Streetcar Named Desire*

Stephanie (STEH-fa-nee)　　　　1984: #6
Popularity: #146

Styles: Surfer '60s, '70s–'80s
Nicknames: Steph, Stevie, Steffi
Variants: Stefanie, Stephany, Estefania, Stephania
Sisters: Melanie, Nicole, Candice, Allison, Danielle, Lauren, Bethany, Andrea
Brothers: Jeremy, Kevin, Brandon, Christopher, Jeffrey, Matthew, Brian, Timothy
✳ Stephanie has joined its male counterpart Steven as an American classic. Neither could be called the peak of fashion these days, but both remain handsome choices that not even the nitpickingest relative could find fault with. Creative spellings like Stefani (or in Stefani Germanotta, aka Lady Gaga) are falling out of favor faster.
In the World: Princess Stéphanie of Monaco; actress Stefanie Powers; "Twilight" author Stephenie Meyer

Sue (SOO) 1946: #61
Popularity: #6765
Styles: Mid-Century,
Nicknames
Variants: Susie   1880 Today
Sisters: Jo, Betsy, Gail, Kay,
Bonnie, Janet, Kathy, Ann
Brothers: Jay, Ted, Larry, Ken, Bill, Alan,
Eddie, Rick
✱ Sweet Sue has been missing from the scene
for decades. It's still heard occasionally as a
nickname, but its cute, plain-Jane style has
nixed it as a stand-alone first name. Approach it
with an open mind, though, and you might find
it an alternative to deft little names like Lily and
Hope.
In the World: Mystery writer Sue Grafton; *Glee*
character Sue Sylvester; song/phrase "Sweet
Sue"

Summer (SUH-mer)   1977: #119
Popularity: #173
Styles: Modern Meanings,
Charms and Graces,
Nickname-Proof, New   1880 Today
Classics
Sisters: Sierra, Brooke, Tessa, Noelle, Scarlett,
Willow
Brothers: Micah, Ian, Lucas, River, Skyler,
Blake
✱ A sunny name, in both meaning and person-
ality. Parents choose a name like Summer as a
big warm hug for their new daughter. It's sweet
but not silly, and can sound adult and sophisti-
cated when required. Read more under Au-
tumn.
In the World: Actress Summer Glau; swimmer
Summer Sanders; film *500 Days of Summer*

Susan (SOO-zən)   1954: #5
Popularity: #781
Styles: Mid-Century
Nicknames: Sue, Susie,
Sukey, Suze, ZuZu   1880 Today
Variants: Susana, Suzanne,
Suzan, Shoshanna, Sanne
Sisters: Linda, Deborah, Janet, Diane, Sharon,
Cathy, Donna, Teresa
Brothers: Mark, Allen, Peter, Dennis, Stephen,
Kenneth, David, Philip
✱ Picture a woman named Susan. Don't you
just want to like her? This is a name that posi-
tively screams "nice." It does not, however,
scream "interesting," and in an era of creative
naming, that has left nice, likable Susan spiral-
ing out of style.
In the World: Suffragist Susan B. Anthony; actor
Susan Sarandon; writer Susan Sontag; Susan G.
Komen Foundation

Susana (soo-ZA-nə)   1993: #472
Popularity: #1213
Styles: Timeless, Biblical,
Latino/Latina, Why Not?
Nicknames: Sue, Susa, Susie, 1880 Today
Suze, Sukey, Zuzu

Variants: Susanna, Suzanna, Susannah,
Shoshana
Sisters: Johanna, Marina, Tabitha, Elise,
Rebecca, Lydia
Brothers: Nathaniel, Simon, Noel, Stephen,
Elliot, Paul
✱ Susana is as familiar and traditional as Susan
but has the graceful flow of trendier names like
Juliana. That makes Susana the most fashion-
able form of the classic name. The spelling Su-
sannah shows off its antique roots and pairs well
with popular Old Testament names.
In the World: Song "Oh! Susanna"; singer Su-
sanna Hoffs; actresses Susannah York and Su-
sana Gimenez

Suzanne (soo-ZAN)   1946: #52
Popularity: #2620
Styles: Mid-Century, French
Nicknames: Suzie, Sue,
Zanna   1880   Today
Variants: Suzann, Suzette,
Susannah, Susana
Sisters: Annette, Maureen, Paula, Yvonne,
Valerie, Connie, Sheryl, Colleen
Brothers: Gregory, Dwight, Randall, Dana,
Gary, Wayne, Jerome, Bruce
✳ Susan is a classic name that reshapes itself to
fit the sound of each generation. In the 1800s,
that meant trimming to Susie, while from the
1940s to '60s it meant extending to the French
Suzanne. Today the antique sound of Susana/
Susannah best fits the moment.
In the World: Author Suzanne Collins; singer
Suzanne Vega; actresses Suzanne Somers and
Suzanne Pleshette

Sybil (SI-bəl)   1919: #282
Popularity: #9023
Styles: Mythological, Ladies
and Gentlemen
Variants: Sibyl, Sibyll, Sybill,   1880   Today
Cybil, Cybill
Sisters: Althea, Beryl, Eudora, Petra, Ione,
Minerva
Brothers: Clement, Jules, Merrill, Bertram,
Willis, Leopold
✳ Sybil has been a rarity for generations. It's
fusty, yet a wee bit funky too. A sibyl was an an-
cient Greek prophetess, the type who would re-
ceive her revelations in an ecstatic frenzy. Harry
Potter's divination professor, Sibyll Trelawney,
is a nod to that tradition. Spellings are a total
crapshoot; even author J. K. Rowling spelled
Professor Trelawney's name differently in differ-
ent editions of the books.
In the World: Actress Cybill Shepherd; Sibyll
Trelawney of the "Harry Potter" series

Sydney (SID-nee)   2000: #23
Popularity: #65
Styles: Last Names First,
Androgynous, Place Names,
Turn of the 21st Century   1880   Today
Nicknames: Syd
Variants: Sidney, Sydnee
Sisters: Aubrey, Morgan, Taylor, Hailey, Shelby,
Jordan, Avery, Kelsey
Brothers: Austin, Tanner, Dillon, Devin,
Hunter, Tucker, Hayden, Tyler
✳ Creative names tend to drift over time from
male to female, and Sydney's a dramatic exam-
ple. A hundred years ago, parents came up with
Sidney as an aristocratic-sounding choice for
their sons. Today it's passé as a boy's name but
red-hot for girls. The Australian city helps make
the spelling Sydney the most contemporary.
In the World: Sydney Bristow of TV series *Alias;*
Sydney Andrews of *Melrose Place;* Sidney
Prescott of film *Scream*

Sylvia (SIL-vee-ə)   1937: #50
Popularity: #554
Styles: Solid Citizens, Ladies
and Gentlemen
Nicknames: Syl, Sylvie   1880   Today
Variants: Silvia, Sylvie
Sisters: Vivian, Rosalie, Sybil, Marian, Barbara,
Stella, Virginia, Frances
Brothers: Vernon, Roland, Warren, Laurence,
Bernard, Clifton, Lionel, Franklin
✳ Smart money is on Sylvia to be one of the
first 1930s names to mount a comeback. The
name is distinctive and melodic, and the magic
letter "v" has a way of breathing new life into old
names. The international spelling Silvia has
particularly smashing associations: a Roman
forest goddess, the queen of Sweden, and
Shakespeare's romantic question, "Who is Silvia?"
In the World: *Sylvia* comic strip; poet Sylvia
Plath

Sylvie (SIL-vee) 2011: #1437
Popularity: #1445
Styles: French, Why Not?
Variants: Silvie, Sylvia, Silvia
Sisters: Amelie, Eloise, Iris,   1880 Today
Elodie, Phoebe, Selene,
Esme
Brothers: Theo, Luc, Tobias, Blaise, Silas,
Felix, Jules
✴ Sylvie may sound like a nickname, but it's the full French version of Sylvia. That makes it a kindred spirit to Sophie, and a promising alternative if you love that name but want something less common. Sylvie was hugely popular in France and Quebec in the 1960s, but American parents don't hear that. Here it's old-fashioned and unexpected with a sense of fun.
In the World: Ballet dancer Sylvie Guillem; model Sylvie van der Vaart; Lewis Carroll book *Sylvie and Bruno*

Tabitha (TA-bi-thə) 1978: #126
Popularity: #676
Styles: '70s–'80s, Biblical
Nicknames: Tabby, Tibby,
Tab   1880 Today
Variants: Tabatha
Sisters: Bethany, Marisa, Candace, Sabrina,
Danielle, Miranda, Jillian, Rebekah
Brothers: Zachary, Justin, Timothy, Jonathan,
Drew, Lucas, Derek, Jared
✴ The creators of the '60s sitcom *Bewitched* had a genius for unearthing names that captured the spirits of their characters. Tabitha is a biblical name, but it wasn't until it appeared as an adorable, otherworldly TV toddler that the name took its current shape. It's classically pretty with an impish streak. In England, Tabitha has been a favorite cat name—note the nickname Tabby.
In the World: Reality TV show *Tabatha's Salon Takeover*; Tabitha Stephens of *Bewitched*

Talia (TAH-lee-ə) 2004: #333
Popularity: #431
Styles: Lacy and Lissome,
Jewish, New Classics, Why
Not?   1880 Today
Nicknames: Tally, Tal
Variants: Talya
Sisters: Ilana, Naomi, Alina, Samara, Tova,
Anya
Brothers: Asher, Nico, Ari, Micah, Myles, Cole
✴ You can call it a short form of Natalia, a modern Hebrew name, or just a contemporary creation. From any direction, Talia sounds fresh yet timeless, with a smart cross-cultural strength.
In the World: Actresses Talia Shire and Talia Balsam

Tamara (TA-mə-rə, 1974: #63
tah-MAHR-ə)
Popularity: #1133
Styles: Surfer '60s, Biblical,
Slavic   1880 Today
Nicknames: Tammy, Mara
Variants: Tamar
Sisters: Sonya, Rochelle, Carla, Angela, Stacy,
Larissa, Belinda, Deanna
Brothers: Geoffrey, Marc, Darren, Craig,
Timothy, Daniel, Randall, Jeremy
✴ This serene biblical name emerged in the '60s as a source for the super-popular nickname Tammy. Tammy is now on the outs, but Tamara remains an attractive possibility. Try Mara for the short form.
In the World: Painter Tamara de Lempicka; actress Tamara Taylor .

Tamika (tah-MEE-kə) 1975: #130
Popularity: #11,952
Styles: African-American
Nicknames: Tami, Mika,
Mimi   1880 Today
Variants: Tameka, Tomika,
Tanika, Tomiko
Sisters: Latasha, Nakia, Tyesha, Latrice, Alisha,
Quiana, Jamila, Keisha
Brothers: Demond, Terrance, Rodrick, Jamaal,
Darnell, Jarrod, Antwan, Terrell
✴ For a time, Tamika was a reigning queen of African-American names. It seems to have come and gone in the blink of an eye. One successor is the slimmed-down version Tamia.
In the World: Basketball player Tamika Catchings; singer Tameka Cottle

Tammy (TA-mee)   1968: #8
Popularity: #2996
Styles: Surfer '60s,
Nicknames
Variants: Tamara, Tammie,   1880   Today
Tammy
Sisters: Marcy, Tina, Cindy, Dawn, Tracy,
Wendy
Brothers: Todd, Robbie, Terry, Kip, Scotty,
Keith
★ Short of Gidget, no name sits more squarely
in the square '60s. Debbie Reynolds's sunny
country gal in the *Tammy* film series made this
nickname a symbol of wholesome sweetness.
In the World: Tammy and the Bachelor; singer
Tammy Wynette; evangelist/TV personality
Tammy Faye Bakker; Senator Tammy Baldwin

Tamsin (TAM-sin)   2005: #8871
Popularity: #13,136
Styles: English, The "-ens,"
Celtic, Why Not?
Nicknames: Tam, Tams,   1880   Today
Tammy
Variants: Tamsyn
Sisters: Davina, Adair, Briony, Emlyn, Ailsa,
Mirren
Brothers: Tiernan, Cormac, Gareth, Trevor,
Piers, Ronan
★ This feminine form of Thomas has been
well used throughout Britain but never crossed
over to the U.S. Its sound is now perfectly cur-
rent, and the name is ripe for discovery.
In the World: Actresses Tamsin Egerton and
Tamsin Greig

Tanith (TA-nith)   [illegible]
Popularity: #11,596
Styles: Exotic Traditional
Variants: Tanis, Tanit
Sisters: Charis, Lorelei, Ione,   1880   Today
Esme, Ariadne, Maris
Brothers: Leander, Tavish, Antony, Caedmon,
Bram, Aldric
★ Tanith was the ancient Phoenician moon
goddess, the patron goddess of Carthage. As a
name, Tanith is highly distinctive but not
showy. The Greek version Tanis has a more
mainstream sound, but Tanith is a slightly more
familiar choice thanks to ice dancer Tanith Bel-
bin and writer Tanith Lee.
In the World: Writer Tanith Lee; ice dancer
Tanith Belbin

Tanya (TAHN-yə)   1974: #46
Popularity: #1105
Styles: '70s–'80s, Nickname-
Proof, Slavic
Variants: Tania, Tonya,   1880   Today
Taniya
Sisters: Shawna, Kerri, Natasha, Erica,
Melinda, Aimee, Janna, Renee
Brothers: Corey, Derrick, Brent, Shane, Jarvis,
Chad, Casey, Byron
★ Tanya is a Russian nickname for Tatiana that
sounds energetically American. (The similar
name Tonya comes from Antonina.) The name
hit a huge peak in the '70s, but today the full
Tatiana is more popular. The spelling Tania has
also emerged as a three-syllable name, like
Taniyah.
In the World: Country singer Tanya Tucker;
skater Tonya Harding

Tara (TAH rə, TA-rə)   1972: #38
Popularity: #877
Styles: '70s–'80s, Nickname-
Proof, Short and Sweet
Sisters: Jenna, Shannon,   1880   Today
Erica, April, Stacy, Krista,
Tanya, Erin
Brothers: Jared, Chad, Brent, Damon, Corey,
Travis, Derek, Kyle
★ The American name Tara was born in Hol-
lywood in 1939, as the O'Hara family plantation
in *Gone with the Wind.* It grew slowly and
steadily to become one of the country's favorite
names. Believe it or not, more 1970s girls were
named Tara than Kristen and Krista combined.
Tara is much less common today, but it could fit
in easily with a generation of Mayas and Jadas.
In the World: Actress Tara Reid; skater Tara
Lipinski; artist Tara Donovan

Tasha (TAH-shə) 1980: #130
Popularity: #3750
Styles: '70s–'80s, African-
American, Nicknames
Variants: Tosha 1880 Today
Sisters: Trina, Keisha, Brandi,
Shana, Nikki, Tanya
Brothers: Derrick, Bryan, Trey, Shaun, Jaime,
Torrey
✶A nickname for a nickname (see Natalia),
Tasha became the center of a mini-style of its
own in the '70s. The core sound still appeals,
but the swirl of Tashas, Natashas, and Latashas
got to be too much. Sasha, the Russian nick-
name for Alexandra, is a more current option
today.
In the World: Actress Tasha Smith; illustrator
Tasha Tudor

Tatum (TAY-tuhm) 2010: #335
Popularity: #345
Styles: Last Names First,
Nickname-Proof
Sisters: Greer, Teagan, 1880 Today
Finley, Willow, Harper,
Rowan
Brothers: Holden, Tucker, Paxton, Kane,
Hudson, Tanner
✶This old English surname made a direct leap
to girl's first name thanks to the example of ac-
tress Tatum O'Neal. Its sound is quite boyish,
and in fact some parents of boys are now turning
to it. (This time, actor Channing Tatum is the
trigger.) But for once, the girls got to the sur-
name first, giving this name a bold female style.
In the World: Actress Tatum O'Neal; (male)
actor Channing Tatum

Tatiana (tah-TYAH-nə) 1999: #213
Popularity: #447
Styles: Lacy and Lissome,
Slavic, Saints
Nicknames: Tanya, Tati, 1880 Today
Tiana
Variants: Tatyana
Sisters: Anastasia, Natalia, Arielle, Katerina,
Melania, Serena
Brothers: Fabian, Dimitri, Tristan, Maximilian,
Krystof, Valentin
✶Tatiana is a perfect choice for residents of
enchanted forests and faerie palaces. Certainly,
this is a serious name—in fact, it's intensely dig-
nified. A classic from the early days of Christi-
anity, Tatiana has been popular in Russia for
hundreds of years. Its sound, though, is the stuff
of daydreams.
In the World: Mexican singer Tatiana; actress
Tatyana Ali; writer Tatyana Tolstaya

Taylor (TAY-ler) 1993: #7
Popularity: #44
Styles: Last Names First,
Androgynous, Turn of the
21st Century 1880 Today
Nicknames: Tay
Variants: Tayla
Sisters: Jordan, Kelsey, Logan, Hunter, Payton,
Haley, Macy, Parker
Brothers: Austin, Carter, Dawson, Tanner,
Dillon, Brady, Trevor, Mason
✶Taylor is the name that opened the flood-
gates on tradesman names for girls. It started
rising in the 1980s, then enjoyed a huge surge in
the '90s after its debut on the soap opera *The
Bold and the Beautiful.* Back then, it was the es-
sence of sleek, modern androgyny. Over the
years that followed it became the familiar sound
of the young American woman, as personified
by singer Taylor Swift.
In the World: Singer Taylor Swift; male Taylors
such as actor Taylor Lautner and singer Taylor
Hicks

Teagan (TEE-gin)   2011: #213
Popularity: #213
Styles: The "-ens," Bell
Tones, Celtic, Androgynous
Variants: Tegan, Teigan   1880   Today
Sisters: Hayden, Ainsley,
Kaya, Taryn, Kenzie, Finley
Brothers: Kieran, Rylan, Cormac, Finnegan,
Rowan, Kane
✷ Teagan, a form of the Irish man's name
Teague, is becoming a feminine favorite in the
U.S. on the model of Megan and Reagan. Un-
like those names, Teagan is almost always pro-
nounced with a long "e," giving it a particularly
bright and modern sound. In the U.K., you're
more likely to encounter Tegan, an unrelated
Welsh name with more varied pronunciations.
In the World: Band Tegan and Sara; Tegan Jo-
vanka of *Doctor Who*

Tenley (TEHN-lee)   2011: #423
Popularity: #424
Styles: Bell Tones, Why Not?
Sisters: Tessa, Kelsey, Tatum,
Lacey, Delaney, Haley   1880   Today
Brothers: Tanner, Logan,
Dalton, Kyle, Trent, Dillon
✷ This name was introduced to the public by
1950s figure skater Tenley Albright. Albright
was an inspiring individual who overcame a
bout with polio to become an Olympic champion and later a successful surgeon. In 2010 a
reality TV contestant reminded parents of the
name Tenley, and many fell in love. It's neither
androgynous nor girly and still sounds perfectly
modern.
In the World: skater Tenley Albright, Bachelor
contestant Tenley Molzahn

Teresa (tə-REE-sə,   1962: #18
teh-RAY-sə)
Popularity: #537
Styles: Mid-Century,
Timeless, Latino/Latina,   1880   Today
Italian
Nicknames: Terry, Tess, Tessa, Tressa, Téa,
Tracy, Reese
Variants: Theresa, Therese, Tereza
Sisters: Cynthia, Pamela, Suzanne, Deborah,
Colleen, Anita, Nina, Kathryn
Brothers: Allen, Douglas, Russell, Mark, Paul,
Stephen, Gregory, Philip
✷ Theresa always seemed like a pure timeless
classic, spelled with or without the "h." In the
past decade, though, it has plummeted out of
style. Mysterious, given that the sound of the
name is still impeccably fashionable. Is the '50s-
style nickname Terry the problem? Switch to
Tess or Téa and you're back in business.
In the World: Mother Teresa of Calcutta; singer
Teresa Brewer; actress Teresa Wright

Terra (TEH-rə)   1980: #378
Popularity: #2196
Styles: Modern Meanings,
Short and Sweet
Variants: Tierra   1880   Today
Sisters: Janna, Brook, Adria,
Misha, Coral, Tama
Brothers: Leif, Tobin, Micah, Brant, Heath,
Tait
✷ Terra first appeared with '70s cuties like Tara
and Tasha, but its meaning—Latin for "earth"—
sets it apart. This can be a contemporary choice
for nature lovers and a match for creative names
from Lyric to Meadow.
In the World: Phrases such as "terra firma,"
"terra nova," and "terra cotta"

Terry (TEH-ree)   1955: #82
Popularity: #7042
Styles: Mid-Century,
Nicknames, Androgynous
Variants: Terri, Teri   1880   Today
Sisters: Randy, Lori, Beth,
Toni, Pam, Sandy
Brothers: Allan, Chris, Gary, Todd, Ricky, Greg
✷ Terry was the queen—and king—of the an-
drogynous nicknames of the '50s and '60s. It was
a tremendous hit for both sexes but has lost its
edge in recent years. Today Terry works best as a
nickname, either for the traditional Theresa or a
new creation like Terra.
In the World: Actresses Teri Hatcher and Teri
Garr

Tess (TEHS) 1993: #480
Popularity: #925
Styles: Guys and Dolls,
Nicknames, Why Not?
Nicknames: Tessie   1880 Today
Variants: Tessa
Sisters: Nell, Evie, Reba, Annie, Sophie, Belle,
Kate, Lena
Brothers: Theo, Charley, Jake, Max, Nate,
Jasper, Luke, Harry
★This nickname (from Teresa) makes a stylish
statement on its own: trim, buoyant, and confi-
dent.
In the World: Thomas Hardy novel *Tess of the
d'Urbervilles*

Tessa (TEH-sə) 2007: #190
Popularity: #229
Styles: Nicknames, Short and
Sweet, New Classics
Nicknames: Tess, Tessie 1880 Today
Sisters: Lia, Audrey, Nika,
Jenna, Molly, Zoe, Lila
Brothers: Drew, Gavin, Cole, Ian, Finn, Miles,
Liam
★As a given name, Tessa borrows virtues from
many forms of Teresa. It's compact and modern
like Tess, lighthearted like Tessie, and feminine
and internationally popular like the full Teresa.
In the World: Ice dancer Tessa Virtue; a Marvel
Comics character (also known as Sage)

Thea (THEE-ə) 1895: #596
Popularity: #1522
Styles: Ladies and
Gentlemen, Nordic, Short
and Sweet, Why Not? 1880 Today
Sisters: Nora, Lucy, Louisa,
Tilda, Mika, Elsa
Brothers: August, Simon, Casper, Reuben,
Niels, Oscar
★This subtle, pretty name is an unconven-
tional choice that sits comfortably alongside fa-
vorites like Ava and Maya. Originally a short
form of Dorothea and Theadora, Thea is simple
but serious enough to stand on its own. It has
already made a huge comeback in fashion-for-
ward Scandinavia.
In the World: Children's book mouse Thea Stil-
ton; nun/educator Sister Thea Bowman

Theda (THEE-də) 1919: #337
Popularity: #19,246
Styles: Ladies and
Gentlemen, Nickname-Proof
Sisters: Viola, Geneva, Sybil,   1880 Today
Ardis, Petra, Althea
Brothers: Bayard, Olin, Rollo, Armand,
Theron, Upton
★Those who are familiar with silent film star
Theda Bara, the original "vamp," will admire
this name for its discreet seductiveness. Those
who've never heard of her may find the name a
bit dowdy. It was traditionally a short form of
Theodora or, as in Ms. Bara's case, Theodosia.
In the World: Actress Theda Bara

Thelma (THEHL-mə) 1911: #27
Popularity: #9040
Styles: Porch Sitters
Sisters: Pauline, Verna,
Arlene, Fern, Bernice, Irma 1880 Today
Brothers: Lester, Cyril,
Duane, Willard, Herbert, Merle
★This is the sort of soft, squishy name that's
currently off the fashion map. Thelma's a rather
nice example of the style, almost like an endear-
ment, but it's still a tough sell.
In the World: Film *Thelma and Louise*; singer
Thelma Houston

Theodora (thee-ə-DOH-rə) 1937: #507
Popularity: #2846
Styles: Ladies and
Gentlemen, Greek
Nicknames: Thea, Theda,   1880 Today
Tea, Dora
Variants: Teodora
Sisters: Eleanora, Philippa, Celestine, Aurelia,
Hermione, Rosamond, Violetta, Wilhelmina
Brothers: Benedict, Albin, Lucius, Ambrose,
Cornelius, Armand, Bartholomew, Leopold
★Theodora is a grand old name, imposingly
distinguished. For a similar but lighter touch,
try reversing the elements to yield Dorothea
("gift of God" versus "God's gift"). Thea and
Dora can serve as nicknames for either.

Therese (teh-REHZ, teh-REES) 1927: #220
Popularity: #3423
Styles: French, Solid Citizens, Saints
Nicknames: Terry, Tess, Reese
Variants: Thérèse, Terese, Theresa
Sisters: Marianne, Louise, Bernadette, Nadine, Helene, Patrice
Brothers: Gerard, Roland, Laurence, Claude, Armand, Jerome
★This intriguing name has two different pronunciations. "Teh-REHZ" is authentically French and elegant, but a bit downbeat. "Teh-REES" is brighter but less exotic. Both are uncommon and handsome.
In the World: Novel and film *Thérèse Raquin*; Massenet opera *Thérèse*

Thomasina (toh-mah-SEE-nə) 1932: #966
Popularity: #16,492
Styles: English
Nicknames: Tommie, Tamsin
Sisters: Philippa, Anthea, Theodosia, Davina, Rosamond, Jessamine
Brothers: Tristram, Ivor, Piers, Tarquin, Bartholomew, Auberon
★Thomasina is a genuine antique that was past its heyday by the year 1700. It's a bit heavy but has a romantic rhythm and a cute tomboy nickname. And given its three centuries of slumber, it is completely free of preconceptions.

Tia (TEE-ə) 1982: #220
Popularity: #917
Styles: Nicknames, Short and Sweet
Sisters: Ali, Tyra, India, Taryn, Mara, Kai
Brothers: Chaz, Tristan, Luca, Noel, Abel, Nico
★Tia used to be a nickname for elaborate Latin creations like Laetitia, but there's no reason not to choose it straight up. It's a little pocketful of cheer.
In the World: Actress Tia Mowry; Spanish for "aunt"

Tiana (tee-AH-nə) 1995: #267
Popularity: #387
Styles: African-American, Bell Tones
Variants: Tianna
Sisters: Ciera, Bianca, Janae, Skyla, Rayna, Jailyn
Brothers: Quinton, Tyson, Donte, Koby, Trevin, Isaiah
★When Disney first scripted an African-American heroine for its film *The Princess and the Frog*, she was going to be a chambermaid named Maddy. After some early grumblings from the public, they went back to the drawing board to cook up something a little more regal. Good-bye, chambermaid, and good-bye Maddy. Enter Tiana, a contemporary African-American favorite with a fairy-dust sparkle that's just a hair's breadth from "tiara."
In the World: Disney Princess Tiana; actress Tiana Benjamin

Tierney (TEER-nee) 1993: #1059
Popularity: #2138
Styles: Celtic, Last Names First, Why Not?
Sisters: Connolly, Keelin, Aislinn, Riley, Tamsin, Shea
Brothers: Teague, Quinlan, Brogan, Cormac, Tynan, Brennan
★Classic movie buffs may associate this name with elegant actress Gene Tierney. Everybody else will just think you've discovered an uncommon Irish name with a fashionable sound. You win either way. Tierney comes from a Gaelic men's name but its usage today is all female. The related name Tiernan is one option for boys.
In the World: Singer Tierney Sutton; actresses Gene Tierney and Maura Tierney

Tiffany (TI-fə-nee) 1988: #13
Popularity: #347
Styles: '70s–'80s
Nicknames: Tif
Variants: Tiffani 1880 Today
Sisters: Brittany, Amber, Ashley, Shanna, Whitney, Crystal
Brothers: Corey, Brandon, Chad, Travis, Shawn, Dustin
★This is the spiritual grandma of all the brand-name names. Tiffany is actually a religious name from the Middle Ages, but its modern use is all about the New York jewelry emporium. Unfortunately, this has given the name a bit of a "downwardly mobile" reputation. The assumption is that people who actually shop at Tiffany's don't name their kids after the store.
In the World: Book and film *Breakfast at Tiffany's*; actress Tiffani Amber Thiessen; singer Tiffany

Tina (TEE-nə) 1968: #18
Popularity: #1332
Styles: Surfer '60s
Sisters: Lisa, Tracy, Julie, Dawn, Sonya, Lori 1880 Today
Brothers: Todd, Chris, Marc, Jeff, Brady, Troy
★This model nickname was one of many propelled to full-name status in the '60s. That style has largely passed, but as a nickname Tina still has classic appeal. If you're at a loss for a full version, consider Bettina, Christina, Justina, Martina, or Valentina.
In the World: Comedian Tina Fey; singer Tina Turner; actress Tina Louise

Tinsley (TINZ-lee) 2011: #1071
Popularity: #1073
Styles: Last Names First
Sisters: Blakely, Taryn, Emerson, Waverly, Leighton, 1880 Today
Hartley
Brothers: Weston, Steele, Tanner, Brantley, Colson, Barlow
★Tinsley Mortimer is a New York socialite whose turn as a reality TV star put her name in the spotlight. Tinsley's sparkly style—"tinselly," you might say—makes it an heir to Tiffany.
In the World: Socialite/reality TV star Tinsley Mortimer

Topaz (TOH-paz) 1989: #5046
Popularity: Very rare
Styles: Charms and Graces
Sisters: Azure, Winter, Lark, Amethyst, Hazel, Briar 1880 Today
Brothers: Birch, Merit, Cyrus, Flint, Sterling, Wolf
★Take the next step past Ruby and Pearl. Topaz was occasionally heard in the heyday of gem names and would be a high-style choice for adventurous parents today. A flamboyant Topaz can be found in the classic young-adult novel *I Capture the Castle*.
In the World: Topaz, a comic-book sorceress

Tori (TOH-ree) 1994: #142
Popularity: #626
Styles: Nicknames, Turn of the 21st Century
Variants: Tory 1880 Today
Sisters: Bria, Carly, Alex, Tessa, Ali, Lexi
Brothers: Trey, Colby, Skylar, Chaz, Trent, Drew
★Tori used to be just a minor nickname for Victoria, but it's well established now as a given name. It's as cute and light as '50s counterpart Vicki, with a '90s spin thanks to singer Tori Amos and *Beverly Hills, 90210* star Tori Spelling.
In the World: Actress Tori Spelling; singer Tori Amos; designer Tori Burch; main character of sitcom *Victorious*

Tova (TOH-və) 1984: #1749
Popularity: #3636
Styles: Short and Sweet, Jewish, Nordic, Nickname-Proof 1880 Today
Variants: Tove
Sisters: Tali, Shira, Dalia, Britta, Riva, Anni
Brothers: Ari, Leif, Jaron, Tal, Aksel, Espen
★Fashionably swift and petite, Tova also has a gentle graciousness. You can picture a Tova zipping masterfully down a ski slope, then baking brownies afterward. The name has both Norse and Hebrew origins for a global sound.
In the World: Writer/illustrator Tove Jansson; actress Tovah Feldshuh

Tracy (TRAY-see)   1970: #10
Popularity: #1880
Styles: Last Names First,
Androgynous, Surfer '60s
Variants: Traci, Tracey,   1880   Today
Tracie
Sisters: Kimberly, Stacy, Robin, Kelly, Tina,
Darcy
Brothers: Todd, Kerry, Brad, Scott, Toby,
Jeffrey
✱ In the film The Philadelphia Story, Katharine Hepburn played glamorous socialite Tracy Lord. That sparkling image sent the name soaring for decades. Tracy's high-society image gradually mellowed, and today it's more often heard on moms than on babies.
In the World: Singer Tracy Chapman; actress Tracy Nelson; writer Tracy Chevalier; Tracy Turnblad of Hairspray

Tricia (TRI-shə)   1971: #109
Popularity: #6279
Styles: '70s–'80s, Nicknames
Nicknames: Trish
Variants: Trisha   1880   Today
Sisters: Tracy, Christa, Leigh,
Tanya, Carrie, Sonia
Brothers: Shawn, Brent, Toby, Scott, Darren,
Todd
✱ A tale of two Patricias: the name Tricia took off just as Patty disappeared from view. Tricia is just as breezy but far less cutesy. Think of the independent spirit of country singer Trisha Yearwood as opposed to the broken-hearted sweetness of predecessor Patsy Cline.
In the World: Actress Tricia Helfer

Trinity (TRI-ni-tee)   2004: #48
Popularity: #77
Styles: Modern Meanings,
Fantastical
Nicknames: Trini, Trina   1880   Today
Variants: Trinidad
Sisters: Genesis, Destiny, Serenity, Nevaeh, Journey, Phoenix, Cadence, Harmony
Brothers: Talon, Maverick, Orion, Tristan, Chance, Jett, Maximus, Zion
✱ Enter The Matrix. . . . That massively popular sci-fi franchise launched the name Trinity, but it has gone on to thrive on its own merits. Trinity has long been identified with the Christian doctrine of the Father, Son, and Holy Spirit. With the new crop of Trinitys, though, it comes across as a modern oomph name akin to Destiny.
In the World: Trinity College; Trinity of The Matrix

Trudy (TROO-dee)   1946: #238
Popularity: #7046
Styles: Mid-Century,
Nicknames
Nicknames: Tru   1880   Today
Variants: Trudie, Trudi
Sisters: Ginny, Kathy, Penny, Sheryl, Glenda, Wendy, Debby, Bonnie
Brothers: Garry, Mickey, Chuck, Dana, Rick, Barry, Ken, Ronnie
✱ Is any nickname further removed from the full name that gave it life? Trudy is cute, perky, and all-American. It's happily rooted in the 1950s and a jolly (if uncommon) choice today. But if you're tempted to use it as a nickname, you have to face the fact that it's short for Gertrude. Or Ermintrude, if that's any help.

Tyler (TIY-ler)   1993: #238
Popularity: #1320
Styles: Last Names First,
Androgynous
Nicknames: Ty   1880   Today
Sisters: Ashton, Hunter,
Logan, Sydney, Jordan, Blake, Skylar, Devin
Brothers: Tanner, Jarret, Bryson, Tucker, Dalton, Brock, Kendall, Spencer
✱ Tyler and Taylor were both on androgynous turf in the '90s, but they agreed to split up the territory. Tyler is now firmly established as a popular choice for boys, Taylor for girls. Tyler still makes a catchy girl's name, but be aware that you'll be courting confusion on two fronts: she'll be called Taylor half the time, and mistaken for a boy the other half.
In the World: Male Tylers include filmmaker Tyler Perry

Tyra (TIY-rə)   1998: #317
Popularity: #2220
Styles: Short and Sweet,
African-American, Bell
Tones, Why Not?   1880   Today
Nicknames: Ty
Sisters: Jada, Mika, Bria, Macy, Anya, Shea, Katya, Tia
Brothers: Keenan, Joah, Devin, Jalen, Taj, Tobin, Kobe, Trey
✱ Most of us find one social niche where we feel comfortable: the jocks, the geeks, the glamour girls. Then there are those enviable few who can move smoothly among groups, fitting in and getting along wherever they go. That's Tyra, a simple but seductive, new but familar name with cross-racial appeal.
In the World: Model and talk show host Tyra Banks

Valentina (va-lin-TEE-na) 2011: #153
Popularity: #153
Styles: Saints, Slavic, Exotic
Traditional, Italian
Nicknames: Val, Tina 1880 Today
Variants: Valentine
Sisters: Donatella, Seraphina, Melania, Alessandra, Dominique, Rafaella, Tatiana, Anastasia
Brothers: Maximilian, Dominik, Leonardo, Emmanuel, Romeo, Blaise, Quentin, Constantin
✷This form of Valentine, used in Italy and Eastern Europe, has the intriguing effect of making the name more feminine yet less girly. Valentina is ravishing but drop-dead serious. It's one of the few names you can picture equally on an executive door and a lingerie label.
In the World: Designer Valentina; Valentina Tereshkova, the first woman in space; daughter of actress Salma Hayek

Valentine (VA-lehn-tiyn) 1885: #695
Popularity: #4521
Styles: Exotic Traditional, Fanciful, Androgynous
Nicknames: Val 1880 Today
Variants: Valentina
Sisters: Evangeline, Raine, Violette, Tempest, Salome, Guinevere
Brothers: Emmanuel, Romeo, Florian, Peregrin, Severin, Constantine
✷Valentine is traditionally a man's name, as in the Saint Valentine whose feast day we celebrate with hearts and candy. Its romantic connotations, though, make it a lavish choice for a girl. The simple nickname Val is a nice antidote to the name's excesses; Valentina is an increasingly popular import.
In the World: Valentine's Day; writer/artist Valentine de Saint-Point

Valeria (vah-LAY-ree-ə) 2009: #72
Popularity: #125
Styles: Lacy and Lissome, Latino/Latina, Shakespearean, Italian, 1880 Today
Slavic
Nicknames: Val, Ria, Valya
Variants: Valerie
Sisters: Natalia, Mariana, Adriana, Viviana, Gabriela, Juliana
Brothers: Marco, Lorenzo, Elias, Antoinio, Diego, Nicolas
✷The French form Valerie has been more familiar in the U.S., but Valeria is a graceful international favorite. It's especially popular in Argentina and Brazil, and a hot choice for U.S. Latinas too.
In the World: Actress Valeria Golino; model Valeria Mazza; singer Valeria Lynch

Valerie (VA-lə-ree) 1959: #60
Popularity: #158
Styles: Mid-Century, French
Nicknames: Val
Variants: Valarie, Valery, 1880 Today
Valeria
Sisters: Jacqueline, Melanie, Vivian, Michele, Danielle, Cynthia, Veronica, Candace
Brothers: Gregory, Randall, Jeffrey, Alan, Gerard, Stephen, Vincent, Mark
✷ Shake off your first reaction to Valerie. It's an old and elegant French name that rolls off your tongue. Plus Val is a smart little nickname, akin to Sam for Samantha but less common. Okay, now we can go back to your first reaction: it sounds like a fifty-year old. Yeah, it may, but I'm betting the other kids in your daughter's class won't think so.
In the World: TV actresses Valerie Harper and Valerie Bertinelli

Vanessa (vah-NEH-sə) 1985: #42
Popularity: #118
Styles: Lacy and Lissome,
New Classics, African-
American 1880 Today
Nicknames: Nessa
Sisters: Cassandra, Miranda, Sabrina, Melanie,
Amanda, Marissa, Christina, Angelica
Brothers: Derek, Brandon, Bryan, Trevor, Erik,
Dylan, Bradley, Aaron
✱The name equivalent of an evening gown,
Vanessa is timeless, lacy luxury. Like many lacy
favorites, it was created by a poet—Jonathan
Swift in the 18th century. Today Vanessa is a
name with strong cross-racial and cross-cultural
appeal.
In the World: Actresses Vanessa Redgrave, Va-
nessa Williams, and Vanessa Hudgens

Vera (VEE-rə) 1899: #69
Popularity: #512
Styles: Ladies and
Gentlemen, Slavic,
Nickname-Proof 1880 Today
Sisters: Alma, Clara, Marion,
Sylvia, Avis, Rhea, Nola, Stella
Brothers: Ellis, Foster, Theo, Emmett, Louis,
Merritt, Porter, Julius
✱Vera is a Slavic name meaning "faith," and it
coincides with the Latin word for "true." That's
a lot of positive energy, and the name's direct,
womanly sound carries the message well. Amer-
icans overindulged in this name a few genera-
tions back, and there's still a lingering hangover,
but a Vera renaissance is on the horizon.
In the World: Gown designer Vera Wang; hand-
maker Vera Bradley; singer Vera Lynn; actress
Vera Farmiga

Verity (VEH-ri-tee) 2010: #3485
Popularity: #3968
Styles: Charms and Graces,
English, Why Not?
Sisters: Briony, Felicity, 1880 Today
Cassia, Arabella, Juniper,
Dahlia, Amity, Jessamyn
Brothers: August, Torin, Jonty, Ivor, Gareth,
Vaughan, Finian, Silvan
✱Verity ("truthfulness") is an uplifting, thor-
oughly unusual meaning name. Usually that
spells flamboyant, yet Verity is modest and lady-
like. It's a familiar name in England and Austra-
lia, but sounds pleasantly surprising in the U.S.

Veronica (və-RAH-ni-kə) 1974: #71
Popularity: #284
Styles: Timeless, Saints,
Latino/Latina
Nicknames: Ronnie, Vera 1880 Today
Variants: Veronika
Sisters: Christina, Valerie, Marina, Camille,
Natalia, Claudia
Brothers: Victor, Raphael, Gregory, Thaddeus,
Nicholas, Vincent
✱Many timeless names are demure and un-
derstated, but Veronica is sizzling. Certainly,
it's a respectable classic, with Latin origins and
early Christian roots. It's just respectably, classi-
cally seductive. *Archie Comics* got this name
just right with their raven-haired dream girl—
compare to Betty.
In the World: TV series *Veronica Mars*; actress
Veronica Lake; Veronica Lodge of *Archie
Comics*

Vickie (VI-kee) 1956: #68
Popularity: #7053
Styles: Mid-Century,
Nicknames
Variants: Vicky, Vicki, Vikki 1880 Today
Sisters: Jan, Debby, Ginny,
Trudy, Sheila, Terri
Brothers: Todd, Ricky, Gary, Ken, Vince,
Donnie
✱Vickie is an adorable nickname that serves a
woman well throughout her lifetime. So go
ahead and call your daughter Vickie . . . but
name her Victoria. Victoria is one of the great
combinations of dignified name and cute nick-
name. Why mess with it?
In the World: Film *Vicky Cristina Barcelona*;
singer Vikki Carr

Victoria (vik-TOH-ree-ə)   1993: #19
Popularity: #23
Styles: Timeless, English,
Antique Charm, Latino/
Latina   1880   Today
Nicknames: Vicky, Tori, Vivi
Variants: Viktoria, Victoire, Vittoria
Sisters: Alexandra, Sophia, Caroline,
Christina, Olivia, Camilla, Charlotte, Amelia
Brothers: Nicholas, James, Nathaniel, Anthony,
Julian, Graham, Oliver, Christopher
★ Victoria is a popular name today, but there's
no chance of its sounding faddish. The image of
Queen Victoria remains too strong to permit
such an undignified fate. The likes of Victoria
Beckham and Victoria's Secret have simply
jazzed up the name, not cheapened it. It's still
classic and elegant.
In the World: The Victorias mentioned above;
Victoria, British Columbia

Violet (VIY-ə-lit)   1919: #74
Popularity: #101
Styles: Charms and Graces,
Antique Charm
Nicknames: Vi   1880   Today
Variants: Violette, Violetta
Sisters: Evelyn, Lydia, Ruby, Hazel, Vivian,
Lily, Josephine
Brothers: Jasper, Everett, Vincent, Theo,
August, Oliver, Finn
★ Violet is a flower petal of a name, velvety and
delicate. It sounds so proper and demure that it's
hard to picture the name making a big splash.
It's coming close, though, with rising popularity
and a rash of Hollywood sightings. Is that
"trendy" label scaring you off a name you love?
Don't let it. Violet is still not very common, and
few names are better at bringing a smile to peo-
ple's faces.
In the World: Violet Baudelaire of Lemony
Snicket's "A Series of Unfortunate Events" series; Violet Beauregarde of *Charlie and the
Chocolate Factory*; a daughter of actors Ben Affleck and Jennifer Garner

Virginia (ver-JIN-yə)   1922: #7
Popularity: #576
Styles: Ladies and
Gentlemen, Place Names,
Country and Western   1880   Today
Nicknames: Ginny, Ginger,
Gina, Gigi
Sisters: Lucinda, Georgia, Marietta, Rosalie,
Annabelle, Charlotte, Veronica, Geneva
Brothers: Charles, Theodore, Porter, Frederick,
Clifton, Houston, Willis, Randolph
★ A grand old dame with a flirtatious side, Vir-
ginia is bubbling over with personality. Yet it's
less common than ever, even as neighbors
Georgia and Carolina climb the charts. Why?
Well, there is that pesky "virgin" problem. Just
accept that during the self-conscious adolescent
years, your daughter may insist on Ginny.
In the World: The Commonwealth of Virginia;
writer Virginia Woolf

Vivian (VI-vee-ən)   1920: #64
Popularity: #154
Styles: Solid Citizens, Saints,
Antique Charm
Nicknames: Viv, Vi, Vivi   1880   Today
Variants: Vivien, Vivienne,
Viviana
Sisters: Audrey, Evelyn, Charlotte, Veronica,
Genevieve, Eleanor
Brothers: Simon, Vincent, Russell, Everett,
Maxwell, Vaughn
★ This polished old favorite is ready to shine
again. The full name Vivian has a no-nonsense
elegance, while the nickname Viv is impish and
contemporary. Angelina Jolie's daughter Vivi-
enne has brought fresh attention to the French
form of the name.
In the World: Actresses Vivien Leigh and Vivian
Vance; designers Vivienne Westwood and Vivi-
enne Tam

Viviana (vi-vee-AH-nə)   2003: #404
Popularity: #462
Styles: Lacy and Lissome,
Latino/Latina, Italian, Saints
Nicknames: Vivi, Viv   1880   Today
Variants: Vivian, Vivianna,
Vibiana, Bibiana
Sisters: Adriana, Liliana, Valentina, Marisol,
Natalia, Serena
Brothers: Cristian, Rafael, Marco, Vincent,
Julian, Sergio
★ What a difference an "-a" makes. Vivian is
stylish but sober; Viviana ardently romantic.
In the World: TV host Viviana Gibelli

Wanda (WAHN-də) 1933: #48
Popularity: #5882
Styles: Mid-Century,
Nickname-Proof, African-
American, Slavic
Variants: Vonda, Vanda

1880   Today

Sisters: Sheila, Anita, Eileen, Paula, Glenda,
Marcia
Brothers: Wayne, Gerald, Darryl, Rodney,
Donald, Gene
★ Wanda is the one global hit name launched
from Poland. It's still popular in its homeland,
but baby Wandas are hard to find outside of Polish borders today. The name's softly nasal English pronunciation has sent it to the back of the
pack. You could try a "v" spelling to echo the
original Polish.
In the World: Singer Wanda Jackson; comedian
Wanda Sykes; film *A Fish Called Wanda*

Waverly (WAYV-er-lee) 2011: #2621
Popularity: #2643
Styles: Last Names First
Nicknames: Wave
Variants: Waverley
Sisters: Connolly, Whitley,
Cadence, Ainsley, Kerrigan, Berkeley

1880   Today

Brothers: Stratton, Bryar, Brannigan, Wilder,
Dyson, Braxton
★ The same strong sound that propels the
name Ava sets Waverly apart from the place
name/surname pack. Waverly sounds cheerful,
even bouncy, rather than buttoned-down
preppy. The nickname Wave adds a bolder kind
of energy.
In the World: TV series *Wizards of Waverly
Place*; Waverly brand home decor products

Wendy (WEHN-dee) 1967: #32
Popularity: #677
Styles: Surfer '60s
Variants: Wendi
Sisters: Cindy, Heidi, Jill,

1880   Today

Lisa, April, Jodi, Dawn, Holly
Brothers: Troy, Craig, Robby, Todd, Darren,
Keith, Chris, Toby
★ Wendy first appeared as the eldest of the
Darling children in *Peter Pan*. That image—a
girl on the verge of growing up—still suits the
name well. It's youthful but responsible. For a
more adventurous take on the name, try it as a
nickname for Gwendolyn.
In the World: Wendy Darling of *Peter Pan*; Wen-
dy's hamburger chain; talk show host Wendy
Williams

Whitney (WIT-nee, 1986: #32
HWIT-nee)
Popularity: #518
Styles: '70s–'80s, Last Names
First, Nickname-Proof
Variants: Whitley

1880   Today

Sisters: Lindsay, Mallory, Justine, Courtney,
Kelsey, Amber, Katrina, Chelsea
Brothers: Dustin, Bryant, Corey, Ryan, Jarrett,
Travis, Logan, Tyler
★ Whitney started out as a swank-sounding
boy's name back when the Whitneys, Morgans,
and Vanderbilts were Gilded Age kingpins.
Once it crossed to the girls' side, it followed the
career arc of singer Whitney Houston. Like
most names of this style, it gets friendlier and
more approachable with age.
In the World: Singer Whitney Houston; sitcom
Whitney, starring Whitney Cummings; Whit-
ney Museum of American Art

Wilhelmina 1884: #215
(wil-heh-MEE-nə)
Popularity: #3112
Styles: Ladies and
Gentlemen, German and
Dutch

1880   Today

Nicknames: Willie, Willa, Billie, Mina,
Minnie, Wilma, Willow
Sisters: Georgina, Alexandra, Philomena,
Henrietta, Eugenie, Lavinia, Celeste, Eleanora
Brothers: Augustus, Frederick, Bertram,
Maximilian, Ferdinand, Basil, Rudolph,
Leopold
★ If we went by sound alone, Wilhelmina
would be in the running. It's expressive and ro-
mantic, with plenty of prime nicknames. Its
regal heritage is as potent as Victoria's. But writ-
ten down, all those consonants can seem like a
heavy load.
In the World: Wilhelmina modeling agency;
multiple queens and empresses

Willa (WI-lə)   1932: #272
Popularity: #991
Styles: Ladies and
Gentlemen, Short and Sweet,
Antique Charm, Literary and   1880 Today
Artistic, Why Not?
Sisters: Rhea, Tessa, Daphne, Gemma, Delia,
Althea, Iris, Calla
Brothers: Silas, Porter, Emerson, Jonas, Grady,
Simon, Bennett, August
★ Willa sounds like a natural hit, combining
the jazzy sweetness of revivals like Lily and Ella
with the airy swiftness of Mia and Skye. Oddly
enough, though, Willa is not a hit: the name
has hardly been heard for generations. It could
be a stylish surprise.
In the World: Author Willa Cather; actress
Willa Holland; model/TV personality Willa
Ford

Willow (WI-loh)   2011: #202
Popularity: #202
Styles: Charms and Graces,
Nickname-Proof
Sisters: Phoebe, Autumn,   1880 Today
Rowan, Marlowe, Violet,
Sienna
Brothers: Holden, Liam, Sawyer, Birch,
Griffin, Lincoln
★ Willow is a thoroughly modern name, yet it's
as graceful and romantic as old-timers like Vio-
let. It also has a simple strength that belies the
image of the "weeping willow." This may be the
biggest crowd-pleaser of all the contemporary
nature names.
In the World: Singer/actress Willow Smith;
newscaster Willow Bay; fantasy film *Willow*

Winifred (WI-ni-frehd)   1917: #141
Popularity: #4758
Styles: Ladies and
Gentlemen, Saints, English
Nicknames: Winnie, Freddie   1880 Today
Variants: Winnifred
Sisters: Gwendolyn, Adelaide, Henrietta,
Beatrice, Clementine, Millicent
Brothers: Leopold, Casper, Benedict, Sylvester,
Ambrose, Ferdinand
★ This Welsh/English old-timer takes you
deep into the territory of maiden great-aunts. So
deep, in fact, that it may have a chance as a
quirky surprise. Winifred's rhythm is delicate
and literary, and nickname Winnie is a cute lit-
tle sprite.
In the World: Princess Winnifred the Woebe-
gone of *Once Upon a Mattress*

Winona (wi-NOH-nə)   1931: #407
Popularity: #6510
Styles: Country and Western
Nicknames: Winnie, Nona
Variants: Wenona, Wynonna   1880 Today
Sisters: Mahala, Tallulah,
Althea, Avis, Rowena, Marietta
Brothers: Chayton, Raleigh, Walden, Bodhi,
Harmon, Crawford
★ If this name only makes you think of actress
Winona Ryder and singer Wynonna Judd, here's
a new perspective. Winona is a classic Ameri-
can Indian name, that of a legendary princess.
Among the Dakota Sioux, it was the traditional
name for a first-born daughter. Doesn't it sound
better already?
In the World: Actress Winona Ryder; singer
Wynonna Judd; activist Winona LaDuke

Winter (WIN-ter)   1979: #703
Popularity: #1041
Styles: Modern Meanings,
Androgynous, Charms and
Graces   1880 Today
Nicknames: Win, Winnie
Variants: Wynter
Sisters: Sage, Indigo, Honor, Phoenix, January,
Willow, Briar, Eden
Brothers: River, Justice, Storm, Ronan, Zephyr,
Lake, Fox, Orion
★ Traditionally, Winter has seemed a little too
chilly for a baby girl's name. More and more,
though, parents are finding the frostiness re-
freshing after a generation of sunny Summers.
It's a gently creative choice. (For more discus-
sion of seasonal names, see Autumn.)
In the World: Phrases like "Winter Olympics"
and "winter is coming"; actress Winter Ave Zoli

Xenia (ZEE-nee-ə,   2011: #2468
KSAYN-yə, SAYN-yə)
Popularity: #2489
Styles: Greek, Slavic, Exotic
Traditional   1880 Today
Variants: Ksenia
Sisters: Alexa, Nika, Ariadne, Elektra, Vika,
Oxana
Brothers: Maxim, Severin, Alexi, Dimitri,
Lazar, Pavel
★ Xenia was the ancient Greek concept of hos-
pitality to travelers. As a name, it's used in
Greece and Russia and is borne by several Or-
thodox saints. That background, coupled with a
simple, feminine sound, makes this your best
bet for an "X" name for girls.
In the World: Actresses Xenia Seeburg and Kse-
nia Solo; singer Xenia

Ximena (hee-MEH-nah, see-MEN-ah)
2011: #215
Popularity: #215
Styles: Latino/Latina
Nicknames: Mena, Meni
Variants: Jimena, Chimène
Sisters: Yaretzi, Fernanda, Nayeli, Alexa, Romina, Luciana
Brothers: Maximo, Emilio, Mateo, Joaquin, Diego, Rodrigo
✱This old name is suddenly sparkling new again. You would have found plenty of Ximenas in Spain back in the 11th century, when it was the name of the wife of El Cid. Today it has come charging back in two equally traditional spellings, Ximena and Jimena. The "X" version is the splashier, more eye-catching choice.
In the World: Singer Ximena Sariñana; Miss Universe Ximena Navarrete

Yael (yah-EHL)
2010: #1804
Popularity: #1881
Styles: Biblical, Jewish
Variants: Yaelle, Jael
Sisters: Adi, Noa, Talia, Tirzah, Merav, Shira
Brothers: Ilan, Ari, Eitan, Boaz, Zev, Noam
✱The Bible is a lot richer in boys' names than in girls' names. So why haven't American parents flocked to Yael, a general-slaying hero from the Book of Judges? Perhaps because the name wasn't used much in olden days, so it doesn't have the antique patina of names like Hannah and Abigail. It is a popular favorite in modern Hebrew, though.
In the World: Singer Yael Naim

Yesenia (yeh-SAY-nee-ə)
1987: #137
Popularity: #881
Styles: Latino/Latina
Nicknames: Yesi
Variants: Yessenia
Sisters: Marisol, Fabiola, Alejandra, Lorena, Araceli, Yadira
Brothers: Rogelio, Gerardo, Marco, Jairo, Jovanni, Osvaldo
✱The name Yesenia bloomed thanks to a pair of popular telenovelas. Actress Adela Noriega's portrayal of a passionate gypsy cemented the name's romantic image, but its sound is dreamy all on its own.
In the World: Telenovela *Yesenia*

Yolanda (yoh-LAHN-də, yoh-LAN-də)
1968: #93
Popularity: #1727
Styles: Mid-Century, African-American, Latino/Latina
Nicknames: Lani, Yoli
Variants: Yolande
Sisters: Anita, Yvette, Regina, Angelia, Rochelle, Benita
Brothers: Darrell, Reynaldo, Roberto, Terrance, Mario, Dion
✱In the '30s and '40s, Yolanda was a romantic exotic, steeped in its French and Hungarian heritage. Later it became an African-American favorite. And all along, it's been used by Spanish-speaking families. Today it's still silky-smooth, but slinking out of style.
In the World: Singer/radio host Yolanda Adams; popular song "Donde Estás, Yolanda?"

Yvette (ee-VEHT)
1967: #125
Popularity: #1244
Styles: Surfer '60s, French, African-American
Nicknames: Yvie
Sisters: Monique, Suzette, Sonya, Janine, Adrienne, Colette
Brothers: Rene, Patrice, Donnell, Michel, Terrence, Andre
✱This French diminutive purrs like a kitten but shows some restraint. You can also use it as a nickname for Yvonne.
In the World: Actresses Yvette Mimieux and Yvette Nicole Brown

Yvonne (ee-VAHN)
1937: #77
Popularity: #1665
Styles: Mid-Century, French, African-American
Nicknames: Vonnie, Yvie
Sisters: Suzanne, Lorelei, Marianne, Ione, Vivienne, Margot
Brothers: Jerome, Regis, Gervase, Cedric, Marcel, Gerard
✱The French classic Yvonne doesn't fit any of the hot current trends, so chances are you haven't even considered the name. But if you take the time, you might find it a pleasant surprise. Yvonne is simple, elegant, and uncommon, and that's a nice combination. The unusual spelling makes it look especially distinguished in print.
In the World: Actresses Yvonne De Carlo and Yvonne Strahovski; singer Yvonne Elliman

Zara (ZAH-rə) 2011: #642
Popularity: #643
Styles: Short and Sweet,
English, Nickname-Proof,
Why Not? 1880 Today
Variants: Zahra
Sisters: Mila, Lyra, Zoe, Paloma, Niko, Esme,
Luna, Isla
Brothers: Roman, Zane, Liam, Gideon, Felix,
Ewan, Theo, Miles
★ Zara sounds exotic, and its origin is mysterious. (The best guess is that it comes from Arabic; see Zaria). Americans might be surprised to learn, then, that the name is most common in England. Zara even broke through the ultratraditional naming patterns of the royal family, in the form of Princess Anne's glamorous daughter, Zara Phillips.
In the World: Zara clothing stores; equestrian and British royal Zara Phillips

Zaria (ZAH-ree-ə) 2000: #479
Popularity: #755
Styles: African-American,
Place Names
Variants: Zahra, Zariah 1880 Today
Sisters: Amaya, Naima, India,
Jada, Zoey, Iyanna
Brothers: Elijah, Zidane, Davon, Josiah, Cairo,
Zander
★ Zaria comes from an Arabic word for "flower" and is best known as the name of a Nigerian city. The variation Zahra is more traditional as a given name. In the U.S., Zaria is the hotter choice, with a sweet sound that nods to African heritage but works well for girls of any background. In the past few years, the spelling Zariah has taken the lead.

Zelda (ZEHL-də) 1911: #376
Popularity: #2327
Styles: Exotic Traditional,
Ladies and Gentlemen,
Nickname-Proof, Literary 1880 Today
and Artistic, Fantastical
Sisters: Nova, Twyla, Zola, Minerva, Eudora,
Avis, Althea, Sibyl
Brothers: Ulysses, Benedict, Link, Roscoe,
Ender, Felix, Otto, Merlin
★ "Z" names may be zesty, but you're not going to choose Zelda for its sound. If you're tempted by this name, it means one of two things: either you're a literary type dreaming of Zelda Fitzgerald and the Roaring Twenties, or a gamer type dreaming of rescuing Princess Zelda from Ganon's evil clutches. Those two images—each, in its way, a romantic fantasy—animate this otherwise old-fashioned name.
In the World: "The Legend of Zelda" video game series; Jazz Age icon Zelda Fitzgerald

Zilla (ZI-lə) 1882: #908
Popularity: Very rare
Styles: Biblical, Exotic
Traditional, Short and Sweet
Variants: Zillah, Tzilla 1880 Today
Sisters: Jemima, Amana,
Beulah, Jael, Avital, Hadassah, Ziva, Tirzah
Brothers: Hosea, Jabez, Elam, Azarel, Reuel,
Raz, Adlai, Zuriel
★ A cool little girl's name starting with "Z"! And it's straight out of the Old Testament! This is great! Yes, it truly is. But it's my duty to point out the potential Godzilla problem. Whether you care is up to you.
In the World: Slang suffix suggesting the monster version of something, e.g., Bridezilla

Zoe (ZOH-ee)   2011: #31
Popularity: #31
Styles: Greek, Short and
Sweet, Nickname-Proof
Variants: Zoë, Zoey, Zoie,   1880   Today
Zoya
Sisters: Mia, Phoebe, Ava, Zara, Piper, Ivy
Brothers: Liam, Zachary, Max, Luke, Dexter,
Zane
✴ If you want to know how surprising the modern popularity of Zoe is, just look at *Sesame Street*. They like to keep their Muppet names far from the mainstream: Kermit, Grover, Elmo. When the character Zoe was created, it seemed a safe bet. But the vitality of this name—which means "life"—was bound to catch on, and it did in a hurry. A lovably quirky hit.
In the World: Actresses Zooey Deschanel and Zoe Saldana; TV series *Zoey 101*; *Sesame Street's* Zoe

Zuzu (ZOO-zoo)   2008: #8084
Popularity: #10,305
Styles: Nicknames, Slavic,
Fantastical
Variants: Zsa Zsa   1880   Today
Sisters: Vivi, Sonnet, Romy,
Zoey, Scout, Zofia, Briar, Maizie
Brothers: Fox, Teo, Atreyu, Zeke, Calder,
Atticus, Axel, Zander
✴ Many Americans get a warm glow from the name Zuzu, thanks to its role in the film *It's a Wonderful Life* ("Zuzu's petals!"). If you're drawn to it but skittish, try it as a nickname. Zuzu comes from Zuzana, a Czech/Slovak form of Susana, and you can use it as a pet form of any name in the Susan family.
In the World: Zuzu's petals in *It's a Wonderful Life*

Zora (ZOH-rə)   1884: #257
Popularity: #2066
Styles: Exotic Traditional,
Slavic, Literary and Artistic,
Nickname-Proof, Why Not?   1880   Today
Variants: Zorah
Sisters: Vera, Zelda, Geneva, Ruby, Octavia,
Cleo
Brothers: Langston, Felix, Zenon, Dashiell,
Ezra, Axel
✴ This jazzy little name commands attention. It peaked in the late 1800s, when acclaimed writer Zora Neale Hurston was born. Yet it sounds exotic enough to be the name of a race of aliens in "The Legend of Zelda" video games.
In the World: Writer Zora Neale Hurston

Zuri (ZOO-ree)   2011: #852
Popularity: #854
Styles: African, African-
American, Short and Sweet,
Androgynous   1880   Today
Sisters: Nia, Amari, Eden,
Thandi, Riya, Isis, Ajani, Zara
Brothers: Jabari, Zion, Kani, Taj, Kobe, Nico,
Zaid, Neo
✴ Zuri is Swahili for "good" and "pretty." That's an impeccable origin, and it's wrapped up in a tidy little package. Zuri is a little bit funky, a little bit unexpected, but simple and cute.

Name Snapshots: Boys

Aaron (A-rən) 1981: #30
Popularity: #50
Styles: Biblical, New Classics, Nickname-Proof
Variants: Aron, Aharon, Haroun
1880 Today
Sisters: Allison, Rachel, Lauren, Hannah, Megan, Natalie, Amanda, Bethany
Brothers: Adam, Jared, Justin, Nathan, Joshua, Andrew, Caleb, Evan
✴ Over the past two generations, Aaron has taken its place among the biblical classics. It fits in smoothly with both traditional and contemporary names, and only an Aaliyah will keep Aaron from being first in every elementary school lineup.
In the World: Composer Aaron Copeland; football player Aaron Rodgers

Abel (AY-bəl) 2011: #238
Popularity: #237
Styles: Biblical, Short and Sweet, Latino/Latina
Nicknames: Abe
1880 Today
Sisters: Mara, Sarai, Lia, Yael, Noemi, Anya, Eden, Phoebe
Brothers: Eli, Saul, Gael, Joah, Noel, Rafael, Ezra, Ruben
✴ The sad fate of the biblical Abel always limited the popularity of this name. Style-wise, it had it all: Old Testament style in a bright, boyish sound. Lately parents have decided they can put the fratricide aside, and Abel has become a surprise hit.
In the World: Actor Abel Ferrara

Abraham (AY-brə-ham) 1911: #124
Popularity: #192
Styles: Biblical, Antique Charm
Nicknames: Abe, Bram, Avi
1880 Today
Variants: Abram, Avraham, Ibrahim
Sisters: Abigail, Miriam, Lydia, Jemima, Hadassah, Annabel, Cecilia, Esther
Brothers: Solomon, Ezra, Moses, Cyrus, Saul, Phineas, Oscar, Judah
✴ Descendants Isaac and Jacob have become youthful hits. Abraham, though, has had a little more trouble shaking its white-beard image. It's worth reconsidering. With its perfect nicknames and presidential pedigree, Abraham could be a dignified standout.
In the World: President Abraham Lincoln

Abram (AY-brəm) 2011: #445
Popularity: #444
Styles: Biblical
Nicknames: Abe, Bram, Avi
1880 Today
Variants: Abraham, Avram
Sisters: Shiloh, Ivy, Hanna, Faith, Annabelle, Sadie, Lilah, Mercy
Brothers: Gideon, Jonas, Levi, Isaak, Asher, Silas, Abel, Tobin
✴ A lot of Old Testament names, like Elijah and Jeremiah, sound like Western pioneers. But Abram (the birth name of Abraham) always used to sound like an old-world Jewish ancestor. Not anymore. Today Abram is a hit with Christians, particularly devout families along a stripe of the country reaching from the deep South across the plains to the mountain West.

Ace (AYS) 2011: #568
Popularity: #567
Styles: Fanciful, Nicknames, Macho Swagger
Sisters: Sky, Vivi, Lux, Scarlet, Liberty, Bree, Star
Brothers: Jett, Duke, Ranger, Cash, Hawk, Jax, Champ

✳ The World War I flying ace; the ace of the pitching staff; the ace of spades; a hole in one. An ace is the best of the best, the coolest customer in town. This used to be a splashy, studly nickname, but too much for a given name. Today, though, it seems that too much is just about right.
In the World: "Ace Ventura" films; rapper Ace Hood; KISS guitarist Ace Frehley

Adam (A-dəm) 1984: #18
Popularity: #81
Styles: Biblical, New Classics, Nickname-Proof
Variants: Adán
Sisters: Rachel, Emily, Sara, Amy, Rebecca, Lauren, Alison
Brothers: Benjamin, Eric, Jonathan, Matthew, Joel, Mark, Andrew

✳ Adam a "new" classic? Yes, the name of the first man wasn't much heard until the '60s, when it suddenly joined the roster of English standards. As a consequence, it's now a rare example of an Old Testament name that doesn't feel like an antique. Adam sounds fresh and modern, despite its obviously ancient origins.
In the World: Comedian Adam Sandler; musician Adam Levine; economist Adam Smith

Adan (ah-DAHN, AY-din) 2005: #287
Popularity: #334
Styles: Latino/Latina
Variants: Adán
Sisters: Perla, Mariana, Dulce, Catalina, Elena, Silvia, Carolina, Ana
Brothers: Esteban, Emilio, Pablo, Marcos, Rodrigo, Cesar, Hugo, Julio

✳ This name has two faces. To a Spanish speaker, it is "ah-DAHN," the fashionable Spanish form of Adam. To many an English speaker, though, it's an alternative spelling of Aidan. Whichever version you're imagining, it's good to be aware of the other. (Note: the sibling suggestions refer to the Spanish Adán. For sibling ideas for the English Adan, see the entries for Ayden and Aidan.)

Addison (A-di-sən) 2000: #514
Popularity: #1003
Styles: Last Names First, Androgynous
Sisters: Delaney, Annabel, Kendall, Adalyn, Ainsley, Sidney, Mckenna, Paige
Brothers: Weston, Campbell, Lawson, Spencer, Garrison, Ashton, Parker, Jamison

✳ Addison is the sort of name that used to sound like a stuffy banker. After a long absence, it has reemerged sounding trendier and more contemporary—especially for girls. Also consider the less common and purely masculine Edison, which gains you a hero namesake and the option of Eddie if the full name turns out to be too much of a mouthful.
In the World: Many distinguished U.S. Addisons born in the 19th century, including judges and congressmen

Adonis (ah-DAW-nis) 2011: #695
Popularity: #694
Styles: Fanciful, Mythological, African-American
Nicknames: Don
Sisters: Isis, Electra, Artemis, Avalon, Selene, Venus, Odyssey, Athena
Brothers: Orion, Apollo, Maximus, Aramis, Phoenix, Titus, Justus, Valentino

✳ Adonis sounds as cool as can be, but it's a gamble. If he's anything but a perfect physical specimen, this name, symbolic of male beauty, could be a burden.
In the World: In Greek mythology, a youth gorgeous enough to make goddesses fight over him

Adrian (AY-dree-ən)   2008: #56
Popularity: #56
Styles: Antique Charm,
Shakespearean, Saints,
Nickname-Proof, Latino/   1880   Today
Latina
Variants: Adrien, Adriano
Sisters: Natalia, Isabella, Giselle, Emilia, Mia,
Ava, Valeria, Sofia
Brothers: Julian, Damian, Xavier, Sebastian,
Rafael, Dominic, Elias, Gabriel
✴ Adrian is an old and dignified name, borne
by popes and emperors. It has always been well
used in Britain but less so in the U.S., where it
used to be confused with the girl's name Adri-
enne. Today, though, the name is both popular
and reliably masculine. A top choice of multi-
lingual families.
In the World: Actor Adrian Grenier; football
player Adrian Peterson

Aidan (AY-din)   2003: #39
Popularity: #107
Styles: Celtic, The "-ens,"
Nickname-Proof, Saints, Bell
Tones   1880   Today
Variants: Aiden, Aden,
Ayden, Aaden
Sisters: Keira, Avery, Mia, Chloe, Ainsley,
Macy, Zoe, Ava
Brothers: Liam, Carson, Declan, Riley, Ronan,
Connor, Ethan, Logan
✴ As recently as the late 1980s, Aidan was an
obscure Irish saint's name. Then its sublimely
clean sound set it soaring. By 2001, when a
heartthrob Aidan appeared on *Sex and the City,*
Aidan was a top-100 boy's name, and 27 other
rhyme-twins (Braden, Cayden, et al.) made the
top 1000. Today Aidan's sound is the sound of a
generation. Alternate spellings like Aiden and
Ayden are equally common but loosen the
name's Irish roots.
In the World: Actors Aidan Quinn and Aidan
Gillen; fictional Aidan Shaw of *Sex and the City*

Aidric (AY-drik)   2011: #3409
Popularity: #3409
Styles: Exotic Traditional,
Saints
Variants: Aidrick, Aedric   1880   Today
Sisters: Avila, Hermione,
Ariadne, Laelia, Sevina, Averil, Imogen,
Sephora
Brothers: Calix, Emeric, Maxim, Phineas,
Severin, Matthias, Caedmon, Cormac
✴ A bona fide exotic, Aidric is not merely un-
common but genuinely unfamiliar. It's a medi-
eval saint's name that still sounds lost in the
mists of time. Twenty years ago, that would have
made the name weird. Today it makes it tempt-
ing. Fellow saint names like Aidan and Domi-
nic are star revivals, and Aidric could hit the
same fashion bull's-eye, from an oblique angle.

Ajax (AY-jaks)   2010: #5003
Popularity: #5413
Styles: Fanciful,
Mythological, Macho
Swagger   1880   Today
Nicknames: Jax
Sisters: Juno, Calliope, Artemis, Io, Aria,
Bellatrix, Indigo, Isis
Brothers: Achilles, Zeus, Arrow, Maximus,
Apollo, Blaze, Thor, Orion
✴ There's powerful potential in this classical
warrior name. The only thing stopping it is the
image of the cleanser. If you're confident that
your little boy will wash all thoughts of scrub-
bing bubbles from people's minds, you might
have a winner in Ajax.
In the World: Trojan War hero Ajax; Ajax house-
hold cleanser

Alan (A-lin) 1951: #40
Popularity: #163
Styles: Timeless, Mid-
Century, The "-ens"
Nicknames: Al 1880 Today
Variants: Allen, Allan, Alain,
Alun
Sisters: Lynn, Diana, Karen, Kathleen, Teresa,
Lana, Janet, Cynthia
Brothers: Neil, Mark, Philip, Byron, Joel,
Kenneth, Stephen, Paul
★ A fine, reliable fellow, that Alan. Sure, he hit
his peak in the middle of the last century, but
he's kept his youthful good looks. The name has
been used in the British Isles since the time of
William the Conquerer and should keep going
strong. Alternative spellings like Allen, once
equally popular in the U.S., are now showing
more age.
In the World: Singer Alan Jackson; actor Alan
Alda; basketball player Allen Iverson; lawyer
Alan Dershowitz

Alban (AL-bin, AHL-bin) 1915: #1601
Popularity: #6549
Styles: The "-ens," Saints,
Why Not?
Nicknames: Albie, Al 1880 Today
Variants: Albin, Alben
Sisters: Aurea, Mabyn, Cecily, Averil, Daria,
Maris
Brothers: Colman, Regis, Tobin, Silvan, Clive,
Florian
★ A nifty old saint's name, Alban has a modern
sound and plenty of history. It has been virtually
unknown in the U.S. except for Harry Truman's
vice president, Alben Barkley, and the tony St.
Albans School for boys in Washington, D.C.
In the World: Musician Dr. Alban; politician
Alben Barkley; boatmaker Albin Marine

Albert (AL-buhrt) 1883: #16
Popularity: #392
Styles: Ladies and Gentlemen
Nicknames: Al, Bert, Albie
Variants: Alberto, Adalbert, 1880 Today
Albrecht
Sisters: Martha, Edith, Frances, Louise,
Esther, Alma, Marion, Harriet
Brothers: Arthur, Louis, Frederick, Ernest,
George, Clarence, Frank, Walter
★ Like many old German and Anglo-Saxon
names, Albert has gone over the style precipice.
(In Albert's case, he may have been pushed. Bill
Cosby's "Fat Albert" is a prime suspect.) Yet it's
a gracious old-school name, and a toddler
named Albert sounds mighty cute, when you
think about it.
In the World: Physicist Albert Einstein; Prince
Albert (husband of Queen Victoria, and pipe
tobacco)

Alden (AHL-din) 1911: #426
Popularity: #864
Styles: Last Names First, The
"-ens," Nickname-Proof, Why
Not? 1880 Today
Sisters: Larkin, Rosemary,
Everly, Afton, Helena, Marlowe, Mercy, Averil
Brothers: Winslow, Truman, Edison, Harris,
Gray, Forrest, Wilson, Carver
★ If you like the prep school aura of surnames,
you can't do better than this Mayflower origi-
nal. It's a gentler, less trendy alternative to Pey-
ton and Chandler.
In the World: Still most familiar as a surname;
pilgrims John and Priscilla Alden

Aldo (AHL-doh, AL-doh) 2007: #430
Popularity: #572
Styles: Italian, Latino/Latina,
Guys and Dolls
Sisters: Clara, Lidia, Roma, 1880 Today
Rubi, Luisa, Perla
Brothers: Oscar, Enzo, Rocco, Gianni, Luca,
Milo
★ Parents are heading up to the attic and shak-
ing the dust off this old-timer. It has a continen-
tal playboy style softened by a whiff of geekiness.
In the World: ALDO shoes; Italian prime minis-
ter Aldo Moro

Alec (AL-ik) 1995: #112
Popularity: #421
Styles: English, Celtic,
Nickname-Proof
Variants: Alick, Alex 1880 Today
Sisters: Victoria, Hope,
Fiona, Daphne, Maeve, Camilla, Ivy, Gillian
Brothers: Colin, Trevor, Duncan, Graham, Ian,
Conor, Gareth, Rhys
✷ Alec is a debonair English/Scottish variation
on Alex. The romance of this name was fixed in
many girls' minds at an early age thanks to the
hero of *The Black Stallion*.
In the World: Actors Alec Baldwin and Alec
Guinness

Alejandro 2001: #87
(ah-lay-KHAHN-droh)
Popularity: #130
Styles: Latino/Latina
Nicknames: Ale, Alex 1880 Today
Variants: Alessandro,
Alexandros
Sisters: Adriana, Gabriela, Valeria, Mariana,
Noemi, Ana, Natalia, Carolina
Brothers: Eduardo, Javier, Antonio, Andres,
Diego, Sebastian, Cesar, Fernando
✷ Like every form of Alexander, this one raced
up the charts starting in the 1990s. An elegant
and fashionable Spanish choice.
In the World: Musicians Alejandro Sanz and
Alejandro Fernández; Lady Gaga song "Alejan-
dro"

Alex (A-liks) 1993: #52
Popularity: #95
Styles: Nicknames, Timeless
Variants: Alec
Sisters: Abby, Leah, Emily, 1880 Today
Hope, Elise, Sara, Katie,
Rachel
Brothers: Jake, Cole, Adam, Ian, Drew, Max,
Evan, Luke
✷ Long a nickname for Alexander, Alex is also
a popular modern choice all on its own. Parents
choose it for simplicity and to emphasize the "x"
sound. The result is a casual, breezy, and confi-
dent name.
In the World: *Jeopardy* host Alex Trebek; "Alex
Rider" adventure novels; baseball player Alex
Rodriguez

Alexander (al-ik-ZAN-der) 1993: #21
Popularity: #8
Styles: Timeless
Nicknames: Alex, Sandy,
Sasha, Xander, Zander, 1880 Today
Sander, Lex
Variants: Alexandre, Alistair, Alejandro,
Alessandro, Alexandros
Sisters: Victoria, Charlotte, Abigail, Lydia,
Catherine, Sophia
Brothers: Nathaniel, Benjamin, Oliver,
Nicholas, Samuel, Maxwell
✷ Alexander has been a classic for thousands of
years. It's lordly, cultured, and valiant. It's also
wildly fashionable around the world, and on the
girls' side you'll find Alexandra, Alexis, Alexa,
Alexandria . . . that, of course, makes for an
awful lot of Alexes. Xander, or the Dutch ver-
sion Sander, is an alternative.
In the World: Alexander the Great; founding fa-
ther Alexander Hamilton; designer Alexander
McQueen

Alfie (AL-fee) 1967: #915
Popularity: #8040
Styles: Nicknames, English
Variants: Alf
Sisters: Daisy, Poppy, Lola, 1880 Today
Tilly, Rosie, Ruby, Elsie, Lucy
Brothers: Archie, Toby, Ollie, Roddy, Tad,
Milo, Davy, Harry
✷ If you flipped right to this name, chances are
you're British, not American. A smash hit in En-
gland, Alfie is not even on the radar in the U.S.
We're two peoples, divided by cuteness. English
parents say, "Ooh, so cute!" Americans say,
"Yikes, so *cute!*"
In the World: 1966 film *Alfie* (with 2004 re-
make) and its popular theme song

Alfred (AL-frid) 1928: #33
Popularity: #917
Styles: Ladies and Gentlemen
Nicknames: Alf, Fred, Al, Alfie 1880 Today
Variants: Alfredo, Avery
Sisters: Edith, Martha, Harriet, Louise, Irene, Frances
Brothers: Frederick, Arthur, Edwin, Gilbert, Harold, Walter
★ If you know a young Alfred, chances are he was named after a relative. American parents just aren't choosing this burly old Saxon name on its own merits anymore. The medieval variation Avery is far trendier.
In the World: Director Alfred Hitchcock; Batman's butler Alfred; *Mad* magazine's Alfred E. Neuman

Alistair (AL-is-tayr, AL-is-ter) 2011: #1487
Popularity: #1486
Styles: Celtic, English, Exotic Traditional
Nicknames: Alec, Alick 1880 Today
Variants: Alastair, Alister, Alasdair
Sisters: Beatrix, Imogen, Ailsa, Iona, Georgina, Annabel, Finola
Brothers: Evander, Colin, Magnus, Dashiell, Gareth, Lachlan, Finlay
★ Alistair has had an uber-genteel image in the U.S., courtesy of longtime *Masterpiece Theatre* host Alistair Cooke. In Scotland it's simply an everyday classic, a form of Alexander. Think of it that way and it may sound more ready for American use. The similar name Alastor comes to us from Greek mythology and means "avenger."
In the World: Masterpiece Theatre host Alistair Cooke; mystic Aleister Crowley; MMA fighter Alistair Overeem

Alonzo (ah-LAHN-zoh) 1882: #111
Popularity: #555
Styles: Exotic Traditional, Shakespearean, African-American, Latino/Latina 1880 Today
Nicknames: Lon, Al, Zo
Variants: Alonso
Sisters: Phoebe, Catalina, Ivy, Helena, Silvia, Zora, Adelina, Viola
Brothers: Oscar, Lorenzo, August, Felix, Orlando, Everett, Hector, Ezra
★ This Latin lover crosses many boundaries. In the 19th century, Alonzo was a stately name for a rural gentleman. More recently, it's become a charismatic African-American favorite. Never common in any guise, Alonzo is an intriguing choice to consider alongside quirky gent names like Felix and Julius.
In the World: Basketball player Alonzo Mourning; comedian Alonzo Bodden

Alton (AHL-tən) 1904: #78
Popularity: #1304
Styles: Last Names First, The "-ens"
Variants: Elton 1880 Today
Sisters: Georgia, Faye, Vivian, Corrine, Regina, Althea
Brothers: Leland, Clifton, Eldon, Stuart, Lowell, Wyman
★ Parents are going to great lengths these days to find new surnames ending in "-n." Meanwhile, the old ones stand by patiently, ready for action. Alton was a favorite for a century but strangely fell out of use just as names like Dalton, Austin, and Grayson hit new heights. *In the World:* TV chef Alton Brown; rocksteady singer Alton Ellis

Alvin (AL-vin) 1927: #66
Popularity: #553
Styles: Solid Citizens
Nicknames: Al, Vin
Variants: Elvin, Alwin 1880 Today
Sisters: Jeanette, Ellen, Sylvia, June, Rita, Rosalyn
Brothers: Edgar, Leon, Vernon, Ray, Ellis, Clifton
★ This is a sweetheart of a name for a little boy, but it carries some baggage. A cloud of geekiness surrounds the name thanks to the squeaky-voiced Alvin and the Chipmunks. But with the growing popularity of Gavin, Devin, and even Calvin, good old Alvin is just a small step away from the mainstream.
In the World: Alvin and the Chipmunks; choreographer Alvin Ailey

Amari (ah-MAH-ree) 2011: #308
Popularity: #307
Styles: African-American, Androgynous
Variants: Amare 1880 Today
Sisters: Zuri, Aliyah, Ayana, Kamaria, Janiyah, Sanai, Naima, Selah
Brothers: Mekhi, Jabari, Semaj, Dakari, Jahir, Malakai, Javion, Amir

✶Amani, with an "n," is Swahili for "peace." Amari, with an "r," is . . . well, you name it. Name "dictionaries" will confidently tell you it's Hebrew, Yoruba, Greek, Hindi, Italian, Japanese, or a generic "African," with a correspondingly wide range of meanings. I'll just tell you it's a smooth but bold name with global appeal, favored by African-American parents. And if you want a traditional origin, feel free to choose one to your liking (or spell it Amare, from the Latin for "to love").
In the World: Basketball player Amar'e Stoudemire; football player Amari Spievey

Ambrose (AM-brohz, 1893: #239
AM-brohs)
Popularity: #2264
Styles: Saints, Ladies and
Gentlemen, English 1880 Today
Nicknames: Broz
Variants: Ambrosio, Ambrosius
Sisters: Augusta, Winifred, Eugenia, Minerva, Adelaide, Leonora
Brothers: Clement, Leopold, Hiram, Godfrey, Armand, Granville

✶Ambrose is like a handlebar mustache, so cheerfully outdated and overblown that it's actually a lot of fun. The name's old-tyme attitude belies its "immortal" origin (think ambrosia, the nectar of the gods). A revival candidate for parents who live on the edge.
In the World: Writer Ambrose Bierce; Civil War general Ambrose Burnside of "sideburns" fame

Amos (AY-məs) 1884: #110
Popularity: #860
Styles: Porch Sitters, Biblical, Namesakes, Nickname-Proof
Sisters: Hester, Adah, 1880 Today
Jemima, Opal, Etta, Dinah
Brothers: Abner, Rufus, Homer, Roscoe, Lemuel, Hiram

✶The racially charged *Amos 'n' Andy Show* casts a long, uncomfortable shadow over this name. That really is too bad, because such unpretentious biblical names are in short supply. A few bold parents are starting to resurrect it.
In the World: The *Amos 'n' Andy Show*; "Famous Amos" cookies; writer Amos Oz; singer Amos Lee

Anderson (AN-der-sən) 2011: #295
Popularity: #294
Styles: Timeless, Last Names
First
Nicknames: Andy 1880 Today
Sisters: Audrey, Caroline, Campbell, Emmaline, Tenley, Annabel
Brothers: Preston, Carter, Nicholson, Bennett, Porter, Jefferson

✶A classic surname, sedate but handsome. Anderson sounds like the bright, diligent type who'll rise quickly up the corporate ladder. Note that this is one surname that still reads like a last name, so tread carefully . . . an Anderson Henry could end up sounding backward.
In the World: News anchor Anderson Cooper

Andre (AHN-dray, 1971: #129
ahn-DRAY)
Popularity: #241
Styles: New Classics,
African-American, French 1880 Today
Nicknames: Dre
Variants: Andrei, Andrés, Andreas, Andrew
Sisters: Adrienne, Nadia, Melanie, Dominique, Kendra, Simone
Brothers: Damon, Antoine, Derek, Fabian, Quentin, Dion

✶Andre has retained the continental flair of its French roots while becoming comfortably American. It's a stylish twist on Andrew, swank but not ostentatious. The Spanish Andrés is equally popular, and the Greek/biblical Andreas is another sophisticated option.
In the World: Musician André 3000; wrestler Andre the Giant; film *My Dinner with Andre*

Andrew (AN-droo) 1987: #6
Popularity: #16
Styles: Timeless, Biblical
Nicknames: Andy, Drew
Variants: Andre, Andreas, 1880 Today
Andrés, Anders
Sisters: Emily, Abigail, Rachel, Jessica, Allison, Lauren
Brothers: Christopher, Matthew, Nicholas, Benjamin, Alexander, Jonathan
✶This classic Scottish-tinged name escapes the stodgy air of most British standards, and parents have noticed. While Charles, George, and Edward are sounding old-fashioned, Andrew remains a steady contemporary favorite. For nicknames, Drew has drawn even with Andy.
In the World: President Andrew Jackson; St Andrews golf course; actors Andrew Garfield and Andrew McCarthy

Angel (AHN-khayl, AYN-jəl) 2006: #30
Popularity: #52
Styles: Latino/Latina, Androgynous
Variants: Ángel, Angelo 1880 Today
Sisters: Alejandra, Natalia, Camila, Alicia, Valeria, Elena, Noelia, Ana
Brothers: Miguel, Diego, Luis, Cesar, Mateo, Carlos, Manuel, Andres
✶Like Jesus, Angel is a Spanish hit that's been virtually taboo for boys in English. The pronunciation is key: said the Spanish way, it's fashionably suave. With an English pronunciation, it's still chiefly for girls and vampires. Note that the name is used even more than its graph suggests because it's popular in two-part names like Miguel Ángel (Michelangelo)
In the World: Vampire TV series *Angel*; golfer Ángel Cabrera

Angelo (AN-jə-loh, 1914: #146
AHN-jeh-loh)
Popularity: #298
Styles: Italian, Shakespearean
Nicknames: Ange, AJ 1880 Today
Variants: Angelino, D'Angelo
Sisters: Lucia, Carmela, Mia, Emilia, Silvia, Claudia, Bianca, Marina
Brothers: Carlo, Orlando, Roman, Bruno, Dominic, Rocco, Antonio, Lorenzo
✶This classic has remained quietly fashionable year after year without losing its grand Italian style. Unlike the popular Spanish version Ángel, Angelo translates to English as 100% masculine.
In the World: Singer D'Angelo; composer Angelo Badalamenti

Angus (ANG-gəs) 1882: #365
Popularity: #2009
Styles: Celtic, Shakespearean
Nicknames: Gus
Sisters: Iona, Maisie, Ailsa, 1880 Today
Muriel, Elspeth, Finola
Brothers: Hamish, Lachlan, Magnus, Duncan, Finlay, Fergus
✶Ready to go *really* Celtic? Angus is pure Scottish, undiluted and unmistakable. It also has a classic nickname that makes the other Celtic-come-lately names green with envy. Many will think of the Angus breed of beef cattle, which originated around Angus County, Scotland. It's an odd but pleasantly brawny association.
In the World: Angus beef; actor Angus T. Jones; film *Angus, Thongs and Perfect Snogging*

Anthony (AN-thə-nee) 1987: #17
Popularity: #11
Styles: Timeless
Nicknames: Tony, Tonio
Variants: Antony, Antonio, 1880 Today
Anton, Antoine, Antonius
Sisters: Theresa, Natalie, Veronica, Anna, Christina, Catherine
Brothers: Victor, Daniel, Michael, Robert, Nicholas, David
✶Robust, timeless—and Italian. Despite generations of steady use across all ethnicities, Tony remains the classic Italian-American name in our cultural imagination. That may account for its continuing freshness in an age when most of the English men's classics are losing steam. In fact, you were probably surprised to learn that Anthony is as popular as it is, since it does not feel overused.
In the World: Actor Anthony Hopkins; chef Anthony Bourdain; rock musician Anthony Kiedis

Antoine (AN-twahn, ahn-TWAN)   1976: #271
Popularity: #879
Styles: French, African-American
Nicknames: Twan
Variants: Antwan, Antwon
Sisters: Monique, Janelle, Angelique, Desiree, Adrienne, Chantal
Brothers: Germaine, Andre, Lamar, Dante, Cedric, Dion
✳ Antoine was one of several French classics embraced by African-American parents starting in the '70s. Many kept the name's sound but cast aside its French roots with spellings like Antwan. All of these variants are now on the wane. For a new look, consider the Russian Anton, Spanish Antonio, or even classical Antonius.
In the World: Basketball player Antoine Walker; writer Antoine de Saint-Exupéry

Anton (AN-tahn)   1880: #171
Popularity: #1014
Styles: Slavic, German and Dutch, Timeless, Why Not?
Nicknames: Tony
Variants: Antony, Antonin
Sisters: Martina, Anya, Elsa, Valentina, Petra, Milena
Brothers: Lukas, Maxim, Bruno, Florian, Dimitri, Roman
✳ Anton's the handsome, exotic stranger on the train . . . mysterious and just a little bit dangerous. It's also a simple and familiar name that won't make your relatives roll their eyes. A delectable combination.
In the World: Actor Anton Yelchin; writer Anton Chekhov

Antonio (ahn-TOH-nee-oh)   1997: #75
Popularity: #118
Styles: Timeless, Italian, Latino/Latina, Shakespearean
Nicknames: Tonio, Tony
Variants: Anthony, Anton, Antonius
Sisters: Elena, Carmen, Marina, Teresa, Valeria, Daniela
Brothers: Alejandro, Lorenzo, Sergio, Orlando, Marco, Roberto
✳ This was Shakespeare's favorite name for characters in exotic, romantic plays. If you're Latino or Italian, Antonio is a handsome classic. If not, it's a flourishy yet familiar possibility.
In the World: Actor Antonio Banderas; composer Antonio Vivaldi; football player Antonio Gates

Apollo (ah-PAH-loh)   2011: #1219
Popularity: #1218
Styles: Fanciful, Saints, Mythological, Macho Swagger
Sisters: Isis, Athena, Venus, Sapphira, Vega, Avalon
Brothers: Ajax, Thor, Samson, Adonis, Triton, Orion
✳ The ultimate in hubris: forget flying too close to the sun, with Apollo you *are* the sun. Fictional boxer Apollo Creed from the *Rocky* films exemplified this name's gaudy, magnetic style in the '70s and '80s; speed skater–turned–reality TV champion Apolo Anton Ohno updated the theme.
In the World: New York's Apollo Theater; Apollo space missions; Apollo Creed of the *Rocky* movies; Apolo Anton Ohno

Aramis (A-rə-mis)   2004: #1670
Popularity: #3033
Styles: Literary and Artistic
Nicknames: Ari
Sisters: Isadora, Charis, Eowyn, Athena, Guinevere, Avalon
Brothers: Romeo, Amadeus, Inigo, Achilles, Orion, Valentino
✳ Aramis was one of the Three Musketeers in the classic adventure novel. That makes the name literary and romantic, in a swashbuckling way. Today, though, many people think of "Three Musketeers" as a candy bar, and Aramis may be most widely recognized as a brand of cologne.
In the World: Baseball star Aramis Ramírez; Aramis cologne

Archer (AHRCH-er)   2011: #448
Popularity: #447
Styles: Last Names First, Why Not?
Nicknames: Archie, Arch
Sisters: Everly, Harper, Willa, Marlowe, Amory, Laney, Blythe, Auden
Brothers: Porter, Gibson, Finley, Deacon, Edison, Sawyer, Ellis, Truman
✳ This long-overlooked name has a light touch befitting a skilled bowman. Too many of the popular "tradesman" names have a counterfeit feeling, a forced heartiness. Archer—with amiable nickname Archie—is far more comfortable in its own skin. It's ready to hit the bull's-eye.
In the World: TV spy spoof *Archer*

Ari (AH-ree) 2011: #510
Popularity: #509
Styles: Short and Sweet,
Jewish, Nickname-Proof,
Why Not? 1880 Today
Variants: Arieh, Are
Sisters: Tova, Ilana, Orly, Dalia, Noa, Romi,
Aviva
Brothers: Eli, Asher, Kai, Liam, Ezra, Ronan,
Nico
✶Ari's light touch is unusual for a male name,
but there's muscle behind it. Think Greek ship-
ping magnates and Israeli fighter pilots. (The
name is Hebrew for "lion," Old Norse for
"eagle," and short for Aristotle.) An underappre-
ciated gem that doesn't take itself too seriously.
In the World: Press secretary Ari Fleischer; busi-
nessman Aristotle ("Ari") Onassis; *Entourage*
agent Ari Gold

Arlo (AHR loh) 2011: #917
Popularity: #918
Styles: Guys and Dolls,
Nickname-Proof 1880 Today
Sisters: Faye, Cleo, Reva,
Roxie, Avis, Lola, Iris, Billie
Brothers: Linus, Benno, Milo, Guy, Felix,
Hugo, Leon, Wiley
✶Arlo is an unassuming old-timer of a name.
It will probably remind your parents of folk
singer Arlo Guthrie. Nonetheless, you can pic-
ture an Arlo being any age from one to 100. He
looks easygoing, trustworthy, and lovable.
In the World: Musician Arlo Guthrie; comic
strip *Arlo & Janis*

Armand (ahr-MAHND, 1918: #289
AHR mahnd)
Popularity: #2524
Styles: Ladies and
Gentlemen, French 1880 Today
Nicknames: Armie
Variants: Armando, Armin
Sisters: Cecile, Leonor, Delphine, Eloise,
Celestine, Marguerite
Brothers: Gaston, Ambrose, Jules, Leopold,
Alphonse, Bertrand
✶This French variant of Herman is impres-
sively genteel but desperately in need of a de-
cent nickname. Not every guy can pull off
Armie the way actor Armie Hammer can.
In the World: Businessman Armand Hammer
and his great-grandson Armie Hammer; actor
Armand Assante

Arnold (AHR-nəld) 1916: #89
Popularity: #1459
Styles: Solid Citizens
Nicknames: Arnie
Variants: Arnaldo, Arno, 1880 Today
Arnaud, Arne, Arendpoli
Sisters: Maxine, Lois, Arlene, Bernice, Pauline,
Verna
Brothers: Willard, Milton, Howard, Myron,
Norman, Leonard
✶Even Arnold Schwarzenegger's muscles
weren't enough to keep this venerable name
from sagging sadly out of fashion. The old Ger-
manic name Arno and the Dutch Arend are
namesake options.
In the World: Actor/politician Arnold Schwarz-
enegger; golfer Arnold Palmer; TV series *Hey
Arnold!*

Arthur (AHR-ther) 1881: #14
Popularity: #338
Styles: Ladies and Gentlemen
Nicknames: Art, Artie
Variants: Artur, Arturo 1880 Today
Sisters: Helen, Edith, Rosa,
Harriet, Louisa, Marion
Brothers: Walter, George, Albert, Harald,
Louis, Frederick
✶My father, as a young boy growing up in the
Great Depression, wished his name were Ar-
thur. It was regal, valiant, and romantic. Today
the name's slightly doughy sound and ani-
mated-aardvark associations keep it out of
vogue. If you conjure up the noble image,
though, the classic might ride again. And how
many names have their own adjective, like Ar-
thurian?
In the World: King Arthur; animated TV series
Arthur; comedy film *Arthur;* writer Arthur
Conan Doyle

Asa (AY-sə) 1881: #178
Popularity: #554
Styles: Biblical, Jewish, Short
and Sweet
Nicknames: Ace 1880 Today
Sisters: Leora, Adah, Lena,
Adina, Edith, Mahala, Clara, Dafna
Brothers: Ezra, Cyrus, Simeon, Saul, Abel,
Joah, Asher, Boaz
✶Bring on the masculine "-a" names! As par-
ents look beyond Jacob and Ethan for more bib-
lical antiques, they're starting to open their
arms to vowel endings. Asa is simple, direct, and
a rare male palindrome. The nickname Ace
gives it a little macho spin.
In the World: Actor Asa Butterfield

Asher (ASH-er)　　　　2011: #113
Popularity: #113
Styles: Biblical, Jewish
Nicknames: Ash
Sisters: Abigail, Delilah, Eve,　　1880　Today
Ariel, Naomi, Lydia
Brothers: Caleb, Judah, Elijah, Levi, Gideon,
Micah
✷ Asher is a one-of-a-kind meeting point for
two opposite name trends: it's a biblical classic
that sounds like a trendy modern surname. That
should help solve naming arguments in plenty
of households.
In the World: Rapper Asher Roth; novel *My
Name Is Asher Lev*

Ashton (ASH-tən)　　　　2004: #76
Popularity: #109
Styles: The "-ens," Last
Names First, Androgynous
Nicknames: Ash　　　　1880　Today
Sisters: Sydney, Taylor,
Addison, Delaney, Ainsley, Bailey
Brothers: Parker, Colton, Landon, Cooper,
Grayson, Brennan
✷ It's safe to call a boy Ash again, as Ashton has
taken up the mantle of the dear departed male
Ashley. Actor Ashton Kutcher helped make the
name a familiar and masculine choice.
In the World: Actor Ashton Kutcher

Atreyu (ah-TRAY-yoo)　　　2010: #1305
Popularity: #1339
Styles: Fantastical
Nicknames: Trey
Variants: Atréju　　　　1880　Today
Sisters: Arwen, Briar, Zuzu,
Arya, Ariadne, Sonnet, Ocean, Lyra
Brothers: Aramis, Strider, Sirius, Zephyr,
Triton, Xander, Caspian, Cloud
✷ Atreyu is the young warrior hero of the book
and film *The Neverending Story*. The name will
require a lot of explanation, but to fans of the
story it carries a message of the unlimited power
of youth and imagination: a dream in name
form.
In the World: Atreyu of *The Neverending Story*;
a heavy-metal band named after him

Atticus (AT-i-kəs)　　　　2011: #463
Popularity: #462
Styles: Exotic Traditional,
Literary and Artistic,
Classical, Nickname-Proof,　　1880　Today
Why Not?
Sisters: Beatrix, Paloma, Oriana, Hermione,
Guinevere, Aurora, Briar, Athena
Brothers: Gideon, Beckett, Sawyer, Cassius,
Soren, Emerson, Tennyson, Phineas
✷ This classical name has long been associated
with intellect and learning, which suits its ex-
alted sound. The best-known example today is
noble Atticus Finch of *To Kill a Mockingbird*.
In the World: Atticus Finch of *To Kill a Mock-
ingbird*

August (AW-guhst)　　　　1882: #74
Popularity: #398
Styles: Ladies and
Gentlemen, Charms and
Graces, Antique Charm　　　1880　Today
Nicknames: Gus, Augie
Variants: Augustus, Augusto
Sisters: Clara, Eleanor, Honor, Georgia,
Aurelia, Violet
Brothers: Emmett, Julius, Theodore, Anders,
Jasper, Solomon
✷ Parents who love names like Max and Sam
are increasingly drawn to the less common Gus.
The full name Augustus is a stretch . . . but
what about August? Simple enough, with a for-
mal, gentlemanly style that's ready to be dusted
off. The name isn't taken from the month; both
are forms of Augustus, meaning "grand" and
"venerable."
In the World: Playwrights August Wilson and
August Strindberg

Austin (AWS-tin)   1995: #10
Popularity: #60
Styles: Last Names First, The
"-ens," Nickname-Proof,
Place Names, Turn of the   1880   Today
20th Century
Variants: Austen, Austyn, Osten
Sisters: Alexis, Jordan, Haley, Taylor, Chelsea,
Shelby
Brothers: Dylan, Mason, Landon, Carter, Tyler,
Dawson
✴A hundred years ago, Austin (a form of Augustine) was a prim, starch-collared name. But it echoes Justin's youthful sound, and when you throw in the Western twang of the capital of Texas and the cheeky Brit style of Austin Powers, you get a name that's cooking on all burners. Austin has fallen some from a sharp peak in the '90s, but it still cooks.
In the World: Austin Powers: International Man of Mystery, actor Austin Butler; Austin, Texas

Avery (AY-və-ree)   2011: #202
Popularity: #201
Styles: Last Names First,
Androgynous, Nickname-
Proof   1880   Today
Sisters: Hanna, Camille,
Alexa, Serena, Ariana, Faith, Olivia, Aubrey
Brothers: Gavin, Parker, Miles, Emerson,
Ashton, Emory, Bennett, Quinn
✴This traditional male name—a medieval form of Alfred—recently climbed to an all-time popularity peak for baby boys. The trick is, it's even more common for girls. Once a name starts to turn feminine, parents of boys usually run in the other direction. But lately, favorites like Jordan and Peyton have been bucking the trend. Cross your fingers that elegant Avery joins them as a two-gender standard.
In the World: Actor Avery Brooks; sitcom son on *Murphy Brown*; basketball coach Avery Johnson

Axel (AK-səl)   2011: #132
Popularity: #132
Styles: Exotic Traditional,
Nordic, Short and Sweet,
Fantastical   1880   Today
Variants: Aksel
Sisters: Eden, Luna, Aeris, Annika, Lyra, Maia,
Tova, Esme
Brothers: Nico, Magnus, Enzo, Odin, Finn,
Ronin, Leo, Maxim
✴A pocket-size powerhouse, Axel is one of the jazziest traditional names going. It was originally Scandinavian, a form of Absalom. The occasional vowel-challenged spelling Axl owes wholly to rock singer Axl Rose (birth name: William).
In the World: rock singer Axl Rose; *Beverly Hills Cop* hero Axel Foley; Axel of the "Kingdom Hearts" video game series

Ayden (AY-dehn)   2011: #70
Popularity: #70
Styles: The "-ens," Bell
Tones, Nickname-Proof
Variants: Aydan, Aydin   1880   Today
Sisters: Kylie, Aubrie,
Addison, Makayla, Hailey, Jayda, Rylee,
Kamryn
Brothers: Keegan, Brady, Rylan, Jaxon, Kyler,
Ashton, Jace, Landon
✴Ayden is the crossroads, the point where the old Irish name Aidan meets the new American names Jayden, Brayden, and Kayden. You can't find a more fashionable spot on the naming map. Like any crossroads, though, this is very well-traveled ground.

Bailey (BAY-lee)   1997: #151
Popularity: #1100
Styles: Last Names First,
Androgynous, Bell Tones,
Turn of the 20th Century   1880   Today
Sisters: Sierra, Maya,
Autumn, Sidney, Lily, Aubrey, Michaela,
Shelby
Brothers: Chandler, Riley, Parker, Skyler,
Keaton, Cody, Taylor, Brady
✴Bailey is perfectly traditional as a boy's name. It's an old surname with a cheerfully preppy outlook and was heard most often in the 1800s. That all changed with a starring role on the '90s TV drama *Party of Five*. Parents leaped on the name . . . then leaped off when it started to become popular for girls too. Today new female Baileys (and Baylees) dominate.
In the World: Bailey Salinger of *Party of Five*

Barack (bah-RAHK) 2009: #2001
Popularity: #5659
Styles: African, Namesakes
Nicknames: Barry
Variants: Baraka, Beracha, 1880 Today
Baruch
Sisters: Zuri, Malaika, Kamaria, Imani, Safiya,
Zahra, Rehema, Thandi
Brothers: Asante, Kofi, Emeka, Bakari, Omari,
Neo, Kwame, Dakarai
✷ The names Barack and Baraka are Swahili,
from an Arabic root meaning "blessing." They
have been used primarily in East Africa—but
that was before Barack Obama. Obama, who
was named after his Kenyan father, made this
name a symbol of a proudly diverse America.
Note that Barack is sometimes confused with
the Hebrew name Barak ("lightning"). The ac-
tual Hebrew equivalent is Beracha ("blessing").
In the World: U.S. president Barack Obama

Barnaby (BAHR-nə-bee) 1974: #2200
Popularity: Very rare
Styles: Exotic Traditional,
English, Biblical
Nicknames: Barney 1880 Today
Variants: Barnabas
Sisters: Jemima, Christabel, Beatrix, Jessamy,
Ariadne, Hermione, Lilias, Bryony
Brothers: Crispin, Auberon, Phineas, Benedict,
Alastair, Ivor, Absalom, Bartholomew
✷ Barnaby is fancified but fun, a playful alter-
native to serious names like Dominic and Se-
bastian. It's also exceptionally rare, given how
comfortable and familiar the name sounds. If
you prefer a dark, brooding style, try the biblical
version Barnabas.
In the World: Comic strip *Barnaby*; '70s TV se-
ries *Barnaby Jones*; *Dark Shadows* vampire
Barnabas Collins

Barney (BAHR-nee) 1898: #204
Popularity: Very rare
Styles: Guys and Dolls,
Nicknames, Namesakes
Sisters: Mae, Della, Rosie, 1880 Today
Mabel, Lily, Nell
Brothers: Harvey, Archie, Nelson, Arlo, Louie,
Roscoe
✷ Barney has vintage charm. In the U.K., par-
ents consider it alongside revivals like Gus and
Charley. In the U.S., though, Fred Flintstone's
buddy Barney Rubble and a certain singing
purple dinosaur have sent the name into deep
freeze. If you're tempted nonetheless, consider
it as a nickname for Barnaby.
In the World: Barney the Dinosaur; Barney
Rubble of *The Flintstones*; Barneys luxury
stores; '70s sitcom *Barney Miller*

Baron (BA-rən) 2008: #996
Popularity: #1305
Styles: Fanciful, The "-ens,"
Nickname-Proof
Variants: Barron 1880 Today
Sisters: Eden, Paisley, Larkin,
Avalon, Lacy, Raven, Emerald, Journey
Brothers: Britton, Ryder, Stone, Major, Talon,
West, Hunter, Bronson
✷ This name risks grandiosity but gets by on its
comfortably classic sound. It's a handsome heir
to earlier grandiose names like Noble and King.
The spelling Barron keeps the sound but adopts
a more modest surname look.
In the World: Basketball player Baron Davis;
hotel heir Barron Hilton; a son of businessman
Donald Trump

Barrett (BAR-rit) 2011: #436
Popularity: #435
Styles: Last Names First,
Timeless, Why Not?
Nicknames: Barry 1880 Today
Sisters: Laney, Aubrey, Elise,
Mercy, Clare, Jillian, Kelsey, Brooke
Brothers: Jamison, Reid, Dexter, Brigham,
Harris, Nolan, Parker, Elliott
✷ This strong surname was popular during the
19th century. It has made a quiet comeback as
an elaboration on Barry. The similar name Ben-
nett has been a faster riser thanks to the more
fashionable nickname Ben.
In the World: Barrett Firearms company; poet
Elizabeth Barrett Browning

Barry (BA-ree)   1962: #61
Popularity: #1389
Styles: Mid-Century
Nicknames: Baz
Variants: Berry   1880   Today
Sisters: Jackie, Sheila, Vicky,
Brenda, Cheryl, Donna
Brothers: Ronnie, Kent, Garry, Troy, Bruce,
Terry
★ The name Barry is a familiar friend, but it
has largely been abandoned as a mid-century
relic. It sounds too much like a nickname, even
though it's not. (Barry is a surname and a form
of an old Irish given name.) The Australian
nickname Baz could give it some new pizzazz.
In the World: Singers Barry White and Barry
Manilow; football player Barry Sanders; politi-
cian Barry Goldwater

Bart (BAHRT)   1959: #249
Popularity: #17,385
Styles: Surfer '60s,
Nicknames
Sisters: Liza, Gwen, Kris,   1880   Today
Dawn, Ginny, Pam, Becky,
Tess
Brothers: Rod, Mitch, Chuck, Rocky, Jed, Nat,
Kip, Brad
★ Bart may be short for Bartholomew, but it's a
world apart from that paragon of gentility. Bart
can be a brash pirate or a star quarterback, or
even a bratty cartoon character. But genteel it
ain't.
In the World: Pirate Black Bart; quarterback
Bart Starr; cartoon character Bart Simpson

Bartholomew   1885: #480
(bahr-THAHL ə myoo)
Popularity: #4803
Styles: Saints, Exotic
Traditional, Biblical   1880   Today
Nicknames: Bart, Bartley,
Batt
Variants: Bartolomé, Bartolomeo
Sisters: Seraphina, Beatrix, Octavia,
Genevieve, Winifred, Ariadne, Philomena
Brothers: Benedict, Thaddeus, Felix, Augustus,
Leopold, Horatio, Lazarus, Barnaby
★ Sure, it's a mouthful, but Bartholomew gives
you both classic refinement and quirky cool. It's
ultra-rare yet familiar, and the cheeky nick-
name Bart offers a dramatic change of pace.
In the World: Dr. Seuss's Bartholomew Cub-
bins; explorer Bartolomeu Dias

Beau (BOH)   1980: #203
Popularity: #350
Styles: Brisk and Breezy,
Country and Western
Variants: Bo   1880   Today
Sisters: Bree, Noelle, Raine,
Blair, Cassidy, Tru, Eden, Bella
Brothers: Blaise, Rhett, Quentin, Bryce, Colt,
Damien, Blake, Lane
★ They may sound alike, but Bo and Beau do
not travel in the same circles. Bo is pure simplic-
ity, and Beau is pure romance. The name is
French for "handsome," for heaven's sake. It's
associated with the Regency dandy Beau Brum-
mel and pulpy Foreign Legion hero Beau Geste.
But it sounds so simple that you can get away
with it.
In the World: Beau Brummel and Beau Geste;
actor Beau Bridges

Beckett (BEH-kit)   2011: #331
Popularity: #330
Styles: Last Names First,
Literary and Artistic
Nicknames: Beck   1880   Today
Sisters: Harper, Campbell,
Scarlett, Emerson, Presley, Marlowe
Brothers: Sawyer, Maddox, Cooper, Wyatt,
Dashiell, Holden
★ Irish playwright Samuel Beckett is an icon of
modernism, and his name has a stylish snap. If
you prefer a different kind of snap, there's always
baseball pitcher Josh Beckett's curveball. To-
gether, they've helped make this a literary name
with a rock-star spirit.
In the World: Playwright Samuel Beckett;
pitcher Josh Beckett; Saint Thomas à Becket

Beckham (BEHK-əm)   2011: #656
Popularity: #655
Styles: Last Names First,
Namesakes
Nicknames: Beck   1880   Today
Sisters: Brooklyn, Presley,
Landry, Aniston, Leighton, Monroe
Brothers: Lennon, Jaxon, Crew, Brigham,
Hendrix, Madden
★ American rock star Beck, British soccer star
David Beckham, and hot literary baby name
Beckett have combined to make Beck one of the
coolest sounds of the generation. It couldn't
have happened to a nicer syllable. The surname
Beckham hews closest to its celebrity origins,
with both a British accent and an athletic kick.
In the World: Soccer star David Beckham; film
Bend It Like Beckham

Benedict (BEHN-ə-dikt) 1914: #447
Popularity: #2242
Styles: Exotic Traditional,
Saints, Shakespearean
Nicknames: Ben 1880 Today
Variants: Bennett, Benoit,
Benito
Sisters: Louisa, Evangeline, Cecily, Rafaela,
Rosamond, Genevieve
Brothers: Edmund, Barnaby, Rowland,
Thaddeus, Carleton, Bartholomew
✱ Frustrated that Dominic and Sebastian are
too common? Have I got a name for you. Bene-
dict is saintly, literary, sophisticated, and ex-
tremely rare. Plus the sturdy nickname Ben
makes this one exotic choice that's virtually
risk-free (unless you still hold a grudge against
the traitorous general Benedict Arnold . . . or
Eggs Benedict).
In the World: Revolutionary War general Benedict Arnold; "Mysterious Benedict Society" series; Eggs Benedict; actor Benedict
Cumberbatch

Benjamin (BEHN-jə-min) 1981: #32
Popularity: #19
Styles: Timeless, Biblical
Nicknames: Ben, Benno,
Benji 1880 Today
Variants: Binyamin
Sisters: Rachel, Abigail, Victoria, Emily,
Rebecca, Lauren, Sarah, Hannah
Brothers: Alexander, Jonathan, Samuel,
Nathaniel, Gabriel, Nicholas, Joshua, Daniel
✱ Benjamin is a name of perfect balance. It's
popular, but not trendy. It's biblical, but not
conspicuously antique. It's manly, but not heavy
or blunt. The full Benjamin is handsome, Benji
is cute, and Ben's an all-around good guy. You're
all set.
In the World: Centuries of Bens from Benjamin
Franklin to Big Ben to Ben Affleck

Bennett (BEH-nit) 2011: #240
Popularity: #239
Styles: Timeless, Last Names
First
Nicknames: Ben 1880 Today
Variants: Bennet, Benedict
Sisters: Juliet, Elise, Claire, Hope, Camilla,
Audrey, Annabelle, Kate
Brothers: Lincoln, Davis, Reid, Preston, Elliott,
Holden, Miles, Grant
✱ An exceptionally flexible name, Bennett
plays well to many audiences. As a crisp sur-
name, it's finding favor in this age of Paytons
and Carters. The nickname Ben appeals to no-
frills traditionalists. And as the medieval form
of Benedict (and surname of *Pride and Prejudice*
heroine Elizabeth Bennet), it wins over the literary romantics.
In the World: Publisher Bennett Cerf; singer
Tony Bennett

Bentley (BEHNT-lee) 2011: #75
Popularity: #75
Styles: Last Names First,
Country and Western
Nicknames: Ben 1880 Today
Variants: Bently
Sisters: Landry, Brinley, Leighton, Brooklyn,
Presley, Shiloh, Savannah
Brothers: Branson, Cooper, Easton, Jameson,
Greyson, Kingsley, Aston
✱ This name has done a total about-face, from
upper-crusty stuffed shirt to down-homey coun-
try boy. Bentley used to conjure up the banker
riding in the back of a Bentley limousine (or
maybe the uniformed driver up front). But
country singer Dierks Bentley helped give the
name a Southern spin, and a Tennessee-born
Bentley on the reality TV series *Teen Mom*
helped cement that new image.
In the World: Bentley luxury cars; singer Dierks
Bentley; "Farnsworth Bentley," flashy valet to
Sean Combs

Bernard (ber-NAHRD, BEHR-nerd) — 1921: #45
Popularity: #1092
Styles: Solid Citizens, Ladies and Gentlemen
Nicknames: Bernie, Barney
Variants: Bernhard, Bernt, Bernardo
Sisters: Maxine, Sylvia, Dorothy, Marion, Loretta, Rita, Jeannette, Arlene
Brothers: Francis, Clifford, Gilbert, Harold, Wallace, Raymond, Stanley, Vernon
✷ Bernard is a proud old Germanic name that has mellowed over time. The burly St. Bernard dog helps make the name warmer and cuddlier than most (and a perfect playmate for Clifford). The nickname Bernie, though, has hit some major road bumps like the crass comedy *Weekend at Bernie's* and Ponzi schemer Bernie Madoff.
In the World: Comedian Bernie Mac; finanical criminal Bernie Madoff; *Weekend at Bernie's* films; St. Bernard dog

Bertram (BER-trəm) — 1895: #337
Popularity: Very rare
Styles: Ladies and Gentlemen, German and Dutch, Shakespearean
Nicknames: Bert
Variants: Bertrand
Sisters: Petra, Leonore, Verena, Winifred, Adele, Rosina, Clarice, Margret
Brothers: Lambert, Bayard, Clement, Leopold, Merritt, Conrad, Rupert, Gerhard
✷ Bertram is uncommon and likely to stay that way. It was never popular enough to be a revival candidate, nor quirky enough to be a glamorous exotic. It's a stately, serious name that charts its own path.
In the World: Boatmaker Bertram Yachts

Bishop (BI-shəp) — 1890: #415
Popularity: #1117
Styles: Fanciful
Sisters: Lacy, Meadow, Ellery, Gracie, Mara, Bellamy, Evie, Shiloh
Brothers: Baron, Major, Deacon, Edison, Turner, Arrow, Shepard, Gibson
✷ Bishop was occasionally heard a century ago during a fad for titles as names. (Major and Judge date to the same era.) Today Bishop has a pleasantly surprising snap when presented on its own as a first name. Paired with a surname, it can create some "name or title?" confusion.

Blaine (BLAYN) — 1884: #209
Popularity: #573
Styles: Brisk and Breezy, Timeless, Celtic, Saints
Variants: Blane, Blayne
Sisters: Ashton, Sydney, Reese, Blythe, Tierney, Sloane
Brothers: Bryce, Cooper, Barrett, Duncan, Grant, Reid
✷ Blaine sounds sharp in all senses of the word: piercing, intelligent, and stylish. It also sounds trendy in this age of Dane, Kane, Lane, and Zane. In fact, though, this old Scottish surname has been used steadily in the U.S. for generations.
In the World: Football player Blaine Gabbert; *Glee* character Blaine Anderson

Blaise (BLAYZ) — 2011: #932
Popularity: #931
Styles: Brisk and Breezy, Saints, French
Sisters: Gisele, Camilla, Soleil, Chantal, Raine, Sabine
Brothers: Xavier, Beau, Valentin, Brice, Maxim, Pierce
✷ A few cutting-edge parents are catching on to this intriguing possibility. It was the name of a French saint, as well as the renowned philosopher-mathematician Blaise Pascal. What could be more respectable? Yet it also sounds like "blaze" of glory. A refined way to indulge your need for speed.
In the World: Philosopher Blaise Pascal; Burkina Faso president Blaise Compaoré

Blake (BLAYK) — 2011: #73
Popularity: #73
Styles: Brisk and Breezy, New Classics
Sisters: Jenna, Paige, Bailey, Brooke, Jocelyn, Aubrey, Jordan, Laine
Brothers: Reid, Cole, Trevor, Drew, Chase, Tate, Grant, Brody
✷ One of the breeziest names for boys. Blake is sleek, confident, and possibly a bit of a rascal. If you're looking for a name with cross-racial appeal, Blake has an unusual pair of origins: it arises from the Old English words for both "black" and "white."
In the World: Singer Blake Shelton; director Blake Edwards; *Dynasty* patriarch Blake Carrington

Bodhi (BOH-dee)   2010: #911
Popularity: #939
Styles: Modern Meanings
Nicknames: Bo
Variants: Bode   1880   Today
Sisters: Sol, Unity, Honor,
Aria, Cielo, Uma
Brothers: River, Taj, Roan, Merit, Reef, Tenzin
✷ The word "bodhi" comes from the Sanskrit for "awakened." It refers to a spiritual awakening to a new level of awareness and enlightenment. That makes Bodhi, the name, a major contrast to the aggressive, even violent, meaning names currently in vogue for boys. The gentleness doesn't appeal to everybody, but it does send a message to your son that you value his *inner* strength the most.
In the World: The Bodhi Tree, under which the Buddha achieved enlightenment; actor Bodhi Elfman

Bond (BAHND)   1920: #3208
Popularity: #7014
Styles: Brisk and Breezy,
Saints, Macho Swagger, Last
Names First   1880   Today
Sisters: Laine, Tanith, Greer,
Winslow, Britt, Esme, Averil, Lise
Brothers: Beck, Reeve, Blaise, Quill, Baldwin, Locke, Rhodes, Steele
✷ The name is Bond . . . yes, just Bond. Bond is indeed a legitimate first name, borne by a seventh-century French saint. It makes a smashing impact in English, with secret-agent-style bravado.
In the World: 007 James Bond; the common word "bond," meaning a link or financial instrument

Boris (BOHR-is, bah-REES)   1923: #961
Popularity: #2527
Styles: Slavic
Nicknames: Borya, Bo, Boro
Sisters: Vera, Olga, Anka,   1880   Today
Natasha, Lida, Svetlana
Brothers: Konrad, Eugene, Viktor, Pavel, Sergei, Igor
✷ Boris is a name that comes across far better in Russian. The English pronunciation conjures up horror king Boris Karloff as well as Rocky and Bullwinkle's nemesis Boris Badenov. That nefarious image could actually work to the name's advantage, though, making it devilish rather than merely drab.
In the World: Horror film star Boris Karloff; tennis player Boris Becker; Russian president Boris Yeltsin

Bowen (BOH-ən)   2011: #724
Popularity: #723
Styles: Last Names First, The
"-ens," Celtic, Why Not?
Sisters: Marley, Kerrigan,   1880   Today
Zoe, Reilly, Bella, Landry
Brothers: Devlin, Bryce, Tobin, Keane, Baylor, Sutton
✷ Picture Owen, wrapped as a surname with a bow on top. (See what I did there? Okay, yeah, I'll stop now.) Bowen is a new name that keeps some of Owen's old-time sound and adds a pinch of cowboy.
In the World: A son of quarterback Drew Brees; Bowen of the film *Dragonheart*

Bowman (BOH-mən)   1884: #971
Popularity: #4968
Styles: Last Names First,
Country and Western, Why
Not?   1880   Today
Nicknames: Bo
Sisters: Carling, Mabry, Adeline, Landry, Bellamy, Gracie, Wallis, Hartley
Brothers: Hawkins, Rourke, Granger, Paxton, Deacon, Harlan, Griffith, Vaughan
✷ Tradesman names ending in "-er" (Carter, Parker) have become so popular that they've started to lose their rustic connotations. Bowman, in contrast, sounds like a true throwback. It has an old-fashioned masculinity, reinforced by the nickname Bo.

Brad (BRAD)   1975: #98
Popularity: #1417
Styles: Surfer '60s,
Nicknames
Sisters: Jodi, Dina, Beth,   1880   Today
Tammy, April, Jill
Brothers: Greg, Robbie, Troy, Randy, Marc, Scott
✷ Brad is pure surfer cuteness. It's direct and masculine, with a breezy, undemanding style. At its best, that translates to actor Brad Pitt. At its worst, think of the ineffectual Brad from *The Rocky Horror Picture Show*. As a nickname, Brad beefs up and remains very popular.
In the World: Actor Brad Pitt; musician Brad Paisley; writer Brad Meltzer

Bradley (BRAD-lee)   1980: #51
Popularity: #179
Styles: New Classics, Last
Names First
Nicknames: Brad   1880   Today
Variants: Bradford
Sisters: Leslie, Alica, Courtney, Melanie,
Monica, Holly
Brothers: Wesley, Bryan, Spencer, Justin,
Timothy, Brett
★This old surname is a longtime American
favorite. Its first surge came in honor of World
War II general Omar Bradley, but it really took
off as a formal version of the hit name Brad.
Bradley adds a little preppy dignity to that '60s
cutie.
In the World: Actors Bradley Cooper and Brad-
ley Whitford

Brady (BRAY-dee)   2007: #93
Popularity: #135
Styles: Last Names First,
Nickname-Proof, Bell Tones
Sisters: Avery, Piper, Peyton,   1880   Today
Brooke, Kennedy, Macy
Brothers: Mason, Bryce, Parker, Colby, Bowen,
Cooper
★Brady has been used quietly for many years,
but it was swept into the limelight with the sur-
name style explosion. Unlike most "-y" names,
it has stayed exclusively masculine. Quarter-
back Tom Brady is a big part of the reason—the
name has been particularly popular within his
New England fan base.
In the World: Quarterback Tom Brady; The
Brady Bunch TV series; baseball player Brady
Anderson

Bram (BRAM)   2005: #2321
Popularity: #3037
Styles: Literary and Artistic,
German and Dutch, Brisk
and Breezy, Why Not?   1880   Today
Variants: Braam
Sisters: Elke, Cilla, Esme, Hedy, Anouk, Meike
Brothers: Soren, Wolf, Gregor, Niels, Carsten,
Pim
★This Dutch version of Abraham is a smart
and coolly tough possibility. *Dracula* author
Bram Stoker is the best-known bearer, giving
the name a dark and stormy undercurrent.
In the World: Writer Bram Stoker; children's
music group Sharon, Lois & Bram

Brandon (BRAN-dən)   1985: #13
Popularity: #47
Styles: The "-ens," '70s–'80s,
Turn of the 20th Century
Nicknames: Bran   1880   Today
Variants: Branden
Sisters: Brooke, Lauren, Allison, Taylor,
Samantha, Lindsey, Megan, Ashley
Brothers: Ryan, Jordan, Kevin, Kyle, Bryan,
Christian, Austin, Tyler
★Brandon sounds dashing, so it's no surprise
that it swept onto the scene as a popular soap
opera name. It also sounds classically mascu-
line, which has given it staying power. The
name is still in the mainstream of fashion, but
down significantly from its '80s and '90s peak.
Even dashing heroes need to rest from time to
time.
In the World: Actor Brandon Lee; musicians
Brandon Flowers and Brandon Boyd

Brannock (BRA-nək)   2006: #9567
Popularity: Very rare
Styles: Celtic, Saints
Nicknames: Bran
Sisters: Emlyn, Niamh,   1880   Today
Wynne, Mabyn, Eleri, Seren
Brothers: Brogan, Maxen, Cadogan, Broderick,
Griffith, Carrick
★This old Welsh saint's name could earn oohs
and aahs as an alternative to Brandon. The "-k"
ending is distinctive today and suggestive of
long-ago heroes.

Brantley (BRANT-lee)   2011: #321
Popularity: #370
Styles: Last Names First,
Country and Western
Nicknames: Brant   1880   Today
Variants: Brentley
Sisters: Landry, Cassidy, Sawyer, Brooklynn,
Shaelyn, Paisley
Brothers: Devlin, Channing, Montgomery,
Branson, Raylan, Westley
★Brantley is one of the new "preppy cowboys."
These are fancy surnames that have made their
way from the yacht club to the rodeo—or onto
the stage at the Grand Ole Opry. (Country
music star Brantley Gilbert helped propel
Brantley's transformation.) The nickname
Brant gives this name some flexibility that Bent-
ley lacks.
In the World: Singer Brantley Gilbert

Name Snapshots: Boys   227

Braxton (BRAKS-tuhn)   2011: #153
Popularity: #153
Styles: Last Names First, The
"-ens," Nickname-Proof
Sisters: Adelyn, Mckenna,   1880   Today
Brooklynn, Reagan, Aubree,
Blakely
Brothers: Ryker, Briggs, Jaxon, Brayden,
Maddox, Kingston
✳ This brawny surname is a recent addition to
the given name ranks, but it's thoroughly famil-
iar to expectant couples who've been reading up
on Braxton Hicks contractions.
In the World: Singer Toni Braxton; Braxton-
Hicks contractions

Brayden (BRAY-dən)   2011: #37
Popularity: #37
Styles: Bell Tones, The "-ens"
Nicknames: Bray, Brade
Variants: Braden, Braeden,   1880   Today
Braiden, Bradyn, Braydon
Sisters: Kaylee, Jayla, Cadence, Brinley,
Teagan, Brooklyn, Ainsley, Gracelyn
Brothers: Rylan, Logan, Bryce, Grayson, Kyler,
Ashton, Landon, Blake
✳ Brayden is one of the trendiest boy's names
in years, with an infectiously confident style. It's
easy to picture a Brayden as an upbeat, self-as-
sured boy. Given the name's many popular
spellings and rhyming options, though, there's a
risk that this will be a name with a "freshness
date" that quickly passes.
In the World: Canadian hockey players Brayden
Schenn, Brayden McNabb, and Braydon Co-
burn (the name caught on earlier in Canada)

Brecken (BREHK-in)   2011: #963
Popularity: #962
Styles: The "-ens," Celtic,
Why Not?
Nicknames: Breck   1880   Today
Variants: Breckin, Breck,
Braec
Sisters: Brielle, Alexis, Kylie, Timber, Adilyn,
Teagan
Brothers: Bevan, Carsten, Cullen, Tanner,
Bridger, Rogan
✳ Brecken is a very rare Irish surname that has
only recently joined the first-name ranks. If it
sounds like a natural with a fresh burst of moun-
tain air, thank the ski resort of Breckenridge,
Colorado.
In the World: Actor Breckin Meyer

Brendan (BREHN-dən)   1999: #96
Popularity: #263
Styles: The "-ens," Celtic,
Nickname-Proof, Turn of the
21st Century   1880   Today
Sisters: Caitlin, Regan,
Maeve, Tierney, Megan, Kiara
Brothers: Colin, Aidan, Garrett, Connor, Liam,
Nolan
✳ What's the difference between Brendan and
Brandon? One little sound, and a world of nu-
ance. Brandon is an English surname, a soap
opera favorite, and an enormously popular mod-
ern name. Brendan is a classic Irish saint's
name, and less common. With an Irish last
name, it has echoes of literary icon Brendan
Behan and the old country.
In the World: Writer Brendan Behan; actors
Brendan Fraser and Brendan Gleeson; hockey
player Brendan Shanahan

Brennan (BREH-nən)   2009: #243
Popularity: #293
Styles: Last Names First, The
"-ens," Celtic, Nickname-
Proof   1880   Today
Variants: Brannon
Sisters: Kendall, Tegan, Kiera, McKenna,
Ashlin, Mallory, Morgan, Finley
Brothers: Griffin, Brady, Dawson, Riordan,
Tanner, Donovan, Shane, Carson
✳ It's Brendan, now with 20% fewer consonant
sounds! Yes, this Irish surname is just a "d" away
from Brendan and Brandon, but that's enough
to make those old friends sound new again. (It's
actually quite separate in origin, from Irish
roots meaning "teardrop" or "raven.")

Brent (BRENT)   1970: #74
Popularity: #775
Styles: '70s–'80s, Brisk and
Breezy
Variants: Brant   1880   Today
Sisters: Kerry, April, Leigh,
Bridget, Tara, Stacy
Brothers: Clint, Brad, Kirk, Derrick, Bryan,
Chad
✳ The '60s and '70s saw a raft of these "blunt
instrument" names: Clint, Dirk, Kurt. They
pack a pile of sounds into a single manly sylla-
ble. The names still have their fans, but they're
losing momentum to a lighter, swifter genera-
tion: Kane, Jace, Trey.
In the World: Actor Brent Spiner; sportscaster
Brent Musberger; military adviser Brent Scow-
croft

Brett (BREHT) 1986: #69
Popularity: #508
Styles: Brisk and Breezy
Variants: Bret
Sisters: Holly, Alison, Kara, 1880 Today
April, Bridget, Katrina
Brothers: Eric, Kyle, Scott, Casey, Brian, Trent
✶ Brett splits the difference between the rock-hard '60s studs like Kirk and Brent and their breezy decendants Tate and Cade. It's clean and solid, but has started to give way to the young upstarts.
In the World: Football player Brett Favre; director Brett Ratner

Brian (BRIY-in) 1973: #8
Popularity: #122
Styles: '70s–'80s, Surfer '60s,
Celtic, Nickname-Proof
Variants: Bryan 1880 Today
Sisters: Amy, Megan, Kelly,
Shannon, Erin, Holly
Brothers: Kevin, David, Patrick, Scott, Jason, Sean
✶ Brian has been an Irish favorite for centuries and an American one since the '50s. It has become one of the "can't miss" names, reliable and teaseproof. Lately, though, Brian has ceded the Irish American crown to the likes of Aiden, Ryan, and Liam.
In the World: Generations of all-American boys, from Beach Boy Brian Wilson to Backstreet Boy Brian Littrell

Bridger (BRI jer) 2009: #865
Popularity: #959
Styles: Country and Western,
Last Names First, Macho
Swagger 1880 Today
Sisters: Oakley, Aspen, Briley,
Sedona, Shiloh, Blakely
Brothers: Branson, River, Archer, Colton, Brecken, Cooper
✶ Bridger is a tradesman surname, which puts it in the company of names like Tanner and Carter. Its use as a baby name, though, owes more to the Bridger Mountains of Montana and Wyoming. That association has made Bridger a rugged regional favorite. It's popular in the mountain West, while in many parts of the country it remains virtually unknown.
In the World: Bridger Bowl ski area

Brock (BRAHK) 2003: #244
Popularity: #325
Styles: Last Names First,
Macho Swagger, New
Classics 1880 Today
Sisters: Lindsay, Blair, Macy,
Tatum, Bailey, Sloane
Brothers: Trent, Drake, Bronson, Hunter, Tyson, Burke
✶ It's always a surprise to encounter a Brock in real life. Shouldn't he be busy saving a soap opera heroine from a burning building, his sculpted muscles glistening in the night? Happily, Brock's decades of steady use have started to humanize the name. It's still ultra-studly, but no longer so showy.
In the World: Wrestler/MMA fighter Brock Lesnar; actor Brock Peters

Brody (BROH-dee) 2008: #70
Popularity: #83
Styles: Last Names First
Variants: Brodie
Sisters: Avery, Macy, Skylar, 1880 Today
Kylie, Brooklyn, Aubrey
Brothers: Logan, Chase, Riley, Blake, Landon, Bryson
✶ This trendy new name has a double appeal: it takes the boyish style of Corey and packages it up as a surname. Choosing an "-ie" ending, which usually makes a name look more feminine, in this case makes it more Scottish. Brodie is the standard spelling of both the first name and surname in Scotland.
In the World: Reality TV personality Brody Jenner (female) singer Brody Dalle

Brogan (BROH-gən) 2011: #778
Popularity: #777
Styles: Celtic, The "-ens,"
Last Names First, Saints,
Why Not? 1880 Today
Sisters: Keelin, Ainsley,
Tierney, Grier, Fallon, Bryn
Brothers: Declan, Ronan, Finnegan, Roarke, Brodie, Killian
✶ Celtic origins? Check. Surname style? Check. Fashionable sound? Big check: it's Brody meets Logan! Brogan certainly has the ingredients of a hit name, but perhaps too much so for some parents. This old Irish saint's name approaches a Hollywood fantasy of Irish manliness.

Brooks (BRUWKS) 2011: #347
Popularity: #346
Styles: Brisk and Breezy,
Timeless, Last Names First
Sisters: Sloan, Finley, Blair, 1880 Today
Claire, Camille, Parker
Brothers: Reid, Westley, Preston, Davis, Grant,
Tate
✱ Brooks has always been the name you choose because you want your son to look good in pinstripes. It has a classic old-money style—a name that doesn't get its hands dirty. In this age of "preppy cowboy" names like Easton and Bentley, though, Brooks could be ready to loosen up.
In the World: Brooks Brothers clothes; country stars Brooks & Dunn and Garth Brooks; baseball player Brooks Robinson

Bruce (BROOS) 1951: #26
Popularity: #470
Styles: Mid-Century
Sisters: Janice, Connie,
Paula, Sharon, Brenda, Sheila 1880 Today
Brothers: Wayne, Dennis,
Barry, Glenn, Rodger, Curtis
✱ The world is full of macho guys named Bruce. Think Bruce Lee, Bruce Willis, Bruce Smith, Bruce Springsteen. Their combined muscle and swagger helps to offset the name's softness. Bruce once conjured up Scotland (à la Robert the Bruce), but the ethnic connection has faded—as demonstrated by the very non-Scottish Bruces listed here.
In the World: Singer Bruce Springsteen; martial artist Bruce Lee; actor Bruce Willis; football player Bruce Smith; Bruce Wayne (Batman)

Bruno (BROO-noh) 1915: #260
Popularity: #828
Styles: Guys and Dolls,
Saints, German and Dutch,
Italian, Macho Swagger 1880 Today
Sisters: Lucia, Inez, Rosa,
Cleo, Gilda, Lola
Brothers: Rocco, Primo, Rex, Mack, Enzo,
Cosmo
✱ Bruno is a brawny name you picture on a barrel-chested man. While the first image that springs to mind may be a bodyguard, the name also has a cuddly teddy bear side. If you come from a family of football linemen, this could be a winner.
In the World: Singer Bruno Mars; Bruno Magli shoes

Bryant (BRIY-int) 1988: #163
Popularity: #446
Styles: Last Names First,
Nickname-Proof
Sisters: Kendra, Mallory, 1880 Today
Whitney, Brenna, Meredith,
Lesley
Brothers: Drake, Mitchell, Brandt, Jarrett,
Kendrick, Tyson
✱ Bryant is a genteel surname, but it's far tougher than most of its ilk. It resembles a power adjective, like "giant" or "defiant." (Okay, "pliant" and "reliant" too, but who's counting?) This is one elegant lad who won't get pushed around.
In the World: TV host Bryant Gumbel; football coach Bear Bryant; New York's Bryant Park

Bryce (BRIYS) 2000: #92
Popularity: #114
Styles: Brisk and Breezy,
Country and Western, Celtic,
New Classics 1880 Today
Variants: Brice
Sisters: Addison, Paige, Sierra, Aspen, Tessa,
Kiley
Brothers: Chase, Blake, Brody, Colton, Ty,
Rylan
✱ Spelled Brice, this is an old French saint's name, used in Scotland for centuries. Spell it with a "y" and it's no longer French—or old. Bryce mixes a pinch of Scottish style with the fresh Western air of landmark Bryce Canyon.
In the World: Bryce Canyon National Park; baseball player Bryce Harper; actress Bryce Dallas Howard

Bryson (BRIY-sən) 2011: #98
Popularity: #98
Styles: The "-ens," Last
Names First
Nicknames: Bryce 1880 Today
Variants: Brycen
Sisters: Mckenna, Brooklyn, Kaylee, Ashlyn,
Lyla, Delaney
Brothers: Keaton, Bennett, Cooper, Rylan,
Maddox, Easton
✱ Bryson seems created by central casting to fit the zeitgeist. It's a surname with a style that's half prep school and half cowboy, which is a hot style recipe today. The spelling Brycen pops up when parents really want Bryce, but think it needs a "formal" version.
In the World: Singer Peabo Bryson; writer Bill Bryson; ancient Greek mathematician Bryson of Heraclea

Byron (BIY-rən) 1967: #196
Popularity: #506
Styles: Timeless, Nickname-
Proof, The "-ens," Literary
and Artistic 1880 Today
Sisters: Darcy, Sonya, Renee,
Teresa, Adrienne, Audra, Vanessa, Brooke
Brothers: Clinton, Darren, Curtis, Wade,
Roderick, Clifton, Dexter, Damon
✖ Byron first joined the name pool in tribute to the poet Lord Byron. It has held up exceptionally well for almost two centuries, even as the literary association has faded. It's a traditional cousin to contemporary favorites like Bryson and Landon.
In the World: Supreme Court justice Byron White; golfer Byron Nelson; basketball player/coach Byron Scott

Cabot (KA-bit) 2004: #3279
Popularity: #9697
Styles: Last Names First,
Why Not?
Nicknames: Cab 1880 Today
Sisters: Mabry, Adair, Maris,
Auden, Holland, Embry
Brothers: Forbes, Winslow, Prescott, Calder,
Hastings, Talbot
✖ Cabot was once the ultimate Boston Brahmin surname, immortalized in the lines: "Where the Lowells speak only to Cabots, and the Cabots speak only to God." In the 21st century, the name's elitist edge has softened to let the stylish sound stand on its own. The nickname Cab trades in high society for high spirits, à la jazzman Cab Calloway.
In the World: Cabot cheese; Senator Henry Cabot Lodge

Cade (KAYD) 2001: #201
Popularity: #347
Styles: Brisk and Breezy
Variants: Kade
Sisters: Reese, Camryn, 1880 Today
Ashlyn, Brynn, Tatum,
Sloane
Brothers: Gage, Beck, Corbin, Trey, Brennan,
Lane
✖ Quarterback Cade McKnown was drafted by the Chicago Bears in 1999. Don't remember him on the field? Surprisingly, his biggest impact was on America's nurseries. The name Cade just struck a nerve. It's tough and cute and contemporary, and it's been gathering attention ever since. Like many other familiar names, Cade has roots as a character in *Gone with the Wind*.
In the World: Quarterback Cade McKnown; Cade Calvert of *Gone with the Wind*

Caden (KAY-din) 2007: #92
Popularity: #136
Styles: The "-ens," Bell Tones
Nicknames: Cade
Variants: Cayden, Caiden, 1880 Today
Kadin, Kaiden, Kayden
Sisters: Adelyn, Rylee, Ainsley, Jayla, Carrigan,
Brooklyn
Brothers: Keegan, Brady, Carson, Rylan, Colby,
Grayson
✖ You can rustle up an Irish origin for Caden, but this name's popularity is about pure sound. You simply cannot get a more fashionable set of phonemes, and the nickname Cade is a winner too. But an entire classroom of rhyming boys is a real risk here. Caden, meet Hayden, Aidan, Jadon, and Braeden. . . . Each name has multiple spellings in the top-1000 list.

Calder (KAHL-der) 2011: #1836
Popularity: #1837
Styles: Literary and Artistic,
Last Names First, Why Not?
Nicknames: Cal 1880 Today
Sisters: Afton, Harper,
Flannery, Auden, Marlowe, Briar, Carson
Brothers: Miles, Cooper, Sawyer, Beckett,
Dashiell, Flynn
✖ Artist Alexander Calder is an icon of creative invention. The beauty of this name is that those who know of the artist will admire the stylish homage, and those who don't will admire the stylish alternative to Carter and Connor.
In the World: Artist Alexander Calder; hockey's Calder Trophy

Cale (KAYL)　　　　　2008: #623
Popularity: #831
Styles: Brisk and Breezy
Variants: Cael, Kale
Sisters: Bree, Mallory, Paige,　1880　Today
Autumn, Bailey, Jordan
Brothers: Rhett, Chase, Carter, Ty, Grayson,
Dalton
✱This speedy little name sounds equally at home on a stock-car driver or a banker. The spelling Cael is a Gaelic up-and-comer that comes from the same source as Kyle (and is sometimes pronounced that way). The equally popular Kale is also a variety of cabbage.
In the World: Auto racer Cale Yarborough; wrestler Cale Sanderson

Caleb (KAY-ləb)　　　　2002: #35
Popularity: #32
Styles: Antique Charm,
Biblical
Nicknames: Cale, Cal, Cab　1880　Today
Variants: Kaleb
Sisters: Abigail, Eliza, Hannah, Chloe,
Annabel, Faith
Brothers: Gabriel, Ethan, Jonas, Isaac, Noah,
Elijah
✱A terrific biblical rediscovery, Caleb is equal parts Puritan antique and soap opera chic. At one time this name seemed like a fresh alternative to the super-popular Jacob, but today it's a hit in its own right.
In the World: Author Caleb Carr; musician Caleb Followill

Callum (KA-luhm)　　　　2011: #848
Popularity: #847
Styles: Celtic, Why Not?
Nicknames: Cal
Variants: Calum, Colm　1880　Today
Sisters: Fiona, Mirren, Isla,
Tegan, Elspeth, Ailsa
Brothers: Liam, Carson, Ewan, Fraser,
Graham, Lachlan
✱This Scots Gaelic name has recently soared in popularity throughout the U.K. and Australia. It's now ready for its U.S. debut. Callum can also be used as a nickname for Malcolm; Colm is the Irish equivalent.
In the World: Actors Callum Blue, Callum Keith Rennie, and Calum Worthy

Calvin (KAL-vin)　　　　1924: #44
Popularity: #209
Styles: Timeless
Nicknames: Cal
Sisters: Joanna, Kathryn,　1880　Today
Theresa, Susana, Elaine,
Lydia
Brothers: Simon, Bennett, Curtis, Neil, Wesley,
Mitchell
✱It used to be that the first Calvin who came to mind was Calvin Coolidge, one of the least exciting men in American history. Now the top Calvin is fashion designer Calvin Klein, with the young hero of the comic strip *Calvin and Hobbes* trailing him. The name has gathered youthful momentum that Coolidge could scarcely have imagined.
In the World: Fashion designer Calvin Klein; comic strip *Calvin and Hobbes*; singer Calvin Harris; President Calvin Coolidge

Camden (KAM-din)　　　　2011: #160
Popularity: #160
Styles: The "-ens," Place
Names, Celtic
Nicknames: Cam　1880　Today
Sisters: Finley, Teagan,
Chloe, Ainsley, Mariah, Sydney
Brothers: Brennan, Mason, Conall, Trenton,
Easton, Ramsay
✱Camden may be most familiar as a city in New Jersey, but it is also an old Scottish boy's name. It has recently attracted attention as a succinct alternative to Cameron.
In the World: Camden Yards ballpark

Cameron (KAM-er-ən, KAM-rin)
2000: #31
Popularity: #53
Styles: Androgynous, Celtic, New Classics
Nicknames: Cam
Variants: Kameron, Camron, Camren, Kamron
Sisters: Jocelyn, Mackenzie, Morgan, Autumn, Brenna, Caitlin
Brothers: Dylan, Connor, Gavin, Parker, Donovan, Logan

✱ Cameron is one of the great Scottish clan names. It has entered the realm of modern American standards, but keeps much of its clan magic—a distinctive brew of romance and swagger. The standard spelling remains mostly masculine, despite the influence of actress Cameron Diaz. Variants like Camryn are more common for girls.
In the World: Director Cameron Crowe; rapper Cam'ron; actor Cameron Boyce

Campbell (KAM-bəl)
2010: #1035
Popularity: #1190
Styles: Last Names First, Androgynous, Why Not?
Nicknames: Cam
Sisters: Darcy, Rowan, Tierney, Ellery, Audra, Larkin
Brothers: Archer, Jameson, Merrick, Channing, Briggs, Prescott

✱ Campbell sounds like a familiar classic, despite the fact that nobody ever uses it. That makes a smashing opportunity for a unique name that will have no trouble fitting in. Note that some parents have started to choose the name for girls, taking advantage of the nickname Cammie.
In the World: Actor Campbell Scott; Campbell's soup

Carl (KAHRL)
1915: #22
Popularity: #591
Styles: Solid Citizens
Variants: Karl
Sisters: Ellen, June, Irene, Marion, Ruth, Nancy
Brothers: Martin, Clark, Lawrence, Roy, Clifton, Lee

✱ Carl is the kind of quiet, sturdy name that many of us take for granted. It may not reach out and grab you, but if you give it your full consideration, you'll be pleasantly surprised. It's strong, masculine, and one of the sharpest old-timers around.
In the World: Astronomer Carl Sagan; track star Carl Lewis; psychiatrist Carl Jung; poet Carl Sandburg

Carlos (KAHR-lohs)
2001: #59
Popularity: #91
Styles: Latino/Latina
Nicknames: Carlitos, Carlito
Variants: Carlo
Sisters: Ana, Elena, Alicia, Adriana, Gabriela, Selena, Maria, Angelica
Brothers: Luis, Antonio, Diego, Jorge, Francicso, Ricardo, Rafael, Alejandro

✱ This Spanish and Portuguese version of Charles is a longtime Latino hit with major crossover potential. It's starting to pop up among non-Latinos looking for a cool and creative classic. The Italian version Carlo is equally stylish.
In the World: Musician Carlos Santana; business magnate Carlos Slim; basketball player Carlos Boozer

Carlton (KAHRL-tən)
1937: #217
Popularity: #1534
Styles: Last Names First, Solid Citizens
Nicknames: Carl
Variants: Carleton
Sisters: Marianne, Rosalyn, Constance, Lorraine, Rosalie, Corrine
Brothers: Stanton, Lawrence, Russell, Winston, Cornell, Stewart

✱ This steady surname may not have the bounce of new hits like Keaton and Bryson, but its grounded style has a lasting appeal, like model trains in the age of air travel. The spelling Carleton is characteristically English.
In the World: Carleton Banks of *The Fresh Prince of Bel Air*; Carlton cigarettes; baseball player Carlton Fisk

Carmelo (kahr-MEHL-oh)   2011: #581
Popularity: #580
Styles: Italian
Nicknames: Melo
Sisters: Melania, Romina,   1880   Today
Alessia, Giada, Luciana,
Graziella
Brothers: Santino, Leandro, Mario, Matteo,
Giancarlo, Orlando
✱This was a barely familiar Sicilian name
until basketball star Carmelo Anthony brought
it to America's attention. He showed off the
name's smooth magnetism to excellent effect.
Some may be reminded of the Caramello choc-
olate bar, but that's a suitably rich, sweet associa-
tion.
In the World: Basketball player Carmelo An-
thony

Carson (KAHR-sən)   2010: #80
Popularity: #85
Styles: Last Names First, The
"-ens," Nickname-Proof,
Celtic, Country and Western   1880   Today
Variants: Karson
Sisters: Camryn, Audrey, Bella, Claire,
Morgan, Riley
Brothers: Jackson, Connor, Logan, Owen,
Gavin
✱Carson has it all: it's a surname, a Celtic
name, and a cowboy name (for Kit Carson). It's
even an MTV name, thanks to TV host Carson
Daly. That's a natural winning combo, and it
makes for a very popular and likable choice.
In the World: TV host Carson Daly; Carson
City, Nevada; football player Carson Palmer;
stylist Carson Kressley

Carsten (KAHR-stin)   2011: #1332
Popularity: #1332
Styles: The "-ens," German
and Dutch, Nickname-Proof,
Why Not?   1880   Today
Variants: Karsten
Sisters: Maren, Sofie, Larkin, Lisbeth, Anja,
Arden
Brothers: Pierson, Stefan, Connor, Evert,
Torin, Finn
✱Carsten is a Germanic form of Christian. Its
sharp, simple sound has all the ingredients of an
American favorite, but some parents have shied
away, fearing confusion with Kristin and
Kirsten.
In the World: Artist Carsten Höller

Carter (KAHR-ter)   2011: #41
Popularity: #41
Styles: Last Names First,
Nickname-Proof
Variants: Karter   1880   Today
Sisters: Avery, Claire, Piper,
Mia, Addison, Marley
Brothers: Mason, Cooper, Bennett, Caleb,
Parker, Jackson
✱This smart surname feels sturdier and less
trendy than most examples of the style. Playful
and brainy, it's a fun name that's not afraid to
grow up.
In the World: President Jimmy Carter; John
Carter of TV show *ER*; multiple Lil Wayne al-
bums titled *Tha Carter*

Cary (KA-ree)   1966: #264
Popularity: #3593
Styles: Mid-Century,
Androgynous, Nickname-
Proof   1880   Today
Sisters: Gail, Margo, Trudy,
Joy, Regina, Charla
Brothers: Dana, Kent, Blaine, Neal, Von,
Robin
✱ On paper, Cary still has much of the breezy,
debonair character it inherited from actor Cary
Grant. Spoken aloud, though, it becomes a con-
fusing match for the girl's name Carrie.
In the World: Actors Cary Grant and Cary Elwes

Case (KAYS)   2011: #665
Popularity: #664
Styles: Brisk and Breezy,
Fantastical, Why Not?
Sisters: Haven, Raine,   1880   Today
Campbell, Emery, Rory,
Quinn
Brothers: Beck, Pryce, Flynn, Calder, Ryker,
Drake
✱ Case sounds natural, doesn't it? It's a name
with a clear image: swift and strong, halfway
between preppy and macho. And yet . . . have
you ever met anyone named Case? Have you
ever even heard of anyone named Case? (Real
world, please; the hero of *Neuromancer* doesn't
count.) This is a creative choice that won't raise
eyebrows.
In the World: The hero of the cyberpunk novel
Neuromancer

Casey (KAY-see) 1988: #83
Popularity: #423
Styles: Celtic, Country and
Western, '70s–'80s,
Androgynous, Last Names 1880 Today
First
Nicknames: Case
Variants: Kasey
Sisters: Kelly, Bridget, Megan, Holly, Lesley,
Erin
Brothers: Jesse, Logan, Cody, Rory, Travis,
Shane
✳ Casey's just as cute as Cody and Corey, but
twice as tough. This Irish/Western favorite has a
rugged disposition closer in spirit to Jack than
Corey. You should know, though, that the name
is used nearly as often for girls today. No matter
how manly the name, a "-y" ending is an invita-
tion to androgyny.
In the World: Railroad engineer Casey Jones;
poem "Casey at the Bat"; radio host Casey
Kasem; actor Casey Affleck

Cash (KASH) 2009: #250
Popularity: #264
Styles: Last Names First,
Brisk and Breezy, Country
and Western, Macho Swagger 1880 Today
Sisters: Scarlet, Piper, Oakley,
Scout, Marley, Presley
Brothers: Ryder, Colt, Deacon, Wyatt, Fox,
Lane
✳ Americans rediscovered this name starting
in 2003, the year country music legend Johnny
Cash died. The name's cowboy aura is much
older, though. You could easily have met a Cash
back in the 1870s in a Western outpost like Kan-
sas.
In the World: Singer Johnny Cash; numerous
phrases from "cash out" to "cash cow"

Cason (KAY-sən) 2010: #478
Popularity: #507
Styles: The "-ens," Last
Names First, Bell Tones,
Why Not? 1880 Today
Nicknames: Case
Variants: Kason
Sisters: Laney, Macy, Kaya, Tatum, Parker,
Ainsley
Brothers: Brennan, Corbin, Barrett, Colt,
Ryland, Keaton
✳ Cason is an English surname, but not a com-
mon one. So while a Dawson or Parker hits you
with surname style first, Cason just sounds like
a fashionable first name. Cason also boasts a
very strong nickname; in fact, Case is catching
up to Cason as a given name.

Casper (KAS-per) 1889: #332
Popularity: #2336
Styles: Ladies and
Gentlemen, Saints,
Namesakes, German and 1880 Today
Dutch
Nicknames: Cap
Variants: Caspar, Kasper, Gaspar, Jasper
Sisters: Louisa, Flora, Ariel, Adelaide, Delia,
Matilda
Brothers: Lucas, Bertram, Quentin, Homer,
Felix, Rudolph
✳ It should take more than one little Friendly
Ghost to scare parents off this name. Casper is
one of the few boys' names with the same light,
nostalgic charm that has made names like Lily
and Sophie such favorites for girls. Granted,
Casper is quirkier than those hits. If you're on
the fence, Jasper is another form of the same
name without the ghost trouble.
In the World: Actor Casper Van Dien; Casper
the Friendly Ghost; a son of model Claudia
Schiffer

Cassius (KA-shəs, KA-see-is)   1880: #425
Popularity: #876
Styles: Exotic Traditional,
Classical, Shakespearean
Nicknames: Cass, Cash   1880   Today
Sisters: Livia, Ariadne,
Sapphira, Lorelei, Paloma, Laelia
Brothers: Titus, Marius, Magnus, Samson,
Tycho, Maximus
✷ A classical contender, very memorable—if a
bit too lean and hungry. (For many, boxer Cassius Clay, who became Muhammad Ali, will
come to mind before any classical or Shakespearean references.) The nickname Cass remains breezily macho on a boy, despite the
many girls with "Cass-" names.
In the World: Boxer Cassius Clay (aka Muhammad Ali)

Cecil (SEH-səl, SEE-sil)   1902: #65
Popularity: #1669
Styles: English, Ladies and
Gentlemen, Nickname-Proof
Variants: Cecilio   1880   Today
Sisters: Muriel, Vera, Clarice,
Inez, Viola, Lenore
Brothers: Basil, Edmund, Wallace, Virgil,
Armand, Clarence
✷ Boys continued to be named Cecil in the
generations after Cecil B. DeMille produced
his Hollywood epics, but the name remains frozen in time. Even with names like August and
Cyrus inching toward comebacks, Cecil is still
determinedly of a time gone by.
In the World: Director Cecil B. DeMille; photographer Cecil Beaton; baseball player Cecil
Fielder

Cedric (SEHD-rik)   1974: #230
Popularity: #751
Styles: Exotic Traditional,
African-American
Nicknames: Rick   1880   Today
Variants: Cedrick
Sisters: Adrienne, Leticia, Gwendolyn, Darcy,
Camille, Serena
Brothers: Duncan, Quincy, Desmond, Lamont,
Orlando, Roderick
✷ A name with Welsh forebears, dashing Cedric was introduced by Sir Walter Scott in his
novel *Ivanhoe*. In the U.S., it has been primarily
an African-American name, with a peak in the
'70s. Its antique style could make it a candidate
for a broader re-revival.
In the World: Comedian Cedric the Entertainer; "Harry Potter" character Cedric Diggory

Cesar (SAY-sahr)   2004: #157
Popularity: #217
Styles: Latino/Latina
Variants: Cezar, Caesar
Sisters: Adriana, Dulce,   1880   Today
Gabriela, Claudia, Alejandra,
Giselle, Karina, Esmeralda
Brothers: Julio, Cristian, Javier, Marco, Sergio,
Jorge, Mario, Hector
✷ Spanish speakers are lucky with this one. As
an English name, Caesar is charismatic but too
flamboyant for comfort. The Spanish Cesar
takes the charisma mainstream. Handsome and
trendy.
In the World: Labor leader Cesar Chavez; actor
Cesar Romero

Chad (CHAD)   1972: #25
Popularity: #568
Styles: '70s–'80s
Variants: Chadd
Sisters: Heather, Shannon,   1880   Today
Tara, Kelly, April, Stacy
Brothers: Brett, Heath, Corey, Shawn, Jamie,
Brent
✷ Chad was the preppy chieftain of the 1970s
and '80s. It's the name you mentally gave to the
rich, handsome rival in every John Hughes teen
movie. That generation of Chads has grown up,
though, so it's time to retire the Izod and the
pastel sport coats. By now, it seems natural that
Chad rhymes with Dad.
In the World: Football player Chad Ochocinco;
actors Chad Everett and Chad Michael Murray;
musician Chad Kroeger

Chaim (KHIYM, HIYM,   2011: #783
KHIY-əm)
Popularity: #782
Styles: Jewish
Variants: Haim, Jaim, Hyam,   1880   Today
Hyman
Sisters: Rivka, Shira, Hadassah, Malka, Chava,
Yael
Brothers: Hillel, Avi, Boaz, Ariel, Noam,
Shimon
✷ A burst of positive energy, Jewish style.
Chaim means "life," as in the traditional toast
l'chaim, "to life!" It's also the preferred way to
honor an ancestor with the luckless name
Hyman. Chaim is a common name among religious Jews, but is seldom heard in secular and
non-Jewish communities.
In the World: Author Chaim Potok; Israeli presidents Chaim Weizmann and Chaim Herzog;
artist Chaïm Soutine

Chance (CHANS) 1996: #154
Popularity: #218
Styles: Brisk and Breezy,
Modern Meanings, Country
and Western 1880 Today
Sisters: Chelsea, Brooke,
Rylee, Cassidy, Autumn, Hayley
Brothers: Trace, Austin, Carter, Weston, Bryce,
Dillon
✶ Like Maverick, Chance is a lone gunman, following the wind and seeking adventure on his own terms. Unlike Maverick, Chance also has a softer side, a reflection of prep school names like Chauncey and Trey. That unlikely combination is a winner, making Chance the top "meaning" name for boys.
In the World: Reality TV star Kamal ("Chance") Givens; Chance the gardener in *Being There*

Chandler (CHAND-ler) 1999: #151
Popularity: #441
Styles: Last Names First,
Turn of the 21st Century
Nicknames: Chan 1880 Today
Sisters: Michaela, Hayley,
Cassidy, Skylar, Sheridan, Chelsea
Brothers: Tanner, Dawson, Colby, Brennan,
Austin, Spencer
✶ Chandler has an offhand elegance that attracts many parents, especially mothers. It probably would have been a popular choice even if it hadn't been featured on the sitcom *Friends*. Probably. If you like the style but balk at the television association, look at Palmer or Schuyler.
In the World: Chandler Bing of *Friends*; football coach Chan Gailey

Channing (CHA-ning) 2010: #645
Popularity: #672
Styles: Last Names First,
Androgynous, Why Not?
Nicknames: Chan 1880 Today
Sisters: Oakley, Sloane,
Audrianna, Everly, Cassidy, Savanna, Callie, Larkin
Brothers: Langston, Campbell, Kingsley, Brigham, Spaulding, Bryce, Travers, Landry
✶ Channing is a surname that breaks out of the sound-alike lineup of "-er" and "-on" names. It has enough first-name history to sound comfortable and even comes with an agreeably masculine nickname. This is probably the biggest crowd-pleaser of all the "-ing" names.
In the World: Actor Channing Tatum; football player Channing Crowder; basketball player Channing Frye

Charles (CHAHRLZ) 1880: #4
Popularity: #62
Styles: Timeless, Solid
Citizens
Nicknames: Charlie, Charley, 1880 Today
Chuck, Chase, Chaz, Cal,
Chick
Variants: Carlos, Carlo, Carl
Sisters: Margaret, Frances, Eleanor, Rose, Catherine, Martha, Alice, Helen
Brothers: Louis, Edward, Willam, Joseph, Philip, James, Henry, George
✶ Charles is stately and dignified, and Charlie is warm and friendly. That sounds like a killer combo, yet the name was in free fall for much of the 20th century. It has stabilized as parents start to turn to Charlie as an attractive alternative to popular nice-guy names like Ben and Sam.
In the World: Author Charles Dickens; naturalist Charles Darwin; England's Prince Charles

Charlie (CHAHR-lee) 1900: #25
Popularity: #236
Styles: Nicknames, Solid
Citizens
Variants: Charley, Charles 1880 Today
Sisters: Sophie, Annie, Tess,
Alice, Molly, Nora, Lucy
Brothers: Max, Leo, Jack, Archie, Sam, Harry, Will
✶ Forget the downtrodden everyman Charlie Brown. Today Charlie is chosen by chic parents as a fashionably fusty revival, simple and lovable. In fact, my informal polling points to Charlie as the single most likable name in America.
In the World: *Charlie and the Chocolate Factory*; "Charlie bit my finger" web video; actors Charlie Chaplin and Charlie Sheen

Chase (CHAYS) 2009: #62
Popularity: #69
Styles: Brisk and Breezy, Last Names First, New Classics
Variants: Chace
Sisters: Macy, Paige, Hailey, Laine, Alexa, Autumn
Brothers: Blake, Cole, Mason, Brody, Cooper, Pryce

1880   Today

✷A breezily wealthy name. Chase doesn't just sound like a banker, it sounds like the bank. Of course, that kind of association with moneyed brand names can end up sending a name downscale . . . just ask Tiffany. But Chase's swift simplicity should keep the name smoothly on track.
In the World: Chase Bank; actor Chace Crawford; baseball player Chase Utley

Chayton (CHAY-tən) 2001: #1287
Popularity: #1807
Styles: The "-ens," Why Not?
Nicknames: Chay
Sisters: Shadi, Larkin, Daelyn, Chenoa, Kateri, Cambrie
Brothers: Dyson, Sakari, Carsten, Callan, Pierson, Torin

1880   Today

✷Chayton sounds like one more preppy cousin to Payton and Clayton. In fact, it's a Sioux name meaning "falcon," a heritage that gives Chayton a little extra loft.

Chester (CHEHS-ter) 1918: #54
Popularity: #1772
Styles: Ladies and Gentlemen
Nicknames: Chet
Sisters: Harriet, Frieda, Pauline, Etta, Florence, Ardell
Brothers: Wallace, Gilbert, Sherman, Webster, Thornton, Baxter

1880   Today

✷Chester is an Old English place name with a proud American history, a name of admirals (Nimitz) and presidents (Arthur). And it's gone. Today Chester would be an unexpected choice, feeble but oddly fetching. It's full of personality in the offbeat style of a picture-book character. Parental advisory: an X-rated comic called *Chester the Molester* has introduced that rhyme to the language.
In the World: President Chester Arthur; singer Chester Bennington; a son of actor Tom Hanks

Chris (KRIS) 1961: #57
Popularity: #461
Styles: Nicknames, Surfer '60s
Variants: Kris
Sisters: Cindy, Terri, Beth, Laurie, Tina, Robin, Lisa
Brothers: Eric, Greg, Matt, Kevin, Scott, Tim, Jeff

1880   Today

✷Typically a nickname, "just Chris" was a common given name in the '60s–'70s, when one-syllable names like Keith and Scott were the rage. The problem is that Chris is still a nickname for a bushel of different boys' and girls' names. A fuller version gives your Chris a clearer identity.
In the World: Singer Chris Brown; comedian Chris Rock; actors Chris Hemsworth and Chris Cooper

Christian (KRIS-tchin) 1996: #24
Popularity: #30
Styles: The "-ens," New Classics
Nicknames: Chris
Variants: Kristian
Sisters: Natalie, Brooke, Abigail, Victoria, Hope, Alison
Brothers: Gabriel, Matthew, Nicholas, Julian, Colin, Lucas

1880   Today

✷This contemporary hit has been bidding to supplant Christopher as the dominant "Chris" name. Parents like the modern two-syllable sound of Christian and the forthright declaration of faith that it represents. Beware alternate spellings that feminize the name.
In the World: Actors Christian Bale and Christian Slater; designer Christian Dior; Christian Grey of *Fifty Shades of Grey*

Christopher (KRIS-tə-fer)   1984: #2
Popularity: #21
Styles: New Classics
Nicknames: Chris, Kit, Kip,
Topher   1880   Today
Variants: Kristofer,
Christophe, Cristobal
Sisters: Stephanie, Jessica, Andrea, Nicole,
Tabitha, Amanda, Samantha, Alison
Brothers: Matthew, Jonathan, Andrew, Jeffrey,
Alexander, Timothy, Adam, Nicholas
✱ Christopher has long epitomized the "new
man" image: masculine but sensitive. Its popu-
larity is declining after decades at the top, but
it's still completely fashionable. The nickname
Chris, though, has vaulted into overuse as
Christophers share the space with Christians,
Christinas, and Crystals. The British nick-
names Kip and Kit offer possible escape.
In the World: Actors Christopher Plummer,
Christopher Reeve, and Christopher Walken;
explorer Christopher Columbus

Chuck (CHUHK)   1961: #218
Popularity: Very rare
Styles: Mid-Century,
Nicknames
Sisters: Penny, Vicki, Pam,   1880   Today
Debbie, Ginny, Jackie, Barb,
Suzy
Brothers: Mitch, Doug, Marty, Cliff, Bart,
Chip, Mickey, Hank
✱ Chuck is the anti-style name. It's not as
much out of fashion as immune to it, a steady
island of everyman in a river of sophisticates
and metrosexuals. Hollywood scriptwriters have
leapt on this everyman sound, using the name
for comic effect in the titles of movies and TV
shows. Parents, though, increasingly stick with
Charlie.
In the World: Action star Chuck Norris; TV series *Chuck*; slang term for "throw" (including
"throw up" and "throw out")

Clarence (KLA-rehns)   1895: #17
Popularity: #1009
Styles: Ladies and
Gentlemen, Nickname-Proof,
African-American   1880   Today
Sisters: Louise, Alma,
Florence, Vera, Marion, Marguerite, Harriet,
Lucille
Brothers: Ernest, Clifford, Albert, Luther,
Horace, Claude, Bernard, Francis
✱ Clarence sounds like a kindly gentleman,
old-fashioned and reliable. It's not a rugged
name, but a friendly one—the guardian angel
in *It's a Wonderful Life* is a fine model. The
name's Achilles' heel is a total lack of nick-
names.
In the World: Clarence the angel in *It's a Won-
derful Life*; Supreme Court justice Clarence
Thomas; musician Clarence Clemons

Clark (KLAHRK)   1881: #175
Popularity: #616
Styles: Solid Citizens,
Timeless, Why Not?
Sisters: Janis, Ellen, Polly,   1880   Today
Martha, June, Constance
Brothers: Ward, Carlton, Hal, Lewis, Clyde,
Stuart
✱ Clark is simple, straightforward, and as
manly as actor Clark Gable. Perhaps more peo-
ple think of Superman's alter ego Clark Kent,
but is that really such a bad image? A mild-man-
nered exterior with surprising inner strength.
In the World: Clark Kent (Superman); actor
Clark Gable; Clark shoes; explorers Lewis and
Clark; consumer advocate Clark Howard

Claude (KLAWD, KLOHD)   1887: #46
Popularity: #2686
Styles: Ladies and
Gentlemen, French
Variants: Claud, Claudio,   1880   Today
Claudius
Sisters: Estelle, Cecile, Marguerite, Leonora,
Louise, Blanche, Adele, Pauline
Brothers: Jules, Clement, Luther, Maurice,
Emile, Edmond, Ambrose, Clarence
✱ The perfect French gentleman, Claude has
been dragged down a bit by the clod-like En-
glish pronunciation of the name. (In French, it
has a long "o" sound.) It's still a distinguished
choice, but not a popular one.
In the World: Painter Claude Monet; composer
Claude Debussy; hockey player Claude Giroux

Clay (KLAY) 1960: #263
Popularity: #727
Styles: Timeless, Brisk and
Breezy
Sisters: Hope, Darcy, 1880 Today
Candace, Blair, Jana, Lea
Brothers: Blaine, Reid, Shaw, Davis, Ty, Drew
✷ You're most likely to find Clay as a nickname
for Clayton these days. On its own, it's friendly
and confident and less likely to get lost in the
surname pack.
In the World: Singers Clay Aiken and Clay
Walker; football player Clay Matthews

Clayton (KLAY-tən) 2000: #151
Popularity: #258
Styles: Timeless, Last Names
First, The "-ens"
Nicknames: Clay 1880 Today
Sisters: Audrey, Claire, Avery,
Maya, Caroline, Jillian, Lesley
Brothers: Preston, Nolan, Mitchell, Wesley,
Davis, Harrison, Spencer
✷ Lots of "-n" surnames are popular today, but
Clayton has been popular for generations. That
helps the name sound polished, substantial, and
ready for grown-up responsibility. It's not a
bucket of laughs . . . but that's where carefree
nickname Clay comes in.

Clifford (KLIF-ferd) 1918: #60
Popularity: #1287
Styles: Ladies and
Gentlemen, Solid Citizens,
Namesakes 1880 Today
Nicknames: Cliff
Sisters: Rosalind, Sylvia, Marion, Loretta,
Marjorie, Jeanette, Dorothy, Roberta
Brothers: Warren, Rudolph, Gilbert, Francis,
Lawrence, Vernon, Sherman, Clarence
✷ Clifford the Big Red Dog has given this
name a shaggy image among kids. Once a
young Clifford makes it past elementary school,
though, he'll be fine. If you're drawn more to
the nickname Cliff, Clifton is another strong
alternative. (Heathcliff just turns the cartoon
dog problem into a cartoon cat problem.)
In the World: Clifford the Big Red Dog; jazz
musician Clifford Brown; *Cheers* mailman
Cliff Clavin

Clifton (KLIF-tən) 1915: #144
Popularity: #1462
Styles: Solid Citizens, Last
Names First
Nicknames: Cliff 1880 Today
Sisters: Marjorie, Corrine,
Vivian, Jeanette, Eileen, Rosemary, Lorraine,
Constance
Brothers: Stanton, Harris, Carlton, Nelson,
Forrest, Marshall, Lowell, Truman
✷ The 1920s gentlemanly surname Clifton is
formal, even a little frosty. The nickname Cliff,
though, is a big gruff teddy bear. Today the full
name is the one with the most fashion potential.
It's like a grown-up big brother to today's trendy
surnames.
In the World: Actors Clifton Webb and Clifton
Collins Jr.; Zydeco musician Clifton Chenier

Clint (KLINT) 1980: #193
Popularity: #1580
Styles: Brisk and Breezy,
Country and Western, Macho
Swagger 1880 Today
Sisters: Leigh, Casey, Jody,
Brooke, Liza, Audra, Christa, Darcy
Brothers: Shane, Curt, Heath, Clay, Jed, Travis,
Craig, Brock
✷ The essence of this name comes straight
from the flinty stare of Clint Eastwood. His
image gives Clint ageless grit. Using Clinton as
a full name gives you a versatile pair, ready for
every occasion from rodeo to black-tie soirée.
In the World: Actors Clint Eastwood and Clint
Walker; soccer player Clint Dempsey

Clinton (KLIN-tən) 1981: #124
Popularity: #923
Styles: Last Names First, The
"-ens," Timeless
Nicknames: Clint 1880 Today
Sisters: Lindsay, Jillian, Sara,
Jocelyn, Joanna, Holly, Lesley, Candice
Brothers: Mitchell, Preston, Nelson, Clayton,
Barrett, Ross, Byron, Stanton
✷ Presidents used to inspire namesakes, but
today they do the opposite. The timeless Clin-
ton fell away after President Bill Clinton took
office, as parents sought to avoid a political
statement. Then Hillary Clinton hit Washing-
ton too. That left the name in a long fashion
limbo, but I wouldn't count this name out. It's a
distinguished choice with a classic nickname
and still sounds timeless. See also Clint.
In the World: Bill and Hillary Clinton; stylist
Clinton Kelly

Clive (KLIYV) 1906: #752
Popularity: #2369
Styles: English, Brisk and Breezy
Variants: Cliff
1880 Today
Sisters: Dulcie, Gemma, Imogen, Tilly, Glynis, Pippa
Brothers: Hugh, Piers, Carleton, Ivor, Niles, Graeme
✶ This smooth, urbane old British name comes from the same root as gruff old buddy Cliff. So far, Americans have left the sleeker cousin on the other side of the Atlantic. It's sounding more usable today, though, as other sleek Brits like Trevor and Sebastian have settled in stateside.
In the World: Actor Clive Owen; writers Clive Barker and Clive Cussler; music executive Clive Davis

Cloud (CLOWD) 2010: #3862
Popularity: #3987
Styles: Modern Meanings, Fantastical
Sisters: Aeris, Poet, Lux, Rogue, Halo, Raine, Serenity, Sol
1880 Today
Brothers: Arrow, Link, Truth, Talon, Jett, Hawk, Jax, Reef
✶ Cloud Strife is a popular protagonist of the "Final Fantasy" video game series. A mercenary, Cloud is recognizable for his massively oversized sword. That fighting image has directed attention to this otherwise gentle name. You can use it in homage to the character or as a unique and purely masculine nature name.
In the World: Cloud Strife of "Final Fantasy" video game series

Clyde (KLIYD) 1905: #53
Popularity: #1175
Styles: Solid Citizens
Sisters: Stella, Faye, Irene, Rhoda, Polly, Maxine
1880 Today
Brothers: Elton, Clifford, Leon, Lewis, Guy, Clark
✶ Between *Bonnie and Clyde* and Walt ("Clyde") Frazier, this name acquired a cocky swagger in the late '60s. It's quite a contrast with the name's natural country-gentleman restraint. The result is an odd but intriguing chimera, part gent and part jive.
In the World: Outlaw Clyde Barrow; basketball players Clyde Drexler and Walt ("Clyde") Frazier

Cody (KOH-dee) 1992: #24
Popularity: #175
Styles: Country and Western, Last Names First, Nickname-Proof, Turn of the 21st Century
1880 Today
Variants: Kody
Sisters: Shelby, Cassidy, Morgan, Kelsey, Sierra, Haley
Brothers: Logan, Casey, Dillon, Jesse, Chad, Austin
✶ Cody is a classic "new cowboy" name, calling up the image of showman Buffalo Bill Cody and the Wyoming city that bears his name. It is distinguished by an eternal boyishness. Like Toby or Corey, Cody is a name that just doesn't want to grow up.
In the World: Buffalo Bill Cody; wrestler Cody Rhodes; singer Cody Simpson; a son of TV host Kathie Lee Gifford

Cohen (KOH-ehn) 2009: #323
Popularity: #336
Styles: The "-ens"
Variants: Kohen, Cowan
Sisters: Emery, Tatum, Presley, Marlee, Hadley, Ainsley, Addyson, Brinley
1880 Today
Brothers: Paxton, Caiden, Zander, Landen, Camden, Brody, Tripp, Weston
✶ Surnames of the British Isles are a hot American name style. Surnames of Jewish tradition are not . . . except for this one. Cohen is a surprising hit name, propelled by its simple, trendy sound (and by comedian Sacha Baron Cohen). Ironically, religious Jews consider Cohen inappropriate as a baby name; it's a title of the ancient priests of Israel and their descendants. Cowan is an unrelated Celtic surname.

Colby (KOHL-bee) 2001: #99
Popularity: #314
Styles: Last Names First, Bell
Tones
Nicknames: Cole 1880 Today
Variants: Kolby
Sisters: Taylor, Sage, Alyssa, Carsyn, Lacey,
Carly
Brothers: Brody, Cooper, Dawson, Tucker,
Grady, Dalton
✷ Colby is a leader of the popular pack of boy-
ish surnames. It's a little preppier than Brady
and Riley, a little more grown-up than Cody
and Corey, and endowed with a side benefit
none of those can offer: a fashionable nick-
name.
In the World: Colby College; Colby cheese; *Dy-
nasty* TV spinoff *The Colbys*

Cole (KOHL) 2002: #69
Popularity: #94
Styles: Brisk and Breezy,
Nicknames, New Classics
Variants: Nicholas 1880 Today
Sisters: Brooke, Carly, Ava,
Ella, Tessa, Claire
Brothers: Grant, Owen, Luke, Chase, Dylan,
Blake
✷ Cole is a politician's dream—a name that
pleases every constituency. It has the bluntness
of a cowboy name, the briskness of a preppy
name, and the sophistication of a Cole Porter
tune. A showstopper.
In the World: Songwriter Cole Porter; actors
Cole Hauser and Cole Sprouse; Cole Haan
shoes; nursery rhyme character Old King Cole;
cole slaw

Coleman (KOHL-min) 1903: #360
Popularity: #912
Styles: Last Names First,
Guys and Dolls, Why Not?
Nicknames: Cole 1880 Today
Variants: Colman
Sisters: Della, Annabel, Cassidy, Adeline,
Ruby, Harlow
Brothers: Walker, Deacon, Truman, Miles,
Turner, Cooper
✷ This lively surname is anchored by the cov-
eted nickname Cole. It's a colorful, rugged an-
tique. Also consider the Irish saint's name
Colman for a Celtic kick.
In the World: Jazz musician Coleman Hawkins;
Coleman camping gear

Colin (KAH-lin, KOH-lin) 2004: #84
Popularity: #120
Styles: New Classics, Celtic,
The "-ens," English,
Nickname-Proof 1880 Today
Variants: Collin
Sisters: Audrey, Claire, Fiona, Jocelyn, Chloe,
Miranda
Brothers: Ian, Graham, Trevor, Brendan,
Gavin, Connor
✷ This Celtic/English favorite is a balanced
choice, contemporary but familiar. You can also
choose it as an old-fashioned nickname for
Nicholas, akin to Robin for Robert. It's a top
choice in the Northeast and upper Midwest.
In the World: Actors Colin Farrell and Colin
Firth; military leader Colin Powell; auto racer
Colin McRae

Colman (KOHL-mən) 1909: #1083
Popularity: #8132
Styles: Celtic, The "-ens,"
Saints
Nicknames: Cole 1880 Today
Variants: Coleman
Sisters: Keyna, Maeve, Kinnia, Mabyn, Nola,
Sian
Brothers: Fintan, Dermot, Tynan, Cormac,
Brogan, Cronan
✷ This spelling is seldom seen in the U.S.—the
surname Coleman is far more common. But
you can get that surname sound with a bonus
Celtic kick by choosing the Irish saint's name
Colman.
In the World: More than 100 different Irish
saints; Colman's mustard

Colt (KOHLT) 2011: #327
Popularity: #326
Styles: Country and Western,
Brisk and Breezy, Macho
Swagger 1880 Today
Variants: Kolt
Sisters: Aspen, Shiloh, Landry, Bree, Scarlett,
Shelby, Cassidy, Ashlyn
Brothers: Cash, Gauge, Maverick, Bridger, Ty,
Jett, Chance, Jarrett
✷ A colt is a spirited young horse, a football
mascot, and an American firearms manufac-
turer. Those combined images have made Colt
a hot name, especially in the West. Some par-
ents lengthen the name to Colton or Colter for
a "formal" version, but the original packs the
strongest punch.
In the World: Football players Colt McCoy and
Colt Brennan; *Fall Guy* TV character Colt
Seavers

Colton (KOHL-tən)   2011: #74
Popularity: #74
Styles: The "-ens," Country
and Western, Last Names
First
Nicknames: Colt
Sisters: Rylee, Cassidy, Kelsey, Carsyn, Shelby,
Sierra
Brothers: Hunter, Cody, Tanner, Cooper,
Landon, Bryce
✳ Colt has a clear image: young, tough, and
feisty. The extended-play-version Colton dresses
the young cowboy up in his Sunday best.

Conan (KOH-nin)   1981: #1151
Popularity: #3301
Styles: Celtic, The "-ens,"
Saints, Fantastical,
Nickname-Proof
Sisters: Morrigan, Enya,
Rhian, Eowyn, Aeris, Niamh
Brothers: Ronin, Payne, Crispin, Lorcan,
Brannock, Taran
✳ If you pronounce it like Conan the Barbar-
ian ("KOH-NAN"), this name is a lot to live up
to. If you pronounce it "KOH-nin," like the Irish
saint (or late-night host Conan O'Brien), you
have an unusual choice that should fit in com-
fortably.
In the World: TV host Conan O'Brien; Conan
the Barbarian; actor Conan Stevens

Connor (KAHN-er)   2004: #38
Popularity: #54
Styles: Celtic, New Classics
Nicknames: Con, Connie
Variants: Conor, Conner,
Konnor, Conchobar
Sisters: Kiera, Morgan, Daniela, Summer,
Fiona, McKenna
Brothers: Dylan, Carson, Riley, Trevor,
Cameron, Garrett
✳ This bold Irish standard has become a favor-
ite of Americans of every heritage. Connor has
some of the flavor of surnames like Tanner but
is a classic first name that has always been well
used in Ireland. The spellings Connor and
Conor are both traditional; Conner adds an
image of con men.
In the World: Singer Conor Oberst; actor Con-
nor Paolo; Connor Cruise, actor son of Tom
Cruise and Nicole Kidman

Conrad (KAHN-rad)   1931: #213
Popularity: #804
Styles: Ladies and
Gentlemen, Shakespearean
Nicknames: Con, Connie
Variants: Konrad
Sisters: Elinor, Greta, Alma, Frances, Cordelia,
Louisa
Brothers: Edmond, Bertram, Rudolph,
Frederick, August, Roland
✳ You'll meet plenty of little boys answering to
"Con," almost all of them Connors. Conrad is a
heavier name but a powerful one. An authority
figure named Conrad is a force to be reckoned
with.
In the World: Hotelier Conrad Hilton; actor
Conrad Bain; writer Joseph Conrad

Cooper (KOO-per)   2011: #82
Popularity: #82
Styles: Last Names First,
Country and Western
Nicknames: Coop
Sisters: Hannah, Riley, Piper,
Ella, Scarlett, Landry
Brothers: Carson, Sawyer, Tucker, Wyatt,
Carter, Brody
✳ Cooper is a trendy name that makes even
skeptical traditionalists smile. The name's in-
fectious good humor helps it stand out among
the many popular tradesman names. (A cooper
was a maker of wooden barrels.) Cooper also
has a frontier feeling thanks to *High Noon* star
Gary Cooper and *Last of the Mohicans* author
James Fenimore Cooper.
In the World: Actor Gary Cooper; writer James
Fenimore Cooper; the college Cooper Union

Corbin (KOHR-bin)   2011: #208
Popularity: #207
Styles: The "-ens"
Nicknames: Cory
Variants: Korbin
Sisters: Macy, Camryn,
Cassidy, Tatum, Kenzie, Brenna
Brothers: Gavin, Cameron, Tucker, Tobin,
Myles, Dawson
✳ Corbin is boyishly attractive, a modern hit in
the mold of Celtic classics. Its emergence in the
'80s was part zeitgeist and part the influence of
L.A. Law star Corbin Bernsen.
In the World: Actors Corbin Bleu and Corbin
Bernsen

Corey (KOH-ree) 1989: #55
Popularity: #312
Styles: '70s–'80s, Bell Tones,
Nickname-Proof
Variants: Cory, Korey, Kory 1880 Today
Sisters: Tara, Whitney,
Kelsey, Shana, Tiffany, Krista
Brothers: Chad, Dustin, Casey, Erik, Torrey,
Brett
★ This was *the* cute boy's name for years, epitomized by Lisa Simpson's mooning over *Corey!* magazine. Corey helped draft a new blueprint for boyishness: not diminutives, but full names with an eternally youthful sound. Corey still sounds young today, even as it passes the torch to the generation of Brody, Colby, and beyond.
In the World: Actors Corey Feldman and Corey Haim; singers Corey Hart and Corey Taylor

Cormac (KOHR-mak, 2011: #1175
KOHR-mik)
Popularity: #1176
Styles: Celtic, Saints, Literary
and Artistic, Why Not? 1880 Today
Nicknames: Mac
Sisters: Aine, Rhian, Kiara, Rory, Sorcha,
Finola
Brothers: Declan, Conall, Aidric, Ronan,
Dermot, Callum
★ It's remarkable that the success of writer Cormac McCarthy (*All the Pretty Horses*) hasn't brought this Irish favorite to America's attention. Cormac's crackling consonants make for a smart, rugged sound. The name has a long and storied history in Ireland, but a disputed origin. Some claim it means "charioteer," others the unappealing "son of defilement."
In the World: Writer Cormac McCarthy

Cornelius (kohr-NEE-lee-əs) 1882: #130
Popularity: #1158
Styles: Ladies and
Gentlemen, Exotic
Traditional, Shakespearean, 1880 Today
Classical, Biblical
Nicknames: Con, Connie, Corny, Neil
Variants: Cornell, Cornelis
Sisters: Eugenia, Minerva, Drusilla,
Clementine, Viola, Ophelia
Brothers: Augustus, Ferdinand, Alonzo,
Tiberius, Bartholomew, Conrad
★ Cornelius is a name straight out of ancient Rome. If you're tempted to pronounce it with an Irish accent, though, you're not alone. The name was popular in Ireland as a variant on the Gaelic Conchobar (much like contemporary favorite Connor). Choose a strong nickname like Con or Neil to counteract the "corny" sound.
In the World: Industrialist Cornelius Vanderbilt; Dr. Cornelius of *Planet of the Apes*

Cosmo (KAWZ-moh) 1913: #930
Popularity: #4357
Styles: Exotic Traditional,
Guys and Dolls
Nicknames: Mo, Cos 1880 Today
Variants: Cosimo, Cosmas
Sisters: Beatrix, Freya, Eloise, Olympia, Clio,
Avis
Brothers: Milo, Tobias, Benno, Rollo, Felix,
Vitus
★ This quirky classic acts as a "personality multiplier." It makes a cool guy seem cooler, a stylish guy snappier, a leader more dynamic. For a geeky or pudgy kid, though, it just adds to the burden. (Fun with etymology: Cosmo derives from the Greek word for "harmonious order," which is the root behind both "cosmos" and "cosmetics.")
In the World: TV characters Cosmo Kramer of *Seinfeld* and Cosmo of *The Fairly OddParents*

Craig (KRAYG)   1960: #42
Popularity: #811
Styles: Surfer '60s, Celtic
Variants: Kraig
Sisters: Belinda, Carla, Jill,   1880   Today
Darcy, Rhonda, Lesley
Brothers: Keith, Neil, Cameron, Scott,
Kenneth, Gregg
✴ Craig came on like gangbusters in the '50s and '60s, but there's no need for it to fade as quickly. Its craggy Scottish sound fits in with current favorites from Bryce to Carson. This is a case where sound and meaning mesh: "Craig" and "craggy" come from the same Gaelic word meaning "rock."
In the World: Website Craigslist.org; TV hosts Craig Ferguson and Craig Kilborn; comedian Craig Robinson

Crispin (KRIS-pin)   2007: #2964
Popularity: #4499
Styles: The "-ens," English,
Saints, Why Not?
Nicknames: Cris   1880   Today
Sisters: Tamsin, Beatrix,
Mabyn, Felicity, Gemma, Davina
Brothers: Corin, Barnaby, Tarquin, Felix,
Dunstan, Ivor
✴ In the past, American parents found Crispin a little too cute for comfort. But now that we have little Devins and Kaydens on every block, Crispin's medieval saintly flavor shines through. This high-impact name will make other parents say, "Ooh, good one!"
In the World: Actor Crispin Glover

Cruz (CROOS, CROOZ)   2011: #301
Popularity: #300
Styles: Latino/Latina, Brisk
and Breezy, Saints
Sisters: Sol, Bianca, Jade,   1880   Today
Reina, Cielo, Lourdes
Brothers: Diego, Jude, Cash, Joaquin, Maximo, Blaise
✴ Spanish for "cross," Cruz is a religious name that comes across as macho in English. It's one part reverence, one part Tom Cruise.
In the World: A son of David and Victoria Beckham

Cullen (KUH-lin)   2010: #413
Popularity: #471
Styles: The "-ens," Last
Names First, Celtic,
Fantastical   1880   Today
Sisters: Lyla, Kendall, Finley,
Maisie, Tierney, Rowan
Brothers: Connor, Finn, Kieran, Brogan,
Griffin, Cameron
✴ Familiar as a last name, Cullen is now poised to join many of its surname brethren as a hot baby name. It has an appealing Celtic lilt and stands a small, fashionable step off the well-beaten path. The Cullen family of the "Twilight" saga has pushed the name's style toward the vampiric for now.
In the World: Olympic swimmer Cullen Jones; Edward Cullen of the "Twilight" series

Curtis (KER-tis)   1962: #73
Popularity: #438
Styles: Timeless,
Shakespearean
Nicknames: Curt   1880   Today
Sisters: Teresa, Yvonne,
Regina, Cynthia, Colleen, Anita
Brothers: Byron, Douglas, Clinton, Ross,
Dwight, Mitchell
✴ Curtis is a quiet, solid man's name that has become an American classic. The nickname Curt gives it toughness, while the full name reflects its origin in the word "courteous."
In the World: Singer Curtis Mayfield; director Curtis Hanson; comic strip *Curtis*

Cyrus (SIY-ruhs)   1886: #220
Popularity: #514
Styles: Antique Charm,
Classical, Biblical, Ladies
and Gentlemen   1880   Today
Nicknames: Cy
Sisters: Augusta, Lydia, Coraline, Viola,
Delilah, Aurelia
Brothers: Jonas, Porter, Abram, Elias, Simeon,
Titus
✴ Cyrus is a genuine surprise. For generations the name nestled in the dustbin with historical curiosities like Hiram and Cyril. Yet it's nudging its way toward a comeback, and once you stop to pay attention, the name does show off some creaky magnetism. Hiram, you're up next!
In the World: Inventor Cyrus McCormick; Secretary of State Cyrus Vance

Dakota (də-KOH-tə)   1995: #56
Popularity: #313
Styles: Place Names,
Androgynous, Country and
Western, Turn of the 21st   1880   Today
Century
Nicknames: Koty, Dak
Variants: Dakotah
Sisters: Cheyenne, Sierra, Montana, Laramie,
Sedona, Cassidy
Brothers: Tanner, Wyatt, Dillon, Phoenix,
Landry, Maverick
✳ This name evokes the wide-open Western
skies. It jumps right out at you because it doesn't
sound like a traditional boy's name. That kind
of distinctive style can backfire, though, when a
name becomes popular. You can meet a dozen
Toms and think nothing of it, but meet a few
Dakotas and you notice the trend.
In the World: Dodge Dakota trucks; soldier Da-
kota Meyer; actress Dakota Fanning

Dale (DAYL)   1958: #46
Popularity: #1115
Styles: Solid Citizens,
Androgynous, Brisk and
Breezy   1880   Today
Sisters: Connie, Elaine, Jo,
Glenna, Therese, Lynn
Brothers: Royce, Lyle, Dean, Wayne, Hale, Roy
✳ Dale, the simple, urbane hit of the '30s and
'40s, now has a rebellious side. It's linked to
"The Intimidator," legendary NASCAR driver
Dale Earnhardt.
In the World: Drivers Dale Earnhardt Jr. and Sr.;
leadership trainer Dale Carnegie; cartoon chip-
munks Chip 'n' Dale

Dallas (DAL-əs)   1995: #214
Popularity: #327
Styles: Place Names, Country
and Western, Timeless,
Nickname-Proof   1880   Today
Sisters: Marley, Savannah,
Cassidy, Darcy, Sierra, Shelby
Brothers: Clayton, Garrett, Walker, Forrest,
Jarvis, Houston
✳ Dallas was originally a Scottish place name
and surname, but today it locates you deep in
the heart of Texas. Unlike other Western place
names, though, Dallas isn't a cowboy throw-
back. It's a name of the new, urban West.
In the World: *Dallas* TV series; football player
Dallas Clark; Dallas Cowboys

Dalton (DAHL-tuhn)   1998: #88
Popularity: #276
Styles: Last Names First, The
"-ens," Nickname-Proof, Turn
of the 21st Century, Country   1880   Today
and Western
Sisters: Shelby, Ashton, Savannah, Kendall,
Sydney, Autry
Brothers: Tanner, Dillon, Chandler, Barkley,
Easton, Dawson
✳ Dalton is one of the old-time surnames, part
of the staid, pipe-smoking world of Palmer,
Sumner, and Winston. But that buttoned-down
look can easily turn youthful today, especially if
there's any Western-style hook to hang it on. For
Dalton, the 1890s Dalton Gang of train robbers
does the trick. In New York and surrounding
areas, Dalton is known as an exclusive prep
school and is seldom used as a name.
In the World: Dalton School; Dalton Gang;
writer Dalton Trumbo

Damian (DAY-mee-ən)   2010: #121
Popularity: #138
Styles: The "-ens,"
Nickname-Proof, Saints, New
Classics   1880   Today
Variants: Damien
Sisters: Nadia, Giselle, Regan, Ariana, Maya,
Daniela
Brothers: Adrian, Devin, Xavier, Dominic,
Sebastian, Ronan
✳ Several decades of steady use haven't robbed
this name of its exotic flair. Damian is hand-
some, elegant, and decidedly devilish. The '70s
horror flick *The Omen* played off the demon-
like sound in naming its hellchild—and oddly
enough, the name's popularity has soared ever
since.
In the World: Damien of *The Omen*; musicians
Damian Marley and Damien Rice; artist
Damien Hirst

Damon (DAY-mən) 1976: #104
Popularity: #414
Styles: New Classics, The
"-ens," Mythological,
Nickname-Proof 1880 Today
Sisters: Sonia, Adrienne,
Tara, Nadia, Meredith, Regan
Brothers: Lance, Quentin, Andre, Devin,
Tobin, Darius
✶ This age-old name has a bold modern sound
that has made it a favorite of American parents.
For extra-positive vibes, the classical Greek tale
of Damon and Pythias celebrates friendship and
loyalty.
In the World: Comedian Damon Wayans; writer
Damon Runyon; singer Damon Albarn

Dana (DAY-nə) 1962: #172
Popularity: #2897
Styles: Androgynous,
Mid-Century
Sisters: Gwen, Lana, Gayle, 1880 Today
Patrice, Lynne, Sonia
Brothers: Cary, Robin, Dale, Kent, Jody, Neal
✶ Dana is a blithe, upscale boy's name, done in
by gender confusion. Try Dane for a contempo-
rary boys-only successor.
In the World: Comedian Dana Carvey; actor
Dana Andrews; actress Dana Delany

Dane (DAYN) 1986: #220
Popularity: #469
Styles: Brisk and Breezy
Variants: Dana, Dean
Sisters: Paige, Avery, Jocelyn, 1880 Today
Reese, Shea, Aubrey
Brothers: Drew, Colt, Tyler, Tate, Evan, Drake
✶ As Dana has lost ground on the boys' side,
this simple variant has taken hold in its place.
Previously a British name, Dane is still on the
preppy side but has picked up some of the cow-
boy aura of similar names Shane and Zane . . .
and the goofy aura of comedian Dane Cook.
In the World: Comedian Dane Cook; actor
Dane DeHaan; Great Dane dogs

Daniel (DAN-yəl) 1985: #5
Popularity: #10
Styles: Timeless, Biblical
Nicknames: Dan, Danny
Variants: Danyel 1880 Today
Sisters: Rachel, Laura, Sarah,
Diana, Rebecca, Stephanie
Brothers: Benjamin, David, Matthew, Thomas,
Jonathan, Michael
✶ Daniel is one of the few Old Testament
names to be a rock-solid American classic. It was
a top hit even back when Jacob and Joshua were
considered ancient relics. As a result, Daniel
sounds less tied to its biblical roots and more
grounded in the modern world. It's friendly,
handsome, and universally liked.
In the World: A global favorite, from pioneer
Daniel Boone to "Harry Potter" actor Daniel
Radcliffe

Dante (DAHN-tay) 1998: #201
Popularity: #268
Styles: Italian, African-
American, Literary and
Artistic, Nickname-Proof, 1880 Today
Fantastical
Variants: Donte, Dontae, Deonte, Durante
Sisters: Gianna, Serena, Daria, Bianca, India,
Paola, Scarlett, Simone
Brothers: Darius, Marco, Dorian, Leonardo,
Vincent, Demetrius, Matteo, Andre
✶ This name was originally bestowed in honor
of Inferno poet Dante Alighieri, an association
that gave the name arty pizzazz. That pizzazz
has stuck around even as the name has become
more popular and less exotic. If you're really in
the market for the unusual, consider that Dante
was a pet form of the poet's given name, Du-
rante.
In the World: Poets Dante Alighieri and Dante
Gabriel Rosetti; protagonist of the "Devil May
Cry" video game series

Darian (DA-ree-ən) 1994: #357
Popularity: #695
Styles: Nickname-Proof, The
"-ens," African-American
Variants: Darien, Darrian, 1880 Today
Darrien, Darrion
Sisters: Ashton, Keely, Jaylen, Tiana, Janae,
Kayla
Brothers: Austen, Kieran, Trevin, Skylar,
Jamison, Keon
✴ An attractive collage of a name, Darian is
part Damian, part Dorian, part the ultra-preppy
Connecticut suburb Darien. For bonus points,
it's even an anagram of another top name. (Got
it yet? Adrian.)

Darius (DA-ree-uhs) 1994: #155
Popularity: #383
Styles: Saints, African-
American, Classical,
Nickname-Proof 1880 Today
Variants: Dario
Sisters: Serena, Lysandra, Octavia, Celeste,
Livia, Alexis
Brothers: Quentin, Damian, Isaias, Trajan,
Xavier, Adrian
✴ This ancient royal name still sounds exotic,
but its rare combination of graces has propelled
it into the mainstream. Antique and creative,
serious and sexy, Darius is a thinking girl's
hunk.
In the World: Singer Darius Rucker; composer
Darius Milhaud; actor Darius McCrary

Darrell (DA-rəl) 1958: #90
Popularity: #689
Styles: Surfer '60s, Mid-
Century, African-American,
Nickname-Proof 1880 Today
Variants: Darryl, Daryl,
Darrel, Daryle, Derrell
Sisters: Denise, Brenda, Sheila, Michelle,
Suzanne, Wanda
Brothers: Randall, Jarrod, Terrence, Dwayne,
Bruce, Dwight
✴ Darrell is a Norman baronial surname that
parents flocked to in the middle of the last cen-
tury. By now its aristocratic aura has worn off,
but the name continues along amiably. The '60s
variant Darryl is aging faster than the original.
In the World: Auto racer Darrell Waltrip; base-
ball player Darryl Strawberry; TV brothers
Larry, Darryl, and Darryl of *Newhart*

Darren (DA-rin) 1965: #52
Popularity: #415
Styles: Surfer '60s, The
"-ens," Nickname-Proof
Variants: Darin, Darrin, 1880 Today
Daren, Darron
Sisters: Carla, Denise, Holly, Lisa, Renee,
Dana
Brothers: Byron, Geoffrey, Marc, Jordan,
Derek, Craig
✴ The "Mack the Knife" singer was Bobby
Darin. The *Bewitched* husband was *Darrin* Ste-
phens. And every spelling of this name you can
dream up hit the charts simultaneously in the
1960s. The name has survived that tumultuous
childhood and is now a smooth, steady choice
for a grown man.
In the World: Actor Darren Criss; director Dar-
ren Aronofsky; *Bewitched* TV husband Darrin
Stephens

Darwin (DAHR-win) 1935: #299
Popularity: #764
Styles: Namesakes, Last
Names First
Variants: Darwen, Derwent 1880 Today
Sisters: Roselyn, Carroll,
Nadine, Marlys, Ilene, Ardith
Brothers: Farrell, Winston, Sherwood, Cornell,
Leland, Newton
✴ This name takes on heavy political connota-
tions from its association with Darwin's theory
of evolution. Perhaps you don't care a whit
about Charles Darwin's studies in the Galápa-
gos Islands, but others do—making this either a
hero name or a guilt-by-association name de-
pending on personal convictions.
In the World: Naturalist Charles Darwin; the
tongue-in-cheek "Darwin Awards"

Dashiell (DASH-əl, DASH-ee-əl) 2010: #1209
Popularity: #1343
Styles: Exotic Traditional, Literary and Artistic, Why Not?
Nicknames: Dash
Sisters: Marlowe, Beatrix, Scarlett, Blythe, Ellery, Briar
Brothers: Langston, Calder, Roman, Finnegan, Atticus, Beckett
✷ Can a name be too cool? With the imprint of Sam Spade creator Dashiell Hammett and the nickname Dash, this one is a veritable dry martini. If you think your kid can pull it off, go for it.
In the World: Writer Dashiell Hammett; a son of actress Cate Blanchett

David (DAY-vid) 1955: #2
Popularity: #18
Styles: Timeless, Biblical
Nicknames: Dave, Davy
Sisters: Rebecca, Susan, Deborah, Sarah, Karen, Diana
Brothers: Michael, Andrew, Daniel, Thomas, Mark, Steven
✷ The classic boys' names always have snappy good-guy nicknames: Mike, Matt, Jim, Jake , , and Dave. But you can get too much of a good-guy thing. The generation raised in the '70s and '80s was surrounded by Daves and is starting to shy away from the name. Of course, that could mean an opportunity for your little David to be the only one in his class. This is also a strong choice for multilingual families, since it's spelled the same in many languages.
In the World: From *David Copperfield* to David Beckham, there are too many examples for any to dominate

Davis (DAY-vis) 2001: #361
Popularity: #436
Styles: Last Names First, Timeless, Why Not?
Nicknames: Dave, Davey
Sisters: Audrey, Claire, Elise, Macy, Caroline, Laine
Brothers: Bennett, Grant, Brooks, Preston, Elliott, Harrison
✷ This handsome name is pleasantly familiar, even though you've probably never met a Davis in person. It's distinctive in a quiet way that appeals across generations.
In the World: Davis Cup tennis competition

Dawson (DAW-sən) 1999: #136
Popularity: #316
Styles: The "-ens," Last Names First, Nickname-Proof
Sisters: Payton, Delaney, Marley, Camryn, Tatum, Macy, Bailey, Regan
Brothers: Tanner, Keegan, Brennan, Easton, Sawyer, Keaton, Parker, Dillon
✷ The TV series *Dawson's Creek* popularized this name. (What, you thought it was Richard Dawson from *Family Feud*?) The name's muscular surname sound has helped it outlive the TV show. Lawson is an up-and-coming alternative.
In the World: *Dawson's Creek*

Dayton (DAY-tən) 2008: #485
Popularity: #610
Styles: Last Names First, The "-ens," Place Names, Nickname-Proof
Sisters: Reilly, London, Dakota, Aubry, Madelyn, Berkeley
Brothers: Brighton, Parker, Canton, Dallas, Hudson, Porter
✷ Like Trenton and Camden—and unlike Paris—this city name is usually chosen for its sound, not its geography. But the Rust Belt is surprisingly fertile ground for contemporary names. (How about Flint while we're at it?)
In the World: Dayton, Ohio; actor Dayton Callie; Dayton Wire Wheels

Deacon (DEE-kən) 2011: #663
Popularity: #662
Styles: Country and Western, Last Names First, Why Not?
Nicknames: Deke
Sisters: Oakley, Larkin, Shiloh, Everly, Harper, Scarlett
Brothers: Truman, Archer, Winslow, Shepard, Gibson, Cooper
✷ A deacon is a cleric or church officer, which sounds like a recipe for laced-up propriety. As a name, though, Deacon has a maverick Western style. When actress Reese Witherspoon chose this name for her son, a lot of parents took note of its stylish throwback sound.
In the World: Football player Deacon Jones; comic-book vampire Deacon Frost

Dean (DEEN)   1961: #84
Popularity: #284
Styles: Brisk and Breezy,
Solid Citizens, Mid-Century
Variants: Deane, Dane   1880   Today
Sisters: Connie, Janet,
Donna, Gwen, Julie, Kathleen
Brothers: Alan, Jay, Troy, Kenneth, Neal, Ross
✳ Dean is an old favorite with a clean sound. It's square in the best way, like a letterman sweater or a formal dinner date. The name wasn't always so clean-cut, though. It peaked in the years immediately following the death of teen-rebel icon James Dean.
In the World: Entertainer Dean Martin; writer Dean Koontz; actor Dean Stockwell

DeAndre (dee-AHN-dray)   1995: #250
Popularity: #511
Styles: African-American,
Turn of the 21st Century
Nicknames: Dre   1880   Today
Variants: D'Andre, Deondre,
D'Ondre, DeAndrae
Sisters: Destiny, Janae, Jasmine, Deja, Amaya,Tianna
Brothers: Darion, Marquis, Tavion, Shamar, DeAngelo, Tyrell
✳ "De-" was the hot prefix of the 1990s, especially for African-American parents. It could transform almost any "ordinary" name into the style of a Romance-language surname like DeMille or DeCaprio. DeAndre was the dean of this style and remains a hit. Many parents have customized the spelling, often with apostrophes (D'Andre) or the popular "Deon-" root (Deondre).
In the World: Basketball player DeAndre Jordan; actor Dondre Whitfield

Declan (DEHK-lahn)   2011: #177
Popularity: #177
Styles: Celtic, Saints
Nicknames: Dec, Dex
Sisters: Fiona, Maeve, Keira,   1880   Today
Aislin, Deirdre, Niamh
Brothers: Eamon, Conor, Ronan, Seamus, Kieran, Finn
✳ Declan was an exclusively Irish name until the '90s. Its handsome, saintly style is now widely in demand, and the name is becoming fashionable in the U.S. That may take a bit of the exotic edge off the name, but it remains distinctive and unmistakably Irish.

Demetrius   1991: #259
(deh-MEE-tree-uhs)
Popularity: #581
Styles: Exotic Traditional,
Saints, Shakespearean,   1880   Today
African-American, Classical
Variants: Dimitrios, Demetrio, Dimitri
Sisters: Serena, Angelique, Lysandra, Athena, Cassandra, Leticia
Brothers: Marcellus, Titus, Quinton, Darius, Emmanuel, Andreas
✳ Classical names have a natural gravity that lets them get away with pushing the style envelope. Case in point: Demetrius, an ornate name that sounds dignified rather than fancified. (Sounds pretty studly too.)
In the World: Football player Demetrius Bell; several ancient kings

Dennis (DEHN-is)   1946: #17
Popularity: #413
Styles: Mid-Century
Nicknames: Denny
Variants: Dennison, Denis   1880   Today
Sisters: Kathleen, Janet,
Sandra, Diane, Bonnie, Sharon
Brothers: Gary, Randall, Steven, Bruce, Gregory, Curtis
✳ It's time to forget about Dennis the Menace. Dennis isn't a little ruffian anymore. He's a stand-up guy, the good-natured, honorable sort you always want on your side. Yet as grown-up as the name sounds, it's still cheery enough for a young boy.
In the World: Comic strip *Dennis the Menace*; actors Dennis Hopper and Dennis Quaid; basketball player Dennis Rodman

Denzel (DEHN-ZEHL)   1993: #310
Popularity: #1152
Styles: African-American,
Namesakes
Variants: Denzil   1880   Today
Sisters: Ciara, Janae, Chantal,
Dasia, Kelis, Asha
Brothers: Keenan, Desmond, Markell, Devin, Vontae, Cortez
✳ A quirky old Cornish surname, now overwhelmingly associated with actor Denzel Washington. As we start to meet more little Denzels, the connection will loosen, but for the time being the name will be taken as an homage to the star.
In the World: Actor Denzel Washington

Derek (DEH-rik)   1987: #54
Popularity: #181
Styles: New Classics,
Nickname-Proof
Variants: Derrick, Deric,   1880   Today
Dietrich, Dirk
Sisters: Vanessa, Holly, Kendra, Jillian, Andrea,
Leslie
Brothers: Trevor, Colin, Jared, Kyle, Garrett,
Devin
✻ To earlier American generations, Derek was
a name like Nigel or Clive: classic British. The
name has now discarded its British image but
kept a grown-up elegance that distinguishes it
from other more boyish '80s favorites. The pop-
ular alternative spelling Derrick (like an oil rig)
is completely American.
In the World: Baseball player Derek Jeter;
dancer Derek Hough; basketball player Derrick
Rose; actor Derek Jacobi

Dermot (DER-mət)   1969. #2046
Popularity: Very rare
Styles: Celtic, Saints
Nicknames: Darby
Variants: Diarmuid   1880   Today
Sisters: Aoife, Liadan,
Niamh, Siobhan, Aine, Riona
Brothers: Colm, Brannock, Lorcan, Niall,
Cormac, Finian
✻ Kermit is a cute Irish name, but it suffers
from a serious frog problem. Not to worry,
there's a non-green relative waiting in the
wings. The related name Dermot gives you Irish
style with a distinctive sound that won't blend in
too much with brothers like Aidan and Kieran.
The Gaelic original Diarmuid is the more pop-
ular spelling in Ireland today; pronounce that
"DEER-mid."
In the World: Actor Dermot Mulroney

Desmond (DEHZ-mənd)   1992: #265
Popularity: #358
Styles: Exotic Traditional,
African-American, Celtic
Nicknames: Des, Dez, Desi   1880   Today
Sisters: Ciara, Margot,
Davina, Zora, Meredith, Tierney
Brothers: Pierce, Bryant, Cedric, Broderick,
Denholm, Carrick
✻ Desmond is one of the most formal of Irish
surname-names. It's sophisticated verging on
stuffy, but the nicknames give it a playful side.
Starting in the 1980s, this name was often cho-
sen to honor Nobel Laureate bishop Desmond
Tutu.
In the World: Bishop Desmond Tutu; Desmond
of *Lost*; musician Desmond Dekker; football
player Desmond Howard

Devin (DEH-vin)   1995: #58
Popularity: #157
Styles: The " ens,"
Nickname-Proof,
Androgynous, Turn of the   1880   Today
21st Century, African-
American
Variants: Devon, Deven, Devan, Devyn
Sisters: Autumn, Morgan, Kiara, Regan, Nadia,
Kayla
Brothers: Austin, Colin, Tyler, Trevin, Damian,
Jaden
✻ Arguably a Celtic name, Devin owes its pop-
ularity more to its coltish sound, like a devilish
Kevin. Like many light, contemporary choices,
Devin shows up as a girl's name as well. See also
Devon.
In the World: Athletes Devin Hester and Devin
Harris; rapper Devin the Dude; musician
Devin Townsend

Devon (DEH-vən, də-VAHN) 1997: #119
Popularity: #352
Styles: The "-ens," African-
American, Place Names,
Turn of the 21st Century 1880 Today
Nicknames: Dev, Von
Variants: Devin, Deven, Devonta, Devonte
Sisters: Macy, Shannon, India, Kendra,
Courtney, Ariana
Brothers: Gavin, Derek, Darius, Trevor,
Desmond, Quinton
✳ Devon is actually two names in one. As an
alternate spelling of Devin, it harkens back to
County Devon in England. But put the stress on
the second syllable and you have an African-
American favorite akin to names like Javon and
Devonte.
In the World: Actor Devon Werkheiser; wrestler
Devon Hughes

Dexter (DEHK-ster) 1968: #262
Popularity: #384
Styles: Timeless, Last Names
First
Nicknames: Dex 1880 Today
Sisters: Darby, Mercy,
Penelope, Quinn, Iris, Ellery
Brothers: Barrett, Quincy, Campbell, Clayton,
Baxter, Mitchell
✳ It's cool. It's geeky. It's geeky-cool? That's
really not a bad niche. If you want to push Dex-
ter firmly into cool territory, the nickname Dex
does the trick.
In the World: Serial killer TV series *Dexter*; ani-
mated series *Dexter's Laboratory*; jazz musician
Dexter Gordon

Diego (dee-AY-go) 2006: #56
Popularity: #99
Styles: Latino/Latina, Saints,
Nickname-Proof
Variants: Diogo, Tiago 1880 Today
Sisters: Sofia, Mariana,
Natalia, Camila, Elena, Catalina, Gabriela,
Carolina
Brothers: Adrian, Mateo, Cesar, Alejandro,
Carlos, Cristian, Marco, Joaquin
✳ Diego is a name familiar to every American,
thanks to the city of San Diego and famous Di-
egos from painters Rivera and Velasquez to soc-
cer star Maradona. In practice, though, the
name has been rare and rather old-fashioned.
That's all changed today. Diego is now a favorite
American name, one you're as likely to encoun-
ter in a schoolyard as on an atlas.
In the World: soccer player Diego Maradona;
painter Diego Rivera; actor Diego Luna; kids'
TV series *Go, Diego, Go!*

Dillon (DI-lən) 1992: #73
Popularity: #345
Styles: Country and Western,
The "-ens," Last Names First,
Turn of the 21st Century 1880 Today
Nicknames: Dill
Variants: Dylan
Sisters: Cassidy, Shelby, Ashton, Sierra,
Mckenzie, Mallory
Brothers: Cameron, Dalton, Tanner, Logan,
Spencer, Austin
✳ Dylan is one of the classic names of Wales.
Dillon is pronounced the same, but its spirit re-
sides a world away. *Gunsmoke's* Marshal Dillon
lends this English/Irish surname a decidedly
Western air.
In the World: Marshal Matt Dillon of *Gun-
smoke*; actors Matt Dillon and Kevin Dillon

Dimitri (di-MEE-tree)   1992: #502
Popularity: #982
Styles: Exotic Traditional,
Slavic, Greek
Nicknames: Dima   1880 Today
Variants: Dmitri, Dimitris,
Demitri, Dimitrios, Demetrius
Sisters: Eleni, Katerina, Xenia, Tatiana,
Anastasia, Dasia, Veronika, Milena
Brothers: Maxim, Dominik, Andreas, Roman,
Damien, Nikolai, Valentin, Alexi
✱ Dimitri is foreign in the best way, mysterious enough to pique our interest but familiar enough to get cozy with. You expect a Dimitri to be intelligent, sophisticated, and easy on the eyes.
In the World: Composer Dmitri Shostakovich; chemist Dmitri Mendeleev; comedian Demetri Martin

Dion (DEE-ahn, dee-AHN)   1970: #344
Popularity: #1227
Styles: African-American,
Shakespearean, Nickname-
Proof   1880 Today
Variants: Deon, Deion
Sisters: Simone, Daria, Sonya, Audra,
Dominique, Tyra, Justine, Bianca
Brothers: Andre, Damon, Gino, Tyron, Darian,
Leon, Fabian, Devin
✱Americans first met Dion in the form of "Runaround Sue" singer Dion Dimucci. The name particularly struck a chord with African-American parents, who embraced it in a variety of spellings (sports star Deion Sanders, for instance). It has a French sound but is actually an English adaptation of the Greek Dionysios.
In the World: Singer Dion Dimucci; athlete Deion Sanders

Dirk (DIRK)   1954: #341
Popularity: #2900
Styles: Surfer '60s, German
and Dutch, Macho Swagger
Variants: Diederik, Derek   1880 Today
Sisters: Heidi, Rhonda, Dana,
Suzette, Mitzi, Shari
Brothers: Rod, Kurt, Barron, Rock, Vance, Bart
✱ Dirk has an exaggerated masculinity that you don't hear much anymore. Macho names today tend toward the playful—Ryder, Madden—rather than the virile. The name is simply a Dutch form of Derek, but many also know it as a Scottish term for a dagger.
In the World: Clive Cussler hero Dirk Pitt; basketball player Dirk Nowitzki; *Boogie Nights* character Dirk Diggler

Dominic (DAHM-i-nik)   2011: #76
Popularity: #76
Styles: Saints, Antique
Charm, Exotic Traditional
Nicknames: Dom, Nic   1880 Today
Variants: Dominick,
Domenic, Dominique, Domingo, Domenico
Sisters: Natalia, Sophia, Madeline, Valentina,
Juliana, Audrey, Raphaela, Angelina
Brothers: Adrian, Raphael, Roman, Xavier,
Vincent, Emmanuel, Quentin, Sebastian
✱An old religious name, Dominic has always had a romantic, mysterious image in the U.S., a curious blend of suave ladies' man and cloistered monk. Today Dominic is as cool and sophisticated as ever, but no longer so exotic. It's one of the new elegant standards.
In the World: Actors Dom DeLuise, Dominic Cooper, and Dominic West; writer Dominick Dunne

Donald (DAHN-əld)   1934: #6
Popularity: #376
Styles: Solid Citizens
Nicknames: Don, Donnie
Variants: Donal   1880 Today
Sisters: Barbara, Elaine,
Gloria, Nancy, Marilyn, Jeanette
Brothers: Gerald, Marvin, Kenneth, Gordon,
Jerome, Raymond
✱ Donald has slipped slowly out of style, while its nickname is still going strong. (Picture TV star Don Johnson as Donald Johnson—suddenly he looks his age.) If you choose Donald for your son, you'll certainly get no objections. But if it's Don you're after, Donovan is now the more popular choice.
In the World: Cartoon character Donald Duck; tycoon/reality TV star Donald Trump

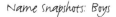

Donovan (DAHN-ə-vin)   2003: #176
Popularity: #254
Styles: Last Names First,
Celtic, Turn of the 21st
Century   1880 Today
Nicknames: Don, Donny, Van
Variants: Donavan
Sisters: Alana, Mckenna, Daniella, Morgan,
Fiona, Jocelyn
Brothers: Brennan, Trevor, Camden, Quinn,
Damian, Griffin
✳ Mmm, mmm . . . that's smooooooth. Name-
sakes like the '60s "Mellow Yellow" singer Don-
ovan and football star Donovan McNabb
reinforce this name's image as a sleek man
about town. Donovan has trendy Irish surname
roots but has been heard as a first name for a
century, making for a modern-sounding classic.
In the World: Singer Donovan Leitch; quarterback Donovan McNabb

Dorian (DOH-ree-ən)   2000: #398
Popularity: #520
Styles: The "-ens,"
Nickname-Proof, Literary
and Artistic, Why Not?   1880 Today
Sisters: Juliana, Regan,
Simone, Aubrey, Serena, Ariana
Brothers: Adrian, Dominic, Holden, Fabian,
Antony, Ronan
✳ This name made its debut as the decadent
title character in Oscar Wilde's *The Picture of
Dorian Gray.* That's not the most attractive ori-
gin, but feel free to ignore the character's short-
comings and enjoy Wilde's perfect ear for
names. Dorian is still unusual and sounds like a
timeless classic.
In the World: *The Picture of Dorian Gray*

Douglas (DUHG-ləs)   1942: #23
Popularity: #513
Styles: Mid-Century, Celtic
Nicknames: Doug
Variants: Douglass   1880 Today
Sisters: Susan, Deborah,
Kathleen, Cynthia, Paula, Cheryl
Brothers: Kenneth, Gregory, Bruce, Stuart,
Phillip, Glenn
✳ Douglas is a classic surname borne by one of
the great families of Scotland. In America, it
acquired a swashbuckling image thanks to the
screen heroics of Douglas Fairbanks Jr. and Sr.
and the real-world heroics of General Douglas
MacArthur. That heroic image has softened
over the past generation. Douglas is still hand-
some, but now more respectable than adventurous.
In the World: Actors Douglas Fairbanks and
Douglas Booth; General Douglas MacArthur;
writer Douglas Adams

Drake (DRAYK)   2010: #199
Popularity: #219
Styles: Brisk and Breezy, Last
Names First, Macho Swagger
Variants: Draco   1880 Today
Sisters: Peyton, Reese, Ava,
Jade, Laine, Tatum
Brothers: Reid, Griffin, Carson, Grant, Chase,
Tate
✳ Parents choose Drake for its lordly sound,
which projects a timeless strength. The name is
not really timeless, of course, but a rising star
taken from the familiar surname. That surname
derives from the same root as the word "dragon";
Draco is a devilishly exotic relative.
In the World: Rapper Drake; sitcom *Drake &
Josh*; sea captain Sir Francis Drake; the word for
a male duck

Draven (DRAY-vən)   2009: #650
Popularity: #729
Styles: The "-ens," Fantastical
Sisters: Jade, Lyra, Echo,
Arwen, Vesper, Aeris   1880 Today
Brothers: Gage, Raiden,
Ryker, Titus, Orion, Mace
✳ If you're not familiar with this name, you
might guess it's Slavic. A brother to Jovan, per-
haps? In fact, its origin is cinematic. The name
was inspired by Eric Draven, the protagonist of
the 1994 dark action film *The Crow.* (Crow,
D'Raven, get it?) The effect is stylishly menac-
ing.
In the World: Eric Draven of *The Crow*

Drew (DROO)
Popularity: #285
Styles: New Classics,
Androgynous, Nicknames,
Brisk and Breezy
Sisters: Tessa, Abby, Kate,
Sabrina, Kara, Paige
Brothers: Alex, Evan, Tyler, Blake, Devin, Trey

1985: #126

1880   Today

✷As a nickname for Andrew, Drew adds a Scottish punch and modern sound. As a given name, it's a preppy jock, akin to Chad but without the '80s aura.
In the World: Comedian Drew Carey; quarterbacks Drew Brees and Drew Bledsoe; talk show host "Dr. Drew"

Duane
(DWAYN, doo-WAYN)
Popularity: #1320
Styles: Mid-Century, Solid
Citizens, Celtic
Variants: Dwayne, Dwain,
Dwane
Sisters: Maureen, Gwen, Darla, Sheila, Eileen, Glenda
Brothers: Darrell, Lyle, Gene, Stuart, Doyle, Gerald

1934: #104

1880   Today

✷Duane was an American standard for 50 years. It started out sounding like a slick young Irish dude and gradually mellowed into a plain-spoken fatherly type (as slick young dudes so often do). It has now mellowed so far that it has fallen out of fashion altogether. See also Dwayne.
In the World: Musicians Duane Eddy and Duane Allman

Dudley (DUHD-lee)
Popularity: #5988
Styles: Porch Sitters, English,
Namesakes
Sisters: Enid, Hester,
Melvina, Eugenia, Fanny,
Dorcas
Brothers: Waldo, Godfrey, Rupert, Elwood, Humphrey, Percival

1907: #313

1880   Today

✷Dudley has never gotten a foothold in the U.S. It used to remind us of Dudley Do-Right, the cartoon Mountie, who at least lent it a prim kind of respectability. But thanks to Harry Potter's oafish cousin Dudley Dursley, it is now virtually off limits.
In the World: cartoon character Dudley Do-Right; Dudley Dursley of the "Harry Potter" series; actor Dudley Moore

Duke (DOOK)
Popularity: #1199
Styles: Guys and Dolls,
Nicknames, Macho Swagger,
Country and Western
Sisters: Dixie, Bess, Queenie,
Roxie, Dolly, Goldie
Brothers: Ike, Dutch, Major, Mack, Rocky, Buzz

1908: #744

1880   Today

✷We're naming kids Princess and Diamond now, so why is Duke such a hard sell? Granted, even the classic American Dukes—Ellington, Snider, and John Wayne—were christened by other names. (Edward, Edwin, and Marion, respectively.) You can follow the same path, using Duke as a nickname for any name you please.
In the World: The icons listed above, plus "Duke Nukem" video games; Duke University; TV series *The Dukes of Hazzard*

Duncan (DUHN-kin)
Popularity: #799
Styles: Celtic, Shakespearean,
Timeless, Nickname-Proof,
Why Not?
Variants: Donagh
Sisters: Fiona, Regan, Esme, Fallon, Orla, Ailsa
Brothers: Lachlan, Ramsay, Ewan, Fraser, Tiernan, Griffin

1997: #377

1880   Today

✷A handsome and dashing Scot, this timeless name is bristling with potential. In some parts of the country, the nickname "Dunkin' Donuts" may occasionally be inevitable.
In the World: Duncan Hines food products; singer Duncan Sheik; furniture maker Duncan Phyfe; director Duncan Jones

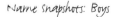

Dustin (DUHS-tin)   1984: #41
Popularity: #371
Styles: '70s–'80s, The "-ens"
Nicknames: Dusty
Sisters: Erin, Jamie, Crystal,   1880   Today
April, Jaclyn, Lindsay
Brothers: Corey, Jared, Brandon, Derrick,
Travis, Shane
✱The name Dustin was a rarity until Dustin
Hoffman's breakout performance in the 1967
film *The Graduate*. The name hit an American
public that was already warming to the more
traditional name Justin. Like a little brother,
Dustin tagged along with Justin to the top of the
name charts by the '80s. And like so many little
brothers, Dustin turned out to have hidden tal-
ents of its own: a fun-loving cowboy style via the
nickname Dusty.
In the World: Actor Dustin Hoffman; golfer
Dustin Johnson; baseball player Dustin Pedroia

Dwayne (DWAYN)   1961: #112
Popularity: #713
Styles: Surfer '60s, African-
American
Variants: Duane, Duwayne,   1880   Today
Dwain, Dwane
Sisters: Tanya, Monica, Rochelle, Angela,
Rhonda, Janine
Brothers: Darryl, Kelvin, Vince, Tyrone,
Kenny, Dexter
✱It may seem like splitting hairs, dividing up
Duane and Dwayne. But the two spellings have
different histories and associations: Irish or
American, white or black, '40s or '60s. Take your
pick—which best fits your family? See also
Duane.
In the World: Actor/wrestler Dwayne ("The
Rock") Johnson; basketball player Dwayne
Wade

Dwight (DWIYT)   1953: #122
Popularity: #1243
Styles: Mid-Century
Nicknames: Dewey
Sisters: Donna, Kathleen,   1880   Today
Janet, Paula, Rosanne, Gayle
Brothers: Stuart, Douglas, Neal, Kent, Roger,
Bruce
✱Dwight is an English surname, and an
American classic. While the name has never
been especially common, you always seem to
find Dwights in positions of prominence in
America. From politicians to athletes to musi-
cians, they somehow rise to the top. Not a fash-
ionable name, but a stronger one than it might
appear at first glance.
In the World: President Dwight David Eisenhower; musician Dwight Yoakam; basketball
player Dwight Howard

Dylan (DI-lən)   2001: #21
Popularity: #33
Styles: Celtic, The "-ens,"
Literary and Artistic
Nicknames: Dyll   1880   Today
Variants: Dillon
Sisters: Morgan, Regan, Paige, Alexis, Lesley,
Bryn
Brothers: Gavin, Logan, Connor, Luke,
Cameron, Trevor
✱Music legend Bob Dylan named himself
after Welsh poet Dylan Thomas, and now those
two Dylans together give the name breadth. A
sensitive Celtic with a rock-and-roll heart. And
yes, in the past generation Dylan has gone elec-
tric. Thank the kids who grew up gazing at Luke
Perry's Dylan on *Beverly Hills, 90210*.
In the World: Musician Bob Dylan; poet Dylan
Thomas; actors Dylan McDermott and Dylan
Sprouse; commentator Dylan Ratigan

Eamon (AY-mən)   2011: #1159
Popularity: #1159
Styles: Celtic, The "-ens,"
Nickname-Proof, Why Not?
Variants: Eamonn, Éamon   1880   Today
Sisters: Teagan, Niamh,
Alannah, Keelin, Riona, Enya
Brothers: Cormac, Torin, Brogan, Seamus,
Declan, Tiernan
✱This is a soulful Irish hit in waiting. The
Gaelic form of Edmund, Eamon has the kind of
artful simplicity that has made Aidan a smash.
The double-"n" spelling is equally traditional.
In the World: Irish President Éamon de Valera;
R&B singer Eamon

Earl (ERL) — 1894: #20

Popularity: #1425

Styles: Solid Citizens, Country and Western, African-American

Variants: Earle

Sisters: Lucille, Faye, Lois, Hazel, Vera, Mae

Brothers: Roy, Leon, Clyde, Vernon, Duke, Clarence

✷ This is a name distinctive to America. Only the land without aristocracy uses aristocratic titles as names. Within that genre, Earl is the most enduring choice. It was a solid hit a century ago, but more recently has become Hollywood's choice for slow-witted hicks and corrupt, beer-bellied sheriffs.

In the World: TV series *My Name Is Earl*; Supreme Court justice Earl Warren; athletes Earl Campbell and Earl Boykins

Easton (EES-tən) — 2011: #102

Popularity: #102

Styles: Last Names First, The "-ens," Nickname-Proof

Sisters: Addison, Macy, Bristol, Sienna, Hadley, Aubrey

Brothers: Garrett, Bentley, Dawson, Landon, Jacoby, Greyson

✷ Easton was once among the preppiest of preppy names, suitable for yacht trips and college a cappella groups. Today it's one of a group of surnames sweeping the Southern U.S. as laid-back country gents — the heirs to names like Harlan and Lamar. Country singer Easton Corbin helped hasten the transition.

In the World: Singer Easton Corbin; novelist Bret Easton Ellis

Edgar (EHD-ger, EHD-gahr) — 1881: #50

Popularity: #243

Styles: Antique Charm, Saints, English, Shakespearean, Latino/Latina

Nicknames: Ed

Variants: Edgardo, Edgard

Sisters: Amelia, Eleanor, Silvia, Adela, Josephine, Clara

Brothers: Oscar, Edmund, Alonzo, Silas, August, Victor

✷ One of the chunky Old English classics, Edgar comes across as sophisticated but self-effacing, like a gentleman with a charming stammer. It owes a good part of its continuing popularity to Latino parents who have adopted this name in large numbers.

In the World: Writer Edgar Allan Poe; painter Edgar Degas; Edgar Awards for mystery writing; SEC EDGAR database

Edison (EHD-i-sən) — 2011: #768

Popularity: #767

Styles: Last Names First, Why Not?

Nicknames: Ed, Eddie, Ned

Sisters: Ashby, Elinor, Harper, Willa, Auden, Marlowe

Brothers: Gibson, Archer, Whitman, Shepard, Egan, Truman

✷ Edison is a handsome, traditional surname that has yet to be rediscovered. Its sound is perfectly current, it has classic nicknames, and it even gives you a historical hero in inventor Thomas Edison. So what's stopping you?

In the World: Inventor Thomas Edison; actor Edison Chen

Edmund (EHD-mənd) 1914: #130
Popularity: #1471
Styles: English, Saints, Ladies
and Gentlemen
Nicknames: Ed, Ned, Ted, 1880 Today
Eddie
Variants: Edmond, Eamon
Sisters: Celia, Elspeth, Marian, Geneva,
Beatrice, Louise
Brothers: Bennett, August, Walter, Hugh,
Bertram, Conrad
✱ Edmund has been lumped in with fusty
gentlemen like Chester and Herman. It's time
for the name to step out on its own. Edmund has
extra refinement, a courtliness closer in spirit to
elegant hits like Julian. Yet it's blessedly unpre-
tentious, especially with nicknames like Ed and
Ned to choose from.
In the World: Explorer Sir Edmund Hillary;
poet Edmund Spenser; Edmund Pevensie of
the "Narnia" books

Edward (EHD-werd) 1882: #11
Popularity: #148
Styles: Timeless, Ladies and
Gentlemen
Nicknames: Ed, Eddie, Ned, 1880 Today
Ted
Variants: Eduardo, Édouard, Eduard, Edvard
Sisters: Margaret, Alice, Elizabeth, Virginia,
Eleanor, Catherine
Brothers: Robert, George, Henry, Joseph,
William, Charles
✱ Edward has always been kingly and sophisti-
cated, a fine choice of fine gentlemen. Its sound,
though, is no longer current. In an age of breezy
names, Edward can seem a little slow. Nonethe-
less, this is too pure of a classic to be discarded.
The nickname Ned is a particularly charming
throwback.
In the World: Eight British kings; "Twilight"
vampire Edward Cullen; actor Edward Norton

Edwin (EHD-win) 1915: #53
Popularity: #235
Styles: Ladies and Gentlemen
Nicknames: Ed, Win
Sisters: Lucille, Edith, Dora, 1880 Today
Agnes, Leona, Inez
Brothers: Edgar, Herman, Alfred, Ernest,
Bernard, Milton
✱ This Old English name has an outdated
sound but has held on admirably. You'll still
meet Edwins of all ages; in the past generation
it has become a favorite of Latino families. It's
the gentlest of gentleman names.
In the World: Astronomer Edwin Hubble; soul
singer Edwin Starr; boxer Edwin Rodriguez

Egan (EE-gən, AY-gahn) 2005: #2395
Popularity: #3109
Styles: Celtic, The "-ens,"
Nickname-Proof, Why Not?
Variants: Eagan, Aogán, 1880 Today
Aodhagán
Sisters: Enya, Keelin, Aisling, Shea, Riona,
Tierney
Brothers: Finian, Cormac, Eamon, Torin,
Keane, Conall
✱ Irish and voguish, Egan may be unfamiliar,
but people will like it when they hear it. It's a
diminutive for an old Gaelic name meaning
"fire," making your child a "little fiery one."
In the World: Poet Egan O'Rahilly

Elam (EE-ləm) 1898: #744
Popularity: #2308
Styles: Biblical, Last Names
First, Why Not?
Sisters: Mara, Shiloh, Oakley, 1880 Today
Atara, Keziah, Mabry
Brothers: Abram, Holt, Japheth, Levi, Joss,
Pryce
✱ Elam is an Old Testament name and, inde-
pendently, an English surname. It could be an
unconventional alternative to Ethan and
Easton, all in one.

Eli (EE-liy)   2011: #58
Popularity: #58
Styles: Biblical, Antique
Charm, Short and Sweet,
Nickname-Proof   1880   Today
Sisters: Leah, Ava, Mia,
Abigail, Ivy, Phoebe, Emma, Molly
Brothers: Noah, Levi, Ethan, Jonas, Seth,
Owen, Luke, Asher
✱ As a rule, to get a gruff, old-time manly
sound you reach for the hard-edged letters. You
want names with a high Scrabble® value: Jake,
Levi, Max. But Eli gives you the same style in a
softer form. No good for Scrabble®, but high-
scoring in the real world.
In the World: Football player Eli Manning; in-
ventor Eli Whitney; pharmaceutical company
Eli Lilly

Elias (ee-LIY-əs, eh-LEE-ahs)   2011: #139
Popularity: #139
Styles: Antique Charm,
Exotic Traditional, Saints,
Greek, Latino/Latina   1880   Today
Nicknames: Eli
Variants: Ellis, Elijah, Elías
Sisters: Natalia, Sofia, Giselle, Mariana, Sarai,
Anastasia
Brothers: Silas, Ezra, Phineas, Alexis, Adrian,
Dominic
✱ Elias is the rarefied Greek form of Elijah. It
may sound like a time traveler from the 18th
century, but this elegant name has made a
smooth leap into contemporary style. The Span-
ish pronunciation is equally fashionable.
In the World: Inventor Elias Howe; actor Elias
Koteas

Elijah (ee-LIY-zhə)   2011: #13
Popularity: #13
Styles: Biblical, African-
American, Antique Charm
Nicknames: Eli   1880   Today
Variants: Eliahu, Elias, Ilya,
Ellis
Sisters: Abigail, Naomi, Sofia, Zoe, Shiloh,
Angelina
Brothers: Josiah, Gabriel, Isaiah, Caleb, Tobias,
Levi
✱ Elijah is one of the most resoundingly bibli-
cal of the popular Old Testament names. De-
spite its soaring modern popularity, it still
conjures up a prophet. That, combined with its
light-as-a-breeze sound, gives Elijah an uplift-
ing spirit.
In the World: Actor Elijah Wood; Nation of
Islam leader Elijah Muhammad; Elijah Mikael-
son of *The Vampire Diaries*

Elisha (ee-LIY-shə)   1883: #253
Popularity: #732
Styles: Biblical, Jewish,
African-American,
Androgynous   1880   Today
Nicknames: Eli
Sisters: Mercy, Hannah, Eden, Jemima, Adah,
Keziah
Brothers: Asa, Cyrus, Isaiah, Ezra, Gideon,
Malachi
✱ The biblical prophet Elisha was Elijah's suc-
cessor, and his name is pronounced similarly.
The name was a no-show in America for genera-
tions, used occasionally for girls as "eh-LEE-
shə." Elisha remained in use for boys chiefly
among religious Jews and in Africa and the Ca-
ribbean. Today the rising interest in Old Testa-
ment names is bringing Elisha back in the U.S.,
with an assist from football star Elisha ("Eli")
Manning.
In the World: Quarterback Elisha ("Eli") Manning

Elliott (EH-lee-ət)   2011: #306
Popularity: #305
Styles: Timeless, Nickname-
Proof
Variants: Elliot, Eliot   1880   Today
Sisters: Camille, Ivy, Daphne,
Juliet, Scarlett, Piper
Brothers: Simon, Bennett, Graham, Maxwell,
Roman, Miles
✱ Elliott has been one of the steadiest names
over time, never really in or out of fashion. Its
snappy double-"t" ending has recently brought
it into the spotlight, but you'd hardly call it
trendy. It's a charmer in the intellectual rather
than brawny vein. Guaranteed to melt girls'
hearts in cafés and college classrooms.
In the World: Singer Elliott Smith; crime fighter
Eliot Ness; writer T. S. Eliot; the boy hero of
E.T.

Elvis (EHL-vis)   1957: #312
Popularity: #904
Styles: Namesakes
Sisters: Janis, Delilah, Everly,
Monroe, Scarlett, Presley   1880   Today
Brothers: Rhett, Jagger, Slade,
Romeo, Hendrix, Axel
✱ This is an American creation of obscure ori-
gin that sounded fancy to parents a hundred
years ago. Elvis is a rare survivor among that
style, with similar names like Clovis long
since . . . pardon me, what was that? Oh, *that*
Elvis! Yes, forget everything else, the King rules
this name absolutely. If your kid is the cool and
confident type, he'll probably revel in the
image.
In the World: Elvis Presley, the "King of Rock
and Roll"; radio host Elvis Duran; singer Elvis
Costello

Ellis (EH-lis)   1899: #154
Popularity: #724
Styles: Solid Citizens, Last
Names First, Celtic,
Nickname-Proof, Why Not?   1880   Today
Sisters: June, Nola, Marjorie,
Celia, Elaine, Corrine
Brothers: Harris, Clifton, Forrest, Murphy,
Archer, Edison
✱ Ellis is the kind of name that nobody ever
thinks of but almost everybody likes. Its sur-
name roots make it an attractive match for con-
temporary favorites like Parker and Jackson.
And as a Welsh derivative of Elijah, it gives you
a Celtic name and biblical name all in one.
In the World: Singer Ellis Paul; immigrant gate-
way Ellis Island

Elmer (EHL-mer)   1895: #34
Popularity: #1057
Styles: Porch Sitters,
Namesakes
Variants: Elmo   1880   Today
Sisters: Wilma, Eunice,
Mamie, Hester, Elvira, Fanny, Maybell, Enid
Brothers: Waldo, Homer, Abner, Lloyd,
Dudley, Orville, Mortimer, Grover
✱ Elmer is buried by the image of cartoon rube
Elmer Fudd. If the name's ultra-retro style grabs
you, your best bet is the closely related name
Elmo. Yes, it just trades in a Looney Toon for a
Muppet, but the "-o" ending shifts the style
from pure fuddy-duddy to potential geek-chic.
In the World: Looney Tunes character Elmer
Fudd; Sinclair Lewis novel *Elmer Gantry*

Emerson (EH-mer-suhn)   2011: #388
Popularity: #387
Styles: Antique Charm,
Literary and Artistic,
Nickname-Proof, Last Names   1880   Today
First, Androgynous
Sisters: Auden, Lilian, Evangeline, Lila,
Annabelle, Harper
Brothers: Everett, Paxton, Whitman, Beckett,
Miles, Truman
✱ If you want a creative but serious-sounding
name for your child, a historical namesake is a
perfect solution. Ralph Waldo Emerson ex-
horted young people to "hitch your wagon to a
star" and "always do what you are afraid to do."
Those could be inspiring messages to grow up
with. Emerson is also attracting parents of girls,
who see "Em-" names as kin to Emily and
Emma.
In the World: Philosopher Ralph Waldo Emerson; race-car driver Emerson Fittipaldi; Emerson Electric Company

Emmanuel (ə-MAN-yoo-əl) 2011: #147
Popularity: #147
Styles: Exotic Traditional,
Biblical, French, Saints
Nicknames: Manny
Variants: Emanuel, Manuel,
Immanuel
Sisters: Seraphina, Angelica, Damaris,
Josefina, Giselle, Evangeline
Brothers: Raphael, Xavier, Sebastian, Gabriel,
Nathanael, Matthias
✹ A classic in other languages, Emmanuel (the
name of the Messiah) was long considered im-
modest as an English name. In recent decades,
though, it has gained new acceptance. The
form Immanuel has a particularly antique and
intellectual flavor.
In the World: Philosopher Immanuel Kant;
Mexican singer Emmanuel

Emmett (EH-mit) 1895: #121
Popularity: #222
Styles: Antique Charm,
Nickname-Proof
Variants: Emmitt, Emmet, 1880 Today
Emmit
Sisters: Violet, Abigail, Celia, Phoebe, Eliza,
Clara
Brothers: Foster, Eli, Jasper, August, Owen,
Wyatt
✹ The perfect little gentleman to accompany
your little lady. Lily, Isabel, Olivia, and friends
have conquered the playground with their gen-
teel femininity, but male counterparts can be
hard to find. If you want the same sweetness in a
neatly masculine form, Emmett is your man.
The name's recent rise had an assist from a
"Twilight" vampire.
In the World: Football player Emmitt Smith;
Emmett Cullen of the "Twilight" series; mur-
der victim Emmett Till; clown Emmett Kelly

Emory (EH-mer-ee) 1902: #242
Popularity: #1073
Styles: Ladies and
Gentlemen, Androgynous,
Nickname-Proof
Variants: Emery
Sisters: Adela, Nola, Jewell, Afton, Leora, Autry
Brothers: Marshall, Forrest, Harley, Palmer,
Dorsey, Warner
✹ Like Avery, Emory started out as a Norman
version of an old Germanic name. Also like
Avery, Emory has built up some momentum
with fans of elegant surnames for boys. And yes,
like Avery again, that rising tide of boy Emorys
has met with an even bigger wave of girls. This
spelling has maintained a closer sex ratio than
the all-"e" Emery. (See Emery under "Snap-
shots: Girls" for more.)
In the World: Emory University; Black Panther
Emory Douglas; actor Emory Cohen

Enzo (EHN-zoh) 2011: #401
Popularity: #400
Styles: Italian, Short and
Sweet
Sisters: Livia, Chiara, Sofia, 1880 Today
Noemi, Mia, Giada
Brothers: Aldo, Matteo, Luca, Massimo,
Gianni, Nico
✹ This Italian name is an old-timer with a
swagger. Enzo Ferrari, the legendary founder of
the sports car company, perfectly captures the
name's combination of jet set and old-country
styles. A fashionable favorite in France, Enzo is
climbing but still uncommon in the U.S.
In the World: Automaker Enzo Ferrari; shoe-
maker Enzo Angiolini

Eoin (OH-in) 2003: #1870
Popularity: #2465
Styles: Celtic
Variants: Ian, Ioan
Sisters: Aoife, Eimear, 1880 Today
Aisling, Meabh, Roisin,
Caoimhe, Saoirse, Niamh
Brothers: Ciaran, Oisin, Fionn, Tadhg, Ronan,
Cillian, Cathal, Niall
✹ If you're an American looking up this name,
it's a good bet your curiosity was piqued by a
particular Eoin. (*Artemis Fowl* author Eoin
Colfer, perhaps?) In that case, the answer to
your question is: it's pronounced "OH-in." If
you're an Irish parent looking up the fashion-
able name Eoin (a form of John), your answer is:
no, most Americans can't pronounce it.
In the World: Author Eoin Colfer; actor Eoin
Macken

Eric (EH-rik) 1972: #16
Popularity: #103
Styles: Nickname-Proof,
Nordic, Surfer '60s, '70s–'80s
Variants: Erik, Erick, Erich, 1880 Today
Eero, Aric

Sisters: Amy, Melissa, Erin, Tara, Kristin, Stacy
Brothers: Adam, Kevin, Matthew, Evan, Marc,
David
✸ Eric is a rare example of an Old Norse name
among the English standards. It was a huge hit
in the '70s and '80s, and it is aging well. The
crisp "-c" ending is as stylish as ever, echoed in
such recent hits as Isaac and Dominic. For a
new look at an old favorite, try the variant Aric.
In the World: Musicians Eric Clapton and Eric
Church; actors Eriq La Salle and Erik Estrada;
illustrator Eric Carle

Ernest (ER-nehst) 1895: #24
Popularity: #851
Styles: Ladies and Gentlemen
Nicknames: Ernie
Variants: Earnest, Ernesto, 1880 Today
Ernst
Sisters: Lenore, Beryl, Alma, Lucille, Vera,
Harriet
Brothers: Clarence, Luther, Hubert, Alfred,
Claude, Walter
✸ Think Ernest Hemingway. Go on, keep
thinking it . . . does it help shake some of the
dust from this name? No? Ah, well, there's no
fighting it: the name Ernest probably won't
come back for another generation. On a young
boy, the name will surprise people, but most
will warm to it quickly. The nickname Ernie is
friendly but strongly linked to *Sesame Street*.
In the World: Writer Ernest Hemingway; actor
Ernest Borgnine; *Sesame Street*'s Bert and
Ernie

Ethan (EE-thin) 2002: #5
Popularity: #7
Styles: Biblical, The "-ens,"
Nickname-Proof
Variants: Eitan 1880 Today

Sisters: Abigail, Hannah,
Chloe, Lila, Olivia, Mia, Emily, Ava
Brothers: Noah, Logan, Eli, Mason, Owen,
Joshua, Luke, Jacob
✸ This biblical classic used to be primarily a
Jewish name, but today the colonial Ethan
Allen associations take the fore. This has been
one of the most fashionable names in America
in recent times, especially in the heartland.
In the World: Ethan Allen (patriot and furniture
company); actor Ethan Hawke; novel *Ethan
Frome*

Eugene (yoo-JEEN, 1928: #20
YOO-jeen)
Popularity: #826
Styles: Ladies and
Gentlemen, Solid Citizens 1880 Today
Nicknames: Gene, Geno,
Zhenya
Variants: Yevgeni, Eugène
Sisters: Phyllis, Sylvia, Maxine, Muriel,
Virginia, Martha
Brothers: Gilbert, Francis, Bernard, Curtis,
Leonard, Ernest
✸ A distinguished classic it may be, but today
Eugene has charisma problems. For Russian
families looking to translate Yevgeni, perhaps
Ewan, Evan, or Egan can stand in.
In the World: Playwright Eugene O'Neill; labor
leader Eugene Debs; comedian Eugene Levy

Evan (EH-vin) 2009: #35
Popularity: #40
Styles: The "-ens,"
Nickname-Proof, New
Classics 1880 Today
Variants: Ifan
Sisters: Audrey, Emma, Megan, Jenna, Mia,
Abby
Brothers: Colin, Ryan, Seth, Carter, Gavin,
Owen
✸ Sean (Irish), Ian (Scottish), and Evan
(Welsh) are all Celtic forms of John that have
become modern American classics. Evan is par-
ticularly upbeat and youthful, one of the friend-
liest-sounding full names around.
In the World: Actor Evan Peters; baseball player
Evan Longoria; film *Evan Almighty*

Evander (ee-VAN-der)   1895: #872
Popularity: #2224
Styles: Celtic, Exotic
Traditional, Mythological,
Why Not?   1880   Today
Nicknames: Van, Andy,
Vander
Sisters: Seraphina, Cassia, Lilias, Ione, Paloma,
Cuinevere, Charis, Liviana
Brothers: Atticus, Gideon, Alistair, Leander,
Desmond, Japheth, Magnus, Simeon
★This romantic name is out of classical leg-
end, filtered through the Scottish Highlands.
It's elegant and colorful, with an extra knockout
punch thanks to heavyweight champion
Evander Holyfield.
In the World: Boxer Evander Holyfield; hockey
player Evander Kane

Everett (EH-ver-it)   1906: #81
Popularity: #257
Styles: Antique Charm, Last
Names First, Nickname-
Proof   1880   Today
Sisters: Hollis, Eleanor,
Adeline, Vivian, Cecelia, Violet
Brothers: Lincoln, Elias, August, Emmett,
Jasper, Truman
★Many of the stately gentleman names seem a
bit sluggish. This one snaps to attention. Everett
is courtly but crisp and full of life, an unbeat-
able combination.
In the World: Actor Everett McGill

Ewan (YOO-in)   2010: #1205
Popularity: #1244
Styles: The "-ens," Celtic,
Nickname-Proof
Variants: Euan, Eoghan,   1880   Today
Eugene
Sisters: Isla, Mirren, Davina, Maisie, Ailsa,
Fiona
Brothers: Callum, Lachlan, Niall, Ramsay,
Torin, Duncan
★This Scottish favorite is much in vogue in its
homeland in two different spellings, Ewan and
Euan. In the U.S., it is primarily known through
actor Ewan McGregor. Despite its resemblance
to names like Evan and Ian, which are forms of
John, Ewan is believed to derive from Eugene.
In the World: Actor Ewan McGregor

Ezekiel (eh-ZEE-kee-əl)   2011: #196
Popularity: #195
Styles: Biblical, Antique
Charm, Exotic Traditional
Nicknames: Zeke   1880   Today
Variants: Ezequiel, Haskell
Sisters: Evangeline, Amelia, Patience, Violet,
Anastasia, Mariah, Delilah
Brothers: Jedidiah, Malachi, Elijah, Josiah,
Ezra, Levi, Tobias
★One of the unlikeliest beneficiaries of the
Old Testament revival. The name Ezekiel was
dead during the middle of the 20th century, a
biblical relic akin to Ebenezer. But the ultra-hip
nickname Zeke has helped carry this quirky an-
tique back into contention.
In the World: Sitcom *Zeke and Luther;* soccer
players Ezequiel Lavezzi and Ezequiel Garay

Ezra (EHZ-rə)   2011: #205
Popularity: #204
Styles: Biblical, Antique
Charm, Exotic Traditional,
Nickname-Proof   1880   Today
Sisters: Ivy, Delilah, Luna,
Penelope, Scarlett, Zoe
Brothers: Eli, Gideon, Levi, Asa, Felix, Micah
★After long years being lumped with losers
like Enoch and Hiram, Ezra's finally coming up
in the world. Creative parents are warming to
the name's unconventional appeal and pocket-
size punch. It's confident, with an eccentric
edge.
In the World: Writers Ezra Jack Keats and Ezra
Pound; band Better Than Ezra; actor Ezra
Miller

Fabian (FAY-bee-ən)   2007: #252
Popularity: #291
Styles: German and Dutch,
Shakespearean, Saints,
Nickname-Proof   1880   Today
Variants: Fabio
Sisters: Mariana, Celeste, Tatiana, Salome,
Candace, Bianca
Brothers: Darius, Gideon, Quentin, Sergio,
Marco, Damian
★For a certain generation, Fabian will forever
mean a teen heartthrob. Yet the '60s icon didn't
inspire many namesakes in his day. The name
Fabian has only entered the mainstream in the
21st century, following in the footsteps of hits
like Damian and Sebastian.
In the World: '60s teen idol Fabian; politician
Fabian Núñez; football player Fabian Washing-
ton

Felix (FEE-liks)
Popularity: #311
Styles: Timeless, Exotic
Traditional, German and
Dutch, Saints, Nickname-
Proof
Variants: Félix, Feliciano
Sisters: Flora, Cleo, Eliza, Phoebe, Hazel, Ivy
Brothers: Milo, Jasper, Linus, Axel, Oscar, Ezra
✷ Tired of Alex? Here's an uncommon classic
with that elusive "-x" ending and an idiosyn-
cratic panache. The '20s cartoon character
Felix the Cat and *The Odd Couple*'s Felix Unger
scared parents off Felix for generations, but
those connotations are fading. The name's brio
should overcome its baggage.
In the World: Felix the Cat; Felix Unger of *The
Odd Couple*; Supreme Court justice Felix
Frankfurter; baseball player Félix Hernández

1895: #141

1880 Today

Finian (FIN-yən)
Popularity: #3610
Styles: Celtic, Saints, Why
Not?
Nicknames: Fin
Variants: Finnian
Sisters: Fiona, Aislin, Niamh, Keelin, Maeve,
Alannah
Brothers: Ronan, Cormac, Callum, Kilian,
Dermot, Tiernan
✷ Finian is 100% Irish, as green as a shamrock,
and remarkably contemporary. A few people
may be reminded of the creaky leprechaun mu-
sical *Finian's Rainbow*, but most will consider
this name fresh and interesting. It also trims
down to the nifty nickname Fin, which gives it
a leg up on the similar choice Kilian.
In the World: *Finian's Rainbow*

2005: #2652

1880 Today

Finley (FIN-lee)
Popularity: #511
Styles: Last Names First,
Celtic, Why Not?
Nicknames: Fin
Variants: Finlay, Findlay,
Finnley, Fionnlagh
Sisters: Maisie, Finola, Elspeth, Isla, Ainsley,
Rhona
Brothers: Ramsey, Duncan, Angus, Carson,
Fraser, Brodie
✷ This Scottish favorite has been an uncom-
mon American choice. Recently, though, par-
ents have caught on to it as a new alternative to
Bailey and Riley—for boys and girls alike. The
spelling Finley dominates in the U.S., based on
the surname. For the fullest Scots flavor as a
given name, go with Finlay. The spelling Finn-
ley means you really want to call your son Finn,
so why not just name him that?

2011: #511

1880 Today

Finn (FIN)
Popularity: #304
Styles: Celtic, Brisk and
Breezy, Nordic
Variants: Fionn
Sisters: Shea, Isla, Maeve,
Malin, Fiona, Rory
Brothers: Owen, Declan, Jude, Leif, Jasper,
Rowan
✷ Finn is a welcome burst of Irish (or Scandi-
navian) energy. It gives you the light touch of a
new, creative name, yet sidesteps the common
traps: it doesn't sound forced or fussy or made
up. The unfussy American icon Huck Finn
helps the cause. As an Irish name, Finn sum-
mons the mythical hero Fionn mac Cumhaill
(Finn McCool); as a Scandinavian name it
means "from Finland."
In the World: mythical Irish hero Finn McCool;
Huckleberry Finn; Finn Hudson of *Glee*

2011: #305

1880 Today

Finnegan (FI-nə-gin) 2011: #479
Popularity: #478
Styles: Last Names First,
Celtic, Why Not?
Nicknames: Finn 1880 Today
Sisters: Kennedy, Fiona,
Felicity, Rory, Kerrigan, Tierney
Brothers: Sullivan, Brogan, Cormac, Quinlan,
Brannigan, Teague
✷ Finn is a high-style full name. Feel free to take it straight. But if that single syllable makes you skittish, you can try extending it into this classic Irish surname (literally "descendant of Finn").
In the World: James Joyce novel *Finnegans Wake*; folk song "Michael Finnegan" ("begin ag'in")

Fletcher (FLEH-cher) 1892: #266
Popularity: #890
Styles: Last Names First,
Guys and Dolls, Why Not?
Nicknames: Fletch 1880 Today
Sisters: Sadie, Harlow,
Adelaide, Cleo, Autry, Clementine
Brothers: Truman, Dexter, Maxwell, Murphy, Porter, Coleman
✷ Amid America's love affair with tradesman names, this old favorite has found few suitors. It has the cheeky confidence of names like Tucker and Cooper but a less trendy style. A Fletcher is an arrow maker, which your son will doubtless find cooler than a cloth finisher (Tucker) or barrel maker (Cooper.)
In the World: Bandleader Fletcher Henderson; Fletcher Christian, leader of the mutiny on the HMS *Bounty*

Floyd (FLOYD) 1897: #48
Popularity: #1708
Styles: Porch Sitters
Variants: Lloyd
Sisters: Gladys, Edna, Muriel, 1880 Today
Eunice, Irma, Bernice
Brothers: Merle, Homer, Lester, Odell, Hoyt, Willard
✷ Floyd is a pure dose of the least trendy sounds of the moment. It's a tough time to be a Floyd, and the tide isn't likely to turn anytime soon. The name began as a valiant attempt to convey the true Welsh pronunciation of Lloyd. (Try the authentic "Ll" yourself by placing your tongue in position to say "L," then hissing air.)
In the World: Boxers Floyd Mayweather and Floyd Patterson; band Pink Floyd

Flynn (FLIN) 2011: #944
Popularity: #946
Styles: Brisk and Breezy, Last
Names First, Celtic, Why
Not? 1880 Today
Sisters: Marlowe, Laine,
Emlyn, Greer, Tierney, Shea
Brothers: Pryce, Archer, Cullen, Case, Penn, Devlin
✷ A popular given name in Australia and Scotland, Flynn hasn't been heard much in the U.S. That's likely to change soon, though, since its swift Irish surname sound couldn't be more fashionable. With its swashbuckling self-assurance, Flynn sounds like a natural playground leader.
In the World: Swashbuckling actor Errol Flynn; Flynn Rider of *Tangled*; a son of actor Orlando Bloom

Forrest (FOH-rist) 1913: #173
Popularity: #1127
Styles: Timeless, Last Names
First, Charms and Graces,
Nickname-Proof, Why Not? 1880 Today
Variants: Forest, Forester
Sisters: Iris, Cecilia, Felicity, Johanna, Mercy, Audra
Brothers: Everett, Sterling, Palmer, Harris, Bennett, Clifton
✷ Nature names for boys are scarce, and sometimes scary. (Thorn, anyone?) Forrest is a happy exception. It's traditional and durable, and the double-"r" surname spelling keeps it understated. Part outdoorsman, part old time gentleman.
In the World: Film *Forrest Gump*; actor Forest Whitaker; MMA fighter Forrest Griffin

Foster (FAHS-ter) 1896: #279
Popularity: #1549
Styles: Ladies and
Gentlemen, Last Names
First, Nickname-Proof, Why 1880 Today
Not?
Sisters: Alma, Leora, Cecile, Louisa, Harriet, Estella
Brothers: Porter, Lofton, Merritt, Harris, Fraser, Palmer
✷ Look backward and forward at the same time with this promising selection. Foster's courteous, old-school ways pair nicely with Lily or Eleanor, while its surname style makes it a natural for the age of Parker and Tanner.
In the World: Foster's lager; foster homes

Francis (FRAN-sis)   1915: #29
Popularity: #618
Styles: Solid Citizens, Ladies
and Gentlemen
Nicknames: Frank, Fran   1880   Today
Variants: Francisco,
Francesco, François
Sisters: Martha, Cecelia, Elaine, Sylvia, Helen,
Marie
Brothers: Bernard, Theodore, Paul, Eugene,
Alfred, Clarence
✹ Francis is a classic name of saints and gentle-
men. You expect a Francis to hold doors for la-
dies and become the leader of his local Elks
lodge. The women's name Frances has compli-
cated the male version, though. It's now the one
gentlemanly standard that sounds androgynous.
In the World: Saint Francis of Assisi; philoso-
pher Francis Bacon; movie quote "Lighten up,
Francis"

Frank (FRANGK)   1880: #6
Popularity: #308
Styles: Solid Citizens
Nicknames: Frankie
Variants: Franco, Franck   1880   Today
Sisters: Helen, Margaret,
Irene, Ruth, Ann, Martha
Brothers: Arthur, Charlie, Fred, Walter, Ed,
George
✹ A name that neatly defines itself: open,
straightforward, and a little bit blunt. While
some prominent Franks have been christened
Francis (or Franklin), Frank is a full and vener-
able given name with a proud history of its own.
In the World: Singer Frank Sinatra; architect
Frank Lloyd Wright; musicians Frank Zappa
and Frank Ocean

Franklin (FRANGK-lin)   1933: #33
Popularity: #504
Styles: Solid Citizens
Nicknames: Frank
Sisters: Jeanette, Marilyn,   1880   Today
Roberta, Constance, Barbara,
Carol

Brothers: Warren, Clifton, Gilbert, Marshall,
Lawrence, Nelson
✹ Franklin is a clean-cut, hardworking name
with a fundamentally American character. The
name is associated with such defining figures as
Benjamin Franklin and Franklin Delano Roo-
sevelt, the latter of whom sparked a wave of
young Franklins in the 1930s.
In the World: Presidents Franklin Roosevelt and
Franklin Pierce; founding father Ben Franklin;
Franklin planners

Fred (FREHD)   1885: #14
Popularity: #1513
Styles: Solid Citizens,
Nicknames
Nicknames: Freddy   1880   Today
Sisters: Annie, Louise, Dora,
Pearl, Fay, Harriet
Brothers: Pete, Frank, Charlie, Ray, Harry, Bert
✹ Frederick has the antique sound, but it's
Fred that's the real old-fashioned name. A hun-
dred years ago, baby Freds outnumbered Fred-
ericks three to one. Today those numbers are
reversed, and Fred sounds rather plain by itself.
In the World: Dancer Fred Astaire; cartoon
caveman Fred Flintstone; actor Fred Savage;
Fred Meyer stores

Frederick (FREHD-rik)   1887: #37
Popularity: #540
Styles: Ladies and
Gentlemen, Shakespearean
Nicknames: Fred, Freddy,   1880   Today
Fritz, Rick
Variants: Frederic, Federico, Friedrich,
Frederik, Fredrick
Sisters: Martha, Eleanor, Harriet, Virginia,
Wilhelmina, Beatrice
Brothers: Conrad, Albert, George, Edmond,
Arthur, Theodore
✹ This German classic has been in a long,
steady decline, but the old boy still has some life
in him. Like a three-piece suit and wingtip
shoes, Frederick carries a timeless air of author-
ity that cuts through fashion. If the nickname
Fred seems too plain, you could give Fritz a try.
In the World: Abolitionist Frederick Douglass;
Frederick the Great of Prussia; Frederick's of
Hollywood lingerie

Fritz (FRITS)   1888: #387
Popularity: #2582
Styles: German and Dutch,
Guys and Dolls
Sisters: Golda, Effie, Mina,   1880   Today
Lotte, Roxie, Frieda
Brothers: Otto, Ernst, Ike, Gus, Emil, Wiley
✹ Fritz has its work cut out for it. There's the
expression "on the fritz," as well as the X-rated
'60s cartoon character Fritz the Cat. And more
importantly, there's the general fashion trend
away from German names. But this name is so
playful and good-humored that it should still
find a few takers—especially as a snappy nick-
name for Frederick.
In the World: Filmmaker Fritz Lang; Fritz the
Cat; the phrase "on the fritz"

Gabriel (GAY-bree-əl)　　　2010: #21
Popularity: #24
Styles: Biblical, Antique
Charm, Latino/Latina,
French
Nicknames: Gabe
Variants: Gavril, Gabriello
Sisters: Abigail, Chloe, Hannah, Isabella, Lily, Sofia
Brothers: Noah, Elijah, Luke, Nathaniel, Adrian, Caleb
✳ This lyrical name is one of the most buoyant biblical choices for boys. It's also one of the most international choices, used in a dozen different languages. Gabriel is currently riding a wave of popularity that takes some of the edge off its impact. That's good news if you're worried that the name's too exotic, bad if you're in search of the unusual.
In the World: Writer Gabriel García Márquez; actor Gabriel Byrne; comedians Gabriel Iglesias and Gabe Kaplan

Gage (GAYJ)　　　2003: #136
Popularity: #154
Styles: Brisk and Breezy, Last
Names First
Variants: Gaige, Gauge
Sisters: Reese, Macy, Kendall, Payton, Piper, Bailey, Brynn, Aubrey
Brothers: Cade, Drake, Cooper, Tate, Jett, Beck, Griffin, Tucker
✳ Like Stone or Chance, this is a name that doesn't quite sound real. It belongs to an impossibly virile hero trapped in the pages of a romance novel. But this style of name is coming on strong, and Gage is a particularly likable example. Oddly, its popularity dates to a not so virile or likable movie character—an undead boy in *Pet Sematary*. See also Gauge.
In the World: Gage of *Pet Sematary*

Galen (GAY-lin)　　　1949: #329
Popularity: #3436
Styles: The "-ens," Classical
Sisters: Livia, Tanis, Oriana, Ione, Thalia, Adria
Brothers: Trajan, Marius, Tycho, Severin, Phineas, Silvan
✳ Galen sounds modern, a happy meeting of Jalen and Gavin. It's also classical, the name of an ancient Greek physician whose writings have taught us much of what we know of ancient medicine. A natural choice for a doctor's child. (Secret bonus: it's an anagram of angel.)
In the World: Many uses in science fiction, including *Babylon 5*, *Battlestar Galactica*, and *Planet of the Apes*

Gannon (GA-nən)　　　2003: #684
Popularity: #1436
Styles: The "-ens," Last
Names First
Sisters: Macy, Alexa, Hadley, Tatum, Sierra, Landry
Brothers: Lawson, Brennan, Gage, Remington, Bridger, Devlin
✳ The Irish surname Gannon started popping up in large numbers when quarterback Rich Gannon was leading the Oakland Raiders to glory (or close enough). It has a macho sound, like the tough big brother of surnames like Brennan and Landon. For an even tougher twist, try Cannon.
In the World: Quarterback Rich Gannon; "Legend of Zelda" archenemy Ganon

Gareth (GA-rehth)　　　1999: #1421
Popularity: #2430
Styles: English, Celtic, Why
Not?
Nicknames: Gary
Sisters: Carys, Bethan, Gemma, Tamsin, Mabyn, Nicola
Brothers: Rhys, Graeme, Hugh, Callum, Morgan, Griffin
✳ Gareth is a Welsh and English classic that Americans have missed out on. It has a familiar, comfortable sound—Gary meets Kenneth—but a refined attitude that makes it a stylish choice. For extra romance, Gareth was a Knight of the Round Table.
In the World: DJ Gareth Emery; soccer player Gareth Bale

Garrett (GA-rit) 2000: #74
Popularity: #190
Styles: Celtic, Country and
Western, New Classics
Nicknames: Garry, Gary   1880 Today
Variants: Garret, Garett,
Gerrit
Sisters: Samantha, Gabrielle, Kendall, Sierra,
Jillian, Cassidy
Brothers: Traver, Gavin, Carson, Mason,
Wyatt, Cameron
★ Garrett combines two popular name styles:
the refined British gentleman and the rugged
cowboy. The latter image comes via Old West
lawman Pat Garrett and the stalwart double-"t"
ending.
In the World: Actors Garrett Hedlund and Gar-
rett Morris; lawman Pat Garrett

Garrison (GAR-i-sən) 1999: #565
Popularity: #1181
Styles: Last Names First
Nicknames: Garry
Sisters: Savannah, Bailey, 1880 Today
Sydney, Gabrielle, Mariah,
Paige
Brothers: Gavin, Emerson, Chandler, Preston,
Remington, Campbell
★ This surname is sometimes chosen for the
son of a man named Gary, but it has the mak-
ings of a broader hit. Abolitionist William Lloyd
Garrison is an appealing namesake.
In the World: Humorist Garrison Keillor; foot-
ball player Garrison Hearst

Garth (GAHRTH) 1954: #445
Popularity: #9911
Styles: Country and Western,
Namesakes
Sisters: Leanne, Andra, 1880 Today
Gwyn, Ronna, Fawn,
Wynona, Delta, Britt
Brothers: Lorne, Waylon, Niels, Rolf, Denver,
Arne, Judd, Dell
★ This used to be a quirky, uncommon name
with a style that was hard to pin down. You
could convince yourself it was exotic, or upper-
crusty, or plodding. But these days it's easy to
pin down: pure country, thanks to the big
shadow of music star Garth Brooks.
In the World: Musicians Garth Brooks and
Garth Hudson; writer Garth Nix; Garth of
Wayne's World

Gary (GA-ree) 1951: #10
Popularity: #494
Styles: Mid-Century
Variants: Garry
Sisters: Sandra, Donna, Judy, 1880 Today
Lynn, Sharon, Connie,
Diane, Gwen
Brothers: Dennis, Bruce, Barry, Gregory, Jay,
Alan, Randall, Dean
★ Most names that end in "-y" end up either
boyish or androgynous. Gary is an exception,
easygoing but reassuringly grown-up. Think
Corey with a cardigan and some pipe tobacco.
Gary has surname roots, and was jump-started
as a first name by actor Gary Cooper. Cooper
took the stage name Gary at the suggestion of
an acquaintance from Gary, Indiana.
In the World: Actors Gary Cooper, Gary Old-
man, Gary Coleman, and Gary Sinise; cartoon-
ists Garry Trudeau and Gary Larson

Gauge (GAYJ) 2009: #721
Popularity: #754
Styles: Modern Meanings,
Country and Western
Variants: Gage 1880 Today
Sisters: Aspen, Landry,
Shiloh, Oakley, Faith, Shyanne
Brothers: Chance, Maverick, Trace, Colt,
Gatlin, Ridge
★ I don't usually give a full entry to alternative
spellings, but Gauge is a spelling with a differ-
ence. Where Gage is a surname, Gauge is a
meaning name. The key meaning in this case is
the measure of the diameter of a gun barrel, as
in a 12-gauge shotgun. That has made this spell-
ing a favorite of hunters and a brother to Western names like Colt and Bridger.

Gavin (GA-vin) 2008: #30
Popularity: #36
Styles: The "-ens," Celtic,
Nickname-Proof
Variants: Gawain 1880 Today
Sisters: Mia, Chloe, Avery,
Fiona, Sofia, Rory
Brothers: Colin, Garrett, Devin, Owen, Carter,
Dylan
★ Gavin has a sophisticated flair that's gallant
rather than showy. And for tradition, you can't
beat a Knight of the Roundtable. (If the name
doesn't sound Arthurian to you, the alternate
version Gawain might ring a bell.)
In the World: Singers Gavin DeGraw and Gavin
Rossdale; politician Gavin Newsom; actor
Gavin MacLeod

Gax (GAKS) rarely used
Popularity: Very rare
Nicknames: FatMan
Sisters: Moo, Spamela, Beer,
Soup, John
Brothers: Flax, Vilx, Clax,
Eleanor, Xax

1880 Today

✳ Gax is a name you should not give to your child at all. It's only in the book because my kids are beside me as I'm writing and they absolutely insisted. Keep this in mind, prospective parents, if you're planning to work from home.

Gene (JEEN) 1937: #61
Popularity: #2147
Styles: Solid Citizens,
Nicknames
Sisters: Elaine, Joyce, Rita,
Sally, Arlene, Nancy
Brothers: Lyle, Ted, Donald, Bill, Dale,
Gordon

1880 Today

✳ Gene was once an American mainstay, borne by icons like singing cowboy Gene Autry and dancing star Gene Kelly. It disappeared hand in hand with the full name Eugene, and few parents today give the name a second thought. It's suffering not rejection so much as neglect.
In the World: Genes (the biological units of heredity); singer Gene Autry; actor/dancer Gene Kelly

Geoffrey (JEF-ree) 1975: #167
Popularity: #1437
Styles: Surfer '60s
Nicknames: Geoff
Variants: Jeffrey, Joffrey
Sisters: Candace, Tamara,
Kimberly, Rochelle, Sonya, Deanna, Adrienne,
Belinda
Brothers: Terence, Gregory, Bradford, Randall,
Brent, Mitchell, Craig, Timothy

1880 Today

✳ The traditional form of Jeffrey, Geoffrey was one of the stylish hits of the Middle Ages. Today that "Middle Ages" vibe is inching toward "middle-aged," but the arcane spelling still romantically echoes the days of Geoffrey Chaucer.
In the World: Actor Geoffrey Rush; designer Geoffrey Beene; poet Geoffrey Chaucer

George (JOHRJ) 1880: #5
Popularity: #165
Styles: Ladies and Gentlemen
Variants: Jorge, Giorgio,
Georg, Georges, Jurgen
Sisters: Margaret, Alice,
Martha, Frances, Mary, Harriet, Rosa, Helen
Brothers: Edward, Arthur, Henry, Frederick,
Walter, Frank, Louis, Charles

1880 Today

✳ Of all the classic kingly names, none has fallen farther than George. In fact, it has fallen far enough to lend it some cachet among upscale, contrarian parents. Political note: The name's use, or lack thereof, is not a reflection on any Republican presidents named George. In fact, the name George is most popular in the most heavily Democratic areas of the country.
In the World: Presidents George Washington, George H. W. Bush, and George W. Bush; actor George Clooney; the phrase "by George!"

Gerald (JEH-rəld) 1939: #19
Popularity: #627
Styles: Solid Citizens,
Mid-Century
Nicknames: Gerry, Jerry
Variants: Jerald, Jerold,
Jerrold, Gerold, Geraldo
Sisters: Eileen, Janice, Gloria, Patrica, Nancy,
Marcia
Brothers: Donald, Richard, Marvin, Jerome,
Kenneth, Roger

✳ A stately old name with a happy-go-lucky nickname, Gerald struck the perfect balance for generations of men. It's a quieter choice today, mainly but mellow.
In the World: President Gerald Ford; basketball players Gerald Wallace and Gerald Green

Gerard (jə-RAHRD, JEH-rahd)
1956: #180
Popularity: #1076
Styles: Solid Citizens, Saints, French
Nicknames: Gerry
Variants: Gérard, Gerardo, Gerhard, Gerrit
Sisters: Therese, Margot, Marianne, Rosalind, Yvonne, Ramona
Brothers: Roland, Stuart, Jerome, Randolph, Cornell, Laurence
✳ Unlike all-American Gerald, Gerard still sounds like the medieval classic it is—if you keep the stress on the last syllable. If you stress the beginning (like Scottish actor Gerard Butler), Gerard rejoins the rest of the Gerry family.
In the World: Actors Gérard Depardieu and Gerard Butler; singer Gerard Way; poet Gerard Manley Hopkins

Gianni (JAH-nee, jee-AH-nee)
2011: #516
Popularity: #515
Styles: Italian
Nicknames: Nino
Variants: Giovanni, Johnny, Gian
Sisters: Giada, Alessia, Mia, Giuliana, Eliana, Chiara
Brothers: Matteo, Luca, Dominick, Enzo, Antonio, Dante
✳ This Italian version of Johnny is pronounced similarly but has a much flashier style. It was seldom used in English before the emergence of fashion designer Gianni Versace.
In the World: Designer Gianni Versace; Puccini opera *Gianni Schicchi*

Gibson (GIB-sən)
2011: #910
Popularity: #909
Styles: Last Names First, Why Not?
Nicknames: Gib
Variants: Gibbs
Sisters: Everly, Oakley, Adelaide, Harlow, Greer, Emmeline, Flannery
Brothers: Sumner, Griffin, Perkins, Cash, Walker, Judson, Truman
✳ Just when you thought you'd heard all the surname names a hundred times, along comes a fresh alternative. Gibson is simple and even a little old-fashioned but shows some swagger, like a classic '50s Gibson guitar.
In the World: Gibson guitars; "Gibson Girl" beauty ideal; Gibson cocktail

Gideon (GI-dee-ən)
2011: #413
Popularity: #412
Styles: Biblical, Exotic Traditional, Antique Charm, Why Not?
Sisters: Shiloh, Naomi, Lydia, Delilah, Eden, Mercy, Violet
Brothers: Samson, Raphael, Judah, Phineas, Asher, Simeon, Tobias
✳ Ladies and gentlemen, may I present a handsome, familiar biblical name that is still unusual! Right now Gideon calls to mind hotel-room Bibles, but soon it may sound like the most stylish boy in town. The lack of a solid nickname is the only thing holding it back.
In the World: Gideons International, distributor of free Bibles

Gilbert (GIL-bert)
1930: #90
Popularity: #869
Styles: Saints, Ladies and Gentlemen, Solid Citizens
Nicknames: Gib, Gil
Variants: Gilberto
Sisters: Arlene, Loretta, Frances, Maxine, Margery, Harriet, Eileen, Lucille
Brothers: Bernard, Herbert, Clifton, Willis, Eugene, Vernon, Stewart, Franklin
✳ There's nothing trendy about Gilbert, and its close resemblance to cartoon antihero Dilbert threatens to send it over the edge to geekdom. Yet its stuffiness is of the charming kind, a sweet dignity. If you're tempted but nervous, Gibson is one option for throwback charm in a trendier package.
In the World: *What's Eating Gilbert Grape*; Gilbert of *Anne of Green Gables*; basketball player Gilbert Arenas

Giles (JIYLZ)
1881: #360
Popularity: #4679
Styles: English, Saints, Exotic Traditional
Nicknames: Gil
Variants: Gilles, Gil, Gyles
Sisters: Beryl, Regina, Flora, Imogen, Lenora, Augusta
Brothers: Basil, Ambrose, Denholm, Guy, Albin, Hugh
✳ Giles is an exceptionally refined name. It's smoothed out to the point where it may be too slick for comfort. If you love the sound, Miles is a handsome, reliable alternative.

Giovanni (joh-VAHN-ee)   2010: #114
Popularity: #117
Styles: Italian
Nicknames: Gianni, Gio
Variants: Jovanni, Jovany   1880   Today
Sisters: Francesca, Giada,
Eliana, Paola, Alessandra, Bianca
Brothers: Orlando, Dante, Sergio, Leonardo,
Giancarlo, Marco
✳Traditionally, Giovanni has been an exclusively Italian name. In the past generation, it has caught on with Spanish speakers, and it's now a solid cross-cultural hit. Giovanni's spirit, though, is still solidly Italiano.
In the World: Mozart opera *Don Giovanni*; Renaissance writer Giovanni Boccaccio; actor Giovanni Ribisi

Glenn (GLEHN)   1962: #55
Popularity: #1121
Styles: Mid-Century, Solid
Citizens, Celtic
Variants: Glen   1880   Today
Sisters: Donna, Susan, Gail,
Janet, Bonnie, Ellen
Brothers: Kenneth, Paul, Allen, Russell, Dean, Mark
✳ Glenn may be Scottish in origin, but it's celebrating a century as the all-American man. Trendy in the days of bandleader Glenn Miller and actor Glenn Ford, it has aged comfortably.
In the World: Bandleader Glenn Miller; commentator Glenn Beck; singer Glen Campbell; pianist Glenn Gould

Gordon (GOHR-dən)   1934: #71
Popularity: #1034
Styles: Solid Citizens
Nicknames: Gordie
Sisters: Eileen, Jeanette,   1880   Today
Roberta, Glenda, Rosalie,
Lorraine
Brothers: Warren, Lewis, Gilbert, Alvin, Roland, Stanley
✳ Gordon feels a little doughy, as if those full, round sounds have gone straight to its waistline. The name has actually held on better than most of its compatriots from the '20s. It sounds manlier than Norman or Howard, just a little outmoded. Gordons can still be found in Canada, where the name is more of a steady classic.
In the World: Chef Gordon Ramsay; singer Gordon Lightfoot; British prime minister Gordon Brown; Gordon's gin

Grady (GRAY-dee)   1911: #179
Popularity: #302
Styles: Last Names First,
Antique Charm
Sisters: Ruby, Willa, Emery,   1880   Today
Annie, Tegan, Laney
Brothers: Leland, Emerson, Murphy, Alden, Dewey, Mason
✳This name, which sounds like one of the trendy new surname hits, was actually most familiar 100 years ago. Grady can hold its own with young preppies like Brody and Colby, but it's just as happy hanging out on the back porch, swapping fish tales with the boys.
In the World: Baseball player Grady Sizemore; Grady-White boats

Graham (GRAM)   2011: #256
Popularity: #255
Styles: Timeless, English,
Celtic
Variants: Graeme   1880   Today
Sisters: Blythe, Camille,
Phoebe, Iris, Juliet, Fiona
Brothers: Elliot, Colin, Miles, Reid, Duncan, Gareth
✳This English and Scottish standard has never fully taken hold in the U.S. Why is a mystery. It's handsome as all get out, sexy but with impeccable manners. Even the graham cracker association really shouldn't hurt: slim, sweet, and snappy. A name on the rise.
In the World: Graham crackers; writer Graham Greene; singer Graham Nash; inventor Alexander Graham Bell

Grant (GRANT)   1997: #115
Popularity: #151
Styles: Brisk and Breezy,
Timeless, Last Names First
Sisters: Laine, Emily, Hope,   1880   Today
Ava, Juliet, Kate
Brothers: Reid, Garrett, Dean, Brooks, Davis, Preston
✳ Ooh . . . that's one fine-looking man! Maybe it's because of Cary Grant, or because it sounds so "grand." Most folks will agree that it's hard to find a name as tall, dark, and handsome as Grant.
In the World: President Ulysses S. Grant; actors Cary Grant and Hugh Grant; basketball player Grant Hill

Grayson (GRAY-sən)   2011: #97
Popularity: #97
Styles: The "-ens," Last
Names First
Nicknames: Gray   1880 Today
Variants: Greyson
Sisters: Aubrey, Laila, Kendall, Hadley, Sienna,
Ainsley
Brothers: Weston, Peyton, Trenton, Gage,
Tucker, Landon
✸ Grayson's sound is a kind of Rosetta stone of modern fashions, connecting the dots from Grace to Mason. Grayson's looks, though, give it a personality all its own: pure preppy elegance. (Doesn't Gracen look like something else entirely?) In the past, this name might have seemed a little *too* elegant, as if it were trying too hard. Today, when names like Bentley and Easton have gone cowboy, it fits right in.
In the World: Singer Greyson Chance; Dick Grayson, the alter ego of Batman's sidekick Robin

Gregory (GREH-gə-ree)   1962: #21
Popularity: #279
Styles: Mid-Century, Surfer
'60s
Nicknames: Greg, Greig,   1880 Today
Grisha
Variants: Gregor, Grigori, Gregorio, Greig
Sisters: Cynthia, Teresa, Valerie, Deborah,
Monica, Kimberly
Brothers: Stephen, Timothy, Douglas,
Kenneth, Geoffrey, Philip
✸ Popes, saints, and Gregory Peck! Can a name get any more distinguished? Except you know he'll go by Greg, which may conjure up Greg Brady's bell bottoms instead. Nonetheless, a can't-miss classic that's not too common.
In the World: Actors Gregory Peck and Greg Kinnear; dancer Gregory Hines; Greg of *The Brady Bunch*

Griffin (GRI-fin)   2011: #229
Popularity: #228
Styles: Celtic, The "-ens,"
Nickname-Proof
Variants: Griffith   1880 Today
Sisters: Regan, Carys,
Bethan, Wynn, Willow, Emlyn
Brothers: Owen, Gavin, Connor, Trevor, Rhys,
Graham
✸ The griffin (or gryphon) is a majestic creature of legend, part eagle and part lion. As a name, Griffin is a form of the Welsh Griffith. It's spirited, traditional, and just plain cute.
In the World: Actor/director Griffin Dunne; actor Griffin O'Neal; the Griffin family of *Family Guy*

Gunnar (GUH-ner)   2011: #503
Popularity: #502
Styles: German and Dutch,
Nordic
Variants: Gunner, Gunther   1880 Today
Sisters: Annika, Lisbeth,
Sofie, Lena, Alexia, Liv
Brothers: Soren, Axel, Rutger, Wolf, Jaeger,
Torben
✸ Americans used to shy away from this Northern European classic because of its warlike sound. These days, that's exactly what draws them to it. (The proof? The spelling Gunner is equally popular.) It's handsome and rugged and makes a fine comrade for Hunter and Rider.

Gus (GUHS)   1888: #121
Popularity: #1411
Styles: Guys and Dolls,
Nicknames
Sisters: Lucy, Hazel, Lottie,   1880 Today
Ruby, Bess, Pearl, Sylvie
Brothers: Abe, Milo, Max, Archie, Leo, Cal,
Roscoe
✸ Gus has a "shabby chic" appeal that's catching the attention of the Max and Gracie crowd. Parents swoon over the name, but don't actually pull the trigger. It's just not serious enough for a birth certificate. So what can you use for a formal version? How about August, Augustus, Gustave, or Angus?
In the World: Director Gus Van Sant; sportscaster Gus Johnson; the phrase "gloomy Gus"

Guy (GIY)   1891: #67
Popularity: #1239
Styles: Solid Citizens, Saints,
Brisk and Breezy, French
Variants: Guido
Sisters: Belle, Cora, May,
Delia, June, Rosa
Brothers: Hugh, Van, Clark, Roy, Jules, Hal

★The obvious problem here is lower-case "guy," the everyday term for a man. "Hey, Guy," you say, and nobody thinks you're using his name. If you can cope with that, the name is utterly charming, a handsome shot of retro chic. Guy was a hot mid-century name in France, where it's pronounced "GHEE."
In the World: Conspirator Guy Fawkes; actor Guy Pearce; restaurateur Guy Fieri; Muppet game show host Guy Smiley

Hal (HAL)   1956: #305
Popularity: #5732
Styles: Solid Citizens,
Nicknames
Sisters: Nan, Alice, June,
Polly, Bess, Reba
Brothers: Lon, Rex, Stewart, Clark, Ned, Hugh

★ Simple but steeped in tradition, Hal should fit in handsomely with the new crop of Charlies and Leos. It can be a strong nickname (or namesake) for a Harry, Henry, or Harold. A young Hal may still receive requests to "open the pod bay doors." Just teach him from toddlerhood to respond, "I'm sorry, Dave."
In the World: HAL 9000, the intelligent computer of *2001: A Space Odyssey*; actor Hal Holbrook

Hamilton (HA-məl-tuhn)   1883: #347
Popularity: #1934
Styles: Last Names First,
Ladies and Gentlemen
Nicknames: Ham
Sisters: Adaline, Louisa,
Cordelia, Lorraine, Harriet, Augusta
Brothers: Watson, Franklin, Crawford, Webster, Richmond, Thornton

★Presidential surnames from Jefferson to Carter are popular choices right now. Hamilton is not technically a presidential surname, but the next best thing (a founding father). This could be a hit if you manage to work around the nickname Ham.
In the World: Founding father Alexander Hamilton; politician Hamilton Jordan; *Perry Mason* DA Hamilton Burger

Hamish (HAY-mish)   2008: #5471
Popularity: #9927
Styles: Celtic
Variants: Seamus
Sisters: Maisie, Ailsa, Iona,
Finola, Mirren, Elspeth
Brothers: Lachlan, Angus, Callum, Tavish, Finlay, Ewan

★A Scottish form of James akin to the Irish Seamus, Hamish is thoroughly charming but inevitably mispronounced. (Use a long "A" sound.) The name is seldom heard outside of Australia, where Scottish name traditions run deep.
In the World: Australian comedian Hamish Blake; actor Hamish Linklater; fictional detective Hamish MacBeth

Harlan (HAR-lan)   1924: #252
Popularity: #1131
Styles: Last Names First,
Nickname-Proof, Country
and Western
Variants: Harland
Sisters: Belle, Virginia, Charlotte, Landry,
Marian, Opal, Faye, Delta
Brothers: Leland, Alton, Boyd, Denver,
Houston, Deacon, Hollis, Winston

★ Harlan is a bygone name that needn't be forgotten. It started off as a form of the surname Harland, but that missing "d" makes it sound more contemporary. Harlan's Southern lilt and easy confidence are a slower paced answer to the zippy new cowboy names like Trace and Colt.
In the World: Writers Harlan Ellison and Harlan Coben; Supreme Court justice Harlan Fiske Stone

Harold (HA-rəld)   1920: #12
Popularity: #843
Styles: Ladies and Gentlemen
Nicknames: Harry, Hal
Variants: Harald
Sisters: Frances, Leona,
Edith, Irene, Doris, Martha
Brothers: Eugene, Leonard, Walter, Bernard,
Ernest, Alfred

★This noble old Anglo-Saxon name has fallen sadly from grace. It could be cute for a little boy and solid for a grown man, but runs into nerd trouble in adolescence. The renewed luster of the nickname Harry could help smooth those bumps.
In the World: Films *Harold and Maude* and *Harold and Kumar Go to White Castle*; children's book *Harold and the Purple Crayon*

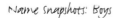

Harris (HA-ris) 1889: #313
Popularity: #1412
Styles: Last Names First,
Solid Citizens, Why Not?
Nicknames: Harry   1880   Today
Sisters: Marian, Nell,
Ramona, Marjorie, Althea, Dorothy
Brothers: Foster, Edison, Walton, Ellis, Clifton,
Fletcher
✴ Harris tweed is the perfect emblem for this name's gentlemanly button-down style. Harris is a great choice to either dress up Harry or mellow down Harrison.
In the World: Harris tweed cloth

Harrison (HA-ri-sən) 1888: #52
Popularity: #197
Styles: Last Names First,
Timeless
Nicknames: Harry   1880   Today
Sisters: Caroline, Elise,
Madeline, Julianna, Cecilia, Isabel
Brothers: Spencer, Bennett, Anderson,
Clayton, Davis, Preston
✴ Harrison is a timeless gentleman's name that has enjoyed a recent wave of popularity. It represents the dignified end of the surname spectrum, a contrast with the jauntier tradesman names. If all that dignity seems a bit frosty, have no fear: the nickname Harry will warm you right up.
In the World: Actor Harrison Ford; presidents Benjamin Harrison and William Henry Harrison

Harry (HA-ree) 1889: #8
Popularity: #709
Styles: Guys and Dolls
Nicknames: Hal
Sisters: Annie, Lena, Molly,   1880   Today
Lucy, Stella, Alice
Brothers: Charlie, Joe, Sam, Teddy, Lewis, Roy
✴ Young wizard Harry Potter has pulled off another dazzling trick: he's made the most unassuming name in English remarkable. Harry is aggressively ordinary, which is a big source of its charm. It's like your favorite, coziest old sweater that you curl up in at the end of the day. If that's not quite enough, it can also be a nickname for Henry, Harold, Harris, or Harrison.
In the World: Wizard Harry Potter; President Harry S Truman; singer Harry Belafonte; magician Harry Houdini

Harvey (HAHR-vee) 1884: #53
Popularity: #862
Styles: Guys and Dolls
Nicknames: Harve
Variants: Hervé   1880   Today
Sisters: Della, Pearl, Harriet,
Mabel, Ruby, Maisie
Brothers: Barney, Sidney, Hugh, Dorsey,
Ernest, Archie
✴ Harvey began as an elegant surname for boys, like androgynous favorites Ashley and Sidney. To Americans today, though, the name is anything but elegant. Harvey comes across as a burly, honest, hardworking guy circa 1940. In the U.K., the name's image has turned the corner from outmoded to charming throwback. It's a Brit hit alongside other cutely clunky names like Archie and Barney.
In the World: Actor Harvey Keitel; politician Harvey Milk; producer Harvey Weinstein; Harvey Wallbanger cocktail

Haskell (HAS-kəl) 1908: #429
Popularity: #12,883
Styles: Last Names First,
Jewish, Guys and Dolls,
Nickname-Proof   1880   Today
Variants: Haskel, Ezekiel
Sisters: Golda, Sadie, Frieda, Sybil, Theda,
Larue
Brothers: Sander, Merrill, Burgess, Herschel,
Gershon, Winslow
✴ Haskell is a Yiddish version of Ezekiel, as well as an English surname. That's an unusual mix with a likable result. Haskell sounds like a fun-loving guy.

Hayden (HAY-dən) 2006: #73
Popularity: #90
Styles: The "-ens," Bell
Tones, Last Names First,
Nickname-Proof   1880   Today
Variants: Haden
Sisters: Hailey, Madelyn, Ava, Sydney, Marley,
Hannah
Brothers: Austin, Dylan, Hunter, Logan, Tyler,
Landon
✴ To your grandparents, this name sounds like a tough old football coach. They'll be shocked to hear that Hayden is now trendy, and used for girls too. Today's parents hear this surname as a pal to Brayden and Cayden, not a grizzled lord of the gridiron.
In the World: Football coach Hayden Fry; TV Coach Hayden Fox; actor Hayden Christensen

Heath (HEETH) 1974: #181
Popularity: #856
Styles: Brisk and Breezy,
Charms and Graces,
'70s–'80s
Sisters: April, Shannon,
Leigh, Holly, Tara, Paige
Brothers: Lance, Shane, Casey, Rhett, Derek,
Birch
✳ Heath was a modest hit in the '70s and '80s,
never common enough to be too trendy. Today
it still sounds contemporary, a nice balance of
preppy, jock, and tree-hugger. For some it will
bring to mind the untimely death of actor Heath
Ledger.
In the World: Actor Heath Ledger; Heath candy
bars

Hector (HEHK-ter) 2005: #166
Popularity: #247
Styles: Latino/Latina,
Classical, Nickname-Proof,
Mythological
Sisters: Leticia, Diana,
Roxana, Celia, Luciana, Silvia
Brothers: Victor, Ruben, Omar, Raul, Hugo,
Cesar
✳ Like many top names from classical litera-
ture, Hector has taken a nosedive as an English
first name. Among Spanish speakers, though,
the name has held on strong as a classic, power-
ful name for boys.
In the World: Actor Héctor Elizondo; singer
Héctor Lavoe

Henry (HEHN-ree) 1881: #8
Popularity: #57
Styles: Timeless, Antique
Charm
Nicknames: Harry, Hank, Hal
Variants: Henri, Henrik,
Enrico, Enrique
Sisters: Charlotte, Eleanor, Lucy, Alice,
Sophia, Grace
Brothers: Samuel, Charles, George, Edward,
Oliver, Joseph
✳ Good old Henry felt a little sluggish in the
second half of the 20th century, when lighter
boy's names dominated. But parents are starting
to come back to the fold, and Henry is now
positively trendy in upscale neighborhoods.
The name's image is warm and friendly, yet ut-
terly respectable.
In the World: Centuries of distinguished Henrys
in every field of endeavor

Herbert (HER-bert) 1929: #25
Popularity: #1786
Styles: Ladies and Gentlemen
Nicknames: Herb, Bert
Sisters: Pauline, Harriet,
Lucille, Muriel, Loretta,
Florence
Brothers: Chester, Wallace, Clarence, Lester,
Vernon, Howard
✳ Starting in the 1800s, Herbert had a century-
long run of popularity. It's unlikely to happen
again soon. Like many names descended from
Old German, it sounded romantic and valiant
circa 1850 but seems simply old-fashioned
today.
In the World: Musician Herb Alpert; U.S. presi-
dent Herbert Hoover

Herman (HER-min) 1893: #44
Popularity: #1674
Styles: Ladies and
Gentlemen, German and
Dutch
Nicknames: Herm, Manny
Variants: Hermann, Armand, Armando, Armin
Sisters: Dora, Harriet, Louise, Hilda, Florence,
Edith
Brothers: Luther, Ernest, Horace, Chester,
Alfred, Walter
✳ One of the hearty German favorites of the
1900s, Herman is a big ol' lunk of a name, too
heavy to be fashionable today. What it does offer
is dignity, a precious commodity that keeps it
safe from the depths of the dust heap. Also con-
sider the related name Armin, a touch lighter
but still serious.
In the World: Monster dad Herman of *The Mun-
sters*; writer Herman Melville; politician Herman Cain

Holden (HOHL-dən)　　2011: #300
Popularity: #299
Styles: The "-ens," Literary
and Artistic, Last Names
First, Nickname-Proof　　1880　Today
Sisters: Harper, Scarlett,
Macy, Maya, Eden, Willow
Brothers: Sawyer, Cooper, Harrison, Mason,
Carter, Beckett
✴ Holden Caulfield, the brooding young protagonist of *The Catcher in the Rye*, makes this name a bit edgier than the many other surname choices. The book has been popular for over 60 years, but the name is thoroughly contemporary.
In the World: Holden Caulfield of *The Catcher in the Rye*; sons of actors Rick Schroder, Brendan Fraser, and Mira Sorvino

Homer (HOH-mer)　　1893: #64
Popularity: #4530
Styles: Porch Sitters,
Namesakes
Sisters: Opal, Wilma, Dolly,　　1880　Today
Zelda, Irma, Olive
Brothers: Waldo, Grover, Roscoe, Elmer,
Amos, Luther
✴ D'oh! In a world without Homer Simpson, this name would be a player. It has the simplicity, roots, literary clout, and surprise factor that avant-garde parents love. But who would want to live in a world without Homer Simpson anyway?
In the World: Homer Simpson of *The Simpsons*; the Greek epic poet Homer; children's book *Homer Price*; home run

Horace (HOH-ris)　　1880: #79
Popularity: #3174
Styles: Ladies and
Gentlemen, Nickname-Proof
Variants: Horatio　　1880　Today
Sisters: Lenore, Henrietta,
Eudora, Cornelia, Maude, Agatha
Brothers: Claude, Luther, Osborne, Roscoe,
Clement, Ambrose
✴ The classical literary icons Horace, Virgil, and Homer share a sad fate in modern namehood. They've lost their literary pedigree and are more likely to show up as comic relief than as a leading man. Of the three, Horace is the gruffest, not a man to be trifled with. This is a name that would sound good with muttonchop whiskers and a gold pocket watch.
In the World: Education advocate Horace Mann; reformer Horace Greeley; "Harry Potter" professor Horace Slughorn

Horatio (hoh-RAY-shee-oh)　　1880: #465
Popularity: #7647
Styles: Exotic Traditional,
Shakespearean, Literary and
Artistic　　1880　Today
Nicknames: Ray, Rash
Variants: Horace
Sisters: Guinevere, Paloma, Portia, Beatrix,
Hermione, Morgana
Brothers: Atticus, Philo, Bartholomew, Albion,
Phineas, Barnabas
✴ Thanks to real-life naval hero Admiral Horatio Nelson and fictional counterpart Horatio Hornblower, this name sounds ready to take to the high seas. It's madly outdated but so vigorous that it seems not to have noticed. An eccentric stud name.
In the World: Horatio Hornblower of C. S. Forester's "Horatio Hornblower" series; Admiral Horatio Nelson; writer Horatio Alger; actor Horatio Sanz

Howard (HOW-erd)　　1912: #25
Popularity: #960
Styles: Solid Citizens
Nicknames: Howie, Ward
Sisters: Irene, Loretta, Eileen,　　1880　Today
Lois, Frances, Pauline
Brothers: Leonard, Milton, Norman, Marvin,
Stanley, Vernon
✴ Once upon a time, Howard sounded like an elegant English surname. Generations of first-name popularity erased that image. Today the name's slow, gentle sound is out of fashion, and the lack of a zippy nickname seals its fate.
In the World: Radio host Howard Stern; tycoon Howard Hughes; Howard Johnson motels; movie *Howard the Duck*

Hudson (HUHD-sən)　　2011: #112
Popularity: #112
Styles: Last Names First,
Place Names
Nicknames: Hud　　1880　Today
Sisters: Harlow, Marley,
Stella, Gracie, Hadley, Larsen
Brothers: Lincoln, Tucker, Preston, Gibson,
Cooper, Paxton
✴ Hudson has an old-fashioned heft that keeps it from disappearing in the current flood of perky surnames. It conjures up the long curves of old Hudson automobiles and the steady flow of the Hudson River. Gruff and reliable.
In the World: Explorer Henry Hudson; Doc Hudson, a vintage Hudson Hornet in the film *Cars*

Hugh (HYOO) 1887: #69
Popularity: #951
Styles: Solid Citizens, Ladies
and Gentlemen, Saints,
English, Why Not? 1880 Today
Nicknames: Hud
Variants: Hugo, Huw, Hughes
Sisters: Delia, Alice, Marian, Dorothea,
Harriet, Nola
Brothers: Guy, Ellis, Clark, Reid, Lewis, Foster
✷ Hugh is a simple classic with a big surprise
factor. It sounds like a standard, but has never
ranked among the top 100 boys' names. That
makes for a nice opportunity to choose a name
that's both familiar and distinctive. If you want
to blow Americans' minds, try the Welsh version
Huw.
In the World: Actors Hugh Jackman, Hugh
Grant, and Hugh Laurie; *Playboy* founder
Hugh Hefner

Hugo (HYOO-goh) 2005: #370
Popularity: #439
Styles: Ladies and
Gentlemen, French, Latino/
Latina 1880 Today
Nicknames: Huey
Sisters: Lola, Ivy, Astrid, Phoebe, Luna, Thea
Brothers: Oscar, Bruno, Felix, Xavier, Milo,
Hector
✷ For most of the 20th century, Hugo was rel-
egated to the dust heap with Amos and Buford.
Eventually, though, parents brushed off the
dust and discovered a funky, charismatic clas-
sic. In its native France, this long-neglected
name has skyrocketed. It's especially adorable
on a toddler.
In the World: 2011 film *Hugo*; actor Hugo Weav-
ing; Venezuelan president Hugo Chávez

Hunter (HUHN-ter) 2000: #35
Popularity: #55
Styles: Last Names First, New
Classics, Macho Swagger
Nicknames: Hunt 1880 Today
Sisters: Autumn, Haley,
Taylor, Payton, Brooke, Aubrey
Brothers: Tanner, Mason, Garrett, Carter,
Sawyer, Jackson
✷ The primal power of the hunt, mixed with
the fearless gonzo style of writer Hunter S.
Thompson, makes this a name with machismo
to burn. Yet the name doesn't look wild or rug-
ged; it's like a guy in a tux throwing a jackknife.
That's turning out to be a killer combination for
today's parents.
In the World: Writer Hunter S. Thompson; actor
Hunter Parrish; singer Hunter Hayes

Ian (EE-ən) 2005: #67
Popularity: #72
Styles: Celtic, New Classics,
Nickname-Proof, Short and
Sweet 1880 Today
Variants: Iain, Ean, Eoin
Sisters: Mia, Claire, Zoe, Jenna, Audrey, Lily
Brothers: Colin, Liam, Gavin, Ramsey, Conor,
Logan
✷ A Scottish form of John, Ian makes a great
match for long Scottish surnames. While no
longer the exotic choice it was a generation ago,
it's still light, fresh, and decidedly Celtic.
In the World: Actors Ian McKellen and Ian
Somerhalder; James Bond creator Ian Fleming

Ike (IYK) 1884: #184
Popularity: #2099
Styles: Guys and Dolls,
Nicknames, Macho Swagger
Sisters: Nora, Elsie, Josie, 1880 Today
Mae, Bess, Mazie, Roxie
Brothers: Gus, Eli, Ezra, Cal, Dock, Fritz, Nate
✷ Ike is traditionally a nickname for Isaac, and
occasionally for other long-"I" names like Ivan
or Isaiah (or, in the case of "I Like Ike" Eisen-
hower, for Dwight). It's tough and playful, like
Spike without the silliness. If you want to make
absolutely certain your son goes by Ike, it's not
out of bounds to choose it as a full name.
In the World: President Dwight Eisenhower;
musician Ike Turner; football player Ike Taylor

Inigo (I-ni-goh)   2009: #7673
Popularity: #11,292
Styles: Exotic Traditional,
Literary and Artistic
Variants: Íñigo, Eneko   1880 Today
Sisters: Ione, Hermione, Clio,
Tanith, Sidony, Lilias
Brothers: Ivor, Ludovic, Horatio, Calix,
Peregrine, Tycho
✳ Inigo is a name that defies cultural pigeon-
holes. It's English, from Spanish, from Basque.
It's dashing like the avenging swordsman Inigo
Montoya of *The Princess Bride*, yet bookish like
the 17th-century British architect Inigo Jones.
That's a splendid combo, but be warned that it
will constantly be mistaken for Indigo, or
stressed on the second syllable on the model of
the movie character.
In the World: Architect Inigo Jones; "My name
is Inigo Montoya. You killed my father. Prepare
to die."

Irving (ER-ving)   1912: #94
Popularity: #1370
Styles: Guys and Dolls, Porch
Sitters, Last Names First
Nicknames: Irv   1880 Today
Variants: Irvine
Sisters: Gladys, Muriel, Irma, Bernice, Pauline,
Frieda
Brothers: Sidney, Morris, Willard, Harvey,
Seymour, Murray
✳ Irving is straight out of the immigrant 1890s.
New Americans chose this Scottish surname
because it sounded dashing and highbrow. Case
in point: songwriter Irving Berlin, born in Rus-
sia as Israel Baline. Ironically, these fancy "aspi-
rational names" now sound antiquated, while
the old-fashioned ethnic names they replaced
(Ike, Molly, Sadie) are back in bloom.
In the World: Songwriter Irving Berlin; photographer Irving Penn; film producer Irving Thal-
berg; writer Irving Wallace

Isaac (IY-zik)   2011: #35
Popularity: #35
Styles: Antique Charm,
Biblical
Nicknames: Ike, Zak   1880 Today
Variants: Isaak, Yitzhak
Sisters: Hannah, Amelia, Phoebe, Abigail,
Leah, Isabel
Brothers: Caleb, Zachary, Samuel, Levi, Noah,
Gabriel
✳ Isaac used to sound forbiddingly ancient.
Today parents are noticing the name's long-
neglected charms. It is simple, familiar, and
handsome. It has strapping nicknames. And
with broader use of the name, Isaac's archaic
image has softened to become glowingly distin-
guished.
In the World: Scientist Isaac Newton; writers
Isaac Asimov and Isaac Bashevis Singer; singer
Isaac Hayes

Isaiah (iy-ZAY-ə)   2006: #39
Popularity: #43
Styles: Biblical, African-
American, Antique Charm
Nicknames: Izzy, Ike   1880 Today
Variants: Isaias
Sisters: Naomi, Isabella, Mariah, Rebekah,
Angelina, Delilah
Brothers: Elijah, Gabriel, Malachi, Jeremiah,
Jonas, Levi
✳ The new popularity of Old Testament names
like Ethan and Noah has opened the doors to
more exotic examples. They're great ways to in-
dulge your taste for elaborate names without
fear that your son will sound flowery or silly.
Like the similar Elijah, Isaiah first caught on
with African-Americans and is now across-the-
board popular.
In the World: Basketball player/coach Isiah
Thomas; philosopher Isaiah Berlin; actor Isaiah
Washington

Ivan (IY-vin, ee-VAHN) 2004: #117
Popularity: #128
Styles: Timeless, Saints,
Slavic, Latino/Latina
Nicknames: Vanya   1880 Today
Variants: Iván
Sisters: Marina, Elena, Natalia, Sasha, Anya,
Nika
Brothers: Victor, Roman, Maxim, Dimitri,
Lukas, Adrian
✴Russian men's names tend to be intriguing
but inaccessible. Ivan, a form of John, is a nota-
ble exception. It's simple, strong, and pleasantly
mysterious. The English version, stressed on the
first syllable, is a little less mysterious and a little
more old-fashioned.
In the World: Czar Ivan the Terrible; writer Ivan
Turgenev; baseball players Iván Nova and Iván
Rodríguez

Ivor (IY-vawr, EE-vawr) 1902: #933
Popularity: Very rare
Styles: English, Celtic, Exotic
Traditional, Why Not?
Variants: Ivar   1880 Today
Sisters: Ione, Adair, Glynis,
Philippa, Averil, Sidony
Brothers: Piers, Clive, Vaughan, Gregor, Kier,
Tarquin
✴Craving the unusual? Drawn to the tradi-
tional? Take a look at Ivor. This simple, distinc-
tive name has dual Norse and Gaelic roots and
a long history in Scotland and Wales. It was
once modestly common in England, but in the
U.S. it's completely fresh.
In the World: Composer Ivor Novello

Jabez (JAY-behz, JAH-behz) 2002: #1306
Popularity: #2698
Styles: Biblical, Exotic
Traditional
Sisters: Keziah, Avital,   1880 Today
Salome, Keturah, Atara, Jael
Brothers: Boaz, Japheth, Eliezer, Aeneas,
Gideon, Azriel
✴Now that Ezra and Zachariah have found
their way into our preschools, the path is clear
for serious biblical rarities. Jabez certainly fits
the bill. It's barely familiar, but short and sweet
with a snazzy "-z" ending. The biblical Jabez
was an honorable man who had his prayers an-
swered, and "the prayer of Jabez" has attracted a
devoted following.

Jace (JAYS) 2011: #106
Popularity: #106
Styles: Brisk and Breezy
Variants: Jayce, Jase
Sisters: Reese, Skylar, Brynn,   1880 Today
Rylee, Eden, Sienna
Brothers: Cade, Gage, Maddox, Bryce, Jair,
Ryder
✴This is the new leaner, meaner version of
Jason. Jace is slick and tough, ready to roll as a
race-car driver or a teen idol.
In the World: Jace Wayland, protagonist of the
"Mortal Instruments" fantasy series

Jack (JAK) 1927: #16
Popularity: #45
Styles: Timeless, Nicknames,
Guys and Dolls
Variants: John, Jake   1880 Today
Sisters: Ella, Kate, Mia, Ruby,
Molly, Lily, Grace
Brothers: Luke, Will, Cole, Henry, Max, Nick,
Joe
✴This traditional nickname for John turns the
classic upside down. John is the strong, silent
type. Alter ego Jack is a tough but fun-loving
bloke, the name of choice for romantic adven-
turers and giant-killers. It's an irresistible image
to parents on both sides of the Atlantic, who
have flocked to Jack as a given name while John
has slipped out of fashion.
In the World: Captain Jack Sparrow of *Pirates of
the Caribbean*; Jack Dawson of *Titanic*; Jack the
Ripper; Jack and Jill

Jackson (JAK-sən) 2011: #23
Popularity: #23
Styles: The "-ens," Last
Names First, Literary and
Artistic   1880 Today
Nicknames: Jack, Jax
Variants: Jaxon
Sisters: Avery, Claire, Addison, Ella, Kennedy,
Harper
Brothers: Mason, Wyatt, Lincoln, Cooper,
Landon, Carter
✴Jackson has history, tradition, and a spot-on
stylish sound. As a firmly masculine surname, it
makes a good sibling match for androgynous
girls like Bailey and Taylor. Painter Jackson Pol-
lock lends the name an extra creative-power
panache.
In the World: Artist Jackson Pollock; President
Andrew Jackson; singer Michael Jackson; Gen-
eral "Stonewall" Jackson

Jacob (JAY-kuhb) 1998: #2
Popularity: #1
Styles: Antique Charm,
Biblical
Nicknames: Jake, Jay, Coby, 1880 Today
Jaco, Cub
Variants: Jakob, Yakov
Sisters: Hannah, Abigail, Emily, Olivia, Chloe,
Sophia
Brothers: Ethan, Caleb, Jonah, Lucas, Noah,
Joshua
★This is the name that unseated Michael
from its longtime perch as America's favorite
boy's name. Jacob has it all: Old Testament ori-
gins; turn-of-the-century style; the popular "j,"
"ay," and "k" sounds; and strong nicknames.
The playgrounds are now crammed with Jakes,
but the name should be enough of a classic to
weather the popularity storm.
In the World: "Twilight" werewolf Jacob Black;
social reformer Jacob Riis

Jacoby (jə-KOH-bee) 2008: #422
Popularity: #487
Styles: Last Names First
Nicknames: Jake, Coby
Variants: Jacobi 1880 Today
Sisters: Brooklyn, Ryleigh,
Hadley, Kennedy, Jasmyn, Addison
Brothers: Skylar, Trey, Finnegan, Bentley,
Lennox, Brady
★Jacoby is a surname meaning "son of Jacob."
Unlike Jacobs or Jacobson, though, Jacoby
turns the name Jacob inside out, changing its
rhythm and making the "o" sound dominant.
That places the name closer to surnames like
McKenzie and new names like Kobe (J'Kobe?)
than to Jacob.
In the World: Singer Jacoby Shaddix; baseball
player Jacoby Ellsbury; football player Jacoby
Jones

Jagger (JA-ger) 2011: #639
Popularity: #640
Styles: Last Names First,
Namesakes, Macho Swagger
Nicknames: Jag 1880 Today
Sisters: Harlow, Presley,
Ember, Marley, Everly, Ripley
Brothers: Lennox, Ryker, Cash, Jett, Madden,
Slater
★Jagger was an old Yorkshire term for a ped-
dler, but you're excused if the only occupation
that comes to mind is rock star. Rolling Stone
Mick Jagger makes this name the cockiest of all
the tradesman names.
In the World: Rock musician Mick Jagger; song
"Moves Like Jagger"

Jake (JAYK) 2004: #98
Popularity: #129
Styles: Guys and Dolls,
Nicknames
Sisters: Ella, Sophie, Molly, 1880 Today
Tess, Jenna, Paige, Abby
Brothers: Alex, Dylan, Max, Luke, Brady, Cole,
Ryan
★Like Jack, this is a brash nickname that par-
ents are choosing on its own, bypassing the
more reserved formal version. But be prepared
to say over and over again, "No, not Jacob, it's
just Jake."
In the World: Actor Jake Gyllenhaal; boxer Jake
LaMotta; singer Jake Owen; football player Jake
Delhomme

Jalen (JAY-lin) 2000: #106
Popularity: #399
Styles: Bell Tones, The
"-ens," African-American
Nicknames: Jay 1880 Today
Variants: Jaylen, Jaylin,
Jaylon, Jalyn, Jaelyn, Jayleen
Sisters: Janae, Makayla, Breanna, Jasmyn, Tyra,
Kiana
Brothers: Braylon, Jaxon, Tyrese, Darian, Kobe,
Keenan
★This contemporary name first became famil-
iar via basketball star Jalen Rose. Today it's a hit
chosen widely for babies of all races and both
sexes. Jalen, Jaylen, and Jaylon are the most reli-
ably masculine spellings.
In the World: Basketball player Jalen Rose

Jamal (jah-MAHL) 1994: #240
Popularity: #677
Styles: African-American,
Muslim, Nickname-Proof
Variants: Jamaal, Jamil 1880 Today
Sisters: Jalisa, Naima,
Jasmine, Dasia, Chantel, Aisha
Brothers: Ahmad, Kareem, Terrell, Jovan,
Rashad, Khalil

✹ From the Arabic word for "beauty," Jamal is a modern African-American standard. It has plenty of company, with such similar-styled names as Jamar and Jajuan, but Jamal is the real deal. Its meaning and roots will keep it around for the long term.
In the World: Basketball players Jamaal Wilkes and Jamal Crawford; actor Malcolm-Jamal Warner

James (JAYMZ) 1944: #1
Popularity: #17
Styles: Timeless, Biblical
Nicknames: Jim, Jamie, Jem,
Jaime, Jimmy 1880 Today
Sisters: Elizabeth, Anna,
Emily, Katherine, Sarah, Julia
Brothers: Thomas, William, Robert, Peter,
Joseph, Charles

✹ James is one of the strongest of all names, an elegant, slashing verbal sword. Jim, on the other hand, is a laid-back sort of guy. And this is a name where you have to pick sides—if a guy is called Jim, he's always only Jim. If you want just an occasional nickname, try Jamie, or go the initials route, à la James ("JT") Taylor, or James ("JC") Penney.
In the World: Countless men named James, Jimmy, and Jim—from President James Madison to rock legend Jimi Hendrix

Jameson (JAY-mə-sən) 2011: #211
Popularity: #210
Styles: Last Names First
Nicknames: Jamie, James
Variants: Jamison 1880 Today
Sisters: Kendall, Larkin,
Aubrey, Harper, Jillian, Marlowe
Brothers: Easton, Remington, Beckett, Preston,
Chase, Jefferson

✹ Jameson is part of a small, thriving genre of names: first names made out of surnames that were made out of first names. Watch it in action: the old favorite Jack yielded Jackson (Jack's son). Elegant Jackson is now a trendy given name . . . with the nickname Jack. Same story for Jameson, which exchanges the regal style of James for a contemporary rhythm.
In the World: Actor Jameson Parker; Jameson Irish whiskey

Japheth (JAY-feth, JA-feth) 2007: #2497
Popularity: #3177
Styles: Biblical, Exotic
Traditional, Why Not?
Nicknames: Japh, Jay 1880 Today
Variants: Jafetz
Sisters: Tirzah, Atara, Damaris, Dinah, Keziah,
Yael
Brothers: Joah, Simeon, Phineas, Boaz,
Gideon, Jabez

✹ Parents are willing to dig deep for biblical names right now—just look at the popularity of Ezekiel and Zechariah. How, then, to explain the neglect of this attractive example? Japheth was the eldest son of Noah, and his name is rare but accessible.

Jared (JEH-rid, JA-rid) 1998: #51
Popularity: #266
Styles: Biblical, '70s–'80s,
Turn of the 21st Century,
Nickname-Proof 1880 Today
Variants: Jarrod, Jarod, Jered,
Jerrod, Jarred
Sisters: Kendra, Bethany, Jenna, Holly, Rachel,
Megan
Brothers: Aaron, Joshua, Trevor, Jeremy, Seth,
Kyle

✹ A modern biblical favorite, Jared is unfussy and comfortably straddles the line between boyish and manly. The popular variation Jarrod transforms the name from biblical to surname. Another surprisingly popular spelling, Jarred, transforms the name into a container of jam.
In the World: Actors Jared Leto and Jared Padalecki; Subway pitchman Jared; author Jared Diamond; Just Jared website

Name Snapshots: Boys 281

Jaron (JA-rən, jə-RAHN)   2001: #440
Popularity: #983
Styles: The "-ens," Jewish,
African-American,
Nickname-Proof   1880   Today
Sisters: Mariah, Ariel, Jada,
Talia, Regan, Mara
Brothers: Micah, Owen, Josiah, Adrian, Devon,
Elijah
✴ With the stress on the first syllable, Jaron is a
modern Hebrew name with an appealing mean-
ing ("to call out" or "to sing") and a contempo-
rary sound. Place the stress on the second
syllable and you have an equally contemporary
African-American name.
In the World: Pop duo Evan and Jaron

Jarrett (JA-rit)   1998: #282
Popularity: #1036
Styles: Last Names First,
'70s–'80s, African-American,
Turn of the 21st Century   1880   Today
Variants: Jarrod, Jarret
Sisters: Lesley, Trista, Lexi, Shayna, Cassidy,
Jenna
Brothers: Tanner, Braxton, Colt, Dalton,
Kendrick, Dillon
✴ Some parents wanted to put their own per-
sonal spin on Jared. Others wanted a rugged-
sounding surname, à la Garrett. Still others
were fans of NASCAR driver Dale Jarrett. To-
gether, they gave birth to a new name with a
sound as familiar as it is modern.
In the World: race-car driver Dale Jarrett; bas-
ketball player Jarrett Jack; Jarret rifles

Jarvis (JAHR-vis)   1989: #358
Popularity: #1264
Styles: '70s–'80s, Country
and Western, Nickname-
Proof, African-American   1880   Today
Variants: Gervase
Sisters: Audra, Lacy, Janelle, Portia, Whitley,
Kendra
Brothers: Lamar, Dexter, Travis, Bryant,
Kendrick, Quincy
✴ Jarvis is either a Texas rabble-rouser or a
proper English butler. Can't reconcile the two?
That might be why this memorable name has
never quite found its footing.
In the World: Musician Jarvis Cocker; football
player Jarvis Green

Jason (JAY-sən)   1974: #2
Popularity: #71
Styles: '70s–'80s,
Mythological, The "-ens"
Nicknames: Jay, Jase   1880   Today
Variants: Jayson
Sisters: Jessica, Amy, Heather, Jennifer, Erin,
Amanda, Melissa, Kelly
Brothers: Kevin, Justin, Christopher, Eric,
Sean, Jonathan, Jeremy, Brian
✴ Jason was everywhere in the '70s and '80s
and is now the quintessential dad name. Yet that
certainly doesn't rule it out for today. This name
is settling into a very comfortable middle age,
with a sound that remains completely current.
Similar-sounding new hits like Jaden and
Mason are tributes to Jason's continuing appeal.
In the World: A generation of actors, singers, and
athletes; the *Friday the 13th* horror villain

Jasper (JAS-per)   1880: #139
Popularity: #282
Styles: Exotic Traditional,
Charms and Graces, Antique
Charm   1880   Today
Nicknames: Jaz
Variants: Casper, Gaspar
Sisters: Phoebe, Eliza, Ivy, Stella, Sadie, Celia,
Luna, Violet
Brothers: Felix, Oliver, Emmett, August, Theo,
Everett, Silas, Foster
✴ Jasper is an old-time favorite that hums
with potential. It's not classically macho, but
has the kind of mischievous charm that makes
all the girls swoon. While Jasper is a gemstone,
the name has a separate origin. It is one of the
names traditionally associated with the three
Magi who visited the infant Jesus.
In the World: Painter Jasper Johns; a member of
the "Twilight" vampire family

Javier (khah-vee-AYR) 2001: #149
Popularity: #194
Styles: Latino/Latina
Nicknames: Javi
Variants: Xavier 1880 Today
Sisters: Ana, Adriana,
Mariana, Natalia, Elena, Silvia, Angelica,
Carolina
Brothers: Sergio, Jorge, Francisco, Julio,
Andres, Miguel, Hector, Roberto
★This sophisticated Spanish and Portuguese
name is both a classic and a contemporary hit.
So far, it has remained an exclusively Latino
name. Families of other backgrounds are jump-
ing on the more "X"-otic version, Xavier.
In the World: Actor Javier Bardem; singers Javier
Solís and Javier Colon; baseball players Javier
López and Javier Vázquez

Jax (JAKS) 2011: #320
Popularity: #319
Styles: Brisk and Breezy,
Fantastical
Variants: Jaxx 1880 Today
Sisters: Aeris, Alexa, Paisley,
Halo, Zoey, Rayne
Brothers: Link, Maddox, Crew, Kane, Raiden,
Slade
★First parents slimmed Jackson down to
Jaxon. Then some trimmed that creation down
to just Jax. Where good old Jack was a giant-
killer, Jax is more apt to battle black magic with
bionic limbs. (It's the name of a popular video
game hero.) The spelling Jaxx is like writing the
name in a heavy metal logo font.
In the World: Major Jackson ("Jax") Briggs of
the "Mortal Kombat" series

Jaxon (JAK-sən) 2011: #86
Popularity: #86
Styles: The "-ens"
Nicknames: Jax
Variants: Jackson, Jaxen, 1880 Today
Jaxton
Sisters: Jazmyn, Lexie, Brooklynn, Kenzie,
Aubree, Skyler
Brothers: Chase, Paxton, Jagger, Maddox,
Zander, Ryder
★Two trends collide . . . "X" is the hottest let-
ter around right now, and surnames like Jackson
are all the rage. So across the country hundreds
of parents simultanously thought up this popu-
lar new creation. The growing use of Jax as both
nickname and given name is helping to make
Jaxon more independent from Jackson.

Jay (JAY) 1960: #78
Popularity: #401
Styles: Timeless, Nicknames,
Mid-Century
Sisters: Kate, Jill, Kim, Diana, 1880 Today
Joy, Leah
Brothers: Neil, Andy, Jon, Dean, Gary, Joel
★This Jay is a rare bird: a timeless nickname.
With its light, sunny style and effortless mascu-
linity, it's a name that can carry you anywhere.
You'd trust the big game to a quarterback
named Jay and your life to a surgeon named Jay.
A baby named Jay is mighty cuddly too. Take it
straight or as a nickname for any name with a
strong "jay" sound, like Jacob or Jayden.
In the World: Rapper Jay-Z; TV host Jay Leno;
writer Jay McInerney

Jayden (JAY-din) 2011: #4
Popularity: #4
Styles: Bell Tones, The
"-ens," African-American,
Androgynous 1880 Today
Variants: Jaden, Jaydon,
Jadon, Jadyn, Jaydan, Jaydin,
Sisters: Kaylee, Brooklyn, Addison, Nevaeh,
Hailey, Jayla
Brothers: Landon, Rylan, Carter, Javion, Brody,
Ashton
★There is a minor Jadon in the Old Testa-
ment, but this is no biblical revival. Cross Jacob
with Aidan and voilà: the sound of the times.
The name's popularity shot up starting in 1998,
when actor parents Will Smith and Jada Pinkett
chose Jaden as a male twist on Mom's name.
The spelling Jayden has since become the dom-
inent choice, boosted by a son of singer Britney
Spears.
In the World: Actor/celebrity child Jaden Smith;
Jayden Federline, son of Britney Spears; Jaden
Yuki of "Yu-Gi-Oh!"

Jebediah (jeh-bə-DIY-ə)   1978: #2072
Popularity: #6352
Styles: Fanciful
Nicknames: Jeb
Variants: Jedediah   1880   Today
★ Public-service announce-
ment: Jebediah is neither a biblical name nor a
traditional name of any kind. I know, there's
founding father Jebediah Springfield from *The
Simpsons* TV show, and a rock band called Jebediah . . . but the band was actually named after
the TV character. You can name your baby after
him too, if you like. But if you want biblical origins, stick with Jedediah, with a "d." And if
you're after the nickname Jeb, it can come from
Jacob or from initials, as in the case of John Ellis
("Jeb") Bush.
In the World: Faux forefather Jebediah Springfield of *The Simpsons*

Jed (JEHD)   1978: #483
Popularity: #1751
Styles: Country and Western,
Nicknames
Variants: Jedidiah   1880   Today
Sisters: Liza, Meg, Ginger,
Edie, Tess, Daisy, Reba
Brothers: Nat, Ty, Hank, Levi, Jake, Kit, Zeke
★ Jed is as plain as Ed and Ted, but feistier. It's
a dandy little cowboy of a name. In the past the
full name Jedidiah would have scared off most
parents, but today it's becoming part of the ap-
peal. If you prefer, though, you can tease the
nickname Jed out of other raw ingredients, like
fictional President Josiah Edward ("Jed") Bart-
let of *The West Wing.*
In the World: Jed Bartlet of *The West Wing*; Jed
Clampett of *The Beverly Hillbillies*

Jedidiah (jeh-di-DIY-ə)   2011: #886
Popularity: #887
Styles: Biblical, Exotic
Traditional, Country and
Western   1880   Today
Nicknames: Jed
Variants: Jedediah
Sisters: Shiloh, Johanna, Delilah, Abigail,
Susannah, Sadie, Keziah, Rebekah
Brothers: Zachariah, Jericho, Matthias, Elijah,
Gabriel, Josiah, Gideon, Jeremiah
★ Jedidiah is an Old Testament name with
full-fledged Puritan flavor. It may be a bit much
for some families, but the cool little moniker
Jed will win many over. See also Jebediah.
In the World: Western trailblazer Jedediah
Strong Smith

Jefferson (JEH-fer-sən)   1891: #251
Popularity: #702
Styles: Timeless, Last Names
First, Why Not?
Nicknames: Jeff   1880   Today
Sisters: Annabel, Campbell,
Mercy, Kennedy, Leighton, Caroline
Brothers: Harrison, Nathaniel, Anderson,
Judson, Turner, Lincoln
★ Jefferson brings Jeffrey into the 21st century,
while summoning images of the 18th. This re-
mains the most presidential of the president
surnames.
In the World: U.S. president Thomas Jefferson;
Confederate president Jefferson Davis

Jeffrey (JEHF-ree)   1966: #9
Popularity: #246
Styles: Mid-Century, Surfer
'60s, '70s–'80s
Nicknames: Jeff   1880   Today
Variants: Geoffrey, Jeffery
Sisters: Kimberly, Lisa, Renee, Melissa, Amy,
Stephanie
Brothers: Timothy, Kevin, Brian, Gregory,
Steven, David
★ Jeffrey was one of the stalwarts of the second
half of the 20th century. Even today it's a basic
feature of our naming landscape: everybody
knows a few Jeffs. The first generation of Jeffreys
is now approaching retirement, though, and
parents are starting to look elsewhere. Despite it
all, the name remains pleasantly youthful.
In the World: A generation of men from actor
Jeff Bridges to Amazon.com founder Jeff Bezos
to killer Jeffrey Dahmer

Jensen (JEHN-sən)   2011: #608
Popularity: #608
Styles: Last Names First, The
"-ens," Androgynous, Why
Not?   1880   Today
Variants: Jenson, Jansen
Sisters: Marley, Claire, Addison, Sienna,
Everly, Larsen
Brothers: Preston, Campbell, Archer, Merrick,
Carlsen, Sutton
★ Names like Mason and Landon have be-
come popular enough that they scarcely show
their surname roots anymore. Jensen still shows
off a full surname style, in a form that's more
banker than cowboy. Its swift, compact sound is
perfectly masculine, though the "Jen-" root
does attract a few parents of girls too.
In the World: Actor Jensen Ackles; auto racer
Jenson Button

Jeremiah (jeh-rə-MIY-ə) 2010: #52
Popularity: #51
Styles: Biblical, African-American
Nicknames: Jerry, Jem 1880 Today
Variants: Jeremy
Sisters: Rebekah, Delilah, Abigail, Aaliyah, Gabriella, Angelina
Brothers: Isaiah, Levi, Josiah, Caleb, Zachariah, Judah
✷ The older brother of Jeremy—much, much older. Jeremiah's antique style is currently the more fashionable of the two. That means this "exotic" variant is actually far more common for babies than the "common" version. That doesn't cost Jeremiah any style points, though, and it might reassure grandparents who can't understand why you don't just choose good old Jeremy.
In the World: Western film *Jeremiah Johnson*; song lyrics "Jeremiah was a bullfrog"; Reverend Jeremiah Wright

Jeremy (JEH-rə-mee) 1977: #15
Popularity: #152
Styles: '70s–'80s, Biblical
Nicknames: Jem, Jerry
Variants: Jeremiah, Jérémie 1880 Today
Sisters: Rachel, Natalie, Stephanie, Amanda, Danielle, Jessica
Brothers: Joshua, Zachary, Adam, Matthew, Kyle, Nathan
✷ A '70s blockbuster, Jeremy has long-term staying power. Its biblical roots are one reason, but the real secret is the name's unusual sound. Unlike Brad and Chad, Eric and Derek, Brian and Ryan, Jeremy has no close competitors. In fact, this name's biggest competition is its own biblical source: see Jeremiah.
In the World: Actors Jeremy Irons and Jeremy Renner; basketball player Jeremy Lin

Jericho (JEH-ri-koh) 2011: #1025
Popularity: #1025
Styles: Biblical, Place Names, Why Not?
Nicknames: Jerry 1880 Today
Sisters: Eden, Shiloh, Sedona, Mercy, Delilah, Abilene
Brothers: Gideon, Deacon, Josiah, Memphis, Jethro, Samson
✷ In the Bible, Jericho was the city where the walls came tumbling down. That's not the cheeriest association. But as a baby name, Jericho is jumping with good cheer. Its bouncing rhythm makes it one of the most energetic biblical names, equally suited for a cowboy, artist, or rock star. Jerry is the obvious nickname, but the kind of parents who are drawn to Jericho aren't likely to use it.
In the World: TV drama *Jericho*; horror video game "Jericho"; football player Jerricho Cotchery

Jermaine (jer-MAYN) 1973: #127
Popularity: #564
Styles: African-American
Variants: Germaine, Jermayne 1880 Today
Sisters: Monique, Janelle, Tamika, Desiree, Keisha, Ericka
Brothers: Antoine, Kendrick, Andre, Terrell, Cedric, Terrance
✷ Jermaine was a top African-American name of the '70s and '80s, created as a twist on the French classic Germaine. (Antwan and D'Andre are similar remixes.) Singer Jermaine Jackson of the Jackson 5 gave this one legs, and it held on to become a standard.
In the World: Musicians Jermaine Jackson and Jermaine Dupri; athletes Jermaine O'Neal and Jermaine Gresham

Jerome (jə-ROHM) 1938: #93
Popularity: #743
Styles: Solid Citizens,
French, African-American
Nicknames: Jerry
Variants: Geronimo,
Hieronymus

1880   Today

Sisters: Teresa, Elaine, Anita, Marianne,
Constance, Yvonne
Brothers: Anthony, Gerard, Roland, Lionel,
Laurence, Bernard
✷ Jerome is a stouthearted teddy bear of a
name. It's smooth and easy—lovable, if not ex-
actly cool. The name's been scarce lately, but it
has the robustness of a classic. Alternative forms
of the name are far more exotic: the Italian
Geronimo and Latin Hieronymus.
In the World: Composer Jerome Kern; director/
choreographer Jerome Robbins; football player
Jerome Bettis

Jerry (JEH-ree) 1941: #14
Popularity: #393
Styles: Mid-Century,
Nicknames
Variants: Gerry
Sisters: Connie, Nancy, Sue,
Janet, Marcia, Jackie
Brothers: Larry, Roger, Steve, Ronnie, Dennis,
Tony
✷ Jerry is a handshake and a smile. The name
isn't especially macho or sophisticated, and it
doesn't try to be. What it tries to be is happy.
From Jerry Mathers "as the Beaver" to Jerry
Garcia of the Grateful Dead, this is a feel-good
name.
In the World: Musicians Jerry Garcia and Jerry
Lee Lewis; comedians Jerry Seinfeld and Jerry
Lewis; Governer Jerry Brown

Jesse (JEH-see) 1981: #37
Popularity: #141
Styles: Timeless, Biblical
Nicknames: Jess
Variants: Jess, Jessie

1880   Today

Sisters: Katie, Rachel, Sara,
Hannah, Maggie, Leah
Brothers: Joshua, Aaron, Wesley, Jonah, Adam,
Casey
✷ Like many Old Testament favorites, Jesse
carries echoes of an earlier America, a land of
farms and frontier. But while Jeremiah and
Joshua were splitting rails and tilling soil, Jesse
was robbing stagecoaches. Timelessly, lawlessly
cool.
In the World: Outlaw Jesse James; singer Jesse
McCartney; athlete Jesse Owens; minister/ac-
tivist Jesse Jackson

Jesús (khay-SOOS, JEE-zəs) 2001: #66
Popularity: #92
Styles: Latino/Latina,
Biblical
Nicknames: Chuy, Chucho
Variants: Jesus

1880   Today

Sisters: Carmen, Ana, Mariana, Guadalupe,
Pilar, Blanca, Rocio, Raquel
Brothers: Juan, Luis, Miguel, Carlos, Manuel,
Javier, Julio, Pedro
✷ In English, the name Jesus has traditionally
been considered an immodest choice. In Span-
ish, though, it's a classic: a heartfelt religious
statement, and an established U.S. hit.
In the World: Jesus of Nazareth

Jethro (JEHTH-roh) 1899: #858
Popularity: #1936
Styles: Biblical, Porch Sitters
Sisters: Jemima, Cleo, Hester,
Elvira, Zilla, Dinah 1880   Today
Brothers: Roscoe, Ezra,
Waldo, Jabez, Amos, Homer
✷ In the Bible, Jethro was the father of Zippo-
rah, wife of Moses. On TV, he was the nephew
of Jed Clampett, Beverly Hillbilly. Guess which
association has won out? The sitcom image of
slow-witted Jethro Bodine has helped keep this
name a funky relic. The confident bounce of
the "-o" ending lends some comeback poten-
tial . . . barely.
In the World: Rock band Jethro Tull; Jethro of
The Beverly Hillbillies

Jett (JEHT)   2011: #332
Popularity: #331
Styles: Brisk and Breezy,
Modern Meanings, Charms
and Graces, Macho Swagger   1880   Today
Variants: Jet
Sisters: Jade, Alexa, Skye, Journey, Quinn,
Eden
Brothers: Drake, Jagger, Cruz, Gage, Jaxon,
Hawk
★ A swaggering rock-and-roll power name.
The spelling Jet is also a deep black mineral and
a magazine—a natural counterpart to *Ebony*.
In the World: TV series *The Famous Jett Jackson*;
singer Joan Jett; late son of actor John Travolta

Joaquin (hwah-KEEN)   2008: #275
Popularity: #328
Styles: Latino/Latina
Nicknames: Quino
Variants: Joachim, Joaquim   1880   Today
Sisters: Mariana, Julia, Sofia,
Jimena, Camila, Catalina, Jazmin, Adriana
Brothers: Javier, Esteban, Julio, Mateo,
Enrique, Armando, Ezequiel, Santiago
★ Joaquin's a Spanish classic that English
speakers used to avoid because its pronuncia-
tion seemed tricky. Now that actor Joaquin
Phoenix has made the name more familiar, its
audience has grown. The less-used English
equivalent is Joachim (JOH-ə-kim).
In the World: Actor Joaquin Phoenix; Domini-
can president Joaquín Balaguer; soccer player
Joaquín Sánchez

Joe (JOH)   1936: #23
Popularity: #491
Styles: Guys and Dolls,
Nicknames
Variants: Jo, JoJo   1880   Today
Sisters: Annie, Jane, Sue,
Molly, Betsy, Mae
Brothers: Ray, Jack, Eddie, Sam, Harry, Pete
★ A good Joe. GI Joe. Heck, even Joe Six-Pack.
For generations, Joe has been the personifica-
tion of the upstanding American everyman.
The name has a warmth and purity that few can
match. But for the birth certificate, why not Jo-
seph? Everyone will be happy to call him Joe
anyway. So just go ahead and give him the more
formal option to use on special occasions.
In the World: The idiom king, as in "an ordinary
Joe," "Joe Cool," and "Say it ain't so, Joe"

Joel (JOHL)   1980: #66
Popularity: #133
Styles: Timeless, Biblical
Sisters: Leah, Natalie, Hope,
Joanna, Rachel, Sara   1880   Today
Brothers: Jared, Seth, Nathan,
Aaron, Daniel, Adam
★ Joel's not flashy. It has been steadily popular
for many years, but not in the top 100. It's bibli-
cal, but unlike the Isaiahs and Ezekiels of the
world, Joel doesn't shout the fact from the roof-
tops. It's quiet and warm, and you'll never tire of
it.
In the World: Performer Joel Grey; singer Joel
Madden; pastor Joel Osteen; filmmaker Joel
Coen

John (JAHN)   1880: #1
Popularity: #27
Styles: Timeless, Biblical
Nicknames: Jack, Johnny
Variants: Jon, Johann, Juan,   1880   Today
Jean, Sean, Ian, Jan
Sisters: Mary, Anna, Catherine, Sarah, Julia,
Margaret, Laura, Elizabeth
Brothers: James, William, Robert, Joseph,
Peter, Charles, Thomas, Paul
★ John is strength in simplicity. The name's
popularity falls further each year, but it's actu-
ally a good match for current tastes. Parents
tempted by the vigorous burst of names like
Trace and Colt might want to reconsider the
classic, which achieves the same force without
trying so hard. And parents lured by the stylish
Jack can go the traditional route, conferring
John with the nickname Jack, à la JFK.
In the World: Too many meanings and references for any one to stick

Jonah (JOH-nə)   2011: #144
Popularity: #144
Styles: Biblical, Antique
Charm
Variants: Jonas   1880   Today
Sisters: Ella, Abigail, Sophie,
Hannah, Lily, Faith
Brothers: Noah, Gabriel, Asher, Eli, Micah,
Ethan
★ Jonah has cute teen-heartthrob style, but
finds strength and gravity in its biblical roots.
While the biblical Jonah had his ups and downs
(most notably down into the belly of a fish), he is
a symbol of personal growth and divine mercy.
Combine that with a light, boyish sound and
you have a hit.
In the World: Actor Jonah Hill; comic-book an-
tihero Jonah Hex

Jonas (JOH-nəs)   2008: #274
Popularity: #493
Styles: Biblical, Antique
Charm
Variants: Jonah   1880   Today
Sisters: Lilian, Ivy, Eliza,
Phoebe, Lydia, Isabel
Brothers: Tobias, Caleb, Ezra, Judah, Cyrus,
Isaiah
✳Jonah is the form of this name that you'll
hear most often today, but the Greek Jonas has
historically been the preferred English version.
That gives Jonas a double punch: it's less common and has a throwback, pioneer style.
In the World: Jonas Brothers band; medical researcher Jonas Salk

Jonathan (JAH-nə-thin)   1985: #17
Popularity: #31
Styles: New Classics, Biblical
Nicknames: Jon, Jonny, Than,
Jonty   1880   Today
Variants: Jonathon, Yonatan
Sisters: Rebecca, Jessica, Allison, Rachel,
Natalie, Samantha
Brothers: Benjamin, Joshua, David,
Christopher, Matthew, Aaron
✳The number of young Johns has been
shrinking for generations. For a long time it was
hard to notice, though, because Jons kept multiplying to keep pace. Both names are unquestioned classics, but Jonathan is more flexible
and, oddly enough, both more antique and less
old-fashioned.
In the World: Writer Jonathan Swift; designer
Jonathan Adler; actor Jonathan Rhys Meyers

Jordan (JOHR-din)   1991: #29
Popularity: #46
Styles: Last Names First,
Androgynous, The "-ens,"
African-American, Place   1880   Today
Names
Nicknames: Jordie, Judd, Jody
Variants: Yarden
Sisters: Sydney, Madison, Kayla, Alyssa, Hailey,
Alexis
Brothers: Dylan, Austin, Parker, Brady, Tyler,
Logan
✳The English name Jordan dates to the Middle Ages, when returning crusaders gave the
name to children baptized with water from the
river Jordan. In modern times, though, this
name owes its style to basketball legend Michael Jordan. The immensely popular athlete
lent the name his macho grace and helped keep
it a masculine favorite even when the number of
female Jordans started rising.
In the World: Basketball star Michael Jordan;
singer Jordan Knight

José (khoh-SAY, zhoh-ZAY)   2002: #30
Popularity: #65
Styles: Timeless, Latino/
Latina
Nicknames: Joe, Pepe,   1880   Today
Chepo, Zé
Variants: Joseph, Xosé
Sisters: Ana, Teresa, Maria, Alicia, Carmen,
Elena
Brothers: Juan, Luis, Miguel, Francisco, Jesús,
Carlos
✳This biblical classic is overwhelmingly popular in the Spanish- and Portuguese-speaking
world, as John once was among English speakers. In fact, in U.S. regions with large Latino
populations, José often tops the overall popularity charts.
In the World: Writer/political theorist José
Martí; musician José Feliciano; soccer coach
José Mourinho

Joseph (JOH-sehf) 1914: #5
Popularity: #22
Styles: Timeless, Biblical,
Biblical
Nicknames: Joe, Joey, Jody, Jo 1880 Today
Jo, Joss
Variants: Josef, José, Yosef, Giuseppe
Sisters: Anna, Catherine, Rebecca, Theresa,
Sarah, Elizabeth
Brothers: Thomas, William, Daniel, James,
Edward, Michael
★ This is the quintessential man's name. A Joe
even means an ordinary guy. While others fal-
ter, Joseph carries on generation after genera-
tion with its dignified, old-world masculinity
firmly intact. As rock-solid a choice as ever.
In the World: Musical *Joseph and the Amazing
Technicolor Dreamcoat*; artist Joseph Cornell;
dictator Joseph Stalin

Joshua (JAH-shoo-ə) 1985: #4
Popularity: #14
Styles: New Classics, Biblical
Nicknames: Josh
Variants: Joshuah, Josue 1880 Today
Sisters: Rachel, Samantha,
Jessica, Allison, Rebekah, Emily
Brothers: Jacob, Zachary, Aaron, Benjamin,
Caleb, Ethan
★ Joshua has joined Jacob at the head of the
pack of wildly popular Old Testament names.
The full name is quaintly rough-hewn, suggest-
ing horse-drawn plows and logs ready for split-
ting, while the nickname Josh is full of fun.
Don't be too scared by the downward trajectory;
the name is still youthful and well liked.
In the World: Actors Josh Hutcherson, Josh Bow-
man, Josh Brolin, and Joshua Jackson; song
"Joshua Fit the Battle of Jericho"

Josiah (joh-ZIY-ə, joh-SIY-ə) 2011: #80
Popularity: #80
Styles: Biblical, Antique
Charm
Nicknames: Jo, Josey, Joss 1880 Today
Variants: Josias
Sisters: Abigail, Mariah, Bella, Bethany,
Angelina, Hannah, Sofia, Delilah
Brothers: Levi, Elijah, Jonas, Isaiah, Tobias,
Jeremiah, Elias, Judah
★ Josiah has a great biblical/cowboy flavor and
flair. It was modestly common in the 1700s and
1800s, then disappeared so completely that its
pioneer style was perfectly preserved. Today the
name is eye-catching but classic and makes a
creative way to name a boy after good old Uncle
Joe.
In the World: Potter Josiah Wedgewood; aboli-
tionist Josiah Henson; founding father Josiah
Bartlett

Joss (JAHS) 2005: #3813
Popularity: #7172
Styles: Country and Western,
Brisk and Breezy, Why Not? 1880 Today
Sisters: Tess, Shea, Landry,
Bay, Brynn, Mercy, Lana,
Romy
Brothers: Beck, Flynn, Deacon, Bo, Colt,
Cooper, Rafe, Cal
★ Joss is simple as can be, with the mellow
Western style of a real cowboy. Either on its own
or as a nickname for Joseph, Jocelyn, or Josiah,
this one grows on you. Female singer Joss (Joc-
elyn) Stone has introduced some androgyny to
the name, but it still sounds masculine on a boy.
In the World: Screenwriter/producer Joss
Whedon

Josué (khoh-SWAY, khoh-soo-AY, zhoh-sway)   2007: #181

Popularity: #213

Styles: Latino/Latina, French

Sisters: Natalia, Mariana, Eliana, Valeria, Catalina, Adriana

Brothers: Joaquin, Diego, Emilio, Jesus, Elias, Marcos

✶ Like its English counterpart Joshua, Josué was unusual until the 1970s, when it suddenly became a beloved favorite in the U.S. (As with many Old Testament names, it's less common in other parts of the world.) Today the name is a handsome Spanish favorite, comfortably familiar but not old-fashioned. Non-Spanish speakers, though, are still prone to mistake it for José.

In the World: Brazilian soccer player Josué Anunciado de Oliveira

Juan (KHWAHN)   2005: #55

Popularity: #89

Styles: Latino/Latina, Timeless

Nicknames: Juanito

Variants: John, João

Sisters: Ana, Maria, Carmen, Elena, Gloria, Alicia, Cristina, Teresa

Brothers: Luis, Jose, Antonio, Manuel, Victor, Miguel, Pedro, Carlos

✶ Like its English counterpart John, Juan is classic, strong, and reliable—but ordinary. So ordinary, in fact, that in major U.S. cities Juan Rodriguezes now easily outnumber John Smiths. It's a solid choice for traditionalists, especially if you have an uncommon surname to set you apart.

In the World: Archetypal womanizer Don Juan; Juan Carlos I, King of Spain; painter Juan Gris

Judah (JOO-də)   2011: #289

Popularity: #288

Styles: Biblical, Antique Charm

Nicknames: Jude, Judd

Variants: Judas, Jude, Yehuda

Sisters: Shiloh, Atara, Delilah, Lydia, Scarlett, Hadassah, Ariel, Naomi

Brothers: Levi, Jericho, Gideon, Ezra, Caleb, Josiah, Boaz, Asher

✶ Judah may be the the most muscular of all the Old Testament favorites, still a warrior in the mold of Judah Maccabee. Judah, Jude, and Judas all point to the same ancient name, but by convention are associated with different biblical figures. Judah typically means the son of Jacob; Jude is the apostle Saint Judas Thaddeus; Judas is the traitor Judas Iscariot.

In the World: The biblical associations still largely dominate

Judd (JUHD)   1973: #689

Popularity: #2055

Styles: Country and Western, Timeless

Variants: Jud

Sisters: Liza, Nell, Britt, Leigh, Dina, Jamie, Liv, Belle

Brothers: Mack, Clint, Rudy, Joss, Rex, Burke, Ned, Cliff

✶ Judd's not light or melodic, but it is strong, timeless, and 100% masculine. It was originally a nickname for the more fluid-sounding Jordan.

In the World: Actors Judd Nelson and Judd Hirsch; producer Judd Apatow; *Oklahoma!* song "Pore Jud Is Daid"

Jude (JOOD)   2011: #155

Popularity: #155

Styles: Saints, Biblical, Brisk and Breezy

Nicknames: Jody

Sisters: Ruby, Eliza, Gemma, Brynn, Piper, Fiona, Anna, Camilla

Brothers: Julian, Cole, Pierce, Jasper, Luke, Finn, Ivan, Graham

✶ This name has a pioneer style and a strong religious heritage that give it impressive gravity. It also has a simple sound that keeps it unpretentious. The one other choice with that same style combo is Luke, which has been a steady hit for decades. Jude is a less common alternative that is finally realizing its breakout potential. See also Judah.

In the World: Beatles song "Hey Jude"; actor Jude Law

Judson (JUHD-sən)   1880: #299
Popularity: #1164
Styles: Last Names First
Nicknames: Jud
Sisters: Landry, Ellery, Belle,   1880   Today
Kelsey, Emlyn, Juniper, Blair,
Oakley
Brothers: Turner, Lawson, Deacon, Gibson,
Briggs, Archer, Walker, Beck
✲ Judson is an appealingly earthy alternative to
the sudsy modern surnames. Even during its
turn-of-the-century peak, it was uncommon
and full of personality. The "Jud" comes from
an old nickname for Jordan, making Judson a
subtle namesake option for a Jordan.

Jules (JOOLZ)   1911: #420
Popularity: #2285
Styles: Ladies and
Gentlemen, French, Why
Not?   1880   Today
Variants: Julius
Sisters: Eloise, Flora, Adele, Genevieve,
Vivien, Belle, Evangeline, Celeste
Brothers: Hugh, Clement, Foster, Regis,
Lucian, Porter, Silas, Pierce
✲ Jules is a dapper gent with a French accent
and a fast punch. The name is polished to a
high sheen, but there's no mistaking the steel
it's made of. This is a smart, sleek choice that's
hot in Paris today.
In the World: Author Jules Verne; cartoonist
Jules Feiffer

Julian (JOO-lee-in)   2011: #49
Popularity: #49
Styles: Timeless, Saints,
Antique Charm, English,
Latino/Latina   1880   Today
Nicknames: Jules
Variants: Julien, Julius, Jolyon
Sisters: Sofia, Victoria, Isabel, Camilla, Anna,
Marina, Phoebe, Lucia
Brothers: Adrian, Sebastian, Dominic, Elias,
Gabriel, Nicholas, Damian, Oliver
✲ In the middle of the 20th century, when
Julie was hugely popular for girls, parents shied
away from Julian. The top boys' names then
were scraggy, like Scott and Keith. Today
smooth and elegant is in, and Julian is back with
all its connotations of saints, emperors, and
gentlemen.
In the World: WikiLeaks founder Julian As-
sange; singers Julian Lennon and Julian Casa-
blancas; actor Julian McMahon

Julius (JOO-lee-əs)   1912: #100
Popularity: #342
Styles: Ladies and
Gentlemen, Antique Charm,
Saints, Classical, African-   1880   Today
American
Nicknames: Jules
Variants: Julian, Jules, Julio
Sisters: Adelaide, Georgia, Hazel, Josephine,
Violet, Esther
Brothers: August, Felix, Cornelius, Solomon,
Casper, Theodore
✲ From Julius Caesar to Julius Erving, this is a
name that rings with grand achievements. It
treads softly, though, with a mild manner that
suits an accountant as comfortably as a con-
querer. Out of vogue since the 1920s, Julius is
making a suitably mild-mannered comeback.
Julian is a sleeker variant.
In the World: Emperor Julius Caesar; basketball
player Julius Erving; football player Julius Pep-
pers

Jupiter (JOO-pi-ter)   2009: #8283
Popularity: #10,096
Styles: Fanciful,
Mythological
Sisters: Isis, Tempest, Avalon,   1880   Today
Vesper, Guinevere, Juno,
Venus
Brothers: Apollo, Thor, Orion, Knight,
Maximus, Triton, Ajax
✲ Jupiter is certainly formidable: the king of
the Roman pantheon, the largest planet in the
solar system. Yet despite all the trappings, this
name comes across as fun and cute. It also has
American roots in poet Jupiter Hammon, the
first published African-American writer.
In the World: Planet Jupiter; Jupiter Jones of the
"Three Investigators" mystery series for kids

Justin (JUHS-tin)   1988: #7
Popularity: #59
Styles: New Classics, The
"-ens," Nickname-Proof
Variants: Justen, Justyn,   1880   Today
Justus, Justinian, Iestyn
Sisters: Jessica, Lauren, Amanda, Megan,
Samantha, Ashley
Brothers: Ryan, Tyler, Brandon, Kevin,
Matthew, Jordan
✴ Justin is the name for the cute boy all the
girls in seventh-grade English class have secret
crushes on. The amazing part is that it has man-
aged to retain that image for over 40 years. (For
the prototypical Justin, see the dashing young
rat hero in the 1971 children's classic *Mrs.
Frisby and the Rats of NIMH.*) Perennially
youthful, but not frivolous.
In the World: Singers Justin Bieber and Justin
Timberlake; baseball player Justin Verlander

Justus (JUHS-təs)   2002: #646
Popularity: #857
Styles: Exotic Traditional,
Saints, Biblical
Variants: Justice   1880   Today
Sisters: Damaris, Paloma,
Danae, Charis, Valentina, Athena
Brothers: Titus, Samson, Josiah, Magnus,
Xavier, Maximilian
✴ This arresting variation on Justin highlights
the name's Latin roots and powerful meaning.
In its traditional spelling, Justus has a historic
force and a saintly pedigree. Spelled Justice, it's
a modern meaning name used equally for boys
and for girls.

Kai (KIY)   2011: #203
Popularity: #202
Styles: Nordic, Brisk and
Breezy, Androgynous, Short
and Sweet, Fantastical   1880   Today
Variants: Kaj
Sisters: Leila, Eden, Zoe, Malia, Ivy, Sage
Brothers: Quinn, Ian, Axel, Jair, Rowan, Taj
✴ Kai has several independent origins, notably
from Northern Europe and Hawaii. You can
sense both styles in the name, and that gives it a
particularly refreshing feel: a ski trip and beach
vacation all in one.
In the World: Radio host Kai Ryssdal; body-
builder Kai Greene; various video game and
anime characters

Kane (KAYN)   2008: #436
Popularity: #505
Styles: Brisk and Breezy,
Celtic, Last Names First,
Fantastical   1880   Today
Variants: Keane, Cathán,
Kain
Sisters: Finley, Hayden, Trinity, Kiera, Rylee,
Marley
Brothers: Gage, Brogan, Wyatt, Slade, Cole,
Roarke
✴ This is the kind of strong, swift name that
you expect to see on the hero of a romance
novel or an action film. Kane is an Anglicized
Irish name (from Cathán) and was exclusively a
surname in the U.S. until recently. Not to be
paired with a brother named Abel.
In the World: Pro wrestler Kane; "Command &
Conquer" and "Legacy of Kain" video game
characters

Kareem (kah-REEM)   1977: #367
Popularity: #740
Styles: African-American,
Muslim
Variants: Karim   1880   Today
Sisters: Yasmin, Samira,
Kamilah, Maryam, Soraya, Amina
Brothers: Hakeem, Jamil, Ahmed, Mahmoud,
Hassan, Ameer
✴ This Muslim name has been favored by Afri-
can-Americans since basketball star Lew Alcin-
dor changed his name to Kareem Abdul-Jabbar
in 1971. For Muslims of other heritages, Karim
is the more common spelling. (This spelling
pattern also holds for other names, such as Ra-
heem/Rahim, Shareef/Sharif.)
In the World: Basketball star Kareem Abdul-
Jabbar

Keane (KEEN)   2007: #2208
Popularity: #2706
Styles: Celtic, Brisk and
Breezy, Last Names First,
Why Not?   1880 Today
Variants: Kean, Kane, Kian,
Cian, Keene
Sisters: Neve, Kerrigan, Greer, Ainsley, Skye,
Tierney
Brothers: Teague, Killian, Blaine, Tynan,
Roarke, Pryce
✶ A traditional English take on the Gaelic
Cian, Keane is a handsome addition to the
growing roster of breezy favorites. It is also an
Irish surname; the English surname Keene
sounds the same but is unrelated in origin.
In the World: English rock band Keane; vampire
Cian in Nora Roberts's "Circle Trilogy"

Keaton (KEE-tən)   2011: #367
Popularity: #566
Styles: The "-ens," Last
Names First, Bell Tones
Sisters: Kiley, Hadley, Tatum,   1880 Today
Marley, Parker, Bailey
Brothers: Payton, Cooper, Tucker, Brennan,
Dawson, Tate
✶ In the year 1983, actor Michael Keaton got
his big break in the film *Mr. Mom*; the Keaton
family of the sitcom *Family Ties* eked out a re-
newal for a second season; and the girl's name
Kaitlyn cracked the top-1000 chart for the first
time. Just like that, the name Keaton was born.
In the decades since, this cheerful surname has
outgrown its '80s origins to fit into a whole new
generation of name style.
In the World: Actors Michael Keaton, Diane
Keaton, and Buster Keaton; the Keaton family
of *Family Ties*

Keegan (KEE-gən)   2008: #223
Popularity: #252
Styles: Last Names First, The
"-ens," Celtic, Nickname-
Proof, Bell Tones   1880 Today
Sisters: Kylie, Sydney,
Mckenna, Kamryn, Lexi, Marley
Brothers: Logan, Kieran, Brennan, Tucker,
Riley, Bryson
✶ Keegan is a common Irish surname, rarely a
first name—until now. This is a completely con-
temporary name that would have been hard to
imagine as recently as the '70s. In style, it's like
the X Games—young and adventurous, with no
patience for convention.
In the World: Golfer Keegan Bradley; comedian
Keegan-Michael Key

Keenan (KEE-nən)   1997: #353
Popularity: #827
Styles: The "-ens," Celtic,
African-American, Bell Tones
Variants: Cianán, Kenan,   1880 Today
Keenen
Sisters: Regan, Shayna, Janae, Brenna,
Morgan, Keely
Brothers: Killian, Conor, Ronan, Desmond,
Kendrick, Donovan
✶ Familiar as a surname, Keenan doesn't miss
a beat as a first name. It's sharp and swift with a
Celtic style—a Kevin for the new millennium.
As a surname, Keenan comes from the Gaelic
name Cian ("ancient"). The spelling Kenan
shifts the origin to biblical Hebrew (Kenan was
a grandson of Adam).
In the World: Actor/comedians Keenen Ivory
Wayans and Kenan Thompson

Keir (KEER)   1970: #1023
Popularity: #6385
Styles: Celtic, Brisk and
Breezy, Why Not?
Variants: Kerr   1880 Today
Sisters: Bryn, Shea, Skye,
Neve, Tierney, Adair, Maeve, Ailsa
Brothers: Blane, Fraser, Keane, Ramsay, Leith,
Teague, Wynn, Niven
✶ How have American parents overlooked this
Scottish favorite? It's simple but bold, and a rare
Brisk and Breezy option that's neither preppy
nor cowboy. It's also a great middle name option
for the many popular two-syllable Celtic names.
In the World: Actors Keir Dullea and Keir
O'Donnell

Keith (KEETH)   1966: #32
Popularity: #367
Styles: Surfer '60s, Celtic
Sisters: Leslie, Denise, Jill,
Deirdre, Carla, Valerie   1880 Today
Brothers: Craig, Scott,
Kenneth, Dean, Timothy, Bruce
✶ This Scottish import has kept a youthful
spirit for generations. There are more Keiths at
retirement age than school age today, but the
name still sounds handsomely boyish—a peren-
nial younger brother to Kenneth.
In the World: Musicians Keith Urban and Keith
Richards; commentator Keith Olbermann; art-
ist Keith Haring

Kellen (KEHL-in) 2011: #345
Popularity: #344
Styles: The "-ens,"
Nickname-Proof
Variants: Kellan   1880 Today
Sisters: Tegan, Finley,
Brenna, Keira, Ainsley, Brynn
Brothers: Kaden, Nolan, Eamon, Kane, Easton,
Brody

✴ Kellen has such a classic sound, you'd think it was a traditional given name . . . perhaps a long-lost Irish saint? (Saint Caolán, maybe? But that turns into the English Kelan, pronounced with a long "lahn" sound like Declan.) In fact, Kellen was almost unknown until football star Kellen Winslow hit the NFL in 1979. "Twilight" actor Kellan Lutz has remade the name for a new generation.

In the World: Actor Kellan Lutz; football players Kellen Winslow Jr. and Sr.

Kelly (KEH-lee) 1967: #102
Popularity: #1508
Styles: Androgynous, Celtic,
Last Names First
Variants: Kelley 1880 Today
Sisters: Sheila, Lesley,
Colleen, Bridget, Sandy, Dina
Brothers: Shannon, Kerry, Jody, Scott, Stacy,
Kyle

✴ Over the course of two generations, girls have taken command of this name. Kelly's Irish surname style is still attractive, but if the girl-boy ratio worries you, consider choices like Riley and Casey, which have maintained a more even gender balance.

In the World: The best-known Kellys are female, including singers Kelly Clarkson and Kelly Rowland and TV host Kelly Ripa

Kelvin (KEHL-vin) 1963: #210
Popularity: #545
Styles: New Classics,
African-American, Celtic,
Nickname-Proof   1880 Today
Sisters: Leslie, Kendra,
Maura, Janelle, Shannon, Karla
Brothers: Bryan, Kendrick, Damon, Keenan,
Terrance, Derek

✴ Kelvin quietly became a classic by appealing to many audiences. It has been a Celtic name, an African-American name, and a way to customize the perennially popular Kevin. It's even a choice if you're looking to raise a young scientist, like the Lord Kelvin who gave his name to a temperature scale.

In the World: A unit of measurement for temperature

Kendall (KEHN-dəl) 1993: #287
Popularity: #606
Styles: Last Names First,
Celtic
Nicknames: Ken   1880 Today
Variants: Kendal
Sisters: Kelsey, Brenna, Meredith, Shea,
Regan, Mckenna
Brothers: Keenan, Donovan, Barrett, Kelvin,
Conor, Reilly

✴ This Ken never achieved the heights of popularity of Kenneth. As a result, it feels a little livelier and more modern and has even been taken up recently as a girl's name.

In the World: Actor/singer Kendall Schmidt of *Big Time Rush*

Kendrick (KEHN-drik) 1991: #329
Popularity: #521
Styles: Last Names First,
African-American, Celtic,
New Classics 1880 Today
Nicknames: Ken, Rick
Variants: Kendric
Sisters: Larissa, Janelle, Adrienne, Natasha,
Whitney, Kendra
Brothers: Derrick, Terrell, Desmond, Keenan,
Roderick, Donavan

✴ This Welsh/Scottish surname made a natural leap to first-name status. Its familar rhythm recalls favorites from Kenneth to Cedric and yields simple, popular nicknames.

In the World: Rapper Kendrick Lamar; Congressman Kendrick Meek; basketball player Kendrick Perkins

Kenneth (KEH-nehth) — 1951: #16

Popularity: #170

Styles: Celtic, Solid Citizens, Mid-Century

Nicknames: Ken, Kenny

Variants: Kent, Kennith

Sisters: Patricia, Kathleen, Sandra, Carolyn, Deborah, Sharon

Brothers: Lawrence, Stephen, Douglas, Paul, Richard, Glenn

★ After a century as a leading man, this handsome Scot is still on the A-list. Kenneth may be showing a bit of silver around the temples, but that simply adds character. Would that we could all age so gracefully.

In the World: Actor Kenneth Branagh; designer Kenneth Cole; singer Kenny Chesney; Barbie's doll pal Ken

Kent (KEHNT) — 1962: #136

Popularity: #1299

Styles: Mid-Century, Surfer '60s, Place Names, Last Names First

Sisters: Karla, Lynn, Sheryl, Jody, Gwen, Diane

Brothers: Brett, Kirk, Darren, Todd, Craig, Dean

★ Kent's prime time was the '50s, but the name feels more modern than that. Its crisp sound fits in with current styles and could make it a strong choice. Be careful matching with last names, though. The final "t" likes to graft onto whatever comes after, turning a name like Kent Oliver into Ken Tolliver.

In the World: Actor Kent McCord; *The Simpsons* news anchor Kent Brockman; Kent, England

Kenyatta (kehn-YAH-tə) — 1975: #533

Popularity: #3634

Styles: African-American, Androgynous, African

Nicknames: Ken

Variants: Kinyatta

Sisters: Maisha, Shani, Akeelah, Tanisha, Ayanna, Kamaria

Brothers: Kwame, Nakia, Asante, Karim, Dakarai, Jelani

★ This name, used for both boys and girls, makes a bold statement of pride in your African origins. Kenyan founding father Jomo Kenyatta (born Kamau Ngengi) adopted the name for its symbolic strength. It has been said to refer to a Masai belt (*kinyata*) he wore, or to the meaning "the light of Kenya."

In the World: Kenya's first president, Jomo Kenyatta

Kermit (KER-mit) — 1909: #175

Popularity: #11,532

Styles: Namesakes, Celtic

Variants: Dermot

Sisters: Ione, Twyla, Glynis, Finola, Avis, Una

Brothers: Erskine, Boyd, Grover, Linus, Elwyn, Denzil

★ Kermit comes from the same Gaelic source as Dermot but has an extra *hop* that keeps it ever *green*. Nonetheless, the name has essentially *croaked* in the U.S., sinking into a *bog* of disuse. Okay, enough frog jokes . . . but that is what most people will think of. At least the association is a positive one, and the name is awfully cute.

In the World: Muppet Kermit the Frog; trumpeter Kermit Ruffins

Kevin (KEH-vin) — 1965: #13

Popularity: #67

Styles: New Classics, Celtic, Nickname-Proof, The "-ens"

Sisters: Kelly, Megan, Alison, Leslie, Kristen, Lauren

Brothers: Ryan, Colin, Sean, Brendan, Kyle, Justin

★ The decades flow by, but Kevin keeps finding some key style point that keeps it fashionable. In the '60s, it was fresh and breezy like Keith. In the '80s, it was cute and sensitive like Justin. Today it's Irish, with the rhythm of favorites like Kieran and Aidan.

In the World: After generations of actors and athletes named Kevin, it's a Teflon name that no single association sticks to

Kian (KEE-in, KEEN) 2010: #576
Popularity: #602
Styles: The "-ens," Celtic,
Short and Sweet, Bell Tones
Variants: Cian, Keane 1880 Today
Sisters: Teagan, Kiara, Nia,
Ainsley, Rory, Eva, Ashlyn, Ayla
Brothers: Ronan, Kieran, Killian, Liam,
Eamon, Conor, Gavin, Declan
✷ Cian was a hero of ancient Celtic legend,
and his name—two brisk, bright syllables—is
one of the top favorites in Ireland today. American
parents usually opt for a "K" spelling to
clarify pronunciation. For a one-syllable version,
go with the Anglicized spelling Keane.
In the World: Singer Kian Egan

Kieran (KEE-rən) 2011: #476
Popularity: #475
Styles: Celtic, Bell Tones,
The "-ens," Saints
Variants: Ciarán 1880 Today
Sisters: Ainsley, Teagan, Nia,
Alannah, Siobhan, Rory
Brothers: Declan, Kilian, Liam, Aidan,
Cormac, Ronan
✷ Ciarán is an old name. It runs deep through
Irish history, a name of saints and heroes dating
back more than 1000 years. In modern Ireland,
it's a popular choice to honor that tradition. To
Americans, though, grand old Ciarán is unfamiliar
and frankly unpronounceable. That's
where Anglicized spelling comes in. Kieran is a
fresh burst of 21st-century sound with strong
Irish underpinnings.
In the World: Actors Ciarán Hinds and Kieran
Culkin

Killian (KI-lee-ən) 2011: #756
Popularity: #756
Styles: Celtic, Saints
Variants: Cillian, Kilian
Sisters: Keira, Alannah, 1880 Today
Kerrigan, Fiona, Aisling,
Brenna
Brothers: Ronan, Cormac, Tiernan, Eamon,
Keane, Finian
✷ Kilian blooms with Irish charm. It's popular
in Ireland, but in the States it's best known as a
beer, Killian's Irish Red, which is actually a domestic
Coors product. This storied old saint's
name deserves a more suitable namesake.
In the World: Actor Cillian Murphy; Killian's
Irish Red beer

Kingston (KING-stən) 2010: #214
Popularity: #226
Styles: Place Names, Last
Names First, The "-ens"
Nicknames: King 1880 Today
Variants: Kingsley
Sisters: Leighton, Marley, Harlow, Winter,
Juno, London
Brothers: Paxton, Drake, Hendrix, Remington,
Bentley, Hawkins
✷ King would be a fun name to call a little
boy—like Duke, only more so. But as a given
name it's too grandiose for many parents. Kingston
not only brings the nickname in line but
sets it to an island beat, courtesy of the capital of
Jamaica. Rock stars Gwen Stefani and Gavin
Rossdale chose this name for their son in 2006,
inspiring a small wave of little Kingstons.
In the World: Kingston Rossdale (son of rock
musicians Gwen Stefani and Gavin Rossdale)

Kip (KIP) 1965: #379
Popularity: #4558
Styles: Surfer '60s, English,
Country and Western, Short
and Sweet 1880 Today
Sisters: Dina, Jody, Lise,
Pippa, Darcy, Marlo
Brothers: Tad, Dirk, Wes, Bart, Toby, Jeb
✷ This good-humored name would be fun to
call out across the playground to a little boy.
While it looks like a nickname, it actually has a
long history as a full given name. If you worry
that it's not enough name, though, you can
make it short for Christopher, Kipling, or even
Kipton.
In the World: Singers Kip Moore and Kip
Winger

Kirk (KERK) 1962: #139
Popularity: #1607
Styles: Surfer '60s, Macho
Swagger, Fantastical
Sisters: Kimberly, Dawn, 1880 Today
Belinda, Kris, Ginger,
Melody
Brothers: Erik, Craig, Blake, Scott, Dirk, Kent
✷ Kirk is an action hero's name. It's emphatically
masculine in a way that goes beyond reality,
like *Star Trek*'s Captain Kirk. In the '60s,
Kirk was the epitome of this style; Drake is a
contemporary equivalent.
In the World: Captain Kirk of *Star Trek*; actors
Kirk Douglas and Kirk Cameron; baseball
player/manager Kirk Gibson

Knox (NAWKS)   2011: #435
Popularity: #434
Styles: Last Names First
Sisters: Everly, Winslow,
Auden, Onyx, Oakley, Sol,   1880   Today
Marlowe, Wren
Brothers: Penn, Locke, Lennox, Cash, Briggs,
Quill, Knight, Lex

✳ When actress Angelina Jolie named her first son Maddox, she set a pattern. All her sons would receive a name ending in "-x." Knox was an unlikely choice, with its curious spelling and "hard knocks" sound, but "x"-loving parents have followed her lead once again. As it becomes more familiar as a given name, the negatives will start to fade.
In the World: Fort Knox; "Mr. Knox, sir," of *Fox in Socks*; son of actors Angelina Jolie and Brad Pitt

Kobe (KOH-bee)   2001: #222
Popularity: #477
Styles: African-American,
Short and Sweet, Turn of the
21st Century   1880   Today
Variants: Koby, Coby
Sisters: Nyla, Kyra, Zaria, Macy, Skyla, Tamia,
Deja, Taya
Brothers: Nico, Taj, Dante, Kai, Axel, Jair,
Rocco, Trae

✳ Kobe Bryant's catchy name and flashy basketball moves inspired thousands of little namesakes when he was winning championships with the Lakers. For what it's worth, Bryant's parents reportedly chose the name from a dinner menu: Kobe is a top-quality Japanese beef. The spelling Coby is also heard as a nickname for Jacob.
In the World: Basketball star Kobe Bryant; Kobe beef

Kurt (KERT)   1966: #110
Popularity: #1474
Styles: Surfer '60s, German
and Dutch
Variants: Curt, Kurtis,   1880   Today
Konrad
Sisters: Jody, Dawn, Beth, Lori, Karla, Toni,
April, Kerry
Brothers: Dirk, Kent, Brad, Marc, Darrell,
Todd, Craig, Keith

✳ Kurt/Curt is name and description wrapped up in one. It's brusque, masculine, and all business, like Kurt Russell in his action hero days. The late Nirvana singer Kurt Cobain briefly lent the name a more emotional edge; more recently, a gay teenage character on the TV series *Glee* made his mark on the name. If you'd like to use it as a nickname, Konrad is a traditional source.
In the World: Musician Kurt Cobain; Kurt Hummel of *Glee*; actor Kurt Russell; writer Kurt Vonnegut Jr.; composer Kurt Weill

Kyle (KIYL)   1990: #18
Popularity: #121
Styles: Celtic, Nickname-
Proof, '70s–'80s, Turn of the
21st Century   1880   Today
Variants: Cael
Sisters: Morgan, Kelsey, Erin, Nicole, Ashley,
Jenna
Brothers: Ryan, Sean, Ian, Jared, Blake, Dylan

✳ This old Scottish surname was a hit ahead of its time. Back when the trendy boys' names were curt and brusque (Scott, Kirk), Kyle was bright and smooth—a glimpse of a generation of names to come. The name has grown into a top modern classic, reflected in spin-offs like Kyler and Kylie.
In the World: Actors Kyle MacLachlan and Kyle Chandler; auto racers Kyle Petty and Kyle Busch

Kyler (KIY-ler)   2011: #253
Popularity: #253
Styles: Bell Tones
Nicknames: Ky
Sisters: Ashlyn, Jacey, Rylee,   1880   Today
Jaylen, Parker, Haylee
Brothers: Rylan, Keegan, Tucker, Raiden,
Bryson, Kolby

✳ Crafty parents have merged the modern classic Kyle with the trendy hit Skyler, producing a sound-alike for the powerhouse Tyler. The result is a name that strikes all the right notes but may blend in *too* well with its surroundings.

Lachlan (LAHK-lən, LAHKH-lən)
Popularity: #1052
Styles: Celtic
Nicknames: Lachie, Lockie
Variants: Lochlan
Sisters: Ailsa, Maisie, Mirren, Iona, Davina, Tamsin
Brothers: Ramsay, Callum, Fraser, Angus, Alistair, Ewan

2011: #1049

1880 Today

★This name fairly shouts its Scottish roots. But if you meet a Lachlan today, chances are he'll hail not from Scotland but from Australia. Lachlan's a classic hit Down Under, thanks to Scottish forebears like Governor Lachlan Macquarie, "The Father of Australia."
In the World: Governor Lachlan Macquarie

Lamar (lah-MAHR)
Popularity: #721
Styles: Country and Western, Nickname-Proof, African-American
Variants: Lamarr
Sisters: Lacy, Whitney, Leanne, Leticia, Yolanda, Carolina, Shelby, Janelle
Brothers: Jarvis, Darnell, Beau, Travis, Harlan, Lamont, Quincy, Marlon

1989: #325

1880 Today

★ Lamar started off as a surname, but given the spread of the "La-" prefix, we no longer hear it that way. Instead, Lamar sounds like a courtly classic of the American South. It's a natural for hardy gentlemen like football coaches and oil barons.
In the World: Sports executive Lamar Hunt; basketball player Lamar Odom; politician Lamar Alexander

Lance (LANS)
Popularity: #467
Styles: Brisk and Breezy, '70s–'80s
Sisters: Amber, Shannon, Leigh, Candace, April, Holly
Brothers: Rex, Shane, Dirk, Heath, Damon, Leif

1970: #76

1880 Today

★ Lance is a name for dashing heroes— modern heirs to Sir Lancelot. Among everyday folks, the name sounds light and windswept, just right for a surfer.
In the World: Cyclist Lance Armstrong; singer Lance Bass; baseball player Lance Berkman

Landon (LAN-dən)
Popularity: #34
Styles: The "-ens," Last Names First, Nickname-Proof, Country and Western
Variants: Landen
Sisters: Addison, Landry, Marley, Payton, Sienna, Avery
Brothers: Mason, Cooper, Logan, Brody, Carson, Jackson

2010: #32

1880 Today

★ With a flick of the wrist, Brandon is softened to a perfect modern surname. Actor Michael Landon's three decades on the air helped give Landon an all-American glow. Its popularity varies enormously by region: it's a huge hit in the deep South and in rural areas, but much less common on the urban coasts.
In the World: Actor Michael Landon; soccer player Landon Donovan

Lane (LAYN)
Popularity: #270
Styles: Brisk and Breezy, Last Names First, Country and Western
Variants: Layne
Sisters: Landry, Cassidy, Brynn, Carly, Parker, Emery
Brothers: Cale, Weston, Reed, Trey, Landon, Chance

2011: #270

1880 Today

★This quiet mid-century favorite has come roaring to life alongside Dane, Kane, Shane, and Zane. Lane sounds like the refined and responsible one of the bunch, but plenty tough. Bull rider Lane Frost was a rodeo legend, and the name is most common today in rodeo country.
In the World: Rodeo rider Lane Frost; football coach Lane Kiffin; singer Layne Staley; Lane Bryant plus-size women's clothing

Larry (LA-ree) 1947: #10
Popularity: #395
Styles: Nicknames,
Mid-Century
Variants: Lawrence, Lars   1880   Today
Sisters: Donna, Nancy,
Linda, Trudy, Peggy, Janice
Brothers: Jerry, Roger, Alan, Barry, Bruce,
Dennis
✳You don't really picture this as a baby
name—a Larry ought to emerge in instant mid-
dle age. But if you are considering Larry for a
new generation, the good news is that it's an af-
fable, easygoing name that's ready to make
friends.
In the World: Actor Larry Hagman; basketball
player Larry Bird; comedian Larry David;
writer Larry Niven

Lawrence (LAW-rchnts) 1949: #32
Popularity: #454
Styles: Solid Citizens
Nicknames: Larry, Lon,
Lorne, Laz, Loz   1880   Today
Variants: Laurence, Lorenzo,
Lorenz, Laurent
Sisters: Constance, Rosalie, Virginia,
Marianne, Gloria, Patricia
Brothers: Russell, Warren, Raymond, Clifton,
Francis, Marshall
✳ Elegant Lawrence belongs to the category of
nickname victims. Larry fell out of fashion and
took Lawrence with it. Imagine Lon or Laz for
your nickname and the whole picture changes.
This name sounds stronger than its plummet-
ing popularity would suggest.
In the World: Lawrence of Arabia; actors Lau-
rence Olivier and Laurence Fishburne; writer
D. H. Lawrence

Lawson (LAW-sən) 2011: #581
Popularity: #582
Styles: Last Names First, The
"-ens," Why Not?
Nicknames: Law, Laz   1880   Today
Sisters: Marin, Laney,
Annabel, Larkin, Hadley, Mercy
Brothers: Archer, Jefferson, Turner, Porter,
Paxton, Coleman
✳This surname has an easy drawl to it. It could
sound like an old-money gent or a rough-and-
tumble cowboy.

Lazarus (LA-zə-ruhs) 1900: #1052
Popularity: #1941
Styles: Biblical, Exotic
Traditional, Saints
Nicknames: Laz   1880   Today
Variants: Lazar, Lazaro,
Eleazar
Sisters: Sapphira, Damaris, Jezebel, Serafina,
Salome, Drusilla
Brothers: Nicodemus, Barnabas, Joachim,
Samson, Aeneas, Eleazar
✳ Lazarus has a fabulously stylish sound and a
perfect nickname. It also has two strong and
separate biblical assocations. There's the Laza-
rus whom Jesus raised from the dead, and then
there's a sore-covered beggar. This last, unfortu-
nate fellow caused the name to become a term
for lepers in the Middle Ages. It's time to get
past that and raise Lazarus up from the ashes
once more.
In the World: Usage inspired by the biblical figures, e.g., a "Lazarus pit" used by a comic-book
villain to regenerate

Leander (lee-AN-der) 1882: #324
Popularity: #2548
Styles: Exotic Traditional,
Saints, Mythological
Nicknames: Lee, Andy, Ander   1880   Today
Variants: Leandro, Lander
Sisters: Aurora, Celeste, Sabina, Ophelia,
Sephora, Ione
Brothers: Matthias, Emerson, Evander,
Thaddeus, Phineas, Lucian
✳ This tragic lover out of Greek myth is an
imaginative and romantic choice with down-to-
earth nickname options.
In the World: Tennis player Leander Paes; poem
"Hero and Leander"

Lee (LEE) 1900: #39
Popularity: #667
Styles: Solid Citizens,
Androgynous, Brisk and
Breezy 1880 Today
Variants: Leigh
Sisters: Lynn, Kim, Denise, Dawn, Ellen,
Laurie, Debbie, Dale
Brothers: Roy, Dean, Allen, Jay, Russell, Mark,
Neal, Glenn
✳ For such a simple name, Lee carries a lot of
nuance. It has a Southern "good ol' boy" angle
thanks to namesakes of Robert E. Lee, but it's
also been a favorite of Jewish families. Lee has
even managed to hold on against an onslaught
of female Lee-annes and Lee-ahs. It's now the
most laid-back option in the high-energy zippy
category.
In the World: Actor Lee Majors; singer Lee
Brice; Lee blue jeans; assassin Lee Harvey Os-
wald

Leif (LAYF, LEEF, LIYF) 1979: #637
Popularity: #1032
Styles: Nordic, Brisk and
Breezy, Exotic Traditional,
Why Not? 1880 Today
Sisters: Liv, Britt, Maren,
Linnea, Thea, Kari
Brothers: Finn, Erik, Rowan, Lars, Bret, Lance
✳ Leif's brisk sound is creative and contempo-
rary, and its Viking heritage makes it an unques-
tioned classic. The name made a brief
appearance in the U.S. during the reign of '70s
heartthrob Leif Garrett, but it remains a ne-
glected gem. It is, however, a magnet for mispro-
nunciations. The first version above is the most
standard.
In the World: Norse explorer Leif Ericson;
singer Leif Garrett

Leland (LEE-lənd) 1921: #171
Popularity: #329
Styles: Last Names First
Nicknames: Lee, Land
Sisters: Angeline, Jewell, 1880 Today
Emory, Iris, Nola, Autry
Brothers: Lowell, Alton, Harland, Linwood,
Palmer, Rowland
✳ This well-mannered surname sounds like a
caption on an old portrait of a company founder
(or a college founder, as in Leland Stanford Ju-
nior University, otherwise known as Stanford).
At least it *did* sound that way until the tattooed
bounty hunter/kickboxer Leland Chapman hit
reality TV. How about "quiet but lethal"?
In the World: Leland Stanford Junior Univer-
sity; reality TV star Leland Chapman

Lennon (LEHN-ən) 2011: #744
Popularity: #745
Styles: Last Names First,
Namesakes, The "-ens,"
Androgynous, Why Not? 1880 Today
Nicknames: Len
Sisters: Marley, Sawyer, Everly, Bowie, Carson,
Abbey
Brothers: Harrison, Lincoln, Gibson, Holden,
Calder, Hendrix
✳ Few babies were named for John Lennon
during the Beatles' heyday. Names were more
conservative back then, and "sounds like Lenin"
was a hard sell during the Cold War. Today the
name is bound for the spotlight. Parents and
even grandparents love the "-n" surname style
and the idea of a rock-and-roll baby ready to give
peace a chance.
In the World: Musician John Lennon

Lennox (LEHN-iks) 2011: #823
Popularity: #823
Styles: Last Names First,
Shakespearean, Why Not?
Nicknames: Len 1880 Today
Variants: Lenox
Sisters: Everly, Tierney, Marlowe, Axelle, Zara,
Leighton
Brothers: Cabot, Quinlan, Hendrix, Kingston,
Sterling, Paxton
✳ This natty Scottish surname could catch on
in an instant. It's powerful but elegant. That
hint of restraint sets it apart in an "x"-name field
that can easily veer into comic-book territory.
In the World: Boxer Lennox Lewis; Lenox china

Leo (LEE-oh)   1903: #37
Popularity: #167
Styles: Guys and Dolls,
Saints, Antique Charm, Short
and Sweet   1880   Today
Sisters: Lucy, Mia, Nora,
Ruby, Clara, Lillie
Brothers: Max, Oliver, Jude, Felix, Milo, Sam
✳ Could "o" be the new "x"? "X" has been the hottest letter in town, lending its offbeat style to powerhouses like Max and Alex. But an "-o" at the end of a name brings you plenty of quirky cool and a less crowded playing field . . . and Leo is a perfect pal for Max.
In the World: Zodiac sign Leo the lion; writer Leo Tolstoy; actors Leonardo ("Leo") DiCaprio and Leo Howard

Leon (LEE-awn)   1918: #77
Popularity: #405
Styles: Solid Citizens,
African-American, German
and Dutch, Fantastical   1880   Today
Sisters: Mabel, Lillie, Rosalie,
Faye, Pearl, Delta
Brothers: Earl, Oscar, Milo, Coleman, Luther, Clyde
✳ This proud name, meaning "lion," has a wealth of colorful namesakes, from boxer Spinks to jazzman Redbone to Bolshevik Trotsky. Leon is a current favorite around the world, but in America it retains—for better and worse—a funky, retro style.
In the World: Rock band Kings of Leon; musician Leon Russell; "Resident Evil" game character Leon Kennedy

Leonard (LEH-nerd)   1920: #38
Popularity: #705
Styles: Solid Citizens
Nicknames: Len, Leo, Lon,
Lenny   1880   Today
Variants: Lenard, Leonardo,
Lennart
Sisters: Frances, Loretta, Estelle, Lucille, Doris, Irene
Brothers: Ernest, Bernard, Stanley, Norman, Milton, Harold
✳ This mighty lion isn't roaring as loud as he used to. The "-nard" sound places Leonard squarely in the last century. Today Leo and Leonardo are more fashionable forms of the name.
In the World: Composer Leonard Bernstein; singer Leonard Cohen; actor Leonard Nimoy; Leonard Hofstadter of *The Big Bang Theory*

Leonardo (lay-oh-NAHR-doh)   2011: #149
Popularity: #149
Styles: Exotic Traditional,
Literary and Artistic, Italian,
Shakespearean   1880   Today
Nicknames: Leo, Nardo
Sisters: Claudia, Donatella, Guinevere, Alessandra, Adriana, Valentina
Brothers: Orlando, Emmanuel, Giovanni, Sebastian, Maximilian, Lorenzo
✳ You can't ask for a finer prototype for a name than Leonardo da Vinci, one of the most creative individuals in history. The Leonardo who did the most for the name, though, was actor Leonardo DiCaprio, who sent this name skyward in the late '90s. All DiCaprio really did was remind America of a magnetic classic that was due for another renaissance.
In the World: Renaissance man Leonardo da Vinci; actor Leonardo DiCaprio

Leopold (LEE-ə-pohld)   1895: #580
Popularity: #2442
Styles: Ladies and
Gentlemen, Exotic
Traditional   1880   Today
Nicknames: Leo
Sisters: Adelaide, Beatrice, Georgina, Cordelia, Rosamund, Augusta
Brothers: Augustus, Theodore, Casper, Ferdinand, Cornelius, Florian
✳ Smashingly distinctive and brimming with confidence, Leopold fairly leaps off the page. To some folks, though, it will sound like a leap off the deep end. Here's a simple test: if you're surrounded by little boys named Julius and Oliver, Leopold should come across as a strong, imaginative choice.
In the World: Film *Kate and Leopold*; Leopold Bloom of *Ulysses*; murderers Nathan Leopold and Richard Loeb

Leroy (LEE-roy, lə-ROY)   1935: #50
Popularity: #1027
Styles: Solid Citizens,
African-American
Nicknames: Roy, Lee   1880   Today
Variants: LeRoy, Leeroy,
LeRoi
Sisters: Laverne, Anita, Maxine, Ardell,
Bernadette, Wanda
Brothers: Leon, Earl, Vernon, Maurice, Lyle,
Clyde
✶ Taken from a French nickname meaning
"the king," Leroy became an American stan-
dard. For African-Americans, in particular, its
popularity helped define a generation of names
with French accents. You won't meet many
young Leroys anymore, though. The king has
stepped down from his throne and now sounds
more like a country boy.
In the World: Song "Bad, Bad Leroy Brown"; artist LeRoy Neiman; composer Leroy Anderson

Levi (LEE-viy, LAY-vee)   2011: #66
Popularity: #66
Styles: Antique Charm,
Biblical, Country and
Western   1880   Today
Nicknames: Lee
Sisters: Lea, Abigail, Bella, Shiloh, Hannah,
Faith
Brothers: Eli, Wyatt, Caleb, Ezra, Luke, Josiah
✶ Levi—a biblical son of Jacob and one of the
12 tribes of Israel—used to be primarily a Jewish
name. Today it's finding a new audience thanks
to its snappy sound and rustic Levi Strauss
image. It's most popular in rural and rugged
parts of the U.S.
In the World: Blue jeans pioneer Levi Strauss;
Levi Johnston, ex-fiancé of political daughter
Bristol Palin

Liam (LEE-əm)   2011: #15
Popularity: #15
Styles: Celtic, Short and
Sweet, Nickname-Proof,
Nicknames   1880   Today
Sisters: Fiona, Sophie, Avery,
Keira, Zoe, Isla
Brothers: Declan, Connor, Aidan, Owen, Riley,
Finn
✶ This Gaelic short form of William only re-
cently made it past the shores of Ireland. (Actor
Liam Neeson led the ocean crossing.) It's now
embraced by American parents looking for an
up-to-date flourish but a trim, simple sound.
Traditionally a nickname, it also works fine as a
full name.
In the World: Actors Liam Neeson and Liam
Hemsworth; singers Liam Gallagher and Liam
Payne

Lincoln (LING-kən)   2011: #178
Popularity: #178
Styles: Last Names First
Nicknames: Linc
Sisters: Annabel, Piper,   1880   Today
Charlotte, Ivy, Juliet, Harper
Brothers: Jefferson, Sawyer, Wyatt, Mason,
Emerson, Cooper
✶ For a long while, the presidential surname
boom mysteriously bypassed Lincoln. It took a
fictional convict (from the TV series *Prison
Break*) to finally turn parents' eyes to one of the
great names in American history. Lincoln has it
all: a fashionable sound, a cool nickname, and
the assurance that the memory of Abe Lincoln
will keep this name from ever sounding like just
a passing fad.
In the World: President Abraham Lincoln; Lincoln automobiles; Lincoln of *Prison Break*

Linus (LIY-nəs) 1882: #611
Popularity: #1347
Styles: Namesakes, Saints,
Mythological, Nordic,
Nickname-Proof
Variants: Lino

1880   Today

Sisters: Astrid, Flora, Britta, Iris, Beatrix, Luna
Brothers: Casper, Felix, Elias, Arlo, Cyrus,
Hugo
✴The specter of a blanket-toting cartoon character has hung over Linus for decades, but the name deserves a fresh chance. It's a stylishly quirky Greek classic and a Scandinavian favorite. Linus has recently gotten more attention thanks to computer programmer Linus Torvalds and his namesake Linux operating system.
In the World: Linus of comic strip *Peanuts*; Linux creator Linus Torvalds; scientist Linus Pauling

Lionel (LIY-ə-nəl) 1933: #294
Popularity: #786
Styles: Solid Citizens,
African-American, Guys and
Dolls
Variants: Leonel

1880   Today

Sisters: Corrine, Rosemary, Twila, Margot,
Lorraine, Ramona
Brothers: Royce, Stewart, Merlin, Gilbert,
Russell, Carlton
✴This is a square name but not old or creaky. Lionel train sets help keep it youthful, with their timeless image of masculinity in training. And when your young Lionel's ready to grow up, the name is ready too. Sophisticated examples abound, from actor Barrymore to jazz legend Hampton.
In the World: Actor Lionel Barrymore; jazz musician Lionel Hampton; singer Lionel Richie; soccer player Lionel Messi

Lloyd (LOYD) 1918: #51
Popularity: #1213
Styles: Porch Sitters, Celtic
Variants: Loyd, Floyd
Sisters: Gladys, Wilma,
Larue, Lois, Irma, Muriel

1880   Today

Brothers: Mervyn, Lyle, Erwin, Merle, Lester,
Boyd
✴This once-classic Welsh name has sunk to the style cellar. One warning sign: it was the name of Jim Carrey's character in *Dumb and Dumber*. Even the rise of a singer and a rapper who both made the name Lloyd their calling card couldn't revive it. Owen, Evan, and Dylan are now the standard-bearers for Welsh-American names. See also Floyd.
In the World: R&B singer Lloyd; rapper Lloyd Banks; actor Lloyd Bridges; writer Lloyd Alexander

Locke (LAWK) 2011: #3029
Popularity: #3069
Styles: Last Names First,
Brisk and Breezy, Fantastical
Sisters: Auden, Berkeley,
Greer, Avonlea, Larkin,
Blythe

1880   Today

Brothers: Penn, Shaw, Beckett, Rhodes,
Whitman, Kane
✴Don't flip past quite yet: this name just might be the solution to your baby name standoff. It's a swift, simple surname that shouldn't give the traditionalists too big of a shock. It's the Enlightenment philosopher John Locke and the video game hero Locke Cole. And the name's very sound gives it a solidity that a lot of creative names lack.
In the World: Video game character Locke Cole

Logan (LOH-gən) 2007: #17
Popularity: #20
Styles: Last Names First, The
"-ens," Celtic, Nickname-
Proof

1880   Today

Sisters: Avery, Camryn,
Chloe, Fiona, Mckenna, Lily
Brothers: Connor, Dylan, Owen, Chase,
Landon, Gavin
✴This name was a rare choice until the 1970s, when the movie and TV series *Logan's Run* raised its profile. Since then, Logan has risen to become one of the hottest names in America. It's Scottish, rakish, and creative without sounding "made up."
In the World: *Logan's Run*; actors Logan Marshall-Green, Logan Henderson, and Logan Lerman

Lon (LAHN)   1880: #192
Popularity: #13,441
Styles: Solid Citizens,
Nicknames
Nicknames: Lonnie   1880   Today
Sisters: Nan, Bess, Meta, Kay,
Gwen, Lina
Brothers: Hal, Rush, Van, Clark, Guy, Rex
✴ Lon is a breezy name of an earlier era,
calmer than today's breezy cowboys like Colt
and Beau. As a nickname, it gives a fresh face to
old friends Lawrence, Leonard, and (as in the
case of actor Lon Chaney) Alonzo.
In the World: Actor Lon Chaney

London (LUHN-dən)   2010: #508
Popularity: #561
Styles: Place Names, The
"-ens"
Nicknames: Don, Lon   1880   Today
Sisters: Siena, Aspen, Shiloh,
Oakley, Lyric, Marley
Brothers: Jensen, Windsor, Kingston, Beckett,
Lennox, Deacon
✴ This place name has a trendy, playful sound
that's just a bit glitzy. It should be a perfect male
counterpart to Paris . . . but be aware that fe-
male Londons are popping up too.
In the World: All things London, England; foot-
ball player London Fletcher

Lorenzo (loh-REHN-zoh)   2007: #293
Popularity: #310
Styles: Italian, Latino/Latina,
Shakespearean, Timeless
Nicknames: Enzo, Lencho   1880   Today
Variants: Laurence
Sisters: Adriana, Bianca, Luciana, Valeria,
Alessandra, Mariana, Viviana, Serena
Brothers: Orlando, Antonio, Leonardo, Fabian,
Sergio, Dante, Alonso, Rodrigo
✴ Need a damsel rescued? A fresco painted? A
swash buckled? This Italian and Spanish
standby has a heroic, artistic style for the ages.
In the World: Renaissance statesman Lorenzo
de' Medici; actor Lorenzo Lamas; a son of real-
ity TV star Snooki

Louis (LOO-is)   1914: #20
Popularity: #332
Styles: Ladies and Gentlemen
Nicknames: Lou, Louie
Variants: Lewis, Luis, Luigi,   1880   Today
Ludwig, Ludovic
Sisters: Rosa, Adele, Helen, Sylvia, Marion,
Clara
Brothers: Arthur, Jules, Edward, George,
Theodore, Charles
✴ Here's a grandly stylish name. Yes, I'm really
talking about Louis. The name has gathered
dust in recent years, but it polishes up nicely to
reveal a name of kingly strength. In England
(and France, where the name's kingly tradition
is strongest), Louis is already making a come-
back. Lewis is a traditional variant that has been
used in England and Scotland for centuries.
In the World: Musician Louis Armstrong; song
"Louie, Louie"; author Lewis Carroll; comedian Louis C.K.

Luca (LOO-kə)   2011: #261
Popularity: #260
Styles: Italian, Short and
Sweet
Variants: Luka   1880   Today
Sisters: Sofia, Lola, Giada,
Francesca, Mia, Livia
Brothers: Matteo, Nico, Gianni, Aldo, Dante,
Enzo
✴ Quite a few classic Italian men's names—
Andrea, Nicola—end in "-a." In English, they've
mostly been used for girls. Luca is the first to
buck the trend. Italian for Luke, Luca is famil-
iar, fashionable, and completely masculine. It is
becoming a global favorite.
In the World: Suzanne Vega song "Luka"; en-
forcer Luca Brasi of *The Godfather;* several ce-
lebrity children

Lucas (LOO-kəs)   2011: #29
Popularity: #29
Styles: Biblical, New Classics
Nicknames: Luke
Variants: Lukas, Luke   1880   Today
Sisters: Natalie, Sofia,
Gabrielle, Chloe, Lily, Lauren, Olivia, Hannah
Brothers: Gabriel, Evan, Zachary, Colin,
Caleb, Julian, Nicholas, Owen
✳ Lucas is the Latin form of Luke, and both
names have soared up the charts. Lucas sounds
more formal and old-fashioned and gives you
the option of Luke as a nickname. It's very pop-
ular with Ivy League grads as both a first and
middle name.
In the World: A global hit name; actor Lucas
Till; *Star Wars* creator George Lucas; Lucas Oil
Stadium

Lucian (LOO-shən)   1881: #289
Popularity: #596
Styles: Saints, Exotic
Traditional
Nicknames: Luke, Lu, Luco   1880   Today
Variants: Luciano, Lucius,
Lucio
Sisters: Lavinia, Cleo, Sabina, Seraphina,
Viorica, Averil
Brothers: Mathias, Ciprian, Felix, Quentin,
Adric, Tudor
✳ Did Harry Potter scare you off Lucius? The
related name Lucian is just as classic, saintly,
and exotic, but its dangerous edge doesn't veer
into "death eater" territory. Like Lucius, it de-
rives from the Latin word for light.
In the World: Painter Lucian Freud; opera
singer Luciano Pavarotti; used most frequently
in Romania

Lucius (LOO-shəs)   1881: #257
Popularity: #1337
Styles: Exotic Traditional,
Saints, Biblical, Classical
Nicknames: Lou   1880   Today
Variants: Lucio, Luciano
Sisters: Augusta, Sabina, Salome, Octavia,
Averil, Verena
Brothers: Silas, Florian, Barnabas, Cassius,
Leander, Albin
✳ Devilishly exotic with a splash of saintly
style, this could be an unexpected alternative to
the popular name Damian. The name's dark
side is underscored by Lucius Malfoy, a smooth
villain in the "Harry Potter" series.
In the World: Lucius Malfoy of the "Harry Pot-
ter" series; Lucius Fox, a *Batman* character

Luis (loo-EES, loo-EEZ)   2000: #49
Popularity: #88
Styles: Latino/Latina
Nicknames: Lucho, Güicho,
Lou   1880   Today
Variants: Luiz, Louis
Sisters: Elena, Ana, Rosa, Adriana, Diana,
Natalia, Rosario, Maria
Brothers: Carlos, Daniel, Jesus, Manuel, Juan,
Antonio, Javier, Miguel
✳ The Spanish Luis is a classic favorite that's
still perfectly contemporary. It has risen steadily
even as the French Louis and English Lewis
have declined.
In the World: Singer Luis Miguel; director Luis
Buñuel; actor Luis Guzmán; baseball player
Luis Tiant

Luke (LOOK)   2005: #41
Popularity: #39
Styles: Biblical, Brisk and
Breezy, Country and Western
Variants: Lucas, Lukas   1880   Today
Sisters: Lily, Brooke, Chloe,
Claire, Ella, Faith
Brothers: Cole, Eli, Nathan, Samuel, Levi, Jake
✳ This New Testament name is bold and tough
and was surprisingly uncommon through much
of the 20th century. The recent generation of
parents raised on Luke Skywalker, *General Hos-
pital*'s Luke and Laura, and *Beverly Hills,
90210*'s Luke Perry changed all that. Luke is
now one of the most popular men's classics. For
a less common alternative, consider Jude.
In the World: Luke Skywalker of *Star Wars*;
General Hospital's Luke; film *Cool Hand Luke*;
actors Luke Wilson and Luke Perry

Luther (LOO-thər)   1887: #63
Popularity: #1819
Styles: African-American,
Ladies and Gentlemen
Nicknames: Lou   1880   Today
Sisters: Leona, Louise, Rosa,
Viola, Alma, Alberta, Blanche, Lucille
Brothers: Claude, Julius, Edmund, Conrad,
Ernest, Horace, Arthur, Lionel
✳ Luther is an old-timer. The name has stayed
marginally more current among African-Amer-
ican families, partially in honor of Martin Lu-
ther King Jr., but parents of any color should
brace for some raised eyebrows if they choose
this classic. Unlike contemporaries Hubert and
Chester, though, Luther has a subtle sexy
groove. The name is a reach, but a potentially
stylish one.
In the World: Singer Luther Vandross

Lyle (LIYL)   1918: #145
Popularity: #1266
Styles: Solid Citizens, Celtic
Sisters: Eileen, Glenna, Faye,
Jeanne, Elaine, Maura, Nola,   1880   Today
Lorraine
Brothers: Glen, Laurence, Roy, Lionel, Yale,
Gene, Vernon, Dale
✶ Lyle is one of the most fluid names for boys.
It dropped out of sight back when names like
Kirk and Todd were the flinty pinnacle of fash-
ion, but it could fit in with the new smoother
favorites.
In the World: Singer Lyle Lovett; Lyle & Scott
apparel; children's book *Lyle, Lyle, Crocodile*

Mack (MAK)   1900: #96
Popularity: #1044
Styles: Guys and Dolls,
Country and Western, Macho
Swagger   1880   Today
Variants: Mac
Sisters: Faye, Roxie, Millie, Nell, Mae, Lucy
Brothers: Cal, Dock, Van, Major, Duke, Ned
✶ Too many Jacks on your block? Do them one
better with Mack, the ultimate smiling tough-
guy name. It can work on its own or as a nick-
name for Macaulay, Cormac, or any "Mac-"
surname. Note that the word "mack" has an
ever-evolving meaning in the hip-hop world.
In the World: Song "Mack the Knife"; Mack
trucks; Big Macs; slang for "a smooth operator"
and, as a verb, "to hit on"

Madden (MA-din)   2011: #541
Popularity: #541
Styles: The "-ens," Last
Names First, Fantastical
Sisters: Landry, Mara, Peyton, 1880   Today
Dempsey, Ellery, Campbell
Brothers: Canton, Raiden, Brady, Gannon,
Kingston, Locke
✶ If you associate this name with the shoe de-
signer Steve Madden or the Madden brothers of
the band Good Charlotte, you're probably not
an adult American male. Quite simply, Madden
is football. It's a hugely popular NFL video
game named for legendary broadcaster and
coach John Madden. Few name trends are
driven by dads, but this is surely one of them.
In the World: "Madden" NFL video games; Joel
and Benji Madden of Good Charlotte

Maddox (MA-dəks)   2011: #169
Popularity: #169
Styles: Last Names First,
Macho Swagger
Variants: Madoc   1880   Today
Sisters: Marley, Larkin,
Quinn, Harlow, Oakley, Monroe
Brothers: Jagger, Lennox, Kingston, Jaxon,
Beckett, Wilder
✶ Most new names created from surnames
sound like they're ready to lounge around at
prep school. This one's too busy skinning bears
and catching bullets with its teeth. The name
was nearly unheard of before actress Angelina
Jolie chose it for her son, but hundreds of par-
ents quickly jumped on the idea. It's macho, yet
surprisingly elegant.
In the World: Maddox Jolie-Pitt, son of actors
Angelina Jolie and Brad Pitt; humor writer
Maddox

Magnus (MAG-nəs)   2010: #1151
Popularity: #1165
Styles: Nordic, Celtic, Exotic
Traditional, Saints
Sisters: Astrid, Lilith, Beatrix, 1880   Today
Signe, Ailsa, Linnea
Brothers: Matthias, Leif, Ramses, Draco,
Xavier, Ronan
✶ You can't ask for a grander name than Mag-
nus, a Latin epithet meaning "great." It's a regal
classic in Scandinavia and an old favorite in
Scotland too.
In the World: Chess grandmaster Magnus
Carlsen; tennis players Magnus Larsson, Mag-
nus Norman, and Magnus Gustafsson

Mahlon (MAY-lən)   1896: #481
Popularity: #2921
Styles: Biblical, The "-ens,"
African-American, Why Not?
Sisters: Bethel, Adah,   1880   Today
Carmel, Dinah, Atara, Sarai
Brothers: Gideon, Lemuel, Rubin, Japheth,
Asa, Elam
✶ This forgotten biblical name has a modern
sound reminiscent of new inventions like Jay-
len. It was once a popular African-American
name, with bearers like 19th-century diplomat
Reverend Mahlon Van Horn and Negro League
ballplayer Mahlon Duckett.

Malachi (MAL-ə-kiy)   2006: #150
Popularity: #164
Styles: Biblical, African-
American, Exotic Traditional
Nicknames: Kai, Mal   1880   Today
Variants: Malachy, Malakai,
Malaki
Sisters: Mariah, Selah, Atara, Jerusha, Havilah,
Keziah
Brothers: Josiah, Ezekiel, Gideon, Zechariah,
Ezra, Nehemiah
✳ Malachi, a biblical prophet name, is coming
on strong in the wake of Elijah and Isaiah. The
name is often confused with Malachy, an Irish
saint's name pronounced "MAL-ə-kee."

Malcolm (MAL-kuhm)   1992: #206
Popularity: #499
Styles: Timeless, African-
American, Celtic, Why Not?
Nicknames: Callum, Mal   1880   Today
Sisters: Nia, Kendra, Fiona,
Brenna, Shea, Lilias, Mirren
Brothers: Duncan, Angus, Desmond, Keenan,
Lachlan, Kendrick
✳ Malcolm is a Scottish perennial bursting
with offbeat charisma. For African-Americans,
it has also been a political statement. Despite
the name's broad familiarity and appeal, it has
remained surprisingly uncommon.
In the World: Activist Malcolm X; actor Mal-
colm McDowell; sitcom *Malcolm in the Mid-
dle*; writer Malcolm Gladwell

Malik (mah-LEEK)   1996: #97
Popularity: #322
Styles: African-American,
Muslim
Sisters: Amani, Kiara, Deja,   1880   Today
Yasmin, Aliyah, Zaria
Brothers: Devon, Tariq, Omar, Malachi,
Trevon, Jaleel
✳ This Arabic name, meaning "king," is heard
throughout the Islamic world. Its trim, powerful
sound has attracted non-Muslim parents in
droves; it has struck a special chord with Afri-
can-Americans.
In the World: Actor Malik Yoba

Manuel (mahn-WEHL)   1929: #111
Popularity: #230
Styles: Latino/Latina, Saints,
Timeless
Nicknames: Manny, Manolo,   1880   Today
Méme
Variants: Manoel, Emmanuel
Sisters: Mariana, Carmen, Rosa, Victoria,
Claudia, Maria, Carolina, Ana
Brothers: Miguel, Victor, Mario, Rafael, Juan,
Carlos, Ramon, Luis
✳ Manuel is such a reliable Spanish classic
that it actually sounds more familiar in America
than the English Emmanuel. Manny, the
world's friendliest nickname, is the icing on the
cake.
In the World: Baseball player Manny Ramirez;
Panama strongman Manuel Noriega; soccer
player Manuel Neuer

Marcel (mar-SEHL)   1992: #557
Popularity: #837
Styles: French, Saints,
Nickname-Proof
Variants: Marcellus, Marcelo   1880   Today
Sisters: Simone, Chantal,
Lucie, Celine, Sabine, Giselle
Brothers: Michel, Olivier, Jules, Noel, Quentin,
Alain
✳ For fans of French names, Marcel's gentle-
manly reserve makes it a handsome choice. In
France it's an old standard, akin to our Warren
or Raymond.
In the World: Writer Marcel Proust; mime Mar-
cel Marceau; artist Marcel Duchamp

Marco (MAHR-koh)   2001: #179
Popularity: #280
Styles: Italian, Latino/Latina
Nicknames: Marc
Variants: Marcos, Marc,   1880   Today
Marcus
Sisters: Adriana, Sofia, Noemi, Eliana, Marisa,
Lidia
Brothers: Carlo, Antonio, Matteo, Sergio,
Emilio, Aldo
✳ A spirited makeover of Marc. Images of
Marco Polo spring to mind, lending the name
an adventurous style and plenty of cross-cul-
tural potential. Marco is one of the most popu-
lar names in Milan, Italy's fashion capital.
In the World: Traveler Marco Polo; politician
Marco Rubio; musician Marco Antonio Solís

Marcus (MAHR-kəs) 1984: #57
Popularity: #145
Styles: Timeless, African-
American, Classical
Nicknames: Marc 1880 Today
Variants: Markus, Mark
Sisters: Christina, Veronica, Simone, Claudia,
Elena, Diana
Brothers: Wesley, Grant, Mitchell, Alexander,
Lucas, Anthony

✴ Marcus is the original Latin form of Mark.
Like Lucas versus Luke, this form of the name is
more elegant but a bit less vigorous. It gains
strength from the imperial style of Marcus Aurelius and the determination of Marcus Garvey.
In the World: Roman emperor Marcus Aurelius;
Black nationalist Marcus Garvey; football
player Marcus Allen

Mario (MAH-ree-oh) 1980: #102
Popularity: #224
Styles: Timeless, Italian,
Latino/Latina, Nickname-
Proof 1880 Today
Variants: Marius
Sisters: Lucia, Eva, Veronica, Carmela,
Daniela, Paola
Brothers: Gino, Roberto, Antonio, Marco,
Carlo, Arturo

✴Americans tend to think of Mario as an Italian name. It is indeed a classic in Italy, as well as
for Italian-Americans, such as Governor Mario
Cuomo and author Mario Puzo (not to mention
Nintendo's pseudo-Italian Mario Brothers). But
Mario is actually used in several different languages and has become a steady favorite of Latino Americans. It's a charismatic, macho
choice.
In the World: Governor Mario Cuomo; Super
Mario Brothers; entertainer Mario Lopez

Marius (MAH-ree-əs) 1881: #866
Popularity: #2213
Styles: Exotic Traditional,
German and Dutch,
Classical, Nordic, Nickname- 1880 Today
Proof
Variants: Mario
Sisters: Livia, Annalie, Maja, Laelia, Charis,
Dania
Brothers: Lucian, Cassius, Axel, Mathias,
Carsten, Anders

✴This ancient Roman name is a favorite in
Northern Europe. It's a sophisticated choice
that pairs well with simple surnames.

Mark (MAHRK) 1960: #6
Popularity: #159
Styles: Mid-Century, Surfer
'60s, Timeless, Biblical
Variants: Marc, Marcus, 1880 Today
Markus, Marco, Marek
Sisters: Karen, Teresa, Julie, Lisa, Christine,
Susan
Brothers: Steven, Paul, Gregory, Alan, Peter,
David

✴ Mark was a '50s and '60s blockbuster and has
inevitably declined from that peak, but it's unlikely to ever go completely out of style. It's
plain, sturdy, and enduringly appealing—and
guaranteed to remain 100% masculine. The
Latin version Marcus is now equally popular.
In the World: Writer Mark Twain; actor Mark
Wahlberg; Facebook founder Mark Zuckerberg;
singer Marc Anthony

Marquis (MAHR-kis, 1993: #282
mahr-KEEZ, mahr-KEE)
Popularity: #697
Styles: Modern Meanings,
African-American 1880 Today
Nicknames: Marc
Variants: Marques, Marquise
Sisters: Raven, Alisha, Deja, Justice, Chantal,
Essence
Brothers: Quinton, Terrell, Cortez, Trevon,
DeAngelo, Stephon

✴This aristocratic-themed riff on Marcus
seems to be pronounced differently by each
family. The variant Marquise actually means
the wife of a marquis, but is better known to
many Americans as a shape of cut diamonds.
In the World: Singer Marques Houston; football
player Marques Colston; the notorious Marquis
de Sade

Marshall (MAHR-shəl) 1908: #147
Popularity: #340
Styles: Timeless, Last Names
First
Variants: Marshal 1880 Today
Sisters: Lesley, Susana,
Meredith, Julianne, Elisa, Joanna
Brothers: Clayton, Forrest, Ellis, Wilson,
Mitchell, Nelson

✴ Marshall is timeless, with the kind of steady
decency you can't manufacture overnight. The
name's rugged history of army generals and
Western lawmen stands in contrast to its gentle
style.
In the World: Marshalls discount stores; Supreme Court justice Thurgood Marshall; U.S.
marshals (law enforcement)

Martin (MAHR-tin) 1883: #46
Popularity: #262
Styles: Solid Citizens,
African-American, Timeless
Nicknames: Marty   1880 Today
Sisters: Kathryn, Theresa,
Ellen, Anita, Martha, Ann
Brothers: Peter, Allen, Lawrence, Mark,
Warren, Philip
✴ Martin is the sort of name that parents tend to ignore today, but it has plenty to offer. It's warmly masculine and gently old-fashioned, and it has never been overused. Squint and you can convince yourself it's kin to the trendier Austin and Mason. Martin is also a possible hero name to honor Martin Luther King Jr.
In the World: Civil rights leader Martin Luther King Jr.; theologian Martin Luther; comedian Martin Lawrence

Marvin (MAHR-vin) 1931: #45
Popularity: #468
Styles: Solid Citizens,
African-American
Nicknames: Marv 1880 Today
Variants: Mervyn
Sisters: Wanda, Anita, Elaine, Corrine,
Roberta, Maxine
Brothers: Donald, Vernon, Jerome, Bernard,
Maurice, Alvin
✴ There's no way around it: the impact of this name depends on the color of your skin. Marvin has remained a perfectly normal, strong name for black men, whereas white Marvins are out of luck.
In the World: Singer Marvin Gaye; boxer Marvin Hagler; Marvin the Martian, Marvin the Paranoid Android

Mason (MAY-sən) 2011: #2
Popularity: #2
Styles: Last Names First, The
"-ens"
Nicknames: Mace 1880 Today
Sisters: Avery, Regan, Mia,
Madison, Chloe, Aubrey
Brothers: Carter, Chase, Logan, Sawyer,
Garrett, Carson
✴ Here's a find: a handsome tradesman name that doesn't end in "-er." That makes Mason a perfect brother for Cooper, Tucker, or Spencer. It's similar in feeling but not sound, to avoid the "butcher, baker, candlestick maker" syndrome. It's also this generation's heir to Jason, and a broad-based hit.
In the World: The Mason-Dixon Line; Masonic lodges; mason jars; a son of reality TV star Kourtney Kardashian

Mateo (mah-TAY-oh) 2011: #171
Popularity: #171
Styles: Latino/Latina
Nicknames: Teo
Variants: Matteo, Matthew 1880 Today
Sisters: Gabriela, Camila,
Lucia, Mariana, Daniela, Estrella, Adriana,
Catalina
Brothers: Mario, Lucas, Sergio, Joaquin, Nico,
Marco, Rafael, Diego
✴ Mateo is a fast-rising Spanish name, and brother to fast-rising names in many languages (see Matthias). Its clean, sophisticated sound makes it a handsome choice that can cut across cultures. Mateo is the Italian version.
In the World: R&B singer Mateo

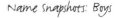

Matthew (MATH-yoo) 1983: #3
Popularity: #12
Styles: New Classics, Biblical
Nicknames: Matt
Variants: Mathieu, Mathew, 1880 Today
Matthias, Mateo, Mats, Thijs,
Mathis
Sisters: Allison, Rachel, Natalie, Amanda,
Melanie, Samantha
Brothers: Daniel, Andrew, Benjamin,
Christopher, Adam, Jonathan
✴ Matthew comes through for parents as a new classic that feels like an old classic. It mingles just as comfortably with John and William as Justin and Brandon. Try bouncing it off your parents, grandparents, nieces, and nephews: nobody has a complaint about the name Matt. In all its global forms, it's one of the most popular names in the world.
In the World: Actors Matthew McConaughey, Matthew Broderick, and Matt Damon; artist Matthew Barney; football player Matt Ryan

Matthias (mah-THIY-is, 2011: #775
mah-TEE-ahs)
Popularity: #774
Styles: Exotic Traditional,
German and Dutch, Biblical, 1880 Today
Saints
Nicknames: Matt
Variants: Mathias, Mathis, Mattias, Matthew
Sisters: Marina, Emilia, Damaris, Seraphina,
Astrid, Sabine
Brothers: Elias, Marius, Benedict, Dominik,
Antony, Raphael
✴ Matthew is a globally fashionable classic. Whether it's Matteo in Italy, Mads in Denmark, or Mathieu in Quebec, the name is uniformly hot. The form Matthias is heard in Germany and in English Bibles. It could also work well for American babies, as kin to scholarly/archaic choices like Isaias and Demetrius.
In the World: '80s amateur aviator Mathias Rust; football player Mathias Kiwanuka

Maurice (moh-REES, 1913: #95
MOH-ris)
Popularity: #460
Styles: African-American,
French 1880 Today
Nicknames: Maury
Variants: Morris, Moritz
Sisters: Yvonne, Corrine, Wanda, Laverne,
Maxine, Clarice
Brothers: Marcus, Byron, Leon, Clarence,
Bernard, Jerome
✴ Maurice comes from the Latin Mauritius and has a long history in England with the pronunciation "Morris." In the U.S., it's generally considered a French name with the stress on the second syllable, thanks in part to *Gigi* star Maurice Chevalier, the ultimate Frenchman. It's been a steady favorite of African-Americans since the '50s.
In the World: Actor Maurice Chevalier; author/illustrator Maurice Sendak; athletes Maurice Cheeks and Maurice Jones-Drew

Maverick (MA-və-rik) 2011: #426
Popularity: #425
Styles: Modern Meanings,
Country and Western, Macho
Swagger 1880 Today
Nicknames: Rick, Mav
Sisters: Liberty, Shiloh, Aspen, Sawyer,
Cheyenne, Oakley
Brothers: Dakota, Maddox, Phoenix, Ranger,
Chance, Jett
✴ Word names can be vessels for parents' own dreams. From Princess to Rocky, we see glimmers of reflected fantasies. Maverick is the cowboy, the rebel, the jet pilot—or nowadays, the upstart entrepreneur. Just be prepared that when you give a boy the name Maverick, you're tacitly approving his decision 20 years later to drop out of college and take his band on the road.
In the World: Maverick Mitchell of *Top Gun*; TV Western *Maverick*; Dallas Mavericks basketball team

Max (MAKS) 2011: #96
Popularity: #96
Styles: Antique Charm,
Nicknames, Guys and Dolls,
Brisk and Breezy 1880 Today
Variants: Maxwell,
Maximilian, Maxim, Maximus, Maximo
Sisters: Sophie, Eva, Tess, Molly, Grace, Zoe
Brothers: Leo, Jack, Rex, Theo, Felix, Eli
✳ The young hero of Maurice Sendak's *Where the Wild Things Are* was named absolutely perfectly. Max is a name that makes you smile, with tons of mischievous life packed into three little letters. It's one of the top choices for Ivy Leaguers and upscale urbanites. Let the wild rumpus start!
In the World: Physicist Max Planck; artist Max Ernst; "Mad Max" films; "Max Payne" games; *Max and Ruby* cartoons

Maxim (MAK-sim) 2011: #722
Popularity: #722
Styles: Exotic Traditional,
Slavic, Saints
Nicknames: Max 1880 Today
Variants: Maxime
Sisters: Mila, Lilia, Katya, Tatiana, Dasia, Vika
Brothers: Roman, Axel, Magnus, Dimitri, Luka, Dominik
✳ This Russian classic is a trim and chic choice for a formal version of Max. It's a hot name in France, as Maxime. It is also, for better or worse, associated with a flashy men's magazine.
In the World: *Maxim* magazine; writer Maxim Gorky

Maximilian 2011: #434
(mak-sə-MIL-yən)
Popularity: #433
Styles: Exotic Traditional,
Saints, German and Dutch 1880 Today
Nicknames: Max
Variants: Maximillian, Maximiliano, Maxim
Sisters: Valentina, Raphaela, Seraphina, Beatrix, Angelique, Victoria, Evangeline, Anastasia
Brothers: Dominik, Antony, Sebastian, Roman, Leonardo, Quinton, Constantine, Emmanuel
✳ This is a showy name with the class and breeding to carry it off. Unlike modern pretenders, Maximilian is exactly what it sounds like: a sophisticated classic with centuries of regal heritage.
In the World: Actor Maximilian Schell; several Habsburg emperors

Maximus (MAK-si-məs) 2011: #213
Popularity: #212
Styles: Classical, Saints,
Macho Swagger
Nicknames: Max 1880 Today
Variants: Maxim, Maximo, Massimo
Sisters: Valentina, Livia, Trinity, Natalia, Harmony, Electa, Serena, Genevieve
Brothers: Titus, Magnus, Apollo, Darius, Maverick, Thor, Maddox, Xavier
✳ Yes, there's a chance everyone will think you're naming your son after Russell Crowe's character in *Gladiator*. But as long as you think that's cool, Maximus is a particularly grand elaboration on Max. It will maintain that grandeur long after the movie's impact has faded. Magnus is a more restrained name in the same vein.
In the World: *Gladiator* hero Maximus; numerous ancient soldiers and philosophers

Maxwell (MAKS-wehl) 1999: #106
Popularity: #134
Styles: Timeless, Antique
Charm, Last Names First
Nicknames: Max 1880 Today
Sisters: Claire, Audrey, Eleanor, Juliana, Jocelyn, Elise
Brothers: Preston, Elliott, Alexander, Grant, Miles, Bennett
✳ Maxwell is a popular name, but the real driving force is the nickname: energetic, lovable Max. Most parents feel that it needs a longer formal version . . . Maximilian? A mouthful. Maxim? A magazine. Maximus? Get serious. Thus Maxwell. It's a handsome name, but if you really just love plain old Max, you hereby have permission to let it stand on its own.
In the World: Maxwell Smart of *Get Smart*; song "Maxwell's Silver Hammer"; Maxwell House coffee

Melvin (MEHL-vin) 1928: #48
Popularity: #622
Styles: Solid Citizens,
African-American
Nicknames: Mel 1880 Today
Variants: Melvyn
Sisters: Maxine, Anita, Gwendolyn, Laverne,
Loretta, Arlene
Brothers: Vernon, Alvin, Bernard, Leon,
Edwin, Eugene
✴ Melvin has been a familiar name since the
1800s, comfortable kin to the fancy surname
Melville and Welsh import Mervyn. It has been
most popular with African-American families
over the past several decades. In fact, if you
meet a man who calls himself Melvin, odds are
he's black or Latino. White Melvins have typi-
cally gone by nicknames, like comedian Mel
Brooks and singer Mel Torme.
In the World: Filmmaker Melvin Van Peebles;
fighter Melvin Guillard; football player Melvin
Ingram

Merlin (MER-lin) 1931: #287
Popularity: #3468
Styles: Literary and Artistic,
Fantastical, Namesakes
Nicknames: Merl 1880 Today
Variants: Myrddin
Sisters: Rowena, Lorna, Ardith, Minerva,
Zelda, Arwen
Brothers: Newton, Felix, Garth, Alastor,
Farrell, Albus
✴ The sound of Merlin is a bit squishy for cur-
rent tastes, but the legendary wizard makes an
enchanting progenitor. The medieval writer
Geoffrey of Monmouth created the name and
character of Merlin from the Welsh prophet/
madman Myrddin.
In the World: Merlin, the wizard of Arthurian
legend; football player/actor Merlin Olsen;
actor Merlin Santana

Messiah (mə-SIY-ə) 2011: #630
Popularity: #629
Styles: Modern Meanings,
Fanciful
Sisters: Epiphany, Trinity, 1880 Today
Nevaeh, Eternity,
Heavenleigh, Shekinah
Brothers: Moses, Wisdom, Josiah, Titus,
Malachi, Zion
✴ As biblical names like Isaiah, Elijah, and
Zachariah became fashionable hits, Messiah
took off as well. It has a similar rhythm and an
unmistakable religious origin. Isaiah and
friends, though, are biblical *names*. Messiah is
the grandest of all titles and was historically
considered inappropriate for a name. You
should be aware that some still hear this name
as immodest, at best.
In the World: Handel's oratorio *Messiah*

Micah (MIY-kə) 2011: #104
Popularity: #104
Styles: Biblical, New Classics
Nicknames: Mike
Sisters: Leah, Ilana, Naomi, 1880 Today
Tessa, Mara, Talia
Brothers: Jonah, Eli, Caleb, Noah, Joshua,
Asher
✴ Micah is a biblical name with a light, cre-
ative touch. It's one of the most youthful and
contemporary of the Old Testament revivals. It
comes with the option of the time-tested nick-
name Mike, but few parents today want that.
Unlike with Michael, the nickname is seldom
forced upon a Micah.

Michael (MIY-kəl) 1969: #1
Popularity: #6
Styles: Timeless, Biblical
Nicknames: Mike, Mickey,
Mick, Mitch 1880 Today
Variants: Micheal, Mikel,
Miguel, Michel, Mikhail
Sisters: Sarah, Diana, Rebecca, Laura, Emily,
Christina
Brothers: David, Matthew, Daniel, Stephen,
Anthony, Thomas
✳The dominant name of the late 20th century, Michael reigned as America's top choice from the '50s until Jacob finally stole the crown in 1999. Its hallmark is versatility: It's Old Testament! It's New Testament! It's black! It's white! It's Mike, it's Mickey, it's Mitch! Michael's immense popularity has only contributed to its standing as a name without boundaries or preconceptions.
In the World: Singer Michael Jackson; basketball player Michael Jordan; actor Michael J. Fox; and many more

Miguel (mee-GEHL) 2002: #89
Popularity: #126
Styles: Latino/Latina
Variants: Michael
Sisters: Cristina, Elena, 1880 Today
Gabriela, Ana, Alejandra,
Carolina, Mariana, Natalia
Brothers: Carlos, Antonio, Javier, Andres,
Gabriel, Ricardo, Rafael, Luis
✳Michael was a huge hit in the middle of the 20th century, but its familiar Spanish counterpart didn't surge along with it. Miguel is just as strong and classic and has finally achieved star status in the U.S.
In the World: Writer Miguel de Cervantes; R&B singer Miguel; boxer Miguel Cotto; baseball player Miguel Cabrera

Miles (MIYLZ) 2011: #115
Popularity: #115
Styles: Antique Charm,
Nickname-Proof, Guys and
Dolls 1880 Today
Variants: Myles, Milo
Sisters: Claire, Lydia, Ivy, Charlotte, Lila, Elise
Brothers: Colin, Elliot, Graham, Wyatt, Isaac,
Julian
✳Miles is a terrific choice if you're drawn to "elegant gentleman" names. A Miles sounds strong, smooth, and unflappable. Despite the surname-styled "-s" ending, this is a classic English given name with a millennium of tradition behind it. In the U.S., it has an eclectic pair of cultural associations: *Mayflower* pilgrim Miles Standish and jazz legend Miles Davis.
In the World: Pilgrim Miles Standish; jazz musician Miles Davis; football player Miles Austin; Miles Morales, comics' second Spider-Man

Milo (MIY-lo) 2011: #362
Popularity: #361
Styles: Antique Charm,
Nickname-Proof, Exotic
Traditional 1880 Today
Variants: Miles
Sisters: Violet, Esme, Lucy, Olive, Luna, Cleo,
Zora
Brothers: Felix, Leo, Oscar, Jasper, Nico,
August, Ezra
✳Milo is cutting-edge cool, an offbeat name that charms crowds but takes a pinch of guts to use. In the Middle Ages, it was the formal Latin form of Miles, but today it's by far the more casual version.
In the World: Characters in *The Phantom Tollbooth*, *Atlantis*, *Catch-22*, and *Milo and Otis*; actor Milo Ventimiglia

Milton (MIL-tən)
Popularity: #1133
Styles: Porch Sitters, Solid Citizens, Last Names First
Nicknames: Milt
Sisters: Pauline, Lois, Arlene, Bernice, Leona, Maxine
Brothers: Sidney, Howard, Norman, Murray, Sherman, Arnold

1912: #64 · 1880 Today

✸ Milton is a cautionary tale for surnames. It's not a bad name by any means, but it's not what the parents who chose it originally intended. Like Grayson or Dalton today, Milton was supposed to sound high-class and elegant. It ended up the king of the Borscht Belt, a world apart from the aristocracy it aspired to join.
In the World: Comedian Milton Berle; game maker Milton Bradley; economist Milton Friedman; poet John Milton

Mitchell (MI-chəl)
Popularity: #420
Styles: Last Names First, Timeless
Nicknames: Mitch
Variants: Mitchel
Sisters: Lindsey, Bridget, Meredith, Audrey, Joanna, Melanie
Brothers: Clayton, Spencer, Wesley, Maxwell, Clinton, Bradley

1994: #71 · 1880 Today

✸ Here's a surname with some heft. Mitchell can dress up spiffy with swells like Preston and Chandler, but when it's time to take the gloves off, good old Mitch will rule the day. In origin, Mitchell is a version of Michael—the two names even share the nickname Mitch.
In the World: Writer Mitch Albom; TV series Sing Along with Mitch

Moe (MOH)
Popularity: #13,566
Styles: Guys and Dolls, Nicknames
Variants: Mo
Sisters: Bess, Mabel, Faye, Flo, Dell, Madge
Brothers: Sol, Gus, Archie, Ike, Nat, Clem

1904: #612 · 1880 Today

✸ Moe is the next step past Sam and Gus for parents who like the "corner barber" style of names. Its hard-luck everyman image was cemented by generations of Three Stooges reruns. To the current generation, this "corner barber" may sound more like a "corner barkeep" thanks to Moe's Tavern on The Simpsons.
In the World: Stooge Moe Howard; bartender Moe of The Simpsons; baseball player/spy Moe Berg

Mohammed (moh-HAH-mehd, moo-HAH-mehd)
Popularity: #562
Styles: Muslim
Variants: Mohammad, Muhammad, Mohamed, Mamadou, Mehmet
Sisters: Khadijah, Samira, Yasmin, Maryam, Fatima, Aisha
Brothers: Ahmed, Ibrahim, Rashad, Hassan, Mustafa, Abdullah

2001: #481 · 1880 Today

✸ The name of the Prophet of Islam, Mohammed is the most popular name on the planet. In English, this classic has a tremendous array of spellings. Variations beginning with "Mo-" are most often favored in the U.S., "Mu-" in the United Kingdom.
In the World: The Prophet Mohammed; over 100 million men and boys around the world today

Montgomery (mahnt-GUHM-ree)
Popularity: #1966
Styles: Last Names First, Exotic Traditional
Nicknames: Monty, Monte
Sisters: Clementine, Oakley, Waverly, Magnolia, Emmeline, Georgiana
Brothers: Carlisle, McKinley, Montague, Conway, Wellington, Kingsley

1883: #720 · 1880 Today

✸ The elegance of this name could sound dreamy—think actor Montgomery Clift—or fusty—think Montgomery Burns from The Simpsons. Montague is a similar choice that also yields the nickname Monty.
In the World: Montgomery Burns of The Simpsons; actor Montgomery Clift; country duo Montgomery Gentry; Montgomery, Alabama

Morgan (MOHR-gin)
Popularity: #539
Styles: Celtic, Androgynous, Nickname-Proof, The "-ens"
Sisters: Megan, Brenna, Regan, Mabyn, Lesley, Brynn
Brothers: Owen, Trevor, Logan, Reese, Griffin, Duncan

1995: #236 · 1880 Today

✸ Morgan is a strapping old Welsh name. When you meet a man named Morgan, the name seems classic and virile. Parents should be aware, though, that it has exploded in popularity as a girl's name. Nine out of ten new Morgans today are female.
In the World: Actor Morgan Freeman; Morgan Stanley financial services; filmmaker Morgan Spurlock

Morris (MOH-ris) 1912: #82
Popularity: #1716
Styles: Last Names First
Nicknames: Mo, Morrie
Variants: Maurice 1880 Today
Sisters: Louise, Marion,
Pauline, Estelle, Maxine, Golda, Frances,
Phyllis
Brothers: Murray, Willis, Sidney, Clifton,
Milton, Nelson, Irving, Sherman

✳ This alternative spelling of Maurice was hot in the 1800s when its surname look was elegant and trendy. It was also a common choice of Jewish parents as an English version of Moshe. Like similar choices Milton and Sidney, it has fallen out of fashion.
In the World: Actor Morris Chestnut; football player Morris Claiborne; book *Tuesdays with Morrie*

Mose (MOHZ, MOHS) 1882: #176
Popularity: #6111
Styles: Guys and Dolls,
Nicknames
Variants: Moss 1880 Today
Sisters: Lula, Etta, Bessie,
Mae, Roxie, Cleo
Brothers: Ike, Archie, Louie, Doc, Lonzo, Abe

✳ This nickname takes Moses downtown. It's a smoky, bluesy throwback with just a hint of hayseed thrown in.
In the World: Jazz musician Mose Allison

Moses (MOH-zis) 1880: #119
Popularity: #522
Styles: Biblical, Timeless
Nicknames: Mo, Mose, Moss
Variants: Moises, Moshe 1880 Today
Sisters: Esther, Miriam,
Flora, Adah, Viola, Naomi, Susannah, Ruth
Brothers: Reuben, Solomon, Cyrus, Asa, Julius, Oscar, Ezra, Abraham

✳ With due respect to Abraham and Noah, Moses is the ultimate Old Testament name. It's also one of the few to resist the recent craze—your best bet to meet a Moses is still in the pages of Exodus, not the neighborhood playground. The ingredients are all there, though. It's simple, old-fashioned, and heartily masculine.
In the World: Basketball player Moses Malone; son of singer Chris Martin and actress Gwyneth Paltrow

Murphy (MER-fee) 1907: #511
Popularity: #1553
Styles: Last Names First,
Celtic, Why Not?
Sisters: Nora, Madigan, 1880 Today
Tierney, Maeve, Orla,
Flannery
Brothers: Griffin, Finlay, Ellis, Forbes,
Colman, Dempsey

✳ Murphy is the #1 surname in Ireland. It was once a steady given-name choice in the U.S. and is ready to step back in without missing a beat. In case you're wondering, the female TV character Murphy Brown did *not* spark a generation of girls named Murphy. The name remains primarily masculine.
In the World: Rapper Murphy Lee; Murphy's Law ("Anything that can go wrong, will go wrong")

Napoleon (nah-POHL-ee-ən) 1887: #294
Popularity: #4740
Styles: Exotic Traditional,
Namesakes
Nicknames: Nap, Leo 1880 Today
Sisters: Magdalene, Ophelia,
Juno, Olympia, Valentine, Guinevere
Brothers: Ferdinand, Lafayette, Columbus,
Horatio, Ulysses, Constantine

✳ First the baggage: Napoleon is highfalutin, imperialist, and popularly associated with insanity. The gawky outcast from the movie *Napoleon Dynamite* makes the whole image even stranger. Still reading on? If so, consider that this historical throwback can hold its own with the gentlemanly revivals like Dominic, make mischief with pals Gus and Max, or strut with newcomers like Maximus and Destiny. Risky but eye-catching.
In the World: French emperor Napoleon Bonaparte; *Napoleon Dynamite*; Napoleon Solo of *The Man from U.N.C.L.E.*

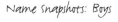

Nathan (NAY-thən)   2004: #20
Popularity: #28
Styles: Biblical, The "-ens,"
Timeless
Nicknames: Nat, Nate   1880   Today
Variants: Natan
Sisters: Leah, Emily, Lauren, Hannah, Natalie,
Rachel
Brothers: Aaron, Benjamin, Owen, Noah,
Andrew, Joshua
✳ Nathan was one of the first Old Testament
revivals to strike a chord with American parents.
Similar choices like Ethan didn't rise until the
'90s, but Nathan has been a favorite for 40 years
now. That familiarity adds to the name's quiet
strength.
In the World: Revolutionary War hero Nathan
Hale; actors Nathan Fillion and Nathan Lane

Nathaniel (nə-THAN-yəl)   2002: #62
Popularity: #84
Styles: Timeless, Biblical,
Shakespearean
Nicknames: Nate, Nat, Than,   1880   Today
Nathan
Variants: Nathanael
Sisters: Rebecca, Caroline, Abigail, Samantha,
Rachel, Victoria
Brothers: Benjamin, Alexander, Samuel,
Zachary, Gabriel, Nicholas
✳ Nathaniel is the perfect understated antique.
It's like that elegant sideboard that's been in the
family for generations. Yes, the name's biblical
style is the height of fashion, but it doesn't make
a fuss about it. It's handsome, confident, and
modest—an American classic. The alternative
spelling Nathanael is standard in the New Tes-
tament.
In the World: Author Nathaniel Hawthorne

Ned (NEHD)   1890: #237
Popularity: #5832
Styles: Guys and Dolls,
Nicknames
Sisters: Nan, Polly, Reba, Sue,   1880   Today
Jo, Nell, Lu, Bess
Brothers: Hal, Abe, Gus, Joe, Sol, Roy, Arlo, Ike
✳ Ned is a merry little nickname that adds zest
to Edward, Edmund, or Edison. It's an uncom-
mon choice with a classic every-guy charm. Un-
like other classic nicknames, though, Ned
remains a pure nickname. Parents almost al-
ways use a formal version on the birth certifi-
cate.
In the World: Ned Flanders of *The Simpsons*;
Ned Stark of *Game of Thrones*

Neil (NEEL)   1933: #149
Popularity: #658
Styles: Timeless, Celtic
Variants: Neal, Niall
Sisters: Diana, Gwen,   1880   Today
Kathleen, Leslie, June,
Laurel
Brothers: Dean, Kenneth, Glyn, Keith,
Malcolm, Craig
✳ Scottish, sturdy, and swift, Neil should be at
the top of many parents' lists. America seems to
have developed a blind spot for the name,
though. It's familar enough to be taken for
granted. If you're after a more eye-catching
style, you can try the Gaelic version Niall,
which pairs up well with trendy hits like Declan
and Liam.
In the World: Astronaut Neil Armstrong; musicians Neil Diamond and Neil Young; writer
Neil Gaiman; playwright Neil Simon

Nelson (NEHL-sən)   1899: #145
Popularity: #559
Styles: Timeless, Last Names
First
Sisters: Kathryn, Nina,   1880   Today
Priscilla, Vivian, Theresa,
Clara
Brothers: Marshall, Clinton, Warren, Clark,
Anderson, Russell
✳ Nelson was first adopted as a given name in
the 1800s in honor of British admiral Horatio
Nelson. Today South African leader Nelson
Mandela is a more likely honoree. In between,
the name was a modest, all-American work-
horse.
In the World: President Nelson Mandela; Admi-
ral Horatio Nelson; bully Nelson of *The Simp-
sons*; politician Nelson Rockefeller

Nicholas (NI-kə-lis) 1995: #6
Popularity: #42
Styles: Timeless, Greek
Nicknames: Nick, Cole, Nico, Niels, Nikos, Colin, Klaus 1880 Today
Variants: Nicolas, Nickolas, Nikolas, Nicholaus, Nils, Niels
Sisters: Victoria, Natalie, Rebecca, Samantha, Caroline, Veronica
Brothers: Alexander, Benjamin, Andrew, Christopher, Nathaniel, Zachary
✳ Nicholas made its big leap in popularity back in the '70s, but it hasn't lost any of its zing. Its crackling rhythm, unusual among classic English boys' names, still rings with its Greek origins. International forms of the name like Niels and Nico are worth considering as nicknames.
In the World: Superhero Nick Fury; Dickens novel *Nicholas Nickleby*; musician Nick Jonas; Nickelodeon/Nick network

Nicholson (NI-kəl-sən) 1994: #5102
Popularity: Very rare
Styles: Last Names First, Why Not?
Nicknames: Nick, Cole, Nico, 1880 Today
Nikos, Colin
Sisters: Sheridan, Mabry, Carrigan, Hollis, Ellery, Afton
Brothers: Richmond, Patterson, Campbell, Forester, Barlow, Robinson
✳ This name is a simple surname twist on the ever-popular Nicholas. Choose it if you love the surname style but also want the great array of nickname choices that come with a classic.
In the World: Writer Nicholson Baker; actor Jack Nicholson

Nico (NEE-koh) 2011: #495
Popularity: #496
Styles: Short and Sweet, Italian, Why Not?
Variants: Niko 1880 Today
Sisters: Lia, Giada, Liv, Siri, Zara, Chiara
Brothers: Luca, Kai, Teo, Dario, Axel, Enzo
✳ An Italian nickname for Nicholas (or Nicola), Nico is suave but cute with no ego problems. It's increasingly used as a full name in various languages, especially English and German. Niko is the popular Finnish version.
In the World: Auto racer Nico Rosberg; Nico di Angelo, son of Hades in the "Percy Jackson" book series

Nigel (NIY-jəl) 1994: #477
Popularity: #1001
Styles: English, Nickname-Proof
Variants: Neil 1880 Today
Sisters: Dahlia, Poppy, Nicola, Philippa, Dulcie, Felicity
Brothers: Clive, Niles, Rupert, Piers, St. John, Neville
✳ To Americans, this is the British name to end all British names. Nigel sounds like the perfect Englishman, despite the fact that the name has been out of favor in England for generations. It's been creeping into use in the States; get ready for little Nigels with Brooklyn and Texas accents.
In the World: Photographer Nigel Barker; fictional rocker Nigel Tufnel of Spinal Tap; auto racer Nigel Mansell

Nils (NEELS) 1888: #815
Popularity: #5098
Styles: Nordic
Variants: Niels, Nicholas
Sisters: Anni, Pia, Signe, 1880 Today
Malin, Tova, Britta
Brothers: Lars, Sven, Anders, Jens, Peder, Olaf
✳ Nils is thoroughly Scandinavian, yet easy to picture on a little American boy. It's ready for import—pronounce it like "kneels." The Danish version Niels makes that pronunciation clearer.
In the World: Guitarist Nils Lofgren; physicist Niels Bohr

Noah (NOH-ə) 2011: #5
Popularity: #5
Styles: Biblical, Nickname-Proof, Short and Sweet,
Antique Charm 1880 Today
Variants: Noé
Sisters: Leah, Abigail, Lily, Molly, Sophie, Bella, Faith, Hannah
Brothers: Eli, Caleb, Jonah, Levi, Seth, Micah, Ethan, Asher
✳ Not long ago, the image of the biblical patriarch herding animals into his ark dominated our image of Noah. Today this former whitebeard name is the toast of the cradle-and-diaper set. It's a lovely rediscovery, and the bevy of young Noahs has lightened up the name so that it's positively cute.
In the World: Actor Noah Wyle; lexicographer Noah Webster

Noam (NOHM, NOH-əm) 2009: #1633
Popularity: #1822
Styles: Jewish, Short and
Sweet
Sisters: Yael, Shira, Tamar, 1880 Today
Lia, Aviva, Adi, Talya
Brothers: Asher, Liam, Eitan, Tal, Avi, Elan,
Boaz
✱ An unconventional pleaser, Noam is a modern Hebrew name from the same root as Naomi. It appropriately means "pleasant." The name is often associated with linguist and political theorist Noam Chomsky.
In the World: Linguist/political theorist Noam Chomsky

Noel (NOHL, NOH-əl, 1938: #266
noh-EHL)
Popularity: #455
Styles: Timeless, French,
Short and Sweet 1880 Today
Variants: Noël
Sisters: Camille, Daphne, Hope, Elise, Eve, Simone, Juliet, Claire
Brothers: Graham, Quentin, Vincent, Blaine, Jules, Reid, Elliot, Vaughn
✱ Noel is globe-trotting and perpetually chic. Its guiding spirit is the British actor and dramatist Noel Coward, whose urbane style shaped the name's modern image. Noel comes from the word for Christmas, but it is commonly pronounced as one syllable, especially in Coward's native England.
In the World: Playwright Noel Coward; musician Noel Gallagher

Nolan (NOH-lin) 2011: #92
Popularity: #93
Styles: The "-ens," Timeless,
Nickname-Proof
Sisters: Madelyn, Avery, 1880 Today
Maya, Aubrey, Jocelyn, Bella
Brothers: Calvin, Maxwell, Gavin, Carson, Parker, Riley
✱ Nolan is a descendant of an old Gaelic name, but it has sounded like a mild-mannered American for generations. Recently parents have started to notice the name's modern sound and Irish roots. It makes for a nice compromise if she wants Aidan and he wants Tom.
In the World: Baseball pitcher Nolan Ryan; basketball coach Nolan Richardson; entrepreneur Nolan Bushnell

Norman (NOHR-mən) 1931: #36
Popularity: #1341
Styles: Solid Citizens
Nicknames: Norm
Sisters: Arlene, Lois, Maxine, 1880 Today
Loretta, Phyllis, Shirley
Brothers: Stanley, Howard, Melvin, Arnold, Eugene, Harold
✱ A slow, steady name of an earlier generation, Norman is now off the beaten track of fashion. The name originally referred to "Northmen": the Vikings who settled Normandy. Today, though, that "norm" comes across more like "normal." The sitcom barfly Norm of *Cheers* typifies the name's everyman image.
In the World: Artist Norman Rockwell; TV producer Norman Lear; writer Norman Mailer; General Norman Schwarzkopf

Oliver (AH-li-ver) 2011: #78
Popularity: #78
Styles: Antique Charm,
Saints, Shakespearean,
English 1880 Today
Nicknames: Ollie
Variants: Olivier
Sisters: Lily, Charlotte, Amelia, Sophie, Violet, Lydia
Brothers: Julian, Leo, Simon, Jasper, Sebastian, Elliot
✱ Oliver seemed a little eccentric a generation ago, but fashion has come around to its charms. Urban professionals in particular are attracted to the name's offbeat elegance. Still, Oliver doesn't even approach the popularity of the girl's name Olivia—except in the U.K., where they've always appreciated unconventional heartthrobs.
In the World: Dickens novel *Oliver Twist*; director Oliver Stone; statesman Oliver Cromwell

Omar (OH-mahr) 2007: #131
Popularity: #193
Styles: Biblical, Latino/
Latina, Muslim, African-
American, Nickname-Proof 1880 Today
Variants: Ömer
Sisters: Sarai, Nadia, Jada, Yasmine, Mariah,
India, Naomi, Selah
Brothers: Jamal, Hector, Eli, Dante, Malik,
Abel, Mario, Taj
✷ Omar is well known as a name of Arabic ori-
gin, thanks to poet Omar Khayyám and actor
Omar Sharif. It's also a biblical name, a Latino
and African-American favorite, and the name of
World War II general Omar Bradley. What do
all those associations add up to? A name that's
completely familiar but uncommonly striking.
In the World: Poet Omar Khayyám; actor Omar
Sharif; General Omar Bradley; reggaeton star
Don Omar; actor Omar Epps

Omari (oh-MAH-ree) 2008: #548
Popularity: #642
Styles: African-American,
African
Variants: Omar, Omarion 1880 Today
Sisters: Imani, Ayana,
Kamaria, Malaika, Aaliyah, Zuri
Brothers: Jabari, Asante, Dakarai, Kwame, Kofi,
Jelani
✷ This popular African name became the seed
for a whole crop of related names. It all started
when young singer Omari Grandberry took the
stage name Omarion. When he hit it big with
the group B2K, the name Omarion briefly sur-
passed Omari in popularity and names like Ja-
marion and Demarion followed. The African
original has staying power, though.
In the World: Singer Omarion; actor Omari
Hardwick

Orion (oh-RIY-ən) 2011: #472
Popularity: #472
Styles: Mythological, The
"-ens"
Sisters: Ivy, Lyra, Athena, 1880 Today
Eden, Ember, Vega
Brothers: Apollo, Lennox, Devin, Sage, Odin,
River
✷ The mythical hunter Orion, immortalized
in a constellation, is a new entry into our name
pantheon. Its celestial style works as a nature
name as well as a mythological name. A young
Orion will feel a special connection with the
night sky.

Orlando (ohr-LAN-doh) 1975: #245
Popularity: #482
Styles: Italian, Latino/Latina,
Exotic Traditional,
Shakespearean 1880 Today
Variants: Rolando
Sisters: Adriana, Silvia, Mariana, Celeste,
Paloma, Bianca
Brothers: Lorenzo, Rodrigo, Antonio,
Demetrius, Rafael, Leonardo
✷ This Italian version of Roland has always
given off a romantic, artistic vibe in English. It
has a prime literary lineage from Shakespeare to
Virginia Woolf. More recently, actor Orlando
Bloom has lent the name a higher profile. Or-
lando, Florida, home to the "Magic Kingdom,"
can dull the literary edge.
In the World: Actors Orlando Bloom and Or-
lando Brown; Virginia Woolf novel *Orlando*;
Orlando, Florida

Oscar (AHS-ker) 1886: #26
Popularity: #162
Styles: Antique Charm,
Latino/Latina, Nordic,
Nickname-Proof 1880 Today
Variants: Oskar, Asger
Sisters: Alice, Eva, Josephine, Eliza, Lucy,
Sofia
Brothers: Victor, Felix, Leo, Edgar, Hugo,
Oliver
✷ This name has so many powerful associa-
tions that they cancel each other out. Yes, your
son would be called Oscar the Grouch and
Oscar Meyer on occasion. And yes, Academy
Award season could be a little disconcerting.
But if you love this cool, quirky name, stick with
it—you won't be sorry.
In the World: Oscar the Grouch from *Sesame
Street*; "the Oscars" (Academy Awards); writer
Oscar Wilde; boxer Oscar De La Hoya

Otis (OH-tis) 1899: #94
Popularity: #1215
Styles: Ladies and
Gentlemen, African-
American 1880 Today
Variants: Ottis
Sisters: Opal, Irma, Vernice, Gladys, Myra,
Eula
Brothers: Leon, Amos, Clyde, Earl, Irvin,
Horace
✷ Otis is cute, punchy, and desperately out of fashion. Prominent bearers like singer Otis Redding helped the name hang on with African-American parents for a time, but it's now settling into nostalgia territory. You can see that in uses like "Otis Spunkmeyer" baked goods, a made-up brand name designed to sound as old-timey and down-homey as possible.
In the World: Singer Otis Redding; Otis Elevator Company; basketball player/executive Otis Smith

Otto (AH-toh) 1889: #65
Popularity: #930
Styles: German and Dutch,
Guys and Dolls, Nickname-
Proof 1880 Today ·
Sisters: Lottie, Greta,
Penelope, Zora, Mabel, Elsa, Hildy
Brothers: Felix, Roscoe, Oscar, Hugo, Axel,
Fritz, Bruno
✷ Otto disappeared in the U.S. during World War I along with other assertively German favorites. Today it's a fun, fresh choice but a bit cartoonish. (Sargeant Snorkel's dog in the comic strip *Beetle Bailey* is, alas, a perfect example.) Nonetheless, stylish parents are starting to tiptoe back toward this name. It's the playful side of the avant-garde.
In the World: German statesman Otto von Bismarck; director Otto Preminger; Otto the dog in *Beetle Bailey*

Owen (OH-ehn) 2011: #44
Popularity: #44
Styles: Antique Charm,
Celtic, Nickname-Proof, The
"-ens" 1880 Today
Variants: Owain, Eóghan
Sisters: Ella, Grace, Hannah, Eliza, Isabel,
Ava, Lily
Brothers: Gavin, Liam, Mason, Eli, Aidan,
Lucas, Noah
✷ The "O" makes Owen sound old-fashioned, and the "-en" keeps it up to date. That elegant compromise makes this Celtic classic one of the most fashionable names of the decade. It's actually a Celt twice over, with two separate origins: Welsh, from Owain, and Irish, from Eóghan.
In the World: Actor Owen Wilson; Western writer Owen Wister

Palmer (PAHL-mer, 1908: #383
PAH-mer)
Popularity: #1630
Styles: Last Names First,
Nickname-Proof 1880 Today
Variants: Palmiro
Sisters: Estella, Avis, Hollis, Everly, Belle,
Auden
Brothers: Foster, Parrish, Sumner, Murphy,
Truman, Porter
✷ Two at one blow: Palmer is both a gentlemanly turn-of-the-century name and a tradesman-style surname. (Tradesman-style, but not really a trade: Palmer comes from a medieval name for a pilgrim to the Holy Land.) It's a distinguished cousin to young rascals like Tucker and Cooper.

Parker (PAHR-ker) 2011: #79
Popularity: #79
Styles: Last Names First,
Androgynous, Nickname-
Proof 1880 Today
Sisters: Aubrey, Piper, Maya,
Avery, Hadley, Chloe, Paige, Hailey
Brothers: Riley, Peyton, Carter, Mason,
Spencer, Preston, Trevor, Carson
✷ Parker was one of the quiet, preppy surnames for generations, but it has exploded in popularity. You can hear both of those phases in the name today. It's part quiet gentleman and part trendy upstart—a split personality, kind of like Peter Parker and Spider-Man. You'll meet an occasional female Parker too, but the name does not sound androgynous on a boy.
In the World: Sitcom *Parker Lewis Can't Lose*; Parker pens; Parker Brothers games

Patrick (PAT-rik) 1968: #30
Popularity: #143
Styles: Timeless, Celtic
Nicknames: Pat, Patsy, Paddy, Rick 1880 Today
Variants: Padraig, Patrice, Patricio
Sisters: Shannon, Leslie, Emily, Bridget, Christina, Kelly
Brothers: Michael, Timothy, Brian, Andrew, Thomas, Sean
✳ Lest you forget that this name represents the patron saint of Ireland, you'll get a convenient reminder every March 17. It's the definitive Irish name, timeless and handsome. Yet parents looking to show off their Irish roots are increasingly turning to more exotic choices. The Gaelic version Padraig (pronounced PAWD-rig or POH-ric) could pull the old favorite toward exotic territory.
In the World: St. Patrick's Day; actors Patrick Dempsey, Patrick Stewart, and Patrick Swayze; *SpongeBob* starfish Patrick

Paul (PAWL) 1964: #16
Popularity: #187
Styles: Timeless, Biblical, Solid Citizens
Nicknames: Pauly 1880 Today
Variants: Pavel, Pablo, Paolo, Pau
Sisters: Anita, Jane, Carolyn, Theresa, Catherine, Patricia, Elaine, Gail
Brothers: Carl, Peter, Mark, Allen, Martin, Russell, Glenn, Neal
✳ Paul is the warmest of the manly classics. It's not soft (think mythical lumberjack Paul Bunyan), but it has an easy gentleness that requires no nickname. The nickname-free angle may be a particular lure if you love names like James and Peter but don't take to the idea of a Jim or Pete.
In the World: Musicians Paul McCartney and Paul Simon; actor Paul Newman; painters Paul Cézanne and Paul Gauguin

Pax (PAKS) 2009: #2880
Popularity: #3077
Styles: Modern Meanings, Brisk and Breezy
Sisters: Tru, Sol, Journey, 1880 Today
Skye, Onyx, Wren, Halo, Dove
Brothers: Lake, Quill, Bodhi, Reef, Fox, Taj, Cloud, Calix
✳ Pax is the Latin word for "peace." Actress and baby-naming queen Angelina Jolie chose it for her second son, and the "x"-starved American populace pricked up its ears. Parents who are tempted but leery often turn it into a nickname for Paxton.
In the World: Pax Jolie-Pitt, son of actors Angelina Jolie and Brad Pitt; the Roman Empire's "Pax Romana"; PAX gaming festivals

Paxton (PAKS-tən) 2011: #274
Popularity: #273
Styles: Last Names First, The "-ens," Fantastical
Nicknames: Pax 1880 Today
Sisters: Emery, Finley, Piper, Avery, Mattea, Rowan
Brothers: Beckett, Sawyer, Griffin, Maddox, Weston, Parker
✳ Paxton combines a lot of hot trends: surnames, "-ton" names, and the uber-stylish letter "x." It's a thoroughly contemporary name. So why does it sound so grown-up? Paxton may be trendy, but it sounds traditional rather than look-at-me creative.
In the World: Paxton Fettel of the "F.E.A.R." video games, actors Bill Paxton and Sara Paxton; singer Tom Paxton

Pedro (PAY-droh) 1999: #202
Popularity: #306
Styles: Latino/Latina, Shakespearean
Nicknames: Pete, Perico, 1880 Today
Pedrinho
Variants: Pietro
Sisters: Rosa, Elena, Ana, Guadalupe, Perla, Maria
Brothers: Jose, Francisco, Pablo, Juan, Miguel, Fernando
✳ Spanish Pedro is much like his English counterpart Peter: a classic that doesn't care much about trends and fashions.
In the World: Filmmaker Pedro Almodóvar; singer Pedro Infante; baseball pitcher Pedro Martinez

Penn (PEHN)   2011: #3214
Popularity: #3273
Styles: Brisk and Breezy, Last Names First, Why Not?
Sisters: Auden, Piper, Willa,   1880   Today
Marin, Sonnet, Emery
Brothers: Briggs, Wilson, Shaw, Price, Edison, Locke
✳ It's hard to get preppier than an Ivy League college (the University of Pennsylvania goes by Penn). Yet the name is agreeably simple, and actor Penn Badgley was named after prosaic Penn tennis balls. William Penn, a champion of freedom and democracy, makes an inspiring model for the name; magician-provocateur Penn Jillette makes a mischievious one.
In the World: Actor Penn Badgley; magician Penn Jillette; abbreviation for Pennsylvania

Percy (PER-see)   1897: #98
Popularity: #2971
Styles: Ladies and Gentlemen
Variants: Percival
Sisters: Delia, Polly, Eugenia,   1880   Today
Dora, Maude, Lenora
Brothers: Emory, Winston, Claude, Chauncey, Basil, Aubrey
✳ Percy is a surname transfer, or occasionally a nickname for Percival. It's also long been the generic name for the prissy kid most likely to get roughed up in the schoolyard. In fact, it's easy to imagine Percy as a girl's name today. But if you want a tougher image, look to the mythological adventure books "Percy Jackson and the Olympians," where it's short for Perseus.
In the World: "Percy Jackson and the Olympians" series; singer Percy Sledge; Percy Weasley of the "Harry Potter" series; football player Percy Harvin

Perrin (PEH-rin)   1899: #1051
Popularity: #2710
Styles: Last Names First, Why Not?
Variants: Pierre   1880   Today
Sisters: Ariane, Mabry, Avril, Elodie, Bellamy, Larsen
Brothers: Edmond, Quill, Yannick, Bastien, Olivier, Aldrin
✳ Perrin is a contemporary-sounding surname, but it started life centuries ago as a French nickname for Pierre (Peter). You might think of it as a male counterpart to Alison, which was similarly a French nickname for Alice. It's a rare choice that fits in well and could also be a nickname option for a young Peter.
In the World: Perrin Aybara of the fantasy book series "The Wheel of Time"

Perry (PEH-ree)   1959: #132
Popularity: #1201
Styles: Mid-Century, Androgynous
Sisters: Vicky, Patti, Darla,   1880   Today
Annette, Cathy, Pam
Brothers: Glenn, Barry, Dell, Guy, Lonnie, Cliff
✳ Perry was the precursor to names like Corey—boyish, nickname-like constructions designed to stand alone. (Actually, Perry can be a nickname for Peregrine. No matter.) The beauty of Perry is that over the years men like Perry Como and Perry Mason have given the youthful name a grown-up style. It still sounds light, but it's not a lightweight.
In the World: Singer Perry Como; fictional attorney Perry Mason; designer Perry Ellis; a cartoon platypus   .

Peter (PEE-ter)   1957: #37
Popularity: #198
Styles: Timeless, Biblical
Nicknames: Pete, Perrin
Variants: Pedro, Pierre, Piet,   1880   Today
Petros, Piers, Pier
Sisters: Susan, Theresa, Donna, Janet,
Kathryn, Patricia
Brothers: Stephen, Paul, Thomas, Allen,
Philip, Martin
✸There will always be Peters, but for now the momentum is moving away from this biblical classic. Pete just sounds a bit out of sync with current tastes—a white-bread name in a low-carb world. Take comfort in knowing, though, that nobody actually dislikes the name. It sounds solid and trend-proof.
In the World: Iconic Peters range from Peter the Great to Peter Rabbit to Peter Parker (Spider-Man)

Peyton (PAY-tən)   2007: #125
Popularity: #166
Styles: Last Names First, The
"-ens," Androgynous,
Nickname-Proof   1880   Today
Variants: Payton
Sisters: Aubrey, Maya, Kennedy, Landry, Paige,
Ashlyn
Brothers: Parker, Nolan, Landon, Bennett,
Preston, Carson
✸Cross the melodrama *Peyton Place* with quarterback Peyton Manning and what do you get? How about a formerly preppy, delicate name that's gained some jock cred. Note, though, that this name is used equally for girls and boys.
In the World: Football players Peyton Manning and Peyton Hillis; *Peyton Place*

Philip (FI-lip)   1948: #54
Popularity: #406
Styles: Timeless, Biblical,
Solid Citizens
Nicknames: Phil, Pip, Flip   1880   Today
Variants: Phillip, Felipe,
Philippe
Sisters: Theresa, Claudia, Jacqueline, Judith,
Veronica, Catherine
Brothers: Thomas, Paul, Michael, Kenneth,
Vincent, Charles
✸ Philip is the handsome, enduring choice for a modern gentleman. So why is the name on its way to becoming an endangered species? Let's lay the blame on nickname Phil, which has acquired a middle-aged talk show host vibe. Just focus on the full name; it's uncommon (for young boys, at least) and classic.
In the World: Countless Philips from hard-boiled detective Philip Marlowe to talk show host Dr. Phil

Phineas (FI-nee-əs)   2010: #1236
Popularity: #1394
Styles: Biblical, Exotic
Traditional
Nicknames: Fin   1880   Today
Variants: Phinehas, Pinchas
Sisters: Genevieve, Beatrix, Lorelei, Phoebe,
Charis, Seraphina
Brothers: Gideon, Atticus, Theodore, Barnaby,
Raphael, Tobias
✸This rare biblical name sounds distinctly old-fashioned, yet the overall effect is smart and jazzy. It's a creative sleeper that could pick up the trail of recent hits like Lucas and Julian.
In the World: Cartoon *Phineas and Ferb*; Phinnaeus, a son of actress Julia Roberts

Phoenix (FEE-nix)   2009: #367
Popularity: #388
Styles: Charms and Graces,
Fantastical, Place Names,
Country and Western,   1880   Today
Androgynous
Sisters: Aurora, Halo, Willow, Scarlett, Lyra,
Serenity
Brothers: Gryphon, Xander, Caspian, Hendrix,
Canyon, Orion
✷ The mythical bird the Phoenix was a symbol
of immortality. Consumed by fire every 500
years, it would rise up reborn from the ashes.
The word is also used to mean a paragon of
beauty or quality. Such fabulous imagery is un-
common for a boy's name, but the capital of
Arizona does ground Phoenix in the real world.
In the World: "Phoenix Wright" video game;
actor Joaquin Phoenix; *Harry Potter and the
Order of the Phoenix*

Pierce (PEERS)   2011: #474
Popularity: #474
Styles: Antique Charm, Brisk
and Breezy, Why Not?
Variants: Piers   1880   Today
Sisters: Charlotte, Fiona,
Julia, Hope, Claire, Daphne
Brothers: Grant, Palmer, Reid, Cole, Duncan,
Blaine
✷ This name is sleek and preppy, but strong as
steel—like Pierce Brosnan's James Bond or
Remington Steele. Pierce makes newer zippy
names like Bryce and Chance look like light-
weights. It's also a presidential surname, an in-
teresting changeup as a brother to a Jackson or
Carter. (History hasn't looked kindly on Presi-
dent Franklin Pierce, though.)
In the World: Actor Pierce Brosnan; science fiction author Piers Anthony; TV host Piers Morgan

Pierson (PEER-sən)   2011: #1388
Popularity: #1395
Styles: Last Names First,
Why Not?
Nicknames: Piers   1880   Today
Variants: Pierce, Pearson
Sisters: Larkin, Hollis, Lilian, Emery, Adeline,
Evelyn
Brothers: Hampton, Merrick, Colson, Brigham,
Quinlan, Preston
✷ Yes, there *are* other names like Jackson and
Greyson that nobody's using yet. Pierson is a
surname based on Piers, a common medieval
form of Peter. You can choose it for style or to
honor a father or grandfather named Peter.

Porter (POHR-ter)   1880: #273
Popularity: #450
Styles: Last Names First,
Antique Charm, Nickname-
Proof, Guys and Dolls, Why   1880   Today
Not?
Sisters: Hadley, Madelyn, Annabel, Harper,
Lila, Audrey
Brothers: Hudson, Turner, Pierce, Mason,
Archer, Preston
✷ Porter pulls off a nice sleight of hand, per-
suading you that it's a stately old gentleman's
name one moment, a trendy new workman
name the next. That kind of versatility can take
you far in life.
In the World: Singer Porter Wagoner; CIA direc-
tor Porter Goss; music producer Porter Robin-
son

Prescott (PRES-kət)   1989: #1890
Popularity: #4595
Styles: Ladies and
Gentlemen, Last Names
First, Why Not?   1880   Today
Nicknames: Pres, Scotty
Sisters: Afton, Bellamy, Christabel, Trilby,
Daphna, Holland, Portia
Brothers: Powell, Winslow, Forbes, Burgess,
Hughes, Spaulding, Prentiss
✷ Prescott is a distinguished, upper-crusty sur-
name, but no softy. Its old-fashioned manliness
stands out in the increasingly androgynous sur-
name field. An uncommon alternative to the
increasingly popular Preston.
In the World: Senator and presidential father
Prescott Bush

Preston (PREHS-tən)   2007: #114
Popularity: #137
Styles: Last Names First,
Antique Charm
Nicknames: Pres   1880   Today
Sisters: Chloe, Harper,
Payton, Piper, Aubrey, Avery, Madelyn, Ellery
Brothers: Parker, Harrison, Grant, Nolan,
Spencer, Clayton, Jameson, Porter
✷ Preston is a fashionable surname with an
old-time courtly quality. It's exceedingly formal
yet doesn't seem stiff—that bowtie and cum-
merbund fit comfortably. And the more Pres-
ton's popularity rises, the more it loosens up.
In the World: Film director Preston Sturges;
Britney Spears's son Sean Preston

Prince (PRINS)   2011: #481
Popularity: #481
Styles: Modern Meanings, African-American, Fanciful
Sisters: Aura, Heaven, Marvel, Paisley, Liberty, Diamond
Brothers: Jett, Orion, Baron, Romeo, Bishop, King
✴This name is linked to the enigmatic one-named musician, but it's been used in the U.S. for many generations. Prince is flamboyant yet more grounded than its Disney-styled counterpart Princess.
In the World: Singer Prince; baseball player Prince Fielder; son of singer Michael Jackson; Prince Charming

Princeton (PRINS-tən)   2011: #978
Popularity: #978
Styles: Place Names
Sisters: London, Shiloh, Vienna, Avalon, Berkeley, Raleigh
Brothers: Kingsley, Parrish, Cornell, Regis, Charleston, Everest
✴The rapid rise of the name Kingston has rubbed off on this close relation. Despite the family resemblance, the effects of the two names are quite different. Where Kingston has a Jamaican lilt, Princeton is pure Ivy League. The name is undeniably elegant, but some may find the Ivy aura a little much. And what happens when your son gets into Harvard?
In the World: Princeton University; Princeton Review test preparation company

Quentin (KWEHN-tin)   1919: #220
Popularity: #408
Styles: The "-ens," Saints, French, Timeless, Nickname-Proof
Variants: Quintinus, Quintus, Quinton
Sisters: Violet, Annabel, Camille, Avril, Serena, Celeste
Brothers: Tristan, Hugh, Vincent, Xavier, Miles, Alexander
✴Quentin is the French form of an old Roman name, and nobody can mistake its traditional elegance. Yet it sounds creative too, thanks to one little letter. The "Q" is this name's calling card and sets it apart, gracefully.
In the World: Filmmaker Quentin Tarantino; illustrator Quentin Blake; writer Quentin Crisp

Quill (KWIL)   rarely used
Popularity: Very rare
Styles: Modern Meanings, Brisk and Breezy, Why Not?
Variants: Quil
Sisters: Blythe, Lark, Prue, Harlow, Sonnet, Bay
Brothers: Frost, Baz, Wilder, Reeve, Watt, Laird
✴The dashing style of Quill makes a convincing case for the pen being mightier than the sword. Many will indeed hear this name as the common word "quill" (a feather, or the writing pen made from one). As a name, though, it's an Irish surname Anglicized from Mac Cuill or Ó Cuill.
In the World: Luann comic-strip character Quill; Quil Ateara, a werewolf in the "Twilight" series

Quincy (KWIN-see)   1977: #274
Popularity: #599
Styles: Last Names First, African-American, Timeless
Nicknames: Quin
Sisters: Noelle, Vanessa, Alexis, Gabrielle, Larissa, Angelique
Brothers: Wesley, Xavier, Jamison, Quentin, Kendrick, Vaughan
✴This surname has a prim colonial style, but it swings nonetheless. The feeling is more Quincy Jones than John Quincy Adams. The "-y" ending occasionally attracts parents of girls, but most people will still hear this name as clearly masculine.
In the World: Musician/producer Quincy Jones; President John Quincy Adams

Quinlan (KWIN-lən)   2006: #1166
Popularity: #1717
Styles: Last Names First, The "-ens," Celtic, Why Not?
Nicknames: Quin
Sisters: Kerrigan, Aislinn, Keelin, Madigan, Mckenna, Waverly, Kendall, Tierney
Brothers: Devlin, Brogan, Riordan, Quill, Killian, Paxton, Brigham, Connor
✴The Irish surname Quinlan is winning fans as an unusual "Q" name that's more elegant than splashy. If that's what you're after, you've hit the target. But if you're just worried that Quinn isn't "formal" enough on its own, put your mind at ease. Quinn is perfectly full, formal, and traditional (and etymologically unrelated to Quinlan).

Quinn (KWIN) 2009: #259
Popularity: #297
Styles: Brisk and Breezy,
Celtic, Last Names First,
Androgynous 1880 Today
Variants: Quin, Conn
Sisters: Kiley, Sage, Fiona, Skye, Isla, Maeve
Brothers: Donovan, Reid, Owen, Finn, Wyatt,
Griffin
★ Quinn is one of the meatiest one-syllable
names around. Equally familiar as a first name
and an Irish surname, it's a dynamic choice that
stands up well to power names of every descrip-
tion. It has become unexpectedly androgynous
due to a crop of female TV characters named
Quinn.
In the World: Song "Quinn the Eskimo (Mighty
Quinn)"; basketball player/commentator Quinn
Buckner

Quinton (KWIN-tən) 1996: #301
Popularity: #531
Styles: Exotic Traditional,
The "-ens," African-American
Nicknames: Quint, Quin 1880 Today
Variants: Quinten, Quintin
Sisters: Alexa, Giselle, Leighton, Serena,
Dominique, Vivian
Brothers: Tristan, Donovan, Vance, Darius,
Xavier, Jamison
★ Assertively classy, Quinton is a name that
demands your attention. It's not quite the re-
fined classic that Quentin is, but it has the ad-
vantage of stronger nicknames. The spelling
Quintin is traditionally used for the fifth son in
a family.
In the World: MMA fighter Quinton ("Ram-
page") Jackson; football player Quinton Coples

Raiden (RAY-din) 2011: #536
Popularity: #535
Styles: Bell Tones, The
"-ens," Fantastical
Nicknames: Ray 1880 Today
Variants: Raijin, Rayden
Sisters: Macy, Avalyn, Jade, Lyra, Ashlyn, Rylee
Brothers: Maddox, Dillon, Ryder, Draven,
Larson, Kane
★ Plenty of names rhyme with Aiden, but only
this one can teleport and shoot lightning bolts.
Raiden is the Japanese thunder god, incarnated
as a character in the "Mortal Kombat" game series. That makes it a gamer name that also fits
neatly with modern fashions. (Pronunciation
note: from its Japanese origin, this name should
be closer to "RIY-DEHN," but the English-lan-
guage games say "RAY-din," and so do American parents.)
In the World: Raiden of "Mortal Kombat" game
series

Ralph (RALF) 1918: #22
Popularity: #953
Styles: Solid Citizens
Variants: Rolf, Raul, Rollo
Sisters: Norma, Doris, 1880 Today
Bernice, Myra, Wilma,
Phyllis
Brothers: Eugene, Leonard, Howard, Earl,
Milton, Leon
★ A dignified classic for generations, Ralph has
fallen on hard times. From Ralph Malph of
Happy Days to Ralph Wiggum of *The Simp-
sons*, the name has been relegated to comic re-
lief. Looking for a twist that might help? You
can try using the British pronunciation "Rafe,"
like actor Ralph Fiennes, but be prepared for
some blank stares.
In the World: Ralph Kramden of *The Honey-
mooners*; designer Ralph Lauren

Ramon (rah-MOHN)   1930: #184
Popularity: #503
Styles: Latino/Latina,
Timeless
Nicknames: Ray   1880 Today
Variants: Ramón, Raymond
Sisters: Carmen, Raquel, Maria, Ana, Cristina,
Alicia
Brothers: Manuel, Ruben, Alfredo, Carlos,
Rafael, Julio
✖ Like its English counterpart Raymond,
Ramón is a timeless workhorse of a name. It's
sturdy, dignified, and couldn't care less about
the vagaries of fashion.
In the World: Musician Ramón Ayala; basket-
ball player Ramon Sessions; silent film star
Ramón Novarro

Ramsey (RAM-zee)   1997: #974
Popularity: #1529
Styles: Last Names First,
Why Not?
Nicknames: Ram   1880 Today
Variants: Ramsay
Sisters: Tierney, Blythe, Lesley, Davina,
Maisie, Everly
Brothers: Finlay, Lachlan, Guthrie, Campbell,
Flynn, Garrick
✖ This underused surname gives you dinner-
party elegance, with the tough-guy nickname
Ram standing by for less domesticated mo-
ments. It's a fun combination, and thoroughly
masculine despite the "-y" ending. The spelling
Ramsay is a Scottish classic.
In the World: Jazz musician Ramsey Lewis; Brit-
ish prime minister Ramsay MacDonald

Rand (RAND)   1950: #676
Popularity: #4431
Styles: Brisk and Breezy,
Literary and Artistic,
Fantastical   1880 Today
Variants: Rance
Sisters: Hollis, Britt, Darcy, Sloane, Amory,
Linley
Brothers: Wynn, Laird, Case, Barron, Locke,
Roark
✖ Between libertarian politician Rand Paul
and novelist Ayn Rand, the mother of objectiv-
ism, this name packs an ideological wallop.
That's not to say it doesn't have other merits.
Rand works as a brawnily preppy name or as a
modernized namesake for a Randy. But if you
choose the name, do so understanding that
some will take it as a statement.
In the World: Politician Rand Paul; writer Ayn
Rand; Rand al'Thor, protagonist of "The
Wheel of Time" fantasy series

Randall (RAN-dəl)   1960: #59
Popularity: #855
Styles: Mid-Century, Surfer
'60s
Nicknames: Randy, Rand   1880 Today
Variants: Randel, Randal
Sisters: Deborah, Robin, Sheryl, Denise,
Suzanne, Pamela
Brothers: Gregory, Darrell, Stephen, Dwight,
Russell, Terrence
✖ The name Randall is an heirloom from the
Middle Ages. Today, though, it's more likely to
remind you of middle age. Most Randalls are
heading into that demographic, and parents
have gradually lost interest in the name. Choos-
ing the nickname Rand instead of Randy helps
bring it up to date.
In the World: Football player Randall Cunning-
ham; cartoonist Randall Munroe; Stephen
King's villain Randall Flagg

Randolph (RAN-dahlf) 1952: #154
Popularity: #2257
Styles: Solid Citizens, Ladies
and Gentlemen
Nicknames: Randy, Dolph, 1880 Today
Rand
Variants: Randolf, Ranulph
Sisters: Virginia, Beverly, Marianne, Rosalind,
Sylvia, Constance
Brothers: Gerard, Carlton, Stewart, Lionel,
Stanton, Cornell
✳ Even when Randy and Randall were atop
the charts, Randolph was left behind. It was per-
haps *too* gentlemanly, a bit heavy-handed for a
modern little boy. It still sounds heavy today,
but that can make a name intriguingly individ-
ual in an age of light, trim names.
In the World: Actor Randolph Scott; Randolph
eyewear

Randy (RAN-dee) 1956: #28
Popularity: #355
Styles: Mid-Century, Surfer
'60s, Nicknames
Variants: Randall, Randolph 1880 Today
Sisters: Cindy, Vicky,
Rhonda, Sandy, Denise, Debby
Brothers: Ricky, Keith, Steve, Kerry, Robby,
Chris
✳ A top-40 name on the 1950s hit parade,
Randy is approaching golden-oldie status today
but has kept its boyish demeanor. That boyish-
ness has a naughtier spin in the U.K., where the
libidinous meaning of "randy" is more standard.
In the World: *American Idol* judge Randy Jack-
son; football player Randy Moss; wrestler Randy
Orton; singer Randy Travis

Ranger (RAYN-jer) 2011: #3289
Popularity: #3330
Styles: Fanciful, Last Names
First, Country and Western,
Macho Swagger 1880 Today
Sisters: Oakley, Sedona,
Cassidy, Sunday, Aspen, Liberty
Brothers: Maverick, Rider, Cannon, Knight,
Cash, Stryker
✳ Ranger sounds perilously close to a cartoon,
until you think of all the boys named Hunter
and Maverick. Boyish and tough, fun and
cocky, Ranger may be ready for the limelight.
In the World: U.S. Army Rangers; park rangers;
The Lone Ranger; Ford Ranger trucks; the
phrase "ranger up"

Raphael (rah-fiy-EHL) 1990: #465
Popularity: #669
Styles: Exotic Traditional,
Timeless, Saints, Biblical,
Why Not? 1880 Today
Nicknames: Raffi, Rafe,
Rafer, Raph, Rafa
Variants: Rafael, Raffaele
Sisters: Lucia, Beatrice, Aurora, Camilla,
Genevieve, Celeste
Brothers: Emmanuel, Gideon, Phineas,
Roman, Tobias, Gabriel
✳ Consider three archangels: Michael was the
most popular name in America for half a cen-
tury. Gabriel is a hot contemporary hit. And
Raphael? Still lurking quietly in the shadows.
Elegant and mildly exotic, Raphael is a promis-
ing choice for adventurous traditionalists.
In the World: Painter Raphael (and his Ninja
Turtle namesake); singer Raphael Saadiq; ten-
nis player Rafael Nadal

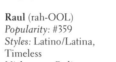

Raul (rah-OOL) 1995: #200
Popularity: #359
Styles: Latino/Latina,
Timeless 1880 Today
Nicknames: Ruli
Variants: Raúl, Raoul, Rollo
Sisters: Raquel, Blanca, Elena, Carmen,
Cristina, Silvia
Brothers: Ruben, Hector, Rafael, Julio, Miguel,
Javier
✳ Raul is timeless and familiar, yet its one-of-a-
kind style still leaps out at you. No other name
matches its syrupy-rich sound, masculine and
mysterious. It's technically a form of Ralph, but
a world removed from that name. For the Span-
ish version, add an accent mark (Raúl); for Por-
tuguese, go without.
In the World: Actor Raúl Juliá; Cuban leader
Raúl Castro; humanitarian Raoul Wallenberg;
soccer player Raúl

Ray (RAY) — 1896: #50
Popularity: #685
Styles: Solid Citizens, Nicknames
Variants: Rey
Sisters: June, Ada, Rosie, Nola, Mae, Rita
Brothers: Rex, Lee, Ellis, Clark, Guy, Joe
★Without the added weight of the full name Raymond, Ray flies surprisingly free. This name could be a Ray of sunshine, or a sting Ray, or a Sugar Ray. It's a Teflon name that will accommodate any image but not stick to it.
In the World: Singers Ray Charles and Ray J; comedian Ray Romano; football player Ray Lewis; writer Ray Bradbury

Raymond (RAY-mənd) — 1919: #14
Popularity: #234
Styles: Solid Citizens
Nicknames: Ray
Variants: Ramon, Raimondo, Raymundo, Reamann, Redmond
Sisters: Carol, Jeanne, Frances, Constance, Barbara, Elaine
Brothers: Donald, Paul, Gordon, Charles, Franklin, Robert
★ If you were asked to compile a top-40 countdown of the most popular baby names of the last century, would Raymond even cross your mind? This name has been a steady soldier, strong but so modest that its decades of popularity went virtually unnoticed. It's now slipping just as modestly out of fashion.
In the World: Sitcom *Everybody Loves Raymond;* writers Raymond Chandler and Raymond Carver; actor Raymond Burr

Raz (RAZ) — 2002: #8446
Popularity: Very rare
Styles: Jewish, Short and Sweet
Variants: Raziel
Sisters: Ziva, Orly, Miri, Bar, Adi, Yael, Tova, Avia
Brothers: Avi, Neo, Boaz, Dov, Teo, Lazar, Joah, Zev
★ Raz comes from a Hebrew word meaning a "spiritual secret" or "mystery." It's most often heard as a full name in Israel, but it can also be used as a short form of Raziel. In the mystical Kabbalah tradition, Raziel was an archangel, the "angel of mysteries" who held much of the secret knowledge of the universe.

Reef (REEF) — 2011: #1927
Popularity: #1944
Styles: Brisk and Breezy, Charms and Graces, Why Not?
Sisters: Juniper, Bay, Briar, Sol, Cassia, Sage, Winter, Lark
Brothers: Lake, Wynn, Falcon, Case, Canyon, River, Penn, Roan
★This unusual name is like a hologram, its image shifting as you look at it from different angles. Now it's a nature name, now a preppie name, now a surfer dude name. The summed effect is cheerful and utterly at ease.
In the World: Reef beach apparel; an occasional shortening of "reefer" (marijuana)

Reese (REES) — 2003: #368
Popularity: #543
Styles: Androgynous, Brisk and Breezy, Last Names First
Variants: Reece, Rhys
Sisters: Paige, Kiley, Brynn, Laney, Regan, Ainsley
Brothers: Luke, Clayton, Owen, Quinn, Gage, Riley
★This old-time preppy classic has been enjoying a burst of popularity. Actress Reese Witherspoon has inspired a crop of female Reeses, but the name is still a solid boy's choice. If you're concerned about confusions, the spelling Reece has remained more consistently masculine, and the traditional Welsh version Rhys almost completely so.
In the World: Actors Reece Thompson and Rhys Ifans

Reginald (REH-ji-nəld) — 1968: #118
Popularity: #652
Styles: Mid-Century, Surfer '60s, African-American
Nicknames: Reggie, Reg
Sisters: Rochelle, Yolanda, Adrienne, Yvette, Demetria, Monique
Brothers: Terrence, Roderick, Darrell, Tyrone, Randolph, Bradford
★The name Reginald is formal and a bit of a dandy. As Reg or Reggie, though, it's bubbling over with good-humored energy. The name was common in Britain early in the 20th century, then was taken up by African-Americans a generation later. Today it's still well liked, but slipping out of use.
In the World: Athletes Reggie Bush, Reggie Jackson, Reggie Miller, Reggie White, and Reggie Lewis

Regis (REE-jis) 1917: #599
Popularity: #7886
Styles: Exotic Traditional,
French, Saints
Sisters: Averil, Romaine, 1880 Today
Loris, Twyla, Avis, Therese
Brothers: Sylvian, Artis, Royce, Vitus, Laurent,
Galen
✳This is an Anglicized version of an old French name with saintly and regal associations. It's elegant, but a bit fussy. For the moment the name is primarily linked with TV host Regis Philbin.
In the World: TV host Regis Philbin

Reid (REED) 2010: #291
Popularity: #296
Styles: Timeless, Brisk and
Breezy, Last Names First,
Celtic 1880 Today
Variants: Reed
Sisters: Laine, Brooke, Avery, Jenna, Riley,
Audrey
Brothers: Grant, Luke, Gavin, Ross, Barrett,
Tate
✳ Reid somehow manages to make preppiness sexy, which is a good recipe for success in life. As a timeless surname, it should age more gracefully than some of its trendier brethren.
In the World: Auto racer Reed Sorenson; entrepreneur Reid Hoffman

Remington (REH-ming-tən) 2011: #479
Popularity: #479
Styles: Last Names First,
Macho Swagger, Country
and Western, Why Not? 1880 Today
Nicknames: Remy
Sisters: Savannah, Oakley, Holliston, Raelynn,
Cassidy, Landry
Brothers: Colton, Jackson, Austin, Brantley,
Lexington, Dalton
✳ In the '80s detective show *Remington Steele*, the title hero was a fiction, a hypermasculine name dreamed up by another character. Yet the name Remington isn't pure fantasy. Its roots include the Remington arms company and Frederic Remington, the great artist of the American West. The TV show is long gone now, but the name has shown staying power.
In the World: *Remington Steele*; Remington arms; Remington shavers

Rene (reh-NAY) 1972: #259
Popularity: #645
Styles: French, Latino/Latina
Variants: René, Renato
Sisters: Lea, Monique, 1880 Today
Raquel, Melanie, Alicia,
Lisette
Brothers: Andre, Raul, Noel, Ramon, Felipe,
Marcel
✳The French male name René was never as popular in the U.S. as its female counterpart Renée, which was a '60s–'70s staple. In fact, you may not hear this name as French at all. That's because René found a second life—as befits its meaning, "rebirth." It became a favorite of Latino parents, picking up a Spanish accent along the way.
In the World: Philosopher René Descartes; actor René Auberjonois; singing duo René & Angela

Reuben (ROO-behn) 1895: #151
Popularity: #942
Styles: Biblical, Timeless,
Jewish, Why Not?
Nicknames: Rube 1880 Today
Variants: Ruben
Sisters: Miriam, Elsa, Sadie, Naomi, Lena,
Esther
Brothers: Solomon, Theo, Monte, Felix, Moses,
Simon
✳The name Reuben is a pure biblical classic, the eldest of Jacob's 12 sons. Yet it remains unpopular, outpaced by even the unlikeliest biblical names, like Ezekiel and Zechariah. Perhaps Reuben's style is a little too mellow. Or perhaps the images it summons are less biblical and more corned-beef-on-rye. The Spanish Ruben is more current.
In the World: Reuben sandwich; musicians Rubén Blades and Ruben Studdard; Rube Goldberg machines

Rex (REHKS) 1951: #171
Popularity: #617
Styles: Brisk and Breezy,
Macho Swagger, Timeless,
Short and Sweet, Why Not? 1880 Today
Sisters: Cleo, Lana, Ruby,
Flora, Scarlett, Eve, Reva, Joy
Brothers: Leo, Vance, Major, Ray, Clark,
Royce, Bond, Von
✴ For too long, parents let Rex go to the dogs.
It took a national love affair with the letter "x"
for this simple yet swaggering name to launch a
comeback, and it's still surprisingly rare. The
name comes from the Latin for "king," as in Ty-
rannosaurus Rex, the tyrant-lizard king.
In the World: Actor Rex Harrison; football
coach Rex Ryan; detective novelist Rex Stout

Rhett (REHT) 2011: #564
Popularity: #563
Styles: Brisk and Breezy,
Country and Western,
Literary and Artistic 1880 Today
Sisters: Shea, Landry, Briar,
Sierra, Faith, Shiloh
Brothers: Shane, Austin, Reid, Wyatt, Beau,
Trace
✴ *Gone with the Wind*'s Rhett Butler makes
and breaks this name. You can't beat him for
roguish charm and grand romance, but his
image lingers around the name like a strong co-
logne. The name isn't pure fiction, though. It
was in fact used in the pre–Civil War South.
In the World: Rhett Butler of *Gone with the
Wind*; singers Rhett Akins and Rhett Miller

Rhys (REES) 2011: #487
Popularity: #486
Styles: Celtic, Brisk and
Breezy, Why Not?
Sisters: Carys, Emlyn, Brynn, 1880 Today
Eleri, Mabyn, Tegan
Brothers: Griffin, Owen, Pryce, Bevan, Wynn,
Vaughn
✴ Americans are more familiar with the Angli-
cized versions of this name: Reese and Reece.
In the rest of the English-speaking world,
though, the Welsh classic Rhys rules. Its look is
distinctive and memorable, and the pronuncia-
tion is getting easier for Americans thanks to
well-known examples like actor Jonathan Rhys
Meyers. Unlike Reese, it's also exclusively mas-
culine.
In the World: Actors Jonathan Rhys Meyers and
Rhys Ifans

Richard (RI-cherd) 1946: #5
Popularity: #127
Styles: Solid Citizens
Nicknames: Dick, Rich, Rick,
Richie, Ricky, Rico 1880 Today
Variants: Ricardo, Rickert
Sisters: Susan, Barbara, Patricia, Nancy,
Gloria, Carol
Brothers: Robert, Kenneth, Paul, James,
Donald, Thomas
✴ The top names of the '30s and '40s are the
names that today's parents just breeze right past.
Richard is fading fast, for no real reason except
the cyclical hunt for something new. It's still a
solid choice, kingly and reliable.
In the World: A defining name of the 20th cen-
tury, from President Richard Nixon to come-
dian Richard Pryor

Riley (RIY-lee, RIY-ə-lee) 2006: #101
Popularity: #111
Styles: Last Names First,
Celtic, Androgynous,
Nickname-Proof 1880 Today
Variants: Rylee, Reilly
Sisters: Avery, Megan, Taylor, Faith, Kennedy,
Tatum
Brothers: Connor, Dylan, Ryder, Brody,
Carson, Parker
✴ This surname transfer has been a favorite
since the 19th century. It's an old-fashioned
name with a young, contemporary sound.
Though Riley is catching on for girls, it's still a
dandy boy's name—just stick to the standard
surname spellings.
In the World: The phrase "living the life of
Riley"; Riley Freeman of comic strip *The Boon-
docks*

River (RI-ver) 2011: #424
Popularity: #424
Styles: Charms and Graces
Variants: Rivers
Sisters: Meadow, Sierra, 1880 Today
Violet, Summer, Hope,
Ember
Brothers: Talon, Sawyer, Canyon, Sage, Orion,
Holden
✴ The late actor River Phoenix left behind
both his first and last names as new options for
boys. River is a pure nature name that can
sound as rugged as whitewater or as gentle as a
shady brook.
In the World: Actor River Phoenix; singer Rivers
Cuomo

Robert (RAW-bert) 1931: #1
Popularity: #61
Styles: Timeless
Nicknames: Bob, Rob, Robin,
Robbie, Bobby, Rab, Dobbin 1880 Today
Variants: Roberto, Rupert
Sisters: Patricia, Margaret, Theresa, Barbara,
Elizabeth, Jane
Brothers: Richard, David, Thomas, Edward,
James, Peter
★ Robert seems to remind many parents of
their own fathers and grandfathers. That's a
natural result of the name's overwhelming pop-
ularity from the '20s to the '60s. But like similar
classics William, Charles, and Richard, Robert
is finding some new life in a shift of nicknames.
The softer Will, Charlie, Rich, and Rob are sup-
planting Bill, Chuck, Dick, and Bob.
In the World: Countless exemplars from author
Robert Louis Stevenson to reggae legend Bob
Marley to actor Robert Pattinson

Roberto (roh-BAYR-toh) 1981: #147
Popularity: #295
Styles: Latino/Latina, Italian,
Timeless
Nicknames: Rob, Robbie, 1880 Today
Beto, Bert, Bob
Variants: Ruperto, Robert
Sisters: Elena, Maria, Ana, Liliana, Marina,
Carmen, Luciana, Rosa
Brothers: Antonio, Mario, Alberto, Carlos,
Ricardo, Lorenzo, Armando, Marco
★ This is a grown-up name in the best sense of
the word. It has an attractively mature, respon-
sible image. Always popular as an Italian name,
Roberto has also become a modern classic
among Latino Americans.
In the World: Baseball legend Roberto Cle-
mente; designer Roberto Cavalli; actor Roberto
Benigni

Robin (RAH-bin) 1956: #143
Popularity: #1571
Styles: Mid-Century, English,
Androgynous, Nicknames
Sisters: Penny, Daphne, Gail, 1880 Today
Trudy, Meg, Lesley
Brothers: Kip, Dana, Stuart, Cary, Colin, Tad
★ Robin was originally a nickname for
Robert—think Robin Hood to get in the swing
of its merry English style. A flock of female Rob-
ins limited the popularity of the boy's name for
years, but that fad has now mostly flown past.
In the World: Robin Hood; Batman and Robin;
comedian Robin Williams; singer Robin Thicke

Robinson (RAH-bin-sən) 1900: #1052
Popularity: #2560
Styles: Last Names First
Nicknames: Rob, Robin
Variants: Robertson, Robbins 1880 Today
Sisters: Laine, Ellery,
Carrington, Laurel, Ashby, Wren, Carey, Hollis
Brothers: Clayton, Anderson, Ramsey, Forester,
Nicholson, Langston, Barrett, Edison
★ This uncommon name contracts neatly into
familiar nicknames. Robinson's cultural roots
run deep, from castaway Robinson Crusoe to
baseball trailblazer Jackie Robinson. A fine
choice to honor a Grandpa Robert.
In the World: Robinson Crusoe; baseball player
Robinson Canó

Rocco (RAH-koh) 2009: #387
Popularity: #402
Styles: Italian, Saints, Guys
and Dolls, Macho Swagger
Nicknames: Rock, Rocky 1880 Today
Sisters: Ruby, Mia, Giada,
Lillie, Lana, Lucia
Brothers: Max, Bruno, Luca, Arlo, Jude, Enzo
★ After a long dry spell, Italian names are mak-
ing a comeback. The suave classics grab most of
the headlines: Giovanni, Dante, Leonardo.
Rocco, in comparison, is a street fighter, rough
and tough, with a twinkle of good humor. Think
of it as the Italian counterpart to Jack.
In the World: Chef Rocco DiSpirito; a son of
singer Madonna and director Guy Ritchie

Roderick (RAH-də-rik) 1971: #224
Popularity: #913
Styles: Timeless, Saints,
English, African-American
Nicknames: Rod, Rory, Rick, 1880 Today
Roddy
Variants: Roderic, Rodrigo, Ruaridh, Rory
Sisters: Cecily, Amabel, Regina, Venetia,
Rosamond, Averill, Jessamy, Elinor
Brothers: Desmond, Reginald, Cedric,
Algernon, Thaddeus, Aldric, Denholm,
Barnaby
★ Parents looking for colorful panache tend to
turn to boys' names from foreign languages.
Here's a chance to get that same impact from an
English classic. Roderick is elegant, easy to pro-
nounce, and chock full of nicknames.
In the World: Actor Roddy McDowall; wrestler
"Rowdy" Roddy Piper

Rodney (RAHD-nee)   1965: #33
Popularity: #548
Styles: Mid-Century,
African-American
Nicknames: Rod   1880   Today
Sisters: Charlene, Yvonne,
Pamela, Wanda, Yolanda, Sherry
Brothers: Darryl, Reginald, Terrance, Kelvin,
Gregory, Curtis

✴ Only a few decades ago, Rodney was in the full height of fashion. It remained a solid favorite of African-American parents for a while longer, but white families largely abandoned the name. (Perhaps the sad-sack image of comic Rodney Dangerfield began to rub off.) If you like the nickname Rod, Roderick is another route to it.
In the World: Comedian Rodney Dangerfield; musicians Rodney Atkins and Rodney Jerkins; Rodney King, flashpoint for 1992 L.A. protest riots

Roger (RAH-jer)   1945: #22
Popularity: #529
Styles: Solid Citizens,
Mid-Century
Nicknames: Rodge, Hodge   1880   Today
Variants: Rodger, Rutger,
Rudiger
Sisters: Janet, Kathleen, Carolyn, Judith,
Donna, Gwen
Brothers: Peter, Allen, Gerald, Glenn, Russell,
Douglas

✴ Roger is an old and noble name that was a great hit in the 12th century. There's nothing medieval about its style, though—Roger sounds like a regular American guy. The name is so disarmingly plain and simple that it could be considered alongside back-to-basics hits like Lucy and Sam. The archaic nickname Hodge is appealingly gruff.
In the World: Jolly Roger pirate flags; "Roger Wilco"; tennis player Roger Federer; film critic Roger Ebert

Rohan (ROH-han, ROH-ən)   2004: #480
Popularity: #575
Styles: The "-ens," Celtic,
African-American
Variants: Rowan   1880   Today
Sisters: Diya, Asha, Regan,
Selah, Rory, Arwen
Brothers: Kiran, Declan, Naveen, Asher, Reilly,
Quinn

✴ The name Rohan is many things to many people. It's a Hindi name, an alternate spelling of the Irish Rowan, and a place name from *The Lord of the Rings*. To top it off, the Hindi version became a standard in the Caribbean thanks to legendary cricket player Rohan Kanhai. Got that? Then you're ready to tackle the pronunciations. If you want an Irish style, say "Rowan"; otherwise, pronounce a hard "h."
In the World: Entrepreneur Rohan Marley (son of singer Bob Marley); writer Rohan Candappa

Roland (ROH-lənd)   1931: #107
Popularity: #749
Styles: Solid Citizens, French
Nicknames: Rollie, Land
Variants: Rolando, Rowland,   1880   Today
Orlando
Sisters: Helene, Marion, Ramona, Constance,
Maxine, Glenna, Margot, Lorraine
Brothers: Jerome, Laurence, Gilbert, Vernon,
Gerard, Eugene, Bernard, Conrad

✴ This venerable, heroic old name has fallen off parents' radar. It's elegant but slow. Roland should make a comeback someday, but while you're waiting, consider two variants that Shakespeare favored: Rowland, which adds a surname flavor, and Orlando, which adds romance.
In the World: Film director Roland Emmerich

Roman (ROH-mən) 2011: #157
Popularity: #158
Styles: Timeless, Exotic Traditional, Slavic, Saints, The "-ens"
1880   Today
Variants: Romain
Sisters: Ivy, Marina, Aurora, Mercy, Juliet, Anya
Brothers: Ivan, Raphael, Miles, Alexander, Maxim, Elias
✳ Roman has an antique, eccentric personality but a modern rhythm, a combo that's perking up the ears of cutting-edge parents. It carries a deeper, darker aura than other "-en" names. The name comes from a Latin byname meaning "Roman." (That may seem obvious, but consider that the similar name German comes from a Latin byname meaning "brother.")
In the World: Director Roman Polanski; hot Hollywood baby name chosen by several celebrities

Romeo (ROH-mee-oh) 2010: #357
Popularity: #360
Styles: Exotic Traditional, Shakespearean, Italian
1880   Today
Sisters: Bianca, Donatella, Luciana, Juno, Valeria, Isis, Giovanna, Serafina
Brothers: Orlando, Titus, Valentino, Fabio, Dante, Leonardo, Orion, Matteo
✳ This lover-boy name, inseparable from Shakepeare's tragic young hero, is a bold choice. On a charismatic, outgoing kid, it will blossom into the coolest name on the block. On a shy bookworm, it could be trouble.
In the World: Romeo and Juliet; rapper Romeo Miller; a son of David and Victoria Beckham

Ronald (RAH-nəld) 1943: #9
Popularity: #341
Styles: Solid Citizens
Nicknames: Ron, Ronnie
Variants: Ronaldo
1880   Today
Sisters: Gloria, Joanne, Nancy, Carole, Joyce, Rosalyn, Barbara, Marilyn
Brothers: Duane, Kenneth, Roger, Gerald, Stuart, Richard, Jerome, Larry
✳ Ronald came in and went out with the 20th century. It was a dashing Scottish name through the '20s, an upstanding guy from the '30s through the '60s, and more and more of a fuddy-duddy after the '70s. The nickname Ron, though, remains timeless. Ronan is one alternate route to it.
In the World: President Ronald Reagan; corporate mascot Ronald McDonald; Ronald Weasley of the "Harry Potter" series

Ronan (ROH-nin) 2011: #457
Popularity: #458
Styles: Celtic, The "-ens," Saints, Why Not?
Nicknames: Ro, Ron
1880   Today
Variants: Rónán, Ronin, Ronen
Sisters: Fiona, Carys, Keira, Maeve, Brenna, Tegan, Tamsin, Anya
Brothers: Eamon, Brogan, Cormac, Brody, Finian, Callum, Egan, Tiernan
✳ In Ireland, the name Ronan is right in the mainstream of fashion. In the U.S., it's just a step to the side, less common but with a mainstream sound. That's a classic recipe for high style. Two unrelated names share the same American pronunciation: Ronin is the Japanese term for "a samurai with no master," a popular figure in comics and film, and Ronen is a modern Hebrew name meaning "song."
In the World: Irish singers Ronan Keating and Ronan Tynan

Roosevelt (ROH-zə-vehlt) 1905: #91
Popularity: #2976
Styles: Namesakes
Nicknames: Rosie
Sisters: Carmela, Jewell, Bernadine, Maryland, Lorna, Garnet, Althea, Germaine
Brothers: Freeman, McKinley, Truman, Llewellyn, Dempsey, Lafayette, Eldridge, Winston
✷ The White House is a huge source of names now, with everyone from Jefferson to Kennedy to Carter well represented in the nursery. Yet Roosevelt, one of the classics of the genre, is out of the picture. If you like the style but want something simpler, consider Hayes or Truman.
In the World: Presidents Franklin Delano Roosevelt and Theodore Roosevelt; musician Roosevelt Sykes

Rory (ROH-ree) 1982: #281
Popularity: #598
Styles: Celtic, Androgynous, Country and Western, Nickname-Proof
Variants: Ruairí, Rúaidhrí, Ruaridh
Sisters: Orla, Maisie, Eva, Moira, Isla, Neve, Keelin, Dara
Brothers: Conor, Shane, Casey, Finn, Ewan, Rhys, Finlay, Shay
✷ This roaring Gaelic favorite has the kind of rascally charm that melts hearts. Handsome Western star Rory Calhoun was a fine example. In the U.S., the name is used for girls as well as for boys. In Ireland and Scotland, it's still strictly a boy's name, popular in both the Anglicized spelling (Rory) and the local Gaelic versions.
In the World: Golfer Rory McIlroy; musician Rory Gallagher; actor Rory Calhoun

Roscoe (RAHS-koh) 1888: #117
Popularity: #2608
Styles: Porch Sitters, Nickname-Proof, Guys and Dolls, Country and Western
Sisters: Lulu, Roxie, Elvira, Selma, Dolly, Goldie, Mamie, Frieda
Brothers: Grover, Jethro, Rufus, Boyd, Gus, Wiley, Otis, Waldo
✷ Roscoe is one of the ultimate country rube names, but unlike most of its kin, it has potential. There's a playful, macho energy to the name that could capture the imagination of adventurous parents.
In the World: Rapper Roscoe Dash; tennis player Roscoe Tanner

Ross (RAHS) 1985: #147
Popularity: #934
Styles: Timeless, Last Names First, Brisk and Breezy
Sisters: Kate, Hillary, Sara, Cassie, Leigh, Joanna, Alison, Lindsay
Brothers: Clay, Marshall, Clinton, Grant, Reid, Mitchell, Vance, Neal
✷ It's cute and brisk and modern, and yet it also sounds like it could be your best friend's dad. Ross is a timeless, mature incarnation of the breezy name style.
In the World: Ross Geller of TV series *Friends*; actor/singer Ross Lynch; businessman Ross Perot

Rowan (ROH-ən) 2011: #310
Popularity: #309
Styles: The " ono," Celtic, Androgynous, Nickname-Proof
Variants: Rohan
Sisters: Maeve, Fiona, Violet, Orla, Tamsin, Brenna
Brothers: Conor, Tobin, Riley, Finn, Eamon, Carson
✷ This nifty Celtic name has a merrier bent than most, well suited to its meaning of "little red." Thanks go in part to comedian Rowan Atkinson, of *Mr. Bean* and *Blackadder* fame. See also Rowan in "Snapshots: Girls."
In the World: Actor Rowan Atkinson; *Rowan & Martin's Laugh-in*; Archbishop of Canterbury Rowan Williams

Roy (ROY) 1897: #19
Popularity: #565
Styles: Solid Citizens, Country and Western
Sisters: Mae, Ruby, Elsie, Rose, Dixie, Nan
Brothers: Lee, Joe, Clyde, Ike, Leo, Ned
✷ Roy is a good ol' boy, a category of names that has been in steady decline for 50 years. But while buddies Earl and Hoyt languish, Roy is a dark-horse candidate for a comeback. It's short and snappy, with the same playful good humor that has brought Max and Gus back to the limelight.
In the World: Singing cowboy Roy Rogers; artist Roy Lichtenstein; singer Roy Orbison; soccer coach Roy Hodgson

Royce (ROYS)   1935: #284
Popularity: #530
Styles: Brisk and Breezy,
Solid Citizens, Why Not?
Sisters: Joy, Margot, Vonda,   1880   Today
Twila, Rochelle, Gwen
Brothers: Myles, Rex, Von, Stanton, Vance,
Glynn
★ This swank surname makes a decorous alternative to brash newcomers like Trace and Zayne. Royce carries the image of old-fashioned luxury: its peak was in the '20s and '30s, when Rolls-Royce motor cars became synonymous with the high life.
In the World: automaker Rolls-Royce; rapper Royce da 5'9"; fighter Royce Gracie; basketball player Royce White

Rudolph (ROO-dahlf)   1927: #111
Popularity: #2711
Styles: Ladies and
Gentlemen, Namesakes
Nicknames: Rudy, Dolph   1880   Today
Variants: Rudolf, Rodolfo,
Rolf
Sisters: Flora, Clarice, Harriet, Geneva,
Rosalie, Estelle
Brothers: Casper, Wallace, Gilbert, Theodore,
Clifford, Bernard
★ To think that a single well-meaning red-nosed reindeer could bring a classic name to its knees! Rudolph is a stylish old-timer, elegant (à la Rudolph Valentino), but with a sense of humor. Among the grade school set, though, it's all about the reindeer. If your little Rudolph can make it through those early Christmas seasons, he'll do fine as an adult.
In the World: Rudolph the Red-Nosed Reindeer; silent film star Rudolph Valentino

Rudy (ROO-dee)   1934: #245
Popularity: #733
Styles: Nicknames, Timeless
Sisters: June, Vicky, Betsy,
Gwen, Margo, Carla, Suzy,   1880   Today
Joy
Brothers: Teddy, Rex, Billy, Dino, Hal, Jay,
Ricky, Cliff
★ If you want a little Mike, you choose Michael; a little Joe, you choose Joseph; a little Rudy, you choose . . . Rudy. Most parents who like this gung-ho boy's name today are skipping over the formal Rudolph. It's perhaps a bit *too* formal, with a lingering whiff of reindeer. If you're desperate for an alternative, try Rudiger, a German form of Roger.
In the World: Underdog sports film *Rudy*; New York City mayor Rudy Giuliani

Rufus (ROO-fəs)   1880: #88
Popularity: #2978
Styles: Porch Sitters, Classical
Nicknames: Ruff
Variants: Ruffin, Rufo   1880   Today
Sisters: Rhoda, Selma,
Hester, Jemima, Eugenia, Dinah
Brothers: Roscoe, Homer, Horace, Grover,
Lucius, Waldo
★ Rufus has some tall mountains to climb before it's a viable name choice for most families. It's both a stereotypical slave name and a stereotypical country bumpkin name. And yes, it rhymes with "doofus." Yet a handful of cool Rufuses, led by singer Rufus Wainwright, have this name creeping onto some parents' lists. It's contrarian and distinctive, but be sure to stop and ponder what happens if your Rufus *isn't* the coolest cat in class.
In the World: Musician Rufus Wainwright; actor Rufus Sewell

Rupert (ROO-pert) 1899: #402
Popularity: #9365
Styles: English, Ladies and
Gentlemen, Saints
Nicknames: Rip, Rupe
Sisters: Dulcie, Beatrice,
Imogen, Winifred, Verity, Portia
Brothers: Edmund, Nigel, Carleton, Tarquin,
Clive, Stuart
✱ For generations, Rupert has sounded to
Americans like a British gent with a stiff upper
lip and even stiffer dance moves. A recent crop
of prominent Ruperts like actors Rupert Everett
and Rupert Grint has been updating the name's
image. Rupert now has a fun and whimsical
side, but is still an unlikely choice for American
parents. The nickname Rip may win a few over.
In the World: Businessman Rupert Murdoch;
actors Rupert Grint, Rupert Friend, and Rupert
Everett

Ryan (RIY-ən) 1985: #12
Popularity: #25
Styles: New Classics, Celtic,
The "-ens," Nickname-Proof
Sisters: Megan, Ashley,
Lauren, Kara, Jessica, Erin
Brothers: Kevin, Sean, Tyler, Brandon, Kyle,
Justin
✱ Once upon a time, Michael and Patrick
were the classic Irish-American names. Then
Brian and Sean rose up to claim the throne.
While all those names are still going strong, it's
Ryan that holds the modern crown. For 30
years, Ryan's bright surname sound has spread
Irish style to every corner of America. (But
psst . . . watch your back, Ryan, here comes
Aidan!)
In the World: Actors Ryan Gosling, Ryan Reyn-
olds, and Ryan O'Neal; TV host Ryan Seacrest;
singer Ryan Adams; NASCAR racer Ryan New-
man

Russell (RUH-səl) 1914: #49
Popularity: #404
Styles: Solid Citizens,
Mid-Century
Nicknames: Russ, Rusty
Sisters: Elaine, Carolyn,
Theresa, Constance, Rosemary, Janice
Brothers: Lawrence, Raymond, Curtis, Warren,
Douglas, Marshall
✱ This reliable old surname is aging grace-
fully. The full name sounds a little slower and
gentler than it used to, but nickname Russ is as
fun-loving as ever. Actor Russell Crowe has
helped to show off the name's tough side.
In the World: Actor Russell Crowe; businessman
Russell Simmons; comic Russell Brand; basket-
ball player Russell Westbrook

Ryder (RIY-der) 2011: #108
Popularity: #108
Styles: Last Names First,
Macho Swagger, Nickname-
Proof
Variants: Rider
Sisters: Marley, Payton, Sienna, Hadley,
Emerson, Rylee
Brothers: Cooper, Hudson, Dylan, Hunter,
Wyatt, Tanner
✱ This swashbuckling surname sounds cus-
tom-made for a sports hero, but its muscular
frame would look pretty spiffy in a suit and tie
too. The international Ryder Cup golf tourna-
ment has helped make this spelling of the name
the most popular. Spelled Rider, it's both more
rugged and more old-fashioned.
In the World: Ryder Cup golf tournament; Ryder
Truck Rental; writer H. Rider Haggard; a son of
actress Kate Hudson

Ryker (RIYK-er)   2011: #268
Popularity: #267
Styles: Last Names First,
Macho Swagger, Fantastical
Variants: Riker   1880   Today
Sisters: Kaydence, Presley,
Layla, Jazlyn, Ripley, Londyn
Brothers: Jaxon, Riddick, Ranger, Cash, Burke,
Maddox
✱ Step aside, all you preppy, elegant surnames:
it's time for Ryker to rappel into the enemy command center, guns blazing. From the '60s army
film *Sergeant Ryker* to the short-lived '80s cop
show *Riker* to *Star Trek's* Commander Riker,
this name has signaled toughness and adventure.
In the World: Commander Riker of *Star Trek*;
Rikers Island jail; fictional Ryker's Island prison
for Marvel Comics supervillains

Rylan (RIY-lin)   2011: #146
Popularity: #146
Styles: The "-ens," Bell Tones
Variants: Rylan
Sisters: Jayla, Teagan, Alexa,   1880   Today
Kylee, Macy, Delaney
Brothers: Corbin, Bryce, Tyson, Landon, Kyler,
Raiden
✱ Nope, Rylan's not a surname; that's Ryland.
Nor is it a place name, or an obscure Irish saint.
It's just a pitch-perfect sound that somehow says
"cowboy." This name has become a soaring hit,
especially in the high plains states up through
Montana.

Samson (SAM-sən)   2011: #875
Popularity: #875
Styles: Exotic Traditional,
Biblical, Saints, Macho
Swagger   1880   Today
Nicknames: Sam
Variants: Sampson
Sisters: Shiloh, Atara, Zena, Paris, Athena,
Tamar, Eden, Scarlett
Brothers: Jericho, Justus, Gideon, Magnus,
Solomon, Jackson, Wolf, Maxim
✱ The nickname Sam is a rugged classic.
Some parents who are drawn to Sam for its
brawn find the full Samuel too tame for their
tastes. The solution for those few is Samson, a
full name that outmuscles the nickname. The
rise of similar-sounding surnames like Jackson
may make the name more approachable.
In the World: The biblical Samson is a symbol of
strength, as in Samsonite luggage

Samuel (SAM-yoo-əl)   1880: #17
Popularity: #26
Styles: Timeless, Biblical,
Antique Charm
Nicknames: Sam   1880   Today
Variants: Shmuel
Sisters: Abigail, Sarah, Lydia, Lily, Hannah,
Isabel
Brothers: Benjamin, Isaac, Nathan, Gabriel,
Henry, Joseph
✱ Samuel is a trendy hit today, but the name
has always been around and always will be. It's
biblical, literary, and rustic, appealing to many
tastes. And most importantly, it has that pure
classic nickname. Lovable Sam is the true engine behind Samuel's popularity.
In the World: Uncle Sam; Samuel Adams
(brewer and patriot); actor Samuel Jackson;
Sam's Club stores; "Sam I Am" of *Green Eggs
and Ham*

Saul (SAWL)   2001: #278
Popularity: #396
Styles: Antique Charm,
Jewish, Biblical
Variants: Saúl   1880   Today
Sisters: Leah, Abigail, Sophie,
Miriam, Sylvia, Esther, Sadie, Ruth
Brothers: Levi, Ezra, Isaac, Asher, Gabe,
Reuben, Jonas, Seth
✱ This is a steady name, never in the limelight
but always quietly present. It is now just as quietly stylish. Back in your parents' and grandparents' time, it was primarily a Jewish name,
which has left an odd aftereffect: a Saul with a
Jewish last name currently sounds decades
older than a non-Jewish Saul.
In the World: Author Saul Bellow

Sawyer (SOY-er, SAW-yer)   2011: #172
Popularity: #172
Styles: Last Names First,
Nickname-Proof, Literary
and Artistic   1880   Today
Sisters: Harper, Scarlett,
Ellery, Auden, Oakley, Marlowe
Brothers: Holden, Archer, Beckett, Shepard,
Tucker, Finn
✴ Sawyer's form fits with preppy surnames like
Parker and Spencer, but its spirit is freer. The
immortal Tom Sawyer lends the name a warm
heart and an eye for mischief. (The word "sawyer," back in Mark Twain's day, referred to sub-
merged trees that made travel down the
Mississippi River a perilous adventure.) This
name was something of a hidden treasure for
years, but a character on the TV series *Lost*
raised its profile. Note that the "SOY-er" pronunciation is dominant; if you prefer "SAW-
yer," prepare for an uphill battle.
In the World: Mark Twain's Tom Sawyer; Sawyer of *Lost*; country band Sawyer Brown

Scott (SKAHT)   1971: #10
Popularity: #372
Styles: Surfer '60s, Last
Names First
Nicknames: Scotty   1880   Today
Variants: Scot
Sisters: Kelly, Tina, Robin, Kimberly, Bridget,
Tracy
Brothers: Todd, Steven, Keith, Brian, Kurt,
Craig
✴ Scott was the granite-jawed man of the '60s.
While the name clearly reflects its original
meaning of "Scotsman," in practical usage it
holds no ethnic associations. Today Scott shines
particularly brightly as a middle name, where its
clipped sound adds a perfect punch to longer,
softer first names.
In the World: Cartoonist Scott Adams; com-
poser Scott Joplin; writer F. Scott Fitzgerald;
singer Scott Weiland

Seamus (SHAY-məs)   2008: #753
Popularity: #840
Styles: Celtic
Nicknames: Shem, Shay
Variants: Séamas, Shamus,   1880   Today
Hamish
Sisters: Aine, Maura, Fiona, Alannah, Rory,
Maeve
Brothers: Declan, Ronan, Finn, Brogan,
Killian, Teague
✴ A Gaelic form of James, Seamus is a hard-
core Irish charmer. The spelling may give
Americans pause, but resist the impulse to spell
this name phonetically. Its Irish quirkiness is
the heart of its charm. Hamish is a close Scot-
tish relative.
In the World: Poet Seamus Heaney; actor Sea-
mus Dever; Seamus Finnigan in the "Harry
Potter" series

Sean (SN)   1986: #37
Popularity: #125
Styles: '70s–'80s, Celtic
Variants: Seán, Shaun,
Shawn, Shane   1880   Today
Sisters: Erin, Sara, Megan,
Shannon, Tara, Kelly
Brothers: Ryan, Kyle, Casey, Brian, Patrick,
Kevin
✴ This Irish Gaelic form of John is now a clas-
sic throughout the English-speaking world. It's
just as clean and simple as John, but softer. The
standard spelling Sean sounds most Irish.
In the World: Actors Sean Connery, Sean Penn,
and Sean Bean; music mogul Sean Combs; en-
trepreneur Sean Parker

Sebastian (seh-BAS-chin)   2011: #68
Popularity: #68
Styles: Shakespearean,
English, Saints
Nicknames: Seb, Baz, Bastien 1880   Today
Variants: Sebastien
Sisters: Natalia, Juliana, Gabriella, Celeste,
Amelia, Victoria, Mariana, Valeria
Brothers: Julian, Nathaniel, Adrian, Xavier,
Tristan, Alexander, Oliver, Maximilian
✴ Sebastian is a refined name that was always a
little too elegant for comfort in the U.S. Your
parents may even call it prissy. You can toss all
that away now, because elegance has gone
mainstream. This paragon of sophistication is
now a global, youthful hit.
In the World: Writer Sebastian Junger; football
player Sebastian Janikowski; Sebastian the crab
in *The Little Mermaid*

Sergio (SAYR-jee-oh) 1995: #157
Popularity: #278
Styles: Italian, Latino/Latina, Saints
Nicknames: Checo
Variants: Serge, Sergei, Sergius
Sisters: Adriana, Bianca, Marina, Silvia, Noemi, Liliana
Brothers: Emilio, Dante, Marco, Dario, Fernando, Armando

1880   Today

✱ Sergio is so smooth, it's almost like a murmured seduction. Yet this name is no fly-by-night Romeo. For all of its seductiveness, Sergio sounds like the timeless, international saint's name it is. It's elegantly serious, and seriously elegant.
In the World: Director Sergio Leone; golfer Sergio Garcia; soccer player Sergio Ramos; designer Sergio Tacchini

Seth (SEHTH) 2000: #63
Popularity: #185
Styles: Biblical, New Classics
Sisters: Leah, Hannah, Molly, Rachel, Abigail, Ruth
Brothers: Joel, Ethan, Noah, Luke, Micah, Aaron

1880   Today

✱ Names like Abraham and Ezekiel are marvelously evocative. They're both patriarchs and pioneers: part Genesis, part Homestead Act. But they're also long and cumbersome. Seth is a plain, soft-spoken alternative (a funny one too, judging from the abundance of comedians named Seth).
In the World: Comedians Seth Rogen, Seth Meyers, Seth MacFarlane, and Seth Green

Shane (SHAYN) 1973: #54
Popularity: #215
Styles: Country and Western, Celtic, Brisk and Breezy, '70s–'80s, Turn of the 21st Century
Variants: Shayne, Sean
Sisters: Brooke, Leslie, Bridget, Sierra, Blair, Shea, Kara, Shannon
Brothers: Casey, Bryce, Rory, Drew, Rhett, Heath, Garrett, Keane

1880   Today

✱ This lone gunslinger has been riding the range for decades now. Shane is an Anglicized form of Sean, with a strong Western flavor from the classic cowboy movie *Shane*. It started out in the U.S. as a purely Western name, but its popularity has slowly spread. Today you could meet a Shane just about anywhere.
In the World: Currently popular in Ireland

Shannon (SHA-nən) 1972: #94
Popularity: #1566
Styles: '70s–'80s, Celtic, Androgynous, Nickname-Proof
Sisters: Kerry, April, Stacey, Krista, Erin, Shauna
Brothers: Torrey, Heath, Derrick, Jared, Shawn, Scottie

1880   Today

✱ This name was a male survivor, hanging on through a storm of female Shannons that swept through a generation back. (See Shannon in "Snapshots: Girls" for more background.) Now Shannon is slowly slipping out of use for both sexes.
In the World: Football player Shannon Sharpe

Sheldon (SHEHL-dən) 1934: #250
Popularity: #1071
Styles: Solid Citizens
Nicknames: Shel, Shelly
Sisters: Nadine, Marlys, Glenda, Darlene, Joyce, Norma
Brothers: Wendell, Sherman, Murray, Gordon, Myron, Arnold

1880   Today

✱ Sheldons everywhere curse the movie *When Harry Met Sally*, in which Billy Crystal's character argues that it's impossible to have great sex with a guy named Sheldon. Then *The Big Bang Theory* chose the name Sheldon as an emblem of geekhood. Despite generations of steady use, these are the kinds of perceptions the name is up against.
In the World: Sheldon Cooper of *The Big Bang Theory*; poet Shel Silverstein; actor Sheldon Leonard

Shepard (SHEH-perd) 2009: #2043
Popularity: #2259
Styles: Last Names First,
Why Not?
Nicknames: Shep 1880 Today
Variants: Shepherd, Sheppard
Sisters: Emeline, Coralie, Bellamy, Harriet,
Lottie, Clementine
Brothers: Gibson, Bowman, Burgess, Hawkins,
Brigham, Tillman
✴ Some surnames sound preppy. Others sound
cute, or modern, or sophisticated. Shepard
doesn't aim for any of those targets. Its appeal is
of the English sheepdog variety: all shaggy, aw-
shucks charm—especially when you use the
nickname Shep. But English sheepdogs are
sharper than they look. Shepard, for all its modest manner, is a high-fashion name.
In the World: Artist Shepard Fairey; newscaster
Shepard Smith; a son of comedian Jerry Seinfeld

Sherman (SHER-min) 1894: #153
Popularity: #2934
Styles: Solid Citizens, Last
Names First
Nicknames: Sherm 1880 Today
Sisters: Rhoda, Helene,
Glenna, Lenore, Pauline, Loretta
Brothers: Willis, Burton, Sanford, Newton,
Rollin, Merrill
✴ Sherman is a tradesman surname. It origi-
nally referred to someone who sheared woolen
cloth (a "shear-man"). If etymology were king,
that would make it a near neighbor to Tucker
and Walker, which are also names for cloth
workers. But in style terms, Sherman is worlds
apart from those trendy choices. Its mild Her-
man-like sound makes it tamer and less fashionable.
In the World: Writer Sherman Alexie; actor
Sherman Hemsley; Sherman tanks

Silas (SIY-ləs) 2011: #184
Popularity: #183
Styles: Antique Charm,
Biblical, Saints
Nicknames: Si 1880 Today
Variants: Silvanus
Sisters: Phoebe, Eliza, Lydia, Annabel, Ivy,
Luna
Brothers: Jonas, Elijah, Gideon, Levi, Titus,
Jasper
✴ Silas sounds handsome and devilish, like a
dapper villain in a silent film. The name eases
up, though, when you transport it to the modern
world. A Silas today looks comfortable in jeans
and is usually seen with a laptop and a Star-
bucks cup.
In the World: Novel *Silas Marner*; Silas in *The
Da Vinci Code*; Silas Botwin in the TV series
Weeds

Silvan (SIL-vin) 1926: #4200
Popularity: #11,956
Styles: Saints, Exotic
Traditional, Charms and
Graces, The "-ens," Why 1880 Today
Not?
Nicknames: Van
Variants: Sylvan, Silvanus, Silvano, Sylvain,
Silas
Sisters: Averil, Mabyn, Cassia, Ariadne,
Verena, Lilias
Brothers: Varian, Aidric, Theron, Alban,
Crispin, Magnus
✴ This is a true Why Not? name—not merely
"Why aren't American parents choosing it
today?" but "Why haven't they ever?" Silvan/
Sylvan is both a traditional name and an adjec-
tive meaning "of the woods." It has a lot of the
ingredients that parents look for, including that
trim "-n" ending, but so far most have ceded the
"sylv-" territory to the girl's name Sylvia.
In the World: Sylvan Learning Centers

Simeon (SI-mee-ən)   1880: #356
Popularity: #1107
Styles: Biblical, Exotic
Traditional, Why Not?
Nicknames: Sim   1880   Today
Variants: Simon
Sisters: Naomi, Hadassah, Aurora, Lydia,
Ketura, Jemima, Delilah
Brothers: Gideon, Ezra, Tobias, Japheth,
Josiah, Raphael, Micah
✳The Old Testament version of Simon,
Simeon has an antique flavor that should go
over well today. So far, though, the name hasn't
caught on. One reason may be the sound-alike
word "simian," meaning "monkey-like." That's
an unfortunate association but an obscure one,
and shouldn't rule the name out.
In the World: Football player Simeon Rice; San
Simeon, California

Simon (SIY-mon)   1888: #141
Popularity: #256
Styles: Timeless, Biblical,
English
Nicknames: Si   1880   Today
Variants: Simeon, Shimon
Sisters: Eve, Lydia, Charlotte, Elise, Daphne,
Claire
Brothers: Jude, Oliver, Owen, Peter, Isaac,
Colin
✳The familiar classic Simon has always been
well used in England. In America, it's been
heard most in nursery rhymes and children's
games. The name is finally getting its due atten-
tion in the U.S., and its British aura adds an
extra level of handsome charm.
In the World: Simon Says game; "Simple
Simon" rhyme; reality TV judge Simon Cowell

Skyler (SKIY-ler)   2002: #222
Popularity: #287
Styles: Last Names First,
Androgynous
Nicknames: Sky   1880   Today
Variants: Schuyler, Skylar
Sisters: Savanna, Tegan, Baylee, Summer,
Kassidy, Makenna
Brothers: Grayson, Spencer, Kolby, Tanner,
Weston, Pryor
✳This name used to be Schuyler, a quirky-
cool surname close in spirit to Dexter. As Skyler,
it is androgynous and aggressively modern.

Solomon (SAH-lə-mən)   1911: #221
Popularity: #449
Styles: Antique Charm,
Biblical
Nicknames: Sol, Solly, Solo   1880   Today
Variants: Zalman, Shlomo,
Sulaiman
Sisters: Esther, Violet, Miriam, Emmeline,
Hadassah, Naomi, Susannah
Brothers: Abraham, Gideon, Silas, Theodore,
Ezra, Isaac, Moses
✳The wisdom of Solomon lends this name an
eternal gravity, even as other biblical classics
turn youthful. It's a sweet solemnity, though,
and the implied wish for wisdom is a lovely mes-
sage for a boy to carry through life.
In the World: King Solomon; singer Solomon
Burke; scholar Solomon Schechter

Soren (SUWR-in, SOH-rin)   2011: #680
Popularity: #680
Styles: Nordic, German and
Dutch, Literary and Artistic,
Fantastical   1880   Today
Variants: Søren, Sören
Sisters: Signe, Ember, Maren, Svea, Aeris,
Ronia
Brothers: Anders, Odin, Ronin, Gunnar, Johan,
Taven
✳The Danish name Søren, pronounced
"SUWR-in," calls up the existential profundity
of philosopher Søren Kierkegaard. But the re-
cent rise of the name Soren (SOH-rin) owes to
some more modern and less human characters:
an owl in the "Guardians of Ga'Hoole" youth
fantasy novels and a mage in the "Fire Emblem"
video game series.
In the World: Philosopher Søren Kierkegaard;
"Fire Emblem" mage Soren

Sparrow (SPA-roh) 2011: #6949
Popularity: #7378
Styles: Charms and Graces,
Fanciful, Fantastical
Sisters: Winter, Eternity, 1880 Today
Cielo, Cortana, Meadow,
Evening, Sonnet, Halo
Brothers: Cloud, Falcon, Canyon, Shadow,
River, Cyan, Phoenix, Indigo
✳ Most bird names migrate to the girls' side of nameland, but Sparrow is chosen for both sexes. A lot of the credit goes to the usually hyper-macho video game industry. Sparrow is the player-controlled hero in "Fable II," whose sex you can choose at the start of the game. How's that for a truly androgynous name?
In the World: Son of Nicole Richie and Joel Madden; "Fable II" hero

Spencer (SPEHN-ser) 1998: #84
Popularity: #227
Styles: New Classics, Last
Names First
Nicknames: Spence 1880 Today
Variants: Spenser, Spence
Sisters: Sabrina, Mallory, Carly, Samantha,
Jocelyn, Kendall, Abby, Bailey
Brothers: Garrett, Parker, Austin, Brendan,
Chandler, Donovan, Riley, Schuyler
✳ Spencer straddled the geeky-cool line for years, but the verdict has come in solidly for cool. The full Spencer now sounds respectably grown-up à la actor Spencer Tracy, with Spence its lively alter ego. The *Spenser: For Hire* TV series helped give the name a slicker style.
In the World: Actor Spencer Tracy; *Spenser: For Hire*; reality TV star Spencer Pratt

Stanley (STAN-lee) 1916: #34
Popularity: #674
Styles: Solid Citizens
Nicknames: Stan
Sisters: Loretta, Eileen, 1880 Today
Jeanette, Roberta, Lois,
Maxine, Virginia, Rita
Brothers: Harold, Gilbert, Leonard, Marvin,
Wallace, Francis, Clifford, Vernon
✳ Over the years, Stanley has evolved from an elegant surname to a tough-luck everyman name. A *Streetcar Named Desire*'s Stanley Kowalski signaled the shift; the hero of the kids' book and movie *Holes*, Stanley Yelnats, is a more recent example.
In the World: Children's book *Flat Stanley*; director Stanley Kubrick; hockey's Stanley Cup championship

Stefan (STEH-fahn, 1991: #338
steh-FAHN)
Popularity: #882
Styles: German and Dutch,
Nordic 1880 Today
Nicknames: Steve, Steff
Variants: Stephan, Stephon, Steffen, Steffan,
Stefanos
Sisters: Katarina, Sofie, Britta, Lisbeth, Greta,
Lena, Mariel, Anke
Brothers: Anders, Gunnar, Markus, Aric,
Johann, Andreas, Tomas, Jurgen
✳ This tweaking of Stephen leaves the basic name intact but soups up its style. Stefan is the German and Scandinavian form, familiar in America but just foreign enough to attract extra notice. The spelling Stephon is an African-American favorite; Steffen is Low German, and Steffan is Welsh.
In the World: Tennis player Stefan Edberg, Stefan of *The Vampire Diaries*; basketball player Stephon Marbury

Stephen (STEE-vehn, 1951: #19
STEHF-ehn)
Popularity: #229
Styles: Biblical, Mid-Century
Nicknames: Steve 1880 Today
Variants: Steven, Stephan,
Stefan, Steffen, Esteban, Istvan, Stefano
Sisters: Diana, Theresa, Christine, Rebecca,
Cynthia, Andrea, Laura, Deborah
Brothers: Michael, Anthony, Philip, Thomas,
Andrew, Daniel, Mark, Matthew
✳ Stephen is the classic spelling of an old favorite. This version stays closest to the name's biblical and 19th-century roots, making it a little heartier and less boyish than Steven.
In the World: Author Stephen King; physicist Stephen Hawking; satirist Stephen Colbert; entertainer Steve Martin

Sterling (STER-ling)   1994: #402
Popularity: #736
Styles: Timeless, Charms and
Graces, Nickname-Proof
Sisters: Willow, Celeste,   1880   Today
Scarlett, Angelica, Jewell,
Genevieve, Serenity, Blythe
Brothers: Forrest, Quincy, Prescott, Fielding,
Maximilian, Quentin, Vaughan, Kingsley
✴ Sterling's a little flashy but leans toward real
luxury rather than mere glitter. It's like setting
out sterling silver flatware at dinnertime. Sure,
stainless is more practical, but there's some-
thing to be said for indulgence.
In the World: Football player Sterling Sharpe;
Mad Men ad agency Sterling Cooper

Steven (STEE-vehn)   1955: #10
Popularity: #124
Styles: Mid-Century, Surfer
'60s, '70s–'80s
Nicknames: Steve   1880   Today

Variants: Stephen, Stephan,
Stefan, Esteban, Istvan, Stefano
Sisters: Amy, Lesley, Melanie, Alison, Monica,
Michelle, Holly, Robin
Brothers: Jeffrey, Kevin, Brian, David,
Timothy, Eric, Patrick, Gregory
✴ Steven is heard less often today, but it re-
mains one of the safest names you can give a
boy. It is universally popular and carries no un-
pleasant baggage. This spelling, influenced by
the nickname Steve, has been the most com-
mon since the '50s. Many parents consider the
unambiguous pronunciation a plus. See also
Stephen.
In the World: Filmmaker Steven Spielberg;
Apple founder Steve Jobs; musician Steven
Tyler

Stone (STOHN)   1999: #627
Popularity: #1099
Styles: Charms and Graces,
Macho Swagger, Brisk and
Breezy, Why Not?   1880   Today

Sisters: Sage, Darby, Winter,
Mercy, Sienna, Bryce, Summer, Willow
Brothers: Storm, Campbell, Gray, Brock,
Steele, Lennox, Forrest, Pierce
✴ You can't mistake the meaning of this name,
an image of enduring strength. But while a
Rock sounds hyper-macho, a Stone sounds dig-
nified. It might be hard to picture the name on
a playful little boy, but it's handsome on a
grown man.
In the World: News anchor Stone Phillips

Strider (STRIY-der)   2003: #4423
Popularity: #9410
Styles: Fantastical, Macho
Swagger
Sisters: Arya, Eowyn, Sonnet,   1880   Today
Rogue, Harper, Aeris,
Sparrow, Phoenix
Brothers: Ryker, Case, Ranger, Locke, Caspian,
Draven, Slater, Knight
✴ Talk about a take-charge guy. Strider is all
energy and action, a name that propels you for-
ward. It matches the machismo of names like
Ranger and Cannon without the comic-book
style. It does, though, have a fantasy-book style.
In *The Lord of the Rings*, the heroic Aragorn is
also known as Strider.
In the World: 1990s video game "Strider"; alias
for Aragorn in *The Lord of the Rings*; Strider
knife company

Stuart (STOO-ert)   1960: #161
Popularity: #1598
Styles: Solid Citizens,
English, Celtic
Nicknames: Stu   1880   Today
Variants: Stewart
Sisters: Marianne, Constance, Janet, Anita,
Elaine, Glenna, Gayle, Rosemary
Brothers: Dwight, Clifton, Kenneth, Douglas,
Carlton, Roger, Wendell, Curtis
✴ Stuart is a playful dash of Scotland, under-
appreciated in the U.S. The name has had a
slightly nerdy image here, especially through its
nickname Stu, but today you'll find that most
people consider it cool and creative. Stewart is a
fine traditional variation.
In the World: Storybook mouse Stuart Little;
drummer Stewart Copeland; shoe designer Stuart Weitzman

Sullivan (SUH-li-vən)   2011: #525
Popularity: #524
Styles: Last Names First,
Celtic
Nicknames: Sully   1880   Today
Sisters: Connolly, Carrigan,
Flannery, Teagan, Hollis, Madigan, Delaney,
McKenna
Brothers: Finnegan, Brennan, Jameson,
McGregor, Fitzgerald, Beckett, Gallagher,
Callahan
✴ With Coopers and Baileys on every corner,
the line between first names and surnames is
blurring. If you're looking for a name that still
gives off a full, classic surname feel, consider
Sullivan.
In the World: Film *Sullivan's Travels*; a son of
actor Patrick Dempsey

Sylvester (sil-VEHS-ter)   1901: #138
Popularity: #2216
Styles: Ladies and
Gentlemen, Saints
Nicknames: Sly, Vet, Syl, Sy   1880   Today
Variants: Silvester
Sisters: Winifred, Henrietta, Penelope,
Clementine, Millicent, Adelaide
Brothers: Leopold, Cornelius, Roosevelt,
Ferdinand, Felix, Archibald
✴ This name manages to sound pompous and
nerdy at the same time. So why even bother
considering it? Because against all odds, Sylves-
ter also has a cool streak a mile wide. (Sylvester
Stallone's nickname Sly helps.) It's a high-stakes
gamble, but if the name fits your son, he'll have
a colorful calling card for life. If you're not quite
ready to roll those dice, consider Silvan, a trim
and traditional alternative from the same root.
In the World: Actor Sylvester Stallone; *Tweety
and Sylvester* cartoons

Tanner (TA-ner)   1997: #82
Popularity: #182
Styles: Last Names First,
Nickname-Proof, Turn of the
21st Century   1880   Today
Sisters: Shelby, Tatum,
Cassidy, Sierra, Kelsey, Taylor
Brothers: Cooper, Hunter, Logan, Dalton,
Austin, Ryder
✴ The upbeat sound of this tradesman name
made it a fast-rising hit. Tanner is one word-
based name that's *not* chosen for its meaning—
tanning hides was always a harsh profession.
In the World: Auto racer/TV host Tanner Foust

Tarquin (TAHR-kwin)   2004: #6131
Popularity: Very rare
Styles: Exotic Traditional,
English, Shakespearean,
Classical   1880   Today
Nicknames: Tark
Sisters: Sidony, Imogen, Beatrix, Araminta,
Hermione, Portia, Amabel, Phyllida
Brothers: Auberon, Ivor, Torquil, Piers, Horatio,
Atticus, Crispin, Tristram
✴ Literary and elegant, Tarquin has the stuff to
win the hearts of everyone from creative namers
to fantasy afficionados to classics buffs. Some,
though, may find it a little too aggressively
"posh." It's also worth noting that not all of the
classical and literary associations are pleasant
ones, including the legendary villain chroni-
cled in Shakespeare's *Rape of Lucrece*.
In the World: Ancient kings of Rome; various
privileged characters in fiction

Tate (TAYT)   2005: #381
Popularity: #394
Styles: Brisk and Breezy, Last
Names First
Variants: Tait   1880   Today
Sisters: Ainsley, Kendall,
Sage, Macy, Logan, Bryn, Laine, Ellery
Brothers: Kane, Reid, Brodie, Keaton, Cole,
Reese, Greyson, Trey
✴ The name Tate is utterly modern, yet you
can convince yourself that it's a traditional
prep-school standard. The Tate Gallery in Lon-
don lends a subtly sophisticated vibe.
In the World: Tate Gallery; actor Tate Donovan;
film *Little Man Tate*

Taylor (TAY-ler)   1992: #52
Popularity: #337
Styles: Last Names First,
Androgynous
Nicknames: Tay   1880   Today
Variants: Tayler
Sisters: Kelsey, Haley, Ashton, Morgan, Baylee,
Cassidy
Brothers: Parker, Tanner, Austin, Carter,
Jordan, Spencer
✴ Hugely popular in the 1990s, this boy's name
has fallen off sharply. The culprits: little girl
Taylors on every block. By the time female
singer Taylor Swift topped the charts, Tyler had
become the preferred choice for boys.
In the World: Actors Taylor Lautner and Taylor
Kitsch; singer Taylor Hanson

Teague (TEEG) 2010: #1726
Popularity: #2020
Styles: Celtic, Brisk and
Breezy
Variants: Tadhg   1880   Today
Sisters: Neve, Aisling,
Madigan, Tatum, Riley, Grier
Brothers: Keane, Riordan, Tiernan, Niall,
Cullen, Finn
★Tadhg (pronounced TIYG) is a classic Irish
name, so common in days long past that "taig"
became a slur term for an Irish Catholic. Mod-
ern Irish families are once again embracing the
name, but the Gaelic spelling tends to scare off
American parents. Try Teague, the Anglicized
version prounounced "TEEG."

Ted (TEHD) 1933: #145
Popularity: #2062
Styles: Solid Citizens,
Nicknames
Nicknames: Teddy   1880   Today
Sisters: Nancy, Kay, Joe,
Libby, Sue, Ellie
Brothers: Carl, Ray, Hal, Rex, Paul, Von
★Ted is a classic nickname for Edward, Theo-
dore, or Edmund. The formality of those names
is worlds away from Ted's sweet bluntness, so
many parents have chosen the nickname
straight up. It's a natural impulse and a lovable
name, but the "nicknamehood" is part of the
charm. For other formal versions, consider
Thaddeus and Edison.
In the World: Senator Ted Kennedy; actor Ted
Danson; businessman Ted Turner; film *Ted*
about a coarse teddy bear

Tenzin (TEHN-zin) 2011: #2023
Popularity: #2041
Styles: Namesakes
Variants: Tenzing
Sisters: Cering, Pema,   1880   Today
Choden, Dawa, Karma,
Khandro, Dechen, Nima
Brothers: Rinchen, Tashi, Kasur, Rabten,
Khenchen, Jampa, Sonam, Kalden
★Tenzin is a Tibetan Buddhist name meaning
"upholder of the Dharma." It is used equally for
boys and for girls. Today it is commonly given to
honor the 14th Dalai Lama, Nobel Laureate
Tenzin Gyatso. In the past, the transliteration
Tenzing was common, but Tenzin is more stan-
dard today.
In the World: Dalai Lama Tenzin Gyatso; Ever-
est-scaling mountaineer Tenzing Norgay

Terrance (TEH-rehns) 1979: #179
Popularity: #585
Styles: African-American,
English, Mid-Century, Surfer
'60s, '70s–'80s   1880   Today
Nicknames: Terry, Teo, Rance
Variants: Terence, Terrence
Sisters: Janelle, Christina, Meredith, Monique,
Lindsey, Candice
Brothers: Geoffrey, Dexter, Kelvin, Roderick,
Cornell, Bradley
★ Did you know that Terrance/Terence is an
old name, stemming from the Latin Terentius?
It hardly sounds it today, since it reemerged in
the 20th century when parents wanted a formal
name to use as a source for the hot nickname
Terry. Today a Terrance is more likely to go by
his full name. The spelling Terence is charac-
teristally British, while Terrance is more often
African-American.
In the World: Actors Terrence Howard and Ter-
ence Stamp; director Terrence Malick; TV host
Terrence J

Terrell (TEH-rəl, tə-REHL) 1989: #258
Popularity: #621
Styles: Last Names First,
African-American
Nicknames: Terry   1880   Today
Variants: Tyrell
Sisters: Larissa, Whitney, Lacey, Shantel,
Kendra, Janae
Brothers: Darnell, Kendrick, Bryant, Keenan,
Quincy, Jarrett
★This handsome surname followed in the
footsteps of Darrell and Terrence. Like those
similar choices, it's especially popular with Afri-
can-American families. Pronunciations with
first- and second-syllable stress are equally com-
mon.
In the World: Football players Terrell Owens,
Terrell Davis, and Terrell Suggs

Terry (TEH-ree) 1954: #27
Popularity: #536
Styles: Mid-Century,
Androgynous, Nicknames
Sisters: Paula, Connie, 1880 Today
Brenda, Vicki, Kathy, Cindy
Brothers: Randy, Barry, Jay, Dana, Bruce,
Danny
✱ In the '50s and '60s, Terry was a ubiquitous name for boys and girls alike. It now seems to have outlived its androgynous period and may be returning to the masculine camp. If you'd like a more formal alternative, Terry is a nickname for either Terrance or Theodore.
In the World: Football player Terry Bradshaw; writer Terry Pratchett; actor Terry Crews

Thaddeus (THA-dee-əs) 1918: #307
Popularity: #910
Styles: Exotic Traditional,
Biblical, Timeless, Why Not?
Nicknames: Tad, Thad 1880 Today
Variants: Tadeo
Sisters: Tabitha, Damaris, Evangeline, Helena, Sapphira, Paloma, Catalina, Aurora
Brothers: Matthias, Titus, Andreas, Gideon, Barnabas, Nathanael, Raphael, Atticus
✱ Thaddeus sounds like a flight of fancy, but it stays grounded thanks to easygoing nicknames and solid biblical roots. A good choice if your tastes are fanciful but you don't want your son to resent you for it.
In the World: The Apostle Thaddeus, generally identified as Jude

Thatcher (THACH-er) 2011: #1109
Popularity: #1113
Styles: Last Names First
Nicknames: Thatch
Sisters: Berkley, Landry, 1880 Today
Shiloh, Leighton, Emerson,
Bristol
Brothers: Watson, Sawyer, Brantley, Tucker, Sutton, Briggs
✱ A tradesman name with a nice crunchy sound, similar to Tucker but without that name's teasing problems. Thatcher does have baggage of its own, though, via former British prime minister Margaret Thatcher. In Britain, the name sounds like a political statement akin to the name Reagan in the U.S.
In the World: Prime Minister Margaret Thatcher; author/illustrator Thacher Hurd

Thelonius (theh-LOH-nee-əs) 1972: #4989
Popularity: Very rare
Styles: Exotic Traditional,
Guys and Dolls
Nicknames: Till, Lon 1880 Today
Variants: Thelonious, Tillo
Sisters: Isadora, Artemisia, Solange, Valentina, Leocadia, Sephora
Brothers: Algernon, Tarquin, Nicodemus, Phineas, Severin, Aldous
✱ An arcane variant of the name of Saint Tillo, Thelonius would be a mere obscurity except for jazz great Thelonious Monk. Monk (who spelled the name with an "-ous" ending, like an adjective) makes it an artsy choice ready to pair with names like Isadora.
In the World: Thelonious Monk

Theo (THEE-oh) 1908: #403
Popularity: #867
Styles: Nicknames, Antique
Charm, Why Not?
Variants: Teo 1880 Today
Sisters: Eva, Annabel, Clara, Lucy, Willa, Nora
Brothers: Oscar, Henry, Charlie, Leo, Felix, Jasper
✱ It took a while, but parents are finally starting to notice that Theo is the perfect solution to the Antique Boy Dilemma. Here's how it goes: you like old-fashioned, traditional names with a light touch. You happily make a list of your 25 favorite girls' names, then stare glumly at a blank page because your friends have already taken Max, Oliver, and Emmett. The answer is Theo.
In the World: Theo of *The Cosby Show*; art dealer Theo van Gogh; actor Theo James; baseball exec Theo Epstein

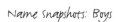

Theodore (THEE-ə-dohr) 1904: #30
Popularity: #231
Styles: Ladies and Gentlemen
Nicknames: Ted, Theo, Teo,
Terry 1880 Today
Variants: Teodoro, Fyodor
Sisters: Eleanor, Beatrice, Virginia, Genevieve,
Emmeline, Josephine
Brothers: Frederick, Edmund, Louis, Everett,
Julius, August
✴This classic name, bristling with gentlemanly vigor, has been surprisingly undiscovered in the recent turn-of-the-century revival. Fine nickname options complete the package: down-to-earth Ted, artistic Theo, and suave Teo.
In the World: President Theodore Roosevelt; writer Theodore Dreiser; cartoon chipmunk Theodore (Alvin's brother)

Thomas (TAH-məs) 1951: #8
Popularity: #63
Styles: Timeless, Biblical
Nicknames: Tom, Tommy
Variants: Tomas, Tommaso 1880 Today
Sisters: Anna, Elizabeth,
Theresa, Susan, Laura, Sarah
Brothers: James, Peter, Robert, David, William,
Joseph
✴Thomas was a monster hit in the '30s and '40s, yet unlike other favorites of that time, it doesn't sound the slightest bit stodgy. It continues to be one of the purest classic names. The everyday use of the full name (instead of Tom or Tommy) for young boys has been boosted by Thomas the Tank Engine.
In the World: Toms and Thomases from President Thomas Jefferson to quarterback Tom Brady to Thomas the Tank Engine

Tiernan (TEER-nin) 2009: #1784
Popularity: #1904
Styles: Celtic, The "-ens,"
Nickname-Proof, Why Not?
Variants: Tiarnan, Tierney 1880 Today
Sisters: Neve, Teagan,
Alannah, Keelin, Aisling, Enya
Brothers: Eamon, Cormac, Dermot, Lorcan,
Finian, Teague
✴Tiernan's an authentic, lively Irish boy's name that has yet to be discovered in the U.S. Catch it while you can!

Timothy (TI-mə-thee) 1967: #11
Popularity: #123
Styles: Surfer '60s, Mid-
Century, Biblical
Nicknames: Tim, Timmy 1880 Today
Variants: Timoteo,
Timotheus, Timo
Sisters: Melanie, Tabitha, Stephanie, Kimberly,
Rebecca, Teresa, Bethany, Cynthia
Brothers: Gregory, Matthew, Cristopher,
Geoffrey, Andrew, Stephen, Nicholas,
Jonathan
✴Timothy has a lyrical sound and is a firmly masculine classic. That's a much-sought-after combination today, so it's surprising to see Timothy's popularity continuing to plummet. Perhaps Tim just sounds too ordinary? If this is why you're hesitating, you could try the Finnish/German Timo instead, à la Nico for Nick.
In the World: Generations of Tims from Tiny Tim of *A Christmas Carol* to football player Tim Tebow

Tobias (toh-BIY-əs) 2007: #472
Popularity: #538
Styles: Antique Charm,
Biblical, German and Dutch,
Why Not? 1880 Today
Nicknames: Toby
Variants: Tobiah, Tobin, Toby, Tevye
Sisters: Bethany, Annalise, Lena, Susannah,
Mariah, Phoebe, Shiloh, Lydia
Brothers: Josiah, Eli, Jonas, Micah, Lukas,
Walker, Gideon, Silas
✴Tobias is a biblical name that echoes centuries past, yet it's hard to hear it as old. The youthful Toby seems to shine through the name's antique shell. That balance is the key to the name's appeal: both sunny and serious. You can go with Toby for your rambunctious toddler, then let him grow into a formidable Tobias.
In the World: Author Tobias Wolff; Tobias Fünke of *Arrested Development*; Tobias Eaton of *Divergent*

Tobin (TOH-bin)   1975: #735
Popularity: #1275
Styles: The "-ens," Last
Names First, Why Not?
Nicknames: Toby   1880   Today
Variants: Tobias
Sisters: Linden, Fiona, Afton, Bellamy,
Tamsin, Marlowe
Brothers: Bowen, Ramsey, Merrick, Flynn,
Tiernan, Galen
★This is an offbeat choice yet plays well to
current fashions. It's an Irish surname as well as
a variant of Tobias and has a young and playful
sound.
In the World: Actor Tobin Bell; son of model
Karolina Kurkova

Toby (TOH-bee)   1975: #190
Popularity: #771
Styles: Surfer '60s,
Shakespearean
Variants: Tobey, Tobias   1880   Today
Sisters: Dara, Heidi, Stacy,
Kara, Tamara, Holly
Brothers: Brad, Jody, Dylan, Jeffery, Kerry,
Brett
★This was one of the '60s–'70s "cute boy"
names. It was ready to fade away until *Spider-
Man* star Tobey Maguire nudged it back into
the spotlight. Toby is a form of Tobias, and with
the renewed popularity of biblical classics, the
most stylish way to use it is as a nickname for
that longer formal version. For a less antique-
styled formal option, consider Tobin.
In the World: Actor Tobey Maguire; singers
Toby Keith and TobyMac

Todd (TAHD)   1968: #28
Popularity: #872
Styles: Surfer '60s
Variants: Tod
Sisters: Jodi, Tracy, Renee,   1880   Today
Dawn, Tina, Jill
Brothers: Scott, Troy, Eric, Bryan, Craig, Brad
★Todd was a favorite for a generation, mascu-
line but not heavy-handed. It ran with a gang of
similar young colts like Scott and Kurt. Today
their sharp crunch is giving way to smooth-
edged names like Bryce and Lane.
In the World: Musician Todd Lundgren; de-
signer Todd Oldham; musical *Sweeney Todd*

Tony (TOH-nee)   1962: #52
Popularity: #409
Styles: Mid-Century,
Nicknames
Sisters: Terri, Kim, Cindy,   1880   Today
Tina, Vicky, Debbie
Brothers: Ricky, Danny, Vince, Dean, Jimmy,
Ronnie
★For generations, scores of parents have left
Anthony, Antonio, and friends by the wayside
and written Tony right on the birth certificate.
The name's rough-and-ready cheer is timelessly
appealing. If you picture the name on a corpo-
rate résumé, though, Anthony still reads better.
In the World: Broadway's Tony Awards; Tonys in
every sphere from skateboarder Tony Hawk to
British PM Tony Blair

Torin (TOHR-in)   2007: #1118
Popularity: #1316
Styles: Celtic, The "-ens,"
Why Not?   1880   Today
Sisters: Tamsin, Alannah,
Keelin, Davina, Carys,
Emlyn
Brothers: Finian, Colton, Tynan, Brodie,
Connal, Ronin
★Torin has a very traditional sound. Picture it
as an old British aristocrat; an Austrian skiing
champion; a Welsh chieftain. It may not actu-
ally be any of those things, mind you, but no-
body's likely to question this name as "made
up." They'll just find it handsome and wonder
why they don't hear it more often. (If you really
want an origin, it may come from the Norse
thunder god Thor by way of Irish mythology.)
In the World: English actor Torin Thatcher; adventure video game "Torin's Passage"

Trace (TRAYS)   1998: #437
Popularity: #577
Styles: Brisk and Breezy,
Country and Western
Sisters: Aspen, Skye, Quinn,   1880   Today
Scarlett, Landry, Sage
Brothers: Rhett, Lane, Bryce, Carson, Tanner,
Chance
★Reclaim the masculinity of Tracy with this
clever creation. Country music star Trace Ad-
kins was one of the many boys to be named
Tracy in the '60s, only to be swamped by the
avalanche of girls with that name. His moniker
Trace neatly clips the name into a male form.
In the World: Singer Trace Adkins

Travis (TRA-vis) 1979: #36
Popularity: #191
Styles: '70s–'80s, Country
and Western, Nickname-
Proof 1880 Today
Sisters: Tara, Alexis, Lindsay,
Tabitha, Courtney, Alicia
Brothers: Derek, Wesley, Shane, Jarvis, Cody,
Trevor
✴Travis is an old surname that once had a
fancy-pants sound. It has toughened up so thor-
oughly that it now sounds like a rowdy cowboy.
The name hit its peak in the '80s but still has
plenty of strength.
In the World: Drummer Travis Barker; country
singers Travis Tritt and Randy Travis; racer Tra-
vis Pastrana

Trent (TRENT) 2001: #208
Popularity: #373
Styles: New Classics, Brisk
and Breezy, Last Names First
Sisters: Tessa, Alana, Carly, 1880 Today
Macy, Lauryn, Sloane
Brothers: Brock, Trevor, Reid, Drake, Troy,
Dane
✴Trent is the blunt weapon of the Brisk and
Breezy names. Let Chase and Cole toss off bon
mots at cocktail parties. Trent has no time for
that frippery. A good name for a man of action,
but tough to cuddle up to.
In the World: Musician Trent Reznor; politician
Trent Lott; football players Trent Richardson
and Trent Dilfer

Trenton (TREHN-tən) 2007: #177
Popularity: #216
Styles: The "-ens," Place
Names
Nicknames: Trent 1880 Today
Variants: Trenten
Sisters: Mckenzie, Sydney, Daniela, Trinity,
Kiley, Brooklyn
Brothers: Camden, Weston, Trevor, Colton,
Brighton, Tucker
✴This place name first became popular as an
elaboration of the hit surname Trent. The effect
is less blunt and more elegant. It's also less dis-
tinctive, though, as Trenton blends in with the
large field of "-ton" names.
In the World: Trenton, the capital of New Jersey;
writer Trenton Lee Stewart

Trevor (TREH-ver) 1998: #58
Popularity: #180
Styles: English, Celtic,
Nickname-Proof, Turn of the
21st Century 1880 Today
Variants: Trever
Sisters: Claire, Jenna, Morgan, Alexa, Jillian,
Paige
Brothers: Colin, Tristan, Garrett, Dylan,
Connor, Austin
✴This name long had a British upper-crusty
ring to it, yet it's not a bit stuffy. On a young boy,
in fact, it sounds playful and rough-and-tumble.
That side of the name has come to the forefront
with a recent flock of young Trevors.
In the World: Actor Trevor Howard; baseball
player Trevor Hoffman

Trey (TRAY) 1999: #189
Popularity: #324
Styles: Brisk and Breezy
Variants: Trae, Tre
Sisters: Carly, Jade, Paige, 1880 Today
Macy, Bryn, Tessa, Abby,
Brooke
Brothers: Drew, Tate, Chase, Reed, Ty, Chaz,
Dane, Brett
✴This name, formed from the word "three," is
a traditional nickname for a "third": for in-
stance, John Smith III, whose dad and grandpa
have already claimed the nicknames Johnny
and Jack. It can also be applied to a third child
or third son in a family. As a given name, it's still
zippy but less preppy.
In the World: Singer Trey Songz; comedy writer
Trey Parker; Phish singer Trey Anastasio

Tristan (TRIS-tin) 1996: #68
Popularity: #87
Styles: The "-ens," English,
French, Literary and Artistic
Nicknames: Tris 1880 Today
Variants: Tristram, Tristen
Sisters: Giselle, Arianna, Fiona, Gabrielle,
Victoria, Natalia, Avery, Jocelyn
Brothers: Sebastian, Colin, Xavier, Julian,
Adrian, Gavin, Trevor, Quentin
✴Until recently, this French/English classic
was one Americans chose to view from afar. El-
egant Tristan was most likely to be spotted gam-
boling through a golden field in a
Merchant-Ivory production. Elegance is in
vogue now, and Tristan has become a U.S. fa-
vorite while keeping its literary style mostly in-
tact.
In the World: Opera *Tristan and Isolde*

Troy (TROY)
Popularity: #244
Styles: Surfer '60s, Brisk and Breezy, Place Names
Sisters: Dawn, Tracy, Kelly, Jill, Dina, Sherry
Brothers: Dean, Kirk, Darren, Scott, Brad, Lance

1968: #40

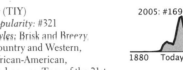

1880 Today

★ In the late '50s, a studio executive suggested that handsome young actor Merle Johnson change his name to Troy Donahue. A heartthrob was born, and so was a glossy hit name. The name is no longer young, but it still has a golden-boy style. The *Simpsons'* "actor Troy McClure" poked fun at that very image.
In the World: Actor Troy Donahue; football star Troy Aikman; the legendary city of the Trojan War

Truman (TROO-mehn)
Popularity: #1039
Styles: Last Names First, Literary and Artistic, Why Not?
Sisters: Elinor, Willa, Flora, Eloise, Nola, June
Brothers: Edison, Foster, Walker, Alden, Fletcher, Winslow

1945: #248

1880 Today

★ Unlike his presidential predecessor Franklin Roosevelt, Harry Truman didn't inspire many namesakes. In fact, the name Truman virtually disappeared after he took office. It's an appealingly genuine name and is worth a fresh look today. As for Harry himself, he's not a bad sort to be linked to: a regular bloke who rose to the occasion and surpassed the world's expectations.
In the World: President Harry S Truman; writer Truman Capote; film *The Truman Show*

Tucker (TUH-ker)
Popularity: #196
Styles: Last Names First
Nicknames: Tuck
Sisters: Camryn, Delaney, Bella, Aubrey, Hailey, Faith, Tatum, Macy
Brothers: Sawyer, Easton, Jackson, Anderson, Tanner, Paxton, Tate, Cooper

2011: #197

1880 Today

★ This tradesman name (it means "cloth finisher") is especially cheerful. Its sound suggests pluck and luck. Of course, it also suggests other "-uck" words, as the kids on the playground will surely point out.
In the World: Commentator Tucker Carlson; 1940s Tucker automobile

Turner (TER-ner)
Popularity: #921
Styles: Last Names First, Nickname-Proof, Why Not?
Sisters: Ellery, Calla, Tessa, Harper, Coral, Jensen
Brothers: Porter, Lawson, Walker, Archer, Hayes, Coleman

1888: #353

1880 Today

★ Turner is just beginning to make its mark as a first name. It has a sly toughness that could keep it climbing. There's no good nickname, though: picture shouting "Turn!" in a crowded room.
In the World: Turner Broadcasting (and founder Ted Turner); singer Tina Turner; slave rebellion leader Nat Turner

Ty (TIY)
Popularity: #321
Styles: Brisk and Breezy, Country and Western, African-American, Nicknames, Turn of the 21st Century
Sisters: Tessa, Carly, Lexi, Sage, Nia, Jade, Bree, Paige
Brothers: Bo, Trey, Chance, Tate, Jace, Taj, Lane, Colt

2005: #169

1880 Today

★ The nickname Ty can come from dozens of different "full" names. Just scan the list: Tyson, Tyrone, Tyler, and Tyree are only a few of the popular options. All of them convey different images and carry different baggage. Many parents are just skipping the choice altogether and leaping straight to merry, rambunctious Ty.
In the World: TV host Ty Pennington; country singer Ty Herndon; football star Ty Law; baseball legend Ty Cobb

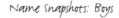

Tyler (TIY-ler)   1994: #5
Popularity: #38
Styles: Last Names First,
Turn of the 21st Century
Nicknames: Ty   1880   Today
Sisters: Haley, Jordan, Kayla,
Sydney, Alexis, Shelby
Brothers: Logan, Tanner, Dylan, Trevor,
Hunter, Austin
★ Tyler is one of the defining names of its generation. It led two fashion charges: tradesman surnames (Cooper, Tanner, Mason) and presidential surnames (Jackson, Madison, Carter). It's even a Texas city, like Austin. While Tyler is no longer a top-10 powerhouse name, it remains solidly beloved, fashionable, and tease-proof.
In the World: Filmmaker Tyler Perry; rapper Tyler, the Creator; Tyler Durden of *Fight Club*; President John Tyler

Tyree (tiy-REE)   1998: #405
Popularity: #958
Styles: African-American
Nicknames: Ty
Sisters: Janae, Tiana, Asha,   1880   Today
Kyah, Daisha, Tyra
Brothers: Donte, Tyrell, Kevon, Jaquan,
Deshawn, Jamar
★ You can't just mention this name casually. It's a blast of energy that demands to be the focus of any sentence. A Scottish surname, Tyree was discovered by African-American parents when Tyrone was at its peak. Today Tyree sounds a bit more youthful than that old favorite.
In the World: Author Omar Tyree

Tyrone (tiy-ROHN)   1970: #132
Popularity: #809
Styles: Celtic, African-
American
Nicknames: Ty   1880   Today
Variants: Tyron
Sisters: Rochelle, Leslie, Yvette, Tanya, Janelle,
Gwendolyn, Regina, Monique
Brothers: Cedric, Terrance, Dwyane, Shannon,
Kelvin, Desmond, Reginald, Darnell
★ Tyrone, a county in Ireland, became a popular name thanks to actors Tyrone Power Sr. and Jr. It originally had a slick Celtic panache, which around 1960 evolved into a slick African-American panache. The name's enduring charisma has spawned a flock of similar Ty names.
In the World: Actors Tyrone Power Sr. and Jr.; football coach Tyrone Willingham

Tyson (TIY-sən)   2010: #237
Popularity: #251
Styles: The "-ens," Last
Names First
Nicknames: Ty   1880   Today
Sisters: Tatum, Alaina,
Summer, Sasha, Mckenna, Alexa
Brothers: Weston, Trent, Braxton, Peyton,
Travis, Jameson
★ This name is a perfect strike at the heart of recent trends. It gives you a crisp surname with the rhythm of Mason and the hot nickname Ty. Tyson is a name that will sit equally naturally on a cowboy, a fashion model, and a corporate raider.
In the World: Basketball player Tyson Chandler; model Tyson Beckford; boxer Mike Tyson; singer Tyson Ritter

Ulysses (yoo-LI-seez)   1895: #269
Popularity: #1053
Styles: Exotic Traditional,
Mythological, Classical,
Nickname-Proof   1880   Today
Variants: Ulises, Odysseus
Sisters: Octavia, Minerva, Ione, Evangeline,
Alethea, Avis, Philomena, Theodosia
Brothers: Horatio, Augustus, Cassius,
Ferdinand, Atticus, Napoleon, Leopold,
Seneca
★ I can already hear the grandparents howling in dismay. "Ulysses? You're naming *my* grandson Ulysses?!!" It's a bold stroke, all right, and even softened by an easy nickname. But if you're looking for classical panache, you've absolutely found it.
In the World: The ancient Greek hero Ulysses; President Ulysses S. Grant; James Joyce novel *Ulysses*

Uriah (yoo-RIY-ə) 2010: #548
Popularity: #584
Styles: Biblical
Nicknames: Uri
Variants: Urijah 1880 Today
Sisters: Shiloh, Mara, Aliya, Delilah, Shekinah, Atara, Selah, Keziah
Brothers: Ezekiel, Joah, Zachariah, Jericho, Abel, Gideon, Malachi, Judah
✱ It's open season on biblical boys' names, and Uriah is finding takers for the first time in living memory. The Old Testament style runs strong in this one, but the opening sound does turn some people off. Urijah, an alternate transliteration, has also taken off, thanks to MMA fighter Urijah Faber.
In the World: Dickens's "yes man" Uriah Heep in *David Copperfield*, after whom rock band Uriah Heep was named; MMA fighter Urijah Faber

Valentino (va-lehn-TEE-noh) 2011: #762
Popularity: #761
Styles: Namesakes, Fanciful, Italian, Saints
Nicknames: Tino, Val 1880 Today
Variants: Valentin, Valentine
Sisters: Viviana, Donatella, Serafina, Guinevere, Francesca, Juliet, Ariadne, Angelina
Brothers: Giancarlo, Carmelo, Alessandro, Romeo, Leonardo, Giovanni, Michelangelo, Orlando
✱ Like Romeo, this name used to be a little too hot for parents to handle. Today, though, the lover boys are a little more approachable. Valentino is actually an old saintly Italian name, as well as a fashion line and a silent-film seducer. Yet it's the seductive image that sticks.
In the World: Actor Rudolph Valentino; Valentino apparel

Van (VAN) 1891: #233
Popularity: #787
Styles: Timeless, Brisk and Breezy, Nicknames
Sisters: Dale, Lana, Vivian, 1880 Today
Lynn, Gail, Aurea, Laurel, Kaye
Brothers: Lon, Guy, Clark, Gil, Ward, Glyn, Rex, Royce
✱ Parents who are drawn to hot new names like Jair and Cael might want to take a look back at this oldie but goodie. It's been used as a full name for generations, but can also be short for any name with the letters "van," such as Ivan, Silvan, or Donovan. In some combinations, it can be mistaken for part of a surname like Van Halen or van Gogh.
In the World: Popular musician Van Morrison; pianist Van Cliburn

Vance (VANS) 1969: #328
Popularity: #752
Styles: Brisk and Breezy, Timeless, Last Names First, Why Not? 1880 Today
Sisters: Lana, Daphne, Virginia, Rosalie, Corinne, Audra
Brothers: Rex, Vaughn, Dexter, Royce, Laird, Pierce
✱ An uncommon name with generations of tradition behind it. Originally a surname, Vance is as brash as newcomers like Bryce and Chance but less faddish. It sounds tough enough for a rodeo, and posh enough for a dinner jacket and martini.
In the World: Musician Vance Gilbert

Varian (VAY-ree-in) 1977: #1447
Popularity: #12,095
Styles: Last Names First, Fantastical, Exotic, Traditional, Why Not? 1880 Today
Sisters: Charis, Averil, Livia, Paloma, Linden, Cortana, Aeris, Adair
Brothers: Perrin, Aldric, Theron, Severin, Regis, Auron, Vitas, Silvan
✱ It's easy enough to identify Varian's sound: elegant, exotic, and a wee bit dangerous. But good luck pinning down its place in the world. Varian is an Irish surname, a "World of Warcraft" king, and the refined, Latinate name of Varian Fry, a privileged young American who risked his life to save hundreds of artists and intellectuals from the Nazis.
In the World: Rescuer Varian Fry; King Varian Wrynn of "World of Warcraft"

Vaughn (VAWN) 1949: #347
Popularity: #903
Styles: Timeless, Celtic, Brisk
and Breezy, Last Names First,
Why Not? 1880 Today
Variants: Vaughan, Von
Sisters: Iona, Elinor, Emlyn, Wynne, Deirdre,
Bronwyn, Maeve, Elise
Brothers: Bayard, Vance, Griffith, Burgess,
Carlise, Hollis, Royce, Graeme
✷This Welsh surname is an elegant choice,
just uncommon enough for an element of sur-
prise. It's smooth and mellow in a gentlemanly
style.
In the World: Composer Ralph Vaughan Wil-
liams

Vernon (VER-nən) 1919: #65
Popularity: #1422
Styles: Solid Citizens,
African-American, Last
Names First 1880 Today
Nicknames: Vern, Verne
Sisters: Maxine, Rosalyn, Corrine, Marion,
Francine, Jeanette
Brothers: Gordon, Bernard, Marvin, Willis,
Jerome, Clifton
✷This fine old surname has slowly slipped into
the ranks of the fusty. Its full version is still ele-
gant, but nickname Vern emphasizes the same
soft sounds that sent names like Merle and
Ernie out of fashion.
In the World: Football player Vernon Davis;
lawyer Vernon Jordan; Harry Potter's Uncle Ver-
non

Victor (VIK-ter) 1918: #63
Popularity: #142
Styles: Timeless, Latino/
Latina, Saints
Nicknames: Vic 1880 Today
Variants: Viktor, Vitor,
Vittorio
Sisters: Marina, Veronica, Claire, Simone,
Natalia, Hope, Celeste, Lucia
Brothers: Ivan, Vincent, Julian, Carlos, Roman,
Nicholas, Anthony, Raphael
✷Truly timeless, never trendy, Victor is the
perfect gentleman. The name deserves more at-
tention for its winning combination of worldly
sophistication and a good old-fashioned nick-
name. Harry Potter's Viktor Krum showed off its
brawny side too. Like Hector, Victor is currently
most popular with Latino parents.
In the World: Viktor Krum of the "Harry Potter"
series; writer Victor Hugo; soap opera hero Victor Newman

Vincent (VIN-sənt) 1963: #61
Popularity: #101
Styles: Timeless, French
Nicknames: Vince, Vinnie,
Vin, Chente 1880 Today
Variants: Vincente, Vicente,
Vincenzo
Sisters: Camille, Diane, Valerie, Christina,
Veronica, Juliet, Daphne, Jaqueline
Brothers: Anthony, Noel, Victor, Julian, Grant,
Dominic, Tristan, Philip
✷Vincent is one of the classic gentlemanly
names, with a devilish elegance that sets it
apart. (Vincent Price was a sterling example.)
Vince and Vinnie are familiar nicknames, but
action star Vin Diesel helps make Vin the most
contemporary choice.
In the World: Painter Vincent van Gogh; horror
film star Vincent Price

Wade (WAYD) 1966: #183
Popularity: #549
Styles: Timeless, Brisk and
Breezy
Sisters: Dale, Angela, Gwen, 1880 Today
Iris, Glenna, Joy
Brothers: Clay, Byron, Ross, Vance, Curtis,
Lane
✷The bad news is that Wade is not in fashion.
The good news is that it has *never* been in fash-
ion. This is a name that doesn't follow trends
but just takes its own quiet path. It's an under-
stated alternative to Cade, Trace, and Gage.
In the World: Baseball player Wade Boggs; foot-
ball coach Wade Phillips

Walden (WAHL-dən) 1908: #1373
Popularity: #5143
Styles: Last Names First,
Place Names, Literary and
Artistic 1880 Today
Nicknames: Wally
Sisters: Linden, Mercy, Auden, Avonlea,
Juniper, Blythe
Brothers: Winslow, Frost, Sawyer, Whitman,
Silvan, Birch
✷Line up, nature and literature lovers: here's a
creative choice that makes a statement, gently.
The nod to Henry David Thoreau's transcen-
dentalist idyll is clear, but Walden sounds so
natural as a boy's name that it's not too big a
stretch.
In the World: Henry David Thoreau's book
Walden; Waldenbooks bookstore chain

Walker (WAH-ker) — 2005: #368
Popularity: #417
Styles: Last Names First, Nickname-Proof, Antique Charm, Country and Western, Why Not?

1880 Today

Sisters: Ivy, Carolina, Ellery, Piper, Julianna, Scarlett
Brothers: Turner, Deacon, Porter, Lawson, Gibson, Archer

✱ Walker offers the surname flair of popular choices like Parker and Tanner without the bandwagon trendiness. Its secret is its long history as an American first name, with forebears like photographer Walker Evans lending depth. And in a name style that tends toward androgyny, Walker is still reliably masculine.
In the World: Photographer Walker Evans; President George Herbert Walker Bush; TV series *Walker, Texas Ranger*

Wallace (WAH-lis) — 1923: #69
Popularity: #1758
Styles: Ladies and Gentlemen
Nicknames: Wally
Sisters: Louise, Frances, Estelle, Muriel, Harriet, Sybil
Brothers: Chester, Claude, Theodore, Holland, Warren, Gilbert

✱ Wallace is a converted surname, first used centuries ago in honor of Scottish hero William Wallace (think *Braveheart*). That warrior association is now, quite literally, history. The name comes across today as a kindly gentleman in an age of rascals. The kindly gentleman many will think of today is an animated one, from the *Wallace and Gromit* films.
In the World: *Wallace and Gromit*; poet Wallace Stevens; actor/playwright Wallace Shawn

Walter (WAL-ter) — 1892: #13
Popularity: #375
Styles: Ladies and Gentlemen
Nicknames: Walt, Wally
Sisters: Martha, Frances, Alice, Esther, Edith, Helen
Brothers: Albert, Frank, Edward, Harold, George, Arthur

✱ On the one hand, Walter is clearly out of style. You expect a Walter to be enjoying his well-earned retirement. On the other hand, if you met a boy named Walt you would think that was pretty darned cool. If you want a Walt but aren't ready to revive Walter, consider Walton.
In the World: Walt Disney Entertainment; Sir Walter Raleigh; newscaster Walter Cronkite; poet Walt Whitman

Walton (WAHL-tən) — 1915: #497
Popularity: #6198
Styles: Last Names First, Why Not?
Nicknames: Walt, Wally
Sisters: Marion, Faye, Rhoda, Autry, Margery, Glenna
Brothers: Tillman, Warren, DeWitt, Barton, Warner, Hilton

✱ Reconfigure Walter to get this attractive surname. It has a trendier sound, but gives you the same friendly nickname Walt.
In the World: *The Waltons* TV series; Walmart founder Sam Walton; actor Walton Goggins

Warren (WAWR-in, WAHR-in) — 1921: #24
Popularity: #501
Styles: Solid Citizens, Nickname-Proof
Sisters: Helene, Gloria, Frances, Eileen, June, Roberta
Brothers: Raymond, Lawrence, Allen, Donald, Vernon, Carl

✱ Warren skyrocketed when Warren G. Harding was elected president in 1920. That's not the brightest star to hitch your wagon to, but Warren had the broad-based appeal to hang on and become an American classic. Today the name is slowly fading into grandpa status but is still a solid, conservative choice.
In the World: Investor Warren Buffet; President Warren Harding; actor Warren Beatty; football player Warren Sapp

Wayne (WAYN) — 1947: #30
Popularity: #704
Styles: Mid-Century, Country and Western
Sisters: Charlene, Wanda, Marsha, Suzanne, Glenda, Marlene, Janette, Sheila
Brothers: Bruce, Roger, Dwight, Larry, Harlan, Glenn, Darryl, Woody

✱ Simple and swift, Wayne is a breezy grandpa name. Its glory days were from the '30s to the '50s, when Western star John Wayne was riding tall. The name is slowing down today, but as a cowboy homage it can still work.
In the World: Film *Wayne's World*; hockey star Wayne Gretzky; rapper Lil Wayne; singer Wayne Newton

Wesley (WEHS-lee, WEHZ-lee)
Popularity: #156
Styles: Timeless, Last Names First
Nicknames: Wes
Variants: Westley
Sisters: Lacey, Christina, Lauren, Joanna, Whitney, Lindsay, Natalie, Elisa
Brothers: Clayton, Davis, Barrett, Bradley, Quincy, Austin, Dexter, Preston

1977: #66

1880   Today

★ Wesley was originally given to honor Methodist Church founder John Wesley, but it's now well established as a secular name with a preppy style. Action movie star Wesley Snipes lent the name a little toughness, and nickname Wes helps tone down the preppiness. The *Princess Bride* hero was the close variant Westley.
In the World: Actor Wesley Snipes; football star Wes Welker; director Wes Anderson

Weston (WEHS-tən)
Popularity: #203
Styles: Last Names First, The "-ens"
Nicknames: West, Wes
Sisters: Tatum, Phoebe, Hailey, Savannah, Macy, Annabel, Sidney, Chelsea
Brothers: Jameson, Drake, Tucker, Grayson, Paxton, Branson, Tate, Dalton

2011: #204

1880   Today

★ As a full name, Weston is like a dream of aristocracy. Unlike the similar choice Austin, Weston's air of privilege isn't tempered by a Texas twang. But the nickname West evens out the balance for the cowboy side: one foot in the stirrup, one on the fast track.
In the World: Photographer Edward Weston; numerous towns in the U.S. and U.K.

Wilbur (WIL-ber)
Popularity: #4779
Styles: Porch Sitters
Nicknames: Willie
Variants: Wilber
Sisters: Eunice, Velma, Hilda, Bernice, Florine, Gladys
Brothers: Elwood, Virgil, Lester, Orville, Hubert, Elmo

1913: #91

1880   Today

★ Wilbur Wright, co-inventor of the airplane, is a pretty dashing model for a name. Unfortunately, the combination of the pig in *Charlotte's Web* and the image of Mr. Ed neighing "Willllburrr" makes this name anything but dashing.
In the World: Aviator Wilbur Wright; Wilbur of *Charlotte's Web*; writer Wilbur Smith

William (WIL-yəm)
Popularity: #3
Styles: Timeless
Nicknames: Bill, Billy, Will, Willy, Liam, Wills, Wim
Variants: Willem, Wilhelm, Liam, Guillaume, Guillermo
Sisters: Anna, Elizabeth, Sarah, Emily, Caroline, Margaret, Julia, Katherine
Brothers: James, Thomas, Edward, Charles, Stephen, Henry, Andrew, Robert

1880: #2

1880   Today

★ Dominant a century ago, William has remained a robust, adaptable classic. It's distinguished but not a bit stuffy. The nickname Bill was among the essential 20th-century names, the smoother Will is the contemporary favorite, and Liam gives the name a popular Celtic spin.
In the World: Centuries of prominent Williams, leading with Shakespeare

Willis (WI-lis)
Popularity: #1924
Styles: Ladies and Gentlemen, Solid Citizens, Last Names First, African-American
Nicknames: Will
Sisters: Adela, Frances, Harriet, Cecile, Rhea, Louisa
Brothers: Clifton, Harris, Foster, Vernon, Nelson, Gilbert

1880: #86

1880   Today

★ Like Wallace, Willis can come across as a well-mannered fellow who's a generation behind the times. But unlike Wallace, Willis has a fashionable nickname (Will versus Wally) that helps bring it up to date. Other strong choices in this vein include Ellis and Harris.
In the World: Football player Willis McGahee; musician Willis Earl Beal; Willis of sitcom *Diff'rent Strokes*

Wilson (WIL-sən) — 1918: #122
Popularity: #603
Styles: Last Names First, Timeless, Why Not?
Nicknames: Will, Wills — 1880 Today
Sisters: Kathryn, Celia, Rose, Marian, Anna, Caroline, Evelyn, Audrey
Brothers: Marshall, Anderson, Truman, Forrest, Porter, Watson, Edison, Harris
✶ Wilson has been a slow but steady American classic. (Its only spike came during Woodrow Wilson's tenure in the White House.) Despite generations of use, it still sounds primarily like a last name.
In the World: R&B singer Wilson Pickett; pop band Wilson Phillips was named for the (female) members' surnames

Winslow (WINZ-loh) — 1907: #999
Popularity: #7981
Styles: Last Names First, Literary and Artistic, Why Not? — 1880 Today
Nicknames: Win
Sisters: Hollis, Verity, Philippa, Everly, Marlowe, Afton
Brothers: Burgess, Truman, Shepard, Woodrow, Prentiss, Carlyle
✶ Winslow is a change of pace from the typical surname. It's quirky, contemplative, and distinctly American. The name takes its cues from the 19th-century American life depicted by painter Winslow Homer.
In the World: Painter Winslow Homer

Winston (WIN-stən) — 1941: #234
Popularity: #742
Styles: Last Names First
Nicknames: Win, Winnie
Sisters: Augusta, Flora, — 1880 Today
Virginia, Rosalie, Margery, Delta
Brothers: Stanton, Truman, Talmadge, Linwood, Hilton, Barclay
✶ The top associations for this name are a British prime minister, a pack of cigarettes, and stock-car racing. The result is a name with a split personality—part prep school boy and part good ol' boy.
In the World: Prime Minister Winston Churchill; Winston cigarettes, the former Winston Cup racing sponsor

Wolf (WUWLF) — 2009: #3707
Popularity: #4070
Styles: Exotic Traditional, German and Dutch, Macho Swagger — 1880 Today
Variants: Wolfe, Vulf, Velvel
Sisters: India, Astrid, Luna, Wren, Paloma, Lisbeth, Esme, Elke
Brothers: Bram, Magnus, Gunnar, Axel, Hawk, Archer, Ivan, Leif
✶ Charisma is not the problem here: this name is loaded with animal magnetism. It's traditional too, and distinguished, in a ferocious sort of way. You just have to decide if you want your son's name to stick out so prominently from the pack.
In the World: TV reporter Wolf Blitzer; the many associations of wolves, from "Big Bad Wolf" to "wolf whistles"

Wyatt (WIY-it) — 2011: #48
Popularity: #48
Styles: Country and Western, Nickname-Proof, Last Names First — 1880 Today
Sisters: Scarlett, Avery, Faith, Piper, Hannah, Oakley, Ivy, Willow
Brothers: Carson, Sawyer, Beckett, Jackson, Levi, Lincoln, Deacon, Cooper
✶ Meet the crossover cowboy. Wyatt's Western bona fides date back to the O.K. Corral, and the name is a big hit in spots like Cheyenne and Oklahoma City. Yet it also strikes a chord with upscale coastal parents who talk about Wyatt in the same breath as Henry and Oliver. That's the kind of crossover appeal politicians dream about.
In the World: Old West lawman Wyatt Earp

Wynn (WIN) — 2011: #2332
Popularity: #2360
Styles: Celtic, Brisk and Breezy, Why Not?
Variants: Wyn, Wynne, — 1880 Today
Gwyn
Sisters: Emlyn, Bryn, Romy, Greer, Carys, Bay, Mabyn, Shea
Brothers: Rhys, Laird, Bevan, Cai, Ellis, Yale, Vaughn, Pryce
✶ This Welsh favorite is a fresh choice in America, yet it sounds pleasantly old-fashioned. That probably reflects the past generations of American Wins, short for Winfield, Winfred, and Winston. The Welsh name comes from *gwyn* ("fair, white"), the familiar root of names like Gwendolyn and Guinevere.
In the World: Wynn resort casinos

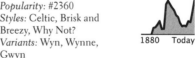

Name Snapshots: Boys 357

Xander (ZAN-der)   2011: #206
Popularity: #205
Styles: Nicknames,
Fantastical
Variants: Zander   1880   Today
Sisters: Lexi, Piper, Kenzie,
Willow, Zoe, Harlow
Brothers: Jaxon, Nico, Kobe, Maddox, Sawyer,
Paxton
★ Start with the surging popularity of the name Alexander. Add a national love affair with the letter "x." Then throw in a character from *Buffy the Vampire Slayer.* The result is a charismatic name sensation. This name charms people, though many will feel it's best as a nickname for the full Alexander.
In the World: Xander Harris of *Buffy the Vampire Slayer;* actor Xander Berkeley

Xavier (ZAY-vyer,   2007: #68
ehk-SAY-vyer)
Popularity: #77
Styles: Latino/Latina,
French, African-American,   1880   Today
Saints
Nicknames: Xavy
Variants: Javier, Xaver, Zavier
Sisters: Ivy, Paloma, Zara, Phoebe, Serena,
Giselle
Brothers: Sebastian, Felix, Elias, Gabriel,
Quentin, Maximilian
★ You love the eye-catching panache of this "x" name. But you're stunned to discover it's a fast-rising hit name! It's even spawning spin-offs, like Alexavier and Xzavier. Yes, Xavier is not as distinctive as it once was, but it's still plenty cooler than the pack. The traditional English pronunciation starts with a "z" sound, the *X-Men* version with an "ex."
In the World: *X-Men* leader Charles Xavier; bandleader Xavier Cugat; actor Xavier Samuel

Zachariah (za-kə-RIY-ə)   1992: #305
Popularity: #465
Styles: Biblical, Exotic
Traditional
Nicknames: Zach, Zack, Zak   1880   Today
Variants: Zechariah,
Zacharias, Zachary
Sisters: Damaris, Keziah, Annabella, Mariah,
Evangeline, Delilah
Brothers: Ezekiel, Jedidiah, Raphael, Phineas,
Zebediah, Matthias
★ This form of Zachary leaves no doubts about the name's biblical roots. Zachariah has the same relationship to Zachary that Jeremiah does to Jeremy: it sounds more antique, and a whisker trendier.

Zachary (ZA-kə-ree)   1993: #15
Popularity: #64
Styles: Biblical, Turn of the
21st Century
Nicknames: Zach, Zack, Zak   1880   Today
Variants: Zachery, Zackary,
Zakary, Zachariah
Sisters: Abigail, Hannah, Bethany, Samantha,
Zoe, Alexandra
Brothers: Nicholas, Joshua, Ethan, Zane,
Jeremy, Nathaniel
★ It's almost hard to believe that in the first half of the 20th century no one was being named Zachary. Zack made an astonishingly quick leap from relic to classic in the United States, becoming the embodiment of biblical cool. Don't let that sharp downward graph upset you unduly. Zachary's deep history and zippy "Z" should keep it from sounding like a trend gone by.
In the World: President Zachary Taylor; actors Zac Efron and Zachary Quinto; musician Zac Hanson

Zane (ZAYN) 2011: #221
Popularity: #220
Styles: Country and Western,
Brisk and Breezy
Variants: Zayne, Zain 1880 Today
Sisters: Sage, Zoe, Quinn,
Savannah, Oakley, Reese
Brothers: Chance, Tucker, Cooper, Bryce,
Devin, Wyatt
★ Wandering the plains in search of a "z," parents have crossed paths with this charming cowboy. It's only surprising that it didn't happen sooner. Zane's Western bona fides come from Zane Grey, the writer whose adventure novels helped create the mythos of the Old West. *In the World:* Writer Zane Grey; comedian/TV host Zane Lamprey

Zayden (Zay-den) 2011: #293
Popularity: #292
Styles: Bell Tones, The "-ens"
Nicknames: Zay
Variants: Zaiden, Xaiden 1880 Today
Sisters: Londyn, Paisley, Kyra,
Lainey, Kenzie, Ily, Cadence, Zoey
Brothers: Jaxon, Zane, Kyler, Keegan, Quinn,
Kolby, Rylan, Zavion
★ This name is the ultimate in Aiden rhymes—literally. Aaden marks the start of that rhyming alphabet, and Zayden the end. It's a name that follows the pack, but with a defiantly individualistic style. Some parents looking for even more eye-catching distinction are using an "X" spelling.

Zeb (ZEHB) 1888: #484
Popularity: #3405
Styles: Biblical, Nicknames
Variants: Zebedee, Zebediah,
Zebulon 1880 Today
Sisters: Selah, Liv, Zella,
Lark, Avis, Atara, Bay, Adah
Brothers: Ike, Rafe, Ezra, Mose, Jabez, Asa,
Dex, Zeke
★ Trim yet audacious, Zeb takes a step past Zach and Zeke into the land of the truly unusual. If you want to take a step even further, use the full name Zebedee.

Zion (ZIY-ahn, ZIY-ən) 2010: #230
Popularity: #245
Styles: Modern Meanings,
Place Names
Sisters: Eden, Selah, Zoey, 1880 Today
Jubilee, Phoenix, Shiloh
Brothers: Malachi, Kingston, Jericho, Zane,
Justice, Asher
★ Zion is a biblical term for the promised land. For Rastafarians, it means a utopia or heaven on earth, and it is also widely associated with the drive for a Jewish homeland and with the ideals of the Mormon Church. Zion wasn't often considered as a name until musicians Lauryn Hill and Rohan Marley (son of Rasta legend Bob Marley) chose it for their son. Scores of parents are now following their example. *In the World:* Varied religious connotations; Zion National Park; musical duos Zion I and Zion & Lennox

Name Styles

*

African

This is an ethnically and linguistically diverse category of names, reflecting the cultures of an entire continent. The origins of specific African names can be challeng- ing to track, with multiple meanings or spellings in different communities. Even the boy/girl division below isn't set in stone, as many of the names are used androgynously in both Africa and America. What you *can* count on is that the names below have genuine African origins as first names and are attractive and easy to pronounce in English. (One pronunciation note: the names beginning with "Th-" are typically pronounced with a hard "t" sound and could be spelled that way for clarity.) Some names are popular short forms of longer names, such as Emeka for Nnaemeka or Chukwuemeka.

If you're interested in English names with an African connection, consider that Old Testament names such as Elisha and Moses and virtue names such as Charity, Gracious, and Rejoice are popular among Christian Africans. For names of Islamic origin that are common in Africa, see the Muslim name section.

GIRLS

Aaliyah	Ayanda	Malaika	Subira
Ajani	Ayanna	Masika	Tanisha
Akilah	Diara	Nakia	Thandeka
Akua	Dineo	Neema	Thandi
Amaka	Imani	Nia	Zuri
Amani	Jinaki	Rehema	
Amari	Kamaria	Safiya	
Aminata	Kenyatta	Shani	
Ashanti	Maisha	Sindi	

BOYS

Abasi	Barack	Jali	Kwame	Shola
Achebe	Baraka	Jelani	Lekan	Sipho
Ade	Bayo	Juma	Mamdou	Tayo
Amachi	Chike	Kabelo	Manzi	Thabo
Amadi	Chima	Kani	Neo	Thulani
Asani	Dakarai	Kenyatta	Nnamdi	Tinashe
Asante	Dumisani	Kijana	Odion	Xolani
Ayo	Emeka	Kimani	Omari	Zuberi
Azuka	Femi	Kofi	Sabelo	
Bakari	Jabari	Kojo	Sekou	

African-American

Pop quiz: which is the African-American name?
A. Devonte
B. Imani
C. Antoine
D. Michael

1880   Today

The answer, of course, would have to be "E: All of the above." Devonte is a modern, uniquely African-American creation. Imani is a Swahili name that many American parents have chosen to reflect their African heritage. Antoine is distinctly French, but an African-American favorite as well. And Michael? That cross-cultural classic has no particular ethnic association at all—but it's the #1 name for African-Americans over the past 50 years.

African-American names are an integral part of America's name tapestry, with styles and traditions that weave in and out of the broader trends around them. Common themes include:

African and Muslim names: A natural choice to honor a child's African ancestry. Favorites include Aaliyah, Malik, Imani, and African place names such as Kenya.

French and Italian names: Names from Romance languages have flourished, often with creative spellings. Top choices: Andre, Monique, Dante/Donte.

Hero names: Names from African-American history are popular choices to encourage children to take pride in their heritage. Booker (T. Washington) and Marcus (Garvey) were common in earlier generations, and Malcolm (X) and Zora (Neale Hurston) are more recent selections.

Combination names: Blending two names to create one has been an African-American tradition. Basketball player Brevin Knight's name, for instance, was taken from his parents Brenda and Melvin. Other prominent examples include Joycelyn (Elders) and Steveland (Morris, better known as Stevie Wonder).

Biblical names: Especially popular for boys. Lyrical favorites include Elijah and Emmanuel.

Meaning names: Uplifting words are chosen to inspire (Justice, Journey) or to sparkle (Diamond, Miracle).

Created names: New inventions abound, often echoing the rhythms of popular African or European names. Name elements tend to sweep in and out of style, creating trademark generational sounds. (Remember all the "La-" names of the '70s?) Recent choices include Janiya, Kamari, and Jamarion.

Such creative, distinctly African-American names have been staples since the rise of the Black Power movement in the late '60s. The names are popular, but they're also controversial. On the positive side, many parents consider inventions like Shanika and Jojuan a joyful form of creative expression. Fans of these names describe them as part of the African-American improvisational tradition, in line with jazz and hip-hop. A created name can also be a special gift from parent to child, a loving statement about the child's uniqueness.

However, others in the African-American community have criticized invented names as rootless and even frivolous. Beyond the issue of style, many worry that such complex and unusual names will be a barrier to success for children who already face obstacles based on the color of their skin. Some studies have suggested that distinctly black names, especially unusual ones, can affect everything from a child's chance of being promoted in school to a job-seeker's chance of getting an interview.

This kind of name-based prejudice is hardly new. Throughout history, names have been scrutinized as markers of race, class, religion, and social standing. Back in the Middle Ages, the name Joan became so popular that it was considered coarse and "common," and well-to-do families turned to Jane instead. In America a century ago, Irish classics like Bridget were shunned as servant names, while Jewish immigrants gave their sons fancy British surnames like Seymour and Milton, hoping they'd be accepted by the Anglo upper classes.

Snap judgments based on names continue today. What's changed is that we're also taking pride in our diverse identities. Parents want their children to find success and acceptance, but they don't want to bury their heritage to achieve it. The latest generation of African-American names includes many that hit both targets. You'll find names with African and Muslim origins that have become cross-cultural power names, such as Nia and Jasmine. And Americans as a whole are naming more creatively. Black parents have been the trendsetters for some of America's hottest name styles, including biblical rediscoveries like Isaiah and affirmation names like Destiny.

The names below have all found favor among African-American parents in the past 40 years. For more ideas in particular style areas, refer to the sections on Muslim names, African names, meaning names, and biblical names.

GIRLS

Aaliyah	Charisse	Jalisa	Lashonda	Sanaa
Adrienne	Charlene	Jaliyah	Latasha	Sanai
Aisha	Ciara	Jamila	Latonya	Saniya
Aiyana	Corrine	Jamya	Latoya	Selah
Aja	Daija	Janae	Laverne	Shalonda
Akeelah	Damita	Janelle	Leticia	Shameka
Alaya	Deasia	Janiya	Lyric	Shani
Alisha	Deja	Jasmine	Makiyah	Shanice
Amani	Demetria	Jayla	Malaika	Shaniya
Amari	Desiree	Justice	Marguerite	Shante
Amiyah	Diamond	Kaliyah	Miesha	Shantel
Anaiya	Dominique	Kamari	Milan	Sharonda
Angel	Ebony	Kamilah	Monique	Shayla
Anita	Ericka	Kayla	Naima	Shekinah
Aniyah	Essence	Keisha	Nakia	Shonda
Aretha	Felecia	Kendra	Natasha	Simone
Ariana	Gwendolyn	Kenya	Nia	Sojourner
Asha	Hadiyah	Khadijah	Nyla	Solange
Ashanti	Iesha	Kiana	Octavia	Taliyah
Asia	Imani	Kiara	Raven	Tamia
Ayanna	India	Kimora	Regina	Tamika
Beyoncé	Iyana	Ladonna	Rihanna	Tanisha
Brandi	Jacquelyn	Lakeisha	Rochelle	Taniya
Brianna	Jada	Laniyah	Rolanda	Taraji
Chantal	Jakayla	Larissa	Sade	Tasha

Tatyana	Trina	Wanda	Zaniyah	Zora
Tawana	Tyra	Yolanda	Zaria	Zuri
Tiana	Vanessa	Yvette	Zina	
Tonya	Venetia	Yvonne	Zion	

BOYS

Adonis	Desmond	Jarvis	Malik	Taj
Ahmad	Devin	Javion	Marcus	Tariq
Akeem	Devon	Javon	Markell	Tavion
Alonzo	Devonte	Jayden	Marlon	Terrance
Amari	Diamond	Jeremiah	Marquis	Terrell
Andre	Dion	Jermaine	Martin	Torrance
Antoine	Dominique	Jerome	Marvin	Trae
Antwan	Donnell	Jordan	Maurice	Tremaine
Asante	Dwayne	Jovan	Mekhi	Trevon
Cairo	Earl	Julius	Melvin	Ty
Cedric	Elijah	Kadeem	Omar	Tyree
Clarence	Elisha	Kamari	Omari	Tyrell
Cortez	Ervin	Kareem	Omarion	Tyrese
Courtney	Freeman	Keenan	Otis	Tyrone
Dakari	Hakeem	Kelvin	Prince	Tyshawn
Damarion	Hezekiah	Kendrick	Quincy	Vernon
D'Angelo	Irvin	Kenyatta	Quinton	Willie
Dante	Isaiah	Keyon	Raheem	Willis
Darian	Jabari	Keyshawn	Rashad	Xavier
Darius	Jaheim	Khalid	Rasheed	Zaire
Darnell	Jahir	Kobe	Reggie	
Darryl	Jakari	Kwame	Reginald	
Davion	Jakobe	Kymani	Roderick	
Davon	Jaleel	Kyree	Rodney	
DeAndre	Jalen	Lamar	Rohan	
Dedrick	Jamal	Latrell	Romare	
Dejuan	Jamar	Leon	Santana	
Demarcus	Jamari	Leroy	Sargent	
Demario	Jamarion	Lionel	Savion	
Demetrius	Jamir	Luther	Semaj	
Denzel	Jaquan	Mahlon	Shamar	
Deonte	Jaquez	Makai	Sharif	
Derrick	Jaron	Malachi	Sincere	
Deshawn	Jarrett	Malcolm	Stephon	

Androgynous

Parents seek out androgynous names—names used for both sexes—for practical, philosophical, and aesthetic reasons. On the practical end, there are expectant parents who choose just one name and plan to use it regard- less of the sex of the baby. Others like the practical idea of a name that, on a document like a résumé, will raise no preconceptions about their child's sex. As a philosophical matter, choosing an androgynous name can be a statement of your belief in gender equality. And as a matter of fashion, parents are attracted by the contemporary flair of these names.

The idea of a one-size-fits-all name, though, has come around before. Back in the '20s and '30s, a little Frankie, Tommie, or Bennie was as likely to be a girl as a boy. For their parents, there was no philosophical debate required—boyish names just sounded modern and fun.

But notice that, even back then, wanting an androgynous name meant wanting a *boyish* name. Androgyny may sound like a move toward equality, but in reality it's usually a move toward the masculine. Historically, male names have been adapted or adopted for girls: Georgia and Josephine, Jamie and Shawn, Leslie and Courtney. The reverse is virtually unheard of. (Even Mario, which looks like a male counterpart of Maria, actually comes from the Latin Marius.)

The blunt truth is that a cross-gender association is perceived as "strong" for girls, but "weak" for boys. As soon as a name starts to tip to the female side, parents of boys abandon it.

For parents seeking equal opportunity for their daughters, choosing a masculine name may send a mixed message. It could point to a world without boundaries or stereotypes, but it could also reinforce the idea that strength has to mean masculinity. Think of the strongest women you've known . . . what were their names? Surely a Margaret or Diana sounds at least as formidable as an Emory or Peyton.

Below is a menu of androgynous name possibilities, new and old. When you choose one, regardless of practical or philosophical concerns, choose it because you love it. A name that stirs a parent's soul is a great start in life for any child, boy or girl.

Adair	Alden	Amani	Angel	Arley
Addison	Alex	Amari	Arden	Arlis
Akira	Alexis	Amory	Ariel	Armani

Ashby	Dana	Jaylin	Lupe	Rowan
Ashley	Darby	Jensen	Lyric	Ryan
Ashton	Devin	Jess	Mackenzie	Rylee
Aubrey	Diamond	Jessie	Madigan	Sage
Auden	Dominique	Jody	Madison	Sammie
Augustine	Drew	Joey	Marley	Sandy
Avery	Eden	Jordan	Meredith	Sawyer
Bailey	Elisha	Joss	Micah	Scout
Berkeley	Ellis	Justice	Mickey	Shannon
Billie	Embry	Kai	Monroe	Shawn
Blair	Emerson	Kamari	Montana	Shea
Blake	Emery	Kayden	Morgan	Skylar
Bobbie	Emlyn	Kelly	Nikita	Stacy
Briar	Emory	Kelsey	Noel	Sydney
Britt	Finley	Kendall	Oakley	Tatum
Brody	Gale	Kennedy	Paris	Taylor
Bryce	Gene	Kenyatta	Parker	Teagan
Cameron	Germaine	Kerry	Perry	Terry
Campbell	Gerry	Kim	Peyton	Tory
Camryn	Gray	Kirby	Phoenix	Tracy
Carrington	Greer	Kolby	Presley	Tristen
Carroll	Guadalupe	Kristian	Quincy	Tyler
Carson	Harley	Laine	Quinn	Val
Cary	Harper	Landry	Raleigh	Valentine
Casey	Haven	Larkin	Reagan	Whitney
Chandler	Hayden	Lee	Reese	Winslow
Channing	Hillary	Leighton	Remy	Winter
Charlie	Hiro	Lennon	Riley	Yael
Clancy	Hollis	Leslie	Ripley	Yancey
Courtney	Indigo	Linden	Robin	Zion
Dakota	Jaime	Logan	Rory	
Dale	Janson	London	Rowan	
Dallas	Jayden	Loren	Rosario	

Antique Charm

What do names like Sophie, Oliver, and Amelia have in common? They're old-fashioned. They're fashionable. And they're fashionable *because* they're old-fashioned.

1880   Today

Alongside the thousands of young Braydens and Brooklyns in America, you'll meet plenty of kids with names straight out of a 19th-century nursery. In part, that reflects a natural generational cycle. Our own generation's names sound ordinary to us; our parents' names sound boring; our grandparents' names sound old. But with our *great*-grandparents' names, things start to get interesting. We view them from enough distance that we can appreciate them anew.

Of course, our great-grandparents' generation of names was every bit as diverse as today's. The names we're reviving are a select group, loaded with sweet, lilting girl's names (Lily yes, Gertrude no) and elegant but lively choices for boys (Jasper yes, Elbert definitely not). The effect is like old tintype portraits in which the past comes to life dressed exclusively in its Sunday best.

Choosing an antique name is choosing to honor the best parts of the past. The sweet names are sweeter and the dignified names more dignified because they're steeped in generations of meaning. The first place to look is in your own family tree. Reviving a great- or great-great-ancestor's name personalizes the connection to the past. For more ideas (or if you happen to come from a long line of Elberts and Gertrudes), here is the *Wizard* list of antiques that are polished and ready for the 21st century.

GIRLS

Abigail	Catalina	Eva	Lila	Sadie
Adela	Cecily	Evangeline	Lillian	Sofia
Adelaide	Charity	Evelyn	Lillie	Sophia
Adeline	Charlotte	Genevieve	Lily	Sophie
Alice	Chloe	Georgia	Lucy	Stella
Amelia	Clara	Grace	Luna	Victoria
Angelina	Cora	Hannah	Lydia	Violet
Anna	Daisy	Hazel	Madeleine	Vivian
Annabella	Eleanor	Helena	Madeline	Willa
Annabelle	Eleanora	Isabel	Mariah	
Annalise	Elinor	Isabelle	Michaela	
Annie	Eliza	Isadora	Molly	
Arabella	Ella	Ivy	Nora	
Ava	Elsa	Josephine	Olivia	
Bella	Emilia	Julia	Patience	
Carolina	Emma	Katharina	Phoebe	
Caroline	Emmaline	Leila	Rhea	
Cassie	Esmeralda	Lena	Ruby	

Abraham	Emerson	Isaiah	Levi	Pierce
Adrian	Emmett	Jacob	Mathias	Porter
August	Everett	Jasper	Max	Preston
Caleb	Ezekiel	Jonah	Maxwell	Samuel
Cyrus	Ezra	Jonas	Miles	Saul
Dominic	Gabriel	Josiah	Milo	Silas
Edgar	Gideon	Judah	Noah	Solomon
Eli	Grady	Julian	Oliver	Theo
Elias	Henry	Julius	Oscar	Tobias
Elijah	Isaac	Leo	Owen	Walker

Spotlight: Golden Age Hollywood

Names like Ava and Olivia owe a lot of their romantic glow to the world's #1 glow producer: Hollywood. Actresses Ava Gardner and Olivia de Havilland connect the names, in our minds, to a glamorous age gone by. More names with that golden aura:

GIRLS

Audrey	Harlow	Lana	Theda
Greer	Hedy	Mae	Veronica
Greta	Ingrid	Monroe	Vivien

BOYS

Bing	Flynn	Kirk	Spencer
Brando	Gable	Montgomery	
Cary	Hudson	Randolph	

Bell Tones

Listen to parents calling out names at your local playground and it may sound like bells chiming. The sharp clang of a consonant launches clear, bright long vowels: "Bay-lee!" "Cay-den!" "Ja-cey!" It's the distinctive chorus of our time.

1880   Today

The Bell Tone names aim for freshness with a clean, light touch. They're 180 degrees removed from the Orvilles and Velmas of the Porch Sitter era. While a few traditional names like Bailey and Hayden fit the new fashion, many parents are striking out on their own to custom-build names for their children.

The handful of most resonant sounds have become like Lego® bricks: a few simple pieces configured into an endless variety of new forms. A dozen currently popular girls' names start with the letters "Jay-," and two dozen more end with the letters "-ee." The similarity of all the sounds is balanced by a tremendous diversity of spellings. You shouldn't be surprised to receive a birth announcement for a Jalen, Jalon, Jailyn, Jalynn, Jaylin, Jaylyn, Jaylon, or Jaelyn. And that child could be either a boy or a girl.

You'll find plenty of admirers for these names, regardless of spelling. But with such a small set of sounds being shaped and reshaped into so many names, they're starting to blur together. Jakayla sounds like a whole generation of kids rolled into one. For the Bell Tone names, though, the rule of thumb is: if it feels good, do it. Take the list of common versions below as a starting point.

GIRLS

Ailey	Brianna	Everleigh	Jalyn	Kaliyah
Ainsley	Brielle	Haley	Janae	Karlee
Ashlyn	Briley	Hayden	Jayda	Katlyn
Ayla	Brinley	Haylee	Jayden	Kaya
Aylin	Brylee	Ily	Jayla	Kayla
Bailey	Cadence	Jacey	Jaylee	Kaylee
Baylee	Caitlin	Jada	Jayleen	Kaylin
Braelyn	Camryn	Jaelyn	Kacie	Keely
Braylee	Corey	Jaidyn	Kaitlyn	Keelyn
Breanne	Daylin	Jakayla	Kaiya	Kelsey

Kenzie	Lacey	Mayra	Shayla	Tiana
Kiana	Laney	Miley	Shaylee	Traeh
Kierra	Macy	Paisley	Shayna	Tylee
Kiley	Maelie	Raelyn	Skyla	Tyra
Kiya	Makayla	Rayna	Tayla	
Kyla	Malia	Rylan	Taylin	
Kylie	Maylee	Rylee	Teagan	
Kyra	Maylin	Shaina	Tenley	

BOYS

Aidan	Cason	Jalen	Kian	Payton
Ayden	Coby	Javen	Kiefer	Raiden
Bailey	Colby	Jayden	Kieran	Rylan
Braden	Corey	Kadin	Kylan	Rylee
Brady	Grayden	Keaton	Kyler	Teagan
Brayden	Hayden	Keegan	Kyson	Zayden
Caden	Jaden	Keon	Layton	

Spotlight: Do-It-Yourself Contemporary Names

Today's parents have tremendous freedom to custom-build names. But not just *anything* goes in name innovation. To create a new name with a trendy sound, try mixing and matching the prefab building blocks below.

Beginning	Middle	End
Am	ber	a
Ana	bree	ah
Aub	d	alia
Aud	k	anna
Av	kay	ee
Ay	l	eigh
Bai	lee	ella
Bree	n	elle

Bry	r	en
Cay	ree	er
Co	s	ett
Col	t	iah
Da	x	iel
Day	z	iella
Hay		in
Ja		lee
Jay		lin
Jo		ly
Ka		on
Ka		ry
Kee		son
Kin		ter
King		ton
Ky		y
La		ya
Ma		yn
Shay		
Sky		
Ty		

Biblical

Biblical roots are so fundamental to our name culture that this may hardly seem like a style at all. The most popular baby name of this generation, Jacob, is straight out of the Bible, as were top names of generations past like John and Mary. But those names have very different histories, and that's where the tale of biblical style turns interesting.

1880   Today

The Bible has two main sections, known to Christians as the Old and New Testaments. (The Christian Old Testament corresponds to the

Jewish Hebrew Bible, or Tanakh.) A handful of New Testament names were dominant favorites in the English-speaking world for centuries. In England, the popularity of a few core names once reached epidemic proportions. During the 1700s, John and Mary alone accounted for one-quarter of all English babies. Those two names lead America's historical popularity list as well, and fellow New Testament names like James and Elizabeth followed close behind.

Now take a look at the top biblical names today: Jacob, Noah, Michael, Ethan, and Elijah. Michael appears in both testaments, while Jacob, Noah, Ethan, and Elijah trumpet their Old Testament origins. John and Mary, meanwhile, are well out of the top 20 and falling fast. Today, what's Old is new.

The rising popularity of Old Testament names has dramatically changed their image. Just a generation or two ago, brothers named Josh and Ethan sounded solidly Jewish—and brothers named Josiah and Ezra positively ancient. Today both pairs sound simply contemporary.

What's the secret to these names' broadened appeal? The Old Testament names are familiar and traditional but were mostly ignored in recent generations. Thus, they sound antique (Jonas) or unconventional (Ezekiel) rather than just plain old. Even among New Testament names, the hottest choices are those that were most neglected early in the 20th century. Matthew and Luke have overtaken John and Mark.

If you love biblical names, you can now feel free to dig deep into your concordance. Names that once sounded clunky or even shocking are finding a whole new life. With Ezekiel and Delilah soaring, almost anything goes.

OLD TESTAMENT GIRLS

Abigail	Delilah	Jerusha	Naomi	Shiloh
Adah	Dinah	Jezebel	Noemi	Susannah
Adina	Elisha	Judith	Rachel	Tamar
Amana	Elisheva	Keren	Rebecca	Tamara
Atara	Esther	Keturah	Rebekah	Tirzah
Avital	Eve	Keziah	Rochelle	Vashti
Bathsheba	Hadassah	Leah	Ruth	Yael
Bethel	Hannah	Mara	Sarah	Zilla
Beulah	Havilah	Mehitabel	Sarai	Zipporah
Carmel	Jael	Michal	Selah	
Deborah	Jemima	Miriam	Shifra	

OLD TESTAMENT BOYS

Aaron	Caleb	Hillel	Jonas	Omri
Abdiel	Cyrus	Hiram	Jonathan	Phineas
Abel	Daniel	Hosea	Joseph	Raphael
Abner	David	Ichabod	Joshua	Reuben
Abraham	Ebenezer	Isaac	Josiah	Ruel
Abram	Ehud	Isaiah	Jotham	Samson
Absalom	Elam	Ishmael	Jubal	Samuel
Adam	Eli	Israel	Judah	Saul
Adlai	Eliam	Jabez	Kenan	Seth
Ahab	Eliezer	Jacob	Laban	Simeon
Ahijah	Elijah	Jamin	Lemuel	Simon
Amasa	Elisha	Japheth	Levi	Solomon
Amon	Elon	Jared	Mahlon	Tobias
Amos	Enoch	Jedidiah	Malachi	Uriah
Ananias	Enos	Jemuel	Matan	Uriel
Aram	Ephraim	Jeremiah	Micah	Zachariah
Asa	Ephron	Jeremy	Michael	Zachary
Asher	Ethan	Jeriah	Mordecai	Zeb
Azarel	Ezekiel	Jericho	Moses	Zedekiah
Azriel	Ezra	Jesaiah	Naphtali	Zeke
Barak	Gabriel	Jesse	Nathan	Zuriel
Baruch	Gershon	Jethro	Nathaniel	
Benjamin	Gideon	Joah	Nehemiah	
Beriah	Gilead	Joel	Noah	
Boaz	Hezekiah	Jonah	Omar	

NEW TESTAMENT GIRLS

Anna	Damaris	Junia	Mary	Susana
Aquila	Dorcas	Lois	Phoebe	Tabitha
Berenice	Drusilla	Lydia	Prisca	Talitha
Bernice	Elizabeth	Magdalena	Priscilla	
Bethany	Eunice	Maria	Rhoda	
Candace	Hosanna	Marie	Salome	
Claudia	Joanna	Martha	Sapphira	

NEW TESTAMENT BOYS

Aeneas	Andrew	Barnabas	Cornelius	Erastus
Alpheus	Artemas	Barnaby	Crispus	Gabriel
Andreas	Balthazar	Bartholomew	Emmanuel	James

Name Styles 373

Jesús	Lucas	Nathanael	Silas	Timothy
Joachim	Lucius	Nathaniel	Silvanus	Titus
John	Luke	Nicodemus	Simon	Zachary
Joseph	Mark	Paul	Stephen	Zebedee
Jude	Matthew	Peter	Thaddeus	Zebediah
Justus	Matthias	Philemon	Theophilus	
Lazarus	Michael	Philip	Thomas	

Brisk and Breezy

Swift, light one-syllable names give off an aura of well-being. Some sound rich and preppy (Blair), while others are windswept cowboys (Shane), but all share a healthy glow to go with their brisk sound.

1880   Today

The prototypical Brisk and Breezy name, in fact, sounds like the word "brisk." Start with the burst of a hard consonant, then settle into a gentle landing. The effect is a name that's vigorous but doesn't overexert itself. You know the type: the straight-A student who never cracks a book, the quarterback who doesn't break a sweat as the game clock winds down. These cool customers make success look easy.

Some parents worry that these names seem a little *too* lightweight. They respond by tacking on extensions to create formal versions like Trey*ton* and Bryc*en*. If it's the Brisk and Breezy name you're really after, though, there's no need for elaborations. Even when they have nickname roots (like Trey), these names feel complete and ageless. Their blithe image has held steady for generations; think of Western stars Dale and Roy riding the range, or Cole Porter's effortless elegance.

Also consider these one-syllable wonders for middle names, where they can lighten up the whole package.

GIRLS

Bay	Brooke	Elle	Joy	Maeve
Belle	Bryce	Faye	June	Neve
Blair	Brynn	Gail	Kaye	Paige
Blake	Claire	Gray	Laine	Paz
Bly	Dale	Greer	Lark	Prue
Blythe	Dawn	Jade	Leigh	Quinn
Bree	Dove	Jill	Lise	Raine
Britt	Drew	Joss	Lynn	Reese

Rue	Shea	Sloane	Tru	Wren
Sage	Skye	Sol	Tyne	Wynne

BOYS

Ames	Cole	Kane	Roarke	Zane
Baird	Colt	Keane	Ross	Zell
Baz	Crew	Keir	Royce	
Beau	Cruz	Laird	Rune	
Beck	Dade	Lake	Ryne	
Bing	Dale	Lance	Sage	
Birch	Dane	Lane	Shane	
Blaine	Dash	Lee	Shaw	
Blair	Dax	Leif	Shea	
Blaise	Dean	Leith	Slade	
Blake	Deuce	Lex	Spence	
Bo	Dex	Locke	Steele	
Bond	Drake	Luke	Stone	
Bram	Drew	Mace	Stowe	
Bran	Fife	Max	Taft	
Brant	Finn	Meade	Taj	
Breck	Flynn	Nash	Tate	
Brent	Frost	Pax	Taye	
Brett	Gage	Payne	Teague	
Brice	Gaines	Pierce	Thane	
Bron	Glyn	Pleis	Till	
Brooks	Graeme	Price	Trace	
Bryce	Grant	Quill	Trent	
Burke	Gray	Quinn	Trey	
Cade	Guy	Rafe	Trip	
Cael	Hale	Rance	Troy	
Cal	Hart	Rand	Ty	
Cale	Hayes	Reef	Tyce	
Case	Heath	Reese	Van	
Cash	Jace	Reeve	Vance	
Chance	Jair	Reid	Vaughn	
Chase	Jax	Rex	Von	
Chaz	Jett	Rhett	Wade	
Clay	Joss	Rhodes	Watt	
Clint	Jude	Rhys	West	
Clive	Kai	Roan	Wynn	

Celtic

By the 1990 U.S. Census, the number of Americans reporting to be of Irish ancestry exceeded the total population of Ireland. The key to that remarkable statistic is the word "reporting." Many American families today have a

1880   Today

mixed ethnic background. If half or even a quarter of that background is Irish (or Scottish or Welsh), chances are that's how people describe themselves. Americans love Celtic traditions, and they love to show it by choosing Celtic baby names.

Just what a Celtic name is, though, is hard to pin down. The ancient Celts gave rise to a whole family of languages and peoples, most prominently the Irish and Scots (who spoke Gaelic) and the Welsh. Many of the names we think of as Celtic, like Patrick and Kathleen, are Anglicized descendants of Celtic originals. In the U.S., longtime favorite Kathleen has now yielded to the old Gaelic version Caitlin, which in Gaelic is pronounced more like . . . Kathleen. And other favorites are Celtic words or surnames that only became given names in America.

In today's Ireland, long-absent Gaelic names have roared back into fashion and now share the stage with English standards. Names like Jack and Katie are hot in Ireland and Scotland, just as in England. But Cian, Darragh, and Oisin are also fashionable for Irish boys, and Aoife, Niamh, and Caoimhe for girls. (If those spellings give you pause, call them Kian, Dara, and Osheen; Eva, Neeve, and Kiva.) In Scotland, Callum and Finlay are popular choices for boys, and Eilidh (Ailey) is hot for girls. Top Welsh names include Dylan and Rhys for boys, Seren and Ffion (FEE-on) for girls.

The list below includes Gaelic revivals, familiar Celtic-styled standards, and Celtic surnames that have been pressed into service as first names. If you're looking for a little Celtic flavor, you're bound to find something to your liking.

GIRLS

Adair	Alannah	Blair	Brynn	Casey
Ailish	Alys	Brenda	Brynna	Catriona
Ailsa	Anwen	Brenna	Caitlin	Cerys
Aine	Aoife	Briallen	Cameron	Ciara
Ainsley	Bedelia	Bridget	Caoimhe	Cliona
Aisling	Bethan	Bronwyn	Carys	Clodagh

Colleen	Gladys	Kinnia	Mhairi	Rowan
Connolly	Glenda	Kirstin	Mina	Ryan
Corrigan	Glynis	Leslie	Mirren	Sadhbh
Dara	Grainne	Liadan	Moira	Saoirse
Davina	Grania	Lilias	Morgan	Seren
Deirdre	Greer	Logan	Morrigan	Shannon
Dilys	Gwendolyn	Lowri	Morven	Shawn
Effie	Gwyneth	Mabyn	Muriel	Shea
Eileen	Iona	Mackenzie	Neve	Sheila
Eilidh	Ione	Madigan	Nia	Sian
Eirlys	Isla	Maëlle	Niamh	Sinéad
Eleri	Kathleen	Maeve	Nora	Siobhan
Elin	Keelin	Máire	Nuala	Skye
Elspeth	Keira	Màiri	Oona	Sorcha
Emlyn	Kelly	Maisie	Orlaith	Tamsin
Erin	Kendall	Maura	Regan	Teagan
Fallon	Kennedy	Maureen	Rhian	Tegan
Ffion	Kennera	Mckenna	Rhiannon	Tierney
Finley	Kerensa	Mckenzie	Riley	Una
Finola	Kerrigan	Mckinney	Riona	Wynne
Fiona	Kerry	Megan	Roisin	
Flannery	Kiara	Merrigan	Rory	

BOYS

Aidan	Broderick	Cathal	Cronan	Duane
Alec	Brodie	Cian	Cullen	Duncan
Alistair	Brogan	Ciaran	Darby	Dylan
Alpin	Bryce	Clancy	Darragh	Eamon
Angus	Cadogan	Colin	Daveth	Egan
Archibald	Cael	Colm	Declan	Emlyn
Baird	Caelan	Colman	Denzil	Eoghan
Bevan	Cai	Coltrane	Dermot	Eoin
Blaine	Callan	Colwyn	Desmond	Evander
Boyd	Callum	Conall	Diarmuid	Ewan
Brannock	Camden	Conan	Donal	Farrell
Brecken	Cameron	Connor	Donovan	Fergus
Brendan	Carrick	Conor	Doran	Fife
Brennan	Carson	Conroy	Dougal	Finbar
Brian	Carwyn	Cormac	Douglas	Finian
Brice	Casey	Craig	Doyle	Finlay

Finn	Kane	Lavin	Niven	Shane
Finnegan	Keane	Lesley	Oisin	Shannon
Fintan	Keegan	Liam	Owen	Shea
Forbes	Keenan	Llewellyn	Patrick	Sian
Gallagher	Keir	Lloyd	Pryce	Steffan
Gareth	Keith	Logan	Quinlan	Struan
Garrett	Kelan	Lorcan	Quinn	Stuart
Gavin	Kelly	Ludovic	Ramsay	Sullivan
Gawain	Kelvin	Lyle	Reid	Tadhg
Glenn	Kendall	Macaulay	Rhodri	Tam
Glyn	Kendrick	Mackenzie	Rhys	Tavis
Graeme	Kennedy	Maclean	Riley	Tavish
Graham	Kenneth	Magnus	Riordan	Teague
Gregor	Kermit	Mahoney	Roarke	Tiernan
Greig	Kerr	Malachy	Rogan	Tomas
Griffin	Kerry	Malcolm	Rohan	Torin
Griffith	Kerwin	Maxen	Ronan	Torquil
Guthrie	Kevin	McCoy	Rory	Trevor
Hamish	Kian	McKay	Rowan	Tynan
Ian	Kieran	Mervyn	Ruairí	Tyrone
Iestyn	Kilian	Morgan	Ryan	Vaughn
Innes	Kyle	Murphy	Seamus	Wylie
Ivor	Lachlan	Neil	Sean	Wynn
Jarlath	Lanigan	Niall	Senan	

Spotlight: *Really* Irish Names

Irish names are hugely popular with American parents. But Irish spellings? Not so much. Few non-Irish parents dare venture into the realm of Tadhg and Aoibheann. For those who'd like to test the waters, here are some Irish Gaelic names that are common in Ireland today.

Áine	Caoimhe	Gráinne	Róisín
(AWN-yə)	(KEE-və,	(GRAWN-yə)	(ROH-sheen)
Aisling	KWEE-və)	Niamh	Sadhbh
(ASH-ling)	Clodagh	(NEEV)	(SIYV)
Aoibheann	(KLOH-dah)	Órlaith	Saoirse
(EEV-een)	Eimear	(OHR-lə)	(SEER-shə)
Aoife (EE-fə)	(EE-mer)		

BOYS

Cathal	Colm	Lorcán	Ruairí
(KA-hal)	(KAWL-m)	(LOHR-kən)	(ROHR-ee)
Cian	Diarmaid	Niall (NIY-əl)	Tadhg
(KEE-ən)	(DEER-mid)	Odhrán	(TIYG)
Ciarán	Dáithí	(OH-rawn)	
(KEER-in)	(DAH-hee)	Oisín	
Cillian	Eoghan	(UHSH-een)	
(KIL-ee-ən)	(OH-in)		

Charms and Graces

The traditional feminine ideals of grace, beauty, and propriety have found natural reflections in girls' names. Propriety was the focus for the Puritans, who favored vir- tue names like Patience and Chastity. In the late Victorian era, the fashion was to celebrate tender beauty with names like Lily, Grace, and May.

1880   Today

The Charms and Graces names slid to the background in the mid-20th century as a cuter, more girlish femininity came into vogue. Today the names are back, in two distinct flavors. The downy Victorian favorites are part of an antique revival, chosen alongside sweet old-timers like Sophie and Annabel. Meanwhile, a new crop of word-based beauties is showing off a bold modern version of the feminine ideal that the Puritans could scarcely imagine. Instead of Pearl and Dove, we have Diamond and Raven. That bolder style inches toward a unisex vision—you'll see a growing crop of nature names for boys as well. For more on contemporary word–names, see the Modern Meanings style.

GIRLS

Acacia	Charity	Golden	Linden	Rowan
Amarantha	Chastity	Grace	Lotus	Ruby
Amaryllis	Cicely	Hazel	Mae	Sage
Amber	Clover	Heather	Magnolia	Senna
Amethyst	Constance	Holly	Mahogany	Serenity
Amity	Coral	Honesty	Marigold	Sienna
April	Crystal	Honor	May	Silver
Aspen	Dahlia	Honorée	Meadow	Summer
Aster	Daisy	Hope	Mercy	Sunday
Autumn	Damiana	Iris	Merry	Tansy
Avril	Dawn	Ivory	Myrtle	Temperance
Azalea	Diamond	Ivy	Olive	Tierra
Azure	Dove	Jade	Opal	Topaz
Bay	Ebony	January	Pansy	Tuesday
Belle	Emerald	Jasmine	Patience	Unity
Beryl	Esperanza	Jessamine	Pearl	Verity
Blossom	Faith	Jewel	Petunia	Violet
Bonnie	Fawn	Joy	Poppy	Willow
Briar	Felicity	June	Primrose	Winter
Briony	Fern	Juniper	Prudence	Wren
Calante	Fleur	Lark	Raven	Zinnia
Calla	Flora	Laurel	Robin	
Camellia	Garnet	Lavender	Rose	
Cassia	Ginger	Lily	Rosemary	

BOYS

August	Diamond	Garnet	Leaf	Silvan
Birch	Dune	Golden	Lion	Sparrow
Blue	Earnest	Hart	Merit	Starling
Bracken	Falcon	Heath	Moss	Sterling
Canyon	Flint	Jasper	Phoenix	Stone
Constant	Forest	Jet	Reef	Storm
Cyan	Frost	Lake	River	

Classical

The glory that was Greece, the grandeur that was Rome! Classical civilizations stand as eternal icons of the heights of human achievement. Whether you aspire to the arts, to philosophy, or to world conquest, the classi- cal world offers plenty of inspiration. Baby names are no exception. You can almost hear the togas rustling when you think of names like Julie and Emily.

What, not catching that rustle? Well, Julie is the French form of Julia, a Latin name that's the feminine form of Julius, as in Caesar. Emily is usually tracked back to the Latin Aemilia/Aemilius. But as with so much of Western civilization, the classical underpinnings have been so well filtered through thousands of years of culture that we scarcely notice them.

Unlike Julie and Emily, the names below still have the power to conjure up the classical world. Their style—be it strong, sophisticated, quirky, or ostentatious—comes to us special delivery straight from antiquity. Note that Roman names commonly had masculine and feminine versions like Julia/Julius, so feel free to mix and match endings. See also the section on Mythological names.

GIRLS

Aelia	Caecilia	Euphemia	Luciana	Sabina
Aeliana	Cassia	Flavia	Lucrece	Serena
Aemilia	Charmian	Gratiana	Lucretia	Severina
Apollonia	Claudia	Junia	Lydia	Sidonia
Aquila	Cleopatra	Laelia	Lysandra	Theodosia
Artemisia	Cornelia	Laetitia	Maxima	Xanthe
Augusta	Drusilla	Livia	Octavia	Zenobia
Aurelia	Eugenia	Liviana	Portia	

BOYS

Aeneas	Amadeus	Ariston	Cassius	Darius
Aeson	Anacletus	Aristotle	Cato	Demetrius
Agathon	Anastasius	Arsenius	Cicero	Erasmus
Albus	Androcles	Atticus	Claudius	Euclid
Alcaeus	Antonius	Augustus	Cornelius	Galen
Alexios	Archimedes	Aurelius	Crispus	Hector
Alphaeus	Aristides	Caesar	Cyrus	Ignatius

Julius	Nicomachus	Severus	Theron	Vitus
Laurentius	Octavian	Silvanus	Theseus	Xenon
Leonidas	Octavius	Socrates	Tiberius	Xerxes
Lucius	Pericles	Solon	Titus	Zeno
Lysander	Philon	Tacitus	Trajan	Zenon
Marcellus	Quintus	Tarquin	Tullius	
Marcus	Rufus	Theodosius	Tycho	
Marius	Seneca	Theophanes	Ulysses	
Maximus	Septimus	Theophilus	Virgil	

Country and Western

Welcome cowpokes, gunslingers, and braves! Home-
steaders, madams, forty-niners—come on in and put your
boots up! There's room for all at the Naming Saloon.

1880   Today

The American West is more than a place; it's a
dream. We close our eyes and imagine wide-open skies, endless prairie,
and men who can mount a horse from a third-story window. We also
picture a world wilder than our own, closer to nature, a place where you
build your home and your livelihood with your own two hands. That
combination of hard work and personal freedom makes for a uniquely
American mythology. The Country and Western names are as varied a
bunch as Faith Hill, Ma Ingalls, and Jesse James, but they're all rooted in
our shared American dreams.

The most popular country names today include Wild West throw-
backs like Wyatt and place names like Aspen. They're the strongest links
to the romance of the frontier and the ideal of boundless opportunity.
But Nashville is adding new wrinkles to the country-western sound, including Southern gent names like Brantley and Easton. These surnames
are updating the roster of Country Belles and Good Ol' Boys, with a
down-home hospitality that's always welcome.

WILD WEST GIRLS

Autry	Casey	Cody	Oakley
Belle	Cassidy	Liberty	

WILD WEST BOYS

Beau	Boone	Boyd	Buzz	Casey
Bo	Bowie	Buck	Carson	Cassidy

Chance	Dusty	Kip	Ridge	Ty
Cimarron	Garrett	Kit	Rory	Walker
Clint	Gatlin	Lane	Rowdy	Wayne
Cody	Gauge	Levi	Roy	Wiley
Colt	Hardy	Luke	Ruff	Woody
Cooper	Hoyt	Mack	Rusty	Wyatt
Dalton	Jeb	Marshal	Shane	Zane
Deacon	Jed	Maverick	Stetson	Zed
Destry	Jedidiah	Paladin	Stoney	
Dillon	Joss	Ranger	Tex	
Duke	Judd	Remington	Trace	

THE LAND GIRLS

Abilene	Dakota	Montana	Shasta	Texanna
Aspen	Dallas	Raleigh	Shenandoah	Virginia
Carolina	Georgia	Savannah	Shiloh	
Cheyenne	Laramie	Sedona	Sierra	

THE LAND BOYS

Bozeman	Canyon	Houston	Phoenix
Branson	Dakota	Macon	Raleigh
Bridger	Dallas	Memphis	Reno
Bryce	Denver	Montana	Ridge

COUNTRY BELLES

Arly	Emmylou	Lucille	Raelynn	Siddalee
Clementine	Faith	Mae	Reba	Susannah
Delta	Landry	Magnolia	Scarlett	Tallulah
Dixie	Larue	Orleanna	Shania	Willodean
Dolly	Leanne	Paralee	Shelby	Winona

GOOD OL' BOYS

Beauregard	Bubba	Gaylon	Landon	Roy
Barkley	Cash	Gentry	Landry	Travis
Bentley	Colton	Harlan	Merle	Waylon
Bowman	Conway	Jarvis	Raylan	
Boyd	Earl	Lafayette	Rhett	
Brantley	Garth	Lamar	Roscoe	

English

Proud sons and daughters of England, prepare to cringe. When I speak of English names, I'm not referring to origins in the Old English language or prominence in English history or culture. I'm not even thinking of names commonly used in England, since those overlap so broadly with American favorites. What is meant here by an English name is a name that by style, tradition, or stereotype sounds English to American ears. This is not the England of geographical reality, it is the England of our imagination.

For the record, the most popular names in the *real* England today tend to be friendly and familiar: Jack and Harry, Sophie and Lily. But what fun is that?

The England of our imagination is a literary place, full of drawing-room mysteries and perfectly proper romances. Historically it cuts across periods from Jane Austen to J. K. Rowling, but its epicenter is a 1920s and '30s world of gentility in decline. (Think Evelyn Waugh meets Agatha Christie.) The men are a mixture of upstanding gentlemen, cads, and aesthetes, but all are dapper. The ladies are, above all, ladylike. Servants scuttle in the background in a mood of muffled discontent.

It may be more *Masterpiece Theatre* than Manchester, England, but it's a potent cultural image with a set of names to match. Some of the names benefit from the association. Sebastian and Graham, for instance, float on a cloud of refinement. Others, like Percival and Dudley, get the short end of the stick as ineffectual milquetoasts. For girls, the choice is typically sweet (Charlotte) or forbidding (Agatha). Sit back to read and enjoy, with some biscuits and clotted cream.

GIRLS

Agatha	Beatrix	Dahlia	Felicity	Henrietta
Alethea	Briony	Daphne	Fiona	Imogen
Amabel	Camilla	Davina	Flavia	India
Amelia	Cecily	Dulcie	Freya	Isla
Anthea	Charlotte	Elspeth	Gemma	Jemima
Arabella	Christabel	Emmeline	Georgina	Jessamine
Araminta	Cordelia	Enid	Gillian	Jessamy
Beatrice	Corinna	Eve	Glynis	Lettice

Nicola	Pippa	Rosamund	Tilly	Ysanne
Penny	Poppy	Sidony	Venetia	Zara
Petula	Portia	Sukey	Verity	
Philippa	Prudie	Tamsin	Victoria	
Phyllida	Romilly	Thomasina	Winifred	

BOYS

Alec	Colin	Gareth	Kit	Rupert
Alfie	Corin	Giles	Neville	Sebastian
Alistair	Crispin	Godfrey	Nigel	Simon
Alwyn	Davy	Graham	Niles	St. John
Ambrose	Denham	Hugh	Oliver	Stuart
Auberon	Denholm	Ivor	Pelham	Tad
Barnaby	Dobbin	Jem	Percival	Tarquin
Basil	Dudley	Jolyon	Piers	Terence
Carleton	Dunstan	Jonty	Pip	Trevor
Cecil	Edgar	Julian	Robin	Tristan
Clive	Edmund	Kip	Roderick	Tristram

The "-ens"

This group of names earned its own category by sheer brute force. If you want to know how mild-mannered Ethan muscled its way to the top of the charts, how Laurens came to outnumber Lauras four to one, or why there are now *nine* spellings of Jaden among the top 1000 boys' names, look to the power of the "-en." (Still reeling over the Jaden? It's Jaden, Jadon, Jaeden, Jaiden, Jaidyn, Jaydan, Jayden, Jaydin, and Jaydon if you're keeping score at home.)

1880   Today

America is in love with two-syllable names ending in "-n." Beyond the nine Jadens, there are dozens of other names rhyming with Aidan on the boy's top-1000 chart. From Aaden to Zayden, you could fill a whole rhyming classroom. All together, a third of American boys now receive a name ending in "-n." We haven't seen this kind of dominant naming sound since Ida, Ada, Ora, Iva, Ola, and a dozen others took the 1900s by storm.

The love affair with "-n" endings cuts across styles, from old-timers like Nathan to new inventions like Kyson. It cuts across races and sexes.

We love the "-en" names because they are compact, upbeat, and accessible. And they are everywhere. If the style speaks to you, you should find your little piece of Heaven, or Eden, below.

GIRLS

Addison	Camryn	Jaidyn	Kiersten	Mirren
Adelyn	Carson	Janson	Kirsten	Morgan
Afton	Daelyn	Jaylin	Kristen	Payton
Alden	Devin	Jazlyn	Larkin	Raelyn
Aniston	Dylan	Jazmyn	Larsen	Raven
Arden	Eden	Jesslyn	Lauren	Reagan
Ashlyn	Emlyn	Jensen	Leighton	Regan
Ashton	Erin	Jillian	Liadan	Rhian
Aspen	Evelyn	Jocelyn	Linden	Rowan
Auden	Fallon	Jordan	London	Ryan
Avalyn	Gracelyn	Joslyn	Mabyn	Seren
Aylin	Haven	Kaitlyn	Madilyn	Tamsin
Braelyn	Hayden	Katlyn	Madison	Taryn
Brooklyn	Heaven	Kayden	Maren	Teagan
Caitlin	Jaden	Kaylin	Maylin	Tegan
Camden	Jaelyn	Keelin	Megan	Tristen

BOYS

Aeson	Bevan	Bronson	Clayton	Damian
Aidan	Boston	Brycen	Clinton	Damon
Akon	Bowen	Bryson	Cohen	Darian
Alan	Braden	Byron	Colin	Darren
Alban	Brandon	Caden	Colman	Davian
Alden	Brannon	Callan	Colton	Davin
Alton	Branson	Camden	Colwyn	Dawson
Alwyn	Braxton	Camron	Conan	Daxton
Arden	Brayden	Canton	Corbin	Dayton
Aston	Braylon	Carson	Corin	Deon
Ashton	Brecken	Carsten	Cowan	Destin
Austin	Brendan	Cason	Crighton	Devin
Axton	Brennan	Caspian	Crispin	Devlin
Ayden	Brenton	Chayton	Cronan	Devon
Balin	Brighton	Christian	Cullen	Dillon
Bannon	Britton	Ciprian	Dallin	Doran
Baron	Brogan	Clarion	Dalton	Dorian

Draven	Griffin	Kian	Nolan	Talan
Duncan	Hayden	Kieran	Olin	Talon
Dunstan	Holden	Kingston	Orion	Taran
Dustin	Jackson	Kipton	Owen	Taven
Dylan	Jaden	Kiran	Patton	Teagan
Dyson	Jalen	Kyan	Paxton	Tevin
Eamon	Jaron	Kylan	Peyton	Theron
Easton	Jason	Kyson	Quentin	Tiernan
Egan	Javen	Landon	Quinlan	Tilden
Eldon	Jaxon	Larson	Quinton	Timon
Elkan	Jaxton	Lavin	Raiden	Tobin
Elton	Jayden	Lawson	Raven	Tomlin
Emlyn	Jensen	Layton	Riordan	Torin
Espen	Jolyon	Lennon	Rogan	Torsten
Ethan	Jordan	Lofton	Rohan	Trenton
Evan	Jurgen	Logan	Roman	Trevin
Ewan	Justin	London	Ronan	Treyton
Faron	Kaden	Lorcan	Rowan	Tristan
Fintan	Keaton	Macon	Ruffin	Triton
Florian	Keegan	Madden	Ryan	Tynan
Florin	Keenan	Mahlon	Rylan	Tyson
Galen	Kellen	Marlon	Silvan	Weston
Gannon	Kelton	Mason	Soren	Zayden
Gavin	Kenton	Maxen	Stellan	
Glendon	Kenyon	Maxton	Stelson	
Grayden	Keon	Morgan	Struan	
Grayson	Kevin	Nathan	Sutton	

Exotic Traditionals

Ordinary is not for you. You want a name that stands out from the pack, that people will associate with your child alone. Yet you roll your eyes at new inventions with wild spellings—you want a name with roots and resonance. Where to turn?

The Exotic Traditionals strike a familiar chord yet have the ability to raise a few eyebrows. Some have artistic or literary pedigrees. Others are foreign names ready for import, or ancients awaiting resurrection. A few are popular, a few downright eccentric, but not a one is merely ordinary.

For more names along these lines, see the Classical, Saints, and Shakespearean sections.

GIRLS

Adelind	Charis	Iolanthe	Monserrate	Talitha
Aida	Christabel	Iole	Octavia	Tallulah
Alethea	Cleo	Ione	Olympia	Tanith
Allegra	Damaris	Isadora	Oona	Theodosia
Amabel	Danae	Isis	Ophelia	Valentina
Amarantha	Delilah	Jacinta	Paloma	Valentine
Angelique	Diantha	Jocosa	Phaedra	Verena
Apollonia	Domicela	Lavinia	Philomena	Violetta
Araminta	Donatella	Leilani	Phyllida	Viva
Ariadne	Drusilla	Leocadia	Portia	Xanthe
Artemisia	Elodie	Lilias	Raphaela	Xanthia
Astrid	Esme	Linnea	Salome	Xenia
Athena	Evangeline	Lorelei	Sapphira	Zelda
Aurora	Eulalia	Lourdes	Sarai	Zena
Avelina	Evadne	Lucretia	Scarlett	Zenobia
Averil	Evangeline	Magdalene	Sephora	Zilla
Avila	Genevieve	Mariamne	Seraphina	Zola
Beatrix	Guinevere	Maris	Severina	Zora
Bronwyn	Hermione	Mehitabel	Sidony	
Caledonia	Honor	Melisande	Solange	
Catalina	Imogen	Minerva	Sophronia	

BOYS

Abelard	Alpheus	Barnaby	Dashiell	Fabio
Absalom	Alphonso	Bartholomew	Demetrius	Falco
Adelard	Anatole	Beauregard	Desmond	Felix
Adolphus	Andreas	Benedict	Dimitri	Ferdinand
Aeneas	Anselm	Caedmon	Dominick	Florian
Aidric	Antony	Calix	Elias	Galen
Alaric	Artemas	Casimir	Eliezer	Gervase
Aldous	Atticus	Cassian	Emmanuel	Gideon
Aldric	Auberon	Cassius	Ephraim	Giles
Algernon	Augustine	Cedric	Erastus	Hannibal
Alistair	Augustus	Constantine	Evander	Horatio
Alonzo	Axel	Cornelius	Ezekiel	Ignatius
Aloysius	Barnabas	Cosmo	Ezra	Ignatz

Inigo	Leif	Montgomery	Romeo	Titus
Isaias	Leonardo	Napoleon	Ruffin	Torquil
Ishmael	Leopold	Nicodemus	Samson	Tristram
Ivo	Lucian	Niels	Severin	Tycho
Ivor	Lucius	Orlando	Silvan	Ulysses
Jabez	Ludovic	Pascal	Simeon	Valerian
Japheth	Magnus	Peregrine	Sinclair	Varian
Jasper	Malachi	Philo	Solon	Vitus
Jedidiah	Marcellus	Phineas	Stanislaus	Wolf
Joachim	Marius	Piers	Tarquin	Zachariah
Justus	Matthias	Quinton	Tavish	Zebedee
Lafayette	Maxim	Raphael	Thaddeus	Zed
Lazar	Maximilian	Regis	Thelonius	Zenon
Lazarus	Milo	Rollo	Theophilus	Zoltan
Leander	Montague	Roman	Theron	

Spotlight: X's and O's

Angelina Jolie may be the world's top baby name style maker. Thousands of parents who normally would never dream of choosing a "celebrity" baby name find themselves gazing longingly at names like Maddox and Shiloh. What other creative names might capture that "x" and "o" magic?

X:

Calix	Hendrix	Lynx	Rex
Dex	Jax	Mannix	
Felix	Lennox	Onyx	
Fox	Lomax	Phoenix	

O:

Amparo	Halo	Marlowe	Willow
Callisto	Harlow	Niko	Winslow
Cielo	Juno	Shadow	
Clio	Lucero	Sparrow	

Fanciful

Are the Exotic Traditionals not exotic enough for you?
Take a step beyond into the realm of the whimsical and
spectacular with the names below.

1880   Today

The Fanciful names come in a variety of breeds: the
heroic (Apollo), the flattering (Charisma), the trademarked (Armani),
and the just plain "out there" (Atom). These names won't please everybody, but they're memorable, with a spirit of freewheeling fun and a will-
ingness to shed everyday constraints and venture into the land of dreams.
(For names that venture into the worlds of science fiction, fantasy, and
video games, see the Fantastical section.)

GIRLS

Abcde	Caress	Fifi	Moon	Sonnet
Aeron	Chanel	Genie	Moxie	Star
Allure	Charisma	Gidget	Nautica	Sunrise
Apple	Chiquita	Heart	Nova	Symphony
Aqua	Cinderella	Heaven	Oceana	Taffeta
Armani	Cinnamon	Honey	Odyssey	Tempest
Aura	Cleopatra	Karma	Paisley	Temple
Avalon	Clover	Lexus	Poet	Treasure
Bambi	Coco	Lotus	Princess	Unique
Bijou	Divine	Lucky	Queen	Valentine
Bliss	Dynasty	Lux	Rainbow	Vanity
Blossom	Echo	Lyric	Riviera	Vega
Breeze	Electra	Madonna	Saffron	Velvet
Calico	Eternity	Marvel	Serenade	Venus
Calliope	Evening	Maxima	Silver	Whisper
Candy	Fantasia	Miracle	Soleil	Wonder

BOYS

Ace	Arrow	Blaze	Crash	Fox
Achilles	Atlas	Blue	Crew	General
Adonis	Atom	Caesar	Denim	Gulliver
Ajax	Axl	Cannon	Diesel	Halston
Aladdin	Banjo	Canyon	Edge	Hawk
Altair	Baron	Casanova	Everest	Heathcliff
Apollo	Bishop	Champion	Falcon	Ivanhoe

Jazz	Major	Phoenix	Rowdy	Talon
Jebediah	Mars	Pilot	Royal	Tank
Judge	Marvel	Prince	Ruger	Triton
Jupiter	Maximus	Prospero	Saber	Truth
Knight	Mercury	Ranger	Seraph	Tyme
Lancelot	Michelangelo	Ransom	Shadow	Valentine
Legend	Noble	Raziel	Sherlock	Wisdom
Loyal	Oberon	Rigel	Sinbad	Zenith
Lynx	Peerless	Ringo	Sparrow	Zephyr
Magic	Peregrine	Rio	Spike	Zeus
Magnum	Pharaoh	Rocket	Squire	Zodiac

Fantastical

Should clones have matching names? Do superpowers give you extra leeway for creative naming? And are there rules of thumb for naming non-carbon-based life forms?

When you dream up a whole world, you get to determine its names. They can be anything under the sun (or under three suns). Yet the names of science fiction, fantasy, and video games do make up a recognizable style.

Many fantasy authors follow the Welsh-inspired stylings of J. R. R. Tolkien. Sci fi and game creators often go for the earthling-only-cooler vibe of *Neuromancer*'s Case, or for descriptive-word names like Sparrow of "Fable II." Even invented names from alien languages can follow patterns, like the popular "ae" vowel combo.

Each name a writer introduces into an alternate world broadens our name options here on Earth. For devoted fanboys and fangirls, there's nothing cooler than a name from a universe that has captured your full imagination. Game players can also develop deep connections to character names they've spent months interacting with, or even inhabiting.

If the name you love is wildly unconventional, though, it's smart to get opinions on it from outside the fan community. Game names in particular can have short life spans as technology changes render their platforms obsolete.

The science fiction and fantasy lists below focus on names from literature, film and TV, with video game names following in a separate list.

SCIENCE FICTION AND FANTASY GIRLS

Aerin	Daine	Harley	Morgaine	Saphira
Amidala	Denna	Kahlan	Mystique	Serenity
Andromeda	Eilonwy	Katana	Primrose	Sookie
Aravis	Elektra	Katniss	Renesmee	Trinity
Arwen	Elora	Katsa	Ripley	Troi
Arya	Eowyn	Leia	Rogue	Vesper
Bellatrix	Evolet	Lyra	Rue	Xena
Brienne	Galadriel	Menolly	Sabriel	Yvaine
Daenerys	Glinda	Minerva	Sansa	Zuzu

SCIENCE FICTION AND FANTASY BOYS

Alastor	Conan	Gandalf	Morpheus	Sirius
Albus	Cullen	Gawain	Nemo	Strider
Aragorn	Cypher	Han	Neo	Sylar
Aslan	Deckard	Indiana	Oz	Taran
Asriel	Draven	Jetson	Paladin	Tarzan
Atreyu	Dune	Kal-El	Pippin	Thor
Auron	Eddard	Kirk	Quaid	Tyrion
Bartimaeus	Ender	Lando	Rand	Xander
Blade	Endymion	Legolas	Riddick	
Bran	Eragon	Lex	Ryker	
Case	Finnick	Mace	Septimus	
Caspian	Fox	Merlin	Severus	

VIDEO GAME GIRLS

Aeris	Delphine	Lara	Rinoa	Yuna
Alyx	Halo	Lyndis	Rosalina	Zelda
Ashe	Kaileena	Mileena	Sakura	
Blaze	Kairi	Navi	Sora	
Cortana	Kitana	Rayne	Vivi	

VIDEO GAME BOYS

Altair	Cyan	Kratos	Phoenix	Sparrow
Alucard	Dante	Leon	Raiden	Stryker
Arthas	Jax	Link	Raziel	Taven
Auron	Kage	Locke	Riku	Tidus
Axel	Kai	Madden	Ronin	Varian
Cloud	Kain	Paxton	Roxas	Zell
Crash	Kane	Payne	Soren	Zidane

French

For Americans, France has always spelled sophistication. Fashions change, but in each age we find French names to capture the moment's ideal of high style. In the early 1900s, that meant stately gentlefolk like Jules and Cecile. In the middle of the century, we created effervescent girls' names by using cute French endings. Voilà, Susan becomes Suzette! A generation later, the favorite feminine forms had a slinkier elegance: Danielle, Monique, Nicole.

What's up next? For American parents today, the most intriguing French names are those that sound the least American. Names like Giselle and Anaïs have no English equivalents, giving them a fresh panache. French names are also a preferred route to lavish romanticism for girls. The smoothness of names like Genevieve and Angelique keeps them light despite their length, and keeps their frills from becoming frivolous.

If your goal is to be in fashion on the streets of Paris, though, you may have to put aside the opulent romance. Current French style favors the short and sweet, with bonus points for quirky style or an imported sound. Tom and Enzo, Emma and Océane are far more fashionable in French nurseries than Jacques or Genevieve.

GIRLS

Adele	Avril	Clarisse	Elodie	Helene
Adrienne	Axelle	Claudette	Eloise	Heloise
Aimee	Babette	Clementine	Emilie	Henriette
Amandine	Beatrice	Clotilde	Emmanuelle	Honorée
Amelie	Bernadette	Colette	Estelle	Inès
Anaëlle	Blanche	Coralie	Eugenie	Isabel
Anaïs	Brigitte	Corinne	Fifi	Isabelle
Angeline	Camille	Danielle	Fleur	Jacqueline
Angelique	Cecile	Delphine	Françoise	Jeanne
Annette	Celeste	Denise	Frederique	Jeannette
Anouk	Celestine	Desiree	Gabrielle	Jeannine
Antoinette	Celine	Diane	Genevieve	Joelle
Ariane	Chantal	Dominique	Germaine	Josette
Augustine	Christine	Eliane	Gigi	Julie
Aurore	Claire	Elise	Giselle	Julienne

Juliette	Lucille	Marine	Oriane	Sophie
Justine	Madeleine	Marion	Patrice	Suzanne
Laure	Maëlle	Marlène	Paulette	Suzette
Laurence	Maëlys	Mathilde	Pauline	Sylvie
Léa	Maeva	Melanie	Raphaëlle	Therese
Léonie	Magalie	Michele	Renée	Valerie
Leonor	Maite	Monique	Romane	Veronique
Leontine	Manon	Nadine	Rosalie	Violette
Lilou	Marceline	Nathalie	Sabine	Virginie
Lise	Marcelle	Nicole	Salome	Vivienne
Lisette	Margot	Nicolette	Sandrine	Yvette
Louise	Marguerite	Noelle	Sidonie	Yvonne
Lucie	Marianne	Noémie	Simone	
Lucienne	Marie	Océane	Solange	

BOYS

Adrien	Denis	Gerard	Lucien	Regis
Alain	Didier	Germaine	Maël	Rémy
Alexandre	Dominique	Gilles	Marcel	Rene
Alphonse	Eloi	Guillaume	Mathias	Roland
Anatole	Emeric	Gustave	Mathieu	Romain
Andre	Emile	Guy	Mathis	Sébastien
Antoine	Emmanuel	Henri	Maurice	Sylvain
Armand	Etienne	Hugo	Maxime	Thibaut
Arnaud	Fabien	Jacques	Nicolas	Thierry
Baptiste	Fabrice	Jean	Noe	Tristan
Bastien	Fernand	Jérémie	Noel	Valentin
Benoit	Florian	Jerome	Octave	Vincent
Bertrand	François	Josué	Olivier	Xavier
Blaise	Gaspard	Jules	Pascal	Yann
Brice	Frederic	Julien	Patrice	Yannick
Christophe	Gabriel	Laurence	Phillipe	Yves
Claude	Gaston	Laurent	Pierre	
Clement	Gautier	Loïc	Quentin	
Damien	Georges	Luc	Raoul	

German and Dutch

A century ago, stout German classics like Bertha and Herman were the height of fashion in America. Today they're not even fashionable in Germany.

1880　　Today

Throughout Europe, names have gravitated toward an international style: smooth classics without any strong ethnic association. Think of them as the name equivalents of the euro. Nowhere is that trend stronger than in the German-speaking world, where almost none of the top baby names are uniquely, unmistakably German. The chart-toppers include Alexander, Paul, and Lukas for boys; Mia, Laura, and Anna for girls. If a name that's trendy in Germany does have an ethnic style, it's as likely to be Italian or French as German. You'll find the same development to a large extent in Austria and Switzerland. The Netherlands is something of an exception, with Dutch names like Daan and Sanne top choices, but international favorites are well represented.

The heaviest Germanic classics are unlikely choices in the U.S. today, but some of the lighter names, unheard in the heyday of Bertha and Herman, make attractive and imaginative selections. Dutch and Flemish names, in particular, have lots of untapped potential. In fact, the more the rest of the world loads up on French and Italian names, the fresher names like Anneliese, Elke, and Bram will sound.

GIRLS

Aleydis	Christiane	Gretchen	Karin	Margot
Alina	Claudia	Hannelore	Katharina	Mariel
Alma	Dagmar	Hedwig	Katja	Marlene
Angela	Elise	Hedy	Katrina	Martina
Anja	Elke	Heidi	Lena	Meta
Anke	Elsa	Heike	Leonie	Mieke
Annalie	Elsbeth	Helga	Liesl	Mina
Anneliese	Eva	Hilde	Lisbeth	Mitzi
Anouk	Femke	Hildegard	Liselotte	Monika
Astrid	Franziska	Ida	Lotte	Petra
Bertha	Gerda	Ilsa	Magdalena	Renate
Bettina	Gertrude	Inge	Manuela	Sabine
Brigitta	Gisela	Ingrid	Margarete	Sanne
Christa	Greta	Johanna	Margit	Saskia

| Sigrid | Stefanie | Ursula | Wilhelmina |
| Sophie | Theresia | Verena | |

BOYS

Adolf	Dominik	Hannes	Ludwig	Sören
Alois	Egon	Hans	Manfred	Stefan
Andreas	Eino	Heinz	Marius	Till
Anton	Emil	Henrik	Markus	Tobias
Armin	Erich	Hermann	Matthias	Tomas
Arno	Ernst	Horst	Maximilian	Torben
Artur	Evert	Ivo	Mees	Torsten
Benno	Fabian	Jakob	Moritz	Ulrich
Bernhard	Felix	Jan	Niels	Volker
Bernt	Florian	Jarne	Otto	Waldemar
Berthold	Franz	Johann	Pascal	Werner
Bertram	Friedrich	Josef	Piet	Wilhelm
Bram	Fritz	Jurgen	Pim	Willem
Bruno	Georg	Karl	Rainer	Wolf
Carsten	Gerhard	Klaus	Reinhold	Wolfgang
Casper	Gerrit	Konrad	Roel	Wouter
Detlef	Gottlieb	Kurt	Rudiger	Xaver
Dieter	Gregor	Lars	Rutger	
Dietrich	Gunnar	Leon	Sander	
Dirk	Günther	Lorenz	Sigmund	

Greek

Greece remains a land of traditional names. The traditions of the Greek Orthodox Church, combined with a custom of family namesakes, keep the classic Greek names on birth certificates generation after generation.

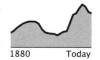

1880   Today

That doesn't mean the naming scene stands still, though. Fashion and fads show up in nicknames, which can be especially important in families where a single given name appears as a grandma, aunt, and cousin.

The current nickname trends in Greece are foreign and exotic. A Greek Anastasia, for instance, may go by the Russian nickname Natasha. To American ears, some Greek nicknames can be surprisingly familiar even when the full names are utterly foreign. Stella, for instance, is a common name in Greece—taken not from the Latin for "star" but from the formal Greek name Styliani. The list below includes a mix of formal names and everyday nicknames that can be used as full names in English.

GIRLS

Aliki	Dimitra	Ioanna	Marina	Styliani
Anastasia	Ekaterini	Irene	Melina	Theodora
Angeliki	Eleni	Irini	Natasa	Vasiliki
Anthi	Elisavet	Kalliopi	Nikoleta	Xenia
Aspasia	Evangelia	Katerina	Olympia	Xristina
Athanasia	Evanthia	Konstantina	Rania	Zoe
Athena	Evdokia	Kyriaki	Roula	
Danae	Fotini	Lina	Sofia	
Demi	Georgia	Maria	Sotiria	
Despina	Iliana	Marilena	Stefania	

BOYS

Achilles	Christos	Ilias	Michalis	Stelios
Agis	Dimitrios	Ioannis	Nicholas	Takis
Alexandros	Dimitris	Konstantinos	Nikos	Thanasis
Alexios	Dimos	Kostas	Panos	Thanos
Anastasios	Elias	Lefteris	Pavlos	Vangelis
Andreas	Evangelos	Leonidas	Petros	Vasilis
Antonios	Fotis	Makis	Savvas	Yannis
Apostolos	Georgios	Manos	Spiros	
Aris	Giannis	Marios	Stavros	
Athanasios	Giorgos	Markos	Stefanos	

Guys and Dolls (and All That Jazz)

Dizzy dames! Stand-up guys! Jazz babies! Gin runners! The Guys and Dolls names remind us that there was a lot more to our great-grandparents' time than just ladies and gentlemen sipping tea in their parlors. Names like Lulu, Roxie, Mack, and Rocco paint a portrait of the saucy side of the early 20th century. They win our hearts with their sheer brio. If you love old-time names but your style is more cheeky than courtly, these are the guys and dolls for you.

For a few names, that Jazz Age style is more literal. Names associated with actual jazz musicians balance a cerebral approach with a wild, free spirit—much like the music itself.

DOLLS

Addie	Effie	Gussie	Mae	Rilla
Allie	Ella	Hallie	Mamie	Rosie
Annie	Ellamae	Hattie	Margie	Roxie
Arlie	Ellie	Jonnie	Mattie	Ruby
Bess	Elsie	Josie	Maxie	Ruthie
Bessie	Emmy	Larue	Maybelle	Sadie
Billie	Etta	Lena	Mazie	Sallie
Birdie	Evie	Lettie	Melba	Sammie
Blossom	Fanny	Libby	Millie	Sophie
Ceil	Faye	Lillie	Minnie	Stella
Charlie	Florida	Lina	Molly	Susie
Clarabelle	Flossie	Liza	Nell	Tess
Cleo	Frankie	Lola	Patsy	Tessie
Dell	Freda	Lottie	Pearl	Tillie
Della	Georgie	Lucy	Pearlie	Tommie
Delta	Gertie	Lula	Queenie	Trixie
Dixie	Gilda	Lulu	Rae	Winnie
Dolly	Goldie	Mabel	Reba	Zadie
Dovie	Gracie	Madge	Reva	

GUYS

Abe	Buck	Earlie	Jimmie	Ned
Aldo	Bud	Eddie	Joe	Otto
Alf	Buddy	Fritz	Judge	Rocco
Arch	Buster	Gus	King	Rocky
Archie	Cab	Harry	Leo	Roscoe
Arlo	Carmine	Harvey	Lonzo	Sal
Arno	Charley	Haskell	Louie	Sammie
Barney	Cosmo	Huey	Mack	Si
Benno	Dee	Ike	Major	Sidney
Benny	Dewey	Ira	Max	Sol
Bernie	Doc	Irving	Meyer	Vito
Bert	Doyle	Jack	Moe	Wiley
Booker	Duke	Jackie	Mose	Willie
Bruno	Dutch	Jake	Nat	

Archie	Cab	Django	Gillespie	Miles
Basie	Chick	Duke	Hampton	Mose
Benny	Cleo	Ella	Hawkins	Porter
Bessie	Coleman	Ellington	King	Thelonius
Billie	Coltrane	Etta	Lionel	Wynton
Bix	Dinah	Fletcher	Louie	

Italian

Italy may be the world's most fashionable name source. Parents around the world are embracing traditional Italian names, thanks to their smooth elegance and boundary-crossing style. Today a little Enzo is likely to be from Paris, Giovanni from Santo Domingo, and Francesca from Berlin. In the U.S., too, baby Leonardos outnumber Leonards, and Gianna is a hot new favorite.

Just as with Italian cuisine, Italian names can have distinctive regional flavors. While a Lorenzo or Luisa could hail from any part of Italy, Gennaro is favored overwhelmingly in Naples, and an Ambrogio is sure to hail from Milan. Owing partly to historical immigration patterns, many names of Italy's South sound old-fashioned in the U.S. Characteristic Southern and Sicilian names like Nunzio, Vito, and Concetta have a grandparent style, while Northern names like Giancarlo, Bianca, and Donatella have a contemporary touch that's more glossy than homey.

GIRLS

Adriana	Carolina	Elisa	Gina	Liliana
Alessandra	Caterina	Emilia	Ginevra	Livia
Alessia	Chiara	Emiliana	Giovanna	Lorenza
Antonella	Claudia	Fabiola	Gisella	Lucia
Antonia	Concetta	Federica	Giulia	Luciana
Antonina	Daniela	Felicita	Giuliana	Luisa
Arianna	Daria	Flavia	Grazia	Maddalena
Assunta	Dina	Francesca	Graziella	Mafalda
Bettina	Domenica	Gabriella	Ilaria	Marcella
Bianca	Donatella	Gemma	Isabella	Margherita
Carla	Elena	Giada	Lia	Maria
Carmela	Eliana	Gianna	Lidia	Mariella

Marietta	Noemi	Rosa	Serena	Valentina
Marilena	Oriana	Rosalba	Silvana	Valeria
Marina	Paola	Rosanna	Silvia	Vincenza
Marisa	Raffaella	Rosaria	Simona	Vittoria
Martina	Renata	Rosella	Sofia	Viviana
Michela	Rita	Sandra	Stefania	
Milena	Roberta	Santina	Teresa	
Mirella	Romina	Serafina	Tiziana	

BOYS

Alberto	Dino	Giacomo	Mario	Rocco
Aldo	Domenico	Gian	Massimo	Romeo
Alessandro	Donato	Giancarlo	Matteo	Salvatore
Alessio	Edoardo	Gianfranco	Mattia	Sandro
Alfredo	Elio	Gianni	Mauro	Santino
Andrea	Emanuele	Gino	Michelangelo	Sergio
Angelo	Emilio	Giovanni	Michele	Silvio
Antonio	Enrico	Giulio	Nico	Stefano
Armando	Enzo	Giuseppe	Nicola	Teodoro
Aurelio	Ernesto	Gregorio	Nunzio	Tommaso
Bernardo	Eugenio	Guido	Orlando	Ugo
Bruno	Ezio	Leonardo	Paolo	Umberto
Camillo	Fabio	Leopoldo	Pasquale	Valentino
Carlo	Fabrizio	Lino	Patrizia	Valerio
Carmelo	Federico	Lorenzo	Pietro	Vincenzo
Cesare	Felice	Luca	Primo	Virgilio
Claudio	Filippo	Luciano	Renato	Vito
Cosimo	Francesco	Lucio	Renzo	Vittorio
Dante	Franco	Luigi	Riccardo	
Dario	Gaetano	Marco	Rico	
Desiderio	Gennaro	Mariano	Roberto	

Jewish

When we talk about a name being "Jewish," the meaning isn't always clear. Compare Irving, a Scottish surname once enthusiastically adopted by American Jews, with Ariel, a biblical Hebrew name that most Americans

1880   Today

think of as a Disney mermaid. Which one's the Jewish name? And why does it matter?

That back-and-forth between cultural and religious influences carries through many facets of the Jewish naming process. In fact, Jews commonly have two different names, the secular *kinnui* and the religious *shem hakodesh* (or "Hebrew name"). Already, that leaves you with twice as many names to pick out. But for an added wrinkle, many families like to choose religious and secular names that are related, to help link the two sides of life and represent a unified identity. Some will simply choose a single Hebrew name to be used in all contexts. Others choose a translation, a shared meaning, or a similar sound—a process that once turned little Moshe into Morris and today might transform a Shlomo into a Shane.

Beyond the meanings and derivations, there is the day-to-day reality of names that are culturally associated with Jews. Even among biblical names, only a select few—150 names—were traditionally considered suitable for a Jewish child. That's why Miriam sounds characteristically Jewish while Vashti does not.

You may be seeking a Jewish-sounding name as a proud cultural calling card for your child. Or you may be avoiding one, fearing discrimination. (For more on name discrimination, see the section on African-American names.) In either case, you're probably weighing the fate of names like Yitzhak and Freydl in a world full of Braydens and Isabellas.

So where do you find names that satisfy both your American style and your Jewish split? The list below is a collection of modern Hebrew names, attractive heirlooms from Jewish heritage, and a few names without religious origins that have been favored by Jewish families. (Consult the "Biblical" section for a list of Hebrew Bible names.) Stylistically, this group runs the gamut. If you're drawn to surnames like Tanner and Haley, check out Asher and Orly. If the old-time names warm your heart, try Hirsch and Leora. And if you're looking for an artistic splash, Raz and Aviva await.

GIRLS

Adi	Allegra	Avital	Bluma	Dalia
Adina	Amira	Aviva	Bracha	Dara
Adira	Ariel	Ayelet	Chava	Dina
Aliyah	Ariela	Bar	Chaya	Eliana
Aliza	Avia	Beth	Dafna	Eliora

Elisheva	Mahala	Raisa	Shani	Tova
Esther	Malka	Resha	Shifra	Yael
Gilia	Margalit	Reyna	Shira	Yaffa
Golda	Michal	Rivka	Shoshana	Zahava
Hadassah	Miri	Romi	Simcha	Ziva
Haia	Miriam	Ronit	Tali	
Ilana	Nava	Sadie	Talia	
Keren	Noa	Sarai	Tehila	
Leora	Orly	Shai	Tirzah	

BOYS

Adin	Boaz	Idan	Moshon	Tal
Adir	Chaim	Iser	Moss	Tamir
Admon	Doron	Israel	Nissim	Tevel
Akiva	Dov	Itai	Noam	Uri
Alon	Ehud	Jaco	Oz	Vidal
Alter	Eitan	Jaron	Pinchas	Yair
Amir	Elan	Lazar	Rahm	Yarden
Anat	Elisha	Leib	Raz	Yehuda
Ari	Elkan	Lev	Reuben	Yosef
Ariel	Gavriel	Liev	Ronen	Yuval
Asa	Gil	Lior	Sander	Zev
Asher	Haskell	Matan	Saul	Zvi
Avi	Herschel	Meir	Shai	
Barak	Hillel	Mordecai	Shia	
Baruch	Hirsch	Moshe	Shimon	

Lacy and Lissome

Femininity takes many forms. It can be sweet or sultry, mature or youthful, bold or demure. And on a really good day, it can be all of them at once.

1880   Today

    The Lacy and Lissome names capture a particular, melodious slice of the feminine spectrum. Even the modern creations among them have an age-old romantic style that could never be mistaken for a male name. These names also, on balance, sound grown-up. No Kitty or Buffy here.

They're old and new, exotic and American-born, but all are clearly and proudly feminine.

Aaliyah	Amiyah	Carissa	Ileana	Maricela
Abrianna	Anastasia	Cassandra	India	Mariela
Abriella	Anaya	Cassia	Isabella	Marietta
Acacia	Andrea	Christiana	Isannah	Marilla
Acadia	Angelia	Clarissa	Janessa	Marisa
Adela	Angelica	Corinna	Janiya	Marissa
Adelia	Angelina	Dahlia	Jordana	Mattea
Adelina	Aniyah	Dalia	Josefina	Melania
Adina	Annabella	Damiana	Juliana	Melia
Adira	Annika	Dania	Karina	Melina
Adria	Antonina	Daniela	Katharina	Molinda
Adriana	Anya	Dariana	Kiana	Melissa
Aelia	Aquila	Davina	Kiara	Miabella
Alana	Arabella	Deanna	Laelia	Miranda
Alannah	Araminta	Eleanora	Larissa	Mischa
Alaya	Aretha	Eliana	Lavinia	Nadia
Alejandra	Aria	Elina	Layla	Natalia
Alessandra	Ariana	Eliora	Leanna	Noelia
Alessia	Ariella	Elisa	Leila	Olivia
Alethea	Artemisia	Elisha	Leticia	Ophelia
Alexa	Arya	Elora	Liana	Oriana
Alexandra	Aryanna	Emilia	Lilia	Orleanna
Alexandria	Aubrianna	Evangelina	Liliana	Rafaela
Alexia	Audriana	Evanthia	Linnea	Raisa
Alia	Audrina	Evelina	Liora	Rianna
Aliana	Aurea	Felicia	Lisandra	Rihanna
Alicia	Aviana	Fiona	Livia	Romina
Alina	Aviva	Francesca	Liviana	Rosabella
Alisa	Ayanna	Gabriela	Luciana	Rosanna
Allegra	Azaria	Galilea	Maddalena	Roxanna
Alyssa	Bedelia	Georgiana	Mahalia	Sabina
Amanda	Belinda	Giovanna	Maira	Samara
Amara	Brianna	Graciela	Malia	Samira
Amarantha	Briella	Gratiana	Marcella	Saniya
Amaya	Calista	Ilana	Mariah	Sariah
Amira	Camila	Ilaria	Mariana	Savanna

Selena	Shoshana	Talia	Valencia	Violeta
Serena	Sienna	Tamara	Valeria	Viviana
Shania	Sierra	Tatiana	Vanessa	Zahara
Shayla	Stefania	Thalia	Venetia	
Shayna	Susanna	Tiana	Verena	

Ladies and Gentlemen

The wealthy industrialist. The stern great-aunt. They're the paragons of stuffy propriety, of heavy gowns and muttonchop whiskers. You may never have met them in person, but they occupy a clear place in your imagina-

1880   Today

tion: they are Ladies and Gentlemen, and you could hardly dream of using one of their names on a sweet little baby. Or could you?

Look through the list below, and you may discover that you don't actually *dislike* these names. The worst that can be said is that they're a bit heavy—baked puddings in an age of sorbet. We've already revived the lightest of the turn-of-the-century names, the Lillies and Isabellas, the Sams and Maxes. But when everything on the menu is light and refreshing, it's the warm and soothing items that start to stand out. And that's the upside of the stout, slow names. They have warmth, plus dignity to spare.

Roll them around in your mind for a while. You might find yourself warming to the idea of raising a true little Lady or Gentleman.

GIRLS

Ada	Audra	Clarice	Eleanor	Frieda
Adelaide	Augusta	Clementine	Eleanora	Geneva
Adele	Aurelia	Cora	Elinor	Georgianna
Adelia	Avis	Coralie	Eloise	Ginevra
Adeline	Beatrice	Coraline	Emelia	Golda
Agatha	Bedelia	Cordelia	Emeline	Greta
Alice	Beryl	Cornelia	Estella	Harriet
Alma	Blanche	Delia	Estelle	Helen
Almeda	Bluma	Delphia	Esther	Heloise
Althea	Caledonia	Diantha	Eudora	Henrietta
Amalia	Cecile	Dora	Eugenia	Hester
Angeline	Celestine	Dorothea	Flora	Honora
Antoinette	Christabel	Dulcie	Florence	Ida
Ardith	Clara	Edith	Frances	Imelda

Imogene	Louisa	Maude	Prudence	Theodora
Inez	Louise	Millicent	Rena	Thora
Iona	Lucille	Minerva	Rosa	Tilda
Iva	Magdalene	Muriel	Rosamond	Vera
Josefa	Maida	Nola	Rose	Viola
Lavinia	Margaret	Odessa	Rowena	Violette
Lenora	Marguerite	Olive	Sidonia	Virginia
Leona	Marilla	Paralee	Sybil	Wilhelmina
Leonor	Marion	Parthenia	Sylvia	Willa
Leontine	Martha	Petra	Thea	Winifred
Leora	Matilda	Philomena	Theda	Zelda

BOYS

Albert	Cecil	Ellsworth	Herbert	Luther
Alfred	Chester	Emil	Herman	Merritt
Ambrose	Clarence	Emory	Hiram	Oswald
Anatole	Claude	Ernest	Hobart	Otis
Ansel	Clement	Eugene	Holland	Percy
Archibald	Clifford	Ferdinand	Horace	Philo
Armand	Conrad	Forest	Hubert	Prescott
Arthur	Cornelius	Foster	Hugh	Randolph
August	Crawford	Francis	Hugo	Rudolph
Augustus	Cuthbert	Franz	Humphrey	Rupert
Bancroft	Cyril	Frederick	Jennings	Sylvester
Basil	Cyrus	George	Jules	Theodore
Bayard	Edmund	Gilbert	Julius	Thornton
Bernard	Edward	Godfrey	Lambert	Virgil
Bertram	Edwin	Granville	Leopold	Wallace
Burgess	Elden	Hamilton	Llewellyn	Walter
Casper	Elgin	Harold	Louis	Willis

Last Names First

Conventional surnames have arrived with a splash as first names. They appeal to creative namers with their freshness, while their familiarity and heritage keep them down to earth. Creative-rustic: it's the perfect new-millennium combo. No wonder these names are just catching on now . . . right?

1880   Today

Actually, what we're seeing today is only the latest wave of last-name crossovers. Starting at the turn of the *last* century, American parents flocked to the classic surnames of English literature and aristocracy. Those parents, including many poor immigrants, had grand dreams for their sons. They wanted to send them into the world with sophisticated names ready to take their places in fine society. Thus, they turned to such historical icons as (John) Milton and (Sir Philip) Sidney. Unfortunately for poor Milt and Sid, the actual aristocrats continued to give their sons names like John and Philip, and the elegance of their surnames quickly faded.

So how are the newly popular surnames different? The new favorites still lean on their British Isles heritage to conjure up a lifestyle, but that style is a far cry from the Oxbridge world of Milton and Sidney. Instead of nobility, we're seeing hardy tradesmen: Coopers, Tanners, and Masons. Parents have also turned away from England to focus on Irish and Scottish traditions: Riley, Mackenzie, Brennan. These new names are rugged and rakish—and they're used for boys *and* for girls.

Parents of boys delight in a new field of names with classically masculine features. The trade names in particular are brisk, direct, and stocked with hard consonants. For parents of girls, surnames present an opportunity to start afresh with names that carry no gender baggage.

So will these names escape the fate of Sid and Milt? Certainly, some portion of the new names will hold their ground over time to join the ranks of the perennials. Russell, for example, is an old surname that we now accept as a classic first name. Yet with any name group experiencing a surge of popularity comes the risk of a "freshness date" that soon passes. To avoid a trendy name with a short shelf life, consider some of the similar but less popular alternatives below. Better yet, search your own family tree for surnames that might be revived. When a name's significance is personal, it has roots that shifting fashions can't sweep away.

TRADE NAMES

Archer	*Bowman*
Bailey	*Bailiff, county officer*
Baker	*Baker*
Barker	*Tanner or shepherd*
Baxter	*Baker*
Bowman	*Archer*
Bridger	*Builder of bridges*

Carter	*Transporter of goods*
Carver	*Carver of wood or stone*
Chancellor	*Administrative officer*
Chandler	*Candle maker*
Chapman	*Merchant or peddler*
Collier	*Coal seller*
Cooper	*Barrel maker*
Coster	*Fruit seller or grower*
Currier	*Leather finisher*
Cutler	*Knife maker*
Deacon	*Deacon or deacon's servant*
Decker	*Builder or roofer*
Dexter	*Dyer*
Draper	*Maker or seller of cloth*
Farrier	*Iron worker*
Faulkner	*Falconer*
Fisher	*Fisherman*
Fletcher	*Arrow maker*
Forester	*Forest warden*
Foster	*Shearer*
Gardner	*Gardener*
Garner	*Keeper of the granary*
Glover	*Maker or seller of gloves*
Granger	*Farm bailiff*
Gunner	*Artillery operator*
Harper	*Harp player*
Hooper	*One who fits hoops on barrels*
Hunter	*Hunter*
Jagger	*Peddler*
Jenner	*Engineer*
Keeler	*Boat builder or pilot*
Keller	*Keeper of cellar stores*
Kingman	*Servant of the king*
Marshall	*Tender of horses/military officer*
Mason	*Stonemason*
Mercer	*Fabric merchant*

Miller	*Miller of grain*
Packer	*Wool packer*
Parker	*Gamekeeper*
Patten	*Clog maker*
Piper	*Piper*
Porter	*Gatekeeper or load-carrier*
Potter	*Pot maker*
Ranger	*Game warden*
Rhymer	*Poet or minstrel*
Ryder	*Mounted soldier or messenger*
Sadler	*Saddle maker*
Sailor	*Sailor*
Sargent	*Servant*
Sawyer	*One who saws wood*
Saylor	*Dancer or acrobat*
Schroeder	*Tailor*
Schuyler	*Scholar*
Shepard	*Shepherd*
Skipper	*Master of a ship*
Slater	*Slate roof maker*
Smith	*Metal worker*
Spearman	*Soldier armed with a spear*
Spellman	*Minstrel*
Spencer	*Pantry servant*
Spurrier	*Spur maker*
Sumner	*Court summoner*
Tanner	*Preparer of hides for leather*
Tasker	*Piece worker*
Taylor	*Tailor*
Thane	*Freeman or feudal baron*
Thatcher	*Straw roof maker*
Tillman	*Farmer*
Tucker	*Dresser of cloth*
Turner	*Lathe operator*
Tyler	*Tile maker*

Walker	Dresser of cloth
Weaver	Weaver
Webster	Weaver
Wheeler	Wheel maker
Wright	Builder or machinist

BRITISH ISLES SURNAMES

Adair	Barlow	Brigham	Casey	Courtney
Addison	Barrett	Briley	Cash	Cowan
Ailey	Barron	Brinley	Cason	Crawford
Ainsley	Barton	Brock	Cassidy	Crighton
Alden	Baylor	Broderick	Channing	Crockett
Aldrin	Beck	Brody	Chase	Cronin
Alton	Beckett	Brogan	Chauncey	Crosby
Ames	Beckham	Bronson	Claiborne	Cullen
Amory	Bellamy	Brooks	Clancy	Curran
Anderson	Bennett	Bryant	Clayton	Dabny
Aniston	Bentley	Bryer	Clemens	Dallin
Ansley	Benton	Bryson	Cleveland	Dalton
Arden	Berkeley	Buckley	Clifton	Daly
Arley	Blakely	Burgess	Clinton	Darby
Ashby	Blythe	Burke	Cody	Darcy
Ashley	Bond	Burton	Colby	Darnell
Ashton	Boone	Cabot	Coleman	Darwin
Aston	Bowen	Cadogan	Coley	Davis
Astor	Braddock	Calder	Colson	Dawson
Atley	Bradford	Callahan	Colton	Dayton
Aubrey	Bradley	Campbell	Connell	Deckard
Auden	Brady	Carey	Connery	Delaney
Austin	Brandt	Carling	Connolly	Dempsey
Autry	Brannigan	Carlisle	Conroy	Dennison
Avery	Brannon	Carlson	Conway	Devlin
Axton	Branson	Carlton	Coolidge	Dewey
Baldwin	Brantley	Carlyle	Copland	Dewitt
Bancroft	Braxton	Carrick	Cornell	Dickinson
Bannon	Breck	Carrigan	Corrigan	Dillon
Barclay	Brennan	Carrington	Cortland	Dixon
Barkley	Briggs	Carson	Coulter	Donnelly

Donovan	Fraser	Hatcher	Keegan	Lennon
Dorsey	Freeman	Hawkins	Kelly	Lennox
Doyle	Frost	Hayden	Kelsey	Lesley
Drake	Gage	Hayes	Kendall	Lincoln
Dwyer	Gaines	Henderson	Kendrick	Lindsay
Dyson	Gallagher	Hendrix	Kennedy	Linley
Eason	Gannon	Henley	Kennison	Locke
Eastman	Garland	Hennessy	Kent	Lofton
Easton	Garnett	Henson	Kenton	Logan
Edgerton	Garrick	Hillary	Kerrigan	Loudon
Edison	Garrison	Hilton	Kerry	Lowell
Elam	Gehrig	Hines	Kiefer	Lyman
Eldridge	Gentry	Hodge	Kiley	Mabry
Ellery	Gibson	Hogan	Kimberlin	Mackenzie
Ellington	Grady	Holden	Kingsley	Macy
Ellis	Grant	Holland	Kingston	Madden
Ellison	Gray	Hollis	Kinley	Maddox
Ellsworth	Grayson	Holliston	Kinsey	Madigan
Elton	Greer	Holt	Kinsley	Madison
Embry	Grover	Houston	Kirby	Maguire
Emerson	Griffith	Hudson	Knight	Mahoney
Emery	Guthrie	Hughes	Knox	Mallory
Emory	Hadley	Hutchison	Kramer	Manning
Ennis	Hailey	Jackson	Lacey	Mannix
Evans	Halston	Jacoby	Laird	Marley
Everett	Hamilton	Jameson	Lamont	Marlowe
Everly	Hampton	Janson	Landon	Maxfield
Everton	Hansen	Jarrett	Landry	Maxwell
Ewing	Hardy	Jarrod	Lane	McArthur
Farrell	Harlan	Jefferson	Laney	McCoy
Finley	Harley	Jennings	Langdon	McKay
Finnegan	Harlow	Jensen	Langston	McKenna
Flannery	Harmon	Jewell	Lanigan	McKinley
Flynn	Harriman	Jordan	Larkin	Meade
Foley	Harris	Judson	Larson	Merrick
Forbes	Harrison	Kane	Lawson	Merrigan
Ford	Hart	Keane	Leighton	Merrill
Forest	Hartley	Kearney	Leith	Merrin
Forrest	Haskell	Keaton	Leland	Merritt

Milton	Pryor	Seaver	Tilden	Wilton
Mitchell	Quaid	Seymour	Tinsley	Windsor
Monroe	Quincy	Shaw	Tobin	Winslow
Montague	Quinlan	Shea	Tomlin	Winston
Montgomery	Quinn	Shelby	Townes	Winton
Morris	Radley	Shelley	Tracy	Worth
Morrison	Rafferty	Shelton	Trent	Wyatt
Morton	Ramsay	Sheridan	Truman	Wylie
Murphy	Rance	Sherman	Tynan	Wyman
Murray	Reagan	Sherwin	Tyson	Yancey
Neilson	Redmond	Sherwood	Upton	York
Nelson	Reese	Sidney	Vance	
Newell	Reeve	Simpson	Varian	
Newman	Reid	Sinclair	Vaughn	
Newton	Reilly	Slade	Vernon	
Nicholson	Remington	Sloane	Vinson	
Norton	Rhodes	Spencer	Walden	
Oakley	Richmond	Stafford	Wallis	
O'Brien	Riddick	Stanford	Walton	
Olin	Ridley	Stanton	Warner	
O'Neill	Riley	Starling	Washington	
O'Rourke	Riordan	Steele	Watson	
Palmer	Ripley	Stewart	Watt	
Parrish	Roarke	Stockman	Waverly	
Patterson	Robinson	Stowe	Wayland	
Patton	Roby	Stratton	Webb	
Paxton	Rockwell	Stryker	Weldon	
Payne	Rodman	Sullivan	Wellington	
Payton	Rogers	Sutton	Wesley	
Pelham	Rollins	Taft	Weston	
Penn	Rooney	Talbot	Wharton	
Perrin	Ross	Talmadge	Whelan	
Pierson	Rowland	Tate	Whitley	
Powell	Ruffin	Tatum	Whitman	
Prentiss	Ryker	Terrell	Whitney	
Prescott	Ryland	Thornton	Wilder	
Presley	Sanders	Thurman	Willard	
Preston	Sanford	Thurston	Willis	
Pryce	Scott	Tierney	Wilson	

Spotlight: Clark Kent Names

With most names, a nickname just softens the full name or helps it loosen up and have fun. Occasionally, though, it offers you two complete and distinct identities, like Clark Kent and Superman. Take the formal, buttoned-down surname Thornton. Peel back its mild-mannered shell and you reveal—*blam!*—the dashing alter ego Thorn, or even the god Thor himself.

Not every name with a super-charged nickname can fit the bill. You can't get the Clark Kent effect by, say, extending Jazz into Jazztyn. The long version (typically a surname) has to be traditional and familiar in its own right, and the nickname has to emerge from it with an ease approaching inevitability. And just as in the world of superheroes, male examples dominate.

Bosley/Boss	Forsyth/Force	Marsden/	Thorn/
Dashiell/	Foxworth/Fox	Mars	Thor
Dash	Hawkins/	Riordan/Rio	Wolford/
Edgerton/	Hawk	Ripley/Rip	Wolf
Edge	Kingsley/King	Thornton/	

Latino/Latina

Luis. Juan. Jesús. Just look through the top 100 boys' names in America, and you'll see it plainly: Spanish names *are* American names, and they're more popular than ever before.

1880   Today

When we talk about Latino names, of course, we're not just referring to Spanish names. Families of Caribbean descent may have different tastes from Mexican-Americans or South Americans. Brazilians add Portuguese variations to the mix. Names of reverence, such as titles of the Virgin Mary (Lourdes, Rosario), are popular choices. And pop culture trends bring whole new surprises. Just look at Shakira, an Arabic name that became a Latina sensation thanks to the Arab-Colombian singer by that name.

The picture gets even more complicated when you consider boys and girls. Notice that all the popular examples we began with were male names. If you looked just at boys, you'd come away convinced that Latino-American parents are very traditional namers. Names like Juan, Carlos, Jorge, and Diego remain high on the charts even as their English counterparts John, Charles, George, and James slip away. Nine classic Spanish boys' names rank among the overall American top 100. But here's the kicker: the only classic Spanish girl's name ranked that high is the cross-cultural favorite Maria, and even that name is falling fast.

So what *are* parents naming girls? Top choices include across-the-board hits like Ashley, Alyssa, and Isabella. In many cases, though, girls are receiving names that were unknown here a few decades ago and that remain unfamiliar outside of Latino communities. Choices like Nayeli, Itzel, and Anahi took off overnight, and celebrities are a huge influence. Current name fashions in Latin America move quickly to the U.S. thanks to Spanish-language television.

The field is wide open for Latino parents, with names old and new— Spanish, Portuguese, English, and beyond. One special consideration for kids who will be growing up in a bilingual environment is choosing names that are attractive and easy to pronounce in both languages. Just try pronouncing Meadow in Spanish, for instance. And Itzel loses a lot of its charm with the English pronunciation "IHT-zul."

The list below includes perennials, rising stars, and a smattering of names that are off the beaten track today. This is a mixed Spanish and Portuguese list, so speakers of either language may find some unfamiliar or unexpected choices.

GIRLS

Abril	Amaya	Araceli	Berenice	Catalina
Adela	Amparo	Arely	Bianca	Catarina
Adelina	Ana	Ariadna	Bibiana	Cielo
Adriana	Anahi	Arleth	Blanca	Citlali
Alejandra	Analía	Aylin	Brisa	Constanza
Alicia	Angela	Azucena	Camila	Consuelo
Alma	Angelica	Azul	Carmela	Cristiana
Alondra	Anita	Beatriz	Carmen	Cristina
Amaris	Antonia	Belen	Carolina	Damaris

Daniela	Ines	Luciana	Odalys	Sofia
Dayana	Isabel	Luisa	Omayra	Sol
Dayanara	Isabela	Lupe	Oriana	Soledad
Dolores	Itzel	Luz	Orly	Sonia
Dora	Ivette	Magdalena	Paloma	Susana
Dulce	Jacinda	Maite	Paulina	Tania
Elena	Jaslene	Manuela	Perla	Teresa
Eliana	Jazmin	Marcela	Pilar	Thalia
Emiliana	Jimena	Marely	Quetzalli	Valencia
Esmeralda	Josefa	Margarita	Rafaela	Valeria
Esperanza	Josefina	Maria	Raquel	Vanessa
Estefania	Juana	Mariam	Reyna	Veronica
Estefany	Juanita	Mariana	Ría	Victoria
Estela	Juliana	Maribel	Rocío	Violeta
Estrella	Julieta	Maricela	Romina	Viviana
Eva	Julissa	Mariela	Rosa	Ximena
Evangelina	Karyme	Marisol	Rosalía	Xiomara
Fabiana	Leticia	Maritza	Rosalinda	Xochitl
Fabiola	Lidia	Martina	Rosario	Yadira
Fátima	Lilia	Mayra	Roselyn	Yahaira
Fernanda	Liliana	Mercedes	Roxana	Yamilet
Francisca	Lisandra	Micaela	Rubi	Yareli
Gabriela	Litzy	Milagros	Salma	Yaritza
Galilea	Lizbeth	Mireya	Sarahi	Yazmin
Genesis	Lizeth	Monserrat	Sarai	Yesenia
Genoveva	Lizette	Natalia	Selena	Yolanda
Giselle	Lluvia	Nayeli	Shakira	Yoselin
Graciela	Lorena	Noelia	Sherlyn	Yuliana
Guadalupe	Lourdes	Noemi	Silvia	Zayra
Iliana	Lucero	Nyasia	Socorro	

BOYS

Abdiel	Aldo	Amador	Arnulfo	Carlos
Abel	Alejandro	Amauri	Arturo	Cesar
Adan	Alexis	Andres	Aurelio	Cristian
Adolfo	Alfonso	Angel	Benito	Cristobal
Adrian	Alfredo	Anibal	Bernardo	Cruz
Adriel	Alonso	Antonio	Blas	Danilo
Agustin	Alonzo	Ariel	Braulio	Diego
Alberto	Álvaro	Armando	Camilo	Dimas

Diogo	Gael	João	Maximo	Ricardo
Domingo	Genaro	Joaquim	Miguel	Rico
Edgar	Gerardo	Joaquin	Misael	Rigoberto
Edgardo	German	Jorge	Moises	Roberto
Eduardo	Gilberto	José	Natanael	Rodolfo
Efrain	Gonzalo	Josué	Neftali	Rodrigo
Efren	Gregorio	Jovani	Nestor	Rogelio
Elian	Guadalupe	Juan	Nicolas	Rolando
Elias	Guillermo	Julian	Nuno	Ronaldo
Elio	Gustavo	Julio	Octavio	Ruben
Eliseo	Hector	Lazaro	Omar	Salvador
Eloy	Heriberto	Leandro	Orlando	Santiago
Emiliano	Hernan	Leonel	Oscar	Santos
Emilio	Horacio	Lisandro	Osvaldo	Sergio
Enrique	Hugo	Lorenzo	Pablo	Tadeo
Ernesto	Humberto	Lucio	Paulo	Tiago
Esai	Ignacio	Luis	Pedro	Ulises
Esteban	Iker	Manuel	Rafael	Vicente
Ezequiel	Isidro	Marcelo	Ramiro	Victor
Federico	Ismael	Marco	Ramon	Wilfredo
Felipe	Ivan	Marcos	Raul	Xavier
Fernando	Jacobo	Mariano	Raymundo	Yadiel
Fidel	Jadiel	Mario	Renato	Yahir
Flavio	Jaime	Mateo	Rene	Yandel
Francisco	Jairo	Mateus	Rey	
Gabriel	Javier	Mauricio	Reyes	
Gadiel	Jesus	Maximiliano	Reynaldo	

Literary and Artistic

Some names can conjure up a whole world. Heidi whisks you to a mountaintop in the Swiss Alps. Rhett drops you into the Civil War South. Holden mires you in adolescent angst. These names create worlds of their own because they exist in worlds of their own: literary worlds, often more intense and evocative than the real thing.

1880　Today

Not every great literary character translates into a literary baby name. Elizabeth Bennet of *Pride and Prejudice* may be the most beloved of all literary heroines, but the name Elizabeth isn't enough to summon up

Georgian England. The name has so many different associations that no single one sticks. But Darcy, now . . . ahh, Darcy. Suddenly, it's 1800 all over again.

You may choose a name like Darcy because you love the book, or the author, or the character and all he represents. Or you may just choose it because you like the sound. Even if that's the case, though, it pays to familiarize yourself with the name's literary associations. You may not think of Jane Austen when you hear the name Darcy, but plenty of others will.

Another name that summons Austen is, of course, Austen. Naming a child after an artist is subtly different from naming him after the artist's creations. It's an homage not just to the works, but to the creative spirit. Whatever the medium—literature, music, painting, dance—names linked to artists call up the power of an individual vision to entertain and to inspire.

For names from Shakespeare plays, see the Shakespearean list; for names from science fiction and fantasy literature, see the Fantastical list.

CHARACTERS/PLACES: GIRLS

Aida	Verdi opera
Avonlea	Prince Edward Island community in the "Anne of Green Gables" series
Briar	Brothers Grimm's fairy tale "Briar Rose"
Camille	Title of a novel, a ballet, and several plays
Carmen	Bizet opera
Coraline	Children's novel *Coraline*
Dagny	Character in *Atlas Shrugged*
Darcy	Surname in *Pride and Prejudice*
Ellery	"Ellery Queen" detective stories
Eloise	Title character in "Eloise" series of children's books
Estella	Character in *Great Expectations*
Guinevere	In Arthurian legend, the wife of King Arthur
Heidi	Johanna Spyri's novel *Heidi*
Hermione	Character in the "Harry Potter" series
Iolanthe	Gilbert and Sullivan comic opera
Isolde	Medieval romance and Wagner opera *Tristan und Isolde*
Lisbeth	Character in *The Girl with the Dragon Tattoo*
Lorna	Title character in novel *Lorna Doone*

Madeline	Ludwig Bemelmans's children's books (note that the literary link holds only if the name is pronounced to rhyme with "two straight lines in rain or shine")
Mehitabel	The cat in Don Marquis's *archy and mehitabel* stories
Ramona	Beverly Cleary "Ramona" series; Helen Hunt Jackson novel *Ramona*
Rilla	Character in *Rilla of Ingleside* ("Anne of Green Gables" series)
Rowena	Character in Sir Walter Scott's *Ivanhoe*
Scarlett	Character in *Gone with the Wind*
Scout	Character in *To Kill a Mockingbird*
Siddalee	Character in *Divine Secrets of the Ya-Ya Sisterhood*
Trilby	Title character of the gothic novel *Trilby*

CHARACTERS/PLACES: BOYS

Ahab	Character in *Moby Dick*
Aramis	One of *The Three Musketeers*
Atticus	Character in *To Kill a Mockingbird*
Bennet	Surname in *Pride and Prejudice*
Dickon	Character in *The Secret Garden*
Dorian	Title character of *The Picture of Dorian Gray*
Gulliver	Title character of *Gulliver's Travels*
Heathcliff	Character in *Wuthering Heights*
Holden	Character in *The Catcher in the Rye*
Horatio	C. S. Forester hero Horatio Hornblower; *Hamlet* character; writer Horatio Alger
Ichabod	Character in "The Legend of Sleepy Hollow"
Ivanhoe	Sir Walter Scott novel
Langdon	Character in *The Da Vinci Code*
Macon	Character in Toni Morrison's *Song of Solomon*
Merlin	Wizard in Arthurian legend
Pip	Character in *Great Expectations*
Rhett	Character in *Gone with the Wind*
Roark	Character in *The Fountainhead*
Sawyer	Title character of *The Adventures of Tom Sawyer*
Sherlock	Arthur Conan Doyle's Sherlock Holmes stories
Tristan	Medieval romance and Wagner opera *Tristan and Isolde*
Tristram	Title character of *Tristram Shandy*
Watson	Character in Sherlock Holmes stories

Anaïs	Writer Anaïs Nin
Artemisia	Painter Artemisia Gentileschi
Auden	Poet W. H. Auden
Carson	Writer Carson McCullers
Colette	Writer Colette
Eudora	Writer Eudora Welty
Flannery	Writer Flannery O'Connor
Frida	Painter Frida Kahlo
Harper	Writer Harper Lee
Isadora	Dancer Isadora Duncan
Jessye	Opera singer Jessye Norman
Mahalia	Gospel singer Mahalia Jackson
Marlowe	Writer Christopher Marlowe; Raymond Chandler's detective Philip Marlowe
Twyla	Dancer/choreographer Twyla Tharp
Willa	Writer Willa Cather
Zelda	Writer/Jazz Age icon Zelda Fitzgerald
Zora	Writer Zora Neale Hurston

Alcott	Writer Louisa May Alcott
Aldous	Writer Aldous Huxley
Amadeus	Composer Wolfgang Amadeus Mozart; play *Amadeus* about him
Anatole	Writer Anatole France
Ansel	Photographer Ansel Adams
Armistead	Writer Armistead Maupin
Austen	Writer Jane Austen
Banjo	Australian poet Banjo Paterson
Beckett	Playwright Samuel Beckett
Bram	Writer Bram Stoker
Byron	Poet Lord Byron
Calder	Artist Alexander Calder
Clemens	Writer Samuel Clemens/Mark Twain
Copland	Composer Aaron Copland
Cormac	Writer Cormac McCarthy
Dante	Writer Dante Alighieri
Dashiell	Writer Dashiell Hammett
Dickinson	Poet Emily Dickinson

Dylan	Poet Dylan Thomas; musician Bob Dylan
Eames	Designers Charles and Ray Eames
Eliot	Writers T. S. Eliot and George Eliot
Ellington	Composer and bandleader Duke Ellington
Ellison	Writer Ralph Ellison
Emerson	Writer Ralph Waldo Emerson
Escher	Artist M. C. Escher
Faulkner	Writer William Faulkner
Frost	Poet Robert Frost
Haydn	Composer Franz Joseph Haydn
Jackson	Painter Jackson Pollock
Kipling	Writer Rudyard Kipling
Langston	Poet Langston Hughes
Leonardo	Renaissance man Leonardo da Vinci
Maxfield	Artist Maxfield Parrish
Melville	Writer Herman Melville
Michelangelo	Artist Michelangelo di Lodovico Buonarroti Simoni
Rand	Writer Ayn Rand
Romare	Artist Romare Bearden
Seeger	Folk singer Pete Seeger
Sinclair	Writers Sinclair Lewis and Upton Sinclair
Søren	Philosopher Søren Kierkegaard
Tennyson	Poet Alfred Lord Tennyson
Truman	Writer Truman Capote
Upton	Writer Upton Sinclair
Wharton	Writer Edith Wharton
Whitman	Poet Walt Whitman
Winslow	Painter Winslow Homer

Long Gone

Admit it. You love bad baby names.

Oh, it's not that you're about to name your twin sons Pink and Dink. But you get a wicked little thrill hearing about celebrities who saddle their kids with outrageous names. Perhaps you even scan birth announcements for evidence that parents in your own neighborhood have lost their minds. Around the water cooler, you swap tales of the wackiest, ugliest, and just plain worst names you've ever heard.

Baby name schadenfreude is part of the fabric of our times. There are whole websites devoted to making fun of the strange names that pop up all around us. Underlying it all is a presumption that names are getting worse. The popularity of luxury brand names like Lexus and Armani, for instance, is taken as a symbol of cultural decay. Whether it's in Hollywood or just down the street, most of us agree: names have gone wild.

Before we proclaim a naming apocalypse, though, a bit of perspective is in order. Allow me to present some of the top 1000 names of the '80s and '90s. The 1880s and 1890s, that is. The boys Pink and Dink? Not so strange back in those days. In fact, Pink ranked as high as #304 among boys back in 1881. And Pink's sisters might well have been called Icy and Dicy . . . or even Spicy and Vicy.

Some of the Long Gone names hearken back to an age of immigrants. Others simply remind us of how fickle fashion really is. They're not necessarily "bad" names—just out of step, out of sight, and out of mind in today's naming culture. Browsing through them may give us some reassurance in this age of lightning-fast fashion change. If our ancestors managed to survive names like Pink and Dink, our kids should do just fine with whatever we choose.

The names below were all, at some point, among the 1000 most popular choices in America. For name thrill-seekers, I've included a special section of some of the most remarkable names ever to hit the charts . . . including a few—marked by an asterisk (*)—that are in the top 1000 today.

LONG-GONE GIRLS

Albina	Fleta	Louvenia	Omie	Vernie
Arvilla	Floy	Lovie	Onie	Versie
Belva	Hassie	Loyce	Osie	Vertie
Bridie	Helma	Ludie	Ozella	Viney
Creola	Hermina	Lugenia	Parthenia	Vesta
Cuba	Hertha	Luzetta	Permelia	Wava
Dezzie	Hildred	Manervia	Sudie	Wilda
Easter	Hortencia	Missouri	Tempie	Zona
Edmonia	Huldah	Mozell	Tennessee	
Electa	Ilo	Myrl	Texanna	
Elva	Izetta	Nova	Velva	
Etter	Izora	Ocie	Verdie	
Eulalie	Lemma	Odie	Vergie	
Exie	Lockie	Olie	Verlie	

Alvah	Delmer	Finis	Loy	Rolla
Arvid	Doctor	Gee	Loyal	Sim
Arvil	Dorman	Golden	Norval	Squire
Author	Duff	Gust	Okey	Urban
Bluford	Durward	Handy	Omer	Vester
Bonnie	Ebb	Helmer	Orlo	Volney
Burley	Egbert	Hosie	Otho	Waino
Chancy	Eloy	Hosteen	Press	Zollie
Clell	Elzie	Junious	Primus	
Commodore	Ezell	Justo	Purl	
Darold	Ferd	Laddie	Reason	

LONG-GONE GIRLS: AND SPECIAL HONORS TO . . .

Chestina	Icy	Media	Ova	Spicy
Dicy	Karma*	Mintie	Pinkie	Tiny
Dimple	Mammie	Mossie	Princess*	Vicy
Fairy	Marvel	Novella	Shelva	

LONG-GONE BOYS: AND SPECIAL HONORS TO . . .

Bee	Flem	Minor	Pleas	Toy
Cloyd	Green	Moody	Primitivo	
Creed	Lemon	Octave	Profit	
Dink	Manly	Orange	Ransom	
Fate	Messiah*	Pink	Sincere*	

Macho Swagger

Snapshots of classic masculinity: a policeman in uniform, a businessman in suit and tie, a father tossing a ball to his kids. Those are all manly images, and there are plenty of names to match. But suppose the image you have in mind is a little more . . . raw. A boxer, say, or a gunslinger. Or perhaps a guy who kills a giant grizzly with his bare hands, then picks his teeth with its bones. That's where the Macho Swagger names come in.

Most of the names below are cheerfully rugged. Some are little more wild, and a few might make you want to cross to the other side of the street. If your son does grow up to be a boxer or a grizzly bear assassin, he'll be in great shape with any of these names. But before you make your final choice, be sure to picture him in other kinds of masculine roles too. If an orthodontist or music teacher named Spike sounds just as good to you, go for it.

Ace	Clint	Ike	Maxx	Sinbad
Ajax	Colt	Jagger	Ranger	Slade
Apollo	Crash	Jaxx	Remington	Slater
Blade	Crew	Jazz	Rex	Spike
Blaze	Crockett	Jetson	Rico	Steele
Bo	Dash	Jett	Rider	Stetson
Bond	Deuce	King	Rocco	Stone
Bridger	Dino	Kirk	Rock	Strider
Brock	Dirk	Knight	Rocket	Stryker
Bronson	Drake	Mace	Rockwell	Tahnk
Bruno	Duke	Mack	Rocky	Thor
Buck	Dutch	Maddox	Rod	Tiger
Butch	Edge	Magnum	Rowdy	Tito
Buzz	Gunner	Major	Ruff	Vito
Cannon	Hawk	Mars	Ryder	Wolf
Cash	Hunter	Maverick	Ryker	Wolfgang
Champ	Hutch	Maximus	Samson	Zeus

Mid-Century America

When you read about the baby boom generation today, it's usually in the context of long-term health care plans or the future of Social Security. Their names, though, reflect the spirit of the days when the boomers really were babies.

1880   Today

The names that surged after World War II tend to be a modest, friendly bunch. They don't try to sound fancy or exotic—compare two of the trendiest boys' names of the time, Larry and Roger, to today's hits like Sebastian and Xavier. The biggest foreign influence you'll see is French endings for familiar girls' names, like Suzanne and Annette.

So what were the parents of the '50s aiming for with their name choices? If you scan the list, the most common theme is that these names sound *happy*. Not breezy and carefree, like the surfer names that followed in the '60s, but happy and relaxed. If the names we give our children represent our hopes for the future, names like Kathie and Jerry, Darlene and

Butch, are dreams of contentment. A comfortable home, good friends, and kids playing in the yard. That's still a dream plenty of us share.

Of course, the generation on which those contented names were bestowed ended up far from content. The little Kathys and Jerrys born in 1950 grew up to be the protesters, free-lovers, and Woodstock attendees of 1969. Their very discontent revolutionized American society.

The '50s names, though, don't care about the politics. They just want to be happy—and happiness never goes out of style.

GIRLS

Annette	Debra	Joanie	Marybeth	Sherry
Barbra	Dee	Jolene	Maureen	Sondra
Becky	Denise	Joy	Merry	Sonja
Betsy	Diane	Judy	Mimi	Sue
Bobbie	Donna	Julie	Mitzi	Suellen
Bonnie	Doreen	Karen	Nanette	Susan
Brenda	Dreama	Kathleen	Pamela	Suzanne
Candace	Francine	Kathy	Patrice	Teresa
Cathie	Gail	Kaye	Patti	Terry
Charlene	Gay	Kim	Paula	Theresa
Cheryl	Ginny	Lana	Paulette	Trudy
Cinda	Glenda	Linda	Peggy	Valerie
Cindy	Glinda	Lucinda	Penny	Vicki
Colette	Gwen	Lynette	Regina	Vonda
Colleen	Jan	Lynn	Ronna	Wanda
Connie	Janet	Marcia	Rosanne	Yolanda
Cynthia	Janice	Margo	Roxanne	Yvonne
Darla	Jayne	Marla	Sandra	
Darlene	Jeannine	Marlene	Sharon	
Debbie	Jerri	Marsha	Sheila	
Deborah	Jo	Maryanne	Shelley	

BOYS

Alan	Cliff	Del	Dwight	Jay
Barry	Dan	Dennis	Frankie	Jeffrey
Bruce	Dana	Denny	Gary	Jerry
Butch	Danny	Dino	Gerald	Jim
Cary	Darrell	Donnie	Glenn	Jimmy
Chip	Davey	Douglas	Gregory	Johnny
Chuck	Dean	Duane	Hank	Jon

Kenneth	Mark	Randall	Rodney	Terrence
Kenny	Marty	Randy	Roger	Terry
Kent	Mel	Reggie	Ron	Timothy
Kerry	Mickey	Reginald	Ronnie	Tony
Kim	Mike	Rich	Russell	Von
Larry	Mitch	Rick	Sandy	Wally
Lenny	Monte	Ricky	Skip	Wayne
Les	Nicky	Robin	Stephen	
Lorne	Perry	Rock	Steve	
Lyndon	Phillip	Rod	Steven	

Modern Meanings

Most names have literal meanings attached to them, if you dig deeply enough. Cameron comes from a Gaelic phrase meaning "crooked nose." Melissa is Greek for "bee." When you hear Cameron and Melissa, though, you simply hear names. Their derivations are historical curiosities that don't have much of an influence on their style.

For some names, though, meaning is everything. These are names whose origins aren't lost in the mist, but come through loud and clear to modern English speakers. For names like Destiny and Maverick, meaning *is* style.

Meaning names are on the rise, with bold, self-affirming words leading the pack. Familiar word-names of generations past were typically gentle souls, like flowers and virtues (see the "Charms and Graces" style section). The Modern Meanings, in comparison, are bursting with confidence. With names like Heaven and Justice, you're making it clear that you expect your children to take on the world, with aplomb.

GIRLS

America	Cadence	Desiree	Emerald	Genesis
Angel	Caprice	Destiny	Epiphany	Glory
Arcadia	Charisma	Diamond	Essence	Golden
Aria	Cherish	Dreama	Eternity	Halcyon
Auburn	Cielo	Dynasty	Evening	Halo
Autumn	Cinnamon	Ebony	Ever	Harmony
Bliss	Clarity	Eden	Fantasia	Haven
Blithe	Crystal	Ember	Gala	Heaven

Honesty	Kyrielle	Odyssey	Serenade	Tempest
Honor	Lark	Onyx	Serene	Terra
Hosanna	Liberty	Paisley	Serenity	Tiara
Ily	Lux	Paz	Shekinah	Tierra
(textspeak	Lyric	Phoenix	Skye	Treah
for "I Love	Madrigal	Poet	Sol	(Heart
You")	Meadow	Prairie	Sonnet	backward)
Indigo	Melody	Precious	Star	Trinity
Jade	Miracle	Princess	Stormy	Unique
Jasmine	Misty	Promise	Story	Unity
Jewel	Mystique	Raine	Summer	Vanity
Journey	Nevaeh	Raven	Sun	Velvet
Jubilee	(Heaven	Saga	Sunshine	Whisper
Justice	backward)	Sage	Swan	Winter
Karma	Ocean	Scarlett	Symphony	Zion
Kyrie	Oceana	Scout	Teal	

BOYS

Amen	Fate	Lyric	Quill	Timber
Arrow	Flint	Marquis	Reason	Truth
Bodhi	Gauge	Marshal	Roan	Tyme
Briar	Hawk	Maverick	Royal	Valor
Chance	Indigo	Merit	Sage	West
Clarion	Ivory	Messiah	Shadow	Winter
Cloud	Jett	Noble	Sincere	Wisdom
Creed	Justice	Pax	Squire	Worth
Deuce	King	Price	Storm	Zephyr
Diamond	Lynx	Prince	Talon	Zion

Spotlight: Siblings for Nevaeh?

So you named your first daughter Nevaeh—"heaven" spelled backward. Now baby #2 is on the way and you want another hidden-message name. Where to turn? It's slim pickings, but here are some anagrammatic and word-play name ideas with help from the readers of the *Baby Name Wizard* blog.

Cloie	Galen	Noel	Sutter	Traeh
(cielo)	(angel)	Dove	(truest)	(heart/
Delia	Ily (I Love	(loved	Tanis	Earth)
(ideal)	You	one)	(saint)	
Evoli	Loah	Reesen		
(I love)	(halo)	(serene)		

Muslim

Names in the Arab and Muslim worlds are typically formed from common Arabic phrases with felicitous meanings. Many popular names represent the values most esteemed in Islam, such as praise (Hamid), purity (Tahira), and service to Allah (Abdullah). Names of the Prophet Mohammed's close associates, such as his daughter Fatima, are also prevalent. And the name Mohammed itself, in many different spellings, is the most common name on the planet.

1880   Today

As with all names, though, the literal origin doesn't tell the full story of the name's popularity. Jamil, for instance, comes from the Arabic word for "beautiful," but it is also popular in non-Arabic-speaking regions of Africa that have Muslim traditions. Many non-Muslim African-Americans, in turn, have adopted the name to reflect their African ancestry.

Arabic and Muslim names are increasingly familiar and popular in the U.S., with dozens among America's top 1000 names. For American-born parents, including Black Muslims, names with a strong "ee" sounds like Kareem and Malik, have been particular favorites. (Double-"e" spellings like Kareem are characteristically American, while "i" spellings like Karim are more common internationally.) The selections below include traditional names with a sound and style attractive to American parents.

GIRLS

Aisha	Anisa	Basma	Fatima	Jamila
Amani	Asma	Dalia	Hadiyah	Khadijah
Amina	Aziza	Faiza	Halima	Latifa
Amira	Azra	Farida	Jalila	Layla

Leila	Nadia	Rania	Shakila	Zahra
Mahala	Nahla	Razia	Shakira	
Malak	Naima	Safiya	Soraya	
Maryam	Nazia	Salima	Tahira	
Nabila	Noor	Samira	Yasmin	

BOYS

Abdullah	Farid	Jamal	Mohammed	Sharif
Ahmad	Habib	Jamil	Muhammad	Syed
Ahmed	Hakeem	Kadir	Mustafa	Taj
Akeem	Hamid	Kamil	Nasir	Tariq
Ali	Hamza	Kareem	Omar	Yusuf
Amir	Hassan	Khalid	Raheem	Zaid
Atif	Ibrahim	Khalil	Rasheed	Zain
Bashir	Imran	Latif	Reza	
Basim	Ismail	Mahmoud	Salim	
Bilal	Jafar	Malik	Salman	
Faisal	Jaleel	Mamadou	Samir	

Mythological

Mythology is a mixture of literature and religion, history and fantasy. Mythological names, in turn, are at once traditional and imaginative. A handful of these names, like Diana and Jason, are familiar enough that their modern associations outweigh their classical origins. Others, like Apollo and Thor, still sound fantastical enough to rule the heavens.

The greatest naming potential may lie with the less familiar deities. Names like Thalia and Clio (Greek muses) echo their fabulous past gently and gracefully. They could be elegant ways to invoke a bit of magic for your child.

The names below include figures from the Celtic, Norse, Egyptian, and (primarily) Greco-Roman traditions.

GIRLS

Aeron	Andromeda	Artemis	Calliope	Chloris
Aine	Aoife	Athena	Callisto	Clio
Althea	Ariadne	Aurora	Cassandra	Dafne

Danae	Freya	Ishara	Melia	Rhiannon
Daphne	Gaia	Isis	Minerva	Selene
Despina	Halcyon	Jocasta	Morrigan	Sibyl
Diana	Halia	Juno	Niamh	Silvia
Doris	Hermione	Larisa	Niobe	Thalia
Echo	Hestia	Lavinia	Pandora	Venus
Electra	Ianthe	Leda	Penelope	Vesper
Eris	Io	Lilith	Persephone	Vesta
Eudora	Ione	Lorelei	Phaedra	Xanthe
Evadne	Irene	Luna	Phyllis	
Flora	Iris	Maia	Rhea	

BOYS

Achilles	Apollo	Hector	Mars	Orpheus
Adonis	Atlas	Hermes	Mercury	Theseus
Ajax	Chiron	Jason	Morpheus	Thor
Alastor	Damon	Jupiter	Odin	Ulysses
Alpheus	Endymion	Leander	Oisin	Vidar
Amon	Evander	Linus	Orion	Zeus

Namesakes

Ever meet a kid named Kermit? It's a quirky Irish classic with a contemporary sound. Shouldn't that make for a hit? But of course, it's also a Muppet frog, and hard to think of any other way. The name, for all its appeal, has disappeared.

Certain characters, real and fictional, simply claim possession of their first names. Elvis *is* Elvis Presley just as Kermit *is* a frog. At least those are positive associations. A young Kermit may be in for a little kidding, but the name remains charming. The situation becomes more serious when a name's associations are sinister. (Adolf is the ultimate example.)

Each of the names on this list is culturally linked to an individual image. Some links are stronger than others, and many of them actually work to the name's advantage. But in each case, the association is something you must make peace with before choosing the name for your child. For more associations, see the names in the "Literary and Artistic" style section.

Adolf (Hitler)
Akon (singer)
Alanis (Morissette)
Amos ('n' Andy)
Anaïs (Nin)
Aretha (Franklin)
Ariel (Disney's *Little Mermaid*)
Avril (Lavigne)
Axl (Rose)
Barack (Obama)
Barbie (doll)
Barney (singing dinosaur)
Beckham (David)
Benito (Mussolini)
Beyoncé (Knowles)
Booker (T. Washington)
Brando (Marlon)
Britney (Spears)
Buffy (Vampire Slayer)
Cary (Grant)

Casper (Friendly Ghost)
Charlize (Theron)
Cher (entertainer)
Coco (Chanel)
Clifford (Big Red Dog)
Coulter (Ann)
Darwin (Charles)
Demi (Moore)
Denzel (Washington)
Dilbert (comic strip)
Django (Reinhardt)
Dolly (Parton)
Dudley (Dursley, Do-Right)
Ebenezer (Scrooge)
Edsel (Ford)
Elmer (Fudd)
Elmo (Muppet)
Elvira (Mistress of the Dark)

Elvis (Presley)
Fabio (model)
Farrah (Fawcett)
Fidel (Castro)
Garth (Brooks)
Gehrig (Lou)
Grover (Muppet)
Gwyneth (Paltrow)
Hannibal (Lecter)
Hendrix (Jimi)
Hester (Prynne)
Homer (Simpson)
Humphrey (Bogart)
Imelda (Marcos)
Jagger (Mick)
Jemima (Aunt)
Jezebel (biblical villain)
John Paul (pope)
Kanye (West)
Katrina (hurricane)

Keanu (Reeves)
Kelis (singer)
Kermit (the Frog)
Kramer (*Seinfeld* character)
LeBron (James)
Lennon (John)
Linus (*Peanuts*)
Lolita (Nabokov's nymphet)
Madonna (entertainer)
Marley (Bob)
Merlin (wizard)
Moby (musician, whale)
Napoleon (Bonaparte)
Oprah (Winfrey)
Osama (bin Laden)
Presley (Elvis)
Rihanna (singer)
Ringo (Starr)

Rudolph (the Red-Nosed Reindeer)
Rush (Limbaugh)
Saddam (Hussein)
Sade (singer)
Satchel (Paige)
Shania (Twain)
Shaquille (O'Neal)
Sinéad (O'Connor)
Siri (iPhone voice)
Sojourner (Truth)
Tallulah (Bankhead)
Tenzin (Gyatso)
Tiger (Woods)
Tupac (Shakur)
Uma (Thurman)
Usher (singer)
Waldo (Where's . . .)

New Classics

This is supposed to be the steadiest of all style categories: the "new reliables." They're the names that have held their ground as American favorites for two generations, but no more than that. As a result, they're too young to sound old, and too established to sound trendy.

1880   Today

When you give your child a name like Evan or Allison, you should be able to breathe easy. No snide comments, no second-guessing. The New Classics should be trend-proof and tease-proof, relaxed and secure. They're youthful, but grow up well.

Notice, though, that I've said the words "should" and "supposed to" a lot. In fact, this category of names is seeing tremendous turnover. The problem is that safe, reliable names don't stand out. Today's parents are increasingly willing to accept some raised eyebrows and wrinkled noses to make sure that their children's names stand apart from the pack.

That means the New Classics list is shrinking. I've had to strike out old friends like Amanda and Megan, Eric and Brandon. Those names are still around, but they're falling fast, victims of their own normalcy. A few new-new classics have risen to take their places; names like Autumn and Chase have stuck around long enough to become adults. But for every new addition, two old favorites move to the retro column.

You can still feel confident that the names on this list are familiar, well liked, and resistant to prejudice and preconceptions. Those are powerful virtues, especially if you fear your child might be vulnerable to prejudice in other ways. But when it comes to predicting the future, even for these steadiest of names, all bets are off.

GIRLS

Abby	Brooke	Jillian	Melanie	Sasha
Adriana	Cara	Jocelyn	Melody	Sonia
Adrienne	Carly	Julianne	Meredith	Summer
Alana	Cassandra	Kara	Miranda	Talia
Alexandra	Clarissa	Kendra	Nadia	Tessa
Allison	Daniela	Lara	Natalie	Vanessa
Amanda	Gabrielle	Laurel	Sabrina	
Andrea	Janelle	Leslie	Samantha	

Aaron	Cameron	Damon	Joshua	Ryan
Adam	Chase	Derek	Justin	Seth
Andre	Christian	Drew	Kelvin	Spencer
Blake	Christopher	Evan	Kendrick	Trent
Bradley	Cole	Garrett	Kevin	
Brendan	Colin	Hunter	Lucas	
Bryan	Connor	Ian	Matthew	
Bryce	Damian	Jonathan	Micah	

Nickname-Proof

The title of this style is false advertising. No name is
100% nickname-proof. There's always the first-initial
approach, such as "T" for Tiernan, or the descriptive
nickname, like Red for a redhead. Or just the total hap-

1880   Today

penstance, like the toddler called Bear because he loves to growl. If it's
really meant to be, that nickname will find its way to your child.

More and more, though, full names are fighting back. It's common
today to meet a little Daniel or James who doesn't answer to Danny or
Jim. The full names sound more fashionable, and parents are insisting on
them. If your dream is raising a little Katherine-not-Kathy, your chances
of success are better than ever.

For the best possible odds of keeping nicknames at bay, here is a collection of multi-syllable names with no common pet forms.

Afton	Autumn	Chelsea	Denise	Giselle
Aida	Ava	Chloe	Devin	Gloria
Ailsa	Avis	Clara	Donna	Gretchen
Alma	Bonnie	Clarice	Dora	Haley
Amber	Brenda	Colleen	Ebony	Hannah
Amy	Brenna	Daisy	Eileen	Harmony
April	Briar	Dalia	Emma	Hayden
Asia	Bristol	Dana	Erica	Hazel
Aspen	Caprice	Daphne	Erin	Heather
Athena	Carmen	Darcy	Fallon	Hillary
Audra	Celeste	Daria	Farrah	Holly
Audrey	Charity	Delia	Flannery	Iris

Isis	Lyra	Myra	Renee	Tanya
Ivy	Mallory	Nadia	Rhoda	Tara
Justice	Mara	Naomi	Robin	Tatum
Justine	Margo	Nia	Ruby	Tegan
Kara	Mariah	Nina	Sarai	Thalia
Karen	Marian	Nora	Scarlett	Theda
Keira	Marion	Norma	Shana	Tova
Keisha	Marley	Paris	Shania	Vera
Kelsey	Marlo	Paula	Shannon	Wanda
Kendra	Maura	Peyton	Sheila	Whitney
Kiara	Maya	Phoebe	Sienna	Willow
Kyra	Mia	Piper	Sierra	Zara
Leslie	Mira	Portia	Simone	Zelda
Lila	Morgan	Rachel	Sonia	Zoe
Lisa	Muriel	Regan	Summer	Zora

BOYS

Aaron	Carter	Dion	Gavin	Linus
Adam	Cary	Dorian	Griffin	Logan
Adrian	Cecil	Duncan	Harlan	Marcel
Aidan	Clarence	Dunstan	Haskell	Mario
Alden	Cody	Eamon	Hayden	Marius
Alec	Colin	Easton	Hector	Miles
Amos	Conan	Egan	Holden	Milo
Ari	Corey	Eli	Horace	Morgan
Arlo	Dallas	Elliott	Ian	Nigel
Atticus	Dalton	Ellis	Jamal	Noah
Austin	Damian	Emerson	Jared	Nolan
Avery	Damon	Emmett	Jaron	Omar
Ayden	Dante	Emory	Jarrett	Oscar
Baron	Darian	Eric	Jarvis	Otto
Brady	Darius	Ethan	Justin	Owen
Braxton	Darrell	Evan	Keegan	Palmer
Brendan	Darren	Everett	Kellen	Parker
Brennan	Darryl	Ewan	Kelvin	Peyton
Brian	Dawson	Ezra	Kevin	Porter
Bryant	Dayton	Fabian	Kyle	Quentin
Byron	Derek	Felix	Lamar	Riley
Carson	Devin	Forrest	Landon	Rory
Carsten	Diego	Foster	Liam	Roscoe

Rowan	Shannon	Theron	Turner	Warren
Ryan	Soren	Tiernan	Ulysses	Wyatt
Ryder	Sterling	Travis	Upton	
Sawyer	Tanner	Trevor	Walker	

Nicknames

You love the nickname Annie, but Ann seems too plain.
You want to name your son after Grandpa Ron . . .
but Ronald? No way.
You're not alone. Plenty of parents start with a nickname they like and work backward from there. A strong nickname can
be the real power behind a full name. Zeke, for instance, has fueled the
resurrection of Ezekiel, and Tess gives Theresa a fresh kick.

Some parents even go a step further, ditching the traditional full
name and bestowing the nickname straight up. A pure nickname gives
parents more control: if you really love Betsy, why choose Elizabeth and
risk your daughter ending up a Liz? It's especially tempting when a cool
nickname derives from a dud full name. But the downside is a loss of
flexibility. Just plain Matt may find himself yearning for the more formal
Matthew on serious occasions. Betsy might seem more like an Elizabeth
(or Eliza, or Liddy) after all. And the occasional use of a longer name
can be a sweet term of endearment . . . or a good way to signal that your
child darned well better come down to dinner by the count of three, or
else!

Below you'll find many familiar nicknames. If you're a nickname
lover, you can just take them straight. But if you're open to full names,
this Nickname Wizard includes a variety of formal starting points for
each name. You might just find a way to honor that beloved, name-im-
paired relative after all.

GIRLS

Nickname	Full Names
Abby	Abigail, Abilene, Abrielle
Addie	Ada, Adelaide, Addison, Adeline, Adriana, Adela, Adele, Adelia, Adina, Adira, Adelia, Ariadne
Alex	Alexandra, Alexa, Alexia, Alexis, Alexandria
Allie, Ali	Allison, Alice, Alexandra, Alexandria, Alana, Aliyah, Alyssa, Alize, Alisa, Allegra, Alexis

Angie	Angela, Angel, Angelica, Angelina, Angeline, Angelique, Angelia
Annie	Ann, Anne, Anna, Annabelle, Annalise, Annika, Annette, Antonia, Anthea, Brianne, Roxanne
Becky	Rebecca, Bianca
Beth, Bess	Elizabeth, Bethany, Lisbeth, Maribeth, Elspeth, Bethan, Bethel
Betsy, Betty	Elizabeth, Bettina
Billie	Wilhelmina, Willa, Sybil, Jubilee, Abilene
Bobbie	Barbara, Roberta, Robin
Bree	Bridget, Brianna, Brittany, Bria, Gabrielle, Sabrina, Brisa, Briony, Aubree, Briella, Abril, Aubrianna
Callie	Caroline, Carolina, Callista, Calla, Calliope
Cammie	Camilla, Camille, Camellia, Campbell, Cambria, Cameron, Camryn, Camdyn
Candy	Candace, Candida
Carly	Carla, Carlotta, Caroline, Carolina, Scarlett, Carmela
Carrie	Caroline, Carolyn, Carissa, Carol, Carmen, Carmela, Carolina, Carys, Carrington
Cassie	Cassandra, Cassia, Cassidy, Catherine
Ceil	Cecilia, Cecile, Celine, Celeste, Celia
Charlie	Charlotte, Charlene, Charlize, Charla
Chrissy, Chris	Christine, Christina, Christa, Christiane, Crystal
Cindy	Cynthia, Lucinda, Cinderella, Cinda, Sinéad
Connie	Constance, Concetta, Consuelo, Cornelia
Corrie	Cora, Coralie, Corazon, Cordelia, Corinna, Corliss, Coral, Coraline
Debbie	Deborah, Debra, Devorah
Dell	Adelaide, Della, Adele, Delphine, Delta, Delilah, Delaney, Delia
Demi	Demitra, Demetria
Dolly	Dorothy, Dolores, Dorothea
Dottie	Dorothy, Dorothea, Donatella
Edie	Edith, Edna, Eden
Ellie, Elle	Ella, Ellen, Eleanor, Elizabeth, Helen, Eloise, Electra, Elena, Eleni, Eliana, Elise
Elsie	Elizabeth, Alice, Elsa, Elspeth, Elise, Eloise
Emmie	Emily, Emmaline, Emma, Emelia, Emory, Embry, Emerald, Emerson

Evie	Eve, Eva, Evelyn, Evita, Evangeline, Genevieve, Evadne
Fifi	Josephine, Sofia, Fiona, Delphine, Seraphina, Saphira
Flo	Florence, Flora, Florida, Flossie
Fran	Frances, Francesca, Francisca, Francine
Georgie	Georgia, Georgina, Georgianna
Gigi	Georgine, Virginia, Giovanna, Ginger, Giselle, Regina, Gina
Ginger	Virginia, Ginevra, Regina
Ginny	Virginia, Ginger, Genevieve, Ginevra, Regina
Gracie	Grace, Graciela, Altagracia, Gracelyn
Hattie	Harriet, Henrietta
Hetty	Harriet, Henrietta, Ester, Hester, Mehitabel
Jan	Janet, Janice, Janine, Jeanette, Jana, Janelle, Janessa, January, Janiyah
Jenny	Jennifer, Jane, Jean, Jenna, Jensen, Genevieve
Jeri, Gerri	Geraldine, Germaine, Jerilyn, Jerrica
Jessie	Jessica, Jane, Jean, Janet, Jessame, Jessamyn
Jo, Joey	Josephine, Josefa, Joanne, Joan, Johanna, Joelle, Jocelyn, Journey, Marjorie
Jodi	Johanna, Joanna, Judith, Josephine
Josie, Joss	Josephine, Josefa, Joselyn
Julie	Julia, Juliana, Julianne, Juliet, Julissa
Kari	Karen, Karina, Katrina, Karissa
Kate, Katie	Katherine, Kaitlyn, Kathleen, Katia, Katarina, Kateri, Katrina
Kathy	Katherine, Kathleen, Kathlyn
Kay	Katherine, Kayla, Kaylee, Kasey, Kaylin, Kaitlyn, Kaydence, Kayden, Makayla
Kiki	Kristina, Kiara, Kimora
Kim	Kimberly, Kimball, Kimberlin, Kimora
Kris, Kristi	Kristina, Kristin, Krista, Kristal, Kristian
Lexi	Alexis, Alexa, Alexia, Alexandra, Alexandria, Lexington
Lillie	Lillian, Lilith, Lilia, Liliana, Lilias
Lindy	Linda, Melinda, Belinda, Rosalind, Linden
Laurie, Lori	Laura, Lauren, Laurel, Loretta, Lorraine, Lorelei, Lorna, Lorena
Liv	Olivia, Lavinia, Olive, Livia, Liviana

Liza	Elizabeth, Louise, Eliza, Lizbeth, Lieselotte, Lizette, Lizeth
Lottie	Charlotte, Lieselotte, Carlotta
Lucy	Lucille, Lucinda, Lucia, Luciana, Lucretia, Lucero
Maddie	Madeline, Madison, Madigan, Maddalena, Madonna, Madrigal
Maggie, Margie	Margaret, Magdalena, Magnolia, Magda, Margery
Maisie	Margaret, Mairead
Mandy	Amanda, Amandine, Manuela, Miranda
Marci	Marcia, Marcelle, Marcella
Mattie	Matilda, Martha, Mattea
Meg	Margaret, Megan, Marguerite
Mel	Melanie, Melinda, Melissa, Melody, Amelia, Carmel, Melba, Melina, Pamela
Millie	Millicent, Mildred, Amelia, Emily, Milla, Melissa, Camille, Emeline, Romilly
Mimi	Maria, Michelle, Miriam, Michaela, Miranda, Madeline, Mirabel
Mindy	Melinda, Miranda
Minnie	Wilhelmina, Minerva, Amina, Jasmine, Yasmin, Araminta, Jessamine
Molly	Mary, Margaret, Mahalia, Amalia
Nan	Nancy, Anne, Susannah, Nanette, Hannah, Fernanda
Nell	Eleanor, Helen, Lenora, Cornelia, Janelle, Penelope
Nikki	Nicole, Nicola, Veronica, Nicolette
Pat, Patsy	Patricia, Martha, Patrice, Patience, Cleopatra
Peggy	Margaret, Margery
Penny	Penelope, Aspen
Polly	Mary, Paula, Paulina
Randi	Miranda
Reba	Rebecca
Ricki	Erica, Patricia, America, Lyric, Richelle
Romy	Rosemary, Roma, Ramona, Romina, Rosamond
Ronnie	Veronica, Rhonda, Rona, Sharon
Rosie	Rose, Rosemary, Rosa, Rosalie, Rosalind, Rosanna, Rosario, Rosetta, Rosita, Roselyn, Rosabella
Sadie	Sarah, Sarai
Sally, Sal	Sarah, Salina, Salma, Salome
Sammie	Samantha, Samara, Samira

Sandy	Alexandra, Sandra, Alessandra, Cassandra, Lisandra, Melisande
Sookie	Susan, Susana
Stevie	Stephanie, Stefania
Sue, Susie	Susan, Suzanne, Susannah, Suzette, Summer
Tammy	Tamara, Tamar, Tamika, Tamia, Tamiko, Tamsin
Tasha	Natasha, Natalia, Latasha
Terry	Teresa, Therese, Terra, Kateri
Tess, Tessa	Teresa, Therese, Tessa, Santesa
Tia	Cynthia, Letitia, Lucretia, Tatiana, Tiana, Tiara
Tilly	Matilda, Clotilde, Tilda
Toni	Antonia, Antoinette, Antonina, Tonya, Payton
Tori	Victoria
Tricia, Trish	Patricia, Patrice, Beatrice, Leatrice, Latricia
Trina	Katrina, Trinity, Trinidad
Trixie	Beatrix, Beatrice, Patricia
Trudy	Gertrude, Ermintrude
Val	Valerie, Valeria, Valencia, Valentine, Valentina, Avalon
Vicky	Victoria, Vicenta
Winnie	Winifred, Winona, Winslow, Gwendolyn
Zuzu	Susana, Zuzana, Azure, Zuleika

BOYS

Nickname	Full names
Abe	Abraham, Abram, Abel, Abdiel
Al	Albert, Alfred, Alan, Alaric, Albin, Alistair, Alphonse, Aldrich, Alexander
Alex	Alexander, Alexi, Alistair
Alf, Alfie	Alfred, Alfredo, Alfonzo, Alphonse
Andy	Andrew, Anderson, Andre, Andreas, Leander
Archie	Archibald, Archer
Art	Arthur, Artis, Arturo, Artem
Barney	Barnabas, Barnaby, Bernard
Bart	Barton, Bartholemew, Bertram
Baz	Barry, Sebastian, Barton, Barron, Barrett
Ben	Benjamin, Benedict, Bennett, Benno, Benton, Bentley, Benson
Bert	Albert, Bertram, Bertrand, Gilbert, Hubert, Robert, Lambert

Bill	William, Willis, Willem
Brad	Bradley, Bradford, Braden, Brady, Braddock
Bram	Abraham, Abram, Bertram
Cab	Cabot, Caleb, Campbell
Cal	Calvin, Caleb, Callum, Callan, Charles, Calder, Pascal
Cam	Cameron, Campbell, Camden, Camilo
Charlie, Chuck	Charles, Charlton, Charleston
Chaz	Charles, Chester
Chet	Chester, Charleston
Chris	Christian, Christopher, Crispin, Cristobal, Christos
Cliff	Clifford, Clifton, Heathcliff
Cole	Nicholas, Colby, Colman, Colin, Colton, Colson, Colston
Con, Connie	Conrad, Connor, Cornelius, Cornell, Constantin, Conan
Curt	Curtis, Courtney
Dan	Daniel, Dante, Danilo, Danner
Dave	David, Davis, Davin, Daveth, Davion
Del	Cordell, Delano, Delton, Delmar, Wardell, Adelard, Adelbert
Denny	Dennis, Denver, Denzel, Dennison, Denholm, Denham
Dex, Des	Dexter, Desmond, Desiderio, Destin
Don	Donald, Donovan, Donal, Donato, Donnell, London
Drew	Andrew
Ed	Edward, Edmund, Edgar, Edison, Edwin, Eduardo
Ernie	Ernest, Ernesto, Ernst
Frank	Francis, Franklin, Francisco
Fred	Frederick, Alfred, Alfredo, Manfred
Gabe	Gabriel
Gene, Gino	Eugene, Genaro, Gentry, Legend
Gil	Gilbert, Giles, Gillespie, Gilead
Greg	Gregory, Gregor, Gregorio
Gus	August, Augustus, Gustave, Gustavo, Angus
Hal	Henry, Harry, Harold, Harley, Halston, Hamilton
Hank	Henry, Hannibal, Hans
Harry	Henry, Harrison, Harris, Harold, Harmon
Ike	Isaac, Isaiah, Dwight
Jack	John, Jackson

Jake	Jacob, John, Jacoby, Jakari
Jamie, Jim	James, Jeremy, Jamison, Jamal
Jay	Jacob, Jason, Jayden, Jalen, James, Japheth
Jed	Jedidiah, Jared, Gerald
Jeff	Jeffrey, Jefferson
Jem	Jeremy, Jeremiah, James
Jerry	Gerald, Jerome, Jeremy, Jered, Jeremiah, Jermaine, Jericho
Jim, Jimmy	James, Jamison
Joe	Joseph, Jonah, Jonas, Jovani, Jordan, Josiah, Joachim
Ken	Kenneth, Kendall, Kendrick, Kennedy, Kenton, Kenyatta, Kenyon, Kenji, Kenzo, Kentrell
Kit	Christopher, Christian
Larry	Lawrence, Lars, Larson, Larkin
Len	Leonard, Lennox, Lennon
Les	Lester, Lesley
Lon	Alonzo, Leonard, Lawrence, London, Waylon, Thelonius
Lou, Lew	Louis, Lewis, Llewellyn, Lucian
Mac	Mackenzie, Macauley, McArthur, McKay, McKinley, McCoy, Macon
Matt	Matthew, Matthias, Matteo, Mathis
Max	Maxwell, Maximilian, Maxim, Maximus, Maximo, Lomax, Maxton
Mel	Melvin, Melton, Melville, Carmelo, Melbourne
Mike, Mickey	Michael, Micah, Michelangelo
Mitch	Mitchell, Michael
Monty	Montague, Montgomery, Lamont, Montana, Montrell, Montez
Mort	Morton, Mortimer, Mordecai
Moss, Moe	Moses, Morris, Maurice, Morrison
Nate, Nat	Nathaniel, Nathan, Donato, Ignatius, Renato
Ned	Edward, Edmund, Edison, Eddard
Nick	Nicholas, Nicholson, Dominick, Nicodemus
Pat	Patrick, Payton, Paxton, Patton, Pasquale
Pete	Peter, Pierre, Pietro, Pedro, Peterson
Phil	Philip, Theophilus, Philippe, Philemon
Randy	Randall, Randolph, Rand, Bertrand
Ray	Raymond, Rayner, Rayburn, Rayford, Rafer, Raymundo, Raynard, Rayshawn, Raylan, Raydan

Reggie	Reginald, Regis
Rich	Richard, Richmond, Richardson
Rick	Richard, Richmond, Ricardo, Frederick, Cedric, Maverick, Patrick, Aldric, Roderick, Derrick, Garrick, Carrick, Broderick
Rico	Ricardo, Enrico, Richard
Rob, Bob	Robert, Roberto, Robin, Robinson, Robertson
Robin	Robert, Robinson
Rod	Rodney, Roderick, Roddick, Rodger, Rodolfo, Rodrigo, Jarod
Ron	Ronald, Ronan, Tyron, Ronaldo, Aaron, Rondell
Sal	Salvatore, Salvador, Absalom
Sam	Samuel, Samson, Sampson, Samir
Sandy	Alexander, Sanford, Santiago, Lisandro, Alessandro
Si	Silas, Seymour, Simon, Sylvester, Simeon, Sinbad
Stan	Stanley, Stanford, Stanton, Dunstan
Steve	Stephen, Steven, Esteban, Steffen, Stefano, Stevenson
Ted	Edward, Theodore, Edmund
Teo	Teodoro, Mateo, Theodore, Terrance, Tadeo
Terry	Terrance, Terrell, Theodore
Than	Ethan, Nathan, Nathaniel, Jonathan
Theo	Theodore, Theophilus, Thelonius, Theron
Tim	Timothy, Timon, Timber
Tom	Thomas, Tomas, Tomlin, Thompson, Tommaso
Tony	Anthony, Antonio, Tonio, Anton
Ty	Tyler, Tyrone, Tyson, Tyrese, Tyrell, Tyree, Tyshawn, Tyrion, Titus
Vin, Vince	Vincent, Calvin, Devin, Gavin, Vincenzo, Vinson
Wally	Walter, Wallace, Walden, Waldo, Walker, Walton
Wes	Wesley, Westley, Weston
Will	William, Willis, Wilson, Wilbur, Wilfred, Wilhelm, Willard, Wilton, Wilder
Xander	Alexander
Zack	Zachary, Zachariah, Isaac
Zeb	Zebediah, Zebedee, Zebulun
Zeke	Ezekiel, Isaac, Hezekiah, Zechariah

Nordic

The names in this category are common in present-day Scandinavia and still carry a Nordic air in America. We associate two different styles with the region. The first is light and crisp, like a breath of wintry air. The second

is weighty and powerful, like the old Norse gods. Both styles are still in evidence in Nordic naming today.

Of course, calling Nordic a single style glosses over the region's naming diversity. While traditions overlap, you're most likely to meet an Alvar in Sweden, a Søren in Denmark, and a Terje in Norway. Finland is another step removed, with Eetu and Veeti top picks for boys and Venla and Aino for girls. Iceland, meanwhile, is where you're likeliest to meet babies with ancient Norse names like Sindri and Gudrun.

If you travel through Denmark, Norway, and Sweden today, though, you'll find that many of the children you meet have names straight out of the "Antique Charm" section of this book. Top choices for girls include international hits like Emma, Hanna, and Sofie. For boys, you'll hear a lot of Lucas, Alexander, and Oliver. In fact, Scandinavia seems to be a few years ahead of the U.S. on the antique revival curve. If you're on the antique trail, you might want to check out some Scandinavian trends that haven't yet caught fire in America. For girls, Alice, Ida, Matilda, Nellie, Frida, and Thea are popular choices. Hot boys' names include Tobias, Emil, August, Anton, Leon, and Victor.

If you're looking for a more distinctively Nordic style, many of the classic names of Norse mythology remain in use. Try Freya, Saga, and Signe for girls; Odin, Sigurd, and Thor for boys. For a more contemporary take, consider the Danish hit Laerke (Lark) or Ronja, a regionwide favorite dreamed up by children's author Astrid Lindgren for her 1981 book *Ronia, the Robber's Daughter*.

GIRLS

Annalie	Birgitta	Disa	Freja	Ida
Anni	Britt	Ebba	Freya	Inge
Annika	Britta	Elin	Frida	Ingrid
Asta	Cecilie	Elina	Greta	Iselin
Astrid	Dagmar	Elisabet	Gudrun	Johanna
Berit	Dagny	Elsa	Hanna	Kaisa
Birgit	Dania	Evelina	Hedda	Kamilla

Karen	Linnea	Marit	Saga	Thea
Kari	Lise	Matilde	Sanni	Thora
Karina	Liv	Meta	Signe	Tilda
Katarina	Lovisa	Mia	Sigrid	Tove
Katrine	Magdalena	Minna	Silje	Tuva
Kiki	Maja	Moa	Siri	Vita
Kirsten	Malin	Noomi	Sofie	Viveka
Kristin	Maren	Pella	Sonja	
Kristina	Margit	Pia	Sunniva	
Laerke	Mari	Ronja	Suvi	
Lina	Marika	Runa	Svea	

BOYS

Aksel	Espen	Josef	Niels	Sigurd
Anders	Finn	Kai	Niko	Sindri
Aric	Gunnar	Knut	Nils	Soren
Arne	Gustav	Kristoffer	Odin	Stefan
Arvid	Hannes	Lars	Olaf	Stellan
Asger	Hans	Lasse	Ole	Sven
Axel	Harald	Leif	Oleg	Thor
Birk	Henrik	Linus	Oscar	Timo
Bjorn	Jan	Mads	Per	Torben
Broder	Jens	Magnus	Ragnar	Torsten
Dag	Jesper	Malthe	Rasmus	Valdemar
Einar	Joar	Marius	Reidar	Vidar
Emanuel	Johan	Mathias	Rolf	Viggo
Emil	Johannes	Mikkel	Rune	
Erik	Jonatan	Miro	Sakari	

Place Names

These days, if you say you've visited Paris and Dakota, there's no telling whether you traveled the world or just dropped in on friends. The boundary between place names and personal names is disappearing, and the range of geographic choices grows every day.

1880   Today

A place name connects a child with the world. When you name a baby Paris, you tap into generations of artistic dreams. With Dakota, you summon the independence of the American West. Even if you've never known anyone by these names, they're familiar and evocative and require no explanation. That makes place names tempting targets for creative parents: brand-new baby names with built-in meanings.

As a place name becomes popular, though, its geographic ties loosen. Just look at Brittany, which no longer reminds anybody of the French coast (try Normandy instead). Some of the less common choices, of course, may be less common for a reason—Paris is a lot catchier than Grenoble. For a name that strikes the right balance, scan a map of your favorite part of the world or try the global list below.

GIRLS

Abilene	Brooklyn	Holland	Milan	Sicily
Acadia	Calais	India	Montana	Siena
Adelaide	Caledonia	Indiana	Nevada	Sierra
Albany	Cambria	Ireland	Normandy	Skye
Alexandria	Carolina	Italia	Odessa	Sonoma
America	Catalina	Jamaica	Paris	Sydney
Arcadia	Chelsea	Jordan	Phoenix	Trinidad
Asia	Cheyenne	Juneau	Raleigh	Valencia
Asmara	China	Kenya	Roma	Venice
Aspen	Dakota	Laramie	Sahara	Verona
Astoria	Dallas	London	Samara	Vienna
Atlanta	Denali	Lorraine	Samaria	Virginia
Augusta	Devon	Madison	Savannah	Zaria
Avonlea	Florence	Malaysia	Sedona	
Berkeley	Florida	Marietta	Shasta	
Bristol	Geneva	Marin	Shenandoah	
Brittany	Georgia	Marseille	Shiloh	

BOYS

Austin	Caspian	Dublin	Kingston	Phoenix
Berkeley	Charleston	Essex	Lexington	Portland
Boston	Cleveland	Everest	London	Princeton
Bozeman	Cody	Holland	Macon	Raleigh
Brighton	Dade	Houston	Melbourne	Reno
Bronx	Dakota	Hudson	Memphis	Rhodes
Cairo	Dallas	Indiana	Milan	Richmond
Camden	Dayton	Jericho	Montana	Rome
Canton	Denver	Jordan	Ontario	Salem
Cardiff	Devon	Kent	Paris	Seattle

Seneca	Torrance	Troy	York	Zion
Stratton	Trenton	Walden	Zaire	

Spotlight: College Names

Call these place names with a PhD. Names of colleges and universities offer the same balance of freshness and familiarity as place names, but their academic style is a world removed from the bright lights of Paris or the badlands of Dakota. A few iconic school names can sound too ivy-covered (yes, I'm talking to you, Harvard). But others put a subtly scholarly spin on surnames and place names.

Bard	Colby	Hopkins	Tulane
Barnard	Cornell	Kenyon	Vassar
Baylor	Creighton	Penn	Wake
Bowdoin	Duke	Princeton	Wellesley
Butler	Emory	Rhodes	Yale
Carleton	Furman	Rollins	
Chapman	Hamilton	Stanford	

Porch Sitters

With due apologies to Gladys and Elmer, this group of names has settled in for a long snooze on the front porch and isn't waking up anytime soon. On television, names from this list signal that a character is strictly comic relief: Floyd and Wilbur never get the girl. Their overwhelming image is rural, outmoded, and ploddingly slow.

You may find a name or two on the list that you take exception to. "But my Grandma Velma was a saint!" you say. I understand, my Grandma Ethel was an absolute peach—but her name wasn't the reason.

Take heart that as they rock in their rocking chairs, the Porch Sitters can dream back to the day when they were in high style. These names do have a distinctive style, favored for its continental elegance a century ago. Note the round, smooth tones that roll around on your tongue, with velvety consonants "l," "m," "r," and "th" and full vowels "o" and "u." And then note how those sounds are out of step in the age of Paytons and Kaylees. Of course, there are now young Paytons and Kaylees in every town. If a name on the Porch Sitter list captures your imagination, it will be a bold and individual choice. For most of us, though, these will remain names looked back on with a smile. So good night, Gladys and Elmer—and sweet dreams.

GIRLS

Agnes	Dolores	Eunice	Luetta	Selma
Albertine	Dorcas	Florine	Lurline	Shirlene
Alvena	Earline	Geraldine	Melva	Thelma
Ardell	Edna	Gertrude	Mildred	Velma
Bernice	Edwina	Gladys	Myrtle	Verna
Bertha	Elvira	Helga	Nadine	Vernell
Beulah	Enid	Hester	Noreen	Vernice
Brunilda	Ernestine	Hilda	Opal	Wilma
Claudine	Ethel	Irma	Pauline	
Delma	Eula	Laverne	Pearline	

BOYS

Abner	Elmer	Lester	Myron	Verl
Amos	Elroy	Lloyd	Norbert	Verne
Buford	Enos	Maynard	Odell	Virgil
Burl	Floyd	Merle	Odie	Waldo
Clem	Homer	Mervin	Orville	Wilbur
Cletus	Hoyt	Millard	Pervis	Wilfred
Delbert	Irving	Milton	Roscoe	Willard
Dillard	Irwin	Mortimer	Rufus	
Elbert	Jethro	Murray	Seymour	

Saints

If you flipped straight to this section of the book, chances are you're already set on choosing a saint's name for your baby. If you're idly reading the Saints section just because it comes before '70s–'80s, you might not think you care about saints' names at all. In either case, you may be in for

1880   Today

some surprises. Because the *Baby Name Wizard* list isn't just saints . . . it's saints with style.

First, some background on saintly names. They're a big, diverse group, and nobody's precisely sure of the membership roster. For the first millennium of Christian history, there was no formal canonization process. The early saints were anointed by public acclaim, or more often by local tradition. Individual communities became memory-keepers for their own local saints, forming a patchwork quilt of piety and community pride across Europe.

Some names recur again and again in any list of saints. Names like Francis and Mary, borne by over 50 saints each, are the bedrock of the Roman Catholic naming tradition. Yet you can explore the farther reaches of name style while still inspiring your children with role models for a spiritual life. The selective list below focuses on less common names, exploring the quirkier corners of 2000 years of religious history. Whether you're Catholic or not, the list is likely to leave you with the realization that saints' names are a lot cooler than you thought.

Some other denominations, such as the Orthodox churches, have their own rosters of saints; see the Greek and Slavic sections for more ideas.

GIRLS

Ada	Ava	Eugenia	Kennera	Melania
Adela	Averil	Fabiola	Keyna	Monica
Adelaide	Avila	Felicity	Kiara	Natalia
Alexis	Baya	Filomena	Kinnia	Paulina
Aleydis	Beatrix	Flavia	Landry	Philomena
Alodia	Belina	Flora	Leocadia	Quiteria
Amalia	Britta	Gemma	Louisa	Raphaela
Amata	Camilla	Genevieve	Lucia	Regina
Anastasia	Cecily	Germaine	Lucilla	Rosalia
Anatolia	Chantal	Gwen	Lucretia	Sabina
Antonia	Chiara	Helena	Mabyn	Savina
Antonina	Cleopatra	Hermione	Marcella	Seraphina
Apollonia	Colette	Ida	Marguerite	Serena
Ariadne	Daria	Josepha	Mariana	Severina
Asteria	Demetria	Josephine	Marina	Silvia
Augusta	Dominica	Juliana	Matilda	Solange
Aurea	Elodie	Justina	Maura	Sophronia
Aurelia	Emiliana	Kateri	Maxima	Tatiana

| Therese | Valentina | Veronica | Viviana | Zita |
| Ursula | Verena | Vivian | Winifred | |

BOYS

Adelard	Caedmon	Elias	Kenelm	Roderick
Adrian	Casper	Emeric	Kieran	Roman
Aedan	Cassian	Emmanuel	Kilian	Ronan
Aidan	Cathal	Erasmus	Lazarus	Rudolf
Aidric	Ciprian	Fabian	Leander	Rupert
Alban	Clement	Falco	Leo	Samson
Aldric	Colman	Felix	Linus	Sebastian
Alexis	Conan	Finian	Lucian	Senan
Aloysius	Cormac	Fintan	Lucius	Sergio
Ambrose	Crispin	Florian	Magnus	Severin
Anselm	Cronan	Gennaro	Malachy	Severus
Antony	Cruz	Gerard	Manuel	Silas
Apollo	Damian	Gilbert	Marcel	Sillan
Baldwin	Dario	Giles	Marcellus	Silvan
Balin	Darius	Guy	Marek	Silvanus
Barnard	Declan	Hermes	Matthias	Stanislaus
Bartholomew	Demetrius	Hugh	Maxim	Sylvan
Benedict	Dermot	Isaias	Maximilian	Sylvester
Bertrand	Diego	Ivan	Maximus	Tarkin
Blaine	Dominic	Ives	Oliver	Tillo
Blaise	Donato	Ivo	Pantaleon	Tychon
Bond	Dunstan	Jarlath	Philo	Valentino
Brannock	Edgar	Jude	Quentin	Victor
Brice	Edmund	Julian	Raphael	Vitus
Brogan	Egon	Julius	Regis	Xavier
Bruno	Elgar	Justus	Rocco	

'70s-'80s

Ah, thanks for stopping by! It gets mighty lonely in this section of the book. You don't meet many parents seeking names to bring back memories of *Charlie's Angels* or *The A-Team*. Not that there's anything remotely objectionable about the baby names of the '70s and '80s . . . but that itself is part of the problem.

For most new parents today, these are the grown-up names you barely notice. You meet a couple named Eric and Kristen and you don't even pause to think about their names because they just seem *normal*. A couple of generations back, they might have been creative, but today they seem like defaults: if you don't choose a name for your daughter, she'll end up Kristen.

Of course, for our children's generation, Madison and Mason will be the defaults. So what will they think of the '70s–'80s hits? If you choose the right names from that group, you'll be tapping into a classic in the making. Your child will have a proven, admired name with cross-generational appeal. But choose unwisely, and the poor kid might sound like— *gulp*—somebody's *mom!* As a rule of thumb, names with a distinctive sound and rhythm (e.g., Jeremy, Amanda) tend to age better than those that travel in a generational pack (Krista-Trista-Christy-Krystal).

GIRLS

Aimee	Cassie	Heather	Kristi	Shana
Alicia	Chandra	Heidi	Latasha	Shannon
Alisa	Chantel	Holly	Lauren	Shawna
Amanda	Cherise	Jaclyn	Leanne	Sheena
Amber	Chrissy	Jamie	Leigh	Shonda
Amy	Christa	Janna	Lindsay	Sonia
Anjanette	Christina	Jennifer	Liza	Stacy
April	Christine	Jessica	Mandy	Stephanie
Ashley	Christy	Jodi	Marisa	Stevie
Audra	Cory	Justine	Marlena	Tabitha
Bethany	Courtney	Kami	Melinda	Tanya
Brandy	Crystal	Kari	Melissa	Tara
Bridget	Danielle	Katrina	Michelle	Tasha
Britney	Deanna	Keisha	Mindy	Tawny
Brittany	Desiree	Kelly	Misty	Tiffany
Buffy	Dionne	Kendra	Monica	Tonya
Candace	Erica	Kerri	Monique	Tricia
Carrie	Erin	Kirsten	Natasha	Trina
Casey	Farrah	Krista	Nikki	Trista
Cassandra	Felicia	Kristen	Rochelle	Whitney

BOYS

Brandon	Brian	Chad	Derrick	Dusty
Brent	Casey	Corey	Dustin	Eric

Heath	Jarrod	Jeremy	Lance	Steven
Jamey	Jarvis	Kristopher	Levar	Terrance
Jared	Jason	Kurtis	Shannon	Torrey
Jarrett	Jeffrey	Kyle	Shawn	Travis

Shakespearean

What's in a name? That which we call a rose
By any other word would smell as sweet.
So Romeo would, were he not Romeo called,
Retain that dear perfection which he owes
Without that title.

Don't believe it for a second.

Say what he may, the immortal bard was fully at-
tuned to the power of names and the meanings they convey. This is a guy who gave his romantic heroes names

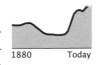

1880   Today

like Romeo and Orlando and his fools names like Dogberry and Elbow.
In some cases he went so far as to invent a name to perfectly capture the
essence of a character. A famous example is Miranda, a classic conjured
up for *The Tempest* from a Latin root meaning "fit to be admired."

The evocative names in Shakespeare's plays still resonate centuries
later, with a distinctive style that merits its own category. This abbrevi-
ated list takes some liberties, including spellings and variants that differ
from those in the plays. (Benedict, for instance, is a more realistic possibility today than Benedick.) It concentrates on names with a literary
flourish and timeless appeal. If you're looking for Falstaff or Fortinbras,
get thee to a library.

GIRLS

Adriana	Desdemona	Isabella	Marina	Rosalind
Amelia	Diana	Jessica	Miranda	Rosaline
Ariel	Emilia	Julia	Nerissa	Silvia
Beatrice	Francisca	Juliet	Olivia	Titania
Bianca	Helena	Juno	Ophelia	Ursula
Celia	Hermia	Katharina	Paulina	Valeria
Charmian	Hermione	Katharine	Phoebe	Viola
Cordelia	Imogen	Luciana	Portia	
Cressida	Iris	Mariana	Regan	

Adrian	Cassio	Duncan	Leonato	Prospero
Alonso	Cassius	Edgar	Lorenzo	Reynaldo
Alonzo	Cato	Fabian	Lysander	Rodrigo
Angelo	Chiron	Ferdinand	Marcellus	Romeo
Angus	Cicero	Francisco	Nathaniel	Sebastian
Antonio	Claudio	Frederick	Nestor	Stefano
Antony	Claudius	Gonzalo	Oberon	Tarquin
Balthazar	Conrad	Horatio	Oliver	Theseus
Belarius	Corin	Iago	Olivier	Timon
Benedict	Cornelius	Laertes	Orlando	Titus
Bernardo	Curtis	Laurence	Paris	Toby
Bertram	Demetrius	Lennox	Pedro	Valentine
Camillo	Dion	Leonardo	Philo	

Short and Sweet

Extremes always make an impact. When you meet a Maximilian or Evangelina, the name's extraordinary length makes it memorable. But you can make your mark at the other extreme too: not super-size, but pocket-size.

1880 Today

Think of those tiny "power" mints that astonish you with their strength. Names like Mia, Ian, and Zoe are perfect, potent miniatures that pack all their style into compact bursts. As strong as they are, these names are never harsh or heavy. And as cute as they are, they don't sound childish, since they're not pet forms but full, self-contained names. These pocket powerhouses are youthful names that will have no problem growing up.

GIRLS

Ada	Avia	Chloe	Eva	Isla
Adi	Avis	Clea	Eve	Iva
Aja	Ayla	Cleo	Fae	Ivy
Anya	Baya	Deja	Gaia	Jada
Arya	Bria	Eden	Gia	Jael
Asta	Britta	Elke	Ila	Janna
Aura	Calla	Elle	Ily	Jenna
Ava	Cara	Esme	Io	Jolie

Kaia	Luna	Mya	Pia	Taya
Kara	Luz	Naia	Pippa	Terra
Kenna	Lyra	Nava	Raya	Tessa
Kia	Macy	Nia	Rhea	Thea
Kira	Maia	Nika	Ría	Tia
Kyra	Mara	Nina	Rika	Tova
Lana	Maya	Noa	Rilla	Tyra
Lea	Meta	Nola	Roma	Una
Leia	Mia	Nova	Romi	Vita
Lela	Mika	Nya	Rue	Willa
Lena	Mila	Nyla	Sela	Zara
Lexa	Milla	Oona	Siri	Zilla
Lia	Mina	Orly	Suri	Ziva
Lida	Mira	Pella	Tai	Zoe
Lila	Misha	Peta	Tali	Zoya
Liv	Moa	Phoebe	Tara	Zuri

BOYS

Abel	Eli	Kai	Luca	Raz
Ari	Enzo	Kian	Neo	Rex
Asa	Gael	Kip	Nico	Rio
Avi	Ian	Kobe	Noah	Taj
Axel	Isai	Koda	Noam	Teo
Cael	Jair	Leo	Noel	Zvi
Elan	Joah	Liam	Raj	

Slavic

The Slavic language family includes a dozen languages of Central and Eastern Europe, each with naming traditions that reflect local culture, history, and religion.
Slavic names are as diverse as the communities they come from, but together they do make up a distinctive style. Common threads can be seen in regional name choices such as Stanislav and Vladimir and in typical versions of international names, such as Pavel for Paul. In the U.S., the most popular Slavic names today tend to be girls' names, including diminutives like Anya, Katia, and Natasha.

Russian is the most widely spoken Slavic language and has had the biggest impact on American names. The following selected list of local and regional favorites focuses on the most common variants of each name.

GIRLS

Alexandra	Elena	Lilia	Oksana	Valentina
Alina	Gabriela	Ludmila	Olga	Valeria
Alisa	Gala	Magdalena	Paulina	Valia
Anastasia	Galina	Margarita	Petrina	Varya
Angela	Halina	Marcela	Polina	Vendula
Aniela	Hana	Martina	Raisa	Vera
Anka	Iliana	Masha	Raya	Verica
Anoushka	Irina	Matea	Renata	Veronika
Antonina	Ivana	Melania	Sasha	Vika
Anya	Jana	Michalina	Severina	Wanda
Basia	Josefa	Mila	Shura	Xenia
Danica	Kamila	Milana	Simona	Yana
Daniela	Katerina	Mira	Sonia	Yuliana
Daria	Katia	Monika	Stanislava	Zlata
Dasia	Lana	Nadezhda	Stefania	Zofia
Denisa	Lara	Nadia	Svetlana	Zora
Domicela	Larissa	Natalia	Tamara	Zoya
Dominika	Lenka	Natasha	Tanya	Zuzana
Ekaterina	Lida	Nika	Tatiana	Zuzu

BOYS

Alexi	Constantin	Jovan	Milos	Viktor
Anatoly	Darko	Kirill	Nikolai	Vitaliy
Andon	Dimitri	Konrad	Oleg	Vladimir
Andrei	Dominik	Krystof	Pavel	Zenon
Anton	Dragomir	Lazar	Rodion	
Antonin	Gavril	Leonid	Roman	
Arkady	Gennadi	Lev	Sergei	
Artem	Goran	Luka	Slobodan	
Artur	Hristo	Lukas	Stanislav	
Bartek	Igor	Marek	Taras	
Bohdan	Ivan	Markian	Tomas	
Boris	Jacek	Maxim	Vaclav	
Bronislav	Jerzy	Mikhail	Vadim	
Casimir	Jiri	Milan	Valentin	

Spotlight: Names Without Borders

Are you looking for a name that is attractive and easy to pronounce in many different languages? Long vowel sounds like "ah," "ee," and "oo" are good bets, while "w," "th," and clusters of consonant sounds are best to avoid. Here are some names that travel particularly well:

GIRLS

Adela	Daria	Lilia	Melania	Sara
Alina	Elena	Liliana	Melina	Shani
Amira	Eliana	Lina	Mika	Sofia
Anika	Elisa	Malia	Mira	Talia
Anna	Emilia	Mari	Nadia	Tova
Ariana	Isabella	Marina	Natalia	Valeria
Ariela	Laura	Maya	Nina	

BOYS

Adam	Dominic	Lev	Noah	Tobias
Adrian	Elias	Lucas	Omar	Victor
Aldo	Erik	Luis	Oscar	
Antonio	Gabriel	Mario	Ruben	
Dario	Gil	Matteo	Sebastian	
David	Ivan	Nico	Simon	

Solid Citizens

Here are the grown-up names of the *Father Knows Best* world. These are the buttoned-down dads, the demure moms in aprons and pearls. Their kids didn't have full names at all, just nicknames: Bud, Kitten, Beaver.

Okay, that's all a "Nick at Nite" illusion, but it's a strong one. After all, we parents of the 21st century weren't there to see the *real* young Vernons and Bettys laugh and bicker and love. But sitcoms are forever, so the Solid Citizens have been firmly established as the squarest names on the block.

Don't turn the page yet, though, because these square standards offer something that the avant-garde can't. The Solid Citizens are comfort names, and like comfort foods they enchant us with their cozy reliability. Everything's okay when you're eating baked macaroni with June and Ward. That warmth is a quality that many of the crisper new hits are lacking. It's also a quality that grows up well, and the world still needs grown-ups. If you find a Solid Citizen name that strikes your fancy, it will make a quiet, understated style statement today with tons of potential for the future.

GIRLS

Anita	Elaine	Jeanette	Marilyn	Rita
Ann	Ellen	Joan	Marion	Roberta
Arlene	Faye	Joanne	Marjorie	Roma
Barbara	Felice	Joyce	Marlys	Rosalie
Bernadette	Frances	Judith	Maryann	Rosalind
Betty	Gayle	June	Mavis	Rosemary
Beverly	Georgette	Kay	Maxine	Roslyn
Carlene	Gloria	Lois	Muriel	Ruth
Carol	Greer	Loretta	Myra	Sally
Carolyn	Gwen	Lorna	Myrna	Shirley
Claudette	Gwendolyn	Lorraine	Nancy	Sylvia
Constance	Helen	Margaret	Norma	Therese
Corrine	Helene	Margarita	Patricia	Twila
Dale	Irene	Margery	Phyllis	Vivian
Darlene	Jane	Margot	Polly	
Doris	Janet	Marian	Ramona	
Dorothy	Janice	Marianne	Rena	
Eileen	Jean	Marie	Rhoda	

BOYS

Allen	Clark	Ellis	Glenn	Lee
Alvin	Clifford	Errol	Gordon	Leon
Arlen	Clifton	Eugene	Guy	Leonard
Arnold	Clyde	Francis	Hal	Leroy
Bernard	Cornell	Frank	Hale	Lewis
Bill	Dale	Franklin	Harris	Lionel
Bob	Dean	Fred	Howard	Lon
Carl	Donald	Gene	Hugh	Loren
Carlton	Duane	Gerald	Jerome	Lyle
Charles	Earl	Gerard	Kenneth	Marlin
Charlie	Eldon	Gilbert	Lawrence	Martin

Marvin	Randolph	Roy	Stewart	Wendell
Melvin	Ray	Royce	Ted	Willis
Milton	Raymond	Russell	Tom	Yale
Norman	Richard	Sheldon	Vernon	
Paul	Roger	Sherman	Ward	
Philip	Roland	Stanley	Wardell	
Ralph	Ronald	Stanton	Warren	

Surfer '60s

Every era has its sound, in names as well as music. For the new wave of names that hit the beach in the 1960s, the sound was brisk, sunny, and windswept. Classic boys' names suddenly felt heavy and old fashioned, and classic girls' names too elaborate. Welcome Gary and Todd, Lori and Tina.

With the benefit of a few decades' distance, the breeziness of this generation of names is a bit surprising. Their era was fraught with social and political upheaval, but the names are resolutely, even aggressively, carefree. Perhaps they are the personification of the "don't trust anyone over 30" mentality: names that break with the past and don't look back. Or perhaps they just remind us that the real '60s were as much about Gidget as Woodstock.

The names below surged in the '60s and held on into the '70s, but most have now lost their steam. They have entered generational limbo because today's parents grew up surrounded by them. "Beth? Nah, half my high school teachers were named Beth, I know a million Beths." Maybe you do . . . but your daughter won't, because Beth has fallen off the popularity charts. So for now, you may not be able to picture yourself raising a little Tracy or Scotty. But in your grandchildren's generation, don't be surprised to see the break-with-the-past '60s names come full circle as old favorites awaiting revival.

GIRLS

Alisa	Belinda	Cherie	Darcy	Denise
Amy	Beth	Chris	Dawn	Dina
Angela	Bobbi	Christine	Deanne	Dionne
Angie	Bridget	Cindy	DeeDee	Dori
Aretha	Candy	Dana	Deena	Fawn
Barbie	Carla	Dara	Deirdre	Gidget

Gina	Kelly	Marcy	Sandy	Tamara
Ginger	Kerry	Marlo	Shari	Tammy
Heidi	Kimberly	Marnie	Sharla	Teri
Holly	Kris	Michele	Shawn	Theresa
Janette	Laurie	Missy	Shelly	Tina
Janine	Leanne	Monica	Sheri	Toni
Jeannie	Lesley	Randi	Sherry	Tracy
Jeri	Lisa	Renee	Sonya	Trina
Jill	Liz	Rhonda	Stacy	Wendy
Jodi	Lori	Robin	Starla	Yvette
Joni	Luann	Rochelle	Stephanie	
Julie	Lynn	Roxanna	Suzette	

BOYS

Ashley	Dirk	Kenny	Randy	Stoney
Barron	Donnell	Kent	Reggie	Tad
Bart	Dwayne	Kerry	Reginald	Terrence
Brad	Eric	Kip	Richie	Thad
Brian	Geoffrey	Kirby	Rob	Tim
Chris	Gregg	Kirk	Robbie	Timothy
Craig	Gregory	Kurt	Russ	Toby
Curt	Jeffrey	Marc	Rusty	Todd
Darin	Jody	Mark	Scott	Tracy
Darrell	Joey	Marty	Scotty	Troy
Darren	Jon	Matt	Stacy	Vince
Darryl	Keith	Randall	Steven	Wes

Timeless

Meet two couples: Lester and Edna, Kody and Brittani. Form images of them in your mind. Chances are you've imagined a vast generation gap. Now meet Alex and Sara. How old are they? If you can't hazard a guess, then 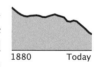 you've just encountered the Timeless name style.

Timelessness is a rare quality in a name, subtler than "classic" or "standard." Many Timeless names are indeed popular classics, but others have never cracked a top-100 list. What they all share is a steadiness from decade to decade that puts them out of the reach of passing trends.

When you hear a Timeless name, you have no inkling whether the person is age 1, 20, 50, or 100. The name holds its own in every generation, alongside names from Bertha to Baylee. That makes the Timeless group the most predictable names in this unpredictable world. It's a good bet that names like Alex and Sara will come across the same way 25 years from now as they do today. They may not win points for creativity, but they'll shelter you from the cruel winds of fashion. These are the names built to last a lifetime.

GIRLS

Ana	Charlotte	Helena	Katie	Nina
Anna	Christina	Hope	Laura	Penelope
Anne	Claire	Ingrid	Lea	Priscilla
Antonia	Clare	Iris	Leah	Rachel
Audrey	Claudia	Ivy	Lina	Rebecca
Aurora	Corinne	Jacqueline	Lucia	Sara
Callie	Daphne	Jane	Lydia	Sarah
Camilla	Diana	Joanna	Maggie	Simone
Camille	Elena	Johanna	Maria	Susana
Carmen	Elisa	Julia	Marina	Teresa
Caroline	Elisabeth	Juliet	Martina	Theresa
Catherine	Elise	Kate	Mary	Veronica
Cecilia	Elizabeth	Katharine	Mercy	Victoria
Celeste	Emily	Katherine	Miriam	
Celia	Eve	Kathryn	Naomi	

BOYS

Alan	Brooks	Dexter	Jay	Manuel
Alex	Byron	Duncan	Jefferson	Marcus
Alexander	Calvin	Edward	Jesse	Mario
Alfonso	Carlo	Eliot	Joel	Mark
Anderson	Charles	Elliott	John	Marshall
Andrew	Clark	Felix	José	Martin
Andy	Clay	Forrest	Joseph	Maxwell
Anthony	Clayton	Graham	Juan	Michael
Anton	Clinton	Grant	Judd	Mitchell
Antonio	Curtis	Harrison	Julian	Moses
Barrett	Dallas	Henry	Julio	Nathan
Benjamin	Daniel	Ivan	Karl	Nathaniel
Bennett	David	Jack	Lorenzo	Neil
Blaine	Davis	James	Malcolm	Nelson

Nicholas	Quentin	Rex	Samuel	Vaughn
Noel	Quincy	Robert	Simon	Victor
Nolan	Rafael	Roberto	Sterling	Vincent
Patrick	Ramon	Roderick	Thaddeus	Wade
Paul	Raphael	Roman	Thomas	Wesley
Peter	Raul	Ross	Tomas	William
Philip	Reid	Ruben	Van	Wilson
Preston	Reuben	Rudy	Vance	

Spotlight: Likable Names

Familiar, timeless names have the special quality of making people feel comfortable—some more than others. What names naturally bring a smile to people's faces? I ran an informal poll at BabyNameWizard.com to find the friendliest, most approachable, and just plain likable baby names.

GIRLS

Amy	Emily	Molly
Annie	Katie	Sadie
Ellie	Laura	Sarah

BOYS

Adam	Charlie	Jake	Tim
Andy	Evan	Sam	Tom
Ben	Jack	Steve	Will

Turn of the 21st Century

This category is new to the third edition of this book. We've reached a turning point where a new generation of names is being defined and written into the record books. These are the names that packed school classrooms across the country through the 1990s and 2000s, but are starting to decline and will be much less common a decade from now.

You may see some of your top name choices on this list. You'll almost certainly see names of your friends' and neighbors' kids—or your own older children. That's as it should be. All of these names are still popular and well liked and would serve your child well. The purpose of the category isn't to dismiss your favorite name as *"so five minutes ago."* The purpose is to give you a kind of preview of the future past. Just as Shawn, Kristie, and Chad spell "'70s" now, these names will be the sound of the turn of the 21st century to coming generations.

GIRLS

Alexandria	Caitlin	Jada	Kirsten	Shania
Alexia	Carissa	Jasmine	Lauren	Shayna
Alexis	Cassandra	Jenna	Lesley	Shelby
Alicia	Cassidy	Jessica	Marissa	Sierra
Alyssa	Chelsea	Jordan	Megan	Sydney
Ashanti	Cheyenne	Kaitlyn	Michaela	Taylor
Asia	Destiny	Karina	Morgan	Tori
Bethany	Gabrielle	Kayla	Nicole	
Bria	Gillian	Kelsey	Paige	
Brianna	Haley	Kiana	Raven	

BOYS

Austin	Cody	Dillon	Kobe	Ty
Bailey	Dakota	Dominique	Kyle	Tyler
Brendan	Dalton	Donovan	Marquise	Tyrese
Brandon	DeAndre	Jared	Shane	Zachary
Cassidy	Devin	Jarrett	Tanner	
Chandler	Devon	Keyshawn	Trevor	

Why Not?

The names below are a hodgepodge of different sounds and styles, with only two things in common: they're perfectly good, and hardly anybody uses them.

1880   Today

Fashion is fickle, picking out certain names for a ride to the top of the charts and leaving other worthy choices behind. Sure, Orval and Hortense died natural deaths, and Kermit and Grover were Muppeted out of contention. But why are there 100 times as many Olivias as Lavinias? Why is Max a smash and Rex an afterthought?

Here, for your consideration, are names seldom heard over the past two decades that have the ingredients to become fashionable. You may quibble over some of the choices ("Rex? Rex is a dog's name!"), but you may also find a neglected gem just waiting to shine.

GIRLS

Ada	Beatrice	Dariana	Graciela	Lilia
Adair	Beatrix	Davina	Greta	Linnea
Adela	Bellamy	Daylin	Halcyon	Lise
Ailsa	Belle	Deirdre	Harlow	Liviana
Alma	Bly	Delia	Haven	Lorelei
Althea	Blythe	Della	Helena	Louisa
Amalia	Bria	Delphine	Holland	Lyra
Amity	Briony	Delta	Ilaria	Mabyn
Amory	Brynna	Donatella	Iliana	Madigan
Annabeth	Calla	Dorothea	Ily	Mae
Annalise	Camellia	Dove	Ione	Maelie
Anne	Carys	Dulcie	Isannah	Maëlle
Anthea	Cassia	Eleni	Jalila	Maeve
Antonia	Cecily	Elle	Jamila	Malaika
Anya	Celeste	Ellery	January	Malin
Arden	Celia	Elodie	Jessamine	Marcella
Ariadne	Charis	Eloise	Jill	Maren
Ariela	Charity	Elsa	Jordana	Margery
Arista	Chiara	Ember	Josefa	Margo
Ashby	Christabel	Embry	Joy	Marian
Asta	Christiana	Emerald	June	Maribel
Audra	Clea	Emlyn	Juniper	Mariela
Aurea	Cleo	Emmeline	Katia	Marilla
Aurelia	Coral	Esme	Keelin	Marin
Autry	Coralie	Estella	Lana	Maris
Avalon	Coraline	Evelina	Landry	Marjorie
Averil	Corinna	Everly	Laney	Marlowe
Aviana	Dagny	Felicity	Lark	Matilda
Avila	Dalia	Flora	Larkin	Mattea
Avis	Damiana	Francesca	Laurel	May
Aviva	Dania	Freya	Lavinia	Melina
Avonlea	Daphne	Geneva	Leora	Melisande
Axelle	Daria	Giovanna	Liana	Mercy

Mika	Orla	Romy	Stefania	Tyra
Milena	Paloma	Ronia	Susana	Valia
Milla	Paralee	Rosabel	Susannah	Verena
Mira	Poppy	Rosemary	Sylvie	Verity
Mirabel	Prairie	Sage	Talia	Vienna
Mirabelle	Promise	Sania	Talitha	Vika
Miri	Rafaela	Sela	Tamsin	Violeta
Mirren	Raine	Serenade	Taryn	Willa
Nell	Rehema	Shea	Taylin	Wren
Nika	Renata	Shira	Tenley	Zara
Nola	Reva	Silvana	Tess	Zia
Oakley	Rhea	Simone	Thea	Ziva
Octavia	Ripley	Soraya	Tierney	Zora
Oriana	Romilly	Stasia	Tyne	

BOYS

Alban	Campbell	Egan	Japheth	Patterson
Alden	Carlo	Elam	Jefferson	Penn
Anton	Carsten	Ellis	Jensen	Perrin
Archer	Case	Emerick	Jericho	Pierce
Ari	Cason	Evander	Joah	Pierson
Atticus	Channing	Finian	Joss	Porter
Axton	Charleston	Finley	Jules	Prescott
Barlow	Chayton	Finnegan	Keane	Pryce
Barrett	Clark	Fletcher	Keir	Quill
Baylor	Coleman	Flynn	Kingsley	Quinlan
Beck	Cormac	Forrest	Lander	Ramsey
Bowen	Crispin	Foster	Lawson	Raphael
Bowman	Crosby	Gareth	Leif	Reef
Bram	Dashiell	Garrick	Lennon	Reeve
Brannigan	Davis	Gibson	Lennox	Remington
Brecken	Deacon	Gideon	Mahlon	Reuben
Britton	Dempsey	Gray	Malcolm	Rex
Brogan	Dennison	Griffith	Merrick	Rhys
Burke	Dorian	Hampton	Merritt	Richmond
Cabot	Duncan	Harris	Murphy	Riddick
Cael	Dyson	Hawkins	Nicholson	Rockwell
Calder	Eamon	Hugh	Nico	Ronan
Callum	Edison	Ivor	Niven	Royce

Seaver	Talbot	Timo	Tynan	Walton
Shepard	Taye	Tobias	Vance	Webb
Silvan	Thaddeus	Tobin	Varian	Wilson
Simeon	Theo	Torin	Vaughn	Winslow
Stanton	Theron	Truman	Vinson	Wynn
Stone	Tiernan	Turner	Walker	

Name Index

Names and page numbers for full "snapshot" descriptions appear in boldface.

Adira, 184, 403, 433
Adlai, 208, 373
Admon, 402
Adolf, 396, 428, 429
Adolfo, 89, 414
Adolphus, 388
Adonis, 43, 115, **211**, 218, 364, 390, 428
Adria, 46, 197, 267, 403
Adrian, 28, 29, 32, 34, 43, 61, 68, 76, 119, 135, 148, 150, 170, 184, **212**, 246, 248, 252, 253, 254, 259, 267, 279, 282, 291, 339, 350, 368, 414, 432, 447, 450, 453
Adriana, 28, **29**, 34, 38, 52, 74, 89, 94, 96, 97, 108, 116, 119, 148, 150, 160, 202, 204, 214, 233, 236, 283, 287, 290, 301, 304, 305, 307, 309, 319, 340, 399, 403, 413, 430, 433, 449
Adrianna, 21, 29, 31
Adrianne, 29
Adriano, 212
Adric, 305
Adriel, 37, 134, 164, 414
Adrien, 65, 212, 394
Adrienne, 29, **29**, 72, 92, 109, 119, 161, 207, 212, 216, 218, 231, 236, 247, 269, 294, 329, 363, 393, 430
Aedan, 447
Aedric, 212
Aelia, 381, 403
Aeliana, 84, 381
Aelianus, 84
Aemilia, 36, 137, 381
Aemilius, 381
Aeneas, 137, 167, 279, 299, 373, 381, 388
Aerin, 392
Aeris, 101, 221, 241, 243, 254, 283, 342, 344, 353, 392
Aeron, 177, 390, 427
Aeson, 381, 386
Afton, **29**, 213, 231, 261, 317, 324, 349, 357, 386, 431
Agata, 29
Agatha, **29**, 46, 276, 384, 404
Agathe, 29
Agathon, 381
Aggie, 29, 30

Agis, 397
Agnes, 29, **30**, 82, 90, 96, 98, 258, 445
Agustin, 149, 150, 158, 414
Ahab, 373, 417
Aharon, 210
Ahijah, 373
Ahmad, 31, 35, 36, 48, 281, 364, 427
Ahmed, 292, 314, 427
Aida, **30**, 388, 416, 431
Aidan, 30, 31, 32, 47, 211, 212, **212**, 221, 228, 231, 251, 256, 283, 295, 296, 302, 318, 320, 337, 370, 377, 385, 386, 432, 447
Aiden, 15, 212, 229, 326, 359
Aidric, 31, 48, **212**, 244, 341, 388, 447
Aidrick, 212
Aileen, 48, 82
Ailey, 369, 376, 409
Ailish, 33, 376
Ailsa, **30**, 75, 189, 195, 215, 217, 232, 255, 263, 273, 293, 298, 306, 376, 431, 460
Ailyn, 48
Aimee, 37, 195, 393, 448
Aine, **30**, 69, 144, 165, 189, 244, 251, 339, 376, 427
Áine, 30, 183, 379
Aino, 441
Ainslee, 30
Ainsley, **30**, 31, 103, 127, 136, 173, **197**, 205, 211, 212, 220, 228, 229, 231, 232, 235, 241, 264, 272, 293, 294, 296, 329, 345, 369, 376, 409
Aiofe, 30
Aïs, 37
Aisha, 27, **31**, 281, 314, 363, 426
Aislin, 250, 264
Aisling, 28, **31**, 44, 134, 258, 261, 346, 348, 376, 379
Aislinn, 29, 31, 189, 199, 325
Aiyana, 48, 363
AJ, 217
Aja, 363, 450
Ajani, 44, 209, 360
Ajax, 109, 120, **212**, 218, 291, 390, 422, 428
Akeelah, 295, 363
Akeem, 364, 427
Akilah, 360
Akira, 365

Akiva, 402
Akon, 386, 429
Aksel, 200, 221, 442
Akua, 360
Al, 213, 215, 437
Aladdin, 390
Alain, 213, 307, 394
Alaina, 31, 83, 352
Alan, 95, 119, 135, 141, 186, 192, 202, **213**, 250, 268, 299, 308, 386, 423, 437, 457
Alana, **31**, 41, 113, 124, 131, 254, 350, 403, 430, 433
Alandra, 34
Alanis, 429
Alanna, 31, 54, 146
Alannah, 31, 111, 256, 264, 296, 339, 348, 349, 376, 403
Alaric, 388, 437
Alasdair, 215
Alastair, 100, 215, 222
Alastor, 215, 312, 392, 428
Alathea, 31
Alaya, 363, 403
Alayna, 31, 83
Alban, 46, 75, **213**, 341, 386, 447, 461
Albany, 443
Alben, 13
Albert, 93, 106, 139, 149, 152, 159, 173, **213**, 219, 239, 266, 355, 405, 437
Alberta, 305
Albertine, 445
Alberto, 99, 168, 175, 213, 332, 400, 414
Albie, 213
Albin, 28, 65, 149, 198, 213, 270, 305, 437
Albina, 420
Albion, 276
Albrecht, 213
Albus, 312, 381, 392
Alcaeus, 381
Alcott, 418
Alden, 44, 50, 105, **213**, 271, 351, 365, 386, 409, 432, 461
Aldo, 96, 99, 137, 159, **213**, 261, 304, 307, 398, 400, 414, 453
Aldous, 347, 388, 418
Aldric, 179, 195, 332, 353, 388, 447
Aldrich, 437
Aldrin, 322, 409

Angelina, 39, 81, 97, 108, 119, 148, 184, 253, 259, 278, 285, 289, 353, 367, 403, 434
Angeline, 39, 41, 300, 393, 404, 434
Angelino, 217
Angelique, 38, 78, 80, 218, 250, 311, 325, 388, 393, 434
Angelita, 147
Angelle, 38
Angelo, 143, 217, 217, 400, 450
Angie, 38, 39, 90, 114, 434, 455
Angus, 166, 217, 264, 272, 273, 298, 307, 377, 438, 450
Ani, 37, 39, 41
Anibal, 414
Aniela, 452
Anika, 33, 41, 56, 126, 137, 146, 453
Anisa, 426
Aniston, 39, 223, 386, 409
Anita, 39, 71, 81, 176, 178, 197, 205, 207, 245, 286, 302, 309, 312, 321, 344, 363, 413, 454
Aniya, 39, 403
Aniyah, 39, 363
Anja, 42, 234, 395
Anjanette, 448
Anka, 42, 226, 452
Anke, 39, 343, 395
Ann, 39, 40, 41, 112, 116, 163, 192, 266, 309, 433, 434, 454
Anna, 39, 40, 41, 42, 64, 85, 87, 90, 99, 119, 122, 148, 165, 183, 217, 281, 287, 289, 290, 291, 348, 356, 357, 367, 373, 395, 434, 453, 457
Annabel, 31, 40, 59, 108, 149, 210, 211, 215, 216, 232, 242, 284, 299, 302, 324, 325, 341, 347, 356, 379, 388
Annabella, 31, 39, 40, 42, 358, 367, 403
Annabelle, 28, 40, 50, 90, 120, 143, 167, 204, 210, 224, 260, 367, 434
Annabeth, 40, 460
Annalie, 308, 395, 441
Annalise, 28, 40, 65, 143,

157, 179, 348, 367, 434, 460
Anne, 33, 37, 39, 40, 110, 152, 436, 457, 460
Anneke, 41
Annelie, 40, 179
Anneliese, 40, 395
Annelisa, 40
Annelise, 40, 88, 99, 176
Annetta, 41, 149
Annette, 40, 41, 71, 176, 180, 193, 322, 393, 422, 423, 434
Anni, 126, 189, 200, 317
Annie, 37, 39, 40, 41, 41, 132, 135, 144, 198, 237, 266, 271, 274, 287, 367, 398, 433, 434, 458
Annika, 31, 32, 41, 121, 122, 154, 158, 165, 221, 272, 403, 434, 441
Annis, 30
Anniston, 39, 129
Annmarie, 132
Annunziata, 143
Anouk, 37, 39, 40, 93, 227, 393, 395
Anoushka, 39, 452
Ansel, 405, 418
Anselm, 388, 447
Ansley, 30, 44, 409
Anthea, 55, 173, 199, 384, 434, 460
Anthi, 397
Anthony, 15, 19, 39, 63, 68, 109, 146, 204, 217, 218, 286, 308, 313, 349, 354, 440, 457
Antoine, 80, 161, 216, 217, 218, 285, 361, 364, 394
Antoinette, 41, 147, 393, 404, 437
Antoinio, 202
Anton, 34, 65, 70, 72, 84, 104, 117, 136, 157, 171, 176, 191, 217, 218, 218, 396, 440, 441, 452, 457, 461
Antonella, 42, 399
Antonia, 42, 65, 70, 104, 146, 174, 399, 413, 434, 437, 446, 457, 460
Antonietta, 41, 42
Antonin, 218, 452
Antonina, 399, 403, 437, 446, 452
Antonio, 29, 43, 83, 94, 214, 217, 218, 218, 233, 270,

290, 304, 305, 307, 308, 313, 319, 332, 349, 400, 414, 440, 450, 453, 457
Antonios, 397
Antonius, 217, 218, 381
Antony, 30, 185, 195, 217, 218, 254, 310, 311, 388, 447, 450
Antwan, 194, 218, 285, 364
Antwon, 218
Anwen, 87, 376
Anya, 30, 39, 41, 42, 74, 122, 134, 158, 160, 162, 164, 165, 166, 167, 194, 201, 210, 218, 279, 334, 403, 450, 451, 452, 460
Aodhagán, 258
Aogán, 258
Aoibheann, 183, 378, 379
Aoife, 90, 93, 134, 165, 183, 189, 251, 261, 376, 379, 427
Apollo, 42, 45, 211, 212, 218, 291, 311, 319, 390, 422, 427, 428, 447
Apollonia, 381, 388, 446
Apostolos, 397
Apple, 390
April, 36, 37, 42, 47, 48, 73, 88, 103, 105, 114, 124, 128, 159, 178, 195, 205, 226, 228, 229, 236, 256, 275, 297, 298, 340, 380, 431, 448
Aqua, 390
Aquila, 120, 373, 381, 403
Arabel, 42
Arabella, 42, 48, 75, 92, 174, 203, 367, 384, 403
Arabelle, 42
Araceli, 150, 185, 207, 413
Aragorn, 392
Aram, 373
Araminta, 31, 43, 345, 384, 388, 403, 436
Aramis, 37, 43, 66, 211, 218, 220, 417
Aravis, 392
Arcadia, 424, 443
Arch, 175, 218, 398
Archer, 29, 59, 66, 102, 120, 135, 218, 229, 233, 249, 257, 260, 265, 284, 291, 299, 324, 339, 351, 355, 357, 406, 437, 461
Archibald, 104, 162, 345, 377, 405, 437
Archie, 30, 51, 71, 77, 81, 90,

Astor, 409
Astoria, 443
Astrid, **45**, 84, 88, 99, 107,
136, 137, 277, 303, 306,
310, 357, 388, 395, 441
Astriel, 392
Atara, 29, 48, 184, 258, 279,
281, 290, 306, 307, 338,
353, 359, 372
Athanasia, 397
Athanasios, 397
Athena, 16, 30, 42, **45**, 47,
78, 109, 155, 168, 185,
211, 218, 220, 250, 292,
319, 338, 388, 397, 427,
431
Atif, 427
Atlanta, 443
Atlas, 390, 428
Atley, 409
Atom, 390
Atréju, 220
Atreyu, 86, 209, **220**, 392
Atticus, 35, 42, 43, 47, 49,
58, 95, 102, 104, 105, 108,
114, 138, 168, 209, **220**,
249, 263, 276, 323, 345,
347, 352, 381, 388, 417,
432, 461
Aubreon, 114, 199, 222, 345,
385, 388
Aubree, 21, 45, 228, 283, 434
Aubrey, 15, 28, 30, 32, **45**,
47, 72, 105, 145, 151, 175,
193, 221, 222, 225, 229,
247, 254, 257, 267, 272,
277, 281, 309, 318, 320,
322, 323, 324, 351, 366,
409
Aubri, 45
Aubriana, 45
Aubrianna, **45**, 403, 434
Aubrie, 45, 221
Aubry, 249
Auburn, 424
Auden, 29, 54, 75, 87, 151,
218, 231, 257, 260, 297,
303, 320, 322, 339, 354,
366, 386, 409, 418
Audra, **45**, 46, 65, 147, 180,
231, 233, 240, 253, 265,
282, 353, 404, 431, 448,
460
Audrey, **46**, 69, 198, 204,
216, 224, 234, 240, 242,
249, 253, 262, 277, 311,
314, 324, 330, 357, 368,
431, 457

Audri, 46
Audriana, 46, 111, 403
Audrianna, 45, 179, 237
Audrina, 29, **46**, 55, 168,
178, 403
Audry, 46
Augie, 220
August, 28, 34, 50, 77, 86,
99, 103, 111, 117, 133, 152,
153, 157, 167, 198, 203,
204, 206, 215, **220**, 236,
243, 257, 258, 261, 263,
272, 282, 291, 313, 348,
368, 380, 405, 438, 441
Augusta, **46**, 72, 159, 167,
171, 216, 245, 270, 273,
301, 305, 357, 381, 404,
443, 446
Augustine, 221, 366, 388,
393
Augusto, 220
Augustus, 31, 46, 72, 131,
159, 205, 220, 223, 244,
272, 301, 352, 381, 388,
405, 438
Aura, 101, 325, 390, 450
Aurea, **46**, 46, 213, 353, 403,
446, 460
Aurelia, 28, 29, 42, 46, **46**,
131, 171, 198, 220, 245,
381, 404, 446, 460
Aurélie, 46
Aurelio, 400, 414
Aurelius, 168, 381
Auron, 353, 392
Aurora, 21, 45, 46, **47**, 75,
93, 120, 138, 141, 159,
168, 184, 220, 299, 324,
328, 334, 342, 347, 388,
427, 457
Aurore, 47, 393
Austen, 221, 248, 416, 418
Austin, 31, 32, 34, 35, 44, 47,
56, 67, 78, 125, 143, 148,
184, 193, 196, 215, **221**,
227, 237, 241, 251, 252,
274, 288, 309, 330, 331,
343, 345, 350, 352, 356,
386, 409, 432, 443, 459
Austyn, 221
Author, 421
Autry, 129, 246, 261, 265,
300, 355, 382, 409, 460
Autumn, 47, 56, 78, 91,
102, 110, 111, 116, 188,
192, 206, 221, 233, 237,
238, 251, 277, 380, 424,
430, 431

Ava, 15, 47, **47**, 48, 68, 85,
90, 97, 128, 133, 154, 157,
167, 198, 205, 209, 212,
242, 254, 259, 262, 271,
274, 320, 367, 368, 431,
446, 450
Avah, 47
Avalon, 37, 60, 86, 211, 218,
222, 291, 325, 390, 437,
460
Avalyn, 99, 326, 386
Avanna, 129
Avelina, 388
Averie, 47
Averil, 48, 212, 213, 226,
279, 305, 330, 341, 353,
388, 446, 460
Averill, 48, 332
Avery, 15, 32, 43, 45, 46, **47**,
49, 57, 77, 87, 124, 173,
178, 189, 193, 212, 215,
221, 227, 229, 234, 240,
247, 261, 268, 279, 298,
302, 303, 309, 318, 320,
321, 324, 330, 331, 350,
357, 366, 409, 432
Avi, 43, 48, 210, 236, 318,
329, 402, 451
Avia, 329, 401, 450
Aviana, 43, 45, **47**, 48, 153,
403, 460
Avianna, 47
Avigail, 27, 67
Avila, 137, 212, 388, 446,
460
Avis, 35, **47**, 71, 92, 107, 138,
162, 171, 172, 203, 206,
208, 219, 244, 295, 320,
330, 352, 359, 404, 431,
450, 460
Avital, 208, 279, 372, 401
Aviva, 29, 33, 36, **48**, 188,
219, 318, 401, 403, 460
Avonlea, 48, 154, 303, 354,
416, 443, 460
Avraham, 210
Avram, 210
Avril, 42, **48**, 322, 325, 380,
393, 429
Axel, 43, 45, 47, 88, 136, 141,
146, 172, 209, **221**, 260,
264, 272, 292, 297, 308,
311, 317, 320, 357, 388,
392, 442, 451
Axelle, 37, 144, 145, 300,
393, 460
Axl, 221, 390, 429
Axton, 386, 409, 461

Ayana, 31, 48, 106, 216, 319
Ayanda, 360
Ayanna, 27, 35, **48**, 295, 360, 363, 403
Ayda, 30
Aydan, 221
Ayden, 19, 211, 212, **221**, 370, 386, 432
Aydin, 110, 221
Ayelet, 401
Ayesha, 31
Ayla, 128, 296, 369, 450
Aylin, 48, 369, 386, 413
Aylín, 48, 82
Ayo, 361
Azalea, 380
Azarel, 208, 373
Azaria, **48**, 403
Azariah, 48
Aziza, 426
Azra, 426
Azriel, 279, 373
Azucena, 413
Azuka, 361
Azul, 413
Azure, 48, 200, 380, 437

Babette, 92, 393
Babs, 49
Bailee, 49, 221
Bailey, **49**, 56, 102, 117, 137, 159, 178, 189, 220, **221**, 225, 229, 249, 264, 267, 268, 279, 293, 343, 345, 366, 369, 370, 406, 459
Baird, 375, 377
Bakari, 44, 222, 361
Baker, 406
Baldwin, 226, 409, 447
Balin, 386, 447
Balthazar, 373, 450
Bambi, 390
Bancroft, 88, 405, 409
Banjo, 390, 418
Bannon, 386, 409
Baptiste, 394
Bar, 329, 401
Barack, **222**, 361, 429
Barak, 222, 373, 402
Baraka, 222, 361
Barb, 49, 239
Barbara, 23, **49**, 61, 98, 116, 118, 169, 188, 193, 253, 266, 329, 331, 332, 334, 434, 454
Barbie, 49, 429, 455
Barbra, 49, 423
Barclay, 357, 409

Bard, 444
Barker, 406
Barkley, 246, 383, 409
Barlow, 200, 317, 409, 461
Barnabas, 43, 156, 222, 276, 299, 305, 347, 373, 388, 437
Barnaby, 31, 49, 55, 65, 92, 106, 113, 114, 120, 155, 172, 179, 222, **222**, 223, 224, 245, 323, 332, 373, 385, 388, 437
Barnard, 444, 447
Barney, 80, 169, 172, 222, **222**, 225, 274, 398, 429, 437
Baron, **222**, 225, 325, 386, 390, 432
Barrett, 33, 52, 129, 131, 157, **222**, 225, 235, 240, 252, 294, 330, 332, 356, 409, 437, 457, 461
Barron, 222, 253, 327, 409, 437, 456
Barry, 41, 53, 60, 66, 67, 71, 75, 100, 116, 122, 123, 153, 168, 169, 171, 181, 187, 201, 222, **223**, 230, 268, 299, 322, 347, 423, 437
Bart, 114, 223, **223**, 239, 253, 296, 437, 456
Bartek, 452
Bartholomew, 46, 120, 131, 198, 199, 222, 223, **223**, 224, 244, 276, 373, 388, 437, 447
Bartimaeus, 392
Bartley, 223
Bartolomé, 223
Bartolomeo, 223
Barton, 105, 355, 409, 437
Baruch, 222, 373, 402
Bashir, 110, 183, 427
Basia, 452
Basie, 399
Basil, 29, 117, 205, 236, 270, 322, 385, 405
Basim, 427
Basma, 163, 426
Bastien, 37, 93, 144, 322, 339, 394
Bathsheba, 115, 372
Batt, 223
Baxter, 238, 252, 406
Bay, 49, 129, 135, 182, 289, 325, 329, 357, 359, 374, 380

Baya, 446, 450
Bayard, 88, 198, 225, 354, 405
Baylee, 49, 55, 110, 112, 182, 342, 345, 369, 457
Bayleigh, 49, 132
Baylor, 103, 154, 226, 409, 444, 461
Bayo, 361
Baz, 223, 325, 339, 375, 437
Bea, 49
Bear, 431
Beatrice, 33, 49, **49**, 70, 72, 81, 83, 86, 96, 147, 148, 152, 206, 258, 266, 301, 328, 337, 348, 384, 393, 404, 437, 449, 460
Beatrix, 42, 46, **49**, 90, 104, 106, 108, 170, 215, 220, 222, 223, 244, 245, 249, 276, 303, 306, 311, 323, 345, 384, 388, 437, 446, 460
Beatriz, 49, 149, 413
Beau, 137, **223**, 225, 298, 304, 331, 375, 382
Beauregard, 383, 388
Beaver, 453
Bebe, 49
Becca, 176
Beck, 56, 66, 179, 223, 226, 231, 234, 267, 289, 291, 375, 409, 461
Beckett, 29, 42, 49, 118, 151, 174, 184, 220, **223**, 231, 249, 260, 276, 281, 303, 304, 306, 321, 339, 345, 357, 409, 418
Beckham, 39, 173, **223**, 409, 429
Becky, 76, 170, 176, 223, 423, 434
Bedelia, 77, 376, 403, 404
Bee, 421
Beer, 269
Bekka, 176
Bel, 50, 115
Belarius, 450
Belen, 413
Belèn, 100
Belina, 50, 446
Belinda, **50**, 60, 73, 76, 194, 245, 269, 296, 403, 435, 455
Bell, 42, 50
Bella, 42, 47, 50, **50**, 98, 99, 108, 155, 177, 179, 223,

226, 234, 289, 302, 317, 318, 351, 367
Bellamy, 50, 91, 93, 225, 226, 322, 324, 341, 349, 409, 460
Bellatrix, 212, 392
Belle, 27, 40, 50, 50, 73, 98, 115, 139, 144, 153, 198, 273, 290, 291, 320, 374, 380, 382, 460
Belva, 420
Ben, 41, 51, 58, 115, 123, 144, 153, 161, 164, 191, 222, 224, 237, 437, 458
Benedick, 449
Benedict, 65, 81, 90, 96, 131, 170, 171, 198, 206, 208, 222, 223, 224, 224, 310, 388, 437, 447, 449, 450
Benita, 207
Benito, 224, 414, 429
Benjamin, 15, 39, 62, 69, 87, 174, 176, 183, 211, 214, 217, 224, 247, 288, 289, 310, 316, 317, 338, 373, 437, 457
Benji, 224
Benjy, 51
Bennet, 55, 75, 224, 417
Bennett, 12, 40, 59, 65, 84, 85, 90, 99, 105, 119, 120, 206, 216, 221, 222, 224, 224, 230, 232, 234, 249, 258, 260, 265, 274, 311, 323, 409, 437, 457
Bennie, 52, 365
Benno, 219, 224, 244, 396, 398, 437
Benny, 398, 399
Benoit, 224, 394
Benson, 437
Bentley, 19, 45, 46, 56, 167, 224, 227, 230, 257, 272, 280, 296, 383, 409, 437
Bently, 224
Benton, 409, 437
Beracha, 222
Berenice, 373, 413
Beriah, 373
Berit, 441
Berkeley, 44, 57, 85, 167, 205, 249, 303, 325, 366, 409, 443
Berkley, 347
Bernadette, 39, 100, 174, 199, 302, 393, 454
Bernadine, 335

Bernard, 113, 153, 170, 180, 193, 225, 239, 258, 262, 266, 270, 273, 286, 301, 309, 310, 312, 333, 336, 354, 405, 437, 454
Bernardo, 225, 400, 414, 450
Bernhard, 225, 396
Bernice, 158, 198, 219, 265, 278, 314, 326, 356, 373, 445
Bernie, 225, 398
Bernt, 225, 396
Berry, 223
Bert, 213, 225, 266, 275, 332, 398, 437
Berta, 50
Bertha, 50, 96, 105, 395, 445, 457
Berthold, 396
Bertie, 50
Bertram, 96, 105, 171, 193, 205, 225, 235, 243, 258, 396, 405, 437, 438, 450
Bertrand, 41, 219, 225, 394, 437, 439, 447
Beryl, 193, 262, 270, 380, 404
Bess, 50, 51, 51, 85, 144, 164, 174, 255, 272, 273, 277, 304, 314, 316, 398, 434
Bessie, 51, 90, 315, 398, 399
Beth, 51, 51, 75, 85, 115, 132, 136, 138, 141, 178, 197, 226, 238, 297, 401, 434, 455
Bethan, 63, 87, 98, 154, 267, 272, 376, 434
Bethany, 27, 50, 51, 60, 63, 109, 116, 157, 164, 176, 182, 191, 194, 210, 281, 289, 348, 358, 373, 434, 448, 459
Bethel, 306, 372, 434
Beto, 332
Betsey, 51
Betsy, 51, 53, 85, 170, 182, 192, 287, 336, 423, 433, 434
Bette, 51, 85
Bettie, 51
Bettina, 70, 200, 395, 399, 434
Betts, 51
Betty, 51, 51, 85, 163, 182, 203, 434, 453, 454
Bettye, 51
Beulah, 50, 208, 372, 445

Bev, 52
Bevan, 63, 82, 228, 331, 357, 377, 386
Beverlee, 52
Beverley, 52
Beverly, 46, 49, 52, 91, 98, 116, 139, 150, 172, 180, 188, 328, 454
Beyoncé, 363, 429
Bianca, 52, 170, 199, 217, 245, 247, 253, 263, 271, 304, 319, 334, 340, 399, 413, 434, 449
Bibi, 52
Bibiana, 41, 204
Bijou, 48, 92, 390
Bilal, 163, 183, 427
Bill, 51, 115, 116, 163, 192, 269, 332, 356, 438, 454
Billie, 52, 66, 205, 219, 366, 398, 399, 434
Billy, 52, 170, 182, 336, 356
Bing, 368, 375
Binyamin, 224
Birch, 111, 129, 135, 200, 206, 275, 354, 375, 380
Birdie, 398
Birgit, 55, 441
Birgitta, 441
Birk, 442
Bishop, 225, 325, 390
Bix, 399
Bjorn, 442
Blade, 392, 422
Blaine, 53, 131, 225, 234, 240, 293, 318, 324, 375, 377, 447, 457
Blair, 52, 85, 128, 189, 223, 229, 230, 240, 291, 340, 366, 374, 375, 376
Blaire, 52
Blaise, 22, 48, 57, 59, 65, 66, 71, 86, 144, 188, 194, 202, 225, 226, 245, 375, 394, 447
Blake, 19, 45, 52, 52, 54, 56, 57, 61, 70, 81, 91, 113, 115, 116, 123, 168, 173, 184, 192, 201, 223, 225, 228, 229, 230, 238, 242, 255, 297, 366, 374, 375, 431
Blakely, 39, 200, 228, 229, 409
Blanca, 52, 53, 81, 286, 328, 413
Blanche, 53, 147, 153, 239, 305, 393, 404
Blane, 99, 225, 293

337, 339, 344, 377, 432, 448, 456
Briana, 54
Brianna, 35, **54**, 56, 57, 58, 60, 101, 123, 145, 150, 178, 186, 363, 369, 403, 434, 459
Brianne, 54, 434
Briar, 48, **54**, 55, 57, 120, 141, 179, 200, 206, 209, 220, 231, 249, 329, 331, 366, 380, 416, 425, 431
Brice, 58, 107, 136, 225, 230, 375, 377, 394, 447
Bridger, 68, 162, 228, **229**, 242, 267, 268, 383, 406, 422
Bridget, **55**, 153, 228, 229, 235, 294, 314, 321, 339, 340, 362, 376, 434, 448, 455
Bridie, 55, 420
Brie, 54
Briella, 55, 112, 403, 434
Brielle, 29, 46, 55, **55**, 68, 111, 168, 228, 369
Brienne, 392
Briggs, 39, 132, 189, 228, 233, 291, 297, 322, 347, 409
Brigham, 222, 223, 237, 324, 325, 341, 409
Brighid, 55
Brighton, 91, 107, 219, 350, 386, 443
Brigid, 55, 76
Brigit, 55
Brigitta, 395
Brigitte, 55, 66
Briley, 30, 57, 127, 229, 369, 409
Brin, 55
Brinlee, 55
Brinleigh, 55
Brinley, **55**, 168, 224, 228, 241, 369, 409
Brionna, 39
Briony, **55**, 65, 92, 114, 179, 195, 203, 380, 384, 434, 460
Brisa, **55**, 413, 434
Bristol, **56**, 57, 158, 257, 347, 431, 443
Britany, 56
Britney, 114, 429, 448
Britt, 55, 56, **56**, 126, 132, 136, 226, 268, 290, 300, 327, 366, 374, 441

Britta, 41, 56, 85, 136, 172, 200, 303, 317, 343, 441, 446, 450
Brittani, 456
Brittanie, 56
Brittany, 36, 44, 51, 54, **56**, 72, 139, 200, 434, 443, 448
Brittney, 56
Brittni, 56
Brittny, 56
Britton, 222, 386, 461
Brock, 102, 161, 201, **229**, 240, 344, 350, 409, 422
Broder, 442
Broderick, 179, 227, 251, 377, 409, 440
Brodie, 28, 30, 189, 229, 264, 345, 349, 377
Brody, 28, 44, 225, 229, **229**, 230, 238, 241, 242, 243, 244, 271, 283, 294, 298, 331, 334, 366, 409
Brogan, 30, 46, 50, 58, 59, 107, 137, 154, 187, 199, 227, **229**, 242, 245, 256, 265, 292, 325, 334, 339, 377, 386, 409, 447, 461
Bron, 375
Bronislav, 152
Bronson, 222, 229, 386, 409, 422
Bronwyn, 98, 100, 177, 354, 376, 388
Bronx, 443
Brook, 56, 57, 197
Brooke, 34, **56**, 61, 69, 115, 130, 164, 168, 192, 222, 225, 227, 231, 237, 238, 240, 242, 277, 305, 330, 340, 350, 374, 430
Brooklyn, 15, 44, 54, **57**, 138, 143, 223, 224, 228, 229, 230, 231, 280, 283, 350, 386, 443
Brooklynn, 21, 57, 141, 227, 228, 283
Brooklynne, 57
Brooks, 44, 45, 52, 87, **230**, 249, 271, 375, 409, 457
Broz, 216
Bruce, 53, 54, 66, 75, 81, 95, 98, 122, 146, 168, 183, 186, 193, 223, 230, 248, 250, 254, 256, 268, 293, 299, 347, 355, 423
Brunilda, 445
Bruno, 71, 146, 217, 218,

230, 277, 320, 332, 396, 398, 400, 422, 447
Bry, 57
Bryan, 33, 129, 153, 155, 156, 196, 203, 227, 228, 229, 294, 349, 431
Bryanna, 54
Bryant, 105, 121, 128, 129, 145, 205, **230**, 251, 282, 346, 409, 432
Bryar, 205
Bryce, 43, 48, 54, **57**, 63, 69, 73, 99, 124, 142, 168, 184, 187, 189, 223, 225, 226, 227, 228, 230, **230**, 237, 243, 245, 279, 324, 338, 340, 344, 349, 353, 359, 366, 374, 375, 377, 383, 431
Brycen, 57, 230, 374, 386
Bryer, 409
Brylee, **57**, 182
Bryleigh, 57
Brylie, 57
Bryn, 52, 54, 55, 57, 63, 187, 189, 229, 256, 293, 345, 350, 357
Brynlee, 21, 55, 57
Brynn, 21, 52, 54, **57**, 93, 99, 141, 144, 176, 181, 231, 267, 279, 289, 290, 294, 298, 314, 329, 331, 374, 376
Brynna, 54, 376, 460
Bryony, 49, 55, 111, 222
Bryson, 44, 57, 112, 127, 201, 229, **230**, 231, 233, 293, 297, 386, 409
Bubba, 383
Buck, 80, 181, 382, 398, 422
Buckley, 409
Bud, 398, 453
Buddy, 52, 79, 398
Buffy, 85, 190, 402, 429, 448
Buford, 277, 445
Burgess, 72, 274, 324, 341, 354, 357, 405, 409
Burke, 229, 290, 338, 375, 409, 461
Burl, 445
Burley, 421
Burton, 341, 409
Butch, 422, 423
Butler, 444
Buzz, 255, 382, 422
Byron, 72, 75, 76, 188, 190, 195, 213, **231**, 240, 245,

248, 310, 354, 386, 418, 432, 457

Cab, 231, 232, 398, 399, 438
Cabot, 50, **231**, 300, 409, 438, 461
Cade, 36, 59, 129, 229, **231**, 267, 279, 354, 375
Caden, 55, 182, **231**, 370, 386
Cadence, 42, 55, **57**, 58, 59, 95, 102, 107, 141, 159, 162, 168, 201, 205, 228, 359, 369, 424
Cadogan, 63, 87, 177, 227, 377, 409
Cady, 57
Caecilia, 381
Caedmon, 31, 42, 100, 104, 185, 195, 212, 388, 447
Cael, 232, 297, 353, 375, 377, 451, 461
Caelan, 377
Caelia, 65
Caesar, 236, 381, 390
Cai, 357, 377
Caiden, 231, 241
Cairo, 44, 125, 158, 208, 364, 443
Cait, 58
Caitlin, 31, **58**, 64, 69, 121, 122, 154, 166, 187, 228, 233, 369, 376, 386, 459
Caitlyn, 58, 121
Cal, 50, 136, 231, 232, 237, 272, 277, 289, 306, 375, 438
Calais, 443
Calante, 380
Calder, 53, 54, 55, 60, 102, 108, 129, 135, 209, 231, **231**, 234, 249, 300, 409, 418, 438, 461
Cale, 232, **232**, 298, 375
Caleb, 27, 68, 91, 101, 143, 148, 157, 210, 220, **232**, 234, 259, 267, 278, 285, 288, 289, 290, 302, 305, 312, 317, 368, 373, 438
Caledonia, 388, 404, 443
Caleigh, 58
Cali, 58
Calico, 107, 390
Calista, **58**, 403
Caliste, 58
Calix, 43, 137, 212, 321, 388, 389
Calla, 50, **58**, 72, 103, 135,

157, 206, 351, 380, 434, 450, 460
Callahan, 143, 345
Callan, 238, 377, 386, 438
Callhan, 409
Callie, **58**, 58, 61, 62, 144, 237, 434, 457
Calliope, 120, 212, 390, 427, 434
Callista, 58, 434
Callisto, 389, 427
Callum, 30, 75, 109, 161, 232, **232**, 244, 263, 264, 267, 273, 298, 307, 334, 376, 377, 438, 461
Calum, 232
Calvin, 46, 108, 180, 215, **232**, 318, 438, 440, 457
Cam, 59, 232, 233, 438
Camaryn, 178
Cambria, 48, 434, 443
Cambrie, 238
Camden, 28, 57, 124, 158, 175, **232**, 241, 249, 254, 350, 377, 386, 438, 443
Camdyn, 434
Camellia, 114, 380, 434, 460
Cameron, **58**, 59, 77, 87, 91, 116, 137, 145, 162, 232, **233**, 243, 245, 252, 256, 268, 366, 376, 377, 424, 431, 434, 438
Cami, 58, 59
Camila, 21, 37, 59, 76, 135, 141, 149, 166, 190, 217, 252, 287, 309, 403, 413
Camilla, 47, 59, **59**, 75, 104, 119, 120, 140, 204, 214, 224, 225, 290, 291, 328, 384, 434, 446, 457
Camille, 28, 41, **59**, 64, 65, 69, 72, 84, 98, 105, 150, 158, 165, 185, 188, 203, 221, 230, 236, 260, 271, 318, 325, 354, 393, 416, 434, 436, 457
Camillo, 400, 450
Camilo, 414, 438
Cammie, 58, 59, 233, 434
Campbell, 40, 57, **59**, 62, 75, 85, 87, 132, 154, 169, 189, 211, 216, 223, **233**, 234, 237, 252, 268, 284, 306, 317, 327, 344, 366, 409, 434, 438, 461
Camren, 233
Camron, 233, 386
Camryn, 44, 58, **59**, 63, 103,

112, 142, 154, 231, 234, 243, 249, 303, 351, 366, 369, 386, 434
Candace, 45, 51, **60**, 70, 72, 76, 116, 119, 130, 147, 156, 194, 202, 240, 263, 269, 298, 372, 423, 434, 448
Candice, 29, 60, 73, 79, 98, 123, 128, 191, 240, 346
Candida, 434
Candis, 60
Candy, 60, 390, 434, 455
Cannon, 328, 344, 390, 422
Canton, 249, 306, 386, 443
Canyon, 106, 154, 162, 324, 329, 331, 343, 380, 383, 390
Caoimhe, 30, 134, 183, 189, 261, 376, 379
Cap, 235
Caprice, **60**, 129, 424, 431
Cara, 4, 121, 131, 430, 450
Caradoc, 100
Cardiff, 443
Caress, 390
Carey, 75, 332, 409
Cari, 62
Carin, 121
Carina, 64, 121, 131
Carissa, **60**, 156, 403, 459
Carl, 92, 104, 107, 112, 120, 149, 180, 181, **233**, 237, 321, 346, 355, 454
Carla, **60**, 74, 79, 97, 169, 178, 181, 187, 194, 245, 248, 293, 336, 399, 434, 455
Carleigh, 132
Carlene, 66, 454
Carleton, 224, 233, 241, 337, 385, 444
Carlie, 61, 64, 142
Carling, 226, 409
Carlise, 354
Carlisle, 314, 409
Carlito, 233
Carlitos, 233
Carlo, 42, 75, 97, 140, 146, 176, 180, 191, 217, 233, 237, 307, 308, 400, 457, 461
Carlos, 19, 83, 217, **233**, 237, 252, 286, 288, 290, 305, 307, 313, 327, 332, 354, 413, 414
Carlotta, 434, 436
Carlsen, 284
Carlson, 409

Cloie, 426
Clotilde, 393, 437
Cloud, 220, 241, 321, 343, 392, 425
Clover, 120, 173, 181, 380, 390
Clovis, 260
Cloyd, 421
Clyde, 138, 162, 170, 239, 241, 257, 301, 302, 320, 335, 454
Coby, 29, 280, 297, 370
Coco, 92, 390, 429
Cody, 64, 68, 109, 123, 188, 221, 235, 241, 242, 243, 350, 382, 383, 409, 432, 443, 459
Cohen, 241, 386
Colby, 60, 78, 121, 128, 142, 186, 200, 227, 237, 242, 244, 271, 370, 409, 438, 444
Cole, 19, 27, 31, 54, 56, 57, 61, 69, 92, 99, 142, 176, 179, 188, 194, 198, 214, 225, 238, 242, 242, 279, 280, 290, 292, 305, 317, 324, 345, 350, 375, 431, 438
Coleman, 242, 242, 265, 299, 301, 351, 399, 409, 461
Colette, 71, 207, 393, 418, 423, 446
Coley, 409
Colin, 19, 31, 59, 74, 92, 95, 97, 113, 154, 160, 164, 182, 214, 215, 228, 238, 242, 251, 262, 268, 271, 277, 295, 305, 313, 317, 332, 342, 350, 377, 385, 386, 431, 432, 438
Colleen, 54, 71, 82, 186, 187, 193, 197, 245, 294, 377, 423, 431
Collier, 407
Collin, 95, 242
Colm, 28, 30, 93, 134, 189, 232, 251, 377, 379
Colman, 65, 213, 242, 242, 315, 377, 386, 438, 447
Colson, 39, 200, 324, 409, 438
Colston, 438
Colt, 62, 129, 137, 223, 235, 242, 243, 247, 268, 273, 282, 287, 289, 304, 351, 375, 422

Colter, 242
Colton, 45, 48, 59, 110, 124, 162, 167, 175, 220, 229, 230, 242, 243, 330, 349, 350, 383, 386, 409, 438
Coltrane, 377, 399
Columbus, 315
Colwyn, 377, 386
Commodore, 421
Con, 243, 244, 438
Conall, 63, 232, 244, 258, 377
Conan, 243, 377, 386, 392, 432, 438, 447
Concetta, 399, 434
Conchobar, 243, 244
Concord, 67
Conn, 326
Connal, 349
Connell, 409
Conner, 243
Connery, 409
Connie, 39, 41, 71, 71, 119, 146, 169, 171, 193, 230, 243, 244, 246, 250, 268, 286, 347, 423, 434, 438
Connolly, 85, 93, 143, 199, 205, 345, 377, 409
Connor, 19, 32, 56, 57, 58, 59, 61, 77, 97, 117, 125, 128, 142, 153, 154, 162, 173, 212, 228, 231, 233, 234, 242, 243, 244, 245, 256, 272, 302, 303, 325, 331, 350, 377, 431, 438
Conor, 31, 47, 54, 58, 63, 69, 109, 165, 176, 188, 214, 243, 250, 277, 293, 294, 296, 335, 377
Conrad, 34, 46, 70, 72, 86, 96, 99, 139, 225, 243, 244, 258, 266, 305, 333, 405, 438, 450
Conroy, 377, 409
Constance, 52, 71, 83, 100, 113, 118, 139, 173, 178, 180, 233, 239, 240, 266, 286, 299, 309, 328, 333, 337, 344, 380, 434, 454
Constant, 67, 380
Constantin, 202, 438, 452
Constantine, 171, 202, 311, 315, 388
Constanza, 413
Consuelo, 80, 413, 434
Conway, 177, 314, 383, 409
Coolidge, 409
Coop, 243

Cooper, 28, 57, 62, 63, 116, 137, 167, 178, 220, 223, 224, 225, 227, 229, 230, 231, 234, 238, 242, 243, 243, 249, 265, 267, 276, 279, 289, 293, 298, 302, 309, 320, 337, 345, 351, 352, 357, 359, 383, 406, 407
Copland, 409, 418
Cora, 16, 21, 34, 69, 71, 72, 98, 106, 132, 273, 367, 404, 434
Coral, 58, 72, 72, 297, 351, 380, 434, 460
Coralie, 341, 393, 404, 434, 460
Coraline, 62, 72, 72, 245, 404, 416, 434, 460
Corazon, 434
Corbin, 112, 119, 231, 235, 243, 338, 386
Cordelia, 29, 46, 72, 77, 88, 169, 243, 273, 301, 384, 404, 434, 449
Cordell, 438
Corey, 36, 44, 53, 72, 110, 121, 127, 159, 186, 191, 195, 200, 205, 229, 235, 236, 241, 242, 244, 256, 268, 322, 369, 370, 432, 448
Cori, 72
Corin, 55, 58, 114, 173, 179, 245, 385, 386, 450
Corina, 84
Corinna, 63, 70, 72, 76, 151, 180, 384, 403, 434, 460
Corinne, 28, 72, 353, 457
Corinne, 393
Corliss, 434
Cormac, 30, 93, 195, 197, 199, 212, 242, 244, 251, 256, 258, 264, 265, 296, 306, 334, 348, 377, 418, 447, 461
Cornelia, 104, 276, 381, 434, 436
Cornelis, 244
Cornelius, 46, 198, 244, 291, 301, 345, 373, 381, 388, 405, 438, 450
Cornell, 149, 233, 244, 248, 270, 325, 328, 346, 409, 438, 444, 454
Corny, 244
Corrie, 71, 72, 137, 434
Corrigan, 377, 409

217, 224, **247**, 249, 287,
289, 305, 310, 313, 343,
373, 431, 438, 457
Daniela, 38, 74, **74**, 83, 94,
116, 160, 162, 168, 170,
180, 191, 218, 243, 246,
308, 309, 350, 399, 403,
414, 430, 452
Daniella, 31, 74, 94, 157, 254
Danielle, 29, 68, 74, **74**, 77,
88, 95, 121, 128, 132, 154,
158, 165, 191, 194, 202,
285, 392, 393, 448
Danika, 74
Danila, 74
Danilo, 414, 438
Danisha, 44
Danner, 438
Danny, 51, 69, 119, 157,
170, 247, 347, 349, 423,
431
Dante, 30, 31, 42, 44, 52,
94, 97, 158, 169, 218, **247**,
270, 271, 297, 304, 319,
332, 334, 340, 361, 364,
392, 400, 418, 432, 438
Danya, 161
Danyel, 247
Daphna, 75, 324
Daphne, 28, 59, 66, 68, **75**,
78, 93, 104, 105, 120, 130,
141, 157, 171, 188, 206,
214, 260, 318, 324, 332,
342, 353, 354, 384, 428,
431, 457, 460
Dara, 76, 335, 349, 376, 377,
401, 455
Darby, 52, 78, 251, 252, 344,
366, 377, 409
Darcie, 75
Darcy, 53, **75**, 129, 132, 174,
191, 201, 231, 233, 236,
240, 245, 246, 296, 327,
409, 416, 431, 455
D'Arcy, 75
Dare, 28
Daren, 248
Daria, 30, 74, **75**, 122, 159,
160, 165, 176, 185, 213,
247, 253, 399, 431, 446,
452, 453, 460
Darian, 33, 48, 89, **248**, 253,
280, 364, 386, 432
Dariana, 403, 460
Darien, 248
Darin, 79, 186, 248, 456
Dario, 43, 97, 137, 191, 248,
317, 340, 400, 447, 453

Darion, 250
Darius, 32, 74, 121, 126,
129, 185, 247, **248**, 250,
252, 263, 311, 326, 364,
381, 432, 447
Darko, 452
Darla, 75, 255, 322, 423
Darleen, 75
Darlene, **75**, 340, 422, 423,
454
Darli, 75
Darline, 75
Darnell, 82, 129, 130, 194,
298, 346, 352, 364, 409
Darold, 421
Darragh, 183, 376, 377
Darrel, 248
Darrell, 153, 168, 207, **248**,
255, 297, 327, 329, 346,
423, 432, 456
Darren, 50, 74, 76, 77, 111,
161, 178, 187, 194, 201,
205, 231, **248**, 295, 351,
386, 432, 456
Darrian, 248
Darrien, 248
Darrin, 75, 97, 248
Darrion, 248
Darron, 248
Darryl, 75, 176, 178, 181,
205, 248, 256, 333, 355,
364, 432, 456
Darwen, 248
Darwin, **248**, 409, 429
Daryl, 248
Daryle, 248
Dash, 249, 375, 412, 422
Dashiell, 48, 54, 72, 88, 105,
108, 209, 215, 223, 231,
249, 388, 412, 418, 461
Dasia, 75, 106, 126, 250,
253, 281, 311, 452
D'asia, 48
Dave, 249, 438
Daveth, 377, 438
Davey, 249, 423
Davia, 75
Davian, 386
David, 15, 51, 73, 75, 76,
121, 136, 148, 176, 192,
217, 229, 247, **249**, 262,
284, 288, 308, 313, 332,
344, 348, 373, 438, 453,
457
Davin, 161, 386, 438
Davina, 65, **75**, 195, 199,
245, 251, 263, 298, 327,
349, 377, 384, 403, 460

Davinia, 75
Davion, 39, 45, 112, 126,
127, 364, 438
Davis, 69, 224, 230, 240,
249, 271, 274, 356, 409,
438, 457, 461
Davon, 208, 364
Davonte, 89
Davy, 75, 214, 249, 385
Dawa, 346
Dawn, **75**, 79, 97, 186, 195,
200, 205, 223, 296, 297,
300, 349, 351, 374, 380,
455
Dawna, 75
Dawson, 59, 103, 189, 196,
221, 228, 235, 237, 242,
243, 246, **249**, 257, 293,
386, 409, 432
Dax, 375
Daxton, 386
Dayana, 37, **76**, 78, 164, 414
Dayanara, 76, 414
Dayane, 76
Daylin, 369, 460
Dayna, 74
Dayton, 127, **249**, 386, 409,
432, 443
Dea, 38
Deacon, 62, 66, 118, 128,
129, 169, 179, 187, 218,
225, 226, 235, 242, **249**,
273, 285, 289, 291, 304,
355, 357, 383, 407, 461
Dean, 41, 71, 95, 118, 123,
141, 157, 246, 247, **250**,
268, 271, 283, 293, 295,
300, 316, 349, 351, 375,
423, 454
Deana, 76
DeAndrae, 250
DeAndre, **250**, 364, 459
Deane, 250
DeAngelo, 250, 308
Deanna, 33, 50, **76**, 92, 156,
180, 194, 269, 403, 448
Deanne, 76, 111, 455
Deasia, 363
Deb, 76
Debbie, 51, 71, **76**, 239, 300,
349, 423, 434
Debby, 76, 201, 203, 328
Debi, 76
Débora, 76
Deborah, 73, **76**, 118, 168,
176, 192, 197, 249, 254,
272, 295, 327, 343, 372,
423, 434

Di, 78, 79
Dia, 79, 86
Diamond, 78, 89, 255, 325, 362, 363, 364, 366, 379, 380, 424, 425
Diamuid, 183
Diana, 16, 61, 74, 76, **78**, 79, 109, 213, 247, 249, 275, 283, 305, 308, 313, 316, 343, 365, 427, 428, 449, 457
Diane, 76, 78, **79**, 81, 85, 111, 135, 141, 168, 183, 186, 192, 250, 268, 295, 354, 393, 423
Dianne, 79, 111
Diantha, 149, 388, 404
Diara, 360
Diarmaid, 379
Diarmuid, 251, 377
Dick, 331, 332
Dickinson, 409, 418
Dickon, 417
Dicy, 420, 421
DiDi, 76
Didier, 394
Diedderik, 253
Diedre, 76
Diego, 19, 28, 55, 76, 163, 202, 208, 214, 217, 233, 245, **252**, 290, 309, 413, 414, 432, 447
Diesel, 390
Dieter, 396
Dietrich, 251, 396
Dilbert, 270, 429
Dill, 252
Dillard, 445
Dillon, 35, 63, 101, 117, 187, 188, 193, 196, 197, 237, 241, 246, 249, **252**, 256, 282, 326, 383, 386, 409, 459
Dilys, 81, 377
Dima, 74, 253
Dimas, 414
Dimitra, 397
Dimitri, 37, 38, 83, 106, 134, 159, 164, 170, 191, 196, 206, 218, 250, **253**, 279, 311, 388, 452
Dimitrios, 250, 253, 397
Dimitris, 253, 397
Dimple, 421
Dina, 29, 60, 75, 79, **79**, 97, 162, 226, 290, 294, 296, 351, 399, 401, 455

Dinah, 79, **79**, 113, 216, 281, 286, 306, 336, 372, 399
Dineo, 360
Dink, 419, 420, 421
Dino, 92, 97, 159, 336, 400, 422, 423
Diogo, 252, 415
Dion, 82, 207, 216, 218, **253**, 364, 432, 450
Dionne, 45, 448, 455
Dionysios, 253
Dirk, 75, 97, 103, 228, 251, **253**, 296, 297, 298, 396, 422, 456
Disa, 441
Divine, 390
Dixie, 52, **79**, 80, 255, 335, 383, 398
Dixon, 112, 409
Diya, 333
Django, 399, 429
Dmitri, 253
Dobbin, 190, 332, 385
Doc, 51, 315, 398
Dock, 277, 306
Doctor, 42
Dodie, 81
Dogberry, 449
Dolly, 80, **80**, 81, 175, 255, 276, 335, 383, 398, 429, 434
Dolores, 80, 414, 434, 445
Doloris, 80
Dolph, 328, 336
Dom, 80, 253
Domenic, 174, 253
Domenica, 143, 399
Domenico, 253, 400
Domicela, 388, 452
Dominga, 80
Domingo, 139, 253, 415
Dominic, 29, 40, 43, 58, 96, 97, 212, 217, 222, 224, 246, **253**, 254, 259, 262, 291, 315, 354, 368, 447, 453
Dominica, 80, 446
Dominick, 90, 253, 270, 388, 439
Dominik, 33, 74, 129, 162, 163, 164, 170, 202, 253, 310, 311, 396, 452
Dominika, 452
Dominique, 66, 78, **80**, 164, 202, 216, 253, 326, 363, 364, 366, 393, 394, 459
Don, 51, 211, 253, 254, 304, 438

Dona, 80, 81
Donagh, 255
Donal, 253, 377, 438
Donald, 23, 49, 61, 81, 98, 116, 118, 150, 169, 172, 178, 188, 205, **253**, 269, 309, 329, 331, 355, 438, 454
Donatella, 80, 202, 334, 353, 388, 399, 434, 460
Donatello, 80, 301, 399
Donato, 191, 400, 438, 439, 447
Donavan, 254
D'Ondre, 250
Donna, 39, 41, 53, 62, 74, 75, 79, **81**, 95, 111, 121, 135, 143, 146, 169, 170, 183, 186, 192, 223, 250, 256, 268, 271, 299, 323, 333, 423, 431
Donnell, 207, 364, 438, 456
Donnelly, 409
Donnie, 203, 253, 423
Donny, 254
Donovan, 46, 54, 58, 63, 77, 91, 112, 121, 125, 142, 150, 154, 175, 187, 228, 233, 253, **254**, 293, 294, 326, 343, 353, 377, 410, 438, 459
Dontae, 247
Donte, 82, 199, 247, 352, 361
Dora, 77, 81, **81**, 90, 108, 179, 198, 258, 266, 275, 322, 404, 414, 431
Doran, 377, 386
Dorcas, 255, 373, 445
Doreen, 423
Dori, 79, 455
Dorian, 30, 75, 119, 247, 248, **254**, 386, 417, 432, 461
Doris, 81, 172, 273, 301, 326, 428, 454
Dorman, 421
Doron, 29, 402
Dorothea, 70, 81, **81**, 83, 86, 96, 159, 198, 277, 404, 434, 460
Dorothy, 51, 80, 81, **81**, 93, 94, 104, 138, 151, 180, 225, 240, 274, 434, 454
Dorrie, 81
Dorris, 81
Dorsey, 261, 274, 410
Dot, 81
Dottie, 81, 172, 434

270, 303, 315, 331, 336,
351, 357, 380, 404, 428,
435, 446, 460
Florence, **93**, 96, 113, 238,
239, 275, 404, 435, 443
Florencia, 93
Florentia, 93
Florian, 77, 93, 137, 156, 171,
202, 213, 218, 301, 305,
387, 388, 394, 396, 447
Florida, 169, 398, 435, 443
Florine, 356, 445
Floris, 93
Florrie, 93
Flossie, 93, 398, 435
Floy, 420
Floyd, 30, 50, 82, **265**, 303,
444, 445
Flynn, 39, 50, 53, 99, 102,
128, 129, 143, 173, 179,
187, 231, 234, **265**, 289,
327, 349, 368, 375, 410,
461
Foley, 410
Forbes, 161, 231, 315, 324,
378, 410
Force, 412
Ford, 410
Forest, 28, 58, 265, 380,
405, 410
Forester, 265, 317, 332, 407
Forrest, 92, 115, 130, 148,
149, 180, 213, 240, 246,
260, 261, **265**, 308, 344,
357, 410, 432, 457, 461
Forsyth, 412
Fortinbras, 449
Fortunato, 143
Foster, 27, 35, 50, 64, 86, 96,
102, 139, 152, 165, 166,
203, 261, **265**, 274, 277,
282, 291, 320, 351, 356,
405, 407, 432, 461
Fotini, 397
Fotis, 397
Fox, 107, 206, 209, 235, 321,
389, 390, 392, 412
Foxworth, 412
Fran, 94, 170, 266, 435
Frances, 94, **94**, 104, 107,
112, 139, 150, 152, 170,
193, 213, 215, 237, 243,
266, 269, 270, 273, 276,
301, 309, 315, 355, 356,
404, 435, 454
Francesca, 23, 31, 94, **94**, 97,
168, 185, 271, 304, 353,
399, 403, 435, 460

Francesco, 266, 400
Francie, 94
Francine, 62, 66, 121, 354,
423, 435
Francis, 225, 239, 240, 262,
266, **266**, 299, 343, 405,
438, 446, 454
Francisca, 94, 414, 435, 449
Francisco, 99, 100, 156, 233,
266, 283, 288, 321, 415,
438, 450
Franck, 266
Franco, 266, 400
François, 266, 394
Françoise, 393
Frank, 107, 149, 168, 181,
213, 266, **266**, 269, 355,
438, 454
Frankie, 52, 66, 94, 266,
365, 398, 423
Franklin, 49, 61, 113, 116,
138, 139, 150, 151, 178,
180, 188, 193, 266, **266**,
270, 273, 329, 438, 454
Franz, 396, 405
Franziska, 94, 395
Fraser, 28, 30, 95, 106, 232,
255, 264, 265, 293, 298,
410
Frazier, 169
Fred, 81, 90, 215, 266, **266**,
438, 454
Freda, 398
Freddie, 206
Freddy, 266
Frederic, 41, 266, 394
Frederick, 49, 81, 94, 102,
106, 117, 159, 204, 205,
213, 215, 219, 243, 266,
266, 269, 348, 405, 438,
440, 450
Frederico, 266
Frederik, 266
Frederique, 393
Fredrick, 266
Freeman, 335, 364, 410
Freia, 94
Freja, 94, 441
Freya, 45, 84, **94**, 95, 146,
179, 189, 244, 384, 428,
441, 460
Freydl, 401
Freyja, 94
Frida, 81, 137, 168, 418, 441
Frieda, 98, 238, 266, 274,
278, 335, 404
Friedrich, 266, 396
Fritz, 181, 266, **266**, 277,

320, 396, 398
Frost, 93, 129, 130, 181, 325,
354, 375, 380, 410, 419
Furman, 144, 444
Fyodor, 348

Gab, 94, 95
Gabby, 95
Gabe, 122, 267, 338, 438
Gabi, 94, 95
Gable, 23, 102, 368
Gabriel, 15, 27, 32, 40, 43,
91, 94, 108, 164, 184, 212,
224, 232, 238, 259, 261,
267, 278, 284, 287, 291,
305, 313, 316, 328, 338,
358, 368, 373, 394, 415,
438, 453
Gabriela, 29, 38, 74, 75,
94, 95, 99, 149, 150, 163,
170, 185, 202, 214, 233,
236, 252, 309, 313, 403,
414, 452
Gabriella, 31, 43, 94, 95, 97,
108, 129, 146, 285, 339,
399
Gabrielle, 70, 94, **95**, 116,
155, 160, 164, 182, 268,
305, 325, 350, 393, 430,
434, 459
Gabriello, 267
Gaby, 94
Gadiel, 415
Gael, 36, 37, 164, 210, 415,
451
Gaetano, 400
Gage, 19, 128, 175, 182, 231,
254, 267, **267**, 268, 272,
279, 287, 292, 329, 354,
375, 410
Gaia, **95**, 428, 450
Gaige, 57, 267
Gail, 27, 85, **95**, 115, 118,
119, 123, 141, 192, 234,
271, 321, 332, 353, 374,
423
Gaines, 375, 410
Gala, 424, 452
Galadriel, 392
Gale, 95, 366
Galen, 106, 164, 173, **267**,
330, 349, 381, 387, 388,
426
Galilea, 36, 47, 58, 106,
403, 414
Galina, 452
Gallagher, 345, 378, 410
Gandalf, 392

220, 259, 263, **270**, 279, 281, 284, 285, 290, 306, 307, 323, 328, 338, 341, 342, 347, 348, 353, 368, 373, 388, 461
Gidget, 195, 390, 455
Gigi, 92, 97, 159, 204, 393, 435
Gil, 270, 353, 402, 438, 453
Gilbert, 102, 133, 172, 174, 180, 215, 225, 238, 240, 262, 266, **270**, 271, 303, 333, 336, 343, 355, 356, 405, 437, 438, 447, 454
Gilberto, 147, 270, 415
Gilda, 230, 398
Gilead, 373, 438
Giles, **270**, 385, 388, 438, 447
Gilia, 402
Gilles, 92, 270, 394
Gillespie, 399, 438
Gillian, 95, **97**, 115, 214, 384, 459
Gilly, 97
Gina, 79, **97**, 176, 178, 204, 399, 435, 456
Ginevra, 96, 399, 404, 435
Ginger, **97**, 146, 204, 284, 296, 380, 435, 456
Ginny, 96, 97, 201, 203, 204, 223, 239, 423, 435
Gino, 253, 308, 400, 438
Gio, 271
Giorgio, 80, 269
Giorgos, 397
Giovanna, 29, 80, 94, 96, 97, **97**, 334, 399, 403, 435, 460
Giovanni, 17, 19, 23, 31, 52, 76, 95, 97, 270, **271**, 301, 332, 353, 399, 400
Gisela, 98, 395
Gisele, 98, 225
Gisella, 399
Giselle, 21, 29, 32, 43, 59, 65, 84, 94, 95, **98**, 145, 190, 212, 236, 246, 259, 261, 307, 326, 350, 358, 393, 414, 431, 435
Giulia, 97, 119, 399
Giuliana, 119, 270, 399
Giulio, 400
Giuseppe, 289, 400
Gladys, 30, 82, 90, **98**, 158, 265, 278, 303, 320, 356, 377, 444, 445

Glen, 98, 271, 306
Glenda, 53, 82, **98**, 100, 146, 153, 174, 187, 201, 205, 255, 271, 340, 355, 377, 423
Glendon, 387
Glenn, 39, 71, 85, 111, 116, 135, 186, 187, 230, 254, **271**, 295, 300, 321, 322, 333, 355, 378, 423, 454
Glenna, 98, 246, 306, 333, 341, 344, 354, 355
Glinda, 98, 392, 423
Gloria, 39, 49, 52, **98**, 112, 118, 138, 150, 163, 169, 172, 253, 269, 290, 299, 331, 334, 355, 431, 454
Glory, 98, 424
Glyn, 98, 316, 353, 375, 378
Glynis, 81, 82, 98, **98**, 241, 279, 295, 377, 384
Glynn, 73, 336
Glynnis, 98
Godfrey, 29, 216, 255, 385, 405
Golda, **98**, 266, 274, 315, 402, 404
Golden, 380, 421, 424
Goldie, 98, 181, 255, 335, 398
Gonzalo, 415, 450
Goran, 452
Gordie, 271
Gordon, 81, 82, 112, 116, 138, 150, 166, 172, 178, 188, 253, 269, **271**, 329, 340, 354, 454
Gottlieb, 396
Grace, 15, 33, 62, 69, 82, 85, 87, 91, 99, **99**, 101, 118, 119, 120, 141, 167, 180, 191, 272, 275, 279, 311, 320, 367, 379, 380
Gracelyn, 29, 44, 45, 55, 57, **99**, 112, 228, 386, 435
Gracelynn, 99
Gracie, 34, 99, **99**, 140, 225, 226, 272, 276, 398, 435
Graciela, 68, 89, **99**, 149, 158, 403, 414, 435, 460
Gracious, 360
Gracyn, 99
Grady, 29, 99, 134, 206, 242, **271**, 368, 410
Graeme, 30, 53, 100, 241, 267, 271, 354, 375, 378
Graham, 59, 69, 75, 93, 120, 150, 204, 214, 232, 242,

260, **271**, 272, 290, 313, 318, 378, 384, 385, 457
Gráinne, 134, 183, 377, 379
Granger, 226, 407
Grania, 93, 377
Grant, 19, 69, 81, 128, 168, 189, 224, 225, 230, 242, 249, 254, **271**, 308, 311, 324, 330, 335, 354, 375, 410, 457
Granville, 216, 405
Gratia, 99
Gratiana, 381, 403
Gray, 28, 57, 99, 130, 166, 213, 272, 344, 366, 374, 375, 410, 461
Grayden, 370, 387
Grayson, 28, 57, 124, 125, 138, 215, 220, 228, 232, **272**, 314, 342, 356, 387, 410
Grazia, 99, 143, 399
Graziella, 80, 99, 234, 399
Green, 421
Greer, 28, 29, 53, **99**, 189, 196, 226, 265, 270, 293, 303, 357, 366, 368, 374, 377, 410, 454
Greg, 51, 69, 114, 115, 116, 122, 138, 146, 197, 226, 238, 272, 438
Gregg, 97, 100, 178, 187, 245, 456
Gregor, 30, 99, 227, 272, 279, 378, 396, 438
Gregorio, 272, 400, 415, 438
Gregory, 16, 38, 67, 68, 73, 76, 77, 78, 79, 95, 99, 121, 126, 130, 168, 193, 197, 202, 203, 250, 254, 268, 269, **272**, 284, 308, 327, 333, 344, 348, 423, 438, 456
Greig, 28, 272, 378
Grenoble, 443
Greta, 41, 45, 86, **99**, 100, 107, 147, 151, 243, 320, 343, 368, 395, 404, 441, 460
Gretchen, 99, **100**, 103, 147, 395, 431
Gretel, 99, 100
Greyson, 124, 224, 257, 272, 324, 345
Grier, 57, 99, 229, 346
Griffin, 74, 99, 129, 172, 176, 181, 189, 206, 228, 245, 254, 255, 267, 270,

Harvey, 134, 139, 170, 222, 274, 278, 398
Haskel, 274
Haskell, 98, 263, 274, 398, 402, 410, 432
Hassan, 91, 183, 292, 314, 427
Hassie, 420
Hastings, 231
Hatcher, 410
Hattie, 102, 104, 398, 435
Haven, 45, 47, 103, 118, 120, 138, 234, 366, 386, 424, 460
Havilah, 307, 372
Hawk, 211, 241, 287, 357, 390, 412, 422, 425
Hawkins, 41, 226, 296, 341, 399, 410, 461
Hayden, 87, 103, 124, 128, 132, 145, 159, 171, 197, 231, 274, 292, 366, 369, 370, 386, 387, 410, 431, 432
Haydn, 419
Hayes, 72, 335, 351, 375, 410
Haylee, 297, 369
Hayley, 35, 101, 121, 186, 237
Haylie, 101
Hazel, 21, 30, 90, 92, 98, 103, 108, 167, 170, 181, 200, 204, 257, 264, 272, 291, 367, 380, 431
Heart, 390
Heath, 36, 37, 42, 91, 103, 105, 110, 125, 130, 186, 197, 236, 240, 275, 298, 340, 375, 380, 449
Heathcliff, 240, 390, 417, 438
Heather, 36, 44, 72, 73, 88, 103, 105, 113, 128, 136, 236, 282, 380, 431, 448
Heaven, 38, 82, 101, 102, 103, 106, 160, 325, 386, 390, 424
Heavenleigh, 48, 312
Hector, 133, 215, 236, 275, 277, 283, 319, 328, 354, 381, 415, 428, 432
Hedda, 441
Hedwig, 395
Hedy, 227, 368, 395
Heidi, 100, 103, 105, 205, 253, 349, 395, 415, 416, 448, 456

Heidrun, 103
Heike, 395
Heinz, 396
Helen, 33, 83, 84, 94, 104, 106, 107, 147, 150, 164, 181, 219, 237, 266, 269, 304, 355, 404, 434, 436, 454
Helena, 40, 42, 59, 65, 89, 104, 104, 117, 132, 213, 215, 347, 367, 446, 449, 457, 460
Helene, 104, 170, 199, 333, 341, 355, 393, 454
Helga, 50, 395, 445
Helma, 420
Helmer, 421
Heloise, 86, 393, 404
Henderson, 410
Hendrix, 91, 102, 223, 260, 296, 300, 324, 389, 410, 429
Henley, 410
Hennessy, 410
Hennie, 104
Henri, 275, 394
Henrietta, 29, 104, 113, 205, 206, 276, 345, 384, 404, 435
Henriette, 104, 393
Henrik, 275, 396, 442
Henry, 33, 36, 62, 64, 67, 69, 83, 84, 87, 88, 90, 91, 94, 96, 99, 119, 134, 135, 140, 141, 147, 161, 191, 237, 258, 269, 273, 274, 275, 279, 338, 347, 356, 357, 368, 438, 457
Henson, 410
Herb, 275
Herbert, 170, 198, 270, 275, 405
Heriberto, 415
Herm, 275
Herman, 50, 82, 96, 105, 158, 219, 258, 275, 341, 395, 405
Hermann, 275, 396
Hermes, 428, 447
Hermia, 449
Hermina, 420
Hermione, 42, 86, 104, 106, 108, 155, 159, 198, 212, 220, 222, 276, 278, 345, 388, 416, 428, 446, 449
Hernan, 415
Herschel, 274, 402
Hertha, 420

Hervé, 274
Hester, 50, 216, 255, 260, 286, 336, 404, 429, 435, 445
Hestia, 428
Hettie, 89, 104, 155
Hetty, 435
Hezekiah, 364, 373, 440
Hieronymus, 286
Hilary, 105, 133
Hilda, 50, 82, 90, 96, 105, 158, 275, 356, 445
Hilde, 105, 395
Hildegard, 395
Hildred, 420
Hildy, 105, 320
Hillary, 105, 128, 136, 335, 366, 410, 431
Hillel, 67, 101, 188, 236, 373, 402
Hilton, 105, 355, 357, 410
Hines, 410
Hiram, 79, 216, 245, 263, 373, 405
Hiro, 366
Hirsch, 401, 402
Hobart, 405
Hodge, 190, 333, 410
Hogan, 44, 410
Holden, 47, 62, 67, 91, 102, 151, 182, 184, 196, 206, 223, 224, 254, 276, 300, 331, 339, 387, 410, 415, 417, 432
Holland, 231, 324, 355, 405, 410, 443, 460
Holli, 105
Hollie, 105
Hollis, 73, 81, 85, 105, 263, 273, 317, 320, 324, 327, 332, 345, 354, 357, 366, 410
Holliston, 330, 410
Holly, 33, 37, 42, 55, 62, 97, 103, 105, 105, 118, 134, 156, 159, 178, 205, 227, 229, 235, 240, 248, 251, 275, 281, 298, 344, 349, 380, 431, 448, 456
Holt, 258, 410
Homer, 30, 113, 216, 235, 260, 265, 276, 276, 286, 336, 429, 445
Honesty, 67, 185, 380, 425
Honey, 390
Honor, 48, 54, 60, 67, 72, 88, 105, 169, 206, 220, 226, 388, 425

Honora, 105, 117, 166, 404
Honorée, 105, 380, 393
Honoria, 105
Hooper, 407
Hope, 38, 90, 91, 105, 122, 131, 153, 157, 178, 192, 214, 224, 238, 240, 271, 287, 318, 324, 331, 354, 380, 457
Hopkins, 444
Horace, 29, 90, 96, 104, 239, 275, 276, 276, 305, 320, 336, 405, 432
Horacio, 415
Horatio, 155, 159, 223, 276, 276, 315, 345, 352, 388, 417, 450
Horst, 396
Hortencia, 420
Hortense, 459
Hosanna, 373, 425
Hosea, 208, 373
Hosie, 421
Hosteen, 421
Houston, 144, 149, 204, 246, 273, 383, 410, 443
Howard, 166, 219, 271, 275, 276, 314, 318, 326, 454
Howie, 276
Hoyt, 265, 335, 383, 445
Hristo, 452
Hubbard, 149, 169
Hubert, 98, 262, 305, 356, 405, 437
Hud, 276, 277
Hudson, 57, 92, 102, 103, 137, 169, 196, 249, 276, 324, 337, 368, 410, 443
Huey, 277, 398
Hugh, 27, 28, 46, 71, 72, 77, 82, 89, 93, 139, 148, 150, 151, 152, 153, 177, 241, 258, 267, 270, 273, 274, 277, 291, 325, 385, 405, 447, 454, 461
Hughes, 277, 324, 410
Hugo, 28, 33, 64, 65, 70, 86, 108, 120, 145, 211, 219, 275, 277, 277, 303, 319, 320, 394, 405, 415
Huldah, 420
Humberto, 415
Humphrey, 255, 405, 429
Hunt, 277
Hunter, 57, 81, 143, 169, 184, 193, 196, 201, 222, 229, 243, 272, 274, 277,

328, 337, 345, 352, 407, 422, 431
Hutch, 422
Hutchison, 410
Huw, 277
Hyam, 236
Hyman, 236

Iago, 450
Iain, 277
Ian, 27, 43, 81, 85, 93, 133, 154, 157, 160, 164, 187, 192, 198, 214, 242, 261, 262, 263, 277, 287, 292, 297, 378, 431, 432, 450, 451
Ianthe, 428
Ibrahim, 210, 314, 427
Ichabod, 155, 373, 417
Icy, 420, 421
Ida, 30, 82, 106, 142, 385, 395, 404, 441, 446
Idalis, 164
Idan, 402
Idris, 82
Iesha, 31, 363
Iestyn, 292, 378
Ifan, 262
Ignacio, 415
Ignatius, 381, 388, 439
Ignatz, 388
Igor, 167, 226, 452
Ike, 51, 138, 139, 174, 181, 255, 266, 277, 278, 314, 315, 316, 335, 359, 398, 422, 438
Iker, 415
Ila, 109, 450
Ilan, 207
Ilana, 29, 36, 43, 48, 67, 74, 188, 194, 219, 312, 402, 403
Ilaria, 105, 399, 403, 460
Ileana, 106, 403
Ilene, 82, 248
Ilia, 106
Iliana, 106, 131, 168, 397, 414, 452, 460
Ilias, 397
Illy, 106
Ilo, 420
Ilsa, 395
Ily, 106, 164, 359, 369, 425, 426, 450, 460
Ilya, 259
Iman, 106
Imani, 44, 106, 222, 319, 360, 361, 363

Imelda, 404, 429
Immanuel, 261
Imogen, 49, 88, 94, 104, 106, 173, 212, 215, 241, 270, 337, 345, 384, 388, 449
Imogene, 106, 162, 405
Imran, 427
India, 44, 107, 125, 185, 199, 208, 247, 252, 319, 357, 363, 384, 403, 443
Indiana, 392, 443
Indigo, 60, 86, 107, 129, 141, 174, 206, 212, 278, 343, 366, 425
Indy, 107
Ines, 414
Inès, 30, 393
Inez, 30, 230, 236, 258, 405
Inga, 107
Inge, 395, 441
Ingrid, 41, 45, 86, 99, 100, 107, 154, 368, 395, 441, 457
Inigo, 104, 108, 218, 278, 389
Íñigo, 278
Innes, 378
Innogen, 106
Io, 212, 428, 450
Ioan, 261
Ioanna, 397
Ioannis, 397
Iolanthe, 156, 388, 416
Iole, 388
Iona, 30, 70, 75, 107, 109, 133, 162, 166, 171, 189, 215, 217, 273, 298, 354, 377, 405
Ione, 35, 42, 47, 68, 71, 107, 108, 120, 177, 193, 195, 207, 263, 267, 278, 279, 295, 299, 352, 377, 388, 428, 460
Ira, 398
Ireland, 56, 107, 443
Irelyn, 107
Irena, 107
Irene, 107, 140, 149, 150, 181, 215, 233, 241, 266, 273, 276, 301, 397, 428, 454
Irie, 184
Irina, 106, 107, 167, 452
Irini, 107, 397
Iris, 46, 47, 81, 103, 108, 109, 153, 163, 165, 167, 178, 194, 206, 219, 252,

Jair, 279, 292, 297, 353, 375, 451
Jairo, 164, 207, 415
Jajuan, 281
Jakari, 39, 364, 439
Jakayla, 129, 363, 369
Jake, 19, 27, 34, 62, 99, 111, 123, 142, 144, 161, 198, 214, 249, 259, 279, 280, **280**, 284, 305, 398, 439, 458
Jakob, 176, 280, 396
Jakobe, 364
Jaleel, 183, 307, 364, 427
Jalen, 126, 201, 267, 280, **280**, 364, 369, 370, 387, 439
Jali, 361
Jalila, 426, 460
Jalisa, 281, 363
Jaliyah, 363
Jalon, 369
Jalyn, 112, 280, 369
Jalynn, 110, 369
Jamaal, 130, 194, 281
Jamaica, 125, 443
Jamal, 31, 44, 82, 125, **281**, 319, 364, 427, 432, 439
Jamar, 281, 352, 364
Jamari, 178, 364
Jamarion, 319, 362, 364
James, 15, 85, 122, 204, 237, 273, 281, **281**, 287, 289, 321, 331, 332, 339, 348, 356, 372, 373, 413, 431, 439, 457
Jamesina, 75
Jameson, 46, 128, 145, 173, 224, 233, **281**, 324, 345, 352, 356, 410
Jamey, 69, 159, 449
Jami, 110
Jamie, 42, 53, 62, **110**, 114, 115, 116, 125, 129, 132, 144, 161, 191, 236, 256, 281, 290, 365, 439, 448
Jamil, 281, 292, 426, 427
Jamila, 31, 106, 110, **110**, 185, 194, 363, 426, 460
Jamilah, 110
Jamin, 373
Jamir, 39, 364
Jamison, 127, 157, 211, 222, 248, 281, 325, 326, 439
Jampa, 346
Jamya, 363
Jan, 111, 114, 141, 171, 203, 287, 396, 423, 435, 442

Jana, 240, 435, 452
Janae, 111, 126, 186, 199, 248, 250, 280, 293, 346, 352, 363, 369
Jane, 40, 104, **110**, 111, 112, 114, 116, 149, 287, 321, 332, 362, 435, 454, 457
Janelle, 156, 180, 218, 282, 285, 294, 298, 346, 352, 363, 430, 435, 436
Janessa, 45, **111**, 403, 435
Janet, 53, 62, 85, **111**, 115, 118, 119, 135, 169, 192, 213, 250, 256, 271, 286, 323, 333, 344, 423, 435, 454
Janette, 111, 113, 355, 456
Janice, 54, 71, 75, 81, 82, **111**, 116, 118, 122, 146, 151, 186, 230, 269, 299, 337, 423, 435, 454
Janie, 110, 111, 182
Janina, 111
Janine, 50, **111**, 121, 181, 207, 256, 435, 456
Janis, 73, 95, 100, 111, 115, 147, 239, 260
Janiya, 112, 129, 216, 363, 403, 435
Janiyah, 39, 178, 362
Janna, 195, 197, 448, 450
Jannette, 113
Jansen, 284
Janson, 366, 386, 410
January, 37, **111**, 120, 130, 206, 380, 435, 460
Japh, 281
Japheth, 138, 185, 258, 263, 279, **281**, 306, 342, 373, 389, 439, 461
Jaquan, 352, 364
Jaqueline, 354
Jaquez, 364
Jared, 51, 67, 74, 88, 105, 113, 115, 121, 125, 146, 161, 165, 186, 194, 195, 210, 251, 256, 281, 282, 287, 297, 340, 373, 432, 439, 449, 459
Jarlath, 378, 447
Jarne, 396
Jarod, 281, 440
Jaron, 36, 126, 200, **282**, 364, 387, 402, 432
Jarred, 281
Jarret, 201, 282
Jarrett, 63, 91, 125, 145, 164,

205, 230, 242, **282**, 346, 364, 410, 432, 449, 459
Jarrod, 124, 186, 194, 248, 281, 282, 410, 449
Jarvis, 45, 132, 161, 195, 246, **282**, 298, 350, 364, 383, 432, 449
Jase, 279, 282
Jaslene, 46, 112, 414
Jaslyn, 112
Jasmin, 112
Jasmine, 32, 35, 44, 47, 78, 89, 110, **112**, 114, 138, 148, 175, 184, 250, 281, 363, 380, 425, 436, 459
Jasmyn, 112, 124, 280
Jason, 113, 114, 128, 229, 279, **282**, 309, 387, 427, 428, 439, 449
Jasper, 36, 49, 66, 67, 72, 77, 84, 109, 117, 118, 120, 134, 141, 171, 191, 198, 204, 220, 235, 261, 263, 264, **282**, 290, 313, 318, 341, 347, 367, 368, 380, 389
Javen, 370, 387
Javi, 283
Javier, 35, 89, 141, 149, 214, 236, **283**, 286, 287, 305, 313, 328, 358, 415
Javion, 216, 283, 364
Javon, 252, 364
Jax, 211, 212, 241, 279, **283**, 283, 375, 389, 392
Jaxen, 283
Jaxon, 55, 112, 145, 189, 221, 223, 228, 279, 280, 283, **283**, 287, 306, 338, 358, 359, 387
Jaxson, 16
Jaxton, 110, 283, 387
Jaxx, 283, 422
Jay, 51, 111, 144, 171, 192, 250, 268, 280, 281, 282, **283**, 300, 336, 347, 423, 439, 457
Jayce, 57, 110, 111, 279
Jaycee, 182
Jayda, 110, 221, 369
Jaydan, 283, 385
Jayde, 110
Jayden, 15, 109, 112, **112**, 221, 283, **283**, 364, 366, 369, 370, 385, 387, 439
Jaydin, 283, 385
Jaydon, 283, 385
Jayla, 110, 112, **112**, 124,

228, 231, 283, 338, 363, 369
Jaylee, 369
Jayleen, 280, 369
Jaylen, 19, 186, 248, 280, 297
Jaylin, 48, 110, 280, 366, 369, 386
Jaylon, 48, 89, 280, 369
Jaylyn, 110, 369
Jaylynn, 110
Jayme, 110
Jayne, 110, 423
Jayson, 282
Jaz, 112, 282
Jazlyn, 111, 112, **112**, 338, 386
Jazlynn, 112
Jazmin, 55, 112, 287, 414
Jazmyn, 110, 283, 386
Jazz, 391, 422
Jazzlyn, 112
Jean, **112**, 113, 114, 115, 116, 178, 186, 287, 394, 435, 454
Jeanette, 43, 52, **113**, 138, 162, 170, 180, 215, 240, 253, 266, 271, 343, 354, 393, 454
Jeanie, 112, 113
Jeanne, 83, 112, 116, 306, 329, 393
Jeannette, 113, 225
Jeannie, 456
Jeannine, 41, 71, 111, 393, 423
Jeb, 284, 296, 383
Jebediah, 284, **284**, 391
Jed, 223, 240, 284, **284**, 383, 439
Jedediah, 73, 185, 284, 373
Jedidiah, 263, 284, **284**, 358, 383, 389, 439
Jeff, 138, 186, 200, 238, 284, 439
Jefferson, 175, 216, 273, 281, **284**, 299, 302, 335, 410, 439, 457, 461
Jeffery, 284, 349
Jeffrey, 33, 37, 38, 51, 55, 60, 68, 103, 113, 119, 124, 126, 136, 156, 158, 177, 178, 187, 191, 201, 202, 239, 269, 284, **284**, 344, 423, 439, 449, 456
Jelani, 35, 106, 295, 319, 361
Jem, 113, 173, 281, 285, 385, 439

Jemima, 77, 79, **113**, 208, 210, 216, 222, 259, 286, 336, 342, 372, 384, 429
Jemma, 95
Jemuel, 373
Jen, 113, 114
Jena, 113, 126
Jenessa, 111
Jenifer, 113
Jenna, 27, 56, 61, 64, **113**, 121, 123, 125, 127, 154, 168, 187, 195, 198, 225, 262, 277, 280, 281, 282, 297, 330, 350, 435, 450, 459
Jenner, 407
Jennie, 113, 114, 115
Jennifer, 96, 100, **113**, 114, 156, 158, 282, 435, 448
Jennings, 405, 410
Jenny, 96, 110, 113, **114**, 435
Jens, 317, 442
Jensen, 105, 151, **284**, 304, 351, 366, 386, 387, 410, 435, 461
Jenson, 284
Jerald, 269
Jered, 281, 439
Jeremiah, 19, 176, 278, 284, 285, **285**, 286, 289, 358, 364, 373, 439
Jérémie, 285, 394
Jeremy, 35, 64, 74, 88, 103, 110, 114, 115, 123, 154, 156, 161, 176, 191, 194, 281, 282, 285, **285**, 358, 373, 448, 449
Jeri, **114**, 187, 435, 456
Jeriah, 373
Jericho, 32, 44, 56, 66, 95, 107, 109, 111, 115, 120, 169, 187, 284, **285**, 290, 338, 353, 359, 373, 439, 443, 461
Jerilyn, 435
Jermaine, 82, 129, 130, **285**, 364, 439
Jermayne, 285
Jerold, 269
Jerome, 39, 66, 71, 109, 151, 162, 174, 193, 199, 207, 253, 269, 270, **286**, 309, 310, 333, 334, 354, 364, 394, 439, 454
Jerri, 114, 423
Jerrica, 435
Jerrie, 114
Jerrod, 281

Jerrold, 269
Jerry, 53, 71, 76, 111, 114, 115, 119, 122, 146, 169, 269, 285, 286, **286**, 299, 422, 423, 439
Jersey, 114
Jerusha, 113, 307, 372
Jesaiah, 373
Jesper, 442
Jess, 114, 115, 164, 286, 366
Jessame, 435
Jessamine, 88, 110, 112, **114**, 179, 199, 380, 384, 436, 460
Jessamy, 114, 222, 332, 384
Jessamyn, 40, 55, 114, 203, 435
Jesse, 61, 62, 115, 123, 132, 235, 241, **286**, 373, 457
Jessi, 115
Jessica, 33, 35, 44, 73, 88, 113, **114**, 115, 130, 156, 165, 183, 217, 239, 282, 285, 288, 289, 292, 337, 435, 448, 449, 459
Jessie, 16, 62, 114, **115**, 286, 366, 435
Jesslyn, 386
Jessye, 115, 418
Jesus, 100, 286, 290, 305, 415
Jesús, 19, **286**, 288, 374, 412
Jet, 287, 380
Jethro, 113, 285, **286**, 335, 373, 445
Jetson, 392, 422
Jett, 78, 110, 141, 169, 175, 201, 211, 241, 242, 267, 280, **287**, 310, 325, 375, 422, 425
Jewel, **115**, 380, 425
Jewell, 115, 261, 300, 335, 344, 410
Jez, 115
Jezebel, **115**, 299, 372, 429
Jill, 51, 97, 115, **115**, 118, 119, 126, 136, 138, 141, 205, 226, 245, 283, 293, 349, 351, 374, 456, 460
Jillian, 34, 97, 113, **115**, 116, 128, 145, 194, 222, 240, 251, 268, 281, 350, 386, 430
Jilly, 115
Jim, 249, 281, 321, 423, 431, 439
Jimena, 207, 287, 414
Jimmie, 52, 398

319, 332, 399, 400, 415, 450, 457
Loreto, 91, 143
Loretta, **138**, 166, 178, 225, 240, 270, 275, 276, 301, 312, 318, 341, 343, 435, 454
Lori, 116, 130, 136, 138, **138**, 139, 146, 197, 200, 297, 435, 455, 456
Loris, 330
Lorna, 118, 162, 174, 180, 312, 335, 416, 435, 454
Lorne, 268, 299, 424
Lorraine, 52, 71, 82, 83, 113, **139**, 153, 180, 233, 240, 271, 273, 303, 306, 333, 435, 443, 454
Lorri, 138
Lotte, 51, 67, 86, 137, 139, 266, 395
Lottie, 67, **139**, 153, 190, 272, 320, 341, 398, 436
Lotty, 139
Lotus, 380, 390
Lou, 139, 304, 305, 439
Loudon, 410
Louie, 52, 90, 172, 222, 304, 315, 398, 399
Louis, 28, 33, 34, 49, 64, 94, 104, 106, 149, 179, 180, 181, 203, 213, 219, 237, 269, 304, **304**, 305, 348, 405, 439
Louisa, 28, 42, 59, 93, 133, 139, **139**, 140, 148, 152, 198, 219, 224, 235, 243, 265, 273, 356, 405, 446, 460
Louise, 93, 139, **139**, 150, 153, 170, 199, 213, 215, 239, 258, 266, 275, 305, 315, 355, 394, 405, 436
Lourdes, **139**, 158, 245, 388, 412, 414
Louvenia, 420
Lovie, 420
Lovisa, 139, 442
Lowell, 215, 240, 300, 410
Lowri, 63, 82, 98, 377
Loy, 421
Loyal, 391, 421
Loyce, 420
Loyd, 303
Loz, 299
Lu, 52, 140, 305, 316
Luann, 456
Luc, 65, 93, 194, 394

Luca, 31, 47, 82, 97, 155, 166, 168, 184, 191, 199, 213, 261, 270, **304**, 317, 332, 400, 451
Lucas, 19, 37, 43, 55, 70, 74, 84, 108, 148, 164, 167, 188, 190, 192, 194, 235, 238, 305, **305**, 308, 309, 320, 323, 374, 431, 441, 453
Luce, 140
Lucero, 389, 414, 436
Lucha, 141
Lucho, 305
Lucia, 42, 83, 97, 99, 117, 140, **140**, 150, 190, 217, 230, 291, 308, 309, 328, 332, 354, 399, 436, 446, 457
Lucian, 46, 291, 299, **305**, 308, 389, 439, 447
Luciana, 76, 135, 140, 207, 234, 275, 304, 332, 334, 381, 399, 403, 414, 436, 449
Luciano, 31, 305, 400
Lucie, 50, 140, 307, 394
Lucien, 77, 86, 394
Lucienne, 41, 394
Lucile, 140
Lucille, 28, 53, 139, **140**, 169, 170, 239, 257, 258, 262, 270, 275, 301, 305, 383, 394, 405, 436
Lucinda, 69, 110, **140**, 204, 423, 434, 436
Lucio, 305, 400, 415
Lucius, 42, 46, 198, 305, **305**, 336, 374, 382, 389, 447
Lucky, 390
Luco, 305
Lucrece, 381
Lucretia, 381, 388, 436, 437, 446
Lucy, 21, 33, 41, 51, 71, 73, 84, 85, 87, 90, 96, 118, 132, 135, 140, **140**, 166, 177, 179, 181, 182, 191, 198, 214, 237, 272, 274, 275, 301, 306, 313, 319, 333, 347, 367, 398, 436
Ludie, 420
Ludmila, 158, 167, 452
Ludovic, 304, 378, 389
Ludwig, 304, 396
Luetta, 445

Lugenia, 420
Luigi, 304, 400
Luigina, 97
Luis, 141, 217, 233, 286, 288, 290, 304, **305**, 307, 313, 412, 415, 453
Luisa, 100, 139, 174, 213, 399, 414
Luise, 139
Luiz, 305
Luka, 42, 158, 304, 311, 452
Lukas, 33, 36, 41, 74, 83, 94, 95, 122, 134, 160, 161, 162, 164, 184, 218, 279, 305, 348, 395, 452
Luke, 45, 46, 68, 69, 81, 85, 91, 96, 122, 131, 135, 136, 198, 209, 214, 242, 256, 259, 262, 267, 279, 280, 290, 302, 304, 305, **305**, 308, 329, 330, 340, 372, 374, 375, 383
Lula, 90, 315, 398
Lulu, 86, 139, 140, 335, 397, 398
Luna, 50, 58, 86, 109, 140, **141**, 158, 172, 188, 208, 221, 263, 277, 282, 303, 313, 341, 357, 367, 428, 451
Lupe, 100, 366, 414
Lupita, 100
Lurline, 445
Luther, 30, 50, 133, 139, 140, 153, 239, 262, 275, 276, 301, **305**, 364, 405
Lux, 140, 211, 241, 390, 425
Luz, 30, 61, 100, 139, **141**, 149, 150, 168, 175, 414, 451
Luzetta, 420
Lydia, 21, 33, 36, 39, 65, 69, 84, 99, 117, 119, 132, **141**, 163, 171, 192, 204, 210, 214, 220, 232, 245, 270, 288, 290, 313, 318, 338, 341, 342, 348, 367, 373, 381, 457
Lyla, 134, 151, 230, 245
Lyle, 70, 81, 82, 138, 153, 162, 178, 246, 255, 269, 302, 303, **306**, 378, 454
Lyman, 410
Lyn, 29, 57, 62, 141
Lynda, 98, 135
Lyndis, 392
Lyndon, 135, 176, 424
Lyndsay, 136

Lynette, 41, 132, 181, 423
Lynn, 51, 75, 79, 115, 126, 135, 141, 213, 246, 268, 295, 300, 353, 374, 423, 456
Lynne, 73, 95, 141, 186, 247
Lynsey, 136
Lynx, 389, 391, 425
Lyra, 30, 42, 43, 86, 95, 106, 120, 141, 141, 208, 220, 221, 254, 319, 324, 326, 392, 432, 451, 460
Lyric, 16, 39, 115, 141, 197, 304, 363, 366, 390, 425, 436
Lysander, 104, 130, 173, 179, 382, 450
Lysandra, 248, 250, 381

Mabel, 51, 77, 142, 170, 222, 274, 301, 314, 320, 398
Mable, 142
Mabry, 226, 231, 258, 317, 322, 410
Mabs, 142
Mabyn, 87, 213, 227, 242, 245, 267, 314, 331, 341, 357, 377, 386, 446, 460
Mac, 52, 244, 306, 439
Macaulay, 306, 378
Macauley, 439
Mace, 254, 309, 375, 392, 422
Macey, 142
Maci, 21, 48, 142
Macie, 128, 142, 182
Mack, 80, 86, 90, 101, 142, 144, 153, 170, 177, 230, 255, 290, 306, 383, 397, 398
Mackenzie, 28, 142, 154, 233, 366, 377, 378, 406, 410, 439
Maclean, 378
Macon, 383, 387, 417, 439, 443
Macus, 190
Macy, 49, 102, 110, 127, 128, 142, 151, 154, 159, 164, 191, 196, 201, 212, 227, 229, 235, 238, 243, 249, 252, 257, 267, 276, 297, 326, 338, 345, 350, 351, 356, 370, 410, 451
Madalyn, 143
Maddalena, 143, 399, 403, 436
Madden, 29, 56, 87, 132,

151, 223, 253, 280, 306, 387, 392, 410
Maddie, 34, 142, 143, 436
Maddison, 143
Maddox, 19, 47, 92, 99, 138, 169, 177, 223, 228, 230, 279, 283, 306, 310, 311, 321, 326, 338, 358, 389, 410, 422
Maddy, 142, 143
Madeleine, 90, 95, 143, 367, 394
Madeline, 28, 40, 86, 91, 108, 135, 142, 143, 155, 157, 167, 253, 274, 367, 417, 436
Madelyn, 27, 29, 87, 99, 115, 249, 274, 318, 324
Madelynn, 143
Madge, 143, 147, 314, 398
Madigan, 30, 39, 50, 93, 132, 143, 154, 315, 325, 345, 346, 366, 377, 410, 436, 460
Madilyn, 386
Madisen, 143
Madison, 15, 28, 66, 79, 104, 116, 142, 143, 143, 150, 153, 175, 288, 309, 352, 366, 386, 410, 436, 443, 448
Madisyn, 5, 143
Madoc, 306
Madonna, 143, 390, 429, 436
Madrigal, 425, 436
Mads, 310, 442
Madyson, 143, 145
Mae, 50, 51, 66, 77, 106, 138, 144, 153, 164, 170, 174, 180, 222, 257, 277, 287, 306, 315, 328, 335, 368, 380, 383, 398, 460
Mael, 144
Maël, 394
Maelie, 370, 460
Maelle, 144
Maëlle, 37, 144, 377, 394, 460
Maëlys, 144, 394
Maeva, 394
Maeve, 21, 30, 144, 153, 214, 228, 242, 250, 264, 293, 315, 326, 334, 335, 339, 354, 374, 377, 460
Mafalda, 152, 399
Magalie, 394
Magda, 436

Magdalena, 132, 373, 395, 414, 436, 442, 452
Magdalene, 151, 315, 388, 405
Maggie, 58, 115, 123, 134, 144, 144, 147, 182, 286, 436, 457
Magic, 391
Magnolia, 46, 53, 144, 166, 314, 380, 383, 436
Magnum, 391, 422
Magnus, 47, 120, 136, 179, 215, 217, 221, 236, 263, 292, 306, 311, 338, 341, 357, 378, 389, 442, 447
Mags, 144
Maguire, 410
Mahala, 113, 122, 206, 219, 402, 427
Mahalia, 108, 403, 418, 436
Mahlia, 145
Mahlon, 79, 149, 306, 364, 373, 387, 461
Mahmoud, 292, 427
Mahogany, 380
Mahoney, 378, 410
Mai, 148, 150
Maia, 55, 94, 136, 141, 154, 158, 221, 428, 451
Maida, 405
Maija, 148
Maile, 132, 145
Maira, 403
Maire, 152
Máire, 153, 377
Mairead, 144, 436
Máirín, 161
Maisha, 295, 360
Maisie, 30, 144, 147, 173, 217, 245, 263, 264, 273, 274, 298, 327, 335, 377, 436
Maisy, 144
Maite, 144, 145, 394, 414
Maïté, 145
Maizie, 209
Maj, 147
Maja, 84, 136, 154, 189, 308, 442
Major, 80, 142, 170, 174, 222, 225, 255, 306, 331, 391, 398, 422
Makai, 364
Makaila, 145
Makani, 132
Makayla, 123, 145, 154, 157, 221, 280, 370, 435
Makenna, 57, 154, 342

Makenzie, 142, 145
Makis, 397
Makiyah, 363
Mal, 307
Malachi, 19, 27, 48, 164,
 259, 263, 278, 307, **307**,
 312, 353, 359, 364, 373,
 389
Malachy, 307, 378, 447
Malaika, 44, 106, **145**, 222,
 319, 360, 363, 460
Malak, 427
Malakai, 39, 184, 216, 307
Malaki, 307
Malaysia, 443
Malcolm, 93, 232, **307**, 316,
 362, 364, 378, 457, 461
Maleah, 145
Maleia, 155
Malia, 21, 31, 126, **145**, 155,
 292, 370, 403, 453
Malik, 44, 106, 110, **307**,
 319, 361, 364, 426, 427
Malin, 84, 134, 136, 146,
 179, 264, 317, 442, 460
Malina, 155
Malinda, 156
Malissa, 156
Malka, 236, 402
Mallory, 61, 67, 105, 115,
 125, **145**, 157, 205, 228,
 230, 232, 252, 343, 410,
 432
Malthe, 442
Mamadou, 314, 427
Mamadou, 361
Mamie, 152, 169, 260, 335,
 398
Mammie, 421
Manda, 35
Mandy, 35, 160, 436, 448
Manervia, 420
Manfred, 151, 396, 438
Mani, 35, 43
Manly, 421
Manning, 410
Mannix, 389, 410
Manny, 261, 275, 307
Manoel, 307
Manolo, 307
Manon, 149, 394
Manos, 397
Manuel, 61, 89, 91, 139, 217,
 261, 286, 290, 305, **307**,
 327, 415, 447, 457
Manuela, 395, 414, 436
Manzi, 361
Mara, 54, **146**, 149, 194,

199, 210, 225, 258, 282,
 306, 312, 353, 372, 432,
 451
Marah, 146
Maranda, 160
Marc, 50, 60, 74, 76, 79, 129,
 177, 194, 200, 226, 248,
 262, 297, 307, 308, 456
Marcel, 65, 66, 71, 72, 80,
 207, **307**, 330, 394, 432,
 447
Marcela, 99, 146, 147, 148,
 414, 452
Marceline, 41, 146, 394
Marcella, 146, **146**, 149,
 180, 399, 403, 436, 446,
 460
Marcelle, 146, 162, 394, 436
Marcellus, 250, 307, 382,
 389, 447, 450
Marcelo, 149, 158, 307, 415
Marci, 146, 174, 436
Marcia, 98, 116, **146**, 169,
 205, 269, 286, 423, 436
Marcie, 75, 103, 146, 152,
 159
Marco, 31, 52, 55, 74, 94,
 96, 97, 135, 148, 168, 174,
 185, 190, 202, 204, 207,
 218, 236, 247, 252, 263,
 271, **307**, 308, 309, 332,
 340, 400, 415
Marcos, 137, 211, 290, 307,
 415
Marcus, 70, 116, 125, 146,
 161, 307, 308, **308**, 310,
 361, 364, 382, 457
Marcy, 97, 115, 138, **146**,
 191, 195, 456
Marek, 159, 165, 308, 447,
 452
Marely, 414
Maren, 94, **146**, 150, 189,
 234, 300, 342, 386, 442,
 460
Margalit, 402
Margaret, 8, 40, 64, 85, 104,
 110, 117, 134, 144, 147,
 147, 151, 152, 153, 154,
 170, 237, 258, 266, 269,
 287, 332, 356, 365, 405,
 436, 454
Margareta, 99, 157
Margarete, 100, 395
Margaretha, 147
Margarita, 61, 147, **147**, 178,
 414, 452, 454
Margaux, 147

Margery, 8, 70, 81, 147, 148,
 151, 270, 355, 357, 436,
 454, 460
Margherita, 147, 399
Margie, 144, 147, 151, 398,
 436
Margit, 107, 147, 395, 442
Margo, 95, 100, 118, 130,
 147, 234, 336, 423, 432,
 460
Margot, 8, 46, 147, 149, 151,
 207, 251, 270, 303, 333,
 336, 394, 395, 454
Margret, 147, 225
Marguerite, 41, 64, 147, **147**,
 154, 167, 219, 239, 363,
 394, 405, 436, 446
Marguita, 147
Mari, 30, 56, 148, 149, 150,
 152, 172, 442, 453
Maria, 61, 115, 148, **148**,
 149, 150, 151, 152, 154,
 233, 288, 290, 305, 307,
 321, 327, 332, 365, 373,
 397, 399, 413, 414, 436,
 457
María, 148
Mariah, 36, 148, **148**, 188,
 232, 263, 268, 278, 282,
 289, 307, 319, 348, 358,
 367, 403, 432
Mariam, 36, 91, 414
Mariamne, 149, 156, 388
Marian, 96, 102, 120, **148**,
 150, 161, 193, 258, 273,
 274, 277, 357, 432, 454,
 460
Mariana, 34, 64, 119, **148**,
 149, 170, 174, 202, 211,
 214, 252, 259, 263, 283,
 286, 287, 290, 304, 307,
 309, 313, 319, 339, 403,
 414, 446, 449
Marianna, 146, 148
Marianne, 83, 109, 113, **149**,
 151, 169, 180, 199, 207,
 233, 270, 286, 299, 328,
 344, 394, 454
Mariano, 400, 415
Maribel, 149, 150, 414, 460
Maribeth, 119, 434
Maricela, 38, 403, 414
Maricris, 145
Marie, 148, **149**, 150, 152,
 266, 373, 394, 454
Mariel, 149, 162, 343, 395
Mariela, 47, 99, 134, **149**,
 155, 156, 403, 414, 460

Mariella, 60, 97, 135, 149, 191, 399
Marieta, 149
Marietta, 90, **149**, 169, 204, 206, 400, 403, 443
Mariette, 149
Marigold, 380
Marika, 442
Marilena, 397, 400
Marilla, 48, **149**, 403, 405, 460
Marillis, 149
Marilyn, 49, 98, **150**, 172, 188, 253, 266, 334, 454
Marilynn, 150
Marin, 129, 136, 146, 158, 299, 322, 443, 460
Marina, 32, 33, 42, 146, **150**, 176, 185, 192, 203, 217, 218, 279, 291, 310, 332, 334, 340, 354, 397, 400, 446, 449, 453, 457
Marine, 394
Mario, 61, 70, 84, 89, 94, 99, 141, 146, 207, 234, 236, 307, 308, **308**, 309, 319, 332, 365, 400, 415, 432, 453, 457
Marion, 28, 64, 139, 148, 149, **150**, 170, 203, 213, 219, 225, 233, 239, 240, 255, 304, 315, 333, 354, 355, 394, 405, 432, 454
Marios, 397
Maris, 63, 195, 213, 231, 388, 460
Marisa, 33, 52, 84, 123, 126, 150, 165, 194, 307, 400, 403, 448
Marisol, 149, **150**, 166, 175, 204, 207, 414
Marissa, 32, 35, 54, 121, 129, 149, **150**, 156, 203, 403, 459
Marit, 442
Marita, 147
Maritza, 150, 414
Marius, 58, 84, 94, 137, 173, 176, 189, 236, 267, 308, **308**, 310, 365, 382, 389, 396, 432, 442
Mariya, 148
Marj, 151
Marja, 148
Marjorie, 138, 139, **151**, 153, 170, 180, 240, 260, 274, 435, 454, 460
Marjory, 151

Mark, 38, 51, 67, 68, 71, 73, 77, 110, 115, 119, 121, 133, 141, 146, 156, 158, 187, 192, 197, 200, 202, 211, 213, 249, 271, 308, **308**, 309, 321, 343, 372, 374, 424, 456, 457
Markell, 250, 364
Markian, 452
Markie, 146
Marko, 126
Markos, 83, 397
Markus, 308, 343, 396
Marla, 423
Marlee, 29, 151, 241
Marlen, 151
Marlena, 151, 448
Marlene, 66, 116, **151**, 355, 395, 423
Marlène, 151, 394
Marley, 45, 103, 127, **151**, 173, 226, 234, 235, 246, 249, 274, 276, 280, 284, 292, 293, 296, 298, 300, 304, 306, 337, 366, 410, 429, 432
Marlin, 162, 174, 454
Marlo, 75, 151, 296, 432, 456
Marlon, 298, 364, 387
Marlowe, 29, 39, 50, 53, 91, 102, 143, **151**, 206, 213, 218, 223, 231, 249, 257, 265, 281, 297, 300, 339, 349, 357, 389, 410, 418, 460
Marly, 151
Marlys, 248, 340, 454
Marni, 150
Marnie, 456
Marques, 308
Marquis, 66, 78, 250, **308**, 364, 425
Marquise, 89, 308, 459
Marquita, 129
Mars, 391, 412, 422, 428
Marsaili, 30
Marsden, 412
Marseille, 443
Marsha, 66, 67, 146, 355, 423
Marshal, 308, 383, 425
Marshall, 240, 261, 266, 299, **308**, 316, 335, 337, 357, 407, 457
Marta, 152
Martha, 94, 110, 146, 147, 152, **152**, 153, 177, 213, 215, 237, 239, 262, 266,

269, 273, 309, 355, 373, 405, 436
Martin, 40, 85, 110, 130, 169, 233, **309**, 321, 323, 364, 454, 457
Martina, 70, 72, 147, **152**, 200, 218, 395, 400, 414, 452, 457
Martine, 152
Marty, 152, 239, 309, 424, 456
Marv, 309
Marvel, 325, 390, 391, 421
Marvin, 138, 153, 166, 253, 269, 276, **309**, 343, 354, 364, 455
Mary, 69, 135, 147, 148, 149, 150, **152**, 153, 161, 172, 190, 267, 269, 287, 371, 372, 373, 436, 446, 457
Maryam, 74, 160, 292, 314, 427
Maryann, 454
Maryanne, 423
Marybeth, 423
Maryjo, 116
Maryland, 335
Marylyn, 150
Masha, 148, 452
Masika, 360
Mason, 15, 32, 45, 47, 68, 119, 142, 143, 157, 171, 189, 196, 221, 227, 232, 234, 238, 262, 268, 271, 272, 276, 277, 279, 282, 284, 298, 302, 309, **309**, 320, 324, 352, 387, 406, 407, 448
Massimo, 80, 261, 311, 400
Matan, 373, 402
Matea, 452
Mateo, 37, 55, 84, 98, 134, 149, 207, 217, 252, **309**, 310, 415, 440
Mateus, 145, 415
Mathew, 310
Mathias, 86, 96, 305, 308, 310, 368, 394, 442
Mathieu, 66, 310, 394
Mathilda, 104, 152
Mathilde, 152, 394
Mathis, 144, 310, 394, 439
Matilda, 86, **152**, 153, 235, 405, 436, 437, 441, 446, 460
Matilde, 442
Mats, 310

Matt, 238, 249, 310, 433, 439, 456
Mattea, 153, 403, 436, 460
Mattea, 321
Matteo, 31, 47, 96, 97, 134, 155, 159, 168, 234, 247, 261, 270, 304, 307, 309, 310, 334, 400, 439, 453
Matthew, 15, 19, 34, 38, 68, 113, 114, 130, 153, 158, 160, 174, 183, 191, 211, 217, 238, 239, 247, 262, 285, 288, 292, 309, 310, 310, 313, 343, 348, 372, 374, 431, 433, 439
Matthias, 40, 42, 90, 95, 109, 120, 168, 169, 174, 185, 212, 261, 284, 299, 306, 309, 310, 310, 347, 358, 374, 389, 396, 439, 447
Mattia, 400
Mattias, 310
Mattie, 66, 152, 153, 398, 436
Maud, 153
Maude, 53, 153, 276, 322, 405
Maudie, 153
Maura, 76, 153, 153, 294, 306, 339, 377, 432, 446
Maureen, 71, 75, 122, 153, 153, 193, 255, 377, 423
Maurice, 140, 147, 170, 239, 302, 309, 310, 315, 364, 394, 439
Mauricio, 150, 415
Maurine, 153
Mauro, 400
Maury, 310
Mav, 310
Maverick, 36, 73, 78, 95, 162, 201, 237, 242, 246, 268, 310, 311, 328, 383, 422, 424, 440
Mavis, 81, 454
Mavrick, 16
Max, 41, 47, 66, 73, 85, 99, 132, 135, 138, 140, 144, 154, 157, 161, 163, 181, 182, 191, 198, 209, 214, 220, 237, 259, 272, 279, 280, 301, 311, 311, 315, 332, 335, 347, 368, 375, 398, 404, 439, 459
Maxen, 87, 177, 227, 378, 387
Maxfield, 410, 419

Maxie, 79, 153, 398
Maxim, 75, 115, 122, 134, 153, 158, 160, 161, 162, 165, 168, 176, 184, 191, 206, 212, 218, 221, 225, 253, 279, 311, 311, 333, 338, 389, 439, 447, 452
Maxima, 381, 390, 446
Maxime, 311, 394
Maximilian, 37, 43, 68, 90, 96, 185, 196, 202, 205, 292, 301, 311, 311, 339, 344, 358, 389, 396, 439, 447, 450
Maximiliano, 311, 415
Maximillian, 311
Maximo, 207, 245, 311, 415, 439
Maximus, 43, 109, 201, 211, 212, 236, 291, 311, 311, 315, 382, 391, 422, 439, 447
Maxine, 81, 138, 153, 162, 219, 225, 241, 262, 270, 302, 309, 310, 312, 314, 315, 318, 333, 343, 354, 454
Maxton, 387, 439
Maxwell, 28, 31, 32, 40, 96, 99, 129, 135, 143, 157, 190, 204, 214, 260, 265, 311, 311, 314, 318, 368, 410, 439, 457
Maxx, 422
May, 42, 47, 120, 142, 144, 147, 152, 153, 178, 273, 379, 380, 460
Maya, 31, 47, 68, 146, 154, 161, 195, 198, 221, 240, 246, 276, 318, 320, 323, 432, 451, 453
Maybell, 260
Maybelle, 142, 398
Maylee, 370
Maylin, 370, 386
Maynard, 445
Mayra, 370, 414
Mayzie, 144
Mazie, 144, 277, 398
McArthur, 410, 439
McCoy, 378, 410, 439
McGregor, 345
McKay, 378, 410, 439
McKayla, 145
McKenna, 228, 243, 345, 410
Mckenna, 30, 77, 99, 121, 127, 142, 145, 154, 189,

211, 228, 230, 254, 293, 294, 303, 325, 352, 377
McKenzie, 142, 280
Mckenzie, 44, 59, 63, 87, 124, 125, 143, 154, 162, 252, 350, 377
McKinley, 21, 127, 154, 314, 335, 410, 439
Mckinney, 377
Meabh, 261
Méabh, 144
Meade, 375, 410
Meadow, 47, 48, 115, 154, 197, 225, 331, 343, 380, 413, 425
Meagan, 154
Meaghan, 154
Meche, 156
Medb, 144
Media, 421
Meeia, 160
Mees, 396
Meg, 115, 137, 144, 154, 284, 332, 436
Megan, 34, 58, 88, 113, 121, 127, 130, 147, 154, 162, 174, 176, 186, 197, 210, 227, 228, 229, 235, 262, 281, 292, 295, 314, 331, 337, 339, 377, 386, 430, 436, 459
Meghan, 154
Mehetabel, 155
Mehitabel, 155, 372, 388, 417, 435
Mehki, 127
Mehmet, 314
Meike, 227
Meir, 403
Mekhi, 27, 35, 44, 178, 216, 364
Mel, 36, 155, 156, 312, 424, 436, 439
Melania, 155, 170, 196, 202, 234, 403, 446, 452, 453
Melanie, 33, 38, 133, 155, 156, 160, 164, 191, 202, 203, 216, 227, 310, 314, 330, 344, 348, 394, 430, 436
Melany, 155
Melba, 79, 398, 436
Melbourne, 439, 443
Melia, 86, 137, 155, 403, 428
Melina, 43, 83, 106, 145, 155, 156, 397, 403, 436, 453, 460
Melinda, 50, 68, 156, 156,

Nainoa, 132
Nakia, 194, 295, 360, 363
Nala, 163
Nalani, 155
Nallely, 164
Nan, 39, 40, 163, 172, 273, 304, 316, 335, 436
Nancie, 163
Nancy, 40, 49, 51, 76, 118, 149, 163, 170, 182, 233, 253, 269, 286, 299, 331, 334, 346, 436, 454
Nanette, 71, 113, 159, 423, 436
Naomi, 134, 154, 160, 163, 166, 194, 220, 259, 270, 278, 290, 312, 315, 319, 330, 342, 372, 432, 457
Nap, 315
Naphtali, 373
Napoleon, 167, 315, 352, 389, 429
Nardo, 301
Nash, 167, 375
Nasir, 427
Nasta, 37
Nat, 51, 71, 101, 153, 164, 175, 223, 284, 314, 316, 398, 439
Natalia, 21, 29, 32, 34, 37, 39, 43, 64, 94, 98, 119, 135, 148, 149, 163, 164, 170, 190, 194, 196, 202, 203, 204, 212, 214, 217, 252, 253, 259, 279, 283, 290, 305, 311, 313, 339, 350, 354, 403, 414, 437, 446, 452, 453
Natalie, 15, 34, 38, 56, 95, 130, 155, 163, 164, 165, 183, 210, 217, 238, 285, 287, 288, 305, 310, 316, 317, 356, 430
Nataly, 164
Natalya, 159, 163
Natan, 316
Natanael, 415
Natasa, 37, 397
Natasha, 78, 82, 92, 129, 161, 163, 164, 195, 196, 226, 294, 363, 396, 437, 448, 451, 452
Nate, 118, 134, 135, 179, 277, 316, 439
Nathalie, 164, 165, 394
Nathan, 27, 51, 87, 131, 146, 174, 176, 183, 210, 285, 287, 305, 316, 316, 338,

373, 385, 387, 439, 440, 457
Nathanael, 176, 261, 316, 347, 374
Nathaniel, 32, 68, 95, 117, 119, 143, 160, 167, 173, 192, 204, 214, 224, 267, 284, 316, 317, 339, 358, 373, 374, 439, 440, 450, 457
Nautica, 43, 390
Nava, 402, 451
Naveen, 333
Navi, 392
Nayeli, 37, 122, 164, 207, 413, 414
Nayely, 164
Nazir, 427
Nea, 136
Neal, 234, 247, 250, 256, 300, 316, 321, 335
Ned, 110, 134, 172, 257, 258, 273, 290, 306, 316, 335, 398, 439
Neema, 360
Neeve, 376
Neftali, 166, 415
Nehemiah, 307, 373
Neil, 118, 122, 213, 232, 244, 245, 283, 316, 317, 378, 457
Neilson, 411
Nell, 51, 80, 83, 85, 92, 101, 132, 137, 142, 164, 170, 174, 175, 198, 222, 274, 290, 306, 316, 398, 436, 461
Nella, 164
Nelle, 164
Nellie, 77, 144, 164, 170, 441
Nelly, 164, 179
Nelson, 222, 240, 266, 308, 315, 316, 356, 411, 457
Nemo, 392
Neo, 86, 209, 222, 329, 361, 392, 451
Nerissa, 449
Nessa, 111, 203
Nessie, 30
Nestor, 139, 185, 415, 450
Netta, 41
Nettie, 41, 104
Nevada, 443
Nevaeh, 21, 38, 103, 106, 164, 201, 283, 312, 425
Neve, 165, 293, 335, 346, 348, 374, 377
Neville, 72, 107, 317, 385

Newell, 411
Newman, 411
Newton, 248, 312, 341, 411
Nia, 35, 54, 69, 164, 165, 166, 176, 209, 296, 307, 351, 360, 363, 377, 432, 451
Niall, 30, 31, 134, 144, 165, 189, 251, 261, 263, 316, 346, 378, 379
Niamh, 30, 31, 93, 109, 134, 144, 164, 165, 177, 183, 189, 227, 243, 250, 251, 256, 261, 264, 376, 377, 379, 428
Nic, 253
Nica, 165
Nicholas, 19, 29, 32, 37, 39, 42, 63, 74, 83, 87, 94, 96, 108, 165, 183, 190, 203, 204, 214, 217, 224, 238, 239, 242, 291, 305, 316, 317, 317, 348, 354, 358, 397, 438, 439, 458
Nicholaus, 317
Nichole, 165
Nicholson, 216, 317, 332, 411, 439, 461
Nick, 157, 279, 317, 348, 439
Nickolas, 317
Nicky, 424
Nico, 42, 47, 96, 97, 134, 137, 141, 153, 158, 164, 172, 194, 199, 209, 219, 221, 261, 297, 304, 309, 313, 317, 317, 348, 358, 400, 451, 453, 461
Nicodemus, 299, 347, 374, 389, 439
Nicola, 75, 165, 173, 174, 267, 304, 317, 385, 400, 436
Nicolas, 74, 98, 119, 145, 148, 165, 202, 317, 394, 415
Nicole, 29, 33, 35, 73, 74, 114, 123, 128, 130, 154, 164, 165, 165, 177, 191, 239, 297, 393, 394, 436, 459
Nicolette, 80, 394, 436
Nicomachus, 382
Niels, 45, 56, 99, 100, 136, 198, 227, 268, 317, 389, 396, 442
Nigel, 251, 317, 337, 385, 432
Nika, 42, 54, 74, 133, 158,

Piper, 21, 46, 47, 68, 102, 169, 171, **172**, 173, 181, 182, 184, 189, 209, 227, 234, 235, 243, 260, 267, 290, 302, 320, 321, 322, 324, 355, 357, 358, 408, 432
Pippa, 144, 172, **172**, 241, 296, 385, 451
Pippi, 172
Pippin, 91, 92, 179, 392
Pita, 100
Pius, 172
Placido, 80
Pleas, 421
Poet, 241, 390, 425
Polina, 452
Polly, 51, 80, 152, **172**, 177, 182, 239, 241, 273, 316, 322, 436, 454
Poppy, 73, 93, 106, 144, 157, 172, **173**, 179, 190, 214, 317, 380, 385, 461
Porter, 28, 71, 87, 104, 203, 204, 206, 216, 218, 245, 249, 265, 291, 299, 320, 324, **324**, 351, 355, 357, 368, 399, 408, 432, 461
Portia, 70, **173**, 276, 282, 324, 337, 345, 381, 385, 388, 432, 449
Portland, 443
Posy, 117
Potter, 408
Powell, 324, 411
Prairie, 181, 425, 461
Precious, **173**, 425
Prentiss, 105, 324, 357, 411
Pres, 324
Prescott, 50, 88, 231, 233, **324**, 344, 405, 411, 461
Presley, 21, 91, 168, 169, **173**, 223, 224, 235, 241, 260, 280, 338, 366, 411, 429
Press, 421
Pressley, 173
Preston, 216, 224, 230, 240, 249, 268, 271, 274, 276, 281, 284, 311, 314, 320, 323, 324, **324**, 356, 368, 411, 458
Price, 63, 87, 322, 375, 425
Primitivo, 421
Primo, 143, 230, 400
Primrose, 380, 392
Primus, 421

Prince, 38, 78, 103, 173, **325**, 364, 391, 425
Princess, 106, 173, 255, 310, 390, 421, 425
Princeton, **325**, 443, 444
Prisca, 173, 373
Priscilla, 109, **173**, 174, 316, 373, 457
Prissy, 173
Profit, 421
Promise, 60, 86, 89, 107, 169, 173, 425, 461
Prospero, 391, 450
Prudence, 105, 118, 380, 405
Prudie, 385
Prue, 325, 374
Pryce, 57, 131, 174, 234, 238, 258, 265, 293, 331, 357, 378, 411, 461
Pryor, 342, 411
Purl, 421

Quaid, 168, 392, 411
Queen, 390
Queenie, 255
Quentin, 29, 59, 66, 72, 84, 96, 150, 165, 185, 188, 202, 216, 223, 235, 247, 248, 253, 263, 305, 307, 318, 325, **325**, 326, 344, 350, 358, 387, 394, 432, 447, 458
Quetzalli, 414
Quiana, 126, 130, 194
Quil, 325
Quill, 86, 105, 107, 141, 181, 226, 297, 321, 322, 325, **325**, 375, 425, 461
Quin, 173, 325, 326
Quincy, 44, 57, 236, 252, 282, 298, **325**, 344, 346, 356, 364, 366, 411, 458
Quinlan, 29, 45, 99, 143, 154, 199, 265, 300, 324, **325**, 378, 387, 411, 461
Quinn, 32, 47, 58, 74, 110, 111, 124, 126, 133, 138, 145, **173**, 176, 187, 189, 221, 234, 252, 254, 287, 292, 306, **326**, 329, 333, 349, 359, 366, 374, 375, 378, 411
Quint, 326
Quinten, 326
Quintin, 326
Quintinus, 325
Quinton, 38, 44, 78, 129,

199, 250, 252, 308, 311, 325, **326**, 364, 387, 389
Quintus, 325, 382
Quiteria, 446

Rab, 332
Rabten, 346
Rachael, 174
Rachel, 51, 87, 116, 131, **174**, 175, 176, 183, 210, 211, 214, 217, 224, 247, 281, 285, 286, 287, 288, 289, 310, 316, 340, 372, 432, 457
Rachelle, 186
Radley, 411
Rae, 78, 174, **174**, 175, 398
Rae Ann, 174
Raegan, 29, 110, 175, 182
Raelyn, 174, 370, 386
Raelynn, 330, 383
Rafa, 328
Rafael, 28, 33, 64, 89, 141, 149, 152, 190, 204, 210, 212, 233, 307, 309, 313, 319, 327, 328, 415, 458
Rafaela, 43, 131, **174**, 224, 403, 414, 461
Rafaella, 202
Rafe, 126, 179, 289, 326, 328, 359, 375
Rafer, 328, 439
Raffaele, 328
Raffaella, 174, 400
Rafferty, 411
Raffi, 328
Rafi, 174
Ragnar, 442
Raheem, 31, 364, 427
Rahim, 292
Rahm, 402
Raiden, 132, 254, 283, 297, 306, **326**, 338, 370, 387, 392
Raijin, 326
Raimondo, 329
Rain, 139, 174
Raina, 36
Rainbow, 390
Raine, 72, 87, 103, 110, 118, **174**, 182, 189, 202, 223, 225, 234, 241, 374, 425, 461
Rainer, 396
Raisa, 402, 403, 452
Raj, 451
Raleigh, 53, 144, 206, 325, 366, 383, 443

Rene, 107, 145, 207, **330**, 394, 415
René, 330
Renee, 50, 75, 77, 177, 178, 195, 231, 248, 284, 349, 432, 456
Renée, 176, 177, **177**, 330, 394
Renesmee, 177, 392
Reno, 383, 443
Renzo, 400
Resha, 402
Reuben, 77, 89, 101, 108, 113, 133, 144, 160, 179, 198, 315, **330**, 338, 373, 402, 458, 461
Reuel, 208
Reva, 137, 175, **177**, 219, 331, 398, 461
Rex, 35, 46, 71, 100, 108, 118, 120, 123, 176, 230, 273, 290, 298, 304, 311, 328, **331**, 336, 346, 353, 375, 389, 422, 451, 458, 459, 460, 461
Rey, 329, 415
Reyes, 415
Reyna, 168, 175, 184, 402, 414
Reynaldo, 207, 415, 450
Reza, 427
Rhea, 34, 71, 77, 93, 171, **177**, 203, 206, 356, 367, 428, 451, 461
Rhett, 48, 223, 232, 260, 275, **331**, 340, 349, 375, 383, 415, 417
Rhi, 177
Rhian, 134, 177, 243, 244, 377, 386
Rhiannon, 91, 100, **177**, 377, 428
Rhoda, 138, 162, **177**, 241, 336, 341, 355, 373, 432, 454
Rhodes, 29, 226, 303, 375, 411, 443, 444
Rhodri, 82, 378
Rhona, 264
Rhonda, 111, **178**, 245, 253, 256, 328, 436, 456
Rhymer, 408
Rhys, 57, 63, 82, 84, 87, 109, 189, 214, 267, 272, 329, **331**, 335, 357, 375, 376, 378, 461
Ria, 46, 148, 202
Ría, 414, 451

Rian, 182
Rianna, 182, 403
Riannon, 177
Ricardo, 100, 233, 313, 331, 332, 415, 440
Riccardo, 400
Rich, 331, 332, 424, 440
Richard, 40, 49, 61, 62, 94, 98, 116, 118, 150, 169, 269, 295, **331**, 332, 334, 440, 455
Richardson, 440
Richelle, 436
Richie, 331, 456
Richmond, 46, 81, 89, 144, 149, 273, 317, 411, 440, 443, 461
Rick, 69, 119, 171, 192, 201, 266, 294, 310, 321, 331, 332, 424, 440
Rickert, 331
Ricki, 36, 436
Ricky, 51, 76, 122, 197, 203, 328, 331, 336, 349, 424
Rico, 331, 400, 415, 422, 440
Riddick, 338, 392, 411, 461
Rider, 272, 328, 337, 422
Ridge, 73, 268, 383
Rigel, 391
Rigoberto, 415
Rihana, 178
Rihanna, 27, 127, **178**, 363, 403, 429
Rika, 451
Riker, 338
Rikki, 114, 174
Riku, 392
Riley, 28, 47, 58, 77, 121, 124, 142, 148, 154, 159, 169, 171, **178**, 182, 191, 199, 212, 221, 229, 234, 242, 243, 264, 293, 294, 302, 318, 320, 329, 330, **331**, 335, 343, 346, 366, 377, 378, 406, 411, 432
Rilla, 149, 181, 398, 417, 451
Rina, 150
Rinchen, 346
Ringo, 391, 429
Rinoa, 86, 392
Rio, 391, 412, 451
Riona, 30, 251, 256, 258, 377
Riordan, 143, 228, 325, 346, 378, 387, 411, 412
Rip, 337, 412
Ripley, 280, 338, 366, 392, 411, 412, 461
Risa, 29

Rissa, 60, 70, 129
Rita, 61, 112, 118, 138, 147, 153, 166, **178**, 215, 225, 269, 328, 343, 400, 454
Riva, 200
River, 45, 48, 54, 86, 95, 103, 105, 118, 120, 134, 154, 174, 182, 185, 206, 226, 229, 319, 329, **331**, 343, 380
Rivers, 331
Riviera, 390
Rivka, 67, 176, 236, 402
Riya, 160, 209
Ro, 179, 181, 334
Roan, 60, 82, 86, 101, 105, 226, 329, 375, 425
Roark, 417
Roarke, 229, 292, 293, 327, 375, 378, 411
Rob, 114, 332, 440, 456
Robbie, 138, 146, 174, 178, 195, 226, 332, 456
Robbins, 332
Robby, 205, 328
Robert, 112, 147, 152, 217, 242, 258, 281, 287, 329, 331, 332, **332**, 348, 356, 437, 440, 458
Roberta, 82, 113, 138, 169, **178**, 240, 266, 271, 309, 343, 355, 400, 434, 454
Roberto, 42, 61, 148, 152, 207, 218, 283, 308, 332, **332**, 400, 415, 440, 458
Robertson, 332, 440
Robin, 37, 75, 77, 97, 105, 115, 136, 177, **178**, 201, 234, 238, 242, 247, 327, 332, **332**, 339, 344, 366, 380, 385, 424, 432, 434, 440, 456
Robinson, 317, **332**, 411, 440
Roby, 411
Robyn, 178, 186
Robyrt, 178
Rocco, 97, 138, 213, 217, 230, 297, 332, **332**, 397, 398, 400, 422, 447
Rochelle, 132, 174, 178, 181, 194, 207, 256, 269, 329, 336, 352, 363, 372, 448, 456
Rocio, 158, 286
Rocío, 55, 89, 141, 414
Rock, 253, 332, 422, 424
Rocket, 391, 422
Rockwell, 411, 422, 461

Rocky, 175, 223, 255, 310, 332, 422
Rod, 41, 126, 223, 253, 332, 333, 422, 424, 440
Roddick, 440
Roddy, 214, 332
Roderic, 332
Roderick, 50, 176, 180, 231, 236, 294, 329, **332**, 333, 346, 364, 385, 440, 447, 458
Rodge, 333
Rodger, 75, 187, 230, 333, 440
Rodion, 452
Rodman, 411
Rodney, 205, **333**, 364, 424, 440
Rodolfo, 147, 336, 415, 440
Rodrick, 194
Rodrigo, 76, 150, 170, 207, 211, 304, 319, 332, 415, 440, 450
Roel, 396
Rogan, 228, 378, 387
Rogelio, 207, 415
Roger, 39, 49, 53, 85, 98, 111, 118, 119, 135, 168, 186, 256, 269, 286, 299, **333**, 334, 344, 355, 422, 424, 455
Rogers, 105, 411
Rogue, 241, 344, 392
Rohan, 69, 107, 126, 145, 164, 177, **333**, 335, 364, 378, 387
Roisin, 165, 261
Róisín, 377, 379
Roland, 70, 80, 83, 113, 151, 162, 180, 193, 199, 243, 270, 271, 286, **333**
Roland, 394, 455
Rolanda, 363
Rolando, 133, 319, 333, 415
Rolf, 268, 326, 336, 442
Rolla, 421
Rollie, 190, 333
Rollin, 341
Rollins, 411, 444
Rollo, 134, 198, 244, 326, 328, 389
Roma, 177, 213, 436, 443, 451, 454
Romain, 334, 394
Romaine, 330
Roman, 28, 33, 37, 42, 47, 70, 74, 88, 96, 138, 140, 150, 162, 163, 165, 176,

184, 190, 208, 217, 218, 249, 253, 260, 279, 311, 328, **334**, 354, 387, 389, 447, 452, 458
Romane, 394
Romare, 364, 419
Rome, 443
Romeo, 120, 202, 218, 260, 325, **334**, 353, 389, 400, 449, 450
Romi, 168, 179, 219, 402, 451
Romilly, 55, **179**, 385, 436, 461
Romina, 76, 149, 207, 234, 400, 403, 414, 436
Romy, 126, 165, 173, **179**, 180, 209, 289, 357, 436, 461
Ron, 334, 424, 433, 440
Rona, 436
Ronald, 66, 98, 111, 116, **334**, 433, 440, 455
Ronaldo, 334, 415, 440
Ronan, 31, 43, 93, 103, 124, 141, 144, 158, 174, 195, 206, 212, 219, 229, 244, 246, 250, 254, 261, 264, 293, 296, 306, 334, **334**, 339, 378, 387, 440, 447, 461
Rónán, 334
Ronda, 178
Rondell, 440
Ronen, 48, 334, 402
Roni, 179
Ronia, 136, 179, 342, 461
Ronin, 221, 243, 334, 342, 349, 392
Ronit, 402
Ronja, 179, 441, 442
Ronna, 268, 423
Ronnie, 178, 201, 203, 223, 286, 334, 349, 424, 436
Ronya, 179
Rooney, 411
Roosevelt, **335**, 345
Rory, 47, 76, 81, 92, 138, 153, 178, 181, 187, 234, 235, 244, 264, 265, 268, 296, 332, 333, **335**, 339, 340, 366, 377, 378, 383, 432
Rosa, 81, 89, 152, **179**, 180, 219, 230, 269, 273, 304, 305, 307, 321, 332, 400, 405, 414, 436
Rosabel, 179, 461

Rosabella, 179, **179**, 403, 436
Rosalba, 43, 400
Rosalia, 28, 35, 181, 446
Rosalía, 414
Rosalie, 113, 172, 193, 204, 233, 271, 299, 301, 336, 353, 357, 394, 436, 454
Rosalina, 392
Rosalind, 140, 149, **180**, 240, 270, 328, 435, 436, 449, 454
Rosalinda, 50, 180, 414
Rosaline, 180, 449
Rosalyn, 52, 150, 180, 215, 233, 334, 354
Rosamond, 180, 198, 199, 224, 301, 332, 405, 436
Rosamund, 385
Rosanna, 45, **180**, 400, 403, 436
Rosanne, 66, 119, 180, 256, 423
Rosaria, 146
Rosario, 100, 139, 305, 366, 400, 412, 414, 436
Roscoe, 50, 79, 90, 142, 181, 208, 216, 222, 272, 276, 286, 320, **335**, 336, 383, 398, 432, 445
Rose, 33, 40, 89, 90, 93, 109, 110, 112, 118, 120, 149, 152, 170, 179, 180, **180**, 181, 237, 335, 357, 380, 405, 436
Roseanna, 180
Roseanne, 180
Rosella, 400
Roselyn, 248, 414, 436
Rosemarie, 180
Rosemary, 71, 81, 100, 118, 130, 139, 151, 170, 179, **180**, 181, 213, 240, 303, 337, 344, 380, 436, 454, 461
Rosetta, 436
Rosie, 66, 73, 80, 99, 172, 179, 180, 182, 214, 222, 329, 335, 398, 436
Rosina, 225
Rosita, 179, 436
Roslyn, 454
Ross, 75, 165, 240, 245, 250, 330, **335**, 354, 375, 411, 458
Roula, 397
Rourke, 44, 226
Rowan, 28, 45, 54, 57, 58,

315, 330, 338, **342**, 368, 373
Solon, 382, 389
Sonam, 346
Sondra, 98, 128, 151, 423
Sonia, 45, 76, 128, 129, 132, 190, 201, 247, 414, 430, 432, 448
Sonja, 147, 190, 423, 442
Sonnet, 107, 209, 220, 322, 325, 343, 344, 390, 425
Sonoma, 443
Sonya, 38, 60, 79, 103, 164, 190, 194, 200, 207, 231, 253, 269, 456
Sookie, **190**, 392, 437
Sophia, 15, 32, 36, 135, 167, 190, **190**, 191, 204, 214, 253, 275, 280, 367
Sophie, 40, 68, 69, 85, 86, 87, 90, 95, 99, 108, 152, 161, 171, 182, 190, **191**, 194, 198, 235, 237, 280, 287, 302, 311, 317, 318, 338, 366, 367, 379, 384, 394, 396, 398
Sophronia, 171, 388, 446
Sora, 392
Soraya, 27, 110, 292, 427, 461
Sorcha, 30, 244, 377
Soren, 30, 37, 41, 42, 58, 84, 86, 126, 136, 137, 146, 172, 179, 189, 220, 227, 272, **342**, 387, 392, 433, 442
Søren, 342, 419, 441
Sören, 342, 396
Sotiria, 397
Soup, 269
Spamela, 269
Sparrow, 101, 107, **343**, 344, 380, 389, 391, 392
Spaulding, 237, 324
Spearman, 408
Spellman, 408
Spence, 343, 375
Spencer, 52, 62, 67, 70, 87, 128, 142, 150, 157, 160, 182, 184, 201, 211, 227, 237, 240, 252, 274, 309, 314, 320, 324, 339, 342, **343**, 345, 368, 408, 411, 431
Spenser, 343
Spicy, 420, 421
Spike, 277, 391, 422
Spiros, 397

Spurrier, 408
Squire, 391, 421, 425
Stacey, 69, 132, 156, 191, 340
Stacie, 125, 191
Stacy, 33, 37, 51, 62, 116, 124, 127, 142, 177, 178, 186, **191**, 194, 195, 201, 228, 236, 262, 294, 349, 366, 448, 456
Stafford, 411
Stan, 343, 440
Stanford, 411, 440, 444
Stanislaus, 389, 447
Stanislav, 451, 452
Stanislava, 452
Stanley, 153, 166, 188, 225, 271, 276, 301, 318, **343**, 440, 455
Stanton, 46, 139, 180, 233, 240, 328, 336, 357, 411, 440, 455, 462
Star, 103, 115, 173, 211, 390, 425
Starla, 456
Starling, 380, 411
Stasi, 37
Stasia, 37, 42, 461
Stavros, 397
Steele, 200, 226, 344, 375, 411, 422
Stefan, 99, 100, 107, 121, 136, 152, 184, 234, 343, **343**, 344, 396, 442
Stefani, 191
Stefania, 37, **191**, 397, 400, 404, 437, 452, 461
Stefanie, 396
Stefano, 343, 344, 400, 440, 450
Stefanos, 343, 397
Steff, 343
Steffan, 63, 87, 98, 343, 378
Steffen, 343, 440
Steffi, 191
Stefi, 191
Stelios, 397
Stella, 41, 89, 96, 103, 118, 132, 135, 139, 140, 141, 166, 181, 182, **191**, 193, 203, 241, 274, 276, 282, 367, 396, 398
Stellan, 45, 136, 179, 387, 442
Steph, 191
Stephan, 343, 344
Stephania, 191
Stephanie, 35, 38, 51, 68, 73, 74, 113, 114, 126, 151, 155,

156, 158, 165, 176, 183, 191, **191**, 239, 247, 284, 285, 348, 437, 448, 456
Stephany, 191
Stephen, 73, 76, 78, 79, 121, 130, 135, 148, 183, 186, 192, 197, 202, 213, 272, 295, 313, 323, 327, 343, **343**, 344, 348, 356, 374, 424, 440
Stephon, 129, 308, 343, 364
Sterling, 114, 115, 200, 265, 300, **344**, 380, 433, 458
Stetson, 383, 387, 422
Steve, 69, 76, 114, 119, 122, 171, 286, 328, 343, 344, 424, 440, 458
Steveland, 362
Steven, 38, 68, 77, 119, 191, 249, 250, 284, 308, 339, 343, **344**, 424, 440, 449, 456
Stevenson, 440
Stevie, 191, 437, 448
Stewart, 52, 73, 140, 177, 180, 233, 270, 273, 303, 328, 344, 411, 455
Stockman, 411
Stone, 63, 72, 181, 222, 267, **344**, 375, 380, 422, 462
Stoney, 161, 383, 456
Storm, 37, 111, 115, 120, 154, 175, 185, 189, 206, 344, 380, 425
Stormy, 425
Story, 425
Stowe, 375, 411
Stratton, 205, 411, 444
Strider, 185, 220, **344**, 392, 422
Struan, 30, 161, 378, 387
Stryker, 328, 392, 411, 422
Stu, 344
Stuart, 82, 83, 92, 98, 100, 116, 118, 149, 174, 188, 215, 239, 254, 255, 256, 270, 332, 334, 337, **344**, 378, 385
Styliani, 397
Subira, 360
Sudie, 430
Sue, 51, 119, 123, 182, 188, 192, **192**, 193, 286, 287, 316, 346, 423, 437
Suellen, 423
Sukey, 179, 190, 192, 385
Suki, 126
Sukie, 190

Viola, 28, 30, 46, 83, 89, 117, 133, 177, 198, 215, 236, 244, 245, 305, 315, 405, 449
Violet, 28, 31, 49, 65, 73, 75, 83, 91, 95, 96, 103, 108, 111, 117, 134, 135, 138, 144, 163, 180, 181, 184, 191, **204**, 206, 220, 261, 263, 270, 282, 291, 313, 318, 325, 331, 335, 342, 367, 380
Violeta, 64, 404, 414, 461
Violetta, 90, 198, 204, 388
Violette, 202, 204, 394, 405
Viorica, 305
Virgil, 82, 236, 276, 356, 382, 405, 445
Virgilio, 400
Virginia, 61, 81, 93, 97, 140, 151, 193, **204**, 258, 262, 266, 273, 299, 328, 343, 348, 353, 357, 383, 405, 435, 443
Virginie, 394
Vita, 442, 451
Vitaliy, 452
Vitas, 353
Vito, 398, 399, 400, 422
Vitor, 354
Vittoria, 204, 400
Vittorio, 354, 400
Vitus, 244, 330, 382, 389, 447
Viv, 48
Viva, 388
Viveka, 442
Vivi, 126, 137, 204, 209, 211, 392
Vivian, 28, 46, 52, 65, 81, 91, 112, 135, 148, 150, 151, 153, 160, 163, 193, 202, 204, **204**, 215, 240, 263, 316, 326, 353, 367, 454
Viviana, 31, 32, 47, 52, 84, 97, 135, 149, 168, 170, 202, 204, **204**, 304, 353, 400, 404, 414, 447
Vivien, 128, 204, 291, 368
Vivienne, 59, 77, 86, 96, 204, 207, 394
Vladimir, 167, 451, 452
Volker, 396
Volney, 421
Von, 73, 100, 118, 126, 149, 234, 252, 331, 336, 346, 354, 375, 424
Vonda, 176, 205, 336, 423

Vonnie, 52, 207
Vontae, 250
Vulf, 357
Wade, 231, **354**, 375, 458
Waino, 421
Wake, 444
Waldemar, 396
Walden, 206, **354**, 411, 440, 444
Waldo, 255, 260, 276, 286, 335, 336, 429, 440, 445
Walker, 27, 40, 61, 96, 171, 175, 242, 246, 270, 291, 341, 348, 351, **355**, 364, 383, 409, 433, 440, 462
Wallace, 70, 138, 162, 225, 236, 238, 275, 336, 343, **355**, 356, 405, 440
Wallis, 226, 411
Wally, 354, 355, 356, 424, 440
Walt, 51, 355
Walter, 93, 104, 152, 213, 215, 219, 258, 262, 266, 269, 273, 275, **355**, 405, 440
Walton, 274, 355, **355**, 411, 440, 462
Wanda, **205**, 248, 302, 309, 310, 333, 355, 364, 423, 432, 452
Ward, 92, 239, 276, 353, 455
Wardell, 438, 455
Warner, 261, 355, 411
Warren, 94, 112, 150, 178, 193, 240, 266, 271, 299, 307, 309, 316, 337, 355, **355**, 433, 455
Washington, 411
Watson, 85, 273, 347, 357, 411, 417
Watt, 325, 375, 411
Wava, 420
Wave, 205
Waverley, 205
Waverly, 50, 200, **205**, 314, 325, 411
Wayland, 411
Waylon, 268, 383, 439
Wayne, 52, 66, 75, 98, 169, 193, 205, 230, 246, **355**, 383, 424
Wayra, 122
Weaver, 409
Webb, 411, 462
Webster, 238, 273, 409
Weldon, 411

Wellesley, 444
Wellington, 314, 411
Wendell, 138, 162, 172, 174, 340, 344, 455
Wendi, 205
Wendy, 100, 103, 195, 201, **205**, 456
Wenona, 206
Werner, 396
Wes, 126, 296, 356, 440, 456
Wesley, 19, 52, 60, 105, 116, 130, 136, 227, 232, 240, 286, 308, 314, 325, 350, **356**, 411, 440, 458
West, 222, 356, 375, 425
Westley, 29, 52, 66, 227, 230, 356, 440
Weston, 128, 132, 200, 211, 237, 241, 272, 298, 321, 342, 350, 352, **356**, 387, 411, 440
Wharton, 411, 419
Wheeler, 409
Whelan, 411
Whisper, 185, 390, 425
Whitley, 205, 282, 411
Whitman, 151, 257, 260, 303, 354, 411, 419
Whitney, 24, 56, 72, 105, 121, 128, 136, 189, 200, **205**, 230, 294, 298, 346, 356, 366, 411, 432, 448
Wilber, 356
Wilbur, 90, **356**, 440, 444, 445
Wilda, 420
Wilder, 35, 205, 306, 411, 440
Wiley, 80, 169, 174, 175, 219, 266, 335, 383, 398
Wilfred, 158, 440, 445
Wilfredo, 415
Wilhelm, 356, 396, 440
Wilhelmina, 29, 104, 198, **205**, 266, 396, 405, 434, 436
Will, 58, 123, 133, 144, 237, 279, 332, 356, 357
Willa, 58, 77, 96, 166, 171, 175, 177, 205, **206**, 218, 257, 271, 322, 347, 351, 367, 405, 418, 434, 440, 451, 458, 461
Willam, 237
Willard, 158, 198, 219, 265, 278, 411, 440, 445
Willem, 356, 396, 438
William, 15, 85, 122, 258,

281, 287, 289, 302, 310, 332, 348, **356**, 438, 440, 458
Willie, 205, 356, 364, 398
Willis, 28, 35, 102, 133, 140, 162, 177, 193, 204, 270, 315, 341, 354, **356**, 364, 405, 411, 438, 440, 455
Willodean, 383
Willow, 21, 45, 47, 54, 66, 74, 102, 109, 111, 130, 132, 154, 172, 181, 182, 187, 188, 192, 196, 205, 206, **206**, 272, 276, 324, 344, 357, 358, 380, 389, 432
Wills, 356, 357
Willy, 356
Wilma, 81, 205, 260, 276, 303, 326, 445
Wilson, 213, 308, 322, **357**, 411, 440, 458, 462
Wilton, 411, 440
Wim, 356
Win, 206, 258, 357
Windsor, 304, 411
Winema, 122
Winfield, 357
Winfred, 357
Winifred, 29, 159, **206**, 216, 223, 225, 337, 345, 385, 405, 437, 447
Winnie, 206, 357, 398, 437
Winnifred, 206
Winona, 144, **206**, 383, 437
Winslow, 29, 55, 86, 102, 151, 177, 187, 213, 226, 231, 249, 274, 297, 325, 351, 354, **357**, 366, 389, 411, 419, 437, 462
Winston, 233, 246, 248, 273, 322, 335, 357, **357**, 411
Winter, 54, 86, 103, 105, 107, 129, 154, 200, **206**, 296, 329, 343, 344, 366, 380, 425
Winton, 411
Wisdom, 173, 312, 391, 425
Wolf, 45, 47, 88, 141, 200, 227, 272, 338, **357**, 389, 396, 412, 422
Wolfe, 357
Wolfgang, 396, 422
Wolford, 412
Wonder, 390
Woodrow, 357
Woody, 79, 355, 383
Worth, 411, 425

Wouter, 396
Wren, 82, 103, 129, 135, 181, 297, 321, 332, 357, 375, 380, 461
Wright, 409
Wyatt, 68, 184, 223, 235, 243, 246, 261, 268, 279, 292, 302, 313, 326, 331, 337, **357**, 359, 382, 383, 411, 433
Wylie, 378, 411
Wyman, 215, 411
Wyn, 357
Wynn, 84, 98, 181, 272, 293, 327, 329, 331, **357**, 375, 378, 462
Wynne, 87, 141, 227, 354, 357, 375, 377
Wynona, 268
Wynonna, 206
Wynter, 206
Wynton, 399

Xaiden, 359
Xander, 32, 45, 126, 133, 190, 214, 220, 324, **358**, 392, 440
Xandra, 32
Xanthe, 12, 381, 388, 428
Xanthia, 388
Xaver, 358, 396
Xavier, 19, 32, 38, 48, 77, 94, 98, 112, 135, 173, 185, 190, 212, 225, 246, 248, 253, 261, 277, 283, 292, 306, 311, 325, 326, 339, 350, **358**, 364, 394, 415, 422, 447
Xavy, 358
Xax, 269
Xena, 392
Xenia, 83, **206**, 253, 388, 452
Xenon, 382
Xerxes, 382
Xia, 32
Ximena, 21, 34, 37, 76, 91, 112, 164, **207**, 414
Xiomara, 414
Xochitl, 414
Xolani, 361
Xosé, 288
Xristina, 397
Xzavier, 358

Yadiel, 415
Yadira, 207, 414
Yael, 29, 48, 101, **207**, 210,

236, 281, 318, 329, 366, 372, 402
Yaelle, 207
Yaffa, 402
Yahaira, 414
Yahir, 37, 164, 415
Yair, 402
Yakov, 67, 280
Yale, 306, 357, 444, 455
Yamilet, 414
Yana, 76, 106, 452
Yancey, 366, 411
Yandel, 415
Yann, 394
Yanni, 48
Yannick, 30, 144, 322, 394
Yannis, 397
Yarden, 288, 402
Yareli, 164, 414
Yaretzi, 207
Yaritza, 414
Yasmeen, 110
Yasmin, 31, 91, 112, 114, 183, 292, 307, 314, 427, 436
Yasmine, 112, 319
Yazmin, 414
Yehuda, 67, 290, 402
Yesenia, 44, 156, 185, **207**
Yesi, 207
Yessenia, 207
Yevgeni, 262
Yitzhak, 278, 401
Yolanda, 61, **207**, 298, 329, 333, 364, 414, 423
Yolande, 207
Yoli, 207
Yonatan, 288
York, 411, 444
Yosef, 289, 402
Yoselin, 116, 414
Ysanne, 385
Yuliana, 37, 414, 452
Yuna, 392
Yusuf, 427
Yuval, 402
Yvaine, 392
Yves, 394
Yvette, 161, 178, 207, **207**, 329, 352, 364, 394, 456
Yvie, 207
Yvonne, 39, 41, 71, 72, 116, 149, 151, 176, 193, 207, **207**, 245, 270, 286, 310, 333, 364, 394, 423

Zach, 358, 359
Zachariah, 176, 282, 285,